The Allyn & Bacon

Sourcebook
for
College Writing Teachers

James C. McDonald
University of Southwestern Louisiana

Allyn and Bacon
Boston · London · Toronto · Sydney · Tokyo · Singapore

CONTENTS

FOREWORD

My first day in a composition class was as a teaching assistant instructing first-year students in 1976, just four months after I had been an undergraduate myself. After two days of orientation, I was teaching two classes and relying on my textbooks, even more than my students would, to make sense of my subject. At the beginning of my first class a student came up to my desk, introduced herself as a sister of a friend of mine, and returned a paper of mine that the friend had once borrowed to -- well -- plagiarize. It was not a good start.

I wasn't comfortable in my role as a teacher, and I didn't know much about how to teach a classroom of writing students. I knew nothing about the writing process movement then well underway, and next to nothing about scholarship on teaching writing. At best I can only vaguely recall some arguments in my weekly teaching-practicum course about *Students' Right to Their Own Language*, only recently endorsed and published by the Conference on College Composition and Communication. My students were bright and well prepared for college English, however, and being supportive of their young instructor , they made up for a lot of the weaknesses in my teaching.

I occasionally looked at scholarship on teaching composition as I worked towards my masters degree, buying a copy of Mina Shaughnessy's *Errors and Expectations* after a semester of teaching basic writing, and attending the 1978 CCCC meeting as I searched for a job. Bit it wasn't until I was an adjunct instructor at another school, and facing four first-year composition classes full of unprepared students, that I realized how inadequate my teaching approaches were. Then I began to look seriously beyond my textbooks to articles and presentations on composition for help in understanding the myriad of problems my students and I were encountering in class. I began to rethink my approach to teaching, really trying to analyze what I was doing for the first time. My reading was not well focused, and finding the time and energy to read articles about composition while instructing over a hundred students a semester was difficult. Improving my teaching was frustratingly slow at first. I began to improve at a quicker pace when I joined a group of adjuncts and teaching assistants at another university a few years later. There we began developing a new first-year writing course for unprepared students, basing our approach on scholarship about writing and composing by such scholars and teachers as Janet Emig, Donald Murray, Peter Elbow, Nancy Sommers, and James Kinneavy.

Those memories as graduate student or adjunct instructor, and the hope of improving the learning curve for others with experience like mine, have guided me as I put together this collection. I wanted *The Allyn & Bacon Sourcebook for College Writing Teachers* to serve as a useful collection of writings on important theories and pedagogies in composition studies. To select the articles I thought would be most useful, I kept thinking back on my struggle to teach too many poorly prepared students while trying to learn more about composition. *The Allyn & Bacon Sourcebook for College Writing Teachers* is directed especially to composition teachers early in their careers who face their first teaching position or are re-examining their teaching goals and methods. At the same time I would hope that experienced teachers will find this material informative.

Some selections here describe general theories and pedagogies for writing instruction. Some describe process-oriented approaches to teaching and discuss what we know and don't know about writers' composing processes. There are also articles on collaborative learning, on audience, on teaching and writing with computers, on organization and style, and on helping students with grammar and editing. Separate sections deal with integrating critical thinking, reading, and writing, or use of sources in research writing, and with argumentation, as well as with writing assignments and evaluating student writing. While reprinted articles could not cover every topic in composition teaching, numerous suggested readings at the end of each section and at the end of the book aim to provide useful leads to other key topics. These include basic writing, writing across the curriculum, teaching international students, teaching students with disabilities, working with writing centers and with student conferencing, and numerous other areas of interest in a fast-growing body of scholarship about college composition.

Acknowledgments. I have a number of people to thank for their assistance with this book. Eileen Barton, Laurie Dever Hook, Beth Maxfield, Mary Alice Trent, and Mary White did some of the library work and helped me sort out selections. Ann Dobie and Nicole Greene made useful suggestions for inclusion. I also thank my editor Allen Workman, who brought this project to me, stayed patiently with a WPA who couldn't always make his deadlines, and labored to make my work easier. I am especially grateful to Doug Day at Allyn & Bacon for recommending me for this project, and to Bill Lalicker of Murray State University for helping to give me a shot at it.

James C. McDonald

A. Perspectives, Theories, and Directions in Composition Teaching

Knowing that many of the readers of this sourcebook are in their first term as a classroom teaching or just about to walk into a classroom as a teacher for the first time, I wanted to begin the readings with an article on the role of the writing teacher, and there may be no one more qualified to write on this subject than Edward P. J. Corbett. One of the most honored and influential teachers and scholars in the past four decades of composition studies, Corbett often mentions how much more he still needs to learn about teaching. I find his modesty as instructive as his advice to teachers in "Mutual Friends: What Teachers Can Learn from Students and What Students Can Learn from Teachers" (originally published in *Balancing Acts: Essays on the Teaching of Writing in Honor of William F. Irmscher*, edited by Virginia A. Chappell, Mary Louise Buley-Meissner, and Chris Anderson, Carbondale: Southern Illinois UP, 1991). The role that Corbett suggests for the teacher requires the modesty to learn from students and to put oneself in the place of a beginning learner in order to address an audience of students effectively. Successful teachers are always learning, about their subjects and about their students, and Corbett suggests that the best way for teachers to get to know their students is with individual conferences. For Corbett, however, the most important challenge that a teacher faces is "to be invariably conscientious, honest, and fair in dealing with students." Corbett asks that we teach with the realization that all teachers have some effect on their students and at times that effect is a profound one.

The rest of the selections in this section are more general and theoretical, looking at writing instruction from various philosophical, historical, and finally technological perspectives ranging from classical rhetoric to postmodernism and networked computer composition classrooms. The next three articles discuss theories and pedagogies from the past and present that inform or perhaps should inform writing instruction today. In "Teaching Writing: The Major Theories" (from *The Teaching of Writing: Eighty-fifth Yearbook of the National Society for the Study of Education, Part II*, ed. Anthony R. Petrosky and David Bartholomae, Chicago: NSSE, 1986), Anne Ruggles Gere gives a brief history of first-year writing courses and classifies modern composition theories into four categories. Gere condemns "current-traditional" rhetoric, the dominant composition pedagogy of the twentieth century, for taking a narrow, dogmatic, "aphilosophical" view of writing dealing only with matters of form, style, and correctness. She describes three general alternatives to current-traditionalism into modern composition instruction: rhetorical instruction, expressivist instruction, and "New Rhetoric," which have made audience, invention, and critical thinking important concerns in writing courses. Gere, however, argues that these pedagogies also lack a philosophical basis and calls for a composition theory and pedagogy built on a philosophical exploration of the relationship between language, reality, and thought and of definitions of truth, knowledge, and logic.

James L. Kinneavy turns to fourth-century BCE Athens and classical rhetoric for different models for uniting theory and pedagogy in composition in "Translating Theory into Practice in Teaching Composition: A Historical View and a Contemporary View" (originally published in *Essays on Classical Rhetoric and Modern Discourse*, edited by Robert J. Connors, Lisa S. Ede, and Andrea A. Lunsford, Carbondale:

Southern Illinois UP, 1984). Kinneavy describes the pedagogies of Plato, Isocrates, and Aristotle, each based on different theories of language, knowledge, and reality, and considers their relevance for composition teaching today. He argues that all three pedagogies treated rhetorical situation as a central concern of the writer.

In contrast, James A. Berlin explores the potential of often controversial postmodern theories and cultural studies for teaching writing today in "Poststructuralism, Cultural Studies, and the Composition Classroom: Postmodern Theory in Practice" (originally published in *Rhetoric Review* 11 [1992]: 16-33). Berlin gives readers an introduction to a number of important concepts of postmodernism and describes a first-year course that he designed that combines the methods of cultural studies and of social-epistemic rhetoric.

The last three articles in this section deal with important recent developments in composition, the increasing importance of collaborative learning, audience, and computers and computer classrooms in writing instruction. Lisa S. Ede and Andrea A. Lunsford, in "The Pedagogy of Collaboration" (a chapter from their book *Singular Texts/Plural Authors: Perspectives on Collaborative Writing*, Carbondale: Southern Illinois UP, 1990), provide readers with an overview of theories and pedagogies of collaborative learning and peer groups for composition. Ede and Lunsford place collaborative learning in a theoretical context grounded in the rejection of the writer as an isolated composer and in a conception of language and writing as intensely social phenomena.

Just as it has become a central concern of writing instruction, audience has become a slippery and contested concept, as the title of Jack Selzer's article, "More Meanings of *Audience*," implies (from *A Rhetoric of Doing: Essays on Written Discourse in Honor of James L. Kinneavy*, edited by Stephen P. Witte, Neil Nakadate, and Roger D. Cherry, Carbondale: Southern Illinois UP, 1992). The many meanings of audience operate at once, states Selzer, who briefly summarizes the different theories of audience. Audience refers to the real people who read a text, to the intended audience that writers construct in their minds to guide the composing of the text, and to the fictionalized, implied, and ideal readers that writers create in the text, roles that writers invite real readers to adopt as they read. The dynamic complexity of addressing audience makes a strong case for classroom pedagogies that frequently involve students in dealing directly with actual readers such as collaborative learning and in reading real texts.

In "Computers and Instructional Strategies in the Teaching of Writing" (first published in *Evolving Perspectives on Computers and Composition Studies: Questions for the 1990s*, edited by Gail E. Hawisher and Cynthia L. Selfe, Urbana, IL: NCTE, 1991), Elizabeth Klem and Charles Moran summarize much of the research on computers and writing and suggest that computers are changing people's writing and reading processes and the nature of texts themselves. Klem and Moran cover many of the implications that student access to word-processing, heuristic software, style checkers, and networked computer classrooms have for writing instruction. Many of these developments seem to support and even encourage process and collaborative pedagogies, but they also present teachers with new concerns, as Klem and Moran's long list of research questions on computers and writing implies.

Mutual Friends:
What Teachers Can Learn from Students and What Students Can Learn from Teachers

Edward P.J. Corbett

We do not always recognize that teaching is a two-way street. Like another familiar analogy--that of the pitcher and the catcher in baseball--the teaching process is often viewed as one in which one of the parties involved in the transaction is doing all of the transmitting and the other party is doing all the receiving. The common concept of the writer-reader relationship is similar: the writer does all the work; the reader just sits back and absorbs--or falls asleep.

Because I am a slow learner, it took me a long time to realize that teaching is a reciprocal process. A lot of sweating goes on on both sides of the podium. Moreover, a lot of learning ensues on both sides of the podium. For a long time, I thought I was the only one in the classroom who was expressing moisture through the pores and the only one in the classroom who was dispensing knowledge. Because I was a slow learner, it took me most of my professional career to realize that all along my students had been teaching me steadily and profusely. It is too late for me to radically alter my own attitudes and methods in the light of the epiphany I have experienced, but I can make some reparation for my persistent myopia by passing on to younger teachers the instant insights I have gained from my revelation.

I might start out by talking first about the dividends that students can reap from contact with the teacher. After all, since most of us think of the teacher-student relationship as a one-way conduit, we might start with the obvious: the teacher has something to give the student.

The simplest and most general answer to the question "what can students learn from the teacher?" is that students can learn whatever the teacher knows that they do not know. Students may regard what the teacher knows as not worth the time or the effort required of them to gain that knowledge. But we all know that the judgments of young people about what is worth acquiring are sometimes erroneous. Even we senior citizens frequently misjudge the worth of the fruits that the world dangles before our eyes, so we cannot fault inexperienced youth for their misappraisals. But what we can say is that if students are not receptive to what the teacher has to offer simply because they have misjudged the value of the plum, they are the losers.

A shorter version of this paper was delivered at the Young Rhetoricians' Conference in Monterey, California, 22-24 June 1989.

Until they learn otherwise, however, students should always presume that the teacher knows something that they do not know. After all, there are circumstances that warrant the presumption: usually the teacher has met certain certification standards; most of the time, the teacher is older and more experienced than the students. Part of the Oriental students' great reverence for the Teacher is due not only to the official certification of the teacher's wisdom but also to the respect that their culture has for older people.

From my vantage point now as an elderly person, I can honestly say that I never had a teacher who made my classroom experience a complete waste of my time and attention. I was frequently bored by a teacher. I was often baffled by a teacher. I was sometimes disenchanted by a teacher. And although today I still know who my memorable teachers were and still can tell you which ones I learned the most from, I still cannot say that I ever came away empty-handed from any teacher I ever had. On the contrary, I could tick off for you many experiences in my life where I felt I had been cheated of the expected dividends- -experiences such as reading a book or seeing a play or going on a trip or viewing a television program.

I acknowledge that the teacher is not the font of all knowledge. The teacher is mainly a conveyor of knowledge and skills and just one of many repositories of knowledge. The big buzzing world around us may be the premier font of knowledge. But we desperately need a guide through the maze of that big buzzing world. There are many guides available to us--parents, clergy, close friends. But maybe the most reliable of the guides for hire is the teacher. We can thank whatever gods that be that in our culture a certain number of years of education are mandatory for all young people and that there are paid, certified teachers to conduct that education. And if those teachers know even a little bit more than we know, our relationship with them is bound to be profitable.

The point I have been trying to make is that we stand to learn something from any relationship where the other party knows something that we do not know. What we learn may be more or less valuable to us. And admittedly there will be times when what we learn from the other party will be deleterious to us. The person, for instance, who knows about and introduces us to the euphoric sensations of a chemical drug may ultimately prove to be a baneful influence on us. But at least we expect teachers to have only good goods to dispense to their charges. There can be some guarantee that the goods dispensed by the teacher will be good if the teacher has the kind of ethos we traditionally associate with the pedagogue.

It is that pedagogical ethos which leads me to a discussion of the second general benefit that students can derive from their contact with a teacher. The second benefit is the set of values- -intellectual or cultural or moral values--that a teacher can convey to the students. I do not mean to suggest that teachers should be deliberate proselytizers. Teachers should exemplify values, not harangue their students about them. Teachers, like other professionals, go through a crucible in order to practice their profession. They want to win the privilege of standing in front of a room full of eager or apathetic students and engaging those students in some sort of intellectual exploration.

Teaching is the most private of the professions. Other professionals--doctors, lawyers, engineers--are exposed ultimately to public scrutiny and assessment. But once the teacher closes the door of the classroom, only God and the students--and maybe the teacher know what goes on behind the closed door. That situation places a tremendous responsibility on teachers. Their integrity--and maybe the ultimate welfare of the students--is on the line. Mind you, they should not take advantage of that closed arena and indoctrinate their students verbally about any particular brand of religion or politics or way of life. However, they can hardly help transmitting some set of values just by their demeanor, their dress, their carriage, their speech patterns, their mere presence on the podium. For that reason, they must be what Quintilian said the ideal orator must be: a good man (or woman) skilled in speaking.

To my mind, being a genuinely good person is the greatest challenge for the teacher. All of us, merely because we are human, are fallible and peccable--and we frequently fall from grace. Nevertheless, when the genuinely good person falls from grace, there is somehow always a residue of nobility and inspiration. I am not suggesting that teachers have to be untarnished saints. Some of the great ones I have known have occasionally cussed like a sailor's parrot when their sensibilities were outraged. But I am asserting that teachers must be unswervingly conscientious, honest, and fair in their dealings with students.

That is the challenge: to be invariably conscientious, honest, and fair in dealing with students. Meeting that challenge may strike some of you as being an easy task, but for most of us, meeting that challenge is the hardest task of all. When I recollect my own practices as a teacher, I simply cringe at the thought of the many times in my career when I was not conscientious or honest or fair in dealing with my students. But I have known a few teachers who hewed unswervingly to that standard.

You have all read or heard somebody's testimony about a person who had profoundly affected his or her life. I have been amazed to discover how often the influential person mentioned in those testimonies has been a former teacher. I have more often heard that it was a teacher rather than a parent or a minister or a boss that turned somebody's life around.

I want all of you now to ask yourselves who had a great influence on the course of your life. Who pushed you in the direction that you eventually took? Who made you what you are today--for better or for worse? I wonder how many of you would answer, as I would, "A teacher."

In my case, it was a teacher of Greek whom I had in high school for at least one class all four years. I want to talk a bit about him because he exemplifies the kind of beneficent ethos I am talking about. He was a Ph.D. who preferred to teach in high school rather than in the university. He was filled with his subject, classical Greek, and he loved it as no other teacher I have ever been exposed to has loved the subject he or she was teaching. An elderly man in his early sixties, he walked two and a half miles to school every morning, and on the way he would recite to himself the hundreds of lines from Homer's *Iliad* or from Xenophon's *Anabasis* that he had committed to memory. If you think that we callow youth were not edified by this display of commitment to learning, you are sadly mistaken. In the breaks between classes, we would frequently exclaim to one another about the wonders of this man's stunning erudition.

This extraordinarily learned man gave us ridiculously high grades on our report cards, not because he was indifferent to intellectual standards but because he had learned along the way that high grades were a powerful incentive for young men to study their Greek. And he was right. We studied harder in that class than we did in the classes where we barely squeaked by with a B-minus. Maybe we *earned* those high grades because we studied hard.

And he was a good man, an exemplary man. I pronounce that judgment about him not because he was a priest but because he fairly exuded, unpretentiously but genuinely, moral and intellectual integrity. What an inspiration he was to us all! He did not preach to us, but by the example of his ethos he made us aspire to be solidly learned, and he made us ashamed of ourselves if we mortally or venially fell from grace in our personal lives. How can one measure what effect such a teacher had on the lives and the fortunes of his students? All I can say is that the effect was as profound as it was unmistakable.

Those are the principal things that students can learn from a teacher: a thirst and a respect for knowledge and a sterling set of intellectual and moral values. I wish I could give you the formula for how a teacher succeeds in promoting those objectives, but the formulation of such a procedure is the subject for another paper, a paper that I am not qualified to present. Instead, let us now consider the other side of the teacher-student relationship: what teachers can learn from students.

I can give a formula that will prepare teachers to learn whatever is to be learned from their students. The formula is easy to articulate but difficult to effectuate, but here it is: attune yourselves to the mind-set of your students. Anyone who has taught for even a few years has had the unsettling experience of alluding in the classroom to some putatively familiar event or personage and meeting with a scrim of glassy-eyed responses from the students. And the older you get as a teacher, the more often you meet with those blank responses. I remember how shocked I was the first time I got that kind of blank response from my students when I alluded to an event that was etched indelibly in my memory: Jack Ruby shooting Lee Harvey Oswald on live television. Now if you were to mention that 1963 world-class event in your classroom, you would not only have to describe the event but have to identify the two men involved in it.

I mention this common experience that teachers have of unresponsive responses from their students because it is the classic example of teachers broadcasting on a frequency quite different from the one their students are tuned to. The frequency metaphor is an apt one here because the baby boomers--and now their children--are, as Marshall McLuhan once reminded us, more "ear-oriented" than "eye-oriented." The private libraries of many of the college students of my generation were stocked with books; the private libraries of most students today are stocked with record albums or compact discs. The difference in what the different generations of college students treasure makes a profound difference in what students readily respond to. I won't go into the different cognitive dispositions brought on by one's repeated exposure to what McLuhan called the "hot media" and the "cool media," but I will mention that if teachers today just want to gain the attention of students in the classroom so that the students can be infused with the instruction prescribed by the syllabus, they are more likely to succeed if they resort to the medium of sound than to the medium of print. Even a message printed in billboard size is not going to distract teenagers from the enchantment of the Walkman cooing in their ears. I do not mean to suggest that older teachers have to abandon what edifies or enchants them and adopt what educates and entertains their young charges, but they do have to make an effort to discover and understand what turns their students on.

It is as natural for a gulf to develop between teachers and students as it is for a gulf to develop between parents and children. But if we do not strive to narrow that gulf, we will diminish our effectiveness as teachers and will foreclose any chance we might otherwise have of learning what our students have to teach us.

Again, I was a slow learner on this score, and I shouldn't have been, because by the time I was ten years into my teaching career, I had had considerable acting experience. It is a commonplace that one of the skills actors have to develop is the ability to put themselves into the shoes of the character they are playing and to act and think the way that character would. I did have some success in making that transformation of personalities on the stage, but it was a number of years before I realized that I had to make a similar kind of transformation in the classroom: I had to make an effort to put myself into the shoes--or, if you don't like that metaphor, into the disposition- -of my students and to imagine how they were responding to what I was preaching or teaching. For a number of years, I kept exclaiming to my students about the mellifluous voice of Bing Crosby emanating from my old 78 rpm records, while they were responding to the rockabilly rhythms and gyrations of Elvis Presley on television. Just the fact that my students and I danced to a different rhythm created a gulf between us.

How do we get on our students' frequency? The surest way I know of is to have frequent conferences with the students. Many teachers, I am sure, have adopted the policy of inviting their students to their office for a conference about anything connected with the class. Some teachers have better luck with that policy than I have had. I have an office across the corridor from a colleague who gets a steady stream of students in response to that kind of standing policy. I must strike my students as an ogre; they do not come to confer with me in my office unless they are absolutely desperate for help.

There are some writing programs in this country that require instructors to hold a specified number of conferences with their students during the term. Don Murray's program at the University of New Hampshire mandated conferences with students on every writing assignment. A teacher in that program told me that when he first began teaching at the University of New Hampshire, he was skeptical about the efficacy of mandated conferences, but now he says that he cannot conceive of teaching a writing course in any other way. I discovered the efficacy of mandated conferences when I began teaching our technical writing course about ten years ago. The curriculum demanded that we require our students to confer with us at least twice in connection with the major report they have to write. I find these conferences so exhausting that I do not set up more than four of them on any one day of the school week.

But I have found these conferences so rewarding for me that I encourage my students to visit me more than twice during the term, and I would definitely establish a system of mandated conferences for any writing course I taught if such a system were not set by the director of the course. What makes these conferences rewarding for me is that they enable me to get a fix on my students: I learn a great deal about their backgrounds, about their strengths and weaknesses in several areas, about their problems, not only in connection with the assignment but in connection with their other classes and commitments, about their aspirations, about their personal lives--although I do not press any of my students for information about their personal lives if they do not want to talk about such matters. One would suppose that the succession of relatively brief conferences with students would soon blur in ones memory, but I have been surprised by how much I remember about each student right up to the end of the term. And best of all, I get so attuned to the mind-set of my students that I no longer exclaim in the classroom about the wonders of Bing Crosby's crooning when they are at that stage of their life where they are turned on by the singing of Madonna.

Another way to get attuned to your students' psyche is to put yourself in a situation where you are once again a beginning learner. Once we ourselves get away from being a student in the classroom, it is very easy for us to forget how baffling and frustrating a teachers lecture or assignment can be for the neophyte. I had an awakening a number of years ago when I decided that I was going to learn how to play the banjo. Instead of going to a music teacher, I decided that I was going to get a book on how to play the banjo and hole up in my room to learn the intricacies of this glorious stringed instrument. I discovered that I had to start at square zero. I had everything to learn and only an instruction book to teach me. I went through a lot of trials and made a lot of errors, and my progress in acquiring the skill was slow and uncertain. I still haven't learned to play the banjo well enough to play for my friends.

But the chief fruit of that humbling experience is that I came to realize how students feel when they venture into a new area of learning, whether it be a class in literature or composition or chemistry or economics. And when I realized the bewilderment and frustration of the beginning learner, I was better able to adjust the level of my teaching to the temper of my audience.

Mimi Schwartz, who teaches at Stockton State College in New Jersey, reported in the Staffroom Interchange section of the May 1989 issue of *College Composition and Communication* about her experience in taking two creative writing courses for credit at Princeton University, one in fiction writing, the other in poetry writing. Like me, she had some salutary epiphanies as a result of becoming a student again. She said about her experience:

> I was surprised at my own vulnerabilities as a writer. Many of my fears, confusions, and needs were not so different from my younger counterparts' as I would have predicted. Remembering "what it was like" as a student writer--and recording in my journal what worked and didn't work for me and for my classmates--has altered my teaching as well as my writing. (203-4)

Already a good teacher of writing, Mimi Schwartz has become a better teacher as a result of her experience, a teacher more sensitive to the needs, the insecurities, the bewilderments of her students. But we don't have to enroll in a formal class in order to renew the experience of a student having to write a paper. We can do what has been frequently recommended in journal articles and in convention talks: we can sit down and write the papers we assign to our students.

Another form of re-experiencing the role of the student is described by Patrick Dias in an article in *English Education*. Dias reported on an experiment in which he teamed up groups of two or three university pre-service teachers with groups of two or three secondary school students and required the pre-service teachers to work collaboratively--as students, not as teachers- -with the students on all assignments. The results of that experiment were amazing to Dias, to his pre-service teachers, and to the high school students. Dias concluded that "a view of the act of teaching from the perspective of what teachers do needs to be complemented by an understanding and an experience of how that teaching is received by students. ... It is the students who teach us about teaching" (208). One of the fruits, Dias claims, of the collaborative experience that he set up is that it forced the pre-service teachers "to recall and re-evaluate their past experiences as students" (207).

At one time, we all were needful, insecure, bewildered students. Furthermore, as students, most of us were far from being hotshots. We handed in some of our papers late: we sometimes gave our homework only a lick and a promise; we were often too proud to ask our teacher to clarify an assignment when we were baffled by it. Since it is easy for us to forget that when we were enrolled in elementary or secondary or college classes, we were no great shakes as students, we would do well to occasionally renew our sympathy and our empathy with our students by really or vicariously projecting ourselves back into the status of students. And then we will have disposed ourselves to learn what the students can teach us.

Our students can give us a new perspective on what we already know and can present us with enticing vistas of other worlds. They can remind us that studying is hard work, that all work and no play is stultifying, that stultification rots the mind. They can make us aware that mercy is frequently a restorative virtue, that intransigence is sometimes nothing more than unconscionable rigidity, and that a mere pat on the back can often be the impetus that impels one toward the finish line. But if we have kept our sensibilities sharp, we already *know* those truisms; we just have to be reminded of them-- and our students are great reminders, if we will just pay attention to them. And if we pay attention to them they can also open up new vistas for us. It is easy for all of us to get locked up in our little circumscribed worlds. One of the ways to break out of those circumscribed worlds is to travel. Another way is to read about other worlds. Still another way for teachers to break out of their circumscribed worlds is to force themselves to become acquainted with the many diverse worlds that their students inhabit. As Terry Dean said in a recent article in *College Composition and Communication,* "Multicultural Classrooms, Monocultural Teachers," "With increasing cultural diversity in classrooms, teachers need to structure learning experiences that both help students write their way into the university and help teachers learn their way into student cultures" (23). Shirley Brice Heath was speaking of much the same thing when she said in her book *Ways with Words,*

> Unless the boundaries between classrooms and communities can be broken and the flow of cultural patterns between them encouraged, the schools will continue to legitimate and reproduce communities of townspeople who control and limit the potential progress of other communities who themselves remain untouched by other values and ways of life. (369)

In short, what students can teach their teachers is the paramount lesson that a rhetorician has to learn: that of all the elements which play a part in the communication process, audience is the most important. Teachers are defined by their students. What do I mean by that curious statement? Well, there are a number of ways in which it is true to say that students define their teachers. For instance, the successes of our students help to validate us as teachers. It is common for people to say of someone who has achieved some honor. "She was a student of so-and-so." That so-and-so teacher not only basks in the glory of that student but acquires a special kind of certification as a teacher.

But teachers are defined also by their ordinary students and by their remedial students. If we remain sensitive to the aspirations that our students entertain, to the stock of knowledge that they command, and to the cognitive skills that they possess, we will be disposed to make those adjustments in our teaching necessary to accommodate their expectations and their capacities. If we don't remain sensitive to the particular population of students that we have in the classroom in a particular semester, we will make unrealistic assignments, we will season our lectures with a sprinkling of jargon, and we will probably make a lot of wounding comments about our students' responses and performances.

What kinds of teachers are we? Our students can define us from the way we manifest ourselves in a particular class of a particular year. It is too bad that we can't eavesdrop on our students when they define us for other students outside the classroom. Hearing some of those definitions might help us to amend our ways. If we don't reach them, if we don't inspirit them, if we don't edify them, all our crudition, all our degrees, all our honors go for naught. We have to observe them, to listen to them, to intuit them. Remember what Patrick Dias said: "It is the students who teach us about teaching." If we keep our antennae tuned to their frequency, we can learn much from them that could convert us from being merely competent teachers to being great teachers. That's what mellowing is: the process whereby ordinariness matures into brilliance. Ripeness is all.

Recently I saw the movie *Dead Poets Society,* in which Robin Williams plays the part of a teacher of English in a New England prep school who uses some very unorthodox methods of teaching. In one scene, he jumps up on his desk in the classroom and asks the students. "Why am I standing up here?" When one of the students answers, "Because you want to be taller," Williams responds that he is standing on his desk not because he wants to be taller but because he wants to get a new perspective on the classroom and on his students. Then he jumps down from the desk and invites all of his students to jump up on the desk in turn and from that perch take a fresh look at the classroom and at their fellow students. Maybe the secret of maximizing the lessons that teachers can learn from students and the lessons that students can learn from teachers is for both parties to change perspectives on each other occasionally so that they can put themselves in a receptive disposition for learning and can become, to use the wonderful tautology. mutual friends.

Teaching Writing: The Major Theories

Anne Ruggles Gere

When the editors of this Yearbook asked me to write a chapter on current models of composition pedagogy, an image came immediately to mind. I would portray the dominant model as King Kong standing on the Empire State Building. Like the beast who swats biplanes away as if they were flies, this model remains impervious to the challenges of other approaches, dispatching them with the brutish power born of preeminence. Or so I thought before I began looking more closely at discussions of what goes on in the majority of composition classes today. First there was the problem of what to call this dominant model. In discussions of research, classes employing experimental procedures are usually contrasted with the "traditional" class, and names for these traditional classes include "formalist," "discipline- centered," and "current-traditional."

Each of these names has a slightly different origin and meaning. The formalist approach was described by Richard Fulkerson, who, moved by Charles Silberman's description of mindlessness in education,[1] considered how to address composition instructors who "either fail to have a consistent value theory or fail to let that philosophy shape pedagogy [and who are] in Silberman's terms ... guilty of mindlessness."[2] As might be expected of one trained in English studies, Fulkerson turned to literary theory for a model and settled upon M.H. Abrams's four theories of literature,[3] claiming that "since the elements in an artistic transaction are the same as those in any communication, it seemed that Abrams's four theories might also be relevant to a composition."[4] Fulkerson shifts Abrams's "objective" criticism to a "formalist" approach. According to Fulkerson's definition, this approach emphasizes certain internal forms, the most commonly valued form being grammar. For the formalist,

> good writing is "correct" writing at the sentence level. In the classroom, one studies errors of form--in order to avoid them. But forms other than grammatical can also be the teacher's key values. I have heard of metaphorical formalists, sentence-length formalists, and topic-sentence formalists, to name a few.[5]

Fulkerson names two major figures in composition (Francis Christensen and E.D. Hirsch) who exemplify the formalist position. Fulkerson offers no evaluation of formalists' effectiveness, but I argue that they take an extremely narrow view of writing. While correctness or at least adherence to conventions makes writing accessible to readers, a model that looks only at this dimension cannot help students see language as a means of communicating with others or as a source of delight.

William Woods takes a slightly broader view as he places composition pedagogy within the context of educational theory. As Woods sees it, two general pedagogical theories--one student- centered and one discipline-centered-have dominated American education since the nineteenth century. Woods claims that discipline-centered teaching accounts for more of the composition curriculum, and he divides this discipline-centered approach into three subcategories emphasizing rhetoric, logic, and language. This leads to a description of three discipline-centered composition pedagogies, one of which is the "discipline-centered/language-based" approach. As Woods describes it, the "discipline-centered/language-based" model

> gives rise to style books, manuals, handbooks and workbooks concerned with grammar, syntax, diction, usage, and style. Two extensions of this theory are the "educational technology" approach, which tends to produce autoinstructional texts, and the approach to teaching writing through various uses of exemplary prose passages.[6]

Woods arrives at this and his other descriptions of discipline-centered and student-centered teaching as a way of describing composition textbooks. According to Woods, each text represents a certain approach to the teaching of writing, and one of the instructor's tasks is to decide which one appeals and choose a text that fits the approach.

The term "current-traditional paradigm" was coined by Richard Young to describe what he saw as a tacit theory dominating composition pedagogy for most of the twentieth century. Borrowing his term from what Daniel Fogarty calls "current-traditional rhetoric."[7] Young described the features of the current-traditional paradigm as

> emphasis on the composed product rather than the composing process; the analysis of discourse into words, sentences, and paragraphs; the classification of discourse into description, narration, exposition, and argument; the strong concern with usage (syntax, spelling, punctuation) and with style (economy, clarity, emphasis); and preoccupation with the informal essay and the research paper.[8]

Although he draws on Thomas Kuhn for the "paradigm" concept, the name for and substance of Young's description derive from the features Daniel Fogarty ascribes to current-traditional rhetoric. Fogarty distinguishes between "a teaching rhetoric and the philosophy of rhetoric" in Aristotle's work.[9] The philosophy includes thought-thing-word relationships, abstraction, definition, logic, and dialectic, while the teaching rhetoric is exemplified in Aristotle's *Rhetoric*. In Fogarty's view, current-traditional rhetoric is essentially Aristotelian, but "time and expediency" have added elements of grammar, syntax, spelling, punctuation, and mechanics; modes of discourse; qualities of style; communication; divisions of words, sentences, and paragraphs; and specialized forms.[10] Fogarty goes on to note that students of Aristotle's day could have easily integrated philosophical concerns with their study of rhetoric, yet "today it is not only quite possible, but quite likely, that the average college student may never make the connection between his philosophy and his composition."[11]

Young does not address the distinction between philosophical and teaching rhetorics, but he identifies as a problem the lack of attention to invention in the teaching rhetoric. For Young, both the delineation of the problem and its solution lie in paradigmatic terms, and he devotes considerable energy to demonstrating the applicability of the paradigm concept to composition or, as Fogarty calls it, the teaching rhetoric.

James Berlin appends the term "positivist" to "current-traditional," arguing that the epistemological basis for the current-traditional model is positivistic because it assumes that writing should assume an uncomplicated correspondence of the faculties and the world in order to "provide the language which corresponds either to the objects in the external world or to the ideas in his or her own mind--both are essentially the same--in such a way that it reproduces the objects and the experience of them in the minds of the heaters."[12] According to Berlin, the current-traditional model "demands that the audience be as `objective' as the writer; both shed personal and social concerns in the interests of the unobstructed perception of empirical reality."[13] Further, he states that "in current-traditional rhetoric the writer must focus on experience in a way that makes possible the discovery of certain kinds of information--the empirical and rational--and the neglect of others--psychological and social concerns."[14]

These different origins--literary theory versus rhetorical history/philosophy of science versus educational theory versus intellectual history--for describing "formalist," "discipline-centered/language-based," and "current-traditional" demonstrate the difficulty of seeing the currently dominant model as a monolith. Satisfyingly dramatic as it is, the King Kong image does not work because the current model is more complex than this colossus suggests.

Closer examination of the definitions offered by Fulkerson, Woods, Young, and Berlin illustrates some of the complexities inherent in the current approach. Fulkerson can be commended for insisting that composition avoid the "value-mode confusion"[15] that results for both instruction and evaluation when instructors fail to think carefully about what they value in composition. And we can thank Fulkerson for recognizing the need to articulate values that have remained inchoate, but his method for solving the problem creates further value conflicts. Rather than looking directly at composition instruction to determine its nature and values, Fulkerson imports literary theory to describe four postures. The awkwardness of this borrowing is evident in the extent to which Fulkerson redefines and renames Abrams's terminology. Abrams's "mimetic" does not mean that "a clear connection exists between good writing and good thinking."[16] and the translation of Abrams's "pragmatic" and "objective" to Fulkerson's "rhetorical" and "formalist" obscures more than it reveals.

Part of the problem with Fulkerson's terminology resides in its sources because terms borrowed from literary criticism fail to capture the essence of composition instruction. The limited definition Fulkerson assigns to formalism bespeaks, however, a greater problem. By concentrating exclusively on issues of form, Fulkerson omits concern with what produces the forms, thereby removing any possibility of connecting this model of instruction with a philosophy of rhetoric.

William Woods has a much less ambitious goal than Young or Fulkerson in that he considers only text selection rather than larger instructional questions. His attempt to connect composition instruction with educational trends such as "life adjustment theory," "academic reform," and the counterrevolution of the Dartmouth Conference suggests the importance of looking, at composition instruction in larger terms, but Wood's analysis does not extend far enough into history. He claims, for example, that "college teaching of writing in America had its official baptism in 1949, when the NCTE founded the Conference on College Composition and Communication."[17] Nor does he explore the educational movements fully enough to demonstrate their philosophical roots.

To the extent that he draws on Fogarty's discussion of rhetorical history, Young offers a useful perspective on current-traditional composition pedagogy, but his attempt to place composition instruction within the scientific tradition is problematical. As Robert Connors has explained so well,[18] there is serious question about the applicability of the paradigm concept to composition, and Young, like others in composition, may have been unduly attracted to the glitter of science. The more serious problem with Young's approach is that it ignores the division between philosophy and composition. Even though he borrows Fogarty's "current-traditional" term, Young fails to develop the philosophy-composition division that Fogarty delineates. In turning to the philosophy of science, Young compounds this neglect.

James Berlin comes closest to making a connection between philosophy and composition pedagogy because he searches for the rhetorical theory underlying the model. In beginning this research Berlin notes that conceptions of writers, reality, audience. and language all contribute to the definition of a model: "To teach writing is to argue for a version of reality, and the best way of knowing and communicating it."[19] As he continues, however, Berlin moves to an advocacy position, claiming superiority for what he calls new rhetoricians, and his argument veers in the direction of intellectual history.

What Fulkerson, Woods, Young, and Berlin share, then, is a failure to connect what Fogarty terms the teaching rhetoric with a philosophy. This is not a problem unique to these four theorists; it has been the continuing problem of composition pedagogy. Because the teaching rhetoric has remained separate from a philosophy of rhetoric, it has been vulnerable to the ravages of "time and expediency."[20] The dominance of mechanical features (syntax, spelling, modes, style, and punctuation) in today's instruction derives from the lack of a coherent philosophy guiding composition pedagogy. When a discipline lacks a coherent philosophy, it can be shaped by the most anti- intellectual forces, and this is precisely what has happened to composition pedagogy over the years.

At the college level, composition instruction began with the introduction of a prescribed full-year freshman course and a half-year sophomore course at Harvard in 1874. These courses, like their predecessors, were stimulated by President Charles Eliot, who at his inaugural in 1869 lamented "the prevailing neglect of the systematic study of the English language"[21] and sought every opportunity to redress this neglect. Francis James Child. Harvard's Boylston Professor of Rhetoric and Oratory when composition courses were first introduced, could have played a major role in articulating the philosophy of these courses, but he did not. Rather, Child resented the composition courses he was asked to teach and devoted his energies to finding a way to escape them. Child's real interest was English literature, and he became this nation's first professor of English in 1874. Child's successor, Adams Sherman Hill, likewise did little to unite the teaching of writing with a philosophy of rhetoric, but he did succeed in building a composition program in the face of significant faculty resistance.

In the 1870s Latin and Greek were the dominant languages on college campuses, and Harvard's faculty, like faculties everywhere, was resistant to English studies. Hill was successful in overcoming this resistance and in instituting a required freshman composition course, English A, in 1885. Hill's influence extended beyond Harvard through his textbooks. The most popular of these, *The Principles of Rhetoric and Their Application,* was published in 1878 and was still in use in the 1930s. This text demonstrates the schism between the teaching rhetoric and a philosophy of rhetoric. Hill's text substituted manner for originality of matter. He borrowed directly from the Scottish rhetoricians Blair, Campbell, and Whateley, simply putting their ideas in more accessible form. While his material was not original and therefore did not profit from new philosophical insights, Hill adopted a dogmatic tone that contributed to the popularity of his text. Pronouncements such as "From the point of view of clearness, it is always better to repeat a noun than to substitute for it a pronoun which fails to suggest that noun"[22] admit no ambiguity and reassure uncertain students and instructors.

Hill's dogmatic tone may have increased the popularity of his text, but it did little to unite philosophy with composition pedagogy. In fact, it worked in the opposite direction. Until very recently teachers of composition at all levels have received no formal training. College composition instructors may have themselves taken a freshman English course, but they had no direct instruction in composition pedagogy, and the same has been true for secondary and elementary school teachers. For example, in 1952 Harold Allen could find only five graduate-level courses on composition in this country, and not all of the five were offered regularly.[23] What composition teachers learned, therefore, came through what I have called the informal curriculum.[24] This informal curriculum, a combination of self-sponsored reading, orientation meetings, and conversations with other instructors, depended heavily upon textbooks. Hill therefore influenced composition pedagogy much more substantially than would have been the case if composition pedagogy had developed its own philosophical and intellectual foundations. Instead, composition instructors, pressured by "time and expediency," clung gratefully to pronouncements about usage and emphasized these in their classes because they discouraged student questions, making teaching easier.

Hill's text was not alone in allowing "time and expediency" to create the current-traditional model of composition pedagogy. There was, in addition, the ongoing resistance of Harvard faculty. When English A became a required course in 1885, the rest of the Harvard curriculum was adopting the German university model of electives, so the one required course stood out. Further, college enrollments expanded over 60 percent during the 1890s, so this requirement directed a high proportion of Harvard's resources toward composition instruction. Predictably, this allocation of resources disgruntled faculty and administrators, leading Harvard's Board of Overseers, in 1891, to appoint a committee to investigate English A.

This committee, composed of three people from c 'de the academic community, issued the first of three "Harvard Reports." This report proposed a simple solution to college composition: It should be taught by high schools. The report stated:

> It is obviously absurd that the College--the institution of higher education--should be called upon to turn aside from its proper functions and devote its means and the time of its instructors to the task of imparting elementary instruction which would be given even in ordinary grammar schools, much more in those higher academic institutions intended to prepare select youth for a university course.[25]

The committee went on to recommend that admission requirements be raised to eliminate students underprepared in composition and to suggest that if schools did not devote more time to teaching writing, they could not expect their students to be accepted at Harvard. While this report may have helped solve Harvard's immediate problems, it had a negative long-term effect on composition instruction in this country.

Harvard's prestige led many other colleges to follow the recommendations of this and the other Harvard Reports. Not only did colleges emulate the position that they should have little responsibility for composition instruction; they also accepted the Committee's narrow definition of writing. This definition was characterized by statements such as it is "little less than absurd to suggest that any human being who can be taught to talk cannot likewise be taught to compose. Writing is merely the habit of talking with the pen instead of with the tongue."[26] This narrow view also emphasizes mechanical correctness in writing above all else. The 1892 report contains many negative comments about students' poor usage and gives special attention to neatness and handwriting. Because composition instructors had no coherent philosophy against which to evaluate such statements, these limited views gained currency and shaped ensuing instruction.

Since a narrow view of writing dominated college composition pedagogy and fostered the development and maintenance of the current-traditional model, it is not surprising that composition pedagogy in secondary and elementary schools followed the same direction. Secondary schools took seriously Harvard's warning that they must prepare students to write mechanically correct papers. Texts used in secondary schools mirrored Hill's *Principles of Rhetoric* in their emphasis on dogmatic statements about correctness, and common school teachers, like their college counterparts, relied on the informal curriculum of texts for their training in the teaching of writing. The nagging Miss Fidditch commonly described as hounding composition classes with details of mechanical correctness can trace her ancestry to the Harvard Reports.

The colossus of current-traditional instruction developed, then, not out of a clearly articulated philosophical tradition but in the absence of same. A convergence administrative, demographic, and prestige concerns created the climate in which composition instructors turned their attention to issues of form, style, and correctness. The aphilosophical emergence of the current-traditional model has been matched by an equally aphilosophical maintenance of it. The extent to which other models have and have not been allowed to coexist or have been partially included by the current-traditional model has resulted from aphilosophical concerns.

One of the earliest challenges to current-traditional instruction emerged in the 1890s. Fred Newton Scott, professor of rhetoric at the University of Michigan from 1889 to 1927, attempted to develop a philosophy of composition pedagogy by drawing on linguistics, psychology, and sociology as well as rhetoric.[27] In trying to foster a fuller conception of rhetoric, one that gave it intellectual breadth as well as social importance, Scott portrayed writing in terms of function rather than mere correctness. According to one of his students, Scott saw correctness as necessary but not the chief purpose of writing. Rather, he "looked on words as a cabinet maker looks on his tools--things that just must be right and unabused throughout or the work will be bad."[28] Although Scott had some brief successes during the reform period of the 1890s, Kitzhaber explains that "most of his ideas were too new, his recommendations for change too fundamental to be generally accepted. Rhetorical instruction fell in behind the Harvard group instead."[29] According to Kitzhaber, composition pedagogy in this country "until well into the 1930s became, for all practical purposes, little more than instruction in grammar and the mechanics of writing, motivated almost solely by the ideal of superficial correctness."[30] The reform movement of the 1890s was followed by a conservative, science-oriented shift in the early decades of this century, and Scott's model could not flourish in this hostile climate.

Had Scott's challenge been successful, the current-traditional colossus might never have reached its current status. Lacking an intellectual base, the current-traditional model fed on Harvard's prestige and grew out of proportion to other models. Scott's work did, however, provide the basis from which models of future generations developed. The contemporary model that owes most to Scott's work has been variously termed "rhetorical" (by Fulkerson), "discipline-centered-rhetoric-based" (by Woods), and neo-Aristotelian or classicist (by Berlin). Richard Young's whole paradigmatic critique of the current-traditional approach derives from his concept of rhetoric, both classical and modern, as including invention as one of its central parts.

Fulkerson describes the rhetorical approach as claiming that "good writing is writing adapted to achieve the desired effect on the desired audience. If the same verbal construct is directed to a different audience, then it may have to be evaluated differently."[31] For Woods the discipline-centered-rhetoric-based approach manifests itself in texts that "reproduce the features of classical rhetoric ... [that offer] a fully developed alternative to classical theory."[32] Berlin explains neo-Aristotelian as "primarily concerned with the provision of inventional devices"[33] and notes that few textbooks adhere closely to this model. Young describes the desired rhetoric as one that "begins with the perception of a social problem and ends with changes in an audience's beliefs and behaviors."[34] Throughout Scott's work, three dimensions--communicator, audience, and language--receive continuing attention, and this emphasis laid the foundation for the contemporary rhetorical model of composition pedagogy. Scott even placed mechanical correctness in a rhetorical context in his textbook: "Presented as a means of meeting definite social needs more or less effectively, of winning attention and consideration, the various devices of grammar and rhetoric make an appeal to self-interest which pupils can understand."[35] Scott's attempt to reconnect the teaching rhetoric with a philosophy of rhetoric failed to succeed because it competed with an aphilosophical and mechanical model in a period when the growing dominance of science reinforced mechanics over philosophy.

Another factor contributing to the eclipse of Scott's model was the separation of rhetoric from English departments, a separation to which Scott himself contributed. Scott sought to create a separate department of rhetoric at the University of Michigan, and in 1903 he succeeded. This move was emulated on many campuses during the next few decades, and in 1914 these shifts were institutionalized by the formation of the Speech Association of America. The majority of these new departments of rhetoric were motivated by the resentments of rhetoricians who felt snubbed and/or overpowered by their colleagues in literature.

Composition pedagogy remained in English departments, isolated from the classical rhetoric that could give it intellectual depth. This separation not only impoverished the philosophical basis of composition pedagogy, but it also contributed to major distinctions between speaking and writing. Composition pedagogy and rhetoric remained distant from one another until the early 1960s.

Writing instruction in the common schools followed a similar pattern. Texts emphasized mechanical correctness, and all but a few exceptional teachers proffered formulaic advice about topic sentences and five-paragraph themes to their students. Compounding philosophical limitations were time constraints which sandwiched writing instruction into a curriculum crowded with language and literature studies. As recently as 1968, a study of exemplary English programs revealed that only 15.7 percent of class time was spent on writing instruction, and most of that was devoted to correcting completed papers.[36] The teaching of writing in secondary schools shared with college classes the liabilities of separating philosophical and teaching rhetorics.

Rhetoric reentered college English departments during the 1940s via the literary criticism developed at the University of Chicago by Richard S. Crane and Richard McKeon. Subsequent to this reentry, a philosophical rhetoric began to exert influence on composition pedagogy. One of the first manifestations of this influence appeared in 1957 in Richard Weaver's textbook, *Composition*, which brought classical rhetoric's enthymeme and topics to the teaching of writing.[37]

This text was followed in 1962 by *Rhetoric: Principles and Usage*. Authors Albert P. Duhamel and Richard E. Hughes made their intentions explicit by stating: "Perhaps the most significant difference between our book and those currently used in composition and rhetoric courses is our attempt to introduce the art of rhetoric as a systematic body of knowledge."[38] Accompanying this text and Edward P.J. Corbett's *Classical Rhetoric for the Modern Student*, which followed in 1965,[39] was a growing intellectual ferment among a small number of composition instructors. The Rhetoric Society of America was founded in 1968 by directors including Edward P.J. Corbett, Wayne Booth, William Irmscher, Ross Winterowd, Richard Larson, Robert Gorrell, Richard Hughes, Harry Crosby, and Owen Thomas. For these individuals and their peers, the reintegration of classical rhetoric and composition pedagogy offered a successful challenge to the current-traditional model.

One offshoot of the revival of classical rhetoric was the development of a modern rhetoric of composition pedagogy. The most notable example appears in the tagmemic theory of Kenneth Pike and his associates. *Rhetoric: Discovery and Change*, the text Pike wrote with Alton Becker and Richard Young,[40] demonstrates how tagmemic linguistics can be used with effect in composition classes. Although the nine-cell matrix of particle, wave, and field combined with contrast, distribution, and variation of tagmemics draws on modern physics, it owes a great deal to Aristotle's topics.

For the majority of composition instructors, however, this reintegration and the resulting scholarship made little difference, and the current-traditional colossus continued its dominance. This lack of effect derived, in large measure, from the training of these composition instructors. The educational expansion of the 1960s gave way to constriction in the 1970s, and secondary and elementary teachers trained in the 1960s were the last group hired in significant numbers. The innovative programs and courses in rhetoric introduced by people such as members of the Rhetoric Society of America had little influence on a stable and aging population of teachers. Courses in the teaching of writing instituted in the past decade have produced college composition instructors who make the intellectual traditions of rhetoric and composition available to future generations of instructors, but the paucity of teaching positions at all levels prevents rapid adoption of this model.

Because training in the rhetorical model has been unavailable to the majority of composition instructors in this country, the informal curriculum has continued to serve as the dominant means of transmitting composition pedagogy. This means that textbooks continue to educate most writing instructors. The small number of textbooks representing the rhetorical tradition and their marginal commercial success demonstrate the relatively small impact of this approach. A second edition of *Rhetoric: Principles and Usage* was issued in 1967, and the book was out of print ten years later. A text such as *Classical Rhetoric for the Modern Student* remains in print, not because it is widely used by composition instructors, but because it is used in courses for graduate students in composition and rhetoric. The rhetorical model of composition pedagogy is not one easily adopted by instructors relying entirely on their own resources. To be effectively assimilated, it requires grounding in an intellectual tradition, something not available in the informal curriculum.

In his discussion of forms of invention, Richard Young separates the tagmemic approach from the rhetorical, explaining:

> classical invention is concerned with finding arguments likely to induce psychological changes in the audience; prewriting, on the other hand, is concerned with the discovery of ordering principles and with changes in the writer. Tagmemic invention is concerned with both. It conceives of invention as essentially a problem-solving activity, the problems being of two sorts: those arising in one's own experience of the world and those arising out of a need to change others.[41]

To make this claim, Young minimizes the ethos of classical rhetoric and emphasizes the individual's experience in tagmemic invention. He also creates two other categories of invention: dramatistic (based on Kenneth Burke's work) and prewriting (to be discussed below). As long as these four--rhetorical, tagmemic, prewriting, and dramatistic--are described as systems of invention, there is no problem, but they are frequently extended to delineate models of composition pedagogy. David Harrington et al., for example, discuss composition texts in terms of Young's four categories, and this discussion waivers between emphasis on invention and immersion in a whole model.[42] For example, in the discussion of texts that adapt principles of classical rhetoric to the teaching of writing, Harrington et al. Include not only works such as those by Duhamel and Corbett, but also books "that adapt principles of classical rhetoric for the teaching of writing."[43] This adaptation includes everything from overviews of principles of invention to a book in which "invention survives, lurking in a chapter on `Development'."[44]

The range of Harrington's inclusions suggests the confusion that results when approaches to invention are substituted for pedagogical models, and this confusion has contributed to the maintenance of the current-traditional model. As Harrington et al. describe it, for example, some texts have adapted principles of classical rhetoric to devices for paragraph and essay development.[45] The focus on paragraph and essay signals a concern with form, an issue much more important to the current-traditional model than to classical rhetoric.

Prewriting, another of Young's categories of invention, has likewise been appropriated by the current-traditional model. As originally described by D. Gordon Rohman,[46] prewriting uses journal writing, meditation, and metaphorical thinking to stimulate writing. The logical pedagogical model for prewriting is the expressivist approach. As Fulkerson describes it, expressivists emphasize the writer and cover a wide range. "from totally accepting and nondirective teachers, some of whom insist that one neither can nor should evaluate writing, to much more directive, experiential teachers who design classroom activities to maximize student self-discovery."[47] Further, expressivists "value writing that is about personal subjects ... [and] desire to have writing contain an interesting, credible, honest, and personal voice."[48]

The most obvious source of the expressivist model is the Dartmouth Conference of 1966. This meeting of American and British educators on the teaching of English brought new theories to this country. As Arthur Applebee puts it, "What the British offered the Americans was a model for English instruction which focussed not on the `demands' of the discipline but on the personal and linguistic growth of the child."[49] The American educators present at this conference were profoundly affected, and their consequent activity helped shape the expressive model of composition pedagogy.

William Woods places the expressivist approach in his "student-directed" category and explains it in terms of a "maturationist" theory of development:

> [H]umankind has in it the seeds of its perfection, which will flower if allowed to grow naturally, uninhibited and unharmed by social or environmental constraints. ... [A]ll aspects of the communication triangle are treated as extensions of the writer's experience. ... Teaching methods guided by this theory encourage such activities as observing, recording, expressing, listening, and reacting.[50]

As this description makes clear, the roots of the expressivist model of composition pedagogy extend past the Dartmouth Conference to the progressive education movement during the first decades of this century. John Dewey, generally credited with giving voice to what became known as the progressive movement, emphasized the learner's experience, interest, and motivation and encouraged teaching that centered on the student rather than on the discipline. Dewey's views influenced many teachers, but the groups shaping the English curriculum, groups such as the Committee of Ten (established in 1892) and the National Conference on Uniform Entrance Requirements in English (active at the turn of the century), operated from the current-traditional model.

The Dartmouth Conference, then, gave new vigor to a progressive movement that had lain dormant for several decades, and it targeted the insights of the progressives toward English instruction specifically. When seen from this perspective, the expressive approach is less tied to the 1960s and is more directly related to larger currents in education. Because the expressive approach has not always been identified with a major educational and intellectual tradition (and sometimes even when it has), it has been subject to appropriation by the current-traditional approach.

One of the terms most commonly appropriated from the expressivist approach is "prewriting." As originally conceived, prewriting denoted methods of enabling writers to explore their own minds. When appropriated by current-traditionalists, however, prewriting has come to mean any activity that occurs at the beginning stages of writing. Accordingly, many current-traditional textbooks include sections on prewriting, but what these sections contain has nothing in common with prewriting as described by expressivists. For example, one text describes prewriting as asking students to make a list of topics they intend to include in their writing. This activity, much closer to outlining than to the kind of exploration described by Rohman, demonstrates the confusions that can result when a practice of one approach is appropriated by practitioners of another approach.

These three approaches--current-traditional, rhetorical, and expressivist--are categories on which theorists such as Young, Woods, Fulkerson, and Berlin agree. There is, however, a fourth category which nearly every theorist expresses differently. Fulkerson borrows Abrams's term "mimetic" to describe instruction that emphasizes correspondence with reality. According to Fulkerson, one manifestation of this approach "says that a clear connection exists between good writing and good thinking. The major problem with student writing is that it is not solidly thought out."[51] The pedagogical solution to this problem is to emphasize the teaching of reasoning and logic as a basis for good writing. Another manifestation of the mimetic approach as Fulkerson describes it is to assume that students do not write well because they do not know enough. Mimetic solutions to this problem include (a) encouragement of more research during the early stages of writing, (b) emphasis on discovery procedures, (c) having students read authors who take different perspectives on the same topic. The result will be writing that is closer to the "real situation."

William Woods's discipline-centered-logic-based approach has much in common with Fulkerson's mimetic category. The emphasis as Woods describes it is on "the art of straight thinking."[52] Texts in this category emphasize the "reciprocal or 'dialectical' relationship between thought and language, the ways in which thought travels back and forth moving from observation to classification, and from generalization back again to specification, in the process of developing and sequencing ideas."[53] Woods explains that texts following the logic-based approach rarely give much space to audiences for writing or to processes of writing, but they focus considerable attention on the dialogue between language and thought in writing.

James Berlin assigns the term "New Rhetoricians" to his version of this fourth category, explaining that it presumes that "knowledge is not simply a static entity available for retrieval. Truth is dynamic and dialectical, the result of a process involving the interaction of opposing elements. It is a relation that is created, not pre-existent and waiting to be discovered."[54] In this view, then, writing aids discovery because writers use language to converse with themselves and thereby discover new ideas. Berlin shares Wood's view that Ann Berthoff's *Forming/Thinking/Writing*[55] exemplifies the New Rhetoricians' approach, but he puts the Young, Becker, and Pike text in the same category. And he argues that audience plays a significant role in the New Rhetoricians' approach. The roots of this fourth approach--New Rhetoricians', mimetic, or logic-based--lie in logic, and the paucity of texts in this category suggests the limited number of instructors who use it. Of the major theories of composition instruction, the New Rhetoricians' logic-based approach is the least widely employed. Perhaps this is because the long-standing split between philosophical and teaching rhetorics has reduced logic's accessibility to composition instructors.

Throughout this discussion I have avoided describing "the writing process" as a model of composition pedagogy. The term "writing process," derived from descriptions of what writers do as opposed to the written products they produce, does not describe a model so much as a way of proceeding within that model. Elements of the writing process, whether they are called prewriting, drafting, and revising or incubating, writing, and reworking, can be adapted to any model discussed here. Indeed, many currently available textbooks graft writing process terminology onto current-traditional, rhetorical, and expressive models.

This grafting has the benefit of reducing emphasis on products in writing, but it also exemplifies one of the problems with current models of composition pedagogy. As the preceding discussion has shown, there is little agreement about the terminology for or exact shape of any of these models. These models can and have been stretched almost beyond recognition because of the continuing separation of the teaching rhetoric from a philosophy of rhetoric. While articulating the shape of models helps reduce vulnerability to the charge of mindlessness, the fact of articulating does not develop a philosophy.

Likewise, attempts to circumvent the issue by drawing on the theoretical foundations of another discipline will only confuse the issue. Richard Young's use of science's "paradigm," for example, finally confounds more than it helps because this term cannot be used accurately with reference to composition studies. Moreover, using such borrowed terminology weakens the models to which it is being applied. Fitting a borrowed term onto an aphilosophical model involves two translations, one from the borrowed field to composition, and a second within the model itself. Just as translations of translations (the King James Bible from the Latin Vulgate, for example) lose accuracy, so models of composition pedagogy lose their integrity when philosophies of another discipline are applied.

When models lose their integrity, they develop fissures into which foreign organisms intrude, and this explaining why it has been so easy for each of the models discussed to borrow from one another and why it is so difficult to find a textbook that adheres to one model exclusively. Another result of operating with aphilosophical models is that arguments about central questions become clouded by extraneous issues. Among the questions facing composition pedagogy recently have been those of grammar instruction, Black English, and remedial studies. Each of these has been dominated by issues of time and expediency because the philosophical basis of existing models remains uncertain.

Grammar instruction, for example, has been dismissed by many theorists and researchers as useless for improving the quality of writing,[56] but it has remained prominent in composition pedagogy, particularly in the current-traditional model. And there are those who take the position that grammar instruction actually does lead to improved writing. What has been lost in this debate is attention to the relationship between language and reality, to ways of knowing the world. Instead, issues of time (teaching grammar is or is not a waste of time) and expediency (grammar instruction does or does not produce better writing) have been argued.

Discussions of Black English have occupied considerable energy in composition pedagogy, and these discussions have likewise strayed from central questions of what constitutes knowledge and the relationship of thought to language. The Black English debate stems from the pragmatic issue of how composition instructors should treat nonstandard dialects. Linguists such as William Labov have demonstrated that nonstandard dialects such as Black English follow a definite grammar of their own. Those who use Black English, therefore, are not erratic or illogical; they simply follow a different system than do users of the standard dialect. An ensuing debate among composition instructors has wrestled with how to respond to nonstandard dialects.

Some people argue that children's concepts of reality are tied to their home dialects and that teachers, especially teachers of composition, need to acknowledge the importance of such dialects. This view is elaborated in a publication of the Conference on College Composition, *Students' Right to Their Own Language.57* Opponents, however, argue that students who use Black English will not be able to succeed in a world that assigns negative connotations to dialects other than standard English.

Likewise, following the model of the Harvard Reports, definition of and response to remedial studies have been shaped almost entirely by questions of time and expediency rather than by philosophical considerations of how students might best arrive at knowledge. Economic incentives, more than philosophical considerations, govern schools' policies. Open admissions programs of colleges in the 1960s resulted from an expanding economy and led to expanded remedial programs, particularly in writing. Secondary schools emulated this expansion by introducing elective programs in writing, among other things. The economic constriction of the late 1970s and early 1980s led to a general shrinking in education and in writing courses particularly. Colleges began to define their missions more narrowly, excluding remedial instruction. Secondary schools likewise retreated from electives to the former pattern of combining composition with language and literature study.

This dominance of time and expediency in composition pedagogy will continue as long as models of instruction fail to have a philosophical basis. Developing such a basis does not require scrapping all current models; it simply means asking different questions about them. These questions should include issues such as thought-word-thing relationships, abstraction, definition, and logic. Put another way, when the teaching rhetoric and philosophy are united, the following questions will become central to each model:

1.   What relationship exists between language and reality?
2.   What relationship exists between thought and language?
3.   How does this model define "truth" or "knowledge"?What system of logic does this model employ to arrive at "truth"?

When such questions are asked and answered, models of composition pedagogy will become more unified and thereby more effective.

FOOTNOTES

1. Charles Silberman, *Crisis in the Classroom* (New York: Random House, 1970).
2. Richard Fulkerson. "Four Philosophies of Composition," *College Composition and Communication* 30 (December 1979): 347.
3. Meyer Howard Abrams, *The Mirror and the Lamp: Romantic Theory and the Critical Tradition* (New York: Oxford University Press, 1953).
4. Fulkerson. "Four Philosophies of Composition" p. 343.
5. Ibid., p. 344.
6. William F. Woods. "Composition Textbooks and Pedagogical Theory 1960-1980," *College English* 43 (April 1981): 396.
7. Daniel Fogarty, *Roots for a New Rhetoric* (New York: Russell and Russell, 1959), p. 118.
8. Richard Young, "Paradigms and Problems: Needed Research in Rhetorical Invention," in *Research on Composing: Points of Departure,* ed. Charles R. Cooper and Lee Odell (Urbana, Ill.: National Council of Teachers of English, 1978), p. 31.
9. Fogarty, *Roots for a New Rhetoric,* p. 117.
10. Ibid., p. 120.
11. Ibid., p. 122.
12. James Berlin, "Contemporary Composition: The Major Pedagogical Theories," *College English* 44 (December 1982): 770.
13. Ibid., p. 775.
14. Ibid., p. 775-76.
15. Fulkerson. "Four Philosophies of Composition." p. 347.
16. Ibid., p. 345.
17. Woods. "Composition Textbooks and Pedagogical Theory 1960-1980," p. 393.
18. Robert Connors. "Composition Studies and Science," *College English* 45 (January 1983): 1-20.
19. Berlin. "Contemporary Composition: The Major Pedagogical Theories," p. 766.
20. Fogarty. *Roots for a New Rhetoric.* p. 120.
21. Charles W. Eliot, *Educational Reform: Essays and Addresses* (New York: Century, 1898), p. 2.
22. Adam Sherman Hill, *The Principles of Rhetoric and Their Application* (New York: Harper, 1878), p. 84.
23. Harold Allen. "Preparing the Teachers of Composition and Communication--A Report," *College Composition and Communication* 3 (May 1952): 3-13.
24. Anne Ruggles Gere, "Teaching Writing Teachers," *College English* 47 (January 1985): 58-65.
25. *Reports of the Visiting Committees of the Board of Overseers of Harvard College* (Cambridge, Mass.: Harvard University Press, 1902), p. 119.
26. Ibid., p. 155.
27. Fred Newton Scott and Joseph Villiers Denney, *Elementary English Composition* (Boston: Allyn and Bacon, 1900).
28. Shirley Smith. "Fred Newton Scott as a Teacher," *Michigan Alumnus,* 1933, p. 279.
29. Albert Kitzhaber. "Rhetoric in American Colleges 1850-1900" (Doct. diss., University of Washington, 1953), p. 114.
30. Ibid., p. 120.
31. Fulkerson. "Four Philosophies of Composition," p. 346.
32. Woods. "Composition Textbooks and Pedagogical Theory 1960-1980," p. 396.
33. Berlin. "Contemporary Composition: The Major Pedagogical Theories," p. 769.
34. Young. "Paradigms and Problems," p. 42.
35. Scott and Denney, *Elementary English Composition,* p. iv.
36. James R. Squire and Roger Applebee, *High School English Instruction Today* (New York: Appleton, 1968), p. 42.
37. Richard M. Weaver, *Composition: A Course in Writing and Rhetoric* (New York: Holt, 1957).
38. Richard E. Hughes and Albert P. Duhamel, *Rhetoric: Principles and Usage* (Englewood Cliffs, N.J.: Prentice, 1962), p. v.
39. Edward P. Corbett, *Classical Rhetoric for the Modern Student* (New York, Oxford University Press, 1965).

40. Richard Young, Alton Becker, and Kenneth Pike, *Rhetoric: Discovery and Change* (New York: Harcourt, 1970)
41. Young. "Paradigms and Problems," p. 39.
42. David V. Harrington, Philip M. Keith, Charles W. Kneupper, Janice A. Tripp, and William F. Woods, "A Critical Survey of Resources for Teaching Rhetorical Invention," *College English* 40 (February 1979): 641-61.
43. Ibid., p. 643.
44. Ibid., p. 644.
45. Ibid.
46. D. Gordon Rohman, "Pre-Writing: The Stage of Discovery in the Writing Process," *College Composition and Communication* 16 (May 1965): 106-112a.
47. Ibid., p. 345.
48. Ibid., p. 345.
49. Arthur Applebee, *Tradition and Reform in the Teaching of English: A History* (Urbana, Ill.: National Council of Teachers of English, 1974), p. 229.
50. Woods. "Composition Textbooks and Pedagogical Theory 1960-1980," p. 397.
51. Fulkerson. "Four Philosophies of Composition," p. 345.
52. Woods. "Composition Textbooks and Pedagogical Theory 1960-1980," p. 396.
53. Ibid., p. 408.
54. Berlin, "Contemporary Composition," p. 774.
55. Ann Berthoff, *Forming/Thinking/Writing* (Montclair, N.J.: Boynton/Cook, 1978).
56. See, for example, Richard Braddock, Richard Lloyd- Jones, and Lowell Schoer, *Research in Written Composition* (Urbana, Ill.: National Council of Teachers of English, 1963).
57. "Students' Right to their Own Language," special issue of *College Composition and Communication,* Fall 1974.

Translating Theory into Practice in Teaching Composition: A Historical View and a Contemporary View

James L. Kinneavy

At the present time a debate which was particularly acute in antiquity has been revived--though with some significant variations, both in the content of the issue and in the motivations which occasion the dispute. The core controversy in the entire educational history of classical *paideia* occurred between 390 and 323 B.C. The argument moved back and forth from the Sophists, to Plato, next to Isocrates, back to Plato, and then to Aristotle. Historically, the decisive winner was Isocrates--but it will be interesting to unravel the layers of the debate over whether theory or practice and how much of each should govern the rhetorical schooling given the young Athenians (and later the entire Mediterranean world).

In many respects the same issue is being fought today in two different terrains. Within English departments, those knowledgeable in rhetorical theory and criticism suddenly find themselves in a position somewhat similar to the situation of new critics in the early forties--in possession of a new body of exciting knowledge and able to influence in a massive way the teaching of English in college and high school circles. How much of this new (and old) theory should be injected into classroom practice is a question being asked across the entire country. And in other areas, especially in existentialism, anthropology, and political theory, the question of theoretical versus practical knowledge is again being waged--and the roots of the debate are replanted from the seeds of the controversy of the fourth century B.C., because the sources of the existentialists and the It Marxists are Isocrates, Aristotle, and Cicero.

I would like to sketch in some detail this curious reincarnation and attempt to see its relevance to the typical English department of the 1980s. I will first outline the controversy in antiquity and then sketch the long classical tradition of education which it engendered. Finally, I will look at the current contest between *theoria and praxis* within and without the English departments.

The Polemic in Antiquity and the Classical Rhetorical Tradition

I have placed the classical debate in the fourth century B.C., but its roots extend back into the fifth with the invention of rhetorical prose by the Sophists. Sequential prose itself, particularly as practiced by historians and philosophers, was the result of a conscious revolt against the inability of poetry to perform these tasks. In the middle of

James L. Kinneavy. "Translating Theory into Practice: A Historical View and a Contemporary View," pp. 69-81 and notes on pp. 269-271, from *Essays on Classical Rhetoric and Modern Disclosure*, edited by Robert J. Connors, Lisa S. Ede, and Andrea A. Lunsford. © 1984 by the Board of Trustees of Southern Illinois University, reprinted by permission of the publisher.

the sixth century B.C., a number of philosophers (Anaximander of Miletus, Pherecydes of Syros. Anaximenes of Miletus) initiated the art of prose and advocated a simple unadorned prose.[1] Anaximander is also called by Bury the first writer of "scientific" prose.[2] Hecataeus, often called the father of history, and his successors, writing in the early half of the fifth century, maintained the same emphasis.

The Sophists of the fifth century, however, were not interested in factual reporting nor in philosophical speculation as such. They trained their students to succeed in law courts and in politics. Rhetoric was born in the courtrooms of Sicily and the assemblies of Greek city-states, and simple, unadorned prose is not the most effective weapon before juries or political assemblies. Consequently, the Sophists introduced into prose the poetic techniques of emotional appeal, of figures of speech, and of rhythmic and rhymic structures which the historians had earlier repudiated. This interesting move from poetry to metaphysics and history and thence to rhetoric has been brilliantly chronicled by Ernst Cassirer in his major works and summarized in his short masterpiece *An Essay on Man.*[3]

It is not inaccurate to represent the movement from philosophic and scientific prose to rhetorical prose as a move from *theoria to praxis,* for the Sophists generally did not accept the epistemological basis of *theoria,* a level of certainty in knowledge, and opted instead for a degree of probability as the best that man could attain in his political and legal activities. This, in fact, became the major issue in the fourth-century debate. Plato and the early Aristotle took over the philosophers' position in the full flowered debate that ensued and Isocrates and the late Aristotle took over the Sophists' position.

Plato: The Dominance of *Theoria*

Plato, following Parmenides, insisted on a certainty in his politics, his ethics, and his rhetoric (both in the earlier *Gorgias* and the later *Phaedrus);* in taking this position he was opposing the relativism and probabilities which the Sophists had advocated. In fact, Plato's epistemology dominated his entire corpus. The locus classicus of the Platonic position can be seen in the *Republic,* where Plato lines up the levels of certainty and probability. In the famous parable of the cave in *Republic* VI, 511D-E, Plato has listed science, thought, belief, and probability as the descending graded relations to truth. And those who live in the cave, chained, with their backs to the light of the fire and who see only shadows created by the light of the fire are those who live by belief and probability. The same hierarchy is outlined in several different places in Plato.

How is this epistemology carried over into Plato's pedagogy? The answer is clear in the *Phaedrus,* a late work in the Platonic corpus, but a work consistent with the middle period epistemology of the *Republic.* Plato still demeans those who live by belief and probability; in discourse such thinking results in rhetoric. A true rhetoric--which he does not see as yet existing--would strive for the certainties of science *(theoria),* the highest level of thinking outlined in the *Republic.* In effect, such a rhetoric would be equivalent to dialectic which would attain truth.

Plato's pedagogical technique in teaching this doctrine can be seen in the organization of the *phaedrus.* In that dialogue, Socrates and Phaedrus successively examine and discuss three speeche's, one by Lysias (allegedly) and two by Socrates. The principles of a Platonic rhetoric are systematically erected by a careful analysis of each of the speeches in turn (each speech, incidentally, representing a level of the epistemological ladder). This fundamentally inductive technique of deriving general principles by examining particular instances thus arrives at the Platonic theory of rhetoric. The truth must be known, the type of audience which is addressed must be known, the nature of the soul-types of the audience must be matched to the type of argument used, and so forth.

The capstone of the Platonic rhetorical system, however, was the notion of *kairos*, the concept of timeliness. Unlike the first component of his rhetorical system, the epistemological level of certainty, this second component of the *kairos*-doctrine, as it has been called, was accepted by most of the Sophists, most notably by Gorgias as well as by Isocrates, by Alcidamas, and by Aristotle.

Let us look at Plato's statement of the doctrine. It occurs close to the end of the dialogue in a section in which Socrates is explaining to Phaedrus how a "writer must go about the business if one intends to be as scientific a writer as possible." Having explained that different arguments must be used with different kinds of audiences, Socrates continues:

> Very well. When a student has attained an adequate grasp of these facts *intellectually*, he must go on to see with his own eyes that they occur in the world of affairs and are operative in *practice*, he must acquire the capacity to confirm their existence through the sharp use of his senses. If he does not do this, no part of the *theoretical* knowledge he acquired as a student is as yet of any help to him. But it is only when he can state adequately what sort of man is persuaded by what sort of speech, when he has the capacity to declare to himself with complete perception in the presence of another, that *here* is the man and *here* the nature that was discussed *theoretically* at school--*here, now, present* to him in *actuality*--to which he must apply this kind of speech in this sort of manner in order to obtain persuasion for this kind of activity--it is only when he can do all of this and when he has, in addition, grasped the concept of *property of time [kairos]*--when to speak and when to hold his tongue, and when to use and when not to use brachylogy, piteous language, hyperbole for horrific effect, and, in a word, each of the specific devices of discourse he may have studied--it is only *then*, and not *until then* that the finishing and perfecting touches will have been given to his science.[4] (my italics)

Unfortunately, this capstone of the Platonic rhetoric has never received the attention it deserves, possibly because it seems to be at variance with the general direction of Plato's thinking.[5] Indeed even in antiquity, no one seems to have analyzed the notion of *kairos* very carefully, as Dionysius of Halicarnassus remarked.[6] This is probably true, despite the fact that Gorgias built his entire system of thought from sense perception through ethics to aesthetics on *kairos* and despite the attention given the concept in medicine.

Summarily, if we were to attempt a graphic representation of Plato's pedagogy of rhetoric incorporating his epistemology, we might represent it as an inductive technique of arriving at theory, which theory is then applied to a given subject matter at the right time and to the right audience. The subject matter is known with a measure of certainty, arrived it by dialectic. The speech might have to be discussed and rewritten-- and the *Phaedrus* itself exemplifies this technique admirably.

I have attempted to incorporate these major facets in the first circle of the figure "Three classical pedagogies for teaching composition."

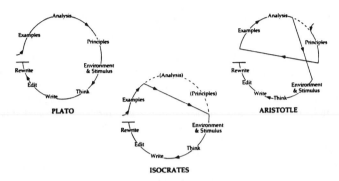

Figure 1 Three classical pedagogies for teaching composition

Isocrates: The Dominance of *Praxis*

On the issue of epistemology Isocrates directly opposed Plato. Like the Sophists, Isocrates was convinced that absolute rules of science, promising certainty, were not a human possibility. In speech after speech he inveighed against the type of theory and science represented by Parmenides and Plato. In particular he used the lessons of the contemporary political scene to warn Athenians against such an absolutism. Twenty-three years of war with Greek states fighting domination by Persia, twenty-seven years with other Greek states fighting Athenian domination, seventeen years of war with Athens and Thebes and other Greek states fighting Spartan domination, and seven years of opposition to Theban domination, with each dominating agency attempting to impose absolutes on the others, have taught Athenians a hard-earned lesson: some compromise was necessary. The issues were not pure falsehood versus pure truth. Opinion, conjecture, and belief were more practically reliable than absolutes, certainty, and science. In his speech to the Assembly "On the Peace" between Athens and her former allies against Persia (Sparta and Thebes), in 355 B.C., he repeatedly pointed to attempts on the part of one or the other of the allies to impose absolute standards on the rest and of the persistent failures of these moves. Early in the speech he told the Athenians that "they ought not to think that they have exact knowledge of what the result will be, but to be minded toward these contingencies as men who indeed exercise their best judgment, but are not sure what the future may hold in store."[7]

In a later speech, he generalizes to all knowledge:

> For since it is not in the nature of man to attain a science by the possession of which we can know positively what we should do or what we should say, in the next resort I hold that man to be wise who is able by his powers of conjecture to arrive generally at the best course, and I hold that man to be a philosopher who

occupies himself with the studies from which he will most quickly gain that kind of insight.[8]

When Isocrates applied his epistemology to rhetoric, some interesting corollaries followed. He adopted a trilogy common enough at the time and made it the fundamental structure of his pedagogy of teaching, a structure which has endured till our time. There are, he says, three factors which have to be taken into consideration in learning how to write: natural talent, theory, and practice. Of the three, he thinks that talent is by far the most important and that practice is of second importance; theory (or rules or study) is of third rank. This trilogy can be seen throughout the history of rhetoric. In Latin, it was referred to as *natura, studium, exercitatio.* Ben Jonson repeats the formula as a given, as do Sidney, Milton, and other Renaissance figures.[9]

His method of practice was to give the student a model of a specific kind of writing and have him imitate it, almost slavishly. The different kinds of writing were compared to the different kinds of gymnastic exercises. In practice, this double methodology (kinds of discourse and imitation) was embodied in the *progymnasmata,* the set of preparatory exercises which the student imitated in his training getting him ready to go into the college equivalent of the time, the *ephebia,* which nearly always was held in the city gymnasium, whence the name *progymnasmata.* The institution of the *ephebia* continued the rhetorical education of the young man and was the central educational experience of all of the city-states of the Mediterranean area for almost seven hundred years (from 300 B.C. to 400 A.D.). It was a required experience for the future citizen of the city-states (some 350 in the Mediterranean area), and the academic core of the experience was further intensive training in rhetoric taught by the Isocratean method.

Cicero and Quintilian refer to these exercises, and some of them have survived from later periods. The sequence was usually the following: fables, tales, edifying stories, proverbs expanded, refutations, confirmations, factual narratives, encomiums, comparisons, impersonations, descriptions, theses, legislations.[10]

The kinds of discourse emphasized in the *ephebia* itself were found in the types of speeches--political, legal, or ceremonial- -or in the issues embodied in the speeches--the matters of fact, or definition, or value. It was through these "kinds" of discourse, learned by an almost mechanical imitation, that most of the writers of western civilization in antiquity, the Middle Ages, and the Renaissance learned to write. Isocrates, in this sense, is the father of western humanism.[11]

The imitation method of Isocrates is graphically represented in the middle circle in the Figure. He exemplified his methodology in the *Antidosis,* using his own speeches for examples, and following them by discussions. We know that he advocated and practiced heavy editing and rewriting. But there was considerably less theory than in Plato, with the consequent dominance of practice. And *practice* in Isocrates meant both the epistemological level of probability (rather than certainty) and the pedagogical level of exercising. In both senses, *praxis* was opposed to *theoria.*

Aristotle: The Synthesis of *Theoria* and *Praxis*

In his youth Aristotle had probably studied rhetoric under Isocrates, but he had transferred to Plato's school, and there he taught rhetoric. In this period of Aristotle's development he wholeheartedly adopted the Platonic basis of *theoria* (scientifically certain axioms) for his theology, his ethics, his politics, and his rhetoric. We know this from the masterly studies of his development by Jaeger, Düring, and Nuyens.[12] Chroust's studies, in particular, support this position for Aristotle's early rhetorical work.[13]

Consequently, we can assume that he followed Plato's emphasis on *theoria*, in contrast to talent and practice. Plato had repeated the same trilogy that Isocrates used, but where Isocrates placed *theoria* last in importance, Plato considered it most important, as *Phaedrus* 269 D--E clearly shows.

Later, however, probably as the result of Isocrates' repeated emphasis on the uncertain character of all thinking in the areas of the human sciences,[14] Aristotle reverted to the Sophistic and Isocratean position that in these disciplines only a measure of probability or belief was possible. He retained a belief in the certainty of theory in some sciences (such as theology, astronomy, metaphysics, and mathematics). But in the human sciences, which more and more occupied his attention, Aristotle settled for the probable. And these were the areas of *praxis* (practical thinking) and *poiesis* (making artifacts).

His treatise on *Rhetoric* thus belongs with his important works in ethics and politics--the human sciences which involve the contingent, the variable, the changeable, *and therefore the free.* The sciences in *theoria*, on the contrary, involve the eternal, the unchangeable, the necessary, and the redetermined. Politics, ethics, rhetoric, and poetics enable us to change some aspect of our life and therefore we can deliberate about the ways we may choose to effect the change. These areas of life more and more preoccupied the mature Aristotle.

Aristotle's *Rhetoric*, therefore, sides with Isocrates in the epistemological debate with Plato. But, like Plato, Aristotle still held on to the importance of rhetorical and psychological principles (though not at a level of certainty) for teaching students the political, legal, and ceremonial types of speeches. Like Plato and Isocrates, Aristotle adopted the notion of training students to a limited number of kinds of discourse. Aristotle's pedagogy of rhetoric, consequently, is a compromise between Plato and Isocrates in pedagogical technique, but an epistemological siding with Isocrates.

In practice, Aristotle assumes that the principles of rhetoric have already been arrived at (by Plato, or Isocrates, or himself), and he teaches by first stating the principles, illustrating them by examples, and then having the students apply them to the subject matter at hand in the right environment. Examples in Aristotle, therefore, are not data for generalizations (as they are in Plato), but illustrations of principles. Aristotle's method is distinctly deductive. And, although Aristotle also believed in the importance of *kairos*, he does not give this notion the central position it had occupied in Plato. In this one sense, he is more theoretical than Plato.

The pedagogical methodology of Aristotle is graphically presented in the third circle in the figure. It attempts to embody the technique of teaching embodied in

Aristotle's *Rhetoric.* Thus the *Phaedrus,* the *Antidosis,* and the *Rhetoric* exemplify different epistemologies and different pedagogical corollaries.[15]

Some Current Concerns with Theory and Practice

The debate among Plato, Isocrates, and Aristotle thus centered around several critical notions: an epistemological controversy between science and probability (*episteme* and *pistis),* the relative importance of environmental situation (*kairos),* and the pedagogical corollaries to be drawn from these positions. Now, I believe that the same basic issues confront contemporary rhetoric. There are two major emphases in the contemporary scene which reincarnate the two concerns of antiquity: a sense of situational context of *kairos,* and a "practical" epistemology that incorporates probabilistic thinking.

In fact, I have recently been progressively tantalized by, impressed with, excited by, and inspired with the realization that important scholars in such diverse areas as philosophy, semiotics, anthropology, theology, and logic exhibit these two important and central tendencies. First, they insist, often shrilly, on the overwhelming importance of situational (and cultural) context in the study of discourse. Secondly, they also insist, despite the impressive advances of symbolic logic, statistics, and computer study in this century, on the distinctive character of the logic of actual discourse.

Situational Context

Some of these scholars take a very comprehensive look at the necessity of some context for interpreting discourse. Others have limited their concerns to more narrow areas. Let us look at some representatives of each tendency.

Certainly one of the most thoroughgoing of the views of the necessity of some context to interpreting anything is that of modern hermeneuticists stemming from the work of Martin Heidegger. Heidegger enlarged the earlier concerns of biblical, legal, and literary hermeneuticists into a position usually called "philosophic hermeneutics." Heidegger's main work, *Being and Time,* poses the hermeneutic problem in its largest dimension: all understanding is a matter of interpretation.[16] Consequently hermeneutics is *the* basic epistemological issue. And in *any* interpretation, man brings to the process a prestructure which incorporates a preholding of the totality of the being to be interpreted, a *preview* of its unity, and a *preconception* of the structural complexity of the object. The German words are *Vorhab, Vorsicht,* and *Vorbegriff,* and they are repeated at many critical junctures in *Being and Time.*[17] Such a prestructure to interpretation is obviously the result of one's cultural and situational context, within which the interpretation is to take place.

For this reason Heidegger emphasizes the unique nature of the interpretive act. Hans-Georg Gadamer, one of Heidegger's contemporaries, has carried this insistence even further. In his many books and articles he continually insists on the necessity of *prejudices* (the German word is *Vorurteil,* prejudgement, but Gadamer prefers the connotations of the English word *prejudice* in the translation precisely because it emphasizes the situational bias).[18]

An important literary and rhetorical critic who takes an equally comprehensive view of the importance of situational context is Kenneth Burke. His pentad--act, agent, agency. purpose. scene--is an attempt to reduce the elements of a situational context to a system. All interpretation must take account of these elements of the dramatistic situation. he insists.[19] In addition, the second critical dimension of Burke's system, the pervasive Hegelian dialectic, is a persistent reminder, throughout the entire Burkean canon. of the noncertainty of any scientific logic in the discourse of the symbolic animal. To use his favorite figure of speech, the synecdoche, Burke can be said to be representative of the entire movement which I am here sketching.

Heidegger's most famous theological disciple was undoubtedly Rudolf Bultmann, possibly the greatest theologian of this century. Bultmann probably takes as comprehensive a view of the importance of prestructure as does Heidegger, but his application of the principle has been mainly in biblical hermeneutics. First, and most dramatically, he contests that the message of the Bible was embodied in the cultural myths of the contemporaries of the biblical authors--this was necessary so that the message could be interpreted at that time. But each age has to separate the essential messages of the Bible from these mythical contexts and not take the myths for the truths of the Bible. To get the message, each age must bring its own cultural and historical prestructures to the interpretation of the Bible.[20] Secondly, Bultmann insists that the genres of the books of the New Testament were also culturally grounded in the life situation (*Sitz im Loben*) of the people of the time.[21] He carried on an intense sociological analysis of these genres, a study which others continue today.

A somewhat less comprehensive, though still far-reaching epistemological principle. also grounded on the importance of situational context, can be seen in the work of some ethnomethodologists. Their basic assumption is that the methodology to be used in describing and analyzing a culture is the methodology which that group itself uses in its internal interactions to accomplish its own goals.[22] One of the major motivations for the technique was the realization on the part of these analysts that much research in the social sciences used the categories of an external science to gauge the actions of a group which was not at all attempting to "do" that kind of science at all. In other words. to understand the "practical reasoning" of the subculture, it was unfair to assess it by the standards of western scientific reasoning."

Consequently, ethnomethodology in one stroke asserts the two approaches we have seen in the other movements--the insistence on situational or cultural context and the difference between much practical reasoning and scientific logic as we usually conceive it.

A very similar position to that of the ethnomethodologists, though with quite different motivations, is that advocated by some Marxists attempting to elaborate on the Aristotelian distinction between *theoria* and *praxis*, a distinction revived by a group of young left Hegelians in the 1840s in order to emphasize the kind of knowledge which leads to action and to change, not just to sterile speculation. This emphasis on *praxis* became a persistent theme throughout the entire Marxist corpus. Neglected for some time. it has recently been reemphasized by some important contemporary Marxists. And in Marx. as well as in these modern disciples, the difference between *theoria* and *praxis* lies in the taking into account of the actual context in any political action. Sartre,

Marcuse, Habermas, Bourdieu, Bernstein, and others all take this direction in analyzing *praxis*.[24]

In the field of rhetorical analysis, a position potentially as comprehensive as that of Heidegger or Burke has been taken by Lloyd Bitzer. His important article on rhetorical situation in *Philosophy and Rhetoric* certainly has been influential in several areas.[25] Even its attackers have acknowledged its impact, particularly in the field of rhetorical analysis.[26]

Logic and Epistemology

It is clear that many of the stances outlined in the previous section have distinct epistemological implications. In some cases, the relation of rhetoric to logic and epistemology has been pointed out. But there are additional voices in this matter which are not so closely allied to an insistence on situational context, theorists to whom the question of *theoria* versus *praxis* is still of vital importance.

In historical and theoretical books which have massive epistemological implications. Ernesto Grassi and Samuel Ijselling have attempted to reintegrate the history of rhetorical thought into that of philosophical thought. Both emphasize important names in the rhetorical tradition which are frequently dismissed as philosophically unimportant by most contemporary professionals in that area--names like those of Isocrates, Cicero, Quintilian, and Vico. Both emphasize the practical basis of rhetorical thought for real-world philosophical applications.[27]

In a somewhat narrower spectrum, some other influential movements ought to be mentioned. Some concern deduction rather in an isolated manner, some deal almost exclusively with inductive generalizations. A few involve both.

In deduction, particularly in the field of ethics, Kurt Baier's moral system, based, as he says, on good reasons, not necessarily on the best reasons, eschews deductive rigorous certainty in its decision inferences. Ethics operates at the level of belief and probability, not at the level of deductive certainty, he maintains--a position remarkably similar to that of Isocrates and of the late Aristotle, as we have seen. Baier's position has been influential in both ethical and rhetorical circles.[28]

Chaim Perelman and L. Olbrechts-Tyteca, analyzing legal and political documents, take a somewhat similar stand. They recognize the probable nature of much deductive reasoning in these fields. Secondly, they also insist on the different types of axioms or premises which different types of audiences will allow for deductive inferences in legal, political, and religious thought.[29]

Some of the philosophers and political scientists mentioned above in connection with situational context also address themselves specifically to the question of scientific logic. Thus Heidegger has attacked the priority of scientific reasoning and the quantifiability of some types of issues.[30] Pollock,[31] Adorno,[32] and Horkheimer[33] have also raised the question of the quantifiability of certain political concepts. Mehan, an ethnomethodologist, has made frontal assaults on some empirical sociological research. He asks why many invalid interviews on the intimacies of divorce relations are any more valid than one such interview: "To think that these `problems' can be resolved by adding this one woman's responses to thousands of others and transforming them all from `sloppy' conversation into numerals seems not so much hopeless as absurd."[34]

It is abundantly clear from even this brief sketch that there are tendencies in modern thought which parallel two of the major motifs in classical rhetoric. These concerns, evident in many varied fields, are too insistent and too frequent to be ignored. And some of them, acknowledged in rhetorical theory, have not yet been carried over into composition practice and rhetorical analysis.

In epistemological assumptions, we may well yet be too Platonic: we teach the logic of certainty borrowed from traditional and modern logic. We have yet to learn from the modern disciples of Isocrates and the later Aristotle. In matters of situational context, we may well not be Platonic enough: we still do not place composition practice and rhetorical analysis into the situational context of the student and modern society. We have much to learn from the modern disciples of the author of the *Phaedrus* in this matter.

FOOTNOTES

1. Kathleen Freeman, *Ancilla to the Pre-Socratic Philosophers: A Complete Translation of the Fragments in Diels' Fragmente der Vorsokratiker* (Cambridge, Mass.: Harvard Univ. Press, 1956), p. 13; J.B. Bury, *The Ancient Greek Historians* (New York: Dover Publications, 1958), p. 5.
2. Bury, *The Ancient Greek Historians*, p. 15.
3. Ernst Cassirer, *An Essay on Man* (New Haven: Yale Univ. Press, 1944), pp. 111-17.
4. Plato, *Phaedrus,* trans. W.C. Helmbold and W.G. Rabinowitz (Indianapolis: Bobbs Merrill Co., 1956), 27 ID-272B.
5. But cf. D. Levi, "Il concetto de *kairos* e la filosofia di Platone," *Rendiconti della Reale Accademia Nazionale dei Lincei, Classe di scienzia morali,* Ser. 5, 33 (1924), 93-118.
6. *On Literary Composition,* trans. W. Rhys Roberts (London: Macmillan and Co., 1910), pp. 12, 84.
7. Isocrates, *Isocrates II,* trans. George Norlin, "On the Peace" (Cambridge: Harvard Univ. Press, Loeb Classical Library, 1968), Sec. 8.
8. Isocrates, "Antidosis", Sec. 271, same edition as cited in note 7.
9. See Ben Jonson, "Timber, or Discoveries," *Ben Jonson,* ed. C.H. Herford, Percy and Evelyn Simpson (Oxford: At the Clarendon Press, 1947), VIII, pp. 637-41.
10. See Donald Lemen Clark, *Rhetoric in Greco-Roman Education* (New York: Columbia Univ. Press, 1957), pp. 177-21 1.
11. Isocrates is also usually given credit for providing the political basis of humanism, which he equated to the intellectual and the cultural. See Isocrates, *Isocrates I,* trans. George Norlin, "Panegyricus" (Cambridge: Harvard Univ. Press, Loeb Classical Library, 1968), Sec. 51: "The man who shares our paideia is a Greek in a higher sense than he who only shares our blood."
12. Werner Jaeger, *Aristotle: Fundamentals of the History of His Development* (Oxford: Oxford Univ. Press, 1948); Ingemar During, *Aristoteles: Darstellung und Interpretation seines Denkens* (Heidelberg: Karl Winter, 1966); Francois Nuyens, *L'Evolution de la psychologie d'Aristote,* trans. from Dutch, no trans. given (Paris: Librairie Philosophique. J. Vrin, 1948).
13. Anton-Hermann Chroust, *Aristotle: New Light on His Life and on Some of His Lost Works, Vol. II: Observations on Some of Aristotle's Lost Works* (Notre Dame, Ind.: Univ. of Notre Dame Press, 1973), pp. 29-42.
14. See René Antoine Gauthier, O.P., and Jean Yves Jolif, O.P., *Aristote: L'Ethique a'Nicomaque* (Louvain: Publications Universitaires de Louvain, 1959), II, 466-67.
15. I do not mean to imply that the inductive method of Plato is a necessary corollary of a *theoria,* nor that the deductive method of Aristotle is a corollary of a modified *theoria.*
16. See Martin Heidegger, *Being and Time,* trans. John Macquarrie and Edward Robinson (New York: Harper & Row, 1962), pp. 148-60, for his basic presentation of the notion of interpretation (pages are from the seventh German edition, glossed in the English translation).
17. See Heidegger, *Being and Time,* pp. 157-58, 233-34, 290-91, 311-13, 327-33.
18. Hans-Georg Gadamer, *Truth and Method,* trans. Barden J. Cumming (New York: Seabury Press, 1979), pp. 241-74.
19. See the introductory section to Kenneth Burke, *A Grammar Of Motives* (Berkeley: Univ. of California Press, 1969).

20. Rudolf Bultmann, "New Testament and Mythology," In Hans Werner Bartsch, ed., *Kerygma and Myth: A Theological Debate*, tmns. Reginald H. Fuller (London: S.P.C.K., 1953),pp. 1-45.
21. See Rudolf Bultmann, *The History of the Synoptic Tradition*, trans. John Marsh (New York: Harper & Row, 1968),p.4.
22. See Roy Turner, ed., *Ethnomethodology Selected Readings* (Baltimore, Md.: Penquin Books, 1975).
23. See the largest section in Turner, *Ethnomethodology*, pp. 21-194.
24. See Jean-Paul Sartre, *The Critique of Dialectical Reason, Vol. 1: The Theory of Practical Ensembles*, trans. Alan Sheridan-Smith, ed. Jonathan Ree (London: NJB, 1976), pp. 79-94; Jurgen Habermas, *Theory and Practice*, trans. John Viertel (Boston: Beacon Press, 1973); Pierre Bourdieu, *Outline of a Theory of Practice*, trans. Richard Nice, ed. Jack Coody, in Cambridge Studies in Social Anthropology, 16 (London: Cambridge University Press, 1977); J. Bernstein, *Praxis and Action: Contemporary Philosophies of Human Activity* (Philadelphia:. Univ. Of Pennsylvania Press, 1971).
25. Lloyd F. Bitzer, "The Rhetorical Situation," *Philosophy and Rhetoric*, 1 (1968),1-14
26. See Richard Vatz, "The Myth of the Rhetorical Situation," *Philosophy and Rhetoric*, 6 (1972), 154-61.
27. Ernesto Grassi, *Rhetoric as Philosophy: The Humanist Tradition*, trans. John Michael Krois and Azizeh Azodi (University Park: Pennsylvania State Univ. Press, 1980); Samuel Ijselling, *Rhetoric and Philosophy in Conflict: An Historic Survey*, trans. Paul Dunphy (The Hague: M. Nijhoff, 1976).
28. See Kurt Baier, *The Moral Point of View: A Rational Basis of Ethics* (Ithaca, N.Y.: Cornell Univ. Press, 1958).
29. Chaim Perelman and L. Olbrechts-Tyteca, *The New Rhetoric: A Treatise on Argumentation*, trans. John Wilkinson and Purcell Weaver (Notre Dame, Ind.: Univ. of Notre Dame Press, 1969).
30. Heidegger, *Being and Time*, pp. 157-59; and "The Question Concerning Technology," trans. William Lovitt, in *Martin Heidegger: Basic Writings*, ed. David Farrell Krell (New York: Harper & Row, 1977), pp. 283-317.
31. Frederich Pollock, "Empirical Research into Public Opinion," trans. Thomas Hall, In *Critical Sociology*, ed. Paul Connerton (New York: Penguin Books, 1976), pp. 225-36.
32. Theodore W. Adorno, "Sociology and Empirical Research," trans. Graham Bartram, in Connerton, *Critical Sociology*, pp. 237-57.
33. Max Horkheimer, "Traditional and Critical Theory," trans. M.J.O. O'Connell, in Connerton, *Critical Sociology*, pp. 206-24.
34. Hugh Mehan, "The Imposition of Reality," in Hugh Mehan and Houston Woods, eds., *The Reality of ethnomethodology* (New York: John Wiley & Sons, 1975), p. 54.

Poststructuralism, Cultural Studies, and the Composition Classroom: Postmodern Theory in Practice

James Berlin

The uses of postmodern theory in rhetoric and composition studies have been the object of considerable abuse of late. Figures of some repute in the field --the likes of Maxine Hairston and Peter Elbow--as well as anonymous voices from the Burkean Parlor section of *Rhetoric Review,*--most recently, TS, a graduate student, and KF, a voice speaking for "a general English teacher audience" (192) have joined the chorus of protest. The charges have included willful obscurity, self-indulgence, elitism, pomposity, intellectual impoverishment, and a host of related offenses. Although my name usually appears among the accused, I won sympathetic with those undergoing the difficulties of the first encounter with this discussion. (I exclude Professor Hairston in her irresponsible charge that its recent contributors in *College English* are "low-risk Marxists who write very badly" [695] and who should be banned from NCTE publications.) I experienced the same frustration when I first encountered the different but closely related language of rhetoric and composition studies some fifteen years ago. I wondered, for example, if I would ever grasp the complexities of Aristotle or Quintilian or Kenneth Burke or I.A. Richards, not to mention the new language of the writing process. A bit later I was introduced to French poststructuralism, and once again I found myself wandering in strange seas, and this time alone. In reading rhetoric, after all, I had the benefit of numerous commentators to help me along--the work of Kinneavy and Lauer and Corbett and Emig, for example. In reading Foucault and Derrida in the late seventies, on the other hand, I was largely on my own since the commentaries were as difficult as the originals, and those few that were readable were often (as even I could see) wrong. Nonetheless, with the help of informal reading groups made up of colleagues and students, I persisted in my efforts to come to terms with this difficult body of thought. I was then, as now, convinced that both rhetorical studies and postmodern speculation offered strikingly convergent and remarkably compelling visions for conducting my life as a teacher and a citizen. It is clear to me that rhetoric and composition studies has arrived as a serious field of study because it has taken into account the best from the past and present, and I have found that postmodern work in historical and contemporary rhetorical theory has done much to further this effort.

I will readily admit that discussants in postmodern theories of rhetoric have been more concerned with advancing this immensely rich vein of speculation than they have with communicating with the novice. But I think it is a mistake to condemn them

James A. Berlin. "Poststructuralism, Cultural Studies, and the Composition Classroom: Postmodern Theory in Practice, *Rhetoric Review*, Vol. 11, No. 1, Fall 1992. Reprinted with permission.

for this. Contrary to what KF, the hard-working general English teacher, has asserted, teaching writing is not a "relatively simple and straightforward task" (192). As the intense effort that has been given this activity in the 2500-year history of Western education indicates, communication is at once extremely important in the life of a society and extremely complex (see the histories of Kennedy or Corbett or Vickers, for example). Those who wish to come to grips with this complexity cannot be expected to write exclusively for the uninitiated, a move that would hopelessly retard the development of any discussion. A new rhetoric requires a new language if we are to develop devices for producing and interpreting discourse that are adequate to our historical moment. I would argue that those working today at the intersections of rhetoric and postmodern theory are beginning to generate rhetorics that in conception and pedagogical application promise to be counterparts to the greatest accomplishments of the past--of an Aristotle (who once sounded strange next to Plato) or an Isocrates (who sounded strange next to Gorgias) or to Campbell (who sounded strange next to Ward). Eventually (and sooner than we might imagine, I expect), those interested in rhetoric will be talking and thinking in the new terminologies emerging today, finding them just as comfortable as the language of cognitive rhetoric or expressionist rhetoric. Still, this does not help the overworked composition teacher or the new graduate student who is eager to explore the significance of this new speculation for theory and the classroom but is not sure where to start.

In this essay I want to present as clearly as I know how some of the central features of postmodern theory that workers in rhetoric have found especially relevant to their efforts. Since covering the field as whole would require more space than I have here, however, I want to restrict myself to considering the ways these postmodern conceptions are counterparts to discussions in social-epistemic rhetoric. I will also include a description of a freshman course I have designed that is the result of my theoretical studies, a course that combines methods of cultural studies (itself a product of postmodern thought coupled with a progressive politics) with the methods of social-epistemic rhetoric in a beginning composition class. My intent is to demonstrate that the complexities of theory have immediate pedagogical applications, and that one of the efforts of composition teachers must be to discover these. Indeed, I will argue that the merger of theory and classroom practice in a uniquely new relation is one of the results of (what I should perhaps now call) postmodern rhetorical theory.

The Postmodern

John Schilb has explained that postmodernism "can designate a critique of traditional epistemology, a set of artistic practices, and an ensemble of larger social conditions" (174). Here the focus will be on the first, particularly on that body of thought that has emerged in what is loosely called structuralist and poststructuralist theory (sometimes called the "language division" of postmodern speculation). In "Rhetoric Programs after World War II: Ideology, Power, and Conflict," I attempt to outline the ways certain branches of rhetorical studies in the US, particularly of the epistemic variety, have paralleled the trajectory of structuralist and poststructuralist developments both at home and abroad. In this section I would like to explore the important features of postmodernism in which this is most apparent; in the next I will trace their uses in social-epistemic rhetoric. The significant postmodern developments fall into three general categories: the status of the subject; the characteristics of signifying practices; the role of master theories in explaining human affairs.

The unified, coherent, autonomous, self-present subject of the Enlightenment has been the centerpiece of liberal humanism. From this perspective the subject is a transcendent consciousness that functions unencumbered by social and material conditions of experience, acting as a free and rational agent who adjudicates competing claims for action. In other words, the individual is regarded as the author of all her actions, moving in complete freedom in deciding how she will live. This perception has been challenged by the postmodern conception of the subject as the product of social and material conditions. Here the subject is considered the construction of the various signifying practices, the uses of language, of a given historical moment (see, for example, Benveniste, Barthes, Foucault). This means that each person is formed by the various discourses, sign systems, that surround her. These include both everyday uses of language in the home, school, the media, and other institutions, as well as the material conditions that are arranged in the manner of languages that is, semiotically (like a sign system), such as the clothes we wear, the way we carry our bodies, the way our school and home environments are arranged. These signifying practices then are languages that tell us who we are and how we should behave in terms of such categories as gender, race, class, age, ethnicity, and the like. The result is that each of us is heterogeneously made up of various competing discourses, conflicted and contradictory scripts, that make our consciousness anything but unified, coherent, and autonomous. At the most everyday level, for example, the discourses of the school and the home about appropriate gender behavior ("Just say `No'") are frequently at odds with the discourse provided by peers and the media ("Go for it"). The result is that we are made up of subject formations or subject positions that do not always square with each other.

Signifying practices then are at the center of the formation of the "subject" and of "subjectivities"--terms made necessary to avoid all the liberal humanist implications of talking about the "individual." But the conception of signifying practices, of language, is itself radically altered in this scheme. A given language is no longer taken to be a transparent medium that records an externally present thing-in-itself, that is, it is not a simple signaling device that stands for and corresponds to the separate realities that lend it meaning. Language is instead taken to be a pluralistic and complex system of signifying practices that construct realities rather than simply presenting or representing them. Our conception of material and social phenomena then are fabrications of signifying, the products of culturally coded signs. Saussure, the prime originator of structuralism in Europe, first demonstrated the ways language functions as a set of differences: Signifiers derive meaning not in relation to signifieds, to external referents, but in relation to other signifiers, the semiotic systems in which they are functioning. For example, just as the sound "t" is significant in English because it contrasts with "d" --making for a difference in meaning between "to" and "do"--a term, such as "man," has significance in a given discourse because it contrasts with another term, such as "woman" or "boy" or "ape." And just as the sounds of a language are culturally variable, so are its terms and their structural relations. A sign thus has meaning by virtue of its position relative to another sign or signs within a given system, not to externally verifiable certainties. Most important, these signs are arranged in a hierarchy so that one is "privileged," that is, considered more important than its related term. For example, Alleen Pace Nilsen has shown that terms in English that are gender specific almost invariably involve positive connotations in the case of males and negative connotation in the case of females (master/mistress, sir/madam, chef/cook, for example). Such hierarchies, once again, are not universal but are culturally specific.

Roland Barthes has shown the ways that signs form systems (semiotic systems) that extend beyond natural language to all realms of a culture, for example, film, television, photography, food, fashion, automobiles, and on and on (see *Mythologies*). He presents a method for analyzing and discussing the semiosis (sign production) of texts as they appear in virtually all features of human behavior. Michel Foucault has indicated the manner in which different "discursive regimes," elaborate systems of signifying systems, forge knowledge/power formations that govern action during successive stages of history. (He does so, furthermore, while denying any master regime or narrative unfolding over time, a matter to be considered shortly.) Finally, Jacques Derrida has shown the attempt of philosophy to establish a foundation, an essential presence, for its systems in a realm outside of language, an effort to avoid the role of signification, of discourse, in all human undertakings. From the postmodern perspective, then, signifying practices shape the subject, the social, and the material--the perceiver and the perceived.

These antifoundational, antiessentialist assaults on Enlightenment conceptions of the subjects and objects of experience are extended to postulates of grand narratives of the past or present--that is, the stories we tell about our experiences that attempt to account for all features of it (its totality) in a comprehensive way. Jean-François Lyotard has been the central figure in denying the possibility of any grand metanarrative that might exhaustively account for human conditions in the past or present. Like Foucault, he renounces the totalizing discourse of such schemes as Hegelianism or Marxism or the faith in scientific progress or the invisible hand of economic law. All are declared language games that are inherently partial and interested, intended to endorse particular relations of power and to privilege certain groups in historical struggles. Against this totalizing move, Lyotard argues for a plurality of particular narratives, limited and localized accounts that attempt to explain features of experience that grand narratives exclude. The structuralist and poststructuralist analyses of sign systems look for the binary opposites of key terms, the marginalized terms that often go unmentioned. (This is why they use the term *foreground:* it refers to putting the concealed and unacknowledged term in a binary structure forward so that the *complete* significance of the term can be examined in a given discourse.) Similarly, postmodern studies of cultures of the past and present look for what is left out, what exists on the unspoken margins of the culture. This moves attention to such categories as class, race, gender, and ethnicity in the unfolding of historical events. This is often history from the bottom up, telling the stories of the people and events normally excluded from totalizing accounts.

Social-Epistemic Rhetoric

Those familiar with social-epistemic rhetoric can readily we its convergence with postmodern conclusions about language and culture. I have discussed this rhetoric at length in *Rhetoric and Reality*, "Rhetoric and Ideology in the Writing Class," and elsewhere. Here I wish to offer a look at the ways in which it converges with postmodern speculation in providing a mutually enriching theoretical synthesis. To say this differently, poststructuralism provides a way of more fully discussing elements of social-epistemic rhetoric that are fully operative within it; at the same time, social-epistemic rhetoric provides poststructuralism with methods for discussing the production and reception of texts--and especially the former--that have been a part of its effort. I will show these convergences in discussing the elements of the rhetorical situation--interlocutor, conceptions of the real, audience, and language--as they are being conceived in social-epistemic rhetoric informed by poststructuralism. I should also mention that this development is bringing social-epistemic rhetoric, particularly, as I will show, in the classroom, very close to the work of cultural studies as it has been discussed by the Birmingham Center for Contemporary Cultural Studies.

We have already seen that the subject of the rhetorical act cannot be regarded as the unified, coherent, autonomous, transcendent subject of liberal humanism. The subject is instead multiple and conflicted, composed of numerous subject formations or positions. From one perspective this is a standard feature of many historical rhetorics in their concern with the *ethos* of the speaker, her presentation of the appropriate image of her character through language, voice, bearing, and the like. For a contemporary rhetoric, the writer and reader, the speaker and listener (and more of their commutability of function shortly), must likewise be aware that the subject (the producer) of discourse is a construction, a fabrication, established through the devices of signifying practices. This means that great care must be taken in choosing the subject position that the interlocutor wishes to present, and equally great care must be taken in teaching students the way this is done. In other words, it will not do to say, "Be yourself," since all of us possess multiple selves, not all of which are appropriate for the particular discourse situation. This is not, it should be noted, to deny that all of us display a measure of singularity. As Paul Smith argues, the unique place of each of us in the network of intersecting discourses assures differences among us as well as possibilities for originality and political agency. This does not mean, however, that anyone can totally escape the discursive regimes, the power/knowledge formations, of the historical moment. Political agency but never complete autonomy is the guiding formulation here.

But if the subject, the sender, is a construct of signifying practices in social-epistemic rhetoric, so are the material conditions to which the subject responds, the prime constituents of the message of discourse. (I am of course relying on Burke's formulation of language as symbolic action to be distinguished from the sheer motion of the material, as well as on the work of Barthes and Foucault). This is not to deny the force of the material in human affairs: people do need to provide for physiological needs, to arrange refuge from the elements, and to deal with eventual physical extinction. However, all of these material experiences are mediated through signifying practices. Only through language do we know and act upon the conditions of our experience. Ways of living and dying are finally negotiated through discourse, the cultural codes that are part of our historical conditions. These conditions are of an economic, social, and political nature, and they change over time. But they too can only be known and acted upon through the discourses available at any historical moment. Thus the subject who experiences and the material and social conditions experienced are discursively constituted in historically specific terms.

The mediation of signifying practices in the relations of subjects to material conditions is especially crucial. From the perspective offered here, signifying practices are always at the center of conflict and contention. In the effort to name experience, different groups are constantly vying for supremacy, for ownership and control of terms and their meanings in any discourse situation. As Stuart Hall, a past director of the Birmingham Center, has pointed out, a given language or discourse does not automatically belong to any class, race, or gender. Following Volosinov and Gramsci, he argues that language is always an arena of struggle to make certain meanings--certain ideological formulations--prevail. Cultural codes thus are constantly in conflict: they contend for hegemony in defining and directing the material conditions of experience as well as consciousness itself. The signifying practices of different groups thus compete in forwarding different agendas for the ways people are to regard their historical conditions and their modes of responding to them, and these signifying practices are thus always scene of battle (Hall, "The Rediscovery of 'Ideology'").

The receiver of messages, the audience of discourse, obviously cannot escape the consequences of signifying practices. The audience's possible responses to texts are in part a function of its discursively constituted social roles. These roles are often constructed with some measure of specificity as membership in a specific discourse community--in a particular union or profession, for example. But these roles are never discretely separate from other subject positions the members of an audience may share or, on the other hand, occupy independent of each other. In other words, members of an audience cannot simply activate one subject position and switch off all others. Thus, audiences must be considered both as members of communities and as separate subject formations. The result is that the responses of the audience as a collective and as separate subjects are never totally predictable, never completely in the control of the sender of a coded message, or of the coded message itself. As Stuart Hall has demonstrated, audiences are capable of a range of possible responses to any message. They can simply accommodate the message, sharing in the codes of the sender and assenting to them. The audience can completely resist the message, rejecting its codes and purposes and turning them to other ends. Finally, the receiver can engage in a process of negotiation, neither accommodating alone nor resisting alone, instead engaging in a measure of both (Hall, "Encoding/Decoding").

The work of rhetoric, then, is to study the production and reception of these historically specific signifying practices. In other words, social-epistemic rhetoric will enable senders and receivers to arrive at a formulation of the conception the entire rhetorical context in any given discourse situation, and this will be done through an analysis of the signifying practices operating within it. Thus in composing a text, a writer will engage in an analysis of the cultural codes operating in defining her role, the roles of the audience, and the constructions of the matter to be considered. These function in a dialectical relation to each other so that the writer must engage in complex decision-making in shaping the text to be presented. By dialectic I mean they change in response to each other in ways that are not mechanically predictable--not presenting, for example, simply a cause-effect relation but a shifting affiliation in which causes and effects are mutually interactive, with effects becoming causes and causes effects simultaneously. The reader of the text must also engage in a dialectical process involving coded conceptions of the writer, the matter under consideration, and the role of the receiver of the text in arriving at an interpretation of the text. Writing and reading are thus both acts of textual interpretation and construction, and both acts of textual interpretation and construction, and both are central to social-epistemic rhetoric. More of this reading/writing relationship will be taken up later. First I would like to consider the role of ideology in rhetoric.

As I have indicated throughout, signifying practices are never innocent: they are always involved in ideological designations, conceptions of economic, social, political, and cultural arrangements and their relations to the subjects of history within concrete power relations. Ideology is not here declared a mystification to be placed in binary opposition to truth or science. The formulation invoked is instead derived from Louis Althusser as elaborated in Goran Therborn's *The Ideology of Power and the Power of Ideology*. This conception places ideology within the category of discourse, describing it as an inevitable feature of all signifying practices. Ideology then becomes closely imbricated with rhetoric, the two inseparably overlapped, however distinguished for purposes of discussion. From this perspective, no claims can be offered as absolute, timeless truths since all are historically specific, arising in response to the conditions of a particular time and place. Choices in the economic, social, political, and cultural are thus based on discursive practices that are interpretations--not mere transcriptions of some external verifiable certainty. Thus the choice is never between ideology and absolute truth, but between different ideologies. Some are finally judged better ("truer") than others on the basis of their ability to fulfill the promises of democracy at all levels of experience--the economic, social, political, and cultural--providing an equal share of authority in decision-making and a tolerance for difference.

Ideology addresses or interpellates human beings. It provides the language to define the subject, other subjects, the material and social, and the relation of all of these to each other. Ideology addresses three questions: what exists, what is good, what is possible? The first, explains Therborn, tells us "who we are, what the world is, what nature, society, men and women are like. In this way we acquire a sense of identity, becoming conscious of what is real and true." Ideology also provides the subject with standards for making ethical and aesthetic decisions: *"what is good*, right, just, beautiful, attractive, enjoyable, and its opposites. In this way our desires become structured and normalized." The very configurations of our desires, what we will long for and pursue, are thus shaped by ideology. Finally, ideology defines the elements of expectation: *"what is possible* and impossible: our sense of the mutability of our being-in-the-world and the consequences of change are hereby patterned, and our hopes, ambitions, and fears given shape." (18). This is especially important since the recognition of the existence of a condition (homelessness, for example) and the desire for its change will go for nothing if ideology indicates that a change is simply not possible (the homeless freely choose to live in the street and cannot be forced to come inside). All three are further implicated in power relations in groups and in society, in deciding who has power and in determining what power can be expected to achieve.

Finally, ideology always brings with it strong social and cultural reinforcement, so that what we take to exist, to have value, and to be possible seems necessary, normal, and inevitable--in the nature of things. And this goes for power as well since ideology naturalizes certain authority regime--those of class, race, and gender, for example--and renders alternatives unthinkable, in this way determining who can act and what can be accomplished. Finally, ideology is always, inscribed in the discourses of daily practice and is pluralistic and conflicted. Any historical moment displays a wide variety of competing ideologies and each subject displays permutations of these conflicts, although the overall effect is to support the hegemony of dominant groups.

All of this has great consequences for the writing classroom. Given the ubiquitous role of discourse in human affairs, instructors cannot be content to focus exclusively on teaching the production of academic texts. Our business must be to instruct students in signifying practices broadly conceived-- see not only the rhetoric of the college essay but the rhetoric of the institution of schooling, of the work place, and of the media. We must take as our province the production--and reception of semiotic codes broadly conceived, providing students with the heuristics to penetrate these codes and their ideological designs on our formation as the subjects of our experience. Students must come to see that the languages they are expected to speak, write, and embrace as ways of thinking and acting are never disinterested, always bringing with them strictures on the existent, the good, the possible, and regimes of power.

If rhetoric is to be a consideration of signifying practices and their ideological involvement--that is, their imbrication in economic, social, political, and cultural conditions and subject formation--then the study of signs will of course be central. A large part of the business of this rhetoric will be to provide methods for describing and analyzing the operations of signification. Just as successive rhetorics for centuries furnished the terms to name the elements involved in text production and interpretation for the past (inventional devices, arrangements, schemes, stylistic labels for tropes and figures), social-epistemic rhetoric will offer a terminology to discuss these activities for contemporary conditions and conceptual formulations. Structuralism, poststruc-turalism, and rhetoric have all begun this effort, and workers in semiotics have profited from them. It is composition teachers, however, who are best situated to develop ways of analyzing and discussing discourse to enable students to become better writers and readers. (After all, most of the important rhetorics of the past were written by teachers: Socrates, Plato, and Aristotle all taught the counterpart of freshman composition.) This leads to a consideration of the relation of reading and writing, of text production and text interpretation.

As I have already indicated, social-epistemic rhetoric demands revised models of reading and writing. Both composing and interpreting texts become instances of discourse analysis and, significantly, negotiation. Indeed, the very acts of writing and reading are themselves verbally coded discursive procedures which guide the production and interpretation of meanings, making a certain range more likely to appear and others more improbable. This exclusionary coding is apparent, for example, in reflecting on the directives for text production and reception provided in certain expressionist rhetorics. For these, only personal and metaphoric accounts can be regarded as authentic discourse, and, unlike current-traditional rhetoric, any attempt to be rational, objective, and dispassionate is considered a violation of the self and of genuine writing. In addition, for social-epistemic rhetoric, writing and reading become acts of discourse analysis as both the sender and receiver attempt to negotiate the semiotic codes in which each is situated-- that is, the signifying practices that make up the entire rhetorical context. Composing and reception are thus interactive since both are performances of production, requiring the active construction of meaning according to one or another coded procedure. The opposition between the active writer and the passive reader is displaced since both reading and writing are considered constructive. It will be the work of rhetoric and composition teachers, then, to develop lexicons to articulate the complex coding activity involved in writing and reading, and this leads us to the classroom.

The Classroom

The recommendations of the new rhetoric proposed here become clearest in considering pedagogy. For social-epistemic rhetoric, teaching is central, not an afterthought through which practice is made to conform with the more important work of theory. Instead, the classroom becomes the point at which theory and practice engage in a dialectical interaction, working out a rhetoric more adequate to the historical moment and the actual conditions of teacher and students. From this perspective, all teachers of rhetoric and composition are regarded as intellectuals engaging in theoretical and empirical research, the two coming to fruition in their interaction within the classroom. Indeed, as Patricia Donahue and Ellen Quandahl have argued, composition teachers are through this interaction striving to create a new variety of academic discourse. The teacher's duty here is to bring to bear rhetorical theory as broadly defined in this essay within the conditions of her students' lives. The teacher will in this act develop methods for producing and moving texts, including strategies for negotiating and resisting signifying practices, that are best suited for the situations of her students. These of course will be recommended to other teachers, but only as example and guideline, not pronouncements from on (theoretical) high. The uses of postmodern theory in rhetoric will then be in the hands of teachers, not prescribed in advance by "outside experts."

This role as intellectual, furthermore, has an important political dimension, involving the transformation and improvement of present social and political arrangements. As I have emphasized elsewhere, social-epistemic rhetoric grows out of the experience of democracy in the US, carrying with it a strong antifoundational impulse *(Rhetoric and Reality,* "Rhetoric and Ideology"). Knowledge/power relationships are regarded as human constructions, not natural and inevitable facts of life. All institutional arrangements are humanly made and so can be unmade, and the core of this productive act is found in democracy and open discussion.

The social-epistemic classroom thus offers a lesson in democracy intended to prepare students for critical participation in public life. It is dedicated to making schools places for individual and social empowerment. Schools after all are places, as Aronowitz and Giroux remind us, "of struggle over what forms of authority, orders of representation, forms of moral regulation, and versions of the past should be legitimated, passed on, and debated" (32). The teacher must then recognize and resist inequities in our society--the economic and social injustices inscribed in race, ethnic, and gender relations, relations that privilege the few and discriminate against the many. This classroom is dialogic, situating learning within the realities of the students' own experience, particularly their political experience. The dialogic classroom is designed to encourage students to transformative intellectuals in their own right. Studying signifying practices will require a "critical literacy." As Ira Shor explains: "Critical literacy invites teachers and students to *problematize* all subjects of study, that is, to understand existing knowledge as historical products deeply invested with the value of those who developed such knowledge." For this teacher, all learning is based in ideology, and signifying practices--the production and reception of texts-- must challenge dominant ideological formations. In Shor's terms, the study of discourse must go "beneath the surface to understand the origin, structure, and consequences of any body of knowledge, technical process, or object under study" (24). Students thus research their own language, their own society, their own learning, examining the values inscribed in them and the ways these values are shaping their subjectivities and their conceptions of their material and social conditions.

The Course

        I would now like to turn to a course in freshman composition that will demonstrate the operations of the social-epistemic rhetoric described here. This effort locates the composing process within its social context, combining the methods of semiotic analysis in considering cultural codes with the recommendations of the rhetoric I have outlined. As will be apparent, it is aimed with attempts to refigure English studies along the lines of cultural studies, a matter I have discussed in "Composition Studies and Cultural Studies" and "Composition and Cultural Studies: Collapsing the Boundaries." Since I devised the syllabus for this course to be shared with teaching assistants in my mentor group at Purdue and since my report here is based on our shared experience over the past three years, I will use the plural pronoun in referring to the effort. (I would also like to thank them for their cooperation throughout.)
        The course is organized around an examination of the cultural codes--the social semiotics--that are working themselves out in shaping consciousness in our students and ourselves. We start with the personal experience of the students, but the emphasis is on the position of this experience within its formative context. Our main concern is the relation of current signifying practices to the structuring of subjectivities--of race, class, and gender formations, for example--in our students and ourselves. The effort is to make students aware of cultural codes, the competing discourses that are influencing their formations as the subjects of experience. Our larger purpose is to encourage students to resist and to negotiate these codes-- these hegemonic discourses-- in order to bring about more democratic and personally humane economic, social, and political arrangements. From our perspective, only in this way can they become genuinely competent writers and readers.
        We thus guide students to locate in their experience the points at which they are now engaging in resistance and negotiation with the cultural codes they daily encounter. These are then used as avenues of departure for a dialogue. It is our hope that students who can demystify the subtle devices of persuasion in these cultural codes will be

motivated to begin the re-forming of subjectivities and social arrangements, a re-forming which is a normal part of democratic political arrangements. We also want to explore the wide range of codes that students confront daily--print, film, television--in order to prepare them to critique their experiences with these codes. As Donald Morton and Mas'ud Zavarzadeh explain, this "critique (not to be confused with criticism) is an investigation of the enabling conditions of discursive practices" (7). Its purpose is to locate the ideological predispositions of the semiotic codes that we encounter and enact in our lives, seeing their commitment to certain conceptions of the existent, the good, and the possible. The course then explores these coded discourses in the institutional forms--the family, the school, the work place, the media--that make them seem natural and timeless rather than historically situated social constructions.

The course consists of six units: advertising, work, play, education, gender, and individuality. Each unit begins with a reading of essays dealing with competing versions of the significance of the topic of the unit. For example, the unit on education includes an analysis of US schools by a diverse range of observers: William Bennett, Jonathon Kozol, John Dewey, and James Thurber. These essays are often followed with a film dealing with school experiences--for example, *Risky Business or Sixteen Candles or The Breakfast Club.* A videotape of a current television program about schools---for example, *Beverly Hills, 90210*--is also often included. The important consideration is not the texts in themselves but the texts in relation to certain methods of interpreting them.

Students are provided a set of heuristics (invention strategies) that grow out of the interaction of rhetoric, structuralism, poststructuralism, semiotics, and cultural studies (again, especially of the Birmingham Center variety). While those outlined here have been developed as a result of reading in Saussure, Peirce, Levi-Strauss, Barthes, Gramsci, Raymond Williams, Stuart Hall, and others, an excellent introduction to them for teachers and students can be found in John Fiske's *Introduction to Communication Studies.* (Diana George and John Trimbur's *Reading Culture* will perform a similar function for composition classrooms.) In examining any text-- print, film, television--- students are asked to locate the key terms in the discourse and to situate these within the structure of meaning of which they form a part. These terms of course are made up of the central preoccupations of the text, but to determine how they are working to constitute experience their functions as parts of coded structures--a semiotic system must be examined. The terms are first set in relation to their binary opposites as suggested by the text itself (This of course follows Saussure's description of the central place of contrast in signification and Lévi-Strauss's application of it.) Sometimes this opposition is indicated explicitly, but often it is not. It is also important to note that a term commonly occupies a position in opposition to more than one other term.

For example, we sometimes begin with a 1981 essay from *The Wall Street Journal,* "The Days of a Cowboy are Marked by Danger, Drudgery, and Low Pay," by William Blundell. (This essay is most appropriate for the unit on work, but its codes are at once so varied and so accessible to students that it is a useful introduction to any unit.) We first consider the context of the piece, exploring the characteristics of the readership of the newspaper and the historical events surrounding the essay's production, particularly as indicated within the text. The purpose of this is to decide what probably acted as key terms for the original readers. The essay focuses on the cowboss, the ranch foreman who runs the cattle operation. The meaning of "cowboss" is established by seeing it in binary opposition to the cowboys who work for him as well as the owners who work away from the ranch in cities. At other times in the essay, the cowboss is grouped together with the cowboys in opposition to office workers. Through the description of labor relations on the ranch, the cowboys are also situated in contrast to urban union workers, but the latter are never explicitly mentioned. Finally, the exclusively masculine nature of ranching is suggested only at the end of the essay when the cowboss's wife is described in passing as living apart from the ranch on the cowboss's own small spread, creating male/female domain binary. All of these binaries suggest others, such as the opposition of nature/ civilization, country/ city, cowboy/ urban cowboy, and the like. Students begin to see that these binaries are arranged hierarchically, with one term privileged over the other. They also see how unstable these hierarchies can be, however, with a term frequently shifting valences as it moves from one binary to another-- for example, cowboy/ union worker but cowboss/ cowboy. It is also important to point out that this location of binaries is of course not an exact operation and that great diversity appears as students negotiate the text differently. Their reasons for doing so become clear at the next level of analysis.

These terms are then placed within the narrative structural forms suggested by the text, the culturally coded stories about patterns of behavior appropriate for people within certain situations. These codes deal with such social designations as race, class, gender, age, ethnicity, and the like. The position of the key terms within these socially constructed narrative codes are analyzed, discussed, and written about. It is not too difficult to imagine how these are at work in the binaries indicated above. The narratives that cluster around the figure of the cowboy in our culture are quickly detected in this essay--for example, of behavior involving individuality, freedom, and independence. These, however, are simultaneously coupled with self-discipline, respect for authority (good cowboys never complain), and submission to the will of the cowboss. Students have little difficulty in pointing out the ways these narratives are conflicted while concurrently reinforcing differences in class and gender role expectations. Of particular value is to see the way the essay employs narratives that at once disparage the *Wall Street Journal* readers because they are urban office workers while enabling them to identify with the rugged freedom and adventure of the cowboys, seeing themselves as metaphorically enacting the masculine narrative of the cowboss in their separate domains. In other words, students discover that the essay attempts to position the reader in the role of a certain kind of masculine subject.

These narrative patterns at the level of the social role are then situated within larger narrative structures that have to do with economic, political, and cultural formulations. Here students examine capitalist economic narratives as demonstrated in this essay and their consequences for class, gender, and race relations and roles both in the work place and elsewhere. They look, for example, at the distribution of work in beef production with its divisions between managers and workers, thinkers and doers, producers and consumers. They also consider the place of narratives of democracy in the essay, discussing the nature of the political relations that are implied in the hierarchies of terms and social relations presented. It should be clear that at these two narrative levels considerable debate results as students disagree about the narratives that ought to be invoked in interpreting the text, their relative worth as models for emulation, and the degree to which these narratives are conflicted. In other words, the discussion emerging from the use of these heuristics is itself conflicted and unpredictable.

Thus, the term as it is designated within a hierarchical binary is situated within narratives of social roles, and these roles are located within more comprehensive narratives of economic and political formations in the larger society. The point of the interpretation is to see that texts--whether rhetorical or poetic--are ideologically invested in the construction of subjectivities within recommended economic, social, and political arrangements. Finally, as should now be clear, this hermeneutic process is open-ended, leading in diverse and unpredictable directions in the classroom. And this is one of its strengths as it encourages open debate and wide-ranging speculation.

After some experience with written and video texts, students apply these heuristics to their personal experiences in order to analyze in essay form the effect of an important cultural code on their lives. The students select the topic and content of the essay, but they must do so within the context of the larger theme of each unit. Thus, in the unit on education, students must choose some feature of their school experience from the past or present that has been of particular personal significance. The students must then locate points of conflict and dissonance in the cultural codes discovered, although they are not expected to resolve them. For example, students often choose to write about their experiences in high school athletics in order to discuss the conflicted codes involved in the emphasis on personal versus team success, winning versus learning to accept defeat, discipline versus play, and the like. The roles the students learn to assume in sports are examined in terms of such categories as gender, age, race, and group membership. Some students have explored the differences in the experiences of male and female athletes. Here they commonly examine the narratives appropriate to the behavior of each as recommended by dominant cultural codes about sports. These role definitions and performances are then placed within larger narratives having to do with life experiences, such as vocational aspirations, career objectives, marriage plans, and the like. Students at this point often discover the parallel between the contrasting experiences of males and females in high school sports and the contrasting experiences of males and females in career tracks. Once again, the various levels of conflict are explored, both within the expectations for each gender and across the genders, although, once again, students are not expected to resolve them. It should also be noted that conflicts also appear as students disagree in discussions about the codes that are being recommended within these sports activities. These incidents reinforce the point that cultural codes are always negotiated so that students produce them as well as simply re-produce them; that is, students do not always simply submit to these codes, often reshaping them to serve their own agendas. And of course incidents of resistance are frequently discussed as students report their defiance of required roles--for example, refusing to engage in some humiliating hazing ritual against those declared "losers."

As students develop material through the use of the heuristic and begin to write initial drafts of their essays, they discover the culturally coded character of all parts of composing. Students must learn to arrange their materials to conform to the genre codes of the form of the essay they are writing--the personal essay, the academic essay, the newspaper essay, for example. (Students could also be asked to create other kinds of texts--short stories, poems, video although we have not done so in our composition course. Here the genre codes of each would again be foregrounded.) These essay genres conform to socially indicated formal codes that students must identify and enact, and they, of course, carry great consequences for meaning. A given genre encourages certain kinds of messages while discouraging others. Next, at the level of the sentence, stylistic form comes into play, and the student must again learn to generate sentence structures and patterns of diction that are expected of the genre employed. It is important that students be made aware of the purposes of these codes, both practical and ideological. In other words, expecting certain formal and stylistic patterns is not always a matter of securing "clear and effective communication." As all writing teachers know, most errors in grammar and spelling do not in themselves interfere with the reader's understanding. The use of "who" for "whom," for example, seldom creates any confusion in reference. These errors instead create interferences of a social and political nature.

Finally, I would like to restate a point on the interchangability of reading and writing made earlier. In enacting the composing process, students are learning that all experience is situated within signifying practices, and that learning to understand personal and social experience involves acts of discourse production and interpretation, the two acting reciprocally in reading and writing codes. Students in the class come to see that interpretation involves production as well as reproduction, and is as constructive as composing itself. At the same time, they discover that the more one knows about a text-- its author, place of publication, audience, historical context-- the less indeterminate it becomes and the more confident the reader can be in interpreting and negotiating its intentions. Similarly, the more the writer understands the entire semiotic context in which she is functioning, the greater will be the likelihood that her text will serve as a successful intervention in an ongoing discussion. After all, despite the inevitable slippages that appear in the production and interpretation of codes, people do in fact communicate with each other daily to get all sorts of work done effectively. At the same time, even these "effective" exchanges can be seen to harbor contradictions that we concealed or ignored. These contradictions are important to discover for the reader and writer because they foreground the political unconscious of decision making, a level of unspoken assumptions that are often repressed in ordinary discourse. It is here that the betrayals of democracy and the value of the individual are discovered despite the more obvious claims to the contrary.

The purpose of social-epistemic rhetoric is finally political, an effort to prepare students for critical citizenship in a democracy. We want students to begin to understand that language is never innocent, instead constituting a terrain of ideological battle. Language--textuality---is thus the terrain on which different conceptions of economic, social, and political conditions are contested with consequences for the formation of the subjects of history, the very consciousness of the historical agent. We are thus committed to teaching writing as an inescapably political act, the working out of contested cultural codes that affect every feature of experience. This involves teachers in an effort to problematize students' experiences, requiring them to challenge the ideological codes they bring to college by placing their signifying practices against alternatives. Sometimes this is done in a cooperative effort with teachers and students agreeing about the conflicts that are apparent in considering a particular cultural formation-- for example, the elitist and often ruthlessly competitive organization of varsity sports in high schools. Students are able to locate points of personal resistance and negotiation in dealing with the injustices of this common social practice. At other times, students and teachers are at odds with each other or, just as often, the students am themselves divided about the operation and effects of conflicting codes. This often results in spirited exchange. The role of the teacher is to act as a mediator while ensuring that no code, including her own, goes unchallenged.

This has been a lengthy introduction to the intersections of postmodern discourse theory and rhetoric. Even so, it only begins to explore the possibilities, as can be seen, for example, in the excellent new collection, *Contending with Words: Composition and Rhetoric in a Postmodern Age,* edited by Patricia Harkin and John Schilb. (This volume arrived while I was putting the finishing touches on this piece.) These essays share with mine the composition as engaged in postmodern speculation has much to offer writing teachers. None, furthermore, suggests that it is a savior come to redeem us from our fallen ways. All see rhetoric and composition as engaged in a dialectic with the new speculation, the result being the enrichment of both. Indeed, these essays confirm what I have long maintained: The postmodern turn in recent discussions in the academy is an attempt to restore the place of rhetoric in the human sciences. In it we find an ally in our work of creating a critically literate citizenry, and we ought not to reject it just because it speaks a nonstandard dialect.

Note on the article's authorship as of 1992. Jim Berlin spent the first six years of his professional career teaching in elementary schools in Detroit and Flint, Michigan. Since receiving his doctorate in nineteenth-century literature at the University of Michigan, he has taught in rhetoric and composition programs at Wichita State University (where he directed the Kansas Writing Project), at the University of Cincinnati (where he directed the freshman English program), and, as a visitor, at the University of Texas at Austin. He now teaches at Purdue University. His published work in the history and theory of rhetoric and composition explores the intersections of rhetorics, poetics, and politics.

[Editorial note from *Rhetoric Review.*]

WORKS CITED

Aronwitz, Stanley, and Henry A. Giroux. *Education Under Siege.* South Hadley, MA: Bergin and Garvey, 1985.

Barthes, Roland *Mythologies.* Trans. Annette Lavers. New York: Hill and Wang 1972.

Benveniste, Emil. *Problems in General Linguistics.* Trans. Mary Elizabeth Meek. Coral Gables: U of Miami P. 1971.

Berlin, James A. "Composition and Cultural Studies." *Composition and Resistance.* Ed. Mark Hurlbert and Michael Blitz. Portsmouth, NH: Heinemann-Boynton/Cook, 1991.47-55.

___."Composition Studies and Cultural Studies: Collapsing the Boundaries." *Into the Field: The Site of Composition Studies.* Ed. Anne Ruggles Gere. New York: MLA, 1992.

___. Rhetoric and Ideology in the Writing Class." *College English* 50 (1988) 477-94.

___. *Rhetoric and Reality: Writing instruction in American Colleges,* 1900-1985. Carbondale, IL: Southern Illinois UP, 1987.

___. "Rhetoric Programs After World War II: Ideology, Power, and Conflict." *Rhetoric and Ideology: Compositions and Criticisms of Power.* Ed. Charles W. Kneupper. Arlington TX: Rhetoric Society of America, 1989.

52   Perspectives, Theories, and Directions in Teaching Composition

Blundell, William E. "The Days of a Cowboy are Marked by Danger, Drudgery, and Low Pay." *Wall Street Journal* 10 June 1981, sec. A: 1+.

Burke, Kenneth. *Language as Symbolic Action.* Berkeley: U of California P, 1966.

Corbett, Edward PJ. *Classical Rhetoric for the Modern Student.* New York: Oxford UP. 1965.

Derrida, Jacques. *Of Grammatology.* Trans. Gayattri Spivak. Baltimore: Johns Hopkins UP, 1976.

Donahue, Patricia, and Ellen Quandahl. *Reclaiming Pedagogy: The Rhetoric of the Classroom.* Carbondale, IL: Southern Illinois UP, 1989.

Dowst, Kenneth. "The Epistemic Approach: Writing, Knowing, and Learning". *Eight Approaches to Teaching Composition.* Ed. Timothy Donovan and Ben W. McClelland. Urbana: NCTE, 1990.

Elbow, Peter. "Reflections on Academic Discourse." *College English* 53 (1991): 135-55.

Fiske, John. *Introduction to Communication Studies.* 2nd ed. London: Routledge, 1990.

Foucault, Michel. *Power/Knowledge: Selected Interviews and Other Writings; 1972-1977.* Ed. Colin Gordon. Trans. Colin Gordon et al. New York: Pantheon, 1980.

George, Diana, and John Trimbur. *Reading Culture.* New York: Harper-Collins, 1992.

Hairston, Maxine. "Comment and Response." *College English* 52 (1990): 694-96.

Hall, Stuart. "Encoding/Decoding." *Culture, Media, Language.* Ed. Stuart Hall et al. London: Hutchinson, 1980.

_____. "The Rediscovery of 'Ideology': Return of the Repressed in Media Studies." *Culture, Society and the Media.* Ed. Michael Gurevitch et al. London: Routledge, 1982.

Harkin, Patricia, and John Schilb, eds. *Contending With Words: Composition and Rhetoric in a Postmodern Age.* New York: MLA, 1991.

Hodge, Robert, and Gunther Kress. *Social Semiotics.* Ithaca, NY: Cornell UP, 1988.

Johnson, Richard. "What is Cultural Studies Anyway?" Social Text 16 (1986-87): 38-80.

Kennedy, George A. *Classical Rhetoric and its Christian and Secular Tradition from Ancient to Modern Times.* Chapel Hill: U of North Carolina P, 1980.

KF. "Putting on the Dog: Heuristics, Paradigms, and Hermeneutics." *Rhetoric Review* 10 (1991): 187-93.

Knoblauch, C.H., and Lil Brannon. *Rhetorical Traditions and the Teaching of Writing.* Upper Montclair, NJ: Boynton/Cook, 1984.

Morton, Donald, and Mas'ud Zavarzadeh. *Theory/Pedagogy/Politics: Texts for Change.* Urbana: U of Illinois P, 1991.

Nilsen, Alleen Pace. "Sexism in English: A Feminist View." *Perspectives: Turning Reading into Writing.* Ed. Joseph J. Comprone. Boston: Houghton, 1987.

Schilb, John. "Cultural Studies, Postmodernism, and Composition." *Contending with Words: Composition and Rhetoric in a Postmodern Age.* Ed. Patricia Harkin and John Schilb. New York: MLA,1991.173-88.

Scott, Robert L. "On Viewing Rhetoric as Epistemic." *Central States Speech Journal* 18 (1967):9-16.

Shor, Ira "Educating the Educators: A Freirean Approach to the Crisis in Education" *Freire for the Classroom.* Ed. Ira Shor. Portsmouth, NH: Heinnemann-Boynton/Cook, 1987. 7-32.

Smith, Paul. *Discerning the Subject.* Minneapolis: U of Minnesota P, 1988.

Therborn, Goran. *The Ideology of Power and the Power of Ideology.* London: Verson, 1980.

TS. "Joining the Conversation." *Rhetoric Review* 10 (1991): 175-86.

Vickers, Brian. *In Defence of Rhetoric.* Oxford: Clarendon, 1988.

The Pedagogy of Collaboration

Lisa Ede and Andrea Lunsford

The concepts of author and authorship, so radically destabilized in contemporary literary theory and current discursive practice, have not surprisingly been problematized in the field of rhetoric and composition, where scholars have challenged the traditional exclusion of student writing from claims to "real writing" and "authorship" and explored the ways in which authority can be established and experienced by students, in spite of the distinction ordinarily drawn-- albeit implicitly-- between literary "authors" and student "writers." In both areas of study, the move to examine processes--either constitutive theories of reading or constitutive theories of writing--reflects shifting epistemological assumptions that foreground the relationship between individuals and social groups. Using the work of Stanley Fish and David Bartholomae as the locus for a discussion of "parallel tracks" in literary and composition studies, Patricia Sullivan notes that both theorists "move from an earlier view of knowledge as an individual construction to the view that knowledge is a function of the linguistic norms of a discourse community." Both fields, she continues, have shifted attention from "extracting truth from autonomous texts" to understanding the "ways that discursive practices constitute knowledge of texts" (in literature) and with the "ways knowledge is constructed by the writing practices of ... various discourse communities" (in composition) (19-20).

In composition studies, interest in discourse communities has gone hand in hand with a growing interest in social construction theories of knowledge--theories which attempt to situate the known in communal contexts. "Writing as a social process" has, in fact, become something of a buzz or catchphrase as articles on small group collaborative efforts, peer response techniques, and the social nature of writing and reading appear in growing numbers. We shall examine this movement, generally referred to as collaborative learning, at a later point in this chapter and will suggest ways in which it still holds an implicit view of solitary, originary authorship.

Historical Perspective on Collaborative Learning

Before doing so, however, we should attempt to situate this discussion of collaborative learning in a historical context that represents a playing out of a persistent tension in American culture--the tension between the individual, the isolated Cartesian self, and the community. This tension is vividly captured by Alexis de Toqueville in his analysis of the American character. To describe this character, he uses a newly coined word *individualism* (which he differentiates from *egoism): "Individualism is a calm and considered feeling which disposes each citizen to isolate himself from the main of his fellows and withdraw into the circle of family and friend; with this little society formed to his taste, he gladly leaves the greater society to look after itself." As such individualism increases, Toqueville notes:

> More and more people who though neither rich nor powerful enough to have much hold over others, have gained or kept enough wealth and enough understanding to look after their own needs. Such folks owe no man anything and hardly expect anything from anybody. They form the habit of thinking of themselves in isolation and imagine that their whole destiny is in their hands. ... Each man is forever thrown back on himself alone, and there is danger that he may be shut up in the solitude of his own heart. (506-8)

Toqueville feared the results of unmediated growth of "individualism" and argued that it could be best countered by a strong tradition of community and of public discourse: "Citizens who are bound to take part in public affairs must turn from private interests and occasionally take a look at something other than themselves" (510). This strong civic involvement with public discourse was, in Toqueville's view, the balancing factor that would keep America from developing into a society of naturally exclusive, autonomous individuals, a society which would not, he feared, easily be able to resist totalitarianism or despotism.

In part, the founding document of America, the Declaration of Independence, reflects both the profound drive toward individualism and the commitment to community and public discourse that Toqueville found in the American character--dual ideals that have been inscribed in our history and that have often been in tension with one another. (These ideals are examined and related to tensions in contemporary America by Bellah and his colleagues in *Habits of the Heart: Individualism and Commitment in American Life.*) So we might expect to find evidence of this tension in American education and, more particularly for our purposes, in the teaching of rhetoric and writing. And indeed we do. As Michael Halloran has demonstrated, the earliest rhetorical instruction in America was influenced by Cicero and Quintilian, and the Roman concept of the "ideal orator" as the public-spirited person speaking well animated such instruction. But this essentially rhetorical emphasis on the Greek and Roman "commune," on communal values and shared meanings, diminished in the nineteenth century as oral discourse was displaced by writing, as new objective methods of testing arose, and as the academy emphasized competition over cooperation, autonomous electives over the classical core curriculum, and the autonomous individual over the social. By the end of the nineteenth century, traditional rhetorical instruction had been largely displaced by emerging English departments heavily imbued with Romantic theories of genius and of originality, with a concept of writing as an individual, solitary act, and with philological and exegetical traditions that emphasized the autonomous writer and text. (See Gerald Graff's recounting of this history in *Professing Literature,* which treats English departments but not rhetorical instruction or theory.)

Nevertheless, some educators resisted the trend toward individualism and isolation in English instruction. Anne Gere's recent monograph on the history of writing groups in America reveals that peer response techniques and small group collaboration have been advocated and enjoyed by some citizens and teachers since the colonial period--in mutual improvement groups such as Benjamin Franklin's Junto, in the Lyceum- and Chautauqua-generated societies, and in the women's clubs and literary societies (see *Writing* 32-54). Fred Newton Scott and his student Gertrude Buck both advocated more natural social conditions for composition instruction and evaluation in schools, while Alexander Bain's *On Teaching English* praised the practice of writing with an eye toward reading draft versions to a society of peers and revising on the basis of discussion. And in the colleges and universities, the great popularity of literary societies and other speaking societies offered an opportunity for cooperation and extensive collaboration.

As Mara Holt has demonstrated, collaborative pedagogy--while never dominant--has a rich history and tradition. Basing her study on an examination of academic journals from 1911 to 1986, Holt traces this collaborative thread, arguing that "the rationales and practices of collaborative pedagogy consistently reflect social and intellectual and economic trends of the sociohistorical movement in which they are located" ("Learning" 235).

As the twentieth century proceeded, the dominant emphasis on individualism, on writing as an individually creative act, and on "objective" testing as a means of evaluating the intellectual property of solitary writers, continued to be questioned by a marginal collaborative pedagogy. Most influential was the work of educational philosopher John Dewey, who argued tirelessly for seeing the education of each individual in a social and communal "context." He notes in *The Public and Its Problems:* "Individuals still do the thinking, desiring, purposing, but *what* they think of is the consequence of their behavior upon that of others and that of others upon themselves" (24). Dewey's calls for "new" or "progressive" education began early in this century; and throughout his career, he insisted that learning occurs in *interaction,* that social context is of utmost importance in the classroom, and that we should reform our traditional model (which privileges the individual) by enhancing "the moving spirit of the whole group ... held together by participation in common activities" (*Public* 54-55).

Dewey influenced generations of teachers and scholars, among them Sterling Andrus Leonard, who argued as early as 1916 in "The Correction and Criticism of Composition Work" that "oral and written composition are developed in a socially organized class to carry out real projects ... in a spirit of hearty cooperation" (598). In his 1917 *English Composition as a Social Problem,* Leonard goes on to say that:

> We must not make the mistake of assuming that training in composition is purely an individual matter. Most self expression is for the purpose of social communication. ... Our whole use of language has a social setting. The futility of much of our past teaching has been due to our mental blinders to the social function of language. One has only to compare the situation of ordinary conversation with that of a class exercise in oral composition to realize how far we have forgotten the social genesis of speech. Worthy social conversation cannot be made at command of any person in authority. Ordinary human beings would not endure hearing the same item of discussion repeated by each person present. Nor would one care to say what everyone else had already said. Yet these are some of the striking characteristics of a composition exercise. If

we are to make our training real, we must naturalize it, which is to say we must socialize our teaching of composition. (viii-ix)

Dewey's interactionist or constructivist approach to learning and knowledge gained increasing support in the 1930s from the work of George Herbert Mead who argued that meaning is not individually wrought but is instead constructed through social interaction, In *Invention as a Social Act,* Karen Burke LeFevre cites Mead's work as providing a theoretical foundation for a view of invention as collaborative, noting that "other social thinkers, such as Martin Buber and Ludwig Wittgenstein, [move from] what have traditionally been regarded as private psychological entities out into the realm of social interaction and contextualization of knowledge" (73). In addition, Jean Piaget's work with children took a social constructivist approach to knowledge and learning as he demonstrated that children learn through interaction with others and with things in their environmental contexts.

Dewey devotees (whose reductivist rendering of Dewey's work seems to have been uncritically accepted by E.D. Hirsch, who uses Dewey as a whipping boy in his cultural literacy argument) did much to rigidify and trivialize his original arguments; his influence faded during the exigencies of the war years. The critique of traditional education, with its teacher-centered classrooms and its emphasis on "working alone" and on "originality" continued, however, primarily in Britain. M.L.J. Abercrombie's *Anatomy of Judgment: An Investigation into the Processes of Perception and Reasoning* (1960) and her later *Aims and Techniques of Group Teaching* (1970), for instance, evolved from her work with groups of medical students. Abercrombie was convinced that small group discussion provided the most effective way to help those students become more sophisticated and accurate at diagnosis and, hence, better physicians. Reacting to a report of a Committee of the Royal College of Physicians that argued: "The average medical graduate ... tends to lack curiosity and initiative; his powers of observation are relatively undeveloped; his ability to arrange and interpret facts is poor; he lacks precision in the use of words" (*Anatomy* 15-16), Abercrombie devised an experimental teaching course that would help students, through collaboration, learn to recognize diverse points of view, diverse interpretations of the results of an experiment, and thus to form more useful and accurate judgments.

My hypothesis is that we may learn to make better judgments if we can become aware of some of the factors that influence their formation. We may then be in a position to consider alternative judgments and to choose from among many instead of blindly and automatically accepting the first that comes; in other words, we may become more receptive or mentally more flexible. The results of testing the effects of the course of [collaborative group] discussions support this hypothesis. (*Anatomy* 17)

Abercrombie's emphasis on contextualizing knowledge and her realization that communally derived diagnoses are generally accurate and effective served as a direct challenge to the traditional individualism and isolated competitiveness endemic to most medical school curricula and higher education in general.

At roughly the same time, Edwin Mason presented a strikingly similar challenge to British secondary schools and, along the way, coined the phrase *collaborative learning.* Charging that "to work in a school day after day and feel that we are doing more harm than good, and that with the best will in the world, is too much to bear" (7), Mason set out to reform the school system, which he believed was "meeting neither the needs of the young nor the demands of the world" (8). As a result, Mason proposed a radical restructuring of this system, one which would replace the current competitive, authoritarian, overly specialized or departmentalized, and hence "alienated" program with one emphasizing interdisciplinary study, small group work, collaboration, and dialogue--largely in the spirit of John Dewey. The remainder of his remarkable book describes such a curriculum and advises teachers on how best to implement it.

As Abercrombie's and Mason's work began to have at least a small impact on pedagogical thinking, so too did that of the Brazilian teacher Paolo Freire, whose *Pedagogy of the Oppressed* appeared in 1968. Arguing that literacy is best taught in the social contexts of people's own lives, Freire faulted traditional education with promoting not genuine public literacy but passivity, alienation, and conformity instead. In his work, Freire aims to empower his student-colleagues to reclaim, reinterpret, and hence reenact their own lives and to gain growing awareness of how social forces work in dialogic relationship with individual experience to enslave--or to liberate--and to create the realities they inhabit "communally." Freire's work has most recently been presented as a challenge to the traditional teaching of writing in Ira Shor's *Freire for the Classroom: A Sourcebook for Liberatory Teaching,* which calls for a commitment to social and political contextualizing of all learning and on a renegotiation of power and authority in all classrooms.

These examples demonstrate that the drive toward individual autonomy, competitiveness, and isolated selfhood has always been countered, often only in a whisper but at other times in a louder, clearer voice, by a call for community, for shared public discourse, for working together for some common good. And, as Gere has shown, we could write part of the history of writing instruction in the twentieth century in just such terms.

Contemporary Composition Studies and the Question of Collaboration

The last twenty years are generally regarded as having witnessed a large shift in writing pedagogy, sometimes as a growing awareness of process and context, sometimes (following the work of pioneers like Moffett, Emig, and Britton) as a move from teacher-centered to student-centered learning models. We wish to acknowledge the effects of these largely positive shifts, most of which in our view run counter to the traditional valorization of autonomous individualism, competition, and hierarchy. But in spite of these pedagogical efforts, most day-to-day writing instruction in American colleges and universities still reflects traditional assumptions about the nature of the self (autonomous), the concept of authorship (as ownership of singly held property rights), and the classroom environment (hierarchical, teacher-centered).

We may look to contemporary composition studies as an illustration in point. Over the past few years, a number of scholars have attempted to understand this emerging field of study by proposing a naming of parts, a taxonomy. Richard Young identifies the two major "groups" in the field as the "new Romanticists" and the "new Classicists," the former stressing the interiority and essential mystery of composing, the latter stressing exteriority and structured procedures for composing. Patricia Bizzell modifies and amplifies this distinction, grouping composition studies into two camps-- those who view composing primarily as "inner-directed" and "prior to social influence" and those who view composing as "outer-directed" and based on "social processes whereby language-learning and thinking capacities are used and shaped in ... communities" ("Cognition" 215). In several essays and a monograph on twentieth-century writing instruction, James Berlin offers a taxonomy of his own, contrasting what he calls "objective" and "subjective" rhetorics with a tripartite division of "transactional" rhetoric.

Similar taxonomic arguments are advanced from differing perspectives by several others, including Lester Faigley and Stephen North, but are probably put most strongly by LeFevre. In *Invention as a Social Act,* LeFevre contrasts what she calls the Platonic view of inventing and composing ("the act of finding or creating that which is ... written as individual introspection; ideas begin in the mind of the individual writer and then are expressed to the rest of the world" [1]) with a social view of inventing and composing. This social view takes a constructivist approach to knowledge and posits that the "self" (in some ways similar to what Wayne Booth calls the "range of selves" or Foucault calls "subject positions") is socially constituted; hence, composing is essentially a social collaborative act.

These taxonomies of composition studies overlap and differ in a number of ways, and as all taxonomies inevitably do, they limit--indeed they often distort--what we perceive about our own field of study. So we mention them here not to endorse any particular taxonomy of rhetoric and composition studies, but to make one point that strikes us as particularly telling: the composition theorists and teachers most often identified with collaborative learning and peer response techniques--James Moffett, Donald Murray, Peter Elbow, Ken Macrorie--are also usually identified with Bizzell's "inner-directed" group or Berlin's "expressionist" group, which posit the uniqueness of individual imagination and see writing as a means of expressing an autonomous self. Ironically, then, the very writers most often associated with collaborative learning hold implicitly to traditional concepts of autonomous individualism, authorship, and authority for texts.

The work of Peter Elbow provides perhaps the best example of the tension and potential contradictions we have been describing. For years, Elbow has encouraged writers to work in groups, reading their work aloud for oral responses, out of which revisions grow. "Elbow grouping" is, in fact, a widespread phenomenon; we have encountered such groups of writers from Hawaii to New York, all expressing the efficacy of group work. Yet in spite of its emphasis on the importance of audience response to revision, Elbow's work rests on assumptions about individualism and individual creativity that fail to problematize traditional conceptions of the author and that deny the social nature of writing. For Elbow, expressing personal authenticity requires not social interaction but mining the depths of the self, searching inside the self for a unique voice. As he says in *Writing Without Teachers,* "The mind's magic. It can cook things instantaneously and perfectly when it gets going. You should expect yourself at times to write straight onto the paper words and thoughts far better than you knew were in you" (69).

In his recent books, *Writing with Power: Techniques for Mastering the Writing Process and Embracing Contraries: Explorations in Learning and Teaching,* Elbow continues to posit the individual self as the essentially mysterious source of creation, frequently calling on the "magical" ways writers discover their unified voices. *Writing with Power,* in fact, ends with a chapter on "Writing and Magic." As Greg Myers notes in a critique of Elbow, "Magic is the only possible source for such [individual] ineffable energies. ... [Such] metaphors prevent any analysis of the social conditions of our writing" (165). Such a stance is reflected in Elbow's recent essays, in which he argues that writers often must ignore audience (or any "others") in order to get to the heart and soul of what they want to say (1987, 1988).

The composition theorist most closely associated with social construction and collaborative learning theories in general and peer group response in particular is Kenneth Bruffee. Bruffee became interested in peer tutoring as a means of helping students "practice judgment collaboratively, through a progressive set of analytical and evaluative tasks applied to each other's academic writing in a context which fosters self-esteem" ("Brooklyn" 450). Yet in his early work on peer tutoring and in his text, *A Short Course in Writing,* Bruffee also holds to the concept of single authorship and individual creativity (students write alone and then revise after getting peer response, much as in the Elbow method) even while acknowledging the degree to which "knowledge is a social phenomenon, and the social context in which we learn permeates what we know and how we know it" (116). In his more recent work, however, Bruffee has moved to resolve the potential contradiction, arguing that our ability to read and write has its roots deep in our "acquired ability to carry on the social symbolic exchanges we call conversation" ("Conversation" 642).

As Bruffee readily notes, only recently has he come to contemplate the full theoretical significance of such an epistemology for the teaching of writing and reading. Drawing on the work of scholars in a number of disciplines--Stanley Fish in literary studies, Lev Vygotsky and Irving Goffman in psychology and sociology, Thomas Kuhn and Richard Rorty in philosophy, and Clifford Geertz in anthropology--Bruffee argues that what and who we are and what we write and know are in large part functions of interaction and of community. Thus writing and reading are, essentially and naturally, collaborative, social acts, ways in which we understand and in which "knowledge is established and maintained in the normal discourse of communities of knowledgeable peers" ("Conversation" 640).

As Berlin points out, Bruffee's later works were "from the start based on a conception of knowledge as a social construction--a dialectical interplay of investigator, discourse community, and material world, with language as the agent of mediation. The rhetorical act is thus implicated in the very discovery of knowledge--a way not merely of recording knowledge for transmissions but of arriving at it mutually for mutual consideration" (*Rhetoric* 175-76). But Bruffee's emphasis on collaboration and consensus, or social context, has been criticized, most recently by Mas'ud Zavarzadeh and Donald Morton, who say that:

There is in Bruffee no sense of the politics of cognition that organizes this socially constructed knowledge. Society and the social for him (as for Rorty) are cognitive domains- -areas in which knowledge somehow appears by means of such apparatuses as agreement and convention and so forth. As a result of such a conservative (cognitive) theory of knowledge, ... the subject is presented as an uncontested category. ... Bruffee's collaborative learning/teaching is, in other words, the latest reproduction of the "management" of the subject and the latest effort to save it through collaborative learning and the *Conversation of Mankind.* The teacher in this model is the manager of the classroom--an agent of social coalescence. (14-15)

Bruffee has also been criticized by Myers, who charges that "while Bruffee shows that reality can be seen as a social construct, he does not give us any way to criticize this construct. Having discovered the role of consensus in the production of knowledge, he takes this consensus as something that just is, rather than as something that might be good or bad" (166).

Myers is insisting that those interested in collaborative learning step back and ask what such learning will be used for, what aims and purposes and motives are served, who will and will not "count" as a collaborator (and why), where power and authority are located. Others in the composition community echo this concern. Richard Ohmann has long criticized composition textbooks for treating student writers as though they were isolated, cut off from any cultural, political, or social contexts. Ohmann's latest work, *Politics of Letters,* extends this critique to most contemporary teaching. Similar critiques of the asocial nature of composition instruction appear in the work of Charles Yarnoff, David Bartholomae, Charles Bazerman, Patricia Bizzell, and James Berlin (see "Rhetoric").

Other work has recently focused on context and communal aspects of learning. In particular, Shirley Brice Heath's ethnographic studies demonstrate how writing and reading must be seen as developing within a social context in which talk plays a major role. David Bleich's *The Double Perspective: Language, Literacy, and Social Relations* examines the ways in which learning is situated in and beyond our classrooms; his chapter on "Collaboration Among Students" offers particularly useful (and concrete) advice. At the Center for the Study of Writing, Linda Flower and her colleagues are working to relate the cognitive factors in composing to their social contexts. Still others, focusing on professional and work-related writing, stress the importance of social and political contexts in such writing (e.g., Lee Odell and Dixie Goswami's collection of essays *Writing in Nonacademic Settings* or Janis Forman and Patricia Katsky's "The Group Report).

The early work of Elbow and Bruffee has been augmented in this decade by a large and growing body of work on collaborative learning, much of it linked to the National Writing Project and to writing across the curriculum movements. (See Trimbur for a review of work on collaborative learning.) In addition to the work of LeFevre and Gere, we now have studies by Colette Daiute and Bridget Dalton on collaboration in young school children, by Anthony Paré on collaboration in the high school setting, and by the authors represented in Bouton and Garth's *Learning in Groups,* to name only a few. This interest in and growing commitment to the principles of collaborative learning grow out of and are informed by the philosophical tradition on which Bruffee's work builds.

Cooperative Versus Collaborative Learning

Paralleling this movement in composition and English studies is one in psychology and education, though its epistemological bases are considerably different. The cooperative learning movement has amassed large amounts of empirical data to support the claim that the strategies and principles they espouse really do enhance learning. The literature in this area is voluminous and grows out of the tradition of research in group dynamics. Robert Slavin says in "An Introduction to Cooperative Learning Research," "cooperative learning methods are based on social psychological research and theory, some of it dating back to the early 1900s ..." In the remainder of this overview article, Slavin describes an "extensively researched and widely used set of cooperative learning methods," structured, systematic instructional strategies capable of being used at any grade level and in most school subjects. All of the methods involve having the teacher assign the students to four- to six-member learning groups composed of high-, average-, and low-achieving students--"boys and girls, black, Anglo, and Hispanic students, and mainstreamed academically handicapped students as well as their non-handicapped classmates" (6-7).

One such method Slavin has developed is Jigsaw II, in which "students are assigned to four- to five-member teams. They read narrative materials, such as social studies chapters, short stories or biographies, and each team member is given a special topic on which to become an expert. The students discuss their topics in 'expert groups,' then return to teach their teammates what they have learned. Finally, the students take a quiz on the material, and the quiz scores are used ... to form individual and team scores" (7-8).

The methods Slavin describes have been tested in numerous projects, including a series of studies conducted by Slavin and others at Johns Hopkins University and by Sharan in Tel Aviv on the effect of cooperative learning on race relations (see DeVries and Edwards, "Student Teams and Learning Games: Their Effect on Cross-Race and Cross-Sex Interaction"; Slavin, "Effects of Biracial Learning Teams on Cross-Racial Friendship Interaction"; and Sharan, "Cooperative Learning in Small Groups: Recent Methods and Effects on Achievement, Attitudes, and Ethnic Relations"). More recently, researchers have focused on analyzing interaction patterns in cooperative groups (Webb, "Student Interaction and Learning in Small Groups") and, particularly, on how to design a classroom conducive to cooperative learning (Graves and Graves, "Creating a Cooperative Learning Environment: An Ecological Approach).

Discrepancies and inconsistencies across these studies certainly exist, and some, such as Michaels, have challenged the claim that cooperative methods improve achievement. On the whole, however, the evidence produced by proponents is impressive. On the basis of a long series of studies, in fact, Johnson and Johnson, of the University of Minnesota Cooperative Learning Center, claim the following "outcomes" for cooperative learning:

1. higher achievement and increased retention
2. greater use of higher level reasoning strategies and increased critical reasoning competencies
3. greater ability to view situations from others' perspectives
4. more positive relations with peers regardless of ethnic, sex, ability, social class, or handicapping differences
5. more positive attitudes toward school learning, and teachers
6. higher self esteem
7. greater collaborative skills and attitudes necessary for working effectively with others (*Learning* 9)

In addition to these advantages, research in cooperative learning poses a strong challenge to the efficacy of tracking, demonstrating that children of differing abilities learn better in mixed groups than they do in "tracks."

Growing as it does out of positivist, empiricist, and behaviorist assumptions, the research on cooperative learning has a different epistemological basis from that of collaborative learning in the Bruffee tradition, one that posits an externally verifiable "reality" which serves as stimulus for various responses. Furthermore, its research agenda demands hypotheses that are confirmed or refuted, problems that are solved, questions that are answered. And the tasks the students collaborate on are rigidly structured and controlled. In spite of these shortcomings, however, this research has important implications, and indeed the methods developed by Slavin, Johnson and Johnson, and others may come close to what George Hillocks, Jr., is calling for as "environmental" tasks in his book *Research on Written Composition: New Directions for Teaching*. Such work deserves to be better known by teachers and researchers in composition if only in order to mount a systematic interrogation of its assumptions.

The Challenge of Collaborative Writing

The work on both cooperative and collaborative learning surveyed here all moves toward contextualizing instruction; the work on collaboration, in particular, emphasizes the ways in which knowledge is constructed among members of communities. The recent attention given to collaborative writing might thus seem a natural extension or a subset of collaborative learning theory. Yet collaborative learning theory has from its inception failed to challenge traditional concepts of individualism and ownership of ideas and has operated primarily in traditional ways. Students may work together on revising or on problem solving, but when they write, they typically write alone in settings structured and governed by a teacher/authority in whom power is vested. Studies of collaborative writing, on the other hand, make such silent accommodations less easy to maintain and as a result offer the potential to challenge and hence re-situate collaborative learning theories.

Much of the work on collaborative writing has focused on the world of work. Studies by Mary Beth Debs, Janis Forman, Stephen Doheny-Farina, Faigley and Miller, and Geoffrey Cross, as well as by the authors of this book, examine collaborative writing in a number of job-related settings. Others, such as Deborah Bosley, Sharon Hamilton-Wieler, Karen Spear, and Charles Cooper, have attempted to build collaborative writing into classroom contexts. In a 1986 survey, Hallie Lemon found that the composition faculty at Western Illinois University use collaboration at every stage of the writing process, including drafting. Extensive research on this kind of "shared document" collaboration is being carried out by a Purdue University research team in an effort to define kinds of collaborative writing and to describe the processes involved in such group writing tasks. Their research includes a case study of collaborative writing groups (see Meg Morgan, et al.). Also at the college level, O'Donnell and colleagues have conducted experiments that support the claim that group-produced documents are perceived as better than those individually produced.

In a study of writers in seven contexts (including junior high, high school upper division undergraduate and doctoral students, a chemist, a general manager, and a civil engineer), Stephen P. Witte has identified four forms of collaborative writing and concludes that across these seven contexts "writing became increasingly more collaborative and collaborative in different ways" (2-3). Thomas L. Hilgers and Daiute have explored the uses of collaborative writing with younger children. Nevertheless, as Nancy Allen and her colleagues point out, because "very little detail is known about collaborative writing processes in general ... there is a need for indepth study of the features of collaborative writing [defined as] a situation in which decisions are made by consensus" ("Shared-Document" 1-2). We would add that much more careful attention needs to be given to just what is meant by consensus and to the ways consensus is or is not achieved.

John Trimbur has begun such exploration in "Consensus and Difference in Collaborative Learning," in which he builds on the work of Habermas to argue that we must "distinguish between consensus as an acculturative practice that reproduces business as usual and consensus as an oppositional one that challenges the prevailing conditions of production" by providing a "critical instrument to open gaps in the conversation through which differences may emerge" (27). Joseph Harris extends this critique of consensus and offers an argument for "community without consensus" in his "Idea of Community in the Study of Writing."

While we clearly need more and better studies on the processes and varieties of collaborative writing, some directions already seem clear. Just as collaborative writing potentially challenges the hegemony of single, originary authorship, so do a mix of historical, social, theoretical, and pedagogical forces all centered on a destabilized author/writer and on context, community, and the social nature of knowledge and learning present a series of challenges to higher education in general and to the teaching of composition in particular. We turn now to examine the pedagogical implications of these challenges.

Closest to home is the challenge to traditional classroom format and to the teacher's role. Our classrooms after all posit power and authority in the teacher. At best, students are in apprenticeship to authority; they do not help constitute it. Ohmann acknowledges this challenge when he probes the issue of student "powerlessness" in our classes: "The writer's situation is heavy with contradictions. She is ... invited both to assume responsibility for her education and to trust the college's plan for it; to build her competence and to follow a myriad of rules and instructions; to see herself as an autonomous individual and to be incessantly judged" (252). As one concrete way of contesting such alienating tensions, Ohmann uses collaborative group interviews, including one of himself. This interview, Ohmann notes, can help establish student "ownership of the writing task in two ways. First, it demystifies my role in the class, opening up my goods and values as a subject for inquiry on the students' terms, taking them off the secret agenda. Second, it changes the relationship of their writing to what I have said in class, turning the latter into material for analysis and criticism rather than the graven words of authority" (256).

But even in the most collaborative of our classrooms, the authority to organize and evaluate rests with the teacher. As Trimbur notes, "Even when I'm not in the room, my authority remains behind, embedded in the very tasks I've asked students to work on. ... If anything, I have never felt more powerful than in the collaborative classroom precisely because I know much more about what's going on, how students are thinking about the issues of the course, what language they are generating to talk about these issues and so on" (Letter). As Foucault's work suggests, collaborative writing itself constitutes a technology of power, one we are only beginning to explore. As we carry out such exploration, as we investigate the ways in which collaborative writing challenges traditional power relationships, we need to bring students into these discussions, asking them to work with us to examine how authority is negotiated, shared, distributed. At least potentially, we would argue, collaborative writing holds out the promise for a plurality of power and of authority among teacher and students, what Ohmann calls an "opening up" of the classroom.

The hierarchical bases of power in our classrooms reflect the larger structure of our educational institutions. Most university calendars, divided neatly into semesters or quarters, reflect a positivistic approach to learning: knowledge is "packaged" into discrete segments and dispensed to passive recipients, fast-food style, through four years. Such a system posits students as isolated units, all of whom learn in similar ways and at similar speeds. The time necessary for group cohesion to occur, for examination of group dynamics involving consensus and dissensus to take place, much less for a consideration of the issues at stake in a seemingly simple question such as "Who is the author of this essay?" is not easily found in such a system. The research and the scholarship reviewed here strongly suggest that just as we must rethink our roles as teachers in a collaborative writing classroom, so also must we rethink our use of time in the college curriculum. At the very least, we must become aware of how such matters as the use of time reflect assumptions and traditions that may no longer fit with our educational goals.

We could of course point out other institutional constraints that mitigate against a pedagogy of collaboration. Most notable is traditional classroom design. Large cavernous lecture halls in which students see only the backs of other students' heads, and classrooms whose bolted down desks face dutifully toward the slightly raised lectern in front present major stumbling blocks to collaborative learning and writing. But ingenious teachers can and will devise ways to change the settings that impede their efforts to undermine traditional teacher-centered pedagogies.

Other institutional practices, bound as they are in ideology, may prove more intractable to change than will classroom settings. Among these we see the examination system as particularly problematic. This system, barely a hundred years old, is rooted solidly in positivistic assumptions: knowledge is objectifiably knowable and can be measured and counted. Such a tradition goes hand in hand with the conception of a solitary, sovereign writer with individually owned property rights. This view of knowledge calls for a controlled testing situation and valorizes the hard data such situations yield as proof of success or failure. Testing as we know it is by definition acontextual, antisocial, anticommunal. And our dependence on testing at all levels of the educational system seems only to be growing. Yet the movements discussed in this book all question the very foundations on which these testing practices rest.

Our sense is that a thorough reexamination of the grounds of testing practices in higher education will have to follow rather than precede curricular reform. And in this area the research on collaborative learning and writing may have a more immediate impact. Our current curriculum is still based on a model of content coverage: classes must clip along, covering a certain number of units in a certain number of days. But this model is under increasing attack on a number of fronts and for a number of reasons. Most obviously, it is simply no longer possible for any one person to cover all the material in any field, even a fairly narrow one. Less obvious but equally important is the growing realization that what we teach in this inexorable drive to cover our content areas is not necessarily or even probably what is learned. Here the research in learning theory is clear and unequivocal: real learning occurs in interaction as students actively use concepts and ideas or strategies in order to assimilate them. The pedagogical implications here are equally clear: less may well yield more in terms of learning.

What follows from this line of reasoning is the need to reconsider course structure in terms of assignments that will engage students in interaction and active collaborative learning. One of the engineer respondents to our survey of collaborative writing remarked: "Perhaps it would be possible for English teachers to pay some attention to collaborative writing in their classrooms." What is much less clear is whether writing teachers are ready and willing to examine their own teaching practices to see in what ways they use collaborative writing (if they use it at all) in traditional, teacher-centered ways and in what ways they use a more liberatory mode of collaborative writing.

Collaborative Writing in the Classroom

As we have indicated already, our vision of this book changed in several important respects during the six years that we worked on it. No discussion has been so substantively reconceived as the following section on pedagogy. When we began our research on collaborative writing, we envisioned developing detailed, specific guidelines for teachers--guidelines that would address such issues as the characteristics of effective collaborative writing assignments and the most efficient ways to organize and evaluate group efforts. We will discuss issues such as these in the following pages, but rather than presenting complete definitive guidelines, our discussion will be much more exploratory.

Why? Our hesitation to proffer definitive guidelines and suggestions to teachers reflects the capacity of collaborative writing to "open out" or problematize both theory and practice. The more we reflected on the data we gathered through our surveys and questionnaires, the more we recognized how deeply embedded and contextualized actual collaborative writing practices are in the world of work. Our reflections on our interviews, in particular, emphasized to us the importance of addressing issues of gender, class, race, and power and of raising questions--hard questions--about collaborative writing in institutional settings: what are the consequences of our interviewees' highly pragmatic, goal-oriented view of collaboration for women and students of color in our classrooms? Can the same activities that might prepare students such as these to write effectively with others in the workplace also empower these students so they can function as full participating members of collaborative writing groups? At present, we have only the vaguest answers to these and similar questions.

Our historical and theoretical explorations of the concept of authorship raised similarly complex issues. If in a Bakhtinian sense all writing, whether drafted by an individual working alone or by a group of persons working together, is collaborative, how can we best help students recognize and build upon this heteroglossic understanding of language? Some carefully structured assignments that enable students efficiently and productively to complete group writing projects may risk-- precisely because they are so carefully structured and sequenced- -silencing or diminishing the polyphony of competing voices that many teachers want to encourage students to hear, and to speak. Which, then, is a better collaborative writing assignment--one that strives to enable students to confront language in all its heteroglossic richness or one that helps students learn how practically and efficiently to get the job of writing together done?

Our inability to resolve questions such as these frustrates us. In a recent essay in *The Chronicle of Higher Education,* Annette Kolodny worries about the tendency of feminist critics to focus less and less on concrete specifics of classroom power and pedagogy and more on esoteric theorizing. Her warning applies, we believe, to those in composition studies as well. In our field, pedagogy has traditionally been the strongest link in our chain; composition theorists could never easily ignore the exigencies of their everyday classrooms. We are concerned that our discussion here may seem to signal a retreat from a concern for pedagogy to the abstruse, but much less challenging, world of theory.

Nothing could be further from the case. Our reluctance here to detail specific, concrete guidelines reflects instead our growing appreciation of the complexity of our rhetorical situation as teachers and our awareness of the profound ways that explorations of collaborative writing challenge not only many traditional classroom practices in English studies but our entire curriculum. Rather than risk premature closure on issues of great significance, we prefer to emphasize the questions rather than the answers.

This in not to say, however, that we have been unable to draw any conclusions based on our research. Our own experiments with collaborative writing assignments, as well as many discussions with colleagues who have generously shared assignments with us, warrant a number of conclusions. Poor collaborative writing assignments are artificial in the sense that one person could really complete the assignment alone: such assignments lead only to busy work and frustration. Poor collaborative writing assignments also fail to provide guidance for students about the processes they might best use to complete the assignment effectively. Students are simply assigned a topic or a project and abandoned to negotiate the minefield of interpersonal and group processes alone.

Successful collaborative writing assignments may vary substantially in goals, methods, and desired outcomes. Most substantial collaborative writing assignments, however, share the following characteristics:

1. They allow time for group cohesion (but not necessarily consensus) to occur and for leadership to emerge.
2. They call for or invite collaboration; students need to work together in order to complete the assignment effectively. The Purdue researchers have tentatively identified three types of tasks which invite such collaboration: "labor-intensive" tasks that need to be divided into smaller subtasks in order to be accomplished effectively and efficiently; "specialization" tasks that call for multiple areas of expertise; and "synthesis" tasks that demand that divergent perspectives be brought together into a solution acceptable to the whole group or an outside group (see Allen et al. "Shared-Document").
3. They allow for the evolution of group norms and the negotiation of authority and responsibility. In a study of a writing group, Rance Conley identifies at least five "bases of authority": in the group itself, from the profession, from the role played in the group, from genre conventions, and from the strength of a member's writing.
4. They allow for and encourage creative conflict and protect minority views. Learning theorists refer to this principle as "inclusiveness," by which they mean recognizing, valuing, and incorporating individual diversity into the whole.
5. They allow for peer and self-evaluation during and after the assignment.
6. They call on students to monitor and evaluate individual and group performance and to reflect on the processes that made for effective--or ineffective--collaboration.

As readers may already have realized, this list does not directly address the question of how teachers should structure collaborative writing assignments other than to indicate the crucial importance of building in opportunities for the evaluation and monitoring of individual and group performance. Should teachers carefully develop collaborative writing assignments so that students are given explicit directions (if not commands) at each stage of the task? Or should teachers rely upon a less hierarchical, teacher-centered approach? The latter may better facilitate empowered, student-directed collaboration. But what about the product that must result from this collaboration and the dissonance, frustration, and inefficiency that can occur when students must take a primary role in instigating and structuring all collaborative activities?

A similar disagreement exists about the best way to form collaborative groups. Some teachers feel strongly that they are best situated and qualified to establish such groups. They may group students on the basis of their students' interests, experiences, majors, and writing skills. Or they may ask students to complete an inventory of their backgrounds, interests, and competencies. Other teachers insist that such careful selection is not necessary--indeed, that it may interfere with the early development of effective group dynamics. Still others argue that no one method of grouping will suffice, that the decision must be made anew with every new class of students.

Groups themselves may vary in size; we ourselves have used groups ranging from two to nine members. The role that groups can play in a class may also vary. Some teachers structure several weeks--at times, an entire course--around one or more group projects; others use them as a means of carrying out more limited and brief activities. And some teachers use them mainly as a means of organizing discussions.

Teachers interested in developing collaborative writing activities for their own classes need to recognize the diverse range of assignments that can engage students. Collaborative writing can be as limited as a twenty-minute group revision of a single paragraph, or it can structure the goals and assignments for an entire term. (In the latter case, not all assignments would be co-written, but all would in some sense involve students in collaborative learning activities. Students might engage in individual research or drafting, for instance, but do so in the context of group-defined goals and projects.) In our travels, we have spoken with teachers who have developed ingenious and exciting collaborative writing projects: a small graduate agriculture class cooperatively producing a textbook for their own course; a group of undergraduates devising a policy statement to use in explaining and justifying American timber and lumber duties to a group of Canadian students; and a group of honors physics students hammering out an "alternative to Armageddon," a proposal they would later present to an open town forum. Certainly one of the most carefully studied assignments we know of is one developed by the Purdue researchers and used in a business writing course. Allen, Morgan, and Atkinson have generously allowed us to reproduce this assignment [in Appendix D of *Singular Texts, Plural Authors*], along with another carefully constructed group-authored assignment from Anthony Paré.

Despite innovative assignments such as these, and despite the efforts of researchers such as Allen, Morgan, and Atkinson, and Paré and colleagues to develop meticulously structured and empirically tested assignments, we are left with many unanswered questions.

1. How should the teacher's role in any particular collaborative classroom be conceived and carried out?

2. What constitutes empowerment of students, both as individuals and as members of a group, in a collaborative project or a classroom?

3. How does--and should--collaboration challenge or re-situate the attitudes, values, beliefs, and ideological assumptions students and teachers bring to the writing class?

4. How do issues of gender, race, and class impinge on collaboration? To what extent can--or should--collaborative activities attempt to highlight or address inequities of gender, race, and class?

5. How are--and should--power and authority be constituted or achieved in collaborative work?

As we hope this discussion demonstrates, much important work has been done to address the pedagogical issues related to collaborative writing and to move toward a compelling pedagogy of collaboration, And yet many challenges remain. Perhaps the greatest--as Kolodny argues and as the set of questions listed above suggests--is to balance theory and practice, to face the full theoretical implications of our practices, to see those practices as embedded in a set of social, political, ideological situations, and to ask our students to attend to and to examine these situations with us. Thus we must not be content to develop- -on our own--individual collaborative writing activities, no matter how carefully worked out and tested they may be. Nor can we be content to address--on our own--provocative unanswered questions. Rather, we must find ways, together with our students, of opening out, of interrogating such assignments, of tracing their implications and assumptions, of building a theory that can account for them and then testing that theory against our practices, and always of making this process part of the very fabric of our classes.

Such a pedagogy may well produce, from time to time, consensually derived singular texts--but singular texts always animated by a self-conscious plurality, a polyphonic chorus of voices, whose difference--as well as sameness--speaks and is heard. Hannah Arendt has said that, "For excellence, the presence of others is always required." We agree. And so, in spite of our many unanswered questions, we believe that working toward a pedagogy of collaboration is worth our efforts, for it holds the potential for allowing, finally and fully, for the presence of others.

WORKS CITED

Abercrombie, M[innie] L[ouie] Johnson. *Aims and Techniques of Group Teaching.* London: Society for Research into Higher Education, 1970.

------------------. *the Anatomy of Judgment: An Investigation into the Processes of Perception and Reasoning.* London: Hutchinson, 1960. Harmondsworth: Penguin, 1969.

Allen, Nancy J., Diane Atkinson, Meg Morgan, Teresa Moore, and Craig Snow. "Shared-Document Collaboration: A Definition and Description." Unpublished paper delivered at Conference for College Composition and Communication. New Orleans: Mar. 1986.

Bain, Alexander. *On Teaching English.* New York: Appleton, 1887.

Bakhtin, Mikhail. *The Dialogic Imagination.* Ed. Michael Holquist. Trans. Caryl Emerson and Michael Holquist. Austin: U of Texas P, 1981.

Bartolomae, David,. "Inventing the University." *When a Writer Can't Write: Studies in Writer's Block and Other Composing-Process Problems.* Ed. Mike Rose. New York: Guilford, 1985. 134-65.

Bazerman, Charles. "Scientific Writing as a Social Act: A Review of the Literature of the Sociology of Science." *New Essays in Technical and Scientific Communication: Research, Theory, Practice.* Ed. Paul V. Anderson, John Brockman, and Carolyn R. Miller. Baywood's Technical Communication Series 2. Farmingdale, NY: Baywood, 1983. 156-84.

Bellah, Robert N., Richard Madsen, William M. Sullivan, Ann Swidler, and Steven M. Tipton. *Habits of the Heart: Individualism and Commitment in American Life.* Berkeley: U of California P, 1985.

Berlin, James A. "Contemporary Composition: The Major Pedagogical Theories." *College English* 44 (1982): 765-77.

------------. "Rhetoric and Ideology." *College English* 50 (Sept. 1988): 477-94.

------------. *Rhetoric and Reality: Writing Instruction in American Colleges, 1900-1985.* Carbondale: Southern Illinois UP, 1987.

Bizzell, Patricia. "Cognition, Convention, and Certainty: What We Need to Know About Writing." *Pre/Text* 3 (1982): 213-43.

------------."Foundationalism and Anti-Foundationalism in Composition Studies." *Pre/Text* 7 (1986): 37-56.

Bleich, David. *The Double Ledger Perspective: Language, Literacy, and Social Relations.* New York: Oxford UP, 1988.

Booth, Wayne C. *Critical Understanding: The Powers of Limits of Pluralism.* Chicago: U of Chicago P, 1979.

Bosley, Deborah. "A National Study of the Uses of Collaborative Writing in Business Communication Courses Among Members of the ABC." Diss. Illinois State U, 1989.

Bouton, Clark, and Russell Y. Garth, eds. *Learning in Groups.* New Directions for Teaching and Learning 14. San Francisco: Jossey-Bass, 1983.

Britton, James N. *Language and Learning.* Coral Gables: U of Miami P; Harmondsworth: Penguin, 1970.

------------, et al. *The Development of Writing Abilities (11-18).* Schools Council Research Studies. London Macmillan Educ., 1975.

Bruffee, Kenneth A. "The Brooklyn Plan: Attaining Intellectual Growth through Peer-Group Tutoring." *Liberal Education* 64 (1978): 447-68.

----------. "Collaborative Learning and the 'Conversation of Mankind.' " *College English* 46 (1984): 635-52.

----------. *A Short Course in Writing.* 2nd ed. Cambridge MA: Winthrop, 1980.

Buck, Gertrude. "Recent Tendencies in the Teaching of English Composition." *Educational Review* 22 (1901): 371-82.

Burke, Kenneth. "Terministic Screens." *Language as Symbolic Action: Essays on Life, Literature, and Method.* Berkeley: U of California P, 1966. 44-62.

Conley, Rance. "Talk About Writing in an Off-Campus Writing Group." Unpublished paper delivered at Conference for College Composition and Communication. Seattle, Mar. 1989.

70   Perspectives, Theories, and Directions in Teaching Composition

Cross, Geoffrey Arthur. "Editing in Context: An Ethnographic Exploration of Editor-Writer Revision at a Midwestern Insurance Company." Diss Ohio State U, 1988.

Daiute, Colette. "Do 1 and 1 make 2 ?: Patterns of Influence by Collaborative Authors." *Written Communication* 3 (1986): 382-408.

-----------, and Bridget Dalton. "Let's Brighten Up a Bit: Collaboration and Cognition in Writing." *The Social Construction of Writing.* Ed. B. Raforth and D. Rubin. Norwood, NJ: Ablex, in press.

Debs, Mary Beth. "Collaboration and Its Effects on the Writer's Process: A Look at Engineering." Unpublished paper delivered at Conference for College Composition and Communication. Detroit, Mar. 1983.

DeVries, D., and K. Edwards. "Student Teams and Learning Games: Their Effect on Cross-Race and Cross-Sex Interaction." *Journal of Educational Psychology* 66 (1974): 741-49.

Dewey, John. *Experience and Education.* New York: Macmillan, 1938; New York: collier, 1963.

---------. *The Public and Its Problems.* Denver: Swallow, 1927.

Doheny-Farina, Stephen. "Writing in an Emerging Organization: An Ethnographic Study."

Elbow, Peter. "Closing My Eyes as I Talk: An Argument against Audience Awareness." *College English* 49 (Jan. 1987): 50-69.

-------------. *Writing Without Teachers.* New York: Oxford UP, 1973.

-------------. *Writing with Power: Techniques for Mastering the Writing Process.* New York: Oxford UP 1981.

Emig, Janet. *The Web of Meaning.* Upper Montclair, NJ: Boynton, 1983.

Faigley, Lester, and Thomas P. Miller. "What We Learn from Writing on the Job." *College English* 44 (1982): 557-69.

Graff, Gerald. *Professing Literature.* Chicago: U of Chicago P, 1987.

Graves, Nancy B., and Theodore D. Graves. "Creating a Cooperative Learning Environment: An Ecological Approach." *Learning to Cooperate, Cooperating to Learn.* Ed. Robert Slavin, et al. New York: Plenum, 1985. 403-36.

Halloran, S. Michael. "Rhetoric in the American College Curriculum: The Decline of Public Discourse." *Pre/Text* 3 (Fall 1982): 245-69.

Hamilton-Wieler, Sharon. "Awkward Compromises and Eloquent Achievements." *English Education* 21 (Oct 1989).

-----------. "How Does Writing Emerge from the Classroom Context? (A Naturalistic Study of the Writing of Eighteen-Year-Olds in Biology, English, Geography, History, History of Art, and Sociology)." ERIC, 1983. ED 284 209.

-----------. "Writing as a thought Process: Site of a Struggle." Unpublished paper delivered at NCTE Convention. San Antonio, Nov. 1986. ED 277 045. Rpt. in *Journal of Teaching Writing* 7 (Fall-Winter 1988): 167-80.

Harris, Joseph. "The Idea of Community in the Study of Writing." *College Composition and Communication* 40 (Feb. 1989): 11-22.

Heath, Shirley Brice. *Ways with Words: Language, Life, and Work ion Communities and Classrooms.* Cambridge, UK: Cambridge UP, 1983.

Hilgers, Thomas L. "On Learning the Skills of Collaborative Writing." Unpublished paper delivered at Conference for College Composition and Communication. New Orleans, 1986.

Hillocks, George, Jr. *Research on Written Composition: New Directions in Teaching.* Urbana, IL: ERIC Clearinghouse on Reading and Communication Skills, National Conference on Research in English, 1986.

Holt, Mara. "Collaborative Learning From 1911-1986: A Sociohistorical Analysis." Diss. U of Texas at Austin, 1988.

Johnson, David W., and Roger T. Johnson. "The Internal Dynamics of Cooperative Learning in Groups." *Learning to Cooperate, Cooperating to Learn.* Ed. Robert Slavin, et al. New York: Plenum, 1985. 103-24.

Kolodny, Annette. "Respectability Is Eroding the Revolutionary Potential of Feminist Criticism." *Chronicle of Higher Education* 4 May 1988: A52.

LeFevre, Karen Burke. *Invention as a Social Act.* Carbondale: Southern Illinois UP, 1987.

Lemon, Hallie S. "Collaborative Strategies for Teaching Composition. Theory and Practice." Unpublished paper delivered at Conference for College Composition and Communication. St.Louis, Mar. 1988.

Leonard, Sterling Andrus. "The Correction and Criticism of Composition Work." *English Journal* 5 (1916): 598-604.

-------------. *English Composition as a Social Problem.* Boston: Houghton, 1917.

Macrorie, Ken. *Telling Writing.* 4th ed. Upper Montclair NJ: Boynton, 1985.

Mason, Edwin. *Collaborative Learning.* London: Ward Locke Educ., 1970.

Mead, George Herbert. *Mind, Self and Society from the Standpoint of a Social Behaviorist*. Ed. Charles W. Morris. Chicago: U of Chicago P, 1934.

Michaels, James W. "Classroom Reward Structures and Academic Performance." *Review of Educational Research* 47 (1977): 87-98.

Moffett, James. *Teaching the Universe of Discourse*. 1968. Boston: Houghton, 1983.

----------, Charles Cooper,, and Miriam Baker. *Active Voices IV*. Upper Montclair, NJ: Boynton, 1986.

Morgan, Meg, Nancy Allen, Teresa Moore, Diane Atkinson, and Craig Snow. "Collaborative Writing in the Classroom." *Bulletin of the Association of Business Communication* 50 (Sept.) 1987): 20-26.

Murray, Donald M. *Learning by Teaching: Selected Articles on Writing and Teaching*. Montclair, NJ: Boynton, 1982.

-----------. "Writing as a Process: How Writing Finds Its Own Meaning." *Eight Approaches to Teaching Composition*. Eds. Timothy R. Donovan and Ben W.McClelland. Urbana, IL: NCTE, 1980. 3-20.

Myers, Greg. "Reality, Consensus, and Reform in the Rhetoric of Composition Teaching." *College English* 48 (1986): 154-74.

Odell, Lee, and Dixie Goswami, eds. *Writing in Nonacademic Settings*. New York: Guilford, 1985.

O'Donnell, Angela M., et al. "Cooperative Writing." *Written Communication* 2 (1985): 307-15.

Ohmann, Richard. *Politics of Letters*. Middletown CT: Wesleyan UP, 1987.

Pare, Anthony. "How It Works: A Group-Authored Assignment." *Inkshed* 7 (Sept. 1988): 5-7.

Piaget, Jean. *The Construction of Reality in the Child*. Trans. Margaret C. Cook. New York: Basic, 1954.

Scott, F[red] N[ewton]. "What the West Wants in Preparatory English." *The School Review* 17 (1909): 10-20.

Sharan, Shlomo. "Cooperative Learning in Small Groups: Recent Methods and Effects on Achievement, Attitudes, and Ethnic Relations." *Review of Educational Research* 50 (1980): 241-71.

Shor, Ira, ed. *Freire for the Classroom: A Sourcebook for Liberatory Teaching*. Portsmouth, NH: Boynton, 1987.

Slavin, Robert E. "Effects of Biracial Learning Teams on Cross-Racial Friendship Interaction." *Journal of Educational Psychology* 71 (1979): 381-87.

----------. "An Introduction to Cooperative Learning Research." *Learning to Cooperate, Cooperating to Learn*. Ed. Robert Slavin, et al. New York: Plenum, 1985. 5-15.

----------, et al. *Learning to Cooperate, Cooperating to Learn*. Ed. Robert Slavin, et al. New York: Plenum, 1985.

Spear, Karen. *Sharing Writing: Peer Response Groups in English Classes*. Portsmouth NH: Boynton, 1988.

Sullivan, Patricia A. "From Student to Scholar: A Contextual Study of Graduate Student Writing in English." Diss. Ohio State U, 1988.

Tocqueville, Alexis de. *Democracy in America*. Trans. George Lawrence. Ed. J.P. Mayer. New York: Doubleday-Anchor, 1969.

Trimbur, John. "Collaborative Learning and Teaching Writing." *Perspectives on Research and Scholarship in Composition*. Ed. Ben W. McClelland and Timothy R. Donovan. New York: MLA, 1985. 87-109.

----------. "Consensus and Difference in Collaborative Learning." Unpublished paper delivered at MLA Convention, San Francisco, Dec. 1987. Rpt. in *College English* 51 (1989): 602-16.

-----------. Letter to authors. 1989.

Webb, Noreen M. "Student Interaction and Learning in Small Groups." *Review of Educational Research* 52 (1982): 421-45.

Witte, Stephen P. "Some Contexts for Understanding Written Literacy." Unpublished paper delivered at Right to Literacy Conference. Columbus OH, Sept. 1988.

Yarnoff, Charles. "Contemporary Theories of Invention in the Rhetorical Tradition." *College English* 41 (1980): 552-60.

Young, Richard. "Arts, Crafts, Gifts, and Knacks: Some Disharmonies in the New Rhetoric." *Reinventing the Rhetorical Tradition*. Ed. Aviva Freedman and Ian Pringle. Ontario: Canadian Council of Teachers of English; Conway, AR: L & S, 1980. 53-60.

Zavarzadeh, Mas'ud, and Donald Morton. "Theory Pedagogy Politics: The Crisis of 'The Subject' in the Humanities." *Boundary 2: A Journal of Postmodern Literature and Culture* 15 (Fall-Winter 1986-87): 1-22.

More Meanings of Audience

Jack Selzer

A major source of frustration--and fascination--within English studies these days is that certain basic concepts once regarded as givens within the profession have come into dispute. *Author, text, literature, genre:* in a postmodern, poststructuralist time, all these terms have become problematic. A quarter century after Roland Barthes in *Image Music Text* declared the "author" dead; two decades after reader-response critics declared the text an event (not an entity) and genre critics found conventional forms to be dynamic organisms rather than static containers; ten years after everyone from Stanley Fish to Terry Eagleton to Robert Scholes concluded that distinctions between *literature* and *nonliterature* cannot survive critique--now all these terms have become the occasion for discussion, dispute, confusion, and loads of commentary.

And so it is with *audience.* Once a stable referent, *audience* has become fractured into *audiences,* into a not-always-peaceable and too-often-fragmented kingdom of terms, complete with colorful relatives, feuding rivals, strange bedfellows, and new arrivals turning up each month. What exactly are the differences and relationships between "evoked" and "invoked" audienccs? Or between "narratees" and "implied readers"? Or between "demographic" and "fictionalized" audiences? Or between "fictionalized," "intended," "ideal," "inscribed," and "universal" audiences? What is the difference between "audience" and "discourse community"? What do technical writing textbooks mean by "multiple audiences"? Is it useful to conceive of audiences and readers as distinct entities? How do texts signal the differences among all of these characters? And how does one devise a pedagogy for "audience" that would improve reading and writing? The aim of this essay is to address these questions, to straighten out some of the current confusion that has converged about the term *audience.* I certainly do not expect to succeed completely in that endeavor--the issues are complex and slippery- -but I do hope to clarify some matters, especially for people who teach rhetoric and writing. Failing that, perhaps I can at least throw into relief the ambiguities involved in understanding the meanings of audience.

Not that there hasn't already been considerable progress made on the question of audience. In the field of rhetoric and composition, two articles have especially clarified and stimulated my own thinking on the subject: Lisa Ede and Andrea Lunsford's "Audience Addressed/Audience Invoked: The Role of Audience in Composition Theory and Pedagogy" and Douglas Park's "The Meanings of `Audience.'"[1] Chiefly in order to influence pedagogical practice, Ede and Lunsford identify, explicate, and finally synthesize the two basic schools of audience study, which they term (after the example of Henry Johnstone) *audience addressed* and *audience invoked.* Those people (often associated with speech departments) who envision audience as "addressed," Ede and Lunsford explain, emphasize the concrete reality of "real people" who receive messages, while those who consider audience as "invoked"

Jack Selzer, "More Meanings of Audience" from *A Rhetoric of Doing: Essays on Written Discourse in Honor of James L. Kinneavy,* edited by Stephen P. Witte, Neil Nakadate, and Roger D. Cherry. Carbondale IL (SIU Press). Copyright 1992 by Jack Selzer. Reprinted with permission of the author.

(often literary theorists) stress the "fictional" audience present in the text itself. Take the case of a recent article in the *Wall Street Journal* by Milton Friedman entitled "An Open Letter to William Bennett, on the subject of legalizing drugs (see the Appendix; I will return to this example throughout this essay). Readers of the *Wall Street Journal* article, including Bennett himself, for instance, are real people--an audience addressed. But the "William Bennett" in the "open letter" itself is a fictional character created by Friedman--an audience invoked. For rhetorical purposes--to win the assent of real readers--writers invoke or create within their texts fictional readers (who correspond to fictional authors, sometimes called "implied authors" or "narrators" or "personae"). Walter Ong and Wayne Booth, among others, contend that all discourse contains invoked (or "fictionalized" or "created" or "implied") audiences cast by means of textual cues into a role that real readers are then invited to assume.

Ede and Lunsford strive for a "synthesis" of the two perspectives that will be useful in the composing process. They seek "a fully elaborated view of audience" that will "balance the creativity of the writer with the creativity of the reader" (169):

> The addressed audience, the actual ... readers of a discourse, exists outside of the text. Writers may analyze these readers' needs, anticipate their biases, even defer to their wishes. But it is only through the text, through language, that writers embody or give life to their conception of the reader. In so doing, they do not so much create a role for the reader--a phrase which implies that the writer somehow creates a mold to which the reader adapts--as invoke it.

Douglas Park's essay, written two years before Ede and Lunsford's, works from their same central distinction and contains their same interest in pedagogy. According to Park, there are "two general directions of meaning of 'audience'-- outside the text and back into the text" (250)--which Park then divides into four more specific meanings: (a) anyone who happens to read a given discourse; (b) external readers or listeners *as* they are involved in the rhetorical situation; (c) the set of conventions that shape the discourse as something to be heard; (d) an ideal conception shadowed forth in the way the discourse itself defines and creates contexts for readers. The first two specify "real" readers outside the text; the last two refer to fictional readers created within the text. While Park does mention the first two, does acknowledge real "people-as-they-are-involved in a rhetorical situation" (244), his main interest is in exploring the latter two, which he claims are "obviously the most important" (250). In his difficult but stimulating analysis, he therefore tends to treat audience essentially as "a metaphor" (252) for the set of conventions, contexts, and aspects of knowledge that writers use to create meaning. He would "replace the idea of 'audience' with a set of questions as to how the work ... establishes or possesses the contexts that make it meaningful" (252). And when he calls for a more systematic and precise "map of the territory of audience" (256), he really means a map of the audience *in the text.*

I want to provide some of this mapping that Park calls for; I want to contribute to "the fully elaborated view of audience" that Ede and Lunsford seek. By way of a general thesis, let me provide a map of my own (fig. 1), a chart of the "meanings of

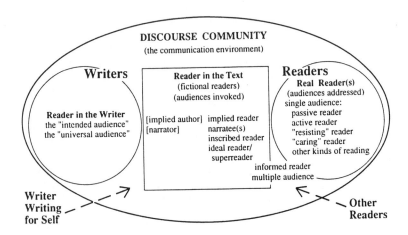

Figure 1 The meanings of __audience__ for and in a given document

audience " as I understand them and as those meanings might relate to each other and as I will discuss them in this essay. My catalogue of the meanings of *audience* includes both the *audiences invoked* in the text ("the reader in the text") and the *audiences addressed* outside it ("real readers"). But audiences in the text may be distinguished: as I will explain, there are implied readers, narratees, inscribed readers, informed readers, and ideal readers (to name some of them). "Real" audiences outside the text may be distinguished, too: there are single (or homogeneous) and multiple (heterogeneous) audiences. But in neither case are real audiences the same thing as a *discourse community,* a broader concept synonymous with *culture* or *environment* or *social setting.* Finally, there is also such a thing as a reader in the writer (the intended audience).   Even this short overview should make my general aim clearer. I mean to rehabilitate some of the elements deemphasized by Park and to problematize some of the constructs used by Ede and Lunsford in their pedagogically oriented synthesis.   I work from their basic distinction between the reader in the text and the reader outside the text (I prefer *reader* to *audience* to make clear that I am discussing audience only in terms of written discourse), but I also consider the reader in the writer as well. Furthermore, I treat audience and reader not as monoliths: I want to call attention to the multiplicity of readers inside and outside the text because puzzling out the distinctions enriches our sense of audience. And I want to clear up some misconceptions about audience, chiefly in connection with the term *discourse community,* that have arisen since Park and Ede and Lunsford wrote. Thus, while my ultimate aim is similar to theirs--to subdue the meanings of audience for the sake of teaching--my perspective is somewhat broader and more abstract. My hope is that this essay might come to be read as a supplement--it is not a correction--to Park and Ede and Lunsford, a gloss and an extension, if you will.

The Reader in the Writer: The "Intended Reader"'''

In all the recent interest in real audiences and in created audiences within texts, it should not be forgotten that audience can also be seen as a writer-based concept. From the writer's point of view, *audience* may have little to do with the identities of the actual people who later actually read the document. An intended audience, in fact, may never even see the document; conversely, some of those who do see the document (e.g., teachers or editors or supervisors or someone in the distant future yet unborn) may not be intended readers. For *intended audience* denotes the mental construct in the writer that aids the act of invention and directs the features of the developing text; it denotes the more or less concrete representation of readers that the writer conceives during composition and then uses to condition his or her developing work. For instance, Milton Friedman's sense of "the people who read the *Wall Street Journal"* was very likely one influence on the composition of his letter. Friedman's internal sense of William Bennett's personality and beliefs may have been another such influence; whether Bennett ever actually read the letter or not, his image may well have affected Friedman during the acts of invention, arrangement, and revision. The same could be true of the Alabama clergymen mentioned in King's famous "Letter from Birmingham Jail": whether those clergymen ever read King's letter or not, they almost certainly served as some of King's intended readers--readers whose image stimulated King during the act of composing. King may have had other readers in mind as well as he planned and drafted and revised.

For we know that writers conceive of audiences as they write; we know that the intended audience[2] does influence the creative process--even if the resulting texts are never actually read. Mikhail Bakhtin insists, for example, that "the listener and his (or her) response are regularly taken into account when it comes to everyday dialogue and rhetoric, but every other sort of discourse as well is oriented toward an understanding that is 'responsive.' ... Responsive understanding is a fundamental force, one that participates in the formulation of discourse" (280). More empirically, Carol Berkenkotter has documented through protocol analysis that a sense of audience influences writers in the process of composition, that "the internal representation or mental sketch a writer makes of the audience is an essential part of the writing process" (396). Peter Elbow concurs: his "argument for ignoring audience" during composing recognizes both implicitly and explicitly that people do regard audience as they write; Elbow would simply advise writers to push audience into the background at certain points in the creative act and especially to disregard any threatening or intimidating audiences that impede the composing process or that diminish the value of writing for the writer. From the perspective of developmental psychology, Barry Kroll, Bennett Rafoth, and Donald Rubin and Gene Piche document how children learn to "decenter"-- to consider the perspective and personalities of others--as they grow as writers. My own favorite example of the writer-based nature of audience comes from the testimony of the eminent British evolutionary biologist John Maynard Smith. He claims that he keeps two readers in mind as he writes: "an intelligent but ignorant 16-year-old ... [i.e.,] myself when young" and "an even more ignorant British Civil Servant, bent on improving his mind" and modeled on "an actual person, [a relative] of mine." In any case, there is plenty of reason to support the writing teacher's perennial exhortation to students, "Consider your audience as you write!"

And there is additional theoretical support for the notion as well, since no less an authority than Chaim Perelman argues that "an orator wishing to persuade a particular audience must of necessity adapt himself to it" (20). Perelman, who gives primary emphasis to the canon of invention, conceives of audience- -particularly his "universal audience"--as a speaker- or writer-based construct. According to Perelman, audience determines the direction and substance that an argument will take. Three such audiences are possible:

> The first such audience consists of the whole of mankind, or at least, of all normal, adult persons; we shall refer to it as the *universal audience.* The second consists of the single *interlocutor* whom a speaker addresses in a dialogue. The third is the *subject himself* when he deliberates or gives himself reasons for his actions. (Perelman 30; quoted in Ray)

Perelman sees audience--and particularly the *universal audience,* a theoretical collection of rational people whose values and beliefs are grounded on rational thought--as more than a real object to which a rhetor directs arguments. It becomes "an active participant in the argumentation process" (Anderson 40), "a mental concept of the speaker" (Ray 363).[3]

The problem is, *how do* and *how should* writers think of audience? Do writers (and should writers) think of concrete persons as they write--as for example Maynard Smith's relative? Or is the representation of audience in the writer's mind an idealization, a creation-like Maynard Smith's "intelligent but ignorant 16-year-old"? Can audience in the writer be "universal" and philosophical, as Perelman maintains? (King's rational, philosophical "Letter" might imply an affirmative answer to that question.) Or is the reader in the writer something more abstract--something like Berkenkotter's "mental sketch"? Or something more abstract still--something closer to the "conventions" of text discussed by Park? Is it, in short, the experience of writers with real readers that tells writers what to include and how? Or is it the experience of writers with reading--with what the reading experience comprises--that enables writers to write, since writing assumes a system of shared conventions?

There is evidence for all these senses of audience within writers. Charlotte Thralls and her colleagues, for instance, found both "real" and "implied" audiences simultaneously in the minds of writers. Their protocol analyses turned up "exophoric referents" that pointed to real readers in the minds of writers as well as "endophoric referents" that pointed to readers as conventional features of texts. Robert Roth found the same range in his student writers' sense of audience as they wrote: some students projected themselves as readers; others incorporated the viewpoints of different (sometimes several) real readers; others had only indefinite and largely text-based senses of audience. Not only that, Roth's students revised their sense of audience as they composed. Audiences expanded, or grew more concrete (or less distinct), or became more realistic or more idealized or more (or less) like their authors or more implicated in the developing text. Like texts themselves in the process of construction, "audience is subject to revision" (Roth 53).

The Reader in the Text

Whatever the status of the reader in the writer, the presence of the intended reader is ultimately manifested in the text itself. In the case of spoken rhetoric, audiences are nearly always "real"--real people on hand for the occasion of the speech. But in the case of writing, audiences are textual presences as well as intended or real ones. But just how are audiences realized in the text?

Answering that question has occupied the energies of several reader-response critics over the past several decades. Walker Gibson and Wayne Booth in the 1950s noticed the presence in fiction of what they called "the mock reader" or "the implied reader"; later, Walter Ong contended that "the writer's audience is always a fiction" no matter what the genre: "the historian, the scholar or scientist, and the simple letter writer all fictionalize their audiences, casting them in a made-up role" (17). According to Gibson, Booth, and Ong, not only does a rhetorical transaction involve a real writer and a real audience; it also involves an implied author distinct from the real author and an implied reader distinct from the real reader--an implied reader created in the text by means of textual conventions. Just as the implied author or persona of this essay is distinct from the "real" Jack Selzer, so the implied reader is distinct from real readers. In Booth's words: "The author creates ... an image of himself and another image of his reader; he makes his reader [i.e., the implied reader], as he makes his second self" (*Rhetoric of Fiction* 138). The implied reader of a particular text, who is distinct from the reader implied by other texts, is known through the background knowledge and assumptions and values and other human characteristics implied by the language of that text. The implied reader created in the first sentences of Friedman's letter, for instance, is an American citizen (implied by the phrase "our foreign policy") who accepts the free-market assumptions apparent in paragraphs three and six, shares the sense of crisis apparent in the second half of the piece, sympathizes with "innocent" victims of current drug policy (paragraphs five, six, and nine), sees the drug problem more pragmatically than morally (note the reference to Billy Sunday), and has the historical knowledge to understand references to "Oliver Cromwell," "Billy Sunday," and "the prohibition of alcoholic beverages." The implied reader, the "we" and "our" and "us" of the letter, has something in common with the "you" and "Bill Bennett," but (as will become further apparent in a moment) is quite distinct nevertheless. By creating implied readers and implied authors like this, authors enact conversations that real readers listen in on.

Implied readers invite a reading behavior that real readers may accept, if they so choose. Gibson, Booth, and Ong all assert that real readers *must* take on the roles implied by a well-written text: they are "called on ... to play the role assigned" (Ong 17); they must "subordinate [their] mind and heart to the book" (Booth, *Rhetoric of Fiction* 138). But that is surely an overstatement. Real readers may or may not identify with the implied reader. Wolfgang Iser's account of the implied reader accordingly allows for more flexible reading behavior on the part of real readers. Though not without its problems (Iser at times conflates the real reader and the reader in the text), his formulation allows for an active reader who may well choose to remain quite distinct from the role suggested by the implied reader: "the concept of the implied reader is ... a textual structure anticipating the presence of a recipient without necessarily defining him [or her]" (*Act of Reading* 34). It is this active yet text-based view of reading and this view of the implied reader that Iser has demonstrated and popularized in his analyses of fiction. And it is this view of reading and the reader in the text that Ede and Lunsford subsume under their heading "audience invoked."

However, the fictional audience created by a text need not be monolithic. In fact, a common mistake is to confuse or conflate the implied reader with other fictional readers that may be created in a text. To put the matter another way, readers may exist in a text in other forms in addition to the implied reader; and real readers therefore might at times be not so much listening in on a conversation between an implied author and implied reader as witnessing a full-fledged drama--a sort of implicit Socratic dialogue--complete with multiple and conflicting speakers and readers representing a range of views. Everyone agrees that a real author can be distinguished from the implied author, and the implied author at times from a dramatized narrator such as Nick Carraway; so, too, a real reader can be distinguished from the implied reader, and the implied reader from other fictional readers. Gerald Prince calls these other fictional readers "narratees," by analogy to the equally fictional narrator.

Narratees rival nartators in their diversity. Prince cites as examples the caliph in *A Thousand and One Nights,* whose threat to execute Scheherazade shapes the stories-within-the-larger-story that we listen in on, and the comrades aboard the *Nellie* who listen to Marlowe tell the events of *Heart of Darkness;* and I immediately think of Chaucer's pilgrims, who listen with all their biases to the Canterbury tales, or of Shreve and Quentin, who swap the roles of narrator and narratee in the course of *Absalom, Absalom!* Friedman's letter in the Appendix can also clarify how fictional audiences in the text can differ from implied readers. I have mentioned how Bennett *might* have figured as one of Friedman's intended readers and how Friedman's "letter" creates an implied reader with certain values and attitudes and knowledge. But the letter also includes a fictional character "Bill Bennett" (distinct from the implied reader and distinct from the real William Bennett), a "you" whose values comprise the straw man created in the opening and closing paragraphs and whose points of view are dismantled in the essay. Or think again of King's "Letter from Birmingham Jail." King creates an implied reader in his text with the values of justice and tolerance, a knowledge of biblical and theological and political texts, and the attitudes of sympathy and generosity; it is this implied reader that King invites his real readers to identify with. But he also creates other fictional readers: the "white moderates" referred to late in the essay that King hopes his real readers will *not* identify themselves with; and of course the eight Birmingham clergymen addressed in the salutation and throughout the essay. Whether those eight clergymen "really" exist is beside the point: almost all real readers know them only as the fictional characters created by King, characters with values at odds with those of the text and those of the implied reader.[4]

Like the intended reader, therefore, and like any other fictional character, narratees and implied readers can be based on real people, can be idealizations of real people, or can be pure creations. Not that every text makes dramatic use of narratees, of course: in Wendell Harris's formulation, "there is always a narrator speaking at least to an assumed narratee, just as there is always an implied author and an implied reader, but in some cases the narrator and implied author and/or the implied reader and narratee are indistinguishable while in other cases ... the members of each pair are quite separate.

In these [latter] cases, the implied author seems almost to be speaking to the implied reader over the heads of the narrator and narratee."

Besides implied readers and narratees, other readers in the text have been identified and described. One is the "inscribed" reader associated with the work of Jonathan Culler. While implied readers and narratees often have a presence in a text that is as concrete as the presence of other "characters" in it, the inscribed reader is something more abstract, something more general: the system of shared conventions and codes and formal devices (what Iser refers to in *The Act of Reading* as the text's "repertoire") that writers and readers deploy to make meaning, the implicit rules that allow a writer to create a text and a reader to comprehend it.[5] "It is his [or her] experience of reading, his [or her] notion of what readers can and will do," says Culler, "that enables the author to write, for to intend meanings is to assume a system of conventions and to create signs within the perspective of that system" ("Prolegomena" 50). The inscribed reader is therefore something close to Park's conception of audience: the "set of conventions ... that shape the discourse," the "totality of the assumptions the discourse makes about context" (251), whether those conventions are generic, lexical, or rhetorical. Inscribed readers are not at all specific or "real"; they are impersonal, a collective. For Culler, "the question is not what actual readers happen to do but what an ideal reader must know implicitly in order to read" (*Structuralist Poetics* 24).

The "ideal reader" is therefore also a textual feature, a set of assumptions inscribed within a document, a fiction implied by the very being of a text but impossible for someone to become in reality. Like many linguistic concepts (Culler here is speaking as a structuralist, after all), the ideal reader is a generalized construct assumed by and in a text; competent in every way, the ideal reader has instantaneous recognition of every rule and convention and signal necessary for deciphering a text. The ideal reader is a "superreader" who is hypersensitive to every formal nuance, who has encyclopedic knowledge to bring to bear on every textual move. As Chomsky puts it in the famous opening paragraphs of *Aspects of the Theory of Syntax*, "linguistic theory is concerned primarily with an ideal speaker-listener, in a completely homogeneous speech community, who knows its language perfectly and is unaffected by such grammatically irrelevant conditions as memory limitations, distractions, shifts of attention and interest, and errors ... in applying his knowledge in actual performance" (3).[7]

More concrete, less theoretical, and more on the way to "real readers" is the *informed reader,* a term suggested by Stanley Fish to denote "neither an abstraction nor an actual living reader but a hybrid--a real reader (me) who does everything within his power to make himself informed" (49). On the one hand, the informed reader is something of a textual ideal that presupposes a general competence ("competence" in Chomsky's and Culler's sense) in the language of the text, an acute awareness of the formal features of all texts, and experience with the properties of every specific kind of discourse, "including everything from the most local of devices (figures of speech, and so on) to whole genres" (48). On the other hand, the informed reader is quite real and quite actively engaged in understanding a particular text--someone living and breathing who is fully involved in becoming what a specific text asks its readers to become ("the informed reader of Milton will not be the informed reader of Whitman"), doing "everything within his [or her] power to make himself [or herself] informed." "Each of us," says Fish, "if we are sufficiently responsible and self-conscious can ... become the informed reader" (49). The informed reader is at once a communal reader predisposed by the linguistic codes and conventions agreed on by an interpretive community and an individual reader in the world who is seeking to understand those codes completely. Or to put it in the terms of linguistic theory, the informed reader is a real reader striving to bring performance into conformity with competence.[8] Informed readers, therefore, like the other fictional readers distinguished in this section, are in one sense literally embodied in texts. But they offer a link with real readers, too. In fact, the text in general (and any sort of reader within that text) may be described as a place where real authors and real readers may meet.

Real Readers

Real readers truly exist. They are a temporal fact, not simply a textual one. Experience with real readers, and experience being real readers, tells writers what to say in a given piece and how to say it; and the actions and responses of real readers provide a most important gauge to the success of any document. When teachers exhort novices to "analyze your audience," therefore, it is to real readers that they are referring. And it is well known that such teachers have a repertoire of techniques to recommend to their novices for the purpose of turning up specific demographic and attitudinal information on real audiences.

Nevertheless, understanding the nature of real readers is by no means uncomplicated. For one thing, real readers may or may not be the ones "intended" by the real author or even the ones "invoked" by the text. All sorts of people may actually read a document who were never "intended" to read it; think of a copyeditor, for instance, or the twentieth-century readers of Keats's letters, or your first reading of the "Letter to Bill Bennett" here. All sorts of people may also read a text who are not "invoked" by it, either; think of that same copyeditor, for example, or recall your first confusing encounter with a Socratic dialogue or medieval allegory or legal brief or some other text whose conventions seemed at first quite alien. To put the matter another way, not all real readers are audiences from the writer's or text's perspective; nor do intended or implied or inscribed audiences always become realized in the flesh.

Nor are real readers any more monolithic than are the readers in the text; in fact, they are so various as to defy any complete classification. It may be useful, however, to consider first a basic distinction between multiple (or heterogeneous) audiences and single (or homogeneous) ones, a distinction commonly made in technical communication to distinguish the readers of documents in complex organizations.[9] Multiple audiences, I would suggest, are not to be defined by their various physical characteristics or by their different places in organizations or by their various roles in relation to the writer or by the different cultural and sexual roles that distinguish real people. They have to do with the multiple *tasks* or *multiple reading behaviors*--that various readers may require of a text, whether those behaviors are implied in texts or assumed in fact by real, empirical readers. That is why in figure 10.1 the term *multiple audience* cuts across boundaries between text and real reader.)

Let me try to clarify by means of an example or two. Consider first the booklet that describes employee benefits at a university or some other large organization. Such a booklet may have multiple uses, may be read in multiple ways: it can be a recruiting device that attracts new employees; once the new employee signs on, it can be read for several informative purposes (as a way of finding out if a particular situation is covered by insurance, for instance, or as a way of learning how to make an insurance claim); it can serve as a model for writers constructing similar documents; or it can become the object of analysis for English teachers and students in a technical writing class. All of these multiple roles are legitimate, of course. Some of them may be implied by the text or intended by the authors; some of the roles perhaps *should* be implied by the text (or should have been intended by the authors), but aren't (that's one reason why people have to phone for additional information on their benefits); and some of those roles are brought to the text "from outside," if you will, sanctioned neither by text nor by authors. A second example: the Friedman letter can intend and invoke a single real audience, but it cannot guarantee that real readers will sit still for a single role. Real readers cannot be completely controlled by a text, though authors may certainly seek such control.[10] Friedman's letter addressing *Wall Street Journal* readers may also be read by social scientists trying to understand the *Wall Street Journal,* for instance, or by someone preparing a biographical essay on Friedman, or by a historian a generation from now, long after the question of legalizing drugs has been resolved. Thus multiple audiences--heterogeneous audiences--can consist of many individuals; or a multiple audience can be one individual who assumes multiple, even conflicting roles over time.

Conversely, even if very different readers (different in a demographic sense) come to a text for the same reason, they may be considered single, not multiple. Single or homogeneous audiences are worth discussing, since they, too, are hardly monolithic. That is, even if a reader approaches a particular text "single-mindedly," that does not imply that the same reader will approach another text in the same way. Readers adjust their reading not only in response to textual cues but also as a result of their own needs and idiosyncracies.

Sometimes readers are "passive"; in the terminology of communication theory, they are "receivers," uncritical receptacles for taking in messages. In one sense, this view of communication sees messages as objects to be consumed and digested in the same way that a computer dispassionately takes in and stores information. In another sense, this view sees writing as a script and reading as a process of accepting cues spelled out, implicitly or explicitly, by a text. Whatever the metaphor, the reader becomes one who passively "processes" a piece of writing. While recent developments in critical theory, reading, and cognitive psychology have quite properly undermined this view of reading, it remains true that to read relatively passively remains an option for readers in certain circumstances. At times it makes sense to subordinate oneself to the text, to try to "process" the text as much as possible. Just think about how you typically read a biology textbook or cookbook, for instance (especially if you are an inexperienced biologist or cook), or any other kind of routine instructions or militantly expository prose.

But most often, of course, readers and reading are more active. The text may be a script, but the actor/reader still has plenty to do, even in the face of the most dictatorial implied author. At the very least, reading means bringing to the text knowledge and experience that enable people to recognize connections and fill in omitted information. At most, reading means shaping the outcome of an encounter with a text--not "processing" but "making meaning." Someplace in the middle it means negotiating meaning--*negotiating* in both senses of the term--with the author through the text. " A reader of Friedman's essay, for instance, may be taking in the text relatively passively, or tentatively, if he or she is unfamiliar (or unconcerned) with the controversy over legalizing drugs. Or the reader might be actively engaged with the argument, taking mental notes, posing possible objections, imagining Bennett's possible responses, supplying analogues or counterinstances, and ultimately being convinced. Or the reader might resist the argument from the outset and examine each sentence with a jaundiced eye.

The use of the word *resist* in connection with the Friedman argument brings to mind people who not only resist the roles set out for them but who resist the entire ideology of a text. Though the term *resisting reader* derives from feminist critical theory [12] and strictly speaking refers to the experience of women readers who resist the masculine ideology of certain texts, the notion of the resisting reader may be implicit in the very notion of persuasion in our culture, a notion that assumes readers who carefully guard--resist--ideological positions that are under siege by a rhetor. Resisting readers resist every kind of textual move; they move through discourse with a kind of skepticism or suspicion, implicitly counter the text at every opportunity, and finally may subjugate it to personal proclivities or counterideologies. It is perhaps a response to this notion of resistance that prompts so many "new rhetoricians" to move toward less agonistic versions of persuasion; consider Burke's concept of identification, Booth's "rhetoric of assent," the notion of "Rogerian" argument, and so forth.

And perhaps that is the motive behind Patrocinio Schweikart's invention of a "caring reader." In an attempt to resolve dualities (is meaning in the text or in the reader? is reading an interaction or a negotiation? are readers "active" or "passive"? is the text a repository of truth or of power?), Schweikart proposes a new model for the reading process that is based on Nel Noddings's work in ethics and education. The caring reader is absorbed by the text but not effaced by it, gains a dual perspective through reading both the self and the text in question, and enacts a reciprocal relationship--an "interanimation"--among author, text, and reader that is mutually respectful and liberating. Schweikart's caring reader has enormous possibilities as a model for writing teachers engaged themselves with student texts and for those who stress collaboration; that is why I emphasize it here. But it can also describe a way of reading a range of other documents in a range of circumstances as well with student texts and for those who stress collaboration; that is why I emphasize it here. But it can also describe a way of reading a range of other documents in a range of circumstances as well.

The possibility of a caring reader does not preclude the existence of resisting readers or of active or passive readers, for that matter. Styles of reading on the part of real audiences are quite various, and those styles may be assumed or discarded, quite legitimately, at different times by the same reader (even in the course of reading a single document) or at the same time by different readers. Whatever the specific facts of a particular reading experience, however, it does seem clear that there is no generic Real Reader, only temporal and situated real readers of various abilities and motivations and backgrounds who exist in differing and dynamic relationships to the texts they are working with.

One last point. A real audience is not the same thing as a discourse community--though *audience* and *discourse* community are sometimes used as synonyms.[13] A discourse community, however it is defined (see Porter, Nystrand, and Fish for definitions), essentially denotes the setting or culture that enables communication within it. As figure 10.1 implies, it refers to the system of rules, conventions, constraints, and beliefs that readers and writers share, and draw upon during the process of communicating. Directing and subtly directed by the whole discourse, the discourse community amounts to the dynamic "rules of the system governing discourse production within [a] community" (Porter 244). As such, a discourse community is something broader than audience, for particular audiences (like particular writers) nearly always exist within a discourse community. (An exception might be a reader who "eavesdrops" for some reason on the conversations, written or oral, of another community.) Many members of a discourse community will never be among the intended or implied or real audience for particular documents. The discourse community for Friedman's letter on drugs, for example, is everyone capable of reading it; but the audience for the letter, as I have noted, consists of those Friedman "intended" it for or those "created" within it or those who really encounter it. To appropriate Roman Jakobson's famous distinction, an *addressee* for a piece of writing should not be confused with the *context* for that writing (see Kinneavy 58-59).

Conclusion

Where does all of this leave the teacher in search of the meanings of *audience?* After all these distinctions have been made among various kinds of audiences and readers, it might be best to end by smoothing over the distinctions a bit. For though it might be useful for teachers or critics or theoreticians to distinguish among the readers in the writer, the readers in the text, and the readers in the real world, in practice, of course, those readers cannot be so nearly separated. In practice the concept of audience is dynamic: it is their experience with addressing real readers and reading real texts that tells writers what to include and how; it is in terms of the reader in the text and the author's intention that real audiences situate themselves (usually) during the act of reading; and it is with reference to real people and to accomplish authorial aims that texts create their fictional readers. Intention and understanding are two ends of the act of reading that meet in a text. Each of those ends, in the words of Stanley Fish, necessarily "stipulates (includes, defines, specifies) the other. To construct the profile of the informed or at-home reader [or any other kind of audience, I would add] is at the same time to characterize the author's intention and vice versa, because to do either is to specify the contemporary conditions of utterance" (161). Writer and audience and text are inextricably patterned in the creation of meaning through discourse. What is needed in understanding discourse, therefore, is what is needed in understanding audience: a tolerance of complexity and a commitment to a pluralism that does justice to the multiple senses of *reader* and *audience.*

Acknowledgments

For their helpful suggestions on this essay in an earlier form, thanks to the members of my seminar on Reader-Response Criticism at Penn State in the spring of 1990, and to those who responded to my presentation on the subject at the Conference on College Composition and Communication in Chicago, 1990. Thanks also to Cynthia Miecznikowski, who served as a research assistant for this project.

Milton Friedman's "Open Letter to Bill Bennett" is reprinted with permission of the *Wall Street Journal,* copyright (c) 1989, Dow Jones and Company, Inc. All rights reserved.

Appendix

An Open Letter to Bill Bennett (*Wall Street Journal,* 19 Sept. 1989)

Dear Bill:

In Oliver Cromwell's eloquent words, "I beseech you, in the bowels of Christ, think it possible you may be mistaken" about the course you and President Bush urge us to adopt to fight drugs. The path you propose of more police, more jails, use of the military in foreign countries, harsh penalties for drug users, and a whole panoply of repressive measures can only make a bad situation worse. The drug war cannot be won by those tactics without undermining the human liberty and individual freedom that you and I cherish.

You are not mistaken in believing that drugs are a scourge that is devastating our society. You are not mistaken in believing that drugs are tearing asunder our social fabric, ruining the lives of many young people, and imposing heavy costs on some of the most disadvantaged among us. You are not mistaken in believing that the majority of the public share your concerns. In short, you are not mistaken in the end you seek to achieve.

Your mistake is failing to recognize that the very measures you favor are a major source of the evils you deplore. Of course the problem is demand, but it is not only demand, it is demand that must operate through repressed and illegal channels. Illegality creates obscene profits that finance the murderous tactics of the drug lords; illegality leads to the corruption of law enforcement officials; illegality monopolizes the efforts of honest law forces so that they are starved for resources to fight the simpler crimes of robbery, theft and assault.

Drugs are a tragedy for addicts. But criminalizing their use converts that tragedy into a disaster for society, for users and non-users alike. Our experience with the prohibition of drugs is a replay of our experience with the prohibition of alcoholic beverages.

I append excerpts from a column that I wrote in 1972 on "Prohibition and Drugs." The major problem then was heroin from Marseilles; today, it is cocaine from Latin America. Today, also, the problem is far more serious than it was 17 years ago: more addicts, more innocent victims; more drug pushers, more law enforcement officials; more money spent to enforce prohibition, more money spent to circumvent prohibition.

Had drugs been decriminalized 17 years ago, "crack" would never have been invented (it was invented because the high cost of illegal drugs made it profitable to provide a cheaper version) and there would today be far fewer addicts. The lives of thousands, perhaps hundreds of thousands of innocent victims would have been saved, and not only in the U.S. The ghettos of our major cities would not be drug-and-crime-infested no-man's lands. Fewer people would be in jails, and fewer jails would have been built.

Colombia, Bolivia and Peru would not be suffering from narco-terror, and we would not be distorting our foreign policy because of narco-terror. Hell would not, in the words with which Billy Sunday welcomed Prohibition, "be forever for rent," but it would be a lot emptier.

Decriminalizing drugs is even more urgent now than in 1972, but we must recognize that the harm done in the interim cannot be wiped out, certainly not immediately. Postponing decriminalization will only make matters worse, and make the problem appear even more intractable.

Alcohol and tobacco cause many more deaths in users than do drugs. Decriminalization would not prevent us from treating drugs as we now treat alcohol and tobacco: prohibiting sales of drugs to minors, outlawing the advertising of drugs and similar measures. Such measures could be enforced, while outfight prohibition cannot be. Moreover, if even a small fraction of the money we now spend on trying to enforce drug prohibition were devoted to treatment and rehabilitation, in an atmosphere of compassion not punishment, the reduction in drug usage and in the harm done to the users could be dramatic.

This plea comes from the bottom of my heart. Every friend of freedom, and I know you are one, must be as revolted as I am by the prospect of turning the United States into an armed camp, by the vision of jails filled with casual drug users and of an army of enforcers empowered to invade the liberty of citizens on slight evidence. A country in which shooting down unidentified planes "On suspicion" can be seriously considered as a drug-war tactic is not the kind of United States that either you or I want to hand on to future generations.

Milton Friedman
Senior Research Fellow
Hoover Institution
Stanford University

NOTES

1. For other accounts of recent work on audience, see Allen; Coney; Keene and Barnes-Ostrander; Kroll ("Writing for Readers").
2. Peter Rabinowitz, speaking of literary discourse, prefers the term *authorial audience:* authors "design their books rhetorically for some more or less specific *hypothetical* audience, which I call the *authorial audience.* Artistic choices are based upon ... assumptions--conscious or unconscious--about readers" *(Before Reading* 21). Though his interest is in narrative art, Rabinowitz's general classification of audiences as *authorial, narrative,* and *actual* roughly correspond to my own classification of audiences as *intended, textual,* and *real.* Gerald Prince's term for the intended reader is the *virtual reader:* the reader the author believes himself or herself to be writing to.
3. For critiques of Perelman's contentions, see Ray and Ede.

4.   King's "Letter" was not really written to or for the eight Alabama clergymen; we know that from its publication history. The "Letter" was never posted to the clergymen but was instead quickly printed by the American Friends Service Committee and later collected in *Why We Can't Wait*. The clergymen are fictions, "narratees": creations used by King to focus his comments and to define his implied audience against. No doubt they were also useful in the process of creating the essay, as I mentioned above. For a discussion of the circumstances of King's "Letter" that is coincidentally quite relevant to a discussion of audience, see Fulkerson.

5.   Many of those conventions are catalogued in Kinneavy's *Theory of Discourse*.

6.   *Superreader* is Michael Riffaterre's term. Though still a structuralist committed to careful analysis of textual conventions, Riffaterre does move beyond strict textual formalism by acknowledging that the superreader brings to the text cultural and historical awareness, not merely a mastery of textual and generic conventions. In that sense, Riffaterre moves beyond strict structuralisms, and in that sense his superreader can be distinguished from the ideal reader assumed by the structuralists.

7.   Quoted in Fish 246. For a helpful short account of distinctions to be made among ideal readers, informed readers, and superreaders, see Iser, *Act* 26-32.

8.   *Ideal* readers and *real* readers--i.e., *competent* and *performative* readers, to continue with the terms of linguistic theory--are also combined in Dell Himes's concept of "communicative competence."

9.   The term *multiple audience* is associated with Mathes and Stevenson.

10. See Roland Barthes's *S/Z*: Barthes classifies texts according to how much they attempt to control the responses of readers.

11. Reader-response critics may be distinguished according to how "active" they see or sanction the process of reading. Ong, Booth, Prince, and Gibson see the text as giving directions to a relatively passive reader; Norman Holland and David Bleich lease relatively more control to active readers than to the texts they experience; and Iser would be in a middle position, with the text providing fixed guides but plenty of gaps, or "indeterminacies," and the reader reducing the indeterminacies. Rather than try to adjudicate among their positions, I would rather see the level of "activity" in a reader as "rhetorically" constrained--as contingent on text and reader and circumstance in a given case.

12. The term seems to have been coined by Judith Fetterley. Feminist readers are not necessarily resisting readers, of course. For a survey of the range of possibilities involved in feminist reader-response theory, see Elizabeth Flynn and Patrocinio Schweikart's *Gender and Reading,* particularly the essays by Flynn and Schweikart themselves.

13. See, for example, James E. Porter, "Reading Presences in Texts: Audience as Discourse Community." It is not just Porter's title that conflates audience and discourse community; throughout the essay the two are treated as ultimately synonymous. I cite Porter not because his is the most egregious example--I could cite many others-- but because his essay remains for me a most thoughtful discussion of the term *discourse community* and its implications, a discussion that I recommend most heartily to others.

WORKS CITED

Allen, Jo. "Breaking with a Tradition: New Directions in Audience Analysis." *Technical Writing: Theory and Practice.* Ed. Bertie Fearing and W. Keats Sparrow. New York: MLA, 1989. 53-62.

Anderson, John R. "The Audience as a Concept in the Philosophical Rhetoric of Perelman, Johnstone, and Natanson." *Southern Speech Communication Journal* 38 (1972): 39-50.

Bakhtin, Mikhail M. *The Dialogic Imagination: Four Essays.* Ed. Michael Holquist; trans. Caryl Emerson and Michael Holquist. Austin: U of Texas P, 1981.

Barthes, Roland. *Image Music Text.* New York: Hill and Wang, 1977.

_____. *S/Z.* Trans. Richard Miller. New York: Hill and Wang, 1974.

Berkenkotter, Carol. "Understanding a Writer's Awareness of Audience." *CCC* 32 (1981): 388-99.

Bleich, David. *Subjective Criticism.* Baltimore: Johns Hopkins UP, 1978.

Booth, Wayne. *Modern Dogma and the Rhetoric of Assent.* Notre Dame, IN: U of Notre Dame P, 1974.

_____. *The Rhetoric of Fiction.* Chicago: U of Chicago P, 1961.

Chomsky, Noam. *Aspects of the Theory of Syntax.* Cambridge: MIT P, 1965.

Coney, Mary. "Contemporary Views of Audience: A Rhetorical Perspective." *Technical Writing Teacher* 14 (1987): 319-36.

Culler, Jonathan. "Prolegomena to a Theory of Reading." *The Reader in the Text.* Ed.

Susan R. Suleiman and Inge Crosman. Princeton: Princeton UP, 1980. 46-66.

_____. *Structuralist Poetics.* Ithaca: Cornell UP, 1975.

Ede, Lisa. "Rhetoric Versus Philosophy: The Role of the Universal Audience in Chaim Perelman's *The New Rhetoric."* *Central States Speech Journal* 32 (1981): 118-25.

Ede, Lisa, and Andrea Lunsford. "Audience Addressed/Audience Invoked: The Role of Audience in Composition Theory and Pedagogy." *CCC* 35 (1984): 155-71.

Elbow, Peter. "Closing My Eyes as I Speak: An Argument for Ignoring Audience." *College English* 49 (1987): 50-69.

Fetterley, Judith. *The Resisting Reading: A Feminist Approach to American Fiction.* Bloomington: Indiana UP, 1978.

Fish, Stanley. *Is There a Text in This Class?* Cambridge: Harvard UP, 1980.

Flynn, Elizabeth, and Patrocinio Schweikart, eds. *Gender and Reading.* Baltimore: Johns Hopkins UP, 1986.

Fulkerson, Richard. "The Public Letter as a Rhetorical Form: Structure, Logic, and Style in King's `Letter from Birmingham Jail.'" *Quarterly Journal of Speech* 65 (1979): 121-36.

Gibson, Walker. "Authors, Speakers, Readers, and Mock Readers." *College English* II (1950):265-69.

Harris, Wendell. *A Dictionary of Literary Concepts.* Westport, CT: Greenwood, in press.

Himes, Del. "On Communicative Competence." *Sociolinguistics: Selected Readings.* Ed. J.B. Pride and Janet Holmes. Harmondsworth: Penguin, 1972.

Holland, Norman. *The Dynamics of Literary Response.* New York: Oxford UP, 1968.

Iser, Wolfgang. *The Act of Reading: A Theory of Aesthetic Response.* Baltimore: Johns Hopkins UP, 1978.

_____. *The Implied Author: Patterns of Communication in Prose Fiction from Bunyan to Beckett.* Baltimore: Johns Hopkins UP, 1974.

Johnston, Henry W. *Validity and Rhetoric in Philosophical Argument.* University Park, PA: Dialogue Press of Man and World, 1978.

Keene, Michael, and Marilyn Barnes-Ostrander. "Audience Analysis and Adaptation." *Research in Technical Communication: A Bibliographic Sourcebook.* Ed. Michael Moran and Debra Journet. Westport, CT: Greenwood, 1985. 163-91.

Kinneavy, James. *A Theory of Discourse.* Englewood Cliffs, NJ: Prentice Hall, 1971.

Kroll, Barry. "Cognitive Egocentrism and the Problem of Audience Awareness in Written Discourse." *Research in the Teaching of English* 12 (1978): 268-81.

_____. "Writing for Readers: Three Perspectives on Audience." *CCC* 35 (1984): 172-85.

Mathes, J.C., and Dwight Stevenson. *Designing Technical Reports.* New York: Bobbs-Merrill, 1976.

Maynard Smith, John. Letter to the Author. 17 Sept. 1989.

Noddings, Nel. *Caring: A Feminine Approach to Ethics and Moral Education.* Berkeley and Los Angeles: U of California P, 1984.

Nystrand, Martin. "Rhetoric's `Audience' and Linguistics `Speech Community': Implications for Understanding Writing, Reading, and Text." *What Writers Know.* Ed. Martin Nystrand. New York: Academic, 1982. 1-28.

Ong, Walter. "The Writer's Audience Is Always a Fiction." *PMLA* 90 (1975): 6-21.

Park, Douglas. "The Meanings of `Audience.'" *College English* 44 (1982): 247-57.

Perelman, Chaim, and L. Olbrechts-Tyteca. *The New Rhetoric: A Treatise on Argumentation.* Trans. John Wilkerson and Purcell Weaver. Notre Dame, IN: U of Notre Dame P, 1969.

Porter, James E. "Reading Presences in Texts: Audience as Discourse Community." *Outspeak/Newspeak: Rhetorical Transformations.* Ed. Charles W. Kneupper. Arlington, TX: Rhetoric Society of America, 1985. 241-56.

Prince, Gerald. "Intoduction to the Study of the Narratee." *Poetique* 14 (1973): 177-93.

Rabinowitz, Peter. *Before Reading: Narrative Conventions and the Politics of Interpretation.* Ithaca: Cornell UP, 1987.

———. "Truth in Fiction: A Reexamination of Audience." *Critical Inquiry* 4 (1977): 121-41.

Rafoth, Bennett. "Audience Adaptation in the Essays of Proficient and Nonproficient Freshman Writers." *Research in the Telling of English* 19 (1985): 237-53.

Ray, John W. "Perelman's Universal Audience." *Quarterly Journal of speech* 64 (1978): 361-75.

Riffaterre, Michael. "Describing Poetic Structures: Two Approaches to Baudelaire's `Les chats.'" *Yale French Studies* 36-37 (1966): 200-242.

Roth, Robert. "The Evolving Audience: Alternatives to Audience Accommodation." *CCC* 38 (1977): 47-55.

Rubin, Donald, and Gene Piche. "Development in Syntactic and Strategic Aspects of Audience Adaptation Skills in Written Persuasive Discourse." *Research in the Teaching of English* 15 (1979): 293-316.

Schweikart, Patrocinio. "Reading, Teaching, and the Ethic of Care." *Gender in the Classroom: Pedagogy and Power.* Ed. Susan L. Gabriel and Isaiah Smithson. Champaign: U of Illinois P, 1990.

Thralls, Charlotte, Nancy Blyler, and Helen Ewald. "Real Readers, Implied Readers, and Professional Writers." *Journal of Business Communication* 25 (1988): 47-M.

Computers and Instructional Strategies
in the Teaching of Writing

Elizabeth Klem and Charles Moran

Research strongly suggests that writing on-line is different from writing with pen and paper. If this is the case, our teaching needs to take account of the difference. How should we teach our students in this new text environment? Existing research has some answers for us. But we are now in a time of rapid technological change, and we are ourselves, moreover, in an amphibious stage, operating as we do partly in print, partly on-screen. Despite the rate of change, and despite the fact that we seem poised between two worlds, we need to discover instructional strategies that will help us cope with the students, and the text environment, we now have.

Overview of Topic and Importance of Area

As our writing students increasingly gain access to computers, they become, to some degree, different students. How can we teach these new writing students? What instructional strategies are best suited to student writers working in this new writing environment? What guidance can the research of the past decade offer us as we attempt to discover how best to teach writing in the 1990s? Should we argue for, and expend our scarce resources on, computer-equipped classrooms? And, if so, how should we best teach in these facilities? Should we argue for public-access, computer-equipped writing labs? And how should our computer classrooms, or computer-writing labs, be equipped? Should we make style-checkers and heuristic programs available in these facilities? Should we install networked writing classrooms, and, if so, what is the best use we can make, as teachers of writing, of these new environments? And, if we teach, as most of us do, in conventional, non-computer-equipped classrooms, how can we best take account in our teaching of the fact that some of our students are composing, outside of class, in the new medium?

As we have read through the research in our field, we have tried to keep before us a realistic vision of the writing teacher in the 1990s. We know that most teachers do not now teach in up-to-date computer environments, and national priorities are such that this situation is likely to continue. As authors of this chapter, we'd like nothing better than to engage in unfettered future-think--imagine that we will all have access to hypertext or multimedia environments--and on the basis of this presumed techno-paradise generate a research agenda that would lead us to the appropriate instructional strategies for such an environment. But we know that while computers are arriving on campuses at an increasing rate, most schools, colleges, and universities do not supply sufficient technological resources for teachers or access for all of their students. In our secondary schools we still see "computer writing labs" in which there are four Apple IIgs computers for twenty-five students--none of whom has an Apple available at home. In our colleges and universities, only those students who can afford computers have them--and postsecondary writing teachers in research universities, chiefly poorly paid teaching assistants or part-time lecturers, are even less likely than their students to have access to the new technology. It is the writing teacher, often a low-status, marginalized worker, who is being asked to cope with this confusing and difficult situation.

Because we have kept this "real" writing teacher in our minds as we thought through the materials of this chapter, we have not given our millennial impulse free rein. We do not, however, want to be seen as neo-Luddites. It is clear to us that the computer as a writing tool is here to stay. Writers who have composed on computers seldom turn back. In addition, the computer holds the promise--elusive as this promise may now seem--of benefits to writers who have been marginalized. To these writers, who have perhaps failed in traditional classrooms, the computer presents a chance for a new beginning. In addition, a networked computer environment may encourage previously unheard voices to enter the discussion and, thus, may be a force for democracy.

Overview of Research

In this section, we review the research now available to us; and, as we can, we make the inferential leap from research findings to their implications for the design of instructional strategies appropriate to the teaching of writing in the 1990s. We need to say that we include under the banner of "research" here both carefully controlled studies and the narratives of teachers who are doing pioneer work in bringing new technologies into their teaching. We do this because we give equal weight to both kinds of report. There is value, certainly, in the well-funded research study. There is also value in the "report from the field," particularly when this report comes from a teacher who has thought long and hard about the implications of the new teaching environment.

For ease of analysis and reading, we have divided the research in the field into five categories: research on writers as they compose on computers, on writers as they read screen-text, on the effects of heuristic programs, on the effects of style-analysis software, and on the effects of networked computer environments. As we describe the research, we will lay out the implications we see in this research for the development of instructional strategies for the 1990s.

Writers Writing the New Text

The most important research in this category suggests that the computer, used as a word-processing tool, alters the nature of text itself and therefore alters the ways in which we write and read this new text. Researchers observe that the word-processing screen presents the writer with a different and perhaps liberating context in which to write. Moving beyond Daiute's (1983) observation that word processing relieves constraints on the writer, Marcus (1984) finds that "seeing words dance around a screen

... generates quite a different sense of the risk involved" (p. 122) in any writing done on a computer. He argues that users "no longer feel their words are `carved in stone'" (p. 122) and sees this freedom as the primary benefit of the new medium. He describes a screen-specific kind of freewriting--"invisible writing"--in which the writer can "turn off" the editor-in-the-head simply by turning down the contrast on the screen. The impact of the new flexibility is seen as a definite asset by Catano (1985), who finds that in computer-writing, composing and revising take place together as the writer shapes the "fluid text," thus affirming in a new way Berthoff's (1984) observation that "revision is not a stage of composition but a dimension" (p. 95).

If the computer-as-word-processing-tool has changed the text and changed its relationship to the writer, then we, as writing teachers, must pay attention. The notion of "draft," which has always been a bit artificial, may be more difficult to sustain in the world of "fluid text." The word *draft* carries with it the sense of "draw," of the pen or pencil making semipermanent lines on paper. The keyboard is tactile, but not graphic: the computer translates a keystroke into a graphic symbol composed of temporarily illuminated phosphor dots. When the students in our computer-equipped classrooms balk at submitting "drafts," are they being lazy? Or are they responding more directly than we do to an aspect of the new text environment?

If the draft *is* an aspect of pen-and-paper composing, then it would be unlikely that we would learn much about students' writing on computers from looking at their drafts--and this has indeed been the case. A significant body of research has been driven by the question "Do students revise more, or less, when using word-processing packages on computers than they do when using pencil-and-paper methods?" To discover the signs of revision, researchers have compared students' drafts in the two modes. Early research argued that student writers would revise more rapidly and easily in the new text environment than they had in the old one (Bean, 1983; Daiute, 1983; Sudol, 1985). Subsequent research suggested that student writers did less revising on-screen than they would have on paper (Collier, 1983; Daiute, 1986; Harris, 1985; Hawisher, 1987). This finding is supported by Lutz's (1987) study of the revising/editing behaviors of professional and experienced writers and by Case's (1985) survey of university faculty.

Often, however, the new text has been presented to students, and handled by the researchers, as if it were the old text. Pufahl (1984) and Curtis (1988) argue that the Harris (1985) and Collier (1983) studies presented the computer to the writers as a fancy typewriter and, thus, discouraged the large-scale revising that the researchers were trying to measure. LeBlanc (1988) notes that Daiute (1986) and Harris (1985) measured changes between the mid-process and the final *drafts* of texts, overlooking much of the early writing. Hawisher's study (1987) also compares fixed drafts and thus, does not discover, as she says, "point-of-utterance shaping and composing" (p. 158).

If we, as teachers, still need to see drafts for our own purposes--to track a student writer's progress, for example, or to measure the quantity and quality of a writer's work, or to make plagiarism more difficult--then we'll have to require drafts in computer environments with a force heretofore unnecessary. Moreover, because many, if not most, of the changes that writers make in their work will not be visible in the new-text drafts- -partly because the changes will have been made on-screen and not recorded on the draft, and partly because the printed draft does not have the crossings-out and marginal scribbling of the handwritten draft--we may need to develop new ways of tracking a writer's progress. We may be able to track and analyze students' keystrokes in the ways suggested by Smith, Rooks, and Ferguson (1989) in their description of the WE (WRITING ENVIRONMENT); or we may want to ask students themselves to tell us, in writing, about the changes and choices they have made as they composed their text.

If we choose to adapt wholly to the new-text environment, we may want to discover instructional strategies that do not involve the submission of a series of drafts. Certainly, we'll want to develop ways of "teaching" composing, ways of enabling students to use the fluidity of the new text to their advantage. These might include emphasizing the block-move functions of a word-processing program, or developing open-ended, short quick-write or free-write writing tasks and factoring them, unedited, into the semester's work.

Writers Reading the New Text

Writers are also readers; they read their own text and, on the basis of this reading, compose, revise, and edit. If the computer and word-processing package presents a new text to the writer, this new "reading" will have implications for the ways in which we teach writers working in the new medium. Haas and Hayes (1986) and Haas (1989b) have found that students working on- screen report less "text-sense." They do not see their whole text as easily in this new medium; they report feeling "lost." To get a global sense of the text, students needed to print their work and see it on paper. Almost certainly related to the screen-reading problem is Haas's (1989a) recent finding that writers using word-processing programs on computers plan less than do writers working with pen and paper only, and that more of the planning writers do on-screen is "sequential planning," or word-and-sentence-level planning that occurs close to the point of utterance. With computers, writers also do less "conceptual planning," by which Haas means the making of plans that "guide the creation of the conceptual meaning and structure of the text" (p. 194). Haas's findings resonate with earlier research that suggests that the word-processing medium draws the writer's attention to the "planning" of smaller units of the text (Collier, 1983).

It may be that we, and our students, need to learn more or better strategies for reading screen-text. For example, word-processing programs offer a "page-down" function, one that moves the text down three lines less than one screen. When the writer positions the cursor at the beginning of the third line from the top of the screen, the cursor becomes a marker for the first word on the next "page," thereby making it possible for the screen-reader's eye to move from screen-page to screen-page without a dislocating search for the beginning of the new text. Perhaps word-processing programs should be considered reading programs as well and should provide text markers independent of the cursor that will facilitate screen-reading. Until they do, as teachers we can "teach our students to read on-screen, using techniques now available and encouraging our students to discover their own.

We know that many professional writers, and journalists in particular, write and edit on screen all day, seldom turning to paper. These writers do seem to be able to "see" their work adequately on-screen. We wonder if the difficulty that student writers now report with screen-text springs from the fact that they work with print-text most of the time and, therefore, have not yet developed the strategies they need to work comfortably with screen-text.

Moreover, student writers compose on-screen, but their work will be read, in almost every instance, in print. We need to be aware that the difference in medium may present rhetorical as well as conceptual complexity that calls for changes in our instructional strategies. As the text approaches publication, does the writer begin to "become" the reader and to read like a print-reader? And is this reader-based perspective more difficult to assume when the writer writes on-screen?

Perhaps until most text is read on-screen, some alternation between screen and paper will have to be managed (Bureau, 1989). It may be that we should teach students to compose on-screen but, as they approach print publication, teach them to bring their screens closer and doser to the 8.5 x 11 double-spaced, black-on- white format in which their work will be read. They can manage this either by printing their text or by using the page-view or printer-display functions of some word-processing programs. When large-screen monitors become less expensive and more widespread, we'll be able to encourage students who need to "see" their pages to move to these monitors at the appropriate point in their composing process.

The Computer as an Aid to Invention

The computer has long been seen as a tool that might facilitate and augment a writer's strategies for invention (Burns & Culp, 1980). There is a widespread sense that invention programs have unrealized potential (Burns, 1984; Rodrigues & Rodrigues, 1984; Spitzer, 1989). Research in this area is chiefly descriptive and anecdotal, as in Schwartz's account (1984) of her work with SEEN. Writers working with invention programs demonstrably produce "ideas," but does this rich mixture somehow find its way to a draft? And are invention strategies best presented via computer? Strickland (1987) has compared the results of invention strategies presented through computers with the results of the same strategies presented in conventional classrooms. He has found no difference either in the quality of writing or in the quantity of ideas generated. Yet he wonders, citing Diane Langston (1986), whether his results are the consequence of "an application of an old paradigm (paper-based invention heuristics) to the new technology (computers)" (p. 18). It seems to us that computer-assisted invention has exposed a problem inherent in the "old paradigm": the separation of writing into stages or steps in a process, and in particular, the separation of "invention" and "writing." Most invention programs now readily available--programs such as MINDWRITER or PRE-WRITE---are stand-alone programs. With these programs, the writer produces a pre-text which then, in some world beyond the program, becomes a draft.

If we accept these stand-alone invention programs, we may want to think of other ways of using them. Perhaps they'd be useful *after* the student has written? Or in mid-process, when the student's own strategies have reached their limit?

An alternative to such programs is a complex and expensive writing environment, with multiple windows that permit the writer to move easily from text to heuristic to text and back again in a seamless, recursive set of moves. Given fiscal reality, only a few sites will be equipped to handle such an environment in the near future, and these sites will be the locus of research in the design of writing environments (see Ross in this collection).

What we'll not want to do, current research suggests, is to stock our labs or networks with a range of invention programs and ask our student writers to choose what works for them (Rodrigues & Rodrigues, 1984). This strategy places an enormous burden on both teachers and students. Teachers must know each program thoroughly-- an investment of time and energy required, as we previously noted, of those who are already overworked and underpaid. The students, according to this model, must learn several programs as well and, having given each a fair trial, must be able to decide which will be most useful at particular points in their composing. Is student writing-time best spent learning how to operate and use a range of invention software? Or could the students' time be better spent writing and re-writing? We are reminded of Moffett's (1968) argument against textbooks, in which he consigns to the fires eternal all "indirect" methods of writing instruction (p. 204).

The Computer as Proofreader

Most powerful word-processing programs have become miniwriting environments, including in their range the ability to check the spelling of words in the writer's text against a list of "good" words. Designers of spell-checking programs find themselves on the horns of a dilemma: if the program checks your text against a massive word list, it will miss many wrong-word errors; if the program checks your text against a short word list, it will flag many perfectly good words. Existing programs do not "read" the text, and it is not likely that programs that parse will be widely available in the next decade. Writing students will therefore need to "learn" to use spell-checking programs. This learning will include learning to proofread after the spell-checking for wrong-word errors and learning to resist the tendency to remove all flagged words and to restrict one's vocabulary to that of the spell-checking program (see Ross in this collection).

We have not found any research on student writers' use of spell-checkers, but we have found a large body of research on text-analysis programs--a fact that surprises us because the programs seem pedagogically retrograde: both limited in application and focused upon the clean, well-proofread print-text. The attraction of these programs may be explained by considering that wordprocessing originated in industry as a computer tool for typing in, correcting, and formatting a document (Bridwell, Nancarrow, & Ross, 1984). The programs may appeal to us because our history makes us focus on errors we make in our use of the King's English. Or perhaps they play into our generation's New Critical training, which produces in us a natural affinity for a machine that can decontextualize discourse and quantify its surface features.

Research in this particular corner of our field divides neatly into two camps: some see the style-checking program as a teacher's and writer's aid, and others see the style-checking program as inaccurate and therefore confusing to the student writer. Kiefer and Smith (1983) suggest that "textual analysis with computers intrigues college writers and speeds learning of editing skills by offering immediate, reliable, and consistent attention to surface features of their prose" (p. 201). In a later piece, Kiefer, Reid, and Smith (1989) sound a more cautious note: the teacher must be careful, they warn, to make sure that the analysis is suited to the writing's genre, to its rhetorical context, and to the needs of the individual writer who is using the program.

Dobrin (1986) believes text-analysis programs are expensive distractions. He points out that the value of the information given by the programs depends on the way in which the user interprets and evaluates the information. He argues that "people who can evaluate the output correctly are the people who don't need the programs in the first place" (p. 23). Collins (1989) matched teachers' perceptions of error with the possible errors flagged by text-analysis programs. His findings are disturbing: excluding the spell-checking function of these programs, the "accuracy rates for finding the same errors as teachers would be 6% for MILLIKEN, 5% for SENSIBLE, and 2% for CONDUIT" (p. 34). Not only, as Dobrin had suggested earlier, can these programs become a second authority in the classroom, but they will generally disagree with the teacher, creating a confusing situation for the student writer.

Some teacher/researchers have gone to extraordinary lengths to make use of text-analysis programs in their writing courses (Smye, 1988). Others have developed what seem to us to be curious arguments for the potential value of quantitative, statistical information on one's own, and on others', writing (Garvey & Lindstrom, 1989). At this moment, however, text-analysis programs seem more likely to confuse than to help most student writers. It seems therefore unlikely that these programs will be widely used in our writing classes, unless we want to prepare our writers for the style-checking programs they may face in their places of employment.

The Networked Writing Classroom

Networks are just now becoming affordable and manageable, so there is little research that bears on the instructional strategies we should adopt in a networked teaching/writing environment. Nor is there evidence that the benefits of a networked writing classroom will outweigh the costs of such an installation, given the level of technical expertise and support that network management requires. Clearly the networked writing room is a wonderful place for research and an exciting place to teach, but an institution considering the installation of networked writing classrooms would need to understand that such a facility requires considerable institutional investment-- not only equipment and technical support, but the staff-development time necessary to learn how to use the network in the service of the teachers' pedagogical goals.

Those who focus on the benefits to be gained from a networked writing classroom generally stress the interactive learning that this arrangement can provide. A networked writing classroom enhances the social, collaborative atmosphere that exists even in classes with stand-alone workstations (Gerrard, 1989; Sudol, 1985; Weiss, 1989). With the arrival of relatively inexpensive networking hardware and software, and with the design of "chat" or "CB" software that permits almost-real-time on-line discussions, we can now engage our students in on-line writing sessions that are dialectical and social. Batson (1989) argues that with a "CB"--Citizen's Band--system, "students and teacher can free-write together, throwing their ideas into a common `pot'" (p. 251). The network's potential for collective, collaborative work carries with it a potential shift in the locus of power and control. As teachers open up the network to their students, they inevitably turn over some of their authority to these same students.

This loss of control can be troubling to the teacher, yet both Batson (1989) and Kremers (1988) recommend that the teacher welcome, not resist, this redistribution of power.

Networks make possible electronic mail (e-mail), which has recently received some attention, partly for its potential as a heuristic device--a new kind of discovery channel for the exchanging of ideas--but also as the new kind of communication form it seems to be. Forman (1987) has examined the use of e-mail in a small corporation and finds it useful for all phases of the writing process--from the initial discussion of ideas through the final distribution of reports. Kinkead (1987) looks at e-mail in a classroom setting and finds it "intrinsically motivating," adding that it "provides a new way of communicating," perhaps more akin to a phone conversation than a letter (p. 341). She has found that, for peer work, "students seem to be able to take more risks in this type of conference than in the face-to-face model" (p. 339) because the written form of their comments encourages students to explain themselves more thoroughly and to become distanced readers.

New Directions for Research

Research gives us the information we need to develop instructional strategies that we may then use to achieve our instructional goals. The research agenda that we see for work in computers and composition during the next decade win blend naturalistic, ethnographic research with the ability of the computer, as a research tool, to count and to remember. The goals of such research will be to discover how writers write in the new medium, how teachers teach in the new medium, and how the computer has entered, and inevitably altered, the system that includes the writer, the text, and the teacher of writing. The trick in this research will be to find research questions that transcend software and hardware boundaries and that, therefore, continue to be useful as the technology evolves.

We list below a range of research questions that we need to begin to explore if we are to find the guidance we need in developing instructional strategies for our writing classrooms in the 1990s and beyond. We note that the focus of most of the research questions that follow is on *students* as they write on computers. This is because our students are not us. They are a different generation, one with a different relationship than ours to computers and to print-text. We may not be able to extrapolate usefully from our own writing/reading experience to theirs. At the least, we must observe our students, ask them questions, and listen to their answers. They will be, perforce, our co-researchers in this venture.

We begin with questions that will fill gaps we have discovered in our review of existing research:

- How do students navigate the "fluid text"? How do they compose in the new medium? And do differing composing procedures produce results that differ in kind? In quality?

- How do students go about reading text on-screen? Are there ways of reading screen-text that seem better than others?

- How do professional writers who work entirely with screen- text adapt to the new medium? Learn to see the text whole? Engage in large-scale planning?

- When students work with invention programs, does the use of a particular heuristic seem to be limited to the context of the program? Or are the questions/prompts to some degree internalized by the student writer? Transferred to other writing tasks, whether on-screen or off?

- How do student writers manage selection and movement of the "useful" material generated with the invention program into their drafts?

- Are there students who benefit from the use of style-checking software? If so, who are they? And what do they perceive these benefits to be? Do their perceptions square with their teachers' perceptions?

- To what extent does the presence of text-analysis software on a system disempower student writers? Or empower them? Do the program's norms become an Orwellian authority? Or do these norms become something like a video game--rules that the writer accepts for the time being but does not generalize.

- Does the norm set by the style-checking program change the students' perceptions of the teacher's role? Of the teacher's authority?

- Does peer interaction on a network differ in its content and character from spoken peer interaction in a conventional classroom?

- What effect does the use of "chat" using a real-time or synchronous conversation program have on the writing of a group of student writers? Can such an environment function as a heuristic?

- In real-time conversations on networks, who writes? Who is silent? Who feels empowered? Who disempowered? What conventions evolve among the participants in such conversations?

- How does the teacher adapt to the change in authority in a networked computer environment?

We conclude with what we think are the most important questions: those that have to do with students', and teachers', equitable access to the new technology.

- Does a student who spends some time writing on a computer, but more time writing with pencil and paper, derive important benefits from working on the computer? Is there transfer of learned skills from one text-environment to the other? Or is the

98 Perspectives, Theories, and Directions in Teaching Composition

student confused by the need to work both with print-text and with screen-text and perhaps, therefore, disadvantaged?

- Does a student who spends a semester in a computer-writing classroom, and who has little or no access to computers thereafter, gain or lose by the experience? What transfer is made between the computer environment and noncomputer environments?

- What is the writing experience of students likely to be after they have left their school/college? To what extent, and in what ways, is computer-writing likely to be useful outside of the academy?

- Does the writing teacher who does not have access to a personal computer at home utilize the school's computers differently from the teacher who does have a personal computer at home?

- Do teachers who have access to personal computers teach their writing students differently, even in conventional classrooms?

- What is the typical "cost" to the teacher in terms of time spent learning the system, of teaching in a computerized writing environment? And what are the perceived benefits?

If writing is really changing, and there seems to be general agreement that it is changing, then developing and testing new instructional strategies is work that writing teachers need to undertake. Yet teachers, schools, and students are, in that order, least likely to have access to new technology. As we wrote this chapter, this fact held in check our pedagogical imagination. Access, it seems to us, is the issue that drives an before it. Who has access, and to what? As teachers and researchers, we will have to come to grips with this mixed situation, where some students have full access, and some do not- -and where those who have access work with different kinds of hardware and software. Discovering how best to teach in this changing and confused environment is our principal instructional challenge for the 1990s.

REFERENCES

Batson, T. (1989). Teaching in networked classrooms. In C.L. Selfe, D. Rodrigues, & W.R. Oates (Eds.), *Computers in English and the language arts* (pp. 247-255). Urbana, IL: National Council of Teachers of English.
Bean, J.C. (1983). Computerized word-processing as an aid to revision. *College Composition and Communication, 34,* 146-148.
Berthoff, A. (1984). Response to Richard Gebhardt. *College Composition and Communication, 35,* 95.

Bridwell, L.S., Nancarrow, P.R., & Ross, D. (1984). The writing process and the writing machine: Current research on word processors relevant to the teaching of composition. In R. Beach & L.S. Bridwell (Eds.), *New directions in composition research* (pp. 381-398). New York: Guilford Press.

Bureau, W.E. (1989). Computers: Catalysts for change at Springfield High School. In C.L. Selfe, D. Rodrigues, & W.R. Oates (Eds.), *Computers in English and the language arts* (pp. 97-110). Urbana, IL: National Council of Teachers of English.

Burns, H.L. (1984). Challenge for computer-assisted rhetoric. *Computers and the Humanities, 18,* 173-81.

Burns, H.L., & Culp, G.H. (1980). Stimulating invention in English composition through computer-assisted instruction. *Educational Technology, 20,* 5-10.

Case, D. (1985). Processing professional words: Personal computers and the writing habits.of university professors. *College Composition and Communication, 36,* 317-322.

Catano, J.V. (1985). Computer-based writing: Navigating the fluid text. *College Composition and Communication, 36,* 309-315.

Collier, R.M. (1983). The word processor and revision strategies. *College Composition and Communication, 34,* 149-155.

Collins, J.L. (1989). Computerized text analysis and the teaching of writing. In G.E. Hawisher & C.L. Selfe (Eds.), *Critical perspectives on computers and composition instruction* (pp. 30-43). New York: Teachers College Press.

Curtis, M.S. (1988). Windows on composing: Teaching revision on word processors. *College Composition and Communication, 39,* 337-344.

Daiute, C.A. (1983). The computer as stylus and audience. *College Composition and Communication, 34,* 134-145.

Daiute, C.A. (1986). Physical and cognitive factors in revising: Insights from studies with computers. *Research in the Teaching of English, 20,* 141-159.

Dobrin, D. (1986). Style analyzers once more. *Computers and Composition; 3* (3), 22-32.

Forman, J. (1987). Computer-mediated group writing in the workplace. *Computers and Composition, 5*(1), 19-30.

Garvey, J.J., & Lindstrom, D.H. (1989). Pros' Prose meets WRITER'S WORKBENCH: Analysis of typical models for first-year writing courses. *Computers and Composition, 6* (2), 81-109.

Gerrard, L. (1989). Computers and basic writers: A critical view. In G.E. Hawisher & C.L. Selfe (Eds.), *Critical perspectives on computers and composition instruction* (pp. 94-108). New York: Teachers College Press.

Haas, C. (1989a). How the writing medium shapes the writing process: Effects of word processing on planning. *Research in the Teaching of English, 23,* 181-207.

Haas, C. (1989b). "Seeing it on the screen isn't really seeing it": Computer writers' reading problems. In G.E. Hawisher & C.L. Selfe (Eds.), *Critical perspectives on computers and composition instruction* (pp. 16-29). New York: Teachers College Press.

Haas, C., & Hayes, J.R. (1986). What did I just say? Reading problems in writing with the machine. *Research in the Teaching of English, 20,* 22-35.

Harris, J. (1985). Student writers and word processing: A preliminary evaluation. *College Composition and Communication, 36,* 323-330.

Hawisher, G.E. (1987). The effects of word processing on the revision strategies of college freshmen. *Research in the Teaching of English, 21,* 145-159.

Kiefer, K.E., Reid, S.D., & Smith, C.R. (1989). Style analysis programs: Teachers using the tools. In C.L. Selfe, D. Rodrigues, & W.R. Oates (Eds.), *Computers in English and the language arts* (pp. 213-225). Urbana, IL: National Council of Teachers of English.

Kiefer, K.E., & Smith, C.R. (1983). Textual analysis with computers: Tests of Bell Laboratories' computer software. *Research in the Teaching of English, 17,*201-214.

Kinkead, J. (1987). Computer conversations: E-mail and writing instruction. *College Composition and Communication, 38,* 337-341.

Kremers, M. (1988). Adam Sherman Hill meets ENFI: An inquiry and a retrospective. *Computers and Composition, 5*(3), 69-77.

Langston, M.D. (1986, March). *New paradigms for computer aids to invention.* Paper presented at the annual convention of the Conference on College Composition and Communication, New Orleans.

LeBlanc, P. (1988). How to get the words just right. *Computers and Composition, 5*(3), 29-42.

Lutz, J.A. (1987). A study of professional and experienced writers revising and editing at the computer and with pen and paper. *Research in the Teaching of English, 21,* 398-421.

Marcus, S. (1984). Real-time gadgets with feedback: Special effects in computer-assisted instruction. In W. Wresch (Ed.), *The computer in composition instruction: A writer's tool* (pp. 120-130). Urbana, IL: National Council of Teachers of English.

Moffett, J. (1968). *Teaching the universal discourse.* New York: Houghton Mifflin.

Pufahl, J. (1984). Response to Richard M. Collier. *College Composition and Communication, 35,* 91-93.

Rodrigues, R.J., & Rodrigues, D.W. (1984). Computer-based invention: Its place and potential. *College Composition and Communication, 35,* 78-87.

Schwartz, H. (1984). Teaching writing with computer aids. *College English, 46* (3), 239-247.

Smith, J., Rooks, M.C., & Ferguson, G.J. (1989). *A cognitive grammar for writing. Version 1.0. TextLab Report.* Chapel Hill, NC: University of North Carolina.

Smye,R. (1988). Style and usage software. *Computers and Composition, 6* (1), 47-61.

Spitzer, M. (1989). Incorporating prewriting software into the writing program. In C.L. Selfe, D.W. Rodrigues, & W.R. Oates (Eds.), *Computers in English and the language arts* (pp. 205-212). Urbana, IL: National Council of Teachers of English.

Strickland, J. (1987). Computers, invention, and the power to change student writing. *Computers and Composition, 4* (2), 7-26.

Sudol, R.A. (1985). Applied word processing: Notes on authority, responsibility, and revision in a workshop model. *College Composition and Communication, 36,* 331-335.

Weiss, T. (1989). A process of composing with computers. *Computers and Composition, 6* (2), 45-59.

Selected Bibliography

Perspectives and Trends

Berlin, James A. *Rhetoric and Reality: Writing Instruction in American Colleges, 1900-1985.* Carbondale: Southern Illinois UP, 1987.

Berthoff, Ann E. *The Making of Meaning: Metaphors, Models, and Maxims for Writing Teachers.* Upper Montclair, NJ: Boynton/Cook, 1981.

Bizzell, Patricia. "Cognition, Convention, and Certainty: What We Need to Know About Writing." *Pre/Text 3* (1982): 213-43.

Bleich, David. "Reconceiving Literacy." *Writing and Response: Theory, Practice, and Research.* Ed. Chris M. Anson. Urbana, IL: National Council of Teachers of English, 1986. 99-114.

Donahue, Patricia, and Ellen Quandahl. *Reclaiming Pedagogy: The Rhetoric of the Classroom.* Carbondale: Southern Illinois UP, 1989.

Enos, T., ed. *A Sourcebook for Basic Writing Teachers.* New York: Random House, 1981.

Knoblauch, C.H., and Lil Brannon. *Rhetorical Traditions and the Teaching of Writing.* Upper Montclair, NJ: Boynton/Cook, 1984.

Lindemann, Erika. *A Rhetoric for Writing Teachers.* 2d ed. New York: Oxford, 1987.

Miller, Susan. *Rescuing the Subject: A Critical Introduction to Rhetoric and the Writer.* Carbondale: Southern Illinois UP, 1989.

Spellmeyer, Kurt. *Common Ground: Dialogue, Understanding, and the Teaching of Composition.* Englewood Cliffs, NJ: Prentice Hall, 1993.

"Symposium on Basic Writing, Conflict and Struggle, and the Legacy of Mina Shaughnessy." Patricia Laurence, Peter Rondinone, Barbara Gleason, Thomas J. Farrell, Paul Hunter, and Min-Zhan Lu. *CE* 55.8 (1993): 879-903.

Tate, Gary, ed. *Teaching Composition: Twelve Bibliographical Essays.* TCU Press, 1987.

Collaboration

Bishop, Wendy. "Helping Peer Writing Groups Succeed." *Teaching College in the Two-Year College* 15 (1988): 120-25.

Bruffee, Kenneth A. "Collaborative Learning and 'the Conversation of Mankind.'" *CE* 46.8 (1984): 635-52.

Bruffee, Kenneth A. *Collaborative Learning: Higher Education, Interdependence, and the Authority of Knowledge.* Baltimore, MD: Johns Hopkins UP (1993).

Gere, Ann Ruggles. *Writing Groups: History, Theory, and Implications.* Carbondale: Southern Illinois UP, 1987.

Grimm, Nancy. "Improving Students' Responses to Their Peers' Essays." *CCC* 37 (1986): 91-94.

Trimbur, John. "Collaborative Learning and Teaching Writing." *Perspectives on Research and Scholarship in Composition.* Eds. Ben W. McLelland and Timothy R. Donovan. New York: MLA, 1985. 87-109.

Trimbur, John. "Consensus and Difference in Collaborative Learning." *CE* 51.6 (1989): 602-16.

B. Composing Processes

Shifting instruction from a "product-centered" pedagogy to "process-centered" pedagogies largely defines the movement that began in the 1960s and 1970s to reform writing instruction and form the academic discipline of composition studies. Instead of a pedagogy that focused on form, style, and correctness where teachers read and commented on only students' finished products, teachers involve themselves and other students in the planning, drafting, revising, and editing of each student's writing, instructing students in strategies of invention and revision and teaching students to analyze, evaluate, and reshape their writing as they reconsider their ideas and purposes, their readers, and their rhetorical situations.

Patricia Bizzell describes the beginnings of the process movement in "Composing Processes: An Overview" (from *The Teaching of Writing: Eighty-fifth Yearbook of the National Society for the Study of Education, Part II*, ed. Anthony R. Petrosky and David Bartholomae, Chicago: NSSE, 1986). Her article provides an excellent survey of process-centered theories since the 1960s and discusses their practical implications for teaching writing. As the process movement continued, Bizzell writes, different theories of writing processes emerged, some stressing the development of a personal style, some building on research into cognitive processes, and others arguing that the character of composing processes depends on the writers' social and cultural contexts. While we still have much to learn about writing processes, Bizzell argues that we now realize that there is no one composing process that works for all writers and writing tasks, that each writer employs several processes for different types of writing, and that writing is a recursive process that cannot be neatly divided into isolated stages of pre-writing, drafting, and revising.

The next piece discusses invention strategies, formal and informal methods with which writers discover and construct what to say. Until the 1960s, composition instruction provided little guidance to student writers for discovering subject matter for their writing beyond observation, reading, and research, and, as W. Ross Winterowd writes, textbooks limited composition mainly to stylistics. In "Rhetorical Invention," from his book *Composition/Rhetoric: A Synthesis*, however, Winterowd argues that invention should be at the heart of composition instruction. Invention systems, like those based on classical rhetoric, tagmemic theory, and Kenneth Burke's pentad, Winterowd explains, tap into the creative powers of the mind and provide writers with perspectives for viewing and "problematizing" the world.

Jeanne H. Simpson has provided some simple, practical instructions on informal invention devices in her book *The Elements of Invention* (Boston: Allyn & Bacon, 1990). She describes strategies for directed freewriting, where students write whatever comes into their heads about a subject as quickly as they can for a given time. Simpson also gives six practical guidelines for getting the most from an invention system:

1. Try to use all the steps in an invention system.
2. Ignore redundancies.
3. Write as much as you can in response to any step in a system.
4. Forget about grammar, punctuation, and spelling for now.
5. Keep going, even if you are drawing a blank.

6. Reward yourself when you've finished a good workout with an invention system.

The last two articles in this section discuss revision.   Lester Faigley and Stephen Witte's "Analyzing Revision"   (originally published in *College Composition and Communication* 32 [1981] 189-204) provides useful categories for discussing types of revision. Revisions may be surface changes or text-based changes. Students usually make only surface revisions, formal changes in grammar and mechanics and meaning-preserving changes such as substituting one word for another, what we normally call editing. Text-based revisions, however, alter the content of the text, some changing the content only of a section of the text, some changing the meaning of the entire text.

In "Recognition, Representation, and Revision" (first published in *Journal of Basic Writing* 3.3 [Fall/Winter 1981] and later included in her book *The Sense of Learning*, Portsmouth, NH: Boynton/Cook, 1990), Ann E. Berthoff vigorously opposes linear models of the composing process and proposes instead a theory of composing and revising consistent with a "pedagogy of knowing." Revision, she writes, "is not a stage but a dimension" of composing. Instructors need to teach students "to take advantage of the allatonceness of composing, to assure that they   continually rediscover how forming, thinking, and writing can be simultaneous and correlative activities." Berthoff describes a way of conceiving and teaching revising that does not separate revising from invention and forming, that takes advantage of the   imaginative powers of the mind, and that takes "seeing relationships" as a crucial part of knowing, thinking, and writing.

Most of the articles in this section make a point of stating that we need to know much more about the complicated, often mysterious natures of writers' composing processes. All, however, agree that if we are to improve students' writing, we must make students' composing processes a central concern of our writing courses.

Composing Processes: An Overview

Patricia Bizzell

What Is "Composing"?

Composition scholars agree that the composing process exists or, rather, that there is a complex of activities out of which all writing emerges. We cannot specify one composing process as invariably successful. Current research in the field is beginning to draw a detailed picture of these composing processes.

"Composing" usually refers to all the processes out of which a piece of written work emerges. During composing, the writer may spend some time musing, rereading notes or drafts, or reading the texts of others, as well as actually putting words on the page herself. In composition research, "writing" usually refers precisely to the scribal act. One focus of composition research examines the extent to which composing occurs during writing, as opposed to the composing that takes place while other tasks, such as those I just listed, are being performed.

Simply to acknowledge that composing processes exist is something of a gain for modern composition studies. My undergraduate students would like to deny this premise: they prefer the fantasy that when they finally become "good writers," they will be able to sit down at the desk and produce an "A" paper in no more time than it takes to transcribe it. Nor are my students alone in this fantasy of instant text production. It is part of a more general notion in our culture a sort of debased Romantic version of creativity wherein verbal artifacts are supposed to be produced as easily and inevitably as a hen lays eggs. This more general fantasy affects Americans' judgment of political orators, for example; we value as "good speakers" those who can think on their feet, apparently producing eloquence in no more time than it takes to utter the words.

The classical rhetoricians knew better. Greek and Roman teachers of effective writing and speaking elaborated a five-stage composing process: invention, or finding ideas; arrangement, or putting
the ideas into persuasive order; style, or dressing the ideas in persuasive language; memory, or memorizing the text of the speech thus prepared; and delivery, or delivering the speech with the most effective use of voice, gesture, and so on. No one supposed that brilliant orators simply opened their mouths and let it flow.

Many of my students, however, have not encountered anything like the classical composing process in school. Until very recently, most language arts instruction in American schools had lost a sense that composing requires complex processes. Instead, students brought their finished products to the teacher for correction and evaluation. The composing of these products was something students had to manage on their own.

Whatever processes they used remained a "black box" to the instructor: the assignment went in at one end, and out came the final paper at the other.

Given that classical rhetoric did emphasize process, how is it that we have inherited such a product-oriented pedagogy? The history is too long to recount here in detail, but let me summarize by saying that over the centuries rhetoric was shorn of four of the five classical stages of composing. In the Renaissance, Ramist rhetoricians, because they sought to develop a purely objective discourse in which to conduct the researches of the new science, redefined invention and arrangement as matters of logic. Rationality, rather than persuasiveness, would be the new standard for judging the soundness and order of ideas. Much later, as English departments were formed in late nineteenth-century American colleges, their avowed focus on literature--on texts to be read--made the study of memory and delivery unnecessary (these elements continued to be studied in the departments of speech which, not coincidentally, split off from English departments at about this time).

As a result of these changes, the study of rhetoric came to focus on only one stage in the classical composing process: style. The tasks of the English department were to analyze the style of canonical literary works, for the purpose of interpreting these works' enduring human values; and to analyze the style of student essays, for the purpose of correcting their errors and encouraging the writers toward the beauties discovered in the canonical works. From the students' viewpoint, the English department thus devoted to the study of style certainly encouraged the fantasy that there are no composing processes. Only finished products were treated in class, whether the accomplished works of literary masters or the mediocre ones of the students themselves. Evidently one could not learn how to compose more effectively, since this was never taught. Evidently one either possessed the inborn ability to produce good texts, or one was out of luck: a cat can't lay eggs.

Rediscovering Composing

Dissatisfaction with this product-centered pedagogy has arisen periodically at least since the early twentieth century in the Progressive Education movement. But a surge of interest in composing developed in the 1960s. It probably received its single greatest impetus from the change in the school population that began to be evident at that time. To summarize this change crudely: more and more students were unable to bring to their teachers essays that needed only stylistic revision. More and more students were producing essays full of errors that were supposed to disappear in the earlier grades and of ideas so ill considered as to call into question the students' cognitive development. Drastic action seemed called for to help these student writers to improve.

It was largely in response to the perceived new needs of students and teachers-- that composition studies began to emerge in the 1960s as an area of specialization within English studies. Literary critics, too, were dissatisfied with the New Criticism's focus on style and began the theoretical debates over a replacement paradigm that have continued to the present. The entire discipline of English studies, in other words, has been undergoing some radical changes. But while literary scholars have focused on problems of reading literary texts, composition scholars have turned to examining writing, the process of composing texts, and particularly the texts of student writers and others who are not literary masters.

Most of the research that shapes our current knowledge of composing has been published since 1970. Composition specialists in the 1960s saw themselves primarily as teachers of writing, not as researchers. Nevertheless, their work has strongly influenced current research, not only in what it tells us about composing but also in the professional agenda it establishes for composition studies.

These first of the modern scholars in composition found themselves at odds with the academy from the beginning. Many academics (not to mention administrators and parents) assumed that the solution to the problem of student writing was simply to correct the ever-more-numerous errors, until by dint of the drill students finally learned not to splice commas, split infinitives, and so on. This assumption informed many early professional decisions made by senior academics about their colleagues in composition. For instance, if teaching grammar need be the only content of the writing class, writing teachers would not require advanced academic training. It became customary (as it still is to this day) to staff the bulk of a school's writing courses with teachers reassigned from other disciplines, voluntarily or not, with graduate students, or with people no longer actively seeking terminal degrees and teaching part-time by choice or necessity. These writing teachers found themselves gaining little professional respect, except, perhaps, that due the person who undertakes a necessary but unpleasant job that nobody else wants. Their senior colleagues assumed, moreover, that there was no serious scholarly work to be done in the field of composition studies, so that the way to professional advancement lay in escape from the writing classroom.

But writing teachers became increasingly convinced, on the basis of their classroom experience, that the initial assumption on the need for grammar drills simply was wrong. Attending closely to the problems students had in writing their papers, rather than merely to the problems that appeared in their finished products, writing teachers became convinced that students needed a better understanding of the whole process of working on a piece of writing, to give adequate time to the task and to make the time spent more productive. To gain this understanding, writing teachers began to work through this along with their students and to try to determine what contributed to a successful, or unsuccessful, writing process.

Some early fruit borne by such study was the model of composing introduced by Gordon Rohman and Raymond Wlecke.[1] Rohman and Wlecke found that successful college-level writers typically traverse three stages in composing: pre-writing, writing, and editing. Most significant here is the concept of "pre-writing," that is, degenerating activities that provide essential preparation for drafting. This was perhaps the first intimation that we needed to study a whole complex of composing processes, of which the actual writing of the paper was only one. Moreover, Rohman suggested that pre-writing activities such as journal keeping and meditation could be taught--that composing processes, rather than grammar drills, could become the actual content of the writing course.

Some academics opposed such activities, however, on grounds that they were not likely to foster the writing of good academic expository prose. This objection was met with even stronger resistance from writing teachers. During this same era, the academy itself began to seem discredited, in the eyes of many students and teachers, by political developments in the nation at large. For one thing, the academy was reluctant to incorporate new methods of responding to these developments, preferring its traditional subjects and methods of inquiry. For another, this reluctance was seen as enforcing discriminatory social sorting, with white middle-class men being educated for positions of power and all others being disenfranchised. Academic expository prose, the mastery of which was a prerequisite for traditional academic work, was implicated in the indictment of the academy as an institution of political oppression.

Hence, many writing teachers came to argue that students could not write good academic expository prose because academic expository prose was bad in itself--it was verbose, indirect, and impersonal to the point of hypocrisy. Instead of forcing students to master it, and the concomitant complexities of formal Standard English, writing teachers began to believe that they should be helping students to free themselves from its baleful influence if ever their writing were to improve. Students should forget their anxieties about correctness, stop trying to sound like someone else, and work to discover and refine their own personal, authentic writing styles.

The study of composing thus came to serve the liberation of each student's personal style, a way of writing that would dearly and sincerely convey her perspective on the world, as uniquely valuable as the student's own humanity. As I have tried to suggest, a combination of professional and historical circumstances made the development of a pedagogy of personal style something of a political crusade for many writing teachers. By fostering students' own styles, instead of forcing conformity to an oppressive institutional standard, writing teachers could feel they were making their own contribution to the reform of oppressive academic and political institutions.

Since the standard for judging a personal style could come only from within the student, who alone could certify its ability to represent her perspective on the world, the pedagogy of personal style aimed mainly to remove barriers to students' perceptions of what they had achieved in their writing. Close-reading, a technique of literary New Criticism, in which many writing teachers were trained, could be adapted for this purpose. Working as a group, teacher and students focused on student writing as the principal text for the course, and by detailed analysis helped each student writer to see whether her choice of words adequately expressed her thoughts. Given the original political agenda of personal-style pedagogy, this process typically worked to eliminate oppressive vestiges of academic writing. A student's personal style was to be characterized by comfortable use of the first person; by focus on a topic the student knows at first hand, typically personal experiences rather than academic subjects' and by exposition relying far more heavily on a detailed account of the writer's perceptions and feelings than on analysis and generalization. Peter Elbow's influential textbook, *Writing Without Teachers,* emphasizes the open-endedness of the composing processes's necessitated by the search for a personal style.[2]

The pedagogy of personal style thus established that composing processes are complex and often lengthy and, hence, that a substantial phenomenon exists for scholarly study. The Rohman-Wlecke model of composing has been faulted for its linearity, that is, for assuming that the successful writer typically moves through the composing process without backtracking or omitting any stage. But, in general, personal-style pedagogy, with its emphasis on rewriting, encouraged the view of composing processes as recursive, which has been confirmed by contemporary research.

In addition to these influential assumptions about composing, personal-style pedagogy helped shape contemporary research through its assumptions about what should go on in the writing classroom: that students and teacher should democratically discuss each student's work, with the teacher acting not as authoritative director but as knowledgeable collaborator and with the goal being each student's accomplishment of self selected writing tasks. Students should not be sidetracked in their search for personal styles by emphasis on standards of correctness set by others, such as the rules of formal Standard English. The teacher's main function, in addition to participating in the class writing workshop, should be to protect students from the academy's oppressive requirements.

Since the great majority of composition scholars have adhered at some time to personal-style pedagogy, it is not surprising that its pedagogical assumptions, as well as its assumptions directly bearing on composing, have influenced our sense of what research projects are worth undertaking. Moreover, this influence is not pernicious, both because all research can only occur under the guidance of assumptions and because these assumptions have guided us toward some fruitful research. It might not be too much to say that we owe all our current knowledge of composing to the early decisions of beleaguered composition scholars to resist the pedagogical agenda being set for them by senior academics, namely teaching grammar, and to seek a pedagogy more responsive to student needs. This pedagogy, in helping students develop their personal styles, brought their composing processes into the classroom and hence into the domain of scholarly inquiry. Moreover, the emphasis of this pedagogy on the personal, on the creative power of the individual writer's mind, helped to legitimate voices silenced in the traditional English classroom, voices of women, ethnic minorities, and other oppressed groups, and so did help to make the academy more responsive to contemporary political issues.

Under the influence of personal-style pedagogy, the first school of thought on composition research, which continues to flourish, encouraged the study of what goes on inside the individual writer's head. Such research is now often referred to as cognitive analyses of composing, because it has borrowed some methods and assumptions from the social sciences. The work of this school has been valuable, as I will explain below; unfortunately, however, until recently, composition research was limited to work in this school by personal-style pedagogy's assumptions about the individual nature of writing ability.

The problem was--and still is, to some extent--that personal-style pedagogy sees the political conflict in schools as between an oppressive institution and individual creative talents. In this view, what the student writer needs to do is to strip away all "outside" influences, such as academic standards of correctness, in order to get down to the thoughts and language that are uniquely, authentically hers. The kind of first-person narrative elicited in personal-style classes was assumed to be such "authentic" writing. The problem with this assumption, however, is illustrated by the fact that this "antiacademic" writing is actually a well-recognized belletristic essay style in itself, as exemplified in writers such as George Orwell and E.B. White, favorites for personal-style classroom reading. To heighten the irony, this style comes much more easily to white middle-and upper-class students than to others, thus preserving in personal-style pedagogy the very social discrimination it sought to combat.

What this example illustrates, however, is not the culpability of writing teachers for failing to free themselves from class-based attitudes, but rather the impossibility of doing so. No one uses language autonomously. One's speaking, reading, and writing are always shaped by one's social and cultural background and by the political relations this background creates with audiences of similar or very different backgrounds. This shaping is as much a matter of what the writer knows as of what she does. For example, a student may fail to produce an acceptable personal-style essay because she comes from a social group that does not value the sort of intense introspection such an essay calls for. Hence, she may either be simply too unfamiliar with introspection to produce it, or too wary with classmates (and teacher) from other social groups to produce it for them to read. As I have argued elsewhere, research into the social and cultural contexts from which the writer's knowledge comes and in which she is addressing an audience is as necessary to our understanding of composing as is research into what goes on in the writer's head.[3] Recently, more research into these contexts of composing has been forthcoming, as I will explain below.

Cognitive Analyses of Composing

The contemporary moment of research on composing may be said to begin with the work of James Britton and Janet Emig. Working independently, but aware of each other's work, Britton and Emig developed strikingly similar pictures of students' composing processes. Perhaps the greatest insight they share is that composing processes vary with the kind of writing the student is doing. Britton distinguishes three kinds: "poetic," which produces literary artifacts; "expressive," in which the student explores a subject and her own feelings about it, for an audience of herself or an intimate friend; and "transactional," in which the student seeks to convey information or argue for a position, for an audience of the teacher in the role of examiner.[4] Emig names two kinds of writing: "reflexive," very similar to Britton's expressive; and "extensive," very similar to Britton's transactional.[5] Britton and Emig agree that student writers' composing processes typically are most truncated and least successful in transactional/extensive writing and most elaborated and most successful in expressive/reflexive writing. Britton and Emig conclude that students should be offered far more opportunities in school for expressive/reflexive writing.

Britton and Emig formed these conclusions about composing by looking at student work, not literary masterpieces. Britton and his colleagues read about 2000 essays by British school children between the ages of eleven and eighteen. Emig interviewed eight American, high school seniors while they composed and produced a case study of one of these writers. This methodology has been widely influential, without being followed to the letter. Although not all researchers base their conclusions on a sample of student essays or on case studies, there is general agreement that composing is best investigated by looking at writers at work.

Emig's and Britton's conclusion, that students need more opportunities in school for expressive/reflexive writing, has also been widely influential, even when their terminology is not used. Indeed, this conclusion formed one of the assumptions of the pervasive pedagogy of personal style. The work of Emig and Britton was thus welcomed because it appeared to provide empirical justification for personal-style pedagogy's political indictment of academic writing. Britton and his colleagues, however, do not see the conflict in terms of academic writing versus individual styles, although their language is sometimes misleading. Rather, it is a battle between the language-using practices of the privileged social class and those of other social classes attempting to gain legitimacy in school. The underlying political agenda of Britton et al. is thus much more radical than that of personal-style pedagogy, calling for a class-based reversal of what constitutes good style rather than for a democracy of styles.

Preferring a focus on the personal, American composition research developed first along lines indicated by Emig, to explore what goes on in the individual writer's head. Some researchers have attempted to make the examination of working writers more rigorous by borrowing methodology from the social sciences. Composition scholar Linda Flower and her colleague, cognitive psychologist John R. Hayes, have pioneered the use of protocol analysis, a cognitive psychology research technique, for studying composing. Flower and Hayes ask writers to describe their thought processes aloud while they are composing. The transcript of what they say is the protocol, which the researchers then analyze for regular features of a composing process.

The Flower-Hayes model divides composing into three main parts: one, the "task environment," subdivided into "rhetorical problem" and "text produced so far"; two, the "writing process," subdivided into "reviewing" (further subdivided into "revising" and "evaluating"), "translating," and "planning" (further subdivided into "generating", so "goal-setting," and "organizing"); and three, the "writer's long-term memory." "Task environment" encompasses the immediate context of a composing situation, such as a school assignment for which a written product must be completed; "long-term memory" encompasses the larger social context for composing to be found, for example, in the writer's knowledge of genre. In the Flower-Hayes model, however, these contexts of composing are treated largely as a ground or frame for the main area of interest, namely the "writing process" (note the much greater number of subdivisions in this part of the model). "Writing process" encompasses activities taking place inside the writer's head.[6]

The most influential arguments propounded in the Flower-Hayes model are, first, that the writer can "access" task environment and long-term memory and switch from one writing subprocess to another at any time while composing: in other words, the composing process typically is recursive, not linear. For instance, the writer typically does not plan first and, that done, go on to write without ever reconsidering her plans. Second, although there is no single natural order in which composing activities do or should occur, there is a sort of natural relationship among them such that some activities are, or should be, subordinated to other activities: in other words, the composing process typically is hierarchical.

The Flower-Hayes model seeks to be comprehensive, that is, to describe all possible composing behaviors, although Flower and Hayes have been careful to point out that not every act of composing will--or should--employ every possible behavior. But in spite of this model's important arguments, which I just mentioned, it can be critiqued precisely on grounds of its claim to comprehensiveness. The problem is that some composition specialists have been prompted by this claim to attempt to explain the differences between successful and unsuccessful writers in terms of how fully they make use of the cognitive activities described in the model. Such research might lead to use of the Flower-Hayes model as a Procrustean bed for students' necessarily diverse composing processes.

For example, some researchers influenced by the Flower-Hayes model have argued that poor writing results from neglecting the recursive quality of the composing process, as did the poor writers in Pianko's study who failed to pause for reflecting on what they were writing.[7] Other researchers have held that poor writing results from misranking activities in the process hierarchy. The poor writers studied by Sondra Perl accorded inordinate importance and time to editing for errors in grammar, spelling, and mechanics.[8] The single most important factor in successful writing, Perl has argued, is to allow the recursive quality of composing by rereading the text as one produces it and waiting for a "felt sense" of structure to emerge and guide planning.[9]

The new importance given to the recursive quality of composing has led some researchers to focus exclusively on revision. Nancy Sommers has argued that the whole composing process, rightly understood, is a process of revision in which the writer does not simply polish her style but, more important, develops her ideas. "Revision" comes to mean the whole complex of activities of rereading, evaluating, and making small-scale and large-scale changes in the text as one produces it. Unsuccessful writers, Sommers argues, do not so understand revision, saving it for the end of the composing process and using it only to make small-scale changes such as in word choice.[10] It follows that the most effective writing pedagogy will be that which creates a climate for continual revising in the classroom, as described, for example, by Lil Brannon.[11]

Interest in revision and a desire to correct some problems with protocol analysis by adapting Emig's case-study method for research on composing have led researchers such as Carol Berkenkotter[12] and Mimi Schwartz[13] to follow the progress of a single text through multiple revisions. This research has emphasized that successful writing, whether by accomplished professionals or beginning students, emerges from recursive composing processes. There must be adequate time for rethinking; a willingness to respond to hunches, word associations, and other seemingly random techniques to trigger revision; and a recurring strong sense of the audience for whom one is writing.

Schwartz, Donald Graves, and others have argued that these factors influence revision even in very young children's writing.[14] Children have a natural proclivity for composing, according to Glenda Bissex and other researchers into the genesis of writing ability.[15] Graves argues in his influential book *Writing: Teachers and Children at Work* that it is vitally important for schools not to stifle children's natural desire to write by constraining them with assignments they are not interested in and intimidating them with constant corrections.[16] Rather, children should be given many opportunities to write on topics they choose and offered help with any aspect of composing only when such help seems necessary to the successful completion of a particular writing project and when it can be offered in such a way as not to make the child feel that she is no longer in control of her own writing. Although Shirley Brice Heath, David Olson, and others have argued that students' readiness to develop their writing in school is greatly influenced by their social and cultural backgrounds, most researchers into children's writing agree that Graves's pedagogy is the most helpful for all students.[17]

It is interesting to note how these various kinds of cognitive research on composing, like the work of Britton and Emig, echo some assumptions of personal-style pedagogy. The work of Pianko, Perl, and Sommers leads to the conclusion that something very like personal-style pedagogy is still the best: the main classroom activity is group revision of student texts, students rewrite to achieve their own expressive goals rather than to satisfy academic requirements, and any insistence on formal correctness is taboo. Graves recommends a similar pedagogy for elementary-school children, with the additional personal-style assumption that the resources they will call on in writing are mainly innate abilities, not knowledge gained in school. Thus, the kind of pedagogy emerging from current cognitive research on composing is open to the same objection that was leveled against personal-style pedagogy, namely, that this new pedagogy does not lead to mastery of academic writing. Personal-style pedagogues, as I noted earlier, were inclined to answer this charge by arguing that mastery of academic writing was undesirable anyway. Those advocating the new pedagogy, however, generally argue that it offers the best route to eventual mastery of academic writing and any other kind of writing the student chooses to do. This view is still open to debate; we have no research evidence that students educated according to this pedagogy develop into more accomplished academic writers than those educated by other means, though the student excerpts typically quoted in works advocating this pedagogy suggest they are accomplished at other kinds of writing. The fact is, however, that curricula designed according to this pedagogy generally do not teach academic writing directly, whatever abilities may be expected of students afterwards.

Research on the Social and Cultural Contexts of Composing

Although, as I suggested earlier, the first contemporary school of thought on composition research focused on the individual writer's mind, more recently a second school has developed to research the social and cultural factors that influence the individual writer's performance. These researchers have been motivated in part by a reluctance to accept the conclusion, forced by personal-style and cognitive-based analyses of composing, that differences in individual performance are due to differences in individual talent. This reluctance sprang from the scholars' observation that performance differences seemed to correlate with social groups; it seemed logical, therefore, to assume that social and cultural, as well as individual, factors influence composing. Moreover, poor performance seemed to correlate with relatively less privileged social groups. Retaining a sympathy with these groups consistent with some assumptions of personal-style pedagogy, these scholars wished to save them from the stigma of personal failure and to seek a pedagogy specific to their needs.

For many of these researchers, mastery of academic writing has become once more an acceptable goal of composition pedagogy, but not as it was traditionally taught. Once, the course teaching academic writing simply laid down its laws, and those who would not or could not conform simply left the academy. Now, composition scholars seek to serve these students particularly-- the ones who have trouble mastering academic writing--so as to give them equal access to the knowledge generated and maintained by the academy. Some scholars may hope that, if academic writing is still a weapon of political oppression, students who master it may be able to turn the weapon against the oppressors. At any rate, many students are now asking for help in mastering academic writing, and writing teachers are responding, just as we responded fifteen years ago when they asked for help in mastering nonacademic, personal styles.

Another influence on the interest in social and cultural contexts of composing has been the new interest in classical rhetoric among composition specialists. Classical rhetoric began to be recovered for English studies in the 1960s, when new collections of original classical texts became available and E.P.J. Corbett's influential *Classical Rhetoric for the Modern Student* suggested contemporary pedagogical applications.[18] At first, classical rhetoric's most important contribution was its multistage composing process, particularly its emphasis on invention, which reinforced the movement in personal-style pedagogy to develop "pre-writing" or idea-generating techniques.

The classical model of composing has been faulted on grounds of excessive linearity. C.H. Knoblauch and Lil Brannon have blamed classical rhetoric, not as recently rediscovered but as embedded in American schooling since the nineteenth century, for influencing teachers to vitiate new pedagogical techniques, such as those encouraging personal style, by inserting them into a curriculum dominated by this linear model of composing.[19] In this way the techniques become mere moments in a rigid progression of stages of composing, rather than, as they should be,periodically useful tools in and open-ended and recursive process. But there is more to the story of classical rhetoric's relevance for the modern student.

As composition specialists have begun to turn to research on the contexts of composing, they have become aware that perhaps the most important contribution of classical rhetoric is precisely its focus on context. Classical rhetoric assumes that the function of writing is not to express oneself but to effect change in the human community in which one lives. Hence, the ability to suit one's style to the particular audience, rather than addressing all in one "personal" register, becomes art, not hypocrisy. Classical rhetoric invites discussion of the social and political uses of writing in ways that personal-style pedagogy, for all its political agenda, never could.

As composition specialists' interest in the contexts of composing has emerged, two seminal theorists have been Ann Berthoff and Mina Shaughnessy. They take two very different approaches, without much reference to each other, but both insist on the crucial connection between individual writer and "outside world." Berthoff has made this point in the strongest terms: human beings use language to make sense of themselves and their world.[20] Hence, if we want to understand composing, we must look at that world with which the writer is in a dialectical relationship, as well as at the writer's individual talents. Berthoff does share some assumptions with personal-style pedagogy concerning all students' innate meaning-making powers. But because she also looks at the context of composing, the world in which and on which they work, she realizes that student writers can be taught to make more personally satisfying use of their meaning-making powers in language--that is, she favors a more directive pedagogy than the personal-style, one that offers what she calls "assisted invitations" to composing. These "invitations" aim not to liberate student writing from the influence of others' styles, but to make students constructively self-conscious about the resources available to their own writing in their society's repertoire of styles. For example, instead of merely keeping a personal journal, Berthoffs students might be encouraged to maintain a "double-entry notebook" in which they periodically reread and critique their own earlier observations. Thus they are made students of their own language-using practices.

While Berthoff's approach is intended, I believe, to be universally applicable, that is, to describe the universal human experience with making meaning in language, Shaughnessy confined her study specifically to the academic community.[21] In her analysis of successive drafts of papers by extremely unskilled college writers, Shaughnessy has found attempts at meaning making where there appears to be no order at all. She understands the composing process as a socialization process, in which gradually bringing one's writing into line with the discourse conventions of one's readers also brings one to share their thinking, their values, in short, their world view. Shaughnessy has argued that student writers are least successful when most ignorant of academic discourse conventions: how the academic audience evaluates evidence, what allusions strike it as elegant, what personae it finds credible, and so on. Shaughnessy has suggested a philosophical critique of personal-style pedagogy in her repudiation of the "honest face" persona for student writers. Nowhere, including the academy, does clear, sincere self-expression win assent unaided.

Shaugnnessy's work gave composition specialists a new perspective on student writing problems. Her analysis allows us to retain the best element of personal-style pedagogy, namely, its sense that students' relationship with the academy is agonistic and requires our mediation if social justice and common humanity are to be served. But she also allowed us to step back from the position that bad student writing was caused by the imposition of bad academic standards on all writing is natural creativity. Rather, if no writing is autonomous, if all writing is situated in some language-using community, then bad student writing, according to Shaughnessy, should be understood as the output of apprentices or initiates into the academic community. The pedagogy they need is not one that excoriates academic discourse, but rather one that mediates their introduction to it while remaining respectful of the language-using practices they bring to school.

Research into the social, cultural, and political influences on composing, particularly as they bear on students attempting to master academic writing, has taken several directions, exploring writing across the curriculum, basic writing, collaborative learning, and reading/writing connections. Questions which remain problematic for this research include the extent to which social, cultural, and political factors determine composing as opposed to merely influencing it, and the pace at which students should be urged toward mastery of academic writing. Assumptions from personal-style pedagogy can be seen playing their part in this school of research, as much as in the cognitive research that this school often seeks to correct or oppose. For example, recommendations for workshop classrooms in which students pursue self-selected writing goals often emerge from this research, as my brief overview will show. Nevertheless, the emphasis on contexts of composing is an essential and unique contribution.

Writing across the curriculum began as a pedagogical movement in Great Britain in the late 1960s. It was fostered by James Britton, Nancy Martin, and their colleagues in response to the discovery, made in the course of their composing process research, that students wrote very little outside the English classroom. Believing that students would write better if given more opportunities to write in school, particularly opportunities for expressive writing, the British researchers published a series of pamphlets explaining how to integrate expressive writing into a wide range of academic disciplines. In effect, these pamphlets argue for teaching a composing process which would begin with expressive writing, for example in class journals, and only later issue in finished academic essays. The British researchers envision a classroom in which much student writing and talking do not issue in finished work at all, but are nevertheless essential for their heuristic value.[22]

Toby Fulwiler[23] and Lil Brannon and C.H. Knoblauch[24] are among the American composition scholars who have adapted for American colleges the work of Britton et al., which is aimed at elementary and secondary level students. In arguing for the efficacy of a journal-centered composing process in college-level academic disciplines, these proponents of writing across the curriculum have focused the British methods more directly toward the production of finished essays, while maintaining that better papers grow from personal interest in the topic that students develop through their journals. This pedagogy, too, has argued that student composing processes may be idiosyncratic and no single composing process can be assumed to be successful for everyone.

Other American work in writing across the curriculum moves away from this focus on the individual writer to look more directly at the academic context and its demands. Composition scholars such as Elaine Maimon have sought to respond to Shaughnessy's call for a taxonomy of academic discourse conventions.[25] Maimon's focus is not merely on formal features of texts, such as laboratory report format. Rather, she analyzes the intellectual framework suggested by the laboratory report and asks: What do the discourse conventions reveal about how scientists define and interact with the world? What kind of thinking does this kind of writing ask students to do or actually make them do as they write? Maimon's work suggests that there may be epistemological constraints on composing. A writer's varying degrees of success with different kinds of writing may not be due to a simple dichotomy of personal writing (good) versus academic writing (bad). Rather, the different kinds of thinking demanded in different disciplines may cause the student's composing process to vary as a function of the different distances between these ways of thinking and that with which the student is originally comfortable.

Thus these two different approaches to writing across the curriculum typically issue in different pedagogies. The centered approach, once again, endorses something very similar to personal-style pedagogy. The classroom is a workshop, students generate their own writing topics and stylistic goals, and emphasis on correctness is avoided. The teacher is likely, however, to encourage writing projects that involve something like traditional academic inquiry--for instance, a topic requiring library research. Moreover, it is not unusual for such a writing course to be linked with a course in some other discipline, so that the students prepare their papers for that course with the aid of the journal-centered pedagogy of the writing course. Typically, however, journal-centered pedagogy spends relatively little time on formal academic expository writing.

In contrast, the approach centered on academic discourse conventions gives first priority to mastery of academic writing and the formal Standard English it employs. Students may well be encouraged to begin front journals and other forms of pre-writing associated with personal-style pedagogy, but they will be urged along more quickly to the production of finished academic essays. Students will be helped to meet academic English standards in the final stages of composing, on grounds that to do so is to observe what counts as polite behavior n the community they are seeking to enter. The classroom atmosphere is likely to be more directive, with the teacher actively seeking to explain academic writing conventions and to demystify the kinds of thinking they make possible.

The academic context has particularly marked effects on students who are least familiar with its discourse conventions and ways of thinking--the students known as "basic writers" who are at the very beginning stages of being able to produce successful academic writing. Much research on the composing processes of basic writers has focused on the extent to which their difficulties are due to the academic context. Mike Rose has argued that a truncated or blocked composing process can result from overly rigid internalization of advice given in writing instruction, rather than from some deficiency in the student's innate ability to compose.[26] David Bartholomae, extending the work of Shaughnessy, has explained the discourse of basic writers as an approximation of the academic discourse whose conventions and world view are unfamiliar to them, rather than merely as a tissue of errors.[27] These readings of the work of basic writers suggest that their composing processes must include a considerable amount of trial-and-error experimentation as they gradually discover how to use academic discourse for their own purposes.

Teaching academic discourse to basic writers has become a particularly sensitive issue because their difficulties with academic writing tend to be a function of the social distance between the academy and their home communities. That is, basic writers typically come from less privileged social groups, where the language-using practices are most unlike those of the academy, which reflect the practices of the privileged groups in our society. Hence, basic writers appear to be in more danger than others of being alienated from their home communities by mastery of academic discourse. Literacy researchers Walter Ong[28] and Thomas J. Farrell[29] have argued in favor of such alienation or assimilation, on grounds that the ways of thinking enabled by the language-using practices of such students' home communities are cognitively inferior to those of the academy. Other scholars, however, see such arguments as unjustly enforcing the social privileges of academic writing.[30] We do not know whether academic ways of thinking are in fact cognitively different from, or superior to, those of other communities; nor do we know to what extent assimilation is unavoidable for basic writers.

As research on writing across the curriculum and on basic writing has emphasized students' adapting to new ways of thinking, many composition researchers have been led to focus on the extent to which learning to compose is a socialization process, a process of initiation into the discourse community's world view. Such a focus immediately brings to the foreground the extent to which composing is a collaborative process. More broadly, the ways we "compose" experience are culturally conditioned, More particularly, all writers are influenced in their composing processes by other writers, other writing, more experienced mentors, and so on. For the student, these are the influences of academic discourse, teachers, and peers. Kenneth Bruffee, a specialist in the "collaborative learning" of writing, has explored these influences and concludes that students who understand something of the academic world view and its discourse are often more effective than teachers in mediating other students' introduction to the academy.

Bruffee has developed a method of training students to tutor their peers that helps them all to become conscious of what they already knew about academic discourse and to improve their knowledge through attention to their own composing processes. Bruffee's writing workshop resembles the personal-style classroom in procedure, with the difference that the main goal is not discovery of one's inmost honest feelings, but rather articulation of a public voice that will allow participation in the academic intellectual community.[31] The greatest contribution of work on collaborative is to emphasize that composing is always in some sense a social process.

Intellectual socialization may be accomplished not only by interacting with people, but also by encountering the writing of others. Thus research on connections between reading and writing also speaks to our knowledge of composing processes. That the writer must be able to read her own text while composing it, we know from such work as that of Sommers and of Flower and Hayes. But Anthony Petrosky and Mariolina Salvatori have suggested that the ability to read the works of others also affects a writer's composing process. Petrosky argues that the successful reading of a literary text is a "transaction" in which the reader must work to make the text meaningful in terms of her own experience, a view influenced by reader-response literary theory. Writing from these perceived correspondences between personal and literary experience helps student writers to elaborate their composing processes where is most needed: in the linking of adequate illustrations to the generalizations that frame their arguments.[32] Similarly, Salvatore has argued that student writers develop intellectually more complex composing processes as they learn to link moments of reading comprehension into larger patterns of meaning and to relate these in turn to their own experience for comparison or critique.[33] In effect, for these researchers, the texts of others become collaborators in the students' composing processes, stimulating critical reflection on composing in much the same way as do peer tutors or the conventions of academic discourse itself, self-consciously viewed.

What We Know: Curricular Implications

We know that the act of composing through writing is a complex process. Although we are beginning to identify characteristic moments or stages in this process, we cannot say exactly what are the relationships of these stages one to another. We can say that we know such relationships exist, that is, the composing process is hierarchical, and also that they are not necessarily ordered serially, that is, the composing process is recursive. We cannot say that there is one composing process invariably successful for all writers, for all purposes. Rather, we know that composing processes vary both as the same writer attempts different kinds of discourse and as different writers attempt the same kind of discourse, and that such variations may be necessary to success in composing. The current state of our knowledge of composing permits the limited generalizations that successful composing results more often from attention to the thinking required by a piece of writing than to its adherence to standard conventions of grammar, spelling, and so on; and that successful composing results more often from a process that allows for rereading, rethinking, and rewriting than from one in which time limitations or other pressures force a rush to closure. I believe that we can also conclude--although this is perhaps more debatable--that "successful" composing results in writing that participates actively in the language-using practices of a particular community, without slavishly imitating them.

This limited understanding of composing processes nevertheless permits some broad recommendations on curriculum. First, learning to write requires writing. Students cannot be expected to master such complex processes if they only practice them two or three times in a school term, or without a teacher's guidance. It follows, then, if students are to be writing frequently and receiving frequent responses from the teacher, that classes in which writing is taught (whether in English or some other discipline) must be kept small. The teacher must be able to get to know the students in order to respond consistently to the thinking they develop in their writing. Moreover, if the emphasis in writing is to be on developing thinking, it follows both that the curriculum should be structured to encourage recursive composing processes and that institutionalized testing of student writing should not set a counteragenda for the writing class, such as mastering a certain number of features of formal grammar.

But in this small class in which students are writing and rewriting frequently, what should they be writing? What should the classroom activities be? These questions, it seems to me, are more open to debate. Some answers can be found in the Position Statement on teaching composition recently promulgated by the Commission on Composition of the National Council of Teachers of English.[34] This document suggests that students should be encouraged "to make full use of the many activities that comprise the act of writing," presumably including various pre-writing and editing techniques as well as the actual drafting of papers. The document also states that writing assignments should reflect the wide variety of purposes for writing, including expressive writing, writing across the curriculum, and writing that would have a place in "the world beyond school." The writing classroom, according to the document, should be organized as a workshop in which students write for each other, as well as for the teacher, and in which writing is used as "a mode of learning" rather than merely "reporting on what has been learned." To accomplish these ends, class size should not be larger than twenty students, and student writing should be the principal text. Tests should allow students "to demonstrate their writing ability in work aimed at various purposes" and should encourage the development of students' self-critical abilities.

The recommendations on class size, testing, and teaching a full range of composing activities, which would necessitate much attention to substantive revision, may be the most politically sensitive of the recommendations, since they at once ask the public for more money for education (more teachers to keep class size small) and deny the public the kind of testing in writing skills that it seems to desire. Yet current research suggests that it is essential to implement these recommendations if student writing is to improve.

It is not equally evident, however, that for good writing to ensue students must always write for each other and make their own writing the principal text. If the curricular goal is to foster mastery of academic discourse, such a classroom organization will not be very productive unless many of the students have already achieved the desired goal and so can teach the others. But it appears that today's students typically do not have enough prior knowledge of academic discourse conventions to help each other to mastery of them. More guidance from the teacher and more reading materials that illustrate and elucidate these practices may be needed (without, however, returning to the traditional, authoritarian classroom).

The Position Statement may be recommending what amounts to a personal-style classroom because the value of this approach is widely acknowledged among composition specialists, while the goal of mastering academic discourse is more problematic. The Commission also finesses the issue of academic discourse by taking a pluralistic view of the kinds of writing assignments it recommends, all the way from personal-style pedagogy's favored expressive writing to some kind of business or technical writing (for "the world beyond school"). In fact, there is no consensus on what kinds of writing students should be doing. Recent anthologies of college student writing, published as textbooks, suggest that personal-style essays still enjoy an edge; indeed, if they did not, there would be no point in publishing such anthologies.[35] But, as I suggested earlier, various kinds of academic writing are mounting a strong challenge. I believe, however, that it is salutary for teachers and students to discuss the problem of what constitutes "good" writing. Thus there is no way to escape the fact the fact that course content choices, with the kinds of writing the valorize, will have political consequences with which we must deal.

Indeed, perhaps the most important conclusion to be drawn from this overview of research on composing is that research results alone not only should not dictate a curriculum, they cannot dictate it. Notice how persistently composition researchers have interpreted their results in light of personal-style pedagogical assumptions, whether about classroom organization or political agenda. But we could not do otherwise. Scholars writing up their research, like students struggling with their first essay assignments, must work within the language- using practices of a particular community, which are in turn shaped by its social, cultural, and political circumstances. The challenge is to be an active participant, to change the community in light of the values that make one's commitment to education professionally and personally meaningful.

Author's note: I would like to thank Bruce Herzberg and David Bartholomae for their careful reading of drafts of this chapter.

FOOTNOTES

1. D. Gordon Rohman, "Pre-Writing: The Stage of Discovery in the Writing Process," *College Composition and Communication 26* (May 1965): 106-12.
2. Peter Elbow, *Writing Without Teachers* (New York: Oxford University Press, 1973).
3. Patricia Bizzell, "Cognition, Convention, and Certainty: What We Need to Know about Writing," *PRE/TEXT* 3 (Fall 1982): 213-44.
4. James Britton, T. Burgess, N. Martin, A. Mcleod, and H. Rosen. *The Development of Writing Abilities (11-18)* (London: Macmillan Education, 1975).
5. Janet Emig, *The Composing Processes of Twelfth Graders* (Urbana, Ill.: National Council of Teachers of English, 1971).
6. Linda Flower and John R. Hayes, "A Cognitive Process Theory of Writing," *College Composition and Communication 32* (December 1981): 365-87.
7. Sharon Pianko, "A Description of the Composing Processes of College Freshman Writers," *Research in the Teaching of English* 13 (February 1979): 5-22.

8. Sondra Perl, "Composing Processes of Unskilled College Writers," *Research in the Teaching of English* 13 (December 1979): 317-36.
9. Sondra Perl, "Understanding Composing," *College Composition and Communication* 31 (December 1980): 363-69.
10. Nancy Sommers, "Revision Strategies of Student Writers and Experienced Adult Writers," *College Composition and Communication* 31 (December 1980): 378-88.
11. Lil Brannon, Melinda Knight, and Vera Neverow-Turk, *Writers Writing* (Montclair, NJ.: Boynton/Cook, 1983).
12. Carol Berkenkotter and Donald Murray, "Decisions and the Planning Strategies of a Publishing Writer, and Response of a Laboratory Rat--or Being Protocoled," *College Composition and Communication* 34 (May 1983): 156-72.
13. Mimi Schwartz, "Two journeys through the Writing Process," *College Composition and Communication* 34 (May 1983): 188-201.
14. Donald Graves, "An Examination of the Writing Processes of Seven-Year-Old Children," *Research in the Teaching of English 9* (Winter 1975): 227-41; Linda Leonard Lamme and Nancy M. Childers, "Composing Processes of Three Young Children," *Research in the Teaching of English 17* (February 1983): 31-50.
15. Glenda L. Bissex, *Gnys at Work: A Child Learns to Write and Read* (Cambridge, Mass.: Harvard University Press, 1980).
16. Donald H. Graves, *Writing: Teachers and Children at Work* (Portsmouth, N.H. and London: Heinemann Educational Books, 1983).
17. Shirley Brice Heath, *Ways With Words: Language, Life, and Work in Communities and Classrooms* (Cambridge, Eng.: Cambridge University Press, 1983); David R. Olson, "The Language of Instruction: The Literate Bias of Schooling," in *Schooling and the Acquisition of Knowledge,* ed. Richard C. Anderson, Rand J. Spiro, and William E. Montague (Hillsdale, N.J.: Lawrence Erlbaum Associates, 1977), pp. 65-90. For a dissenting view, see Margaret Donaldson, "Speech and Writing and Modes of Learning," in *Awakening to Literacy. The University of Victoria Symposium of Children's Response to a Literate Environment: Literacy before Schooling,* ed. Hillel Goelman, Antoinette A. Oberg, and Frank Smith (Exeter, N.H. and London: Heinemann Educational Books, 1984), pp. 174-84.
18. Edward P.J. Corbett, *Classical Rhetoric for the Modern Student,* 2d edition (New York: Oxford University Press, 1971).
19. C.H. Knoblauch and Lil Brannon, *Rhetorical Traditions and the Teaching of Writing* (Montclair, NJ.: Boynton/Cook, 1984).
20. Ann E. Berthoff, *The Making of Meaning: Metaphors, Models and Maxims for Writing Teachers* (Montclair, N.J.: Boynton/Cook, 1981).
21. Mina P. Shaughnessy, *Errors and Expectations: A Guide for the Teacher of Basic Writing* (New York: Oxford University Press, 1977).
22. Nancy Martin, editor, *Writing across the Curriculum: Pamphlets from the Schools Council/London Institute of Education W.A.C Projects* (Montclair,N.J.: Boynton/Cook, 1984).
23. Toby Fulwiler, "The Personal Connection: Journal Writing across the Curriculum," in *Language Connections: Writing and Reading across the Curriculum,* ed. Toby Fulwiler and Art Young (Urbana, Ill.: National Council of Teachers of English, 1982), pp. 15-32.
24. C.H. Knoblauch and Lil Brannon, "Writing as Learning through the Curriculum," *College English 45* (September 1983): 465-74.
25. Elaine Maimon, "Maps and Genres: Exploring Connections in the Arts and Sciences," in *Composition and Literature: Bridging the Gap,* ed. Winifred Bryan Horner (Chicago: University of Chicago Press, 1983) pp. 110-25.
26. Mike Rose, "Rigid Rules, Inflexible Plans and the Stifling of Language: A Cognitivist Analysis of Writer's Block," *College Composition and Communication* 31 (December 1980): 389-400.
27. David Bartholomae, "The Study of Error," *College Composition and Communication* 31 (October 1980): 253-69.
28. Walter J. Ong, "Literacy and Orality in Our Times," in *Composition and Literature: Bridging the Gap,* ed. Horner, pp. 126-140.
29. Thomas J. Farrell, "I.Q. and Standard English," *College Composition and Communication* 34 (December 1983): 470-84.
30. See rebuttals to Farrell by Karen Greenberg, Patrick Hartwell, Margaret Himley, and R.E. Stratton in *College Composition and Communication* 35 (December 1984): 455-77.
31. Kenneth A. Bruffee "Collaborative Learning and the 'Conversation of Mankind,'" *College English 46* (November 1984): 635-52.

32. Anthony R. Petrosky, "From Story to Essay: Reading and Writing," *College Composition and Communication* 33 (February 1982): 19-36.
33. Mariolina Salvatori, "Reading and Writing a Text: Correlations between Reading and Writing," *College English* 45 (November 1983): 657-66.
34. Commission on Composition of the National Council of Teachers of English "Teaching Composition: A Position Statement," (Urbana, Ill.: National Council of Teachers of English, 1983). I should note that as a member of the Commission I participated in the drafting of this document and endorsed its publication.
35. See, for example, William E. Coles, Jr., and James Vopat, editors, *What Makes Writing Good: A Multiperspective* (Lexington, Mass. and Toronto: D.C. Heath Co., 1985); Nancy Sommers and Donald McQuade, editors, Student Writers at Work: The Bedford Prizes (New York: Bedford Books of St. Martin's Press, 1984)

Rhetorical Invention
W. Ross Winterowd

Aristotle and Extrapolation

In *The Philosophy of Composition* (1977), E.D. Hirsch, Jr. argued that composition and rhetoric are separate fields, and it was this argument that led Hirsch into what I have called neo-Ramism, the exclusion of invention from composition. In fact, Hirsch's "philosophy" reduced composition to stylistics. But as practitioners, we know positively that style is not all, not even our central concern when we teach composition.

Favorable or unfavorable, each of our responses to student texts falls into one of four categories: content, organization, style, or editing. We react to logic, semantic intention, development of ideas; to the order in which the ideas are presented; to sentence structure, figurative language, tone; and to "mechanics" such as punctuation and verb agreement. If this spectrum does represent what we can say about a text, then we must have methods for teaching *invention, arrangement, style,* and mechanics.

The traditional departments of rhetoric are invention, arrangement, style, delivery, and memory, but since we are dealing with written discourse, not spoken, delivery and memory become irrelevant.

Obviously, then, composition and rhetoric are *not* identical, in just the same way that cardiology and medicine are not: one is a branch of the other. Just as a cardiologist must be a physician, so a compositionist must be a rhetorician. Aristotle and his successors wrought better than they could have imagined. Much better.

A schematic of the field of composition/rhetoric appears below. I will use the diagram--which captures something of the elegance of rhetoric, either traditional or modern--as the basis for this and the two subsequent chapters.

Rhetorical invention concerns the generation of subject matter: any process--conscious or subconscious, heuristic or algorithmic--that yields something to say about a subject, arguments for or against a case. Inartificial arguments are simply the facts of the "case," discoverable
through research if they are not immediately obvious. (Aristotle lists such evidence as contracts, testimony of witnesses, statements under torture and so on. Artificial arguments are more subtle, arising from the character of the speaker *(ethos),* the nature of the audience *(pathos),* or the integrity of the argument itself *(logos).* And, of course, logical arguments can be either deductive or inductive.

"Brain, Rhetoric, and Style" (pp. 129-57) is, in fact, a contemporary reaction to the deduction-induction dichotomy in rhetoric and logic. It is perhaps dangerous to boil the argument down to its simplest terms, but for the sake of clarity: the left hemisphere of the brain works deductively, and the right hemisphere works inductively. Western

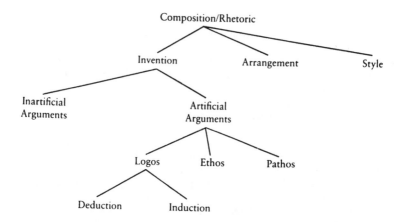

rationalist that he was, Aristotle had little to say about induction, the mode of reasoning most congenial to the "intuitive" right hemisphere, and rhetoric throughout its history has not paid attention to the alternative, right hemispheric processes of logos. Currently, however, the situation is changing: a great deal of work in rhetoric proper, linguistics, psychology, neurophysiology, anthropology, and other fields is concerned with cognitive and discourse modes of the right hemisphere, and certainly this work will be a major influence on composition theory and teaching in the next decades. (See Benderly, 1981; Emig, 1978; Freed, 1981; Glassner, 1981; Miner, 1976.)

It is a useful oversimplification to point out that in literary criticism, mimetic theories focus on "truth" value (logos); expressive, on the poet (ethos); pragmatic, on the reader (pathos); and objective, on the text itself (arrangement and style). However, as chapters 2 and 3 should have demonstrated, a theory of language, a hermeneutic method, or a set of evaluative criteria will be unsatisfactory unless it squares with the classical theory of rhetoric, dealing with all factors as they interrelate. Thus, it can be argued that a literary theory (or any other theory of discourse) will be adequate just to the degree that it squares with the classical theory of rhetoric. (See "The Three R's: Reading, Reading, and Rhetoric," pp. 253-63.) I am not claiming that modern rhetoric is simply a new application of the same old stuff, though I would argue strongly that modern work in linguistics, psycho-linguistics, speech act theory, anthropology, and other fields gives a more penetrating conception of the triad ethos-pathos-logos, but does not supersede it.

Invention, Lost and Found

As composition became a massive, if not respectable, enterprise in American schools and universities, the emphasis was squarely on style and structure, to the virtual exclusion of invention. (See Berlin, 1984.)

Inside the front cover of my edition of *The Foundations of Rhetoric,* by Adams Sherman Hill, Boylston Professor of Rhetoric and Oratory in Harvard University (Harper and Brothers Publishers, 1897)--owned once by Julian U. Siegel of Baltimore- -are these ghostly wisps of humor: "Shake well before using!" and "Take in small doses!" This, from the preface:

> Differ as good writers may in other respects, they are all distinguished by the judicious and the skillful placing of words. They all aim (1) to use no word that is not established as a part of the language. in the sense in which they use it, and no word that does not say what they wish it to say so clearly as to be understood at once, and either so strongly as to command attention or so agreeably as to win attention; (2) to put every word in the place fixed for it by the idiom of the language, and by the principles which govern communication between man and man--the place which gives the word its exact value in itself and in its relations with other words; (3) to use no more words than are necessary to effect the purpose in hand. If it be true that these simple principles underlie all good writing, they may properly be called *The Foundations of Rhetoric.*

In short, for A.S. Hill as for E.D. Hirsch, Jr., almost a century later, stylistics was virtually the all.

The *Foundations of Rhetoric* is by no means a bad book; it is not schlock mindlessly and quickly produced to capitalize on a G.I. Bill or a Baby Boom or a Sputnik. For our purposes, it is merely a typical book, and the highest praise we can give it is to say it is an admirable example of an era that stretched from the latter part of the nineteenth century to, roughly, 1964, when Rohman and Wlecke published their landmark study of invention: *Pre-Writing: The Construction and Application of Models for Concept Formation in Writing.* It was the genius of these scholars to understand that the compositionist must deal with substance, for a composition has meaning as well as style and structure. No doubt Adams Sherman Hill would have agreed, but he was caught in a rhetorical paradigm which implied that his colleagues in the substantive fields had a corner on the content market, Brothers Hunt who, in the educational marketplace, controlled logos: "Save the fuss; leave the thinking to us."

A kind of antiquarian passion leads me from one old composition text to another, those solidly bound, magisterial books with now-fading notations of students from generations ago; the ignominy of the old texts--none of them classics, all of them forgotten--is a melancholy but salubrious commentary on the profession that we share. Our best works, composition texts that do give students the ability to write (and hence a powerful tool of cognition), are as doomed as is *Composition and Rhetoric,* by Alfred M. Hitchcock (Henry Holt, 1923; copyright 1906, 1908, 1909, 1913, 1914, 1917). In the margin on page 270 (chapter 21 "Adjectives and Adverbs"), the penciled enigmatic word "Lymerick." What drowsy lecture inspired Rina White, 849 Genesee Ave. (telephone Wasatch 7079), to make the inscription? We can be certain that on that day in the 1910s or 1920s--in Salt Lake City--there was a lecture in the composition class, and probably some exercises on adjectives and adverbs. And looming somewhere was a theme for Rina to compose; when it was turned in, the lecturer would become a correcter. (A Saturday afternoon in May. The trees are lacy green, and the peonies are almost ready for their Memorial Day duty. The lecturer-correcter sits at her dining-room table, "marking" papers. She is unmarried, necessarily so, lest students in her high school think of- -fantasize about--her libido, thus losing respect for the virginal purity of her nunlike mediation between the doctrine according to Saint Alfred Hitchcock-- presumably no relation--and their imperfect attempts to achieve correctness.) No doubt this digression is invidious, but let it stand. As a corrective, assume that Hitchcock, lecturer-correcter, and Rina were decent, intelligent folk doing the best they knew how within the paradigm and educational system that they inherited. Assume the same about us and our students. With this healthier, at least more charitable, attitude, let us proceed with our delineation of the enlightened present, hoping that our successors will be at least as mellow as we.)

After a long, disastrous hiatus, composition once again became rhetorical, starting, as I have said, in about 1964 with the Rohman Wlecke study. (*Writing Instruction in Nineteenth-Century American Colleges,* by James A. Berlin [1984], is essential reading.) In 1965, Edward P.J. Corbett reintroduced students and teachers to the tradition with *Classical Rhetoric for the Modern Student,* and second and third editions of even the most conservative texts began to include sections on prewriting and invention. William Irmscher's enormously successful *Holt Guide to English* (1972) included an extensive introduction to Kenneth Burke's Pentad.

In his important essay "Invention: A Topographical Survey" (1976), Richard Young outlines current "methodologies": neo-classical invention, adapted from the classical tradition, as in Corbett (1965); Burke's dramatism, as in Irmscher (1972); prewriting (Rohman and Wlecke, 1964); and tagmemic invention, as in Young, Becker, and Pike (1970); to which I would subjoin the variety of heuristics to be found in the second edition of my own textbook (1981).

Heuristics

In "'Topics' and Levels in the Composing Process" (1973), I have explained a system for classifying and evaluating heuristics; however, my purpose now is to discuss their usefulness for composition teachers.

We find ourselves uncomfortably on the spot when we claim that we're trying to teach people to think or to think creatively, for we are hardly philosophers or psychologists, and yet we find ourselves equally in an uncomfortable position (since being on the spot whether we are standing or sitting is not an optimum sort of repose) when we must respond to student texts with "You need to develop your ideas" or "Your ideas are unoriginal"--though, of course, in more tactful ways, less scarifying terms, for we attempt to give sympathetically helpful reactions to texts that we must, as teachers, take seriously. As teachers! What are we to advise students? "Think, and you'll discover ideas!" "Be original, and you'll be original!" We are constrained, in fact, to teaching thinking or methods thereof.

The fashionable word "heuristics" is broad enough to cover the field of methods available to the comp teacher faced with the problem of a student who either seems unable to generate ideas concerning a topic or inscribes platitudes--and my dour tone here simply obscures my respect for every student's potential to write amply and originally, though I find myself, for the strategic purposes of this essay, too often assuming the negative stance, which, of course, is always disastrous in teaching: the sort of attitude that implies bare tolerance of the acne-essays submitted by our composition students, the bubble-gum writings of juveniles who will never mature to the suave literacy and keen thinking of their mentors. As mentors, nonetheless, we must respect our charges enough to believe that maturity and a healthy diet will cure the acne and that our guidance will overcome the taste for bubble gum.

In his 1976 essay, Richard Young provides an apposite account of heuristics:

> It is important to distinguish between rule-governed procedures (i.e., algorithms) and heuristic procedures lest we make the error of thinking that because invention is a systematic activity it is necessarily a mechanical one. A rule-governed procedure specifies a finite series of steps which can be carried out consciously and mechanically without the aid of intuition or special ability and, if properly carried out, infallibly produces a correct result- -for example, the procedure for making valid inferences in syllogistic reasoning. A heuristic procedure provides a series of questions or operations whose results are provisional; it helps us guess more effectively--for example, the procedure used by journalists for gathering information for an article, the familiar who? what? when? where? how? and why? It does not infallibly lead to a comprehensive and useful account but it makes data gathering more efficient and increases the likelihood that the account will be adequate. Although systemic, heuristic search is neither purely conscious nor mechanical, intuition, relevant experience and skill are necessary for effective use. The use of heuristic procedures is, by implication, an acknowledgment that the psychological processes involved in invention are too unpredictable to be controlled by rule-governed procedures. (P. 2)

In more homely terms, heuristics are procedures that encourage the writer to "walk around" his or her subjects, viewing them from different angles--the problem with invention frequently being the head-on, unwavering approach that the writer takes.

The subject of heuristics is properly a branch of creativity theory, the literature of which is massive, fascinating and sometimes fatuous, often commonsensical but frequently outlandish, useful to some degree though often just plain esoteric. "Creativity and the Comp Class" (pp. 205-20) provides an entry into the field and a bibliography.

If I were asked to recommend the single best discussion of heuristics in general, I would unhesitatingly cite Chapter 7, "Plans Up Front," from *The Mind's Best Work,* by D.N. Perkins (1981). In three propositions, Perkins sums up his points regarding heuristics:

> The broad organization of behavior does not necessarily take care of itself once contributing performances are mastered. Both particular heuristic advice and the more general heuristics of managerial strategies may be helpful. Most of all, one's big plans for conducting various activities deserve critical scrutiny and creative revision. (P. 200)

People often modify considerably the heuristics they are taught. But they may gain anyway, by improving poor heuristics, learning to think about how they think, and in many other roundabout ways. (P. 106)

Of course, one needs particular knowledge and experience to function at all in a field. But beyond that, knowing the informal rules of the game is more important than knowing very general heuristics. (P. 213)

The "translation" of these propositions for composition teachers yields productive advice and an understanding of what heuristics can be expected to do (or not to do).

Heuristics are obviously prompts, aids to "natural" cognitive processes in problem solving. We would expect, then, that various procedures--such as brainstorming, clustering, the Pentad, the tagmemic grid--would have differing appeal and utility for various writers working on various topics. In other words, we have strong reason to believe that some writers prefer and are more successful with some heuristics than with others, and we know for a fact that heuristics function well or poorly, depending on the subject matter. (See Adams, 1979, PP. 83-101.) And, of course, hemisphericity is a factor. In discussing cerebral organization and function, Jerry Levy (in Wittrock, ed., 1980) might well have been presenting an argument in favor of heuristics:

> Neither the nature of stimuli, choices, nor responses, or even actual hemispheric capacity, determines hemispheric dominance. Rather a hemisphere's propensity to control behavior seems to be a function of how it perceives the cognitive requirements for a given task. If those requirements call for literal encoding of sensory information or visualization of spatial relations, the right hemisphere assumes and maintains control, even if it turns out that the particular task is poorly processed by the controlling hemisphere. If there appears to be a requirement for speaking, phonetic analysis, semantic decoding of words, or for the derivation of conceptual categories, the left hemisphere assumes and maintains control, even if on the particular task, the right hemisphere is as competent as the left. (P. 258)

We are, of course, interested in teaching skills--for instance, those of syntactic fluency and accessibility in style. The Christensen (1967) free modifiers (illustrated on pp. 52-53) are a heuristic for the development of style, giving students possibilities to elaborate their sentences; in Perkins' terms, the system of free modifiers constitutes "particular heuristic advice." However, the ability to elaborate sentences is one thing, and knowing when to do so is quite another, a decision that might be facilitated by "the more general heuristics of managerial strategy"--for instance, Roman Jakobson's schema for the discourse act, which places style in relation to purpose (emotive, referential, phatic, and conative), which imply various relationships with audiences. (Jakobson, 1960; see Winterowd, 1981, pp. 86-93.)

In a sense, heuristics such as the Jakobson schema, the Pentad, and the tagmemic procedure are what Kenneth Burke calls "terministic screens." If you view the world through the Pentad, all acts are dramas--scenes, purposes, agents, and agencies being foregrounded--whereas tagmemics brings one to look at features, contrasts, processes, organizations. It seems obvious that the Pentad is more useful as an instrument for understanding literature but that tagmemics could be valuable for developing a critique of, say, an organization such as a college cafeteria.

When Perkins talks about "knowing the informal rules of the game," he is getting at one of the central points of language skills learning. By and large, we acquire those skills--i.e., do not learn them through conscious effort--and our knowledge of them is tacit. (See pp. 95-101; also "Developing a Composition Program," pp. 281-97; and "From Classroom Practice to Psycholinguistic Theory," pp. 299-306.) Heuristics can help us acquire them by calling them to our attention, and can help us bring them into performance once acquired. You could never teach students to write expository essays by using heuristics alone; writers gain a sense of genre only through immersion in it, acquiring the informal rules of the game, but once some acquisition has taken place, heuristics can be extremely useful as teaching methods. For instance, I find the Jakobson schema helpful when I am attempting to help a student create a satisfactory essay. Using the schema as a guide, I can teach the student to ask questions about *audience,* the *writer* and his or her intentions, the *content* of the piece, its *structure,* its *format,* and its *style.* In Chapter 9 (pp. 104-6), I give an extended example of how this heuristic works.

These sets of questions are no panacea, but they do provide useful points of departure for instruction, and they do make students aware of the manifold problems involved in producing a successful text. The heuristic itself is of no value, however, if students have not at least partially internalized the informal rules of the game. Perkins summarizes:

> This might seem to say that general heuristics are useless. Indeed to a degree it says just that. There is no substitute for knowledge--experience, familiarity with a field, knowing the ins and outs, the rules of the game, whether explicit or tacit. Yet for all that, general heuristics have their place. When genre-specific principles are used, general strategies can add to their power. Moreover, we do not always operate in familiar problem domains. In fact, we encounter new kinds of problems constantly not only as we explore novel subject areas but as we go further in a familiar field. General strategies provide an initial approach that will give way to genre-specific understanding as experience accumulates. Finally, remember that the deliberate search for and use of genre-specific strategies can itself be a potent general strategy. (P. 213)

It is important to realize, however, that Perkins is talking about heuristics in specialized fields such as mathematics or botany. In composition, we are concerned with those areas of knowledge that constitute liberal education; the thinking and writing that we are interested in is nonspecialist; we attempt to create *bricoleurs,* not engineers. Perkins deals with the use of heuristics for "engineers"; we are concerned about the analytic and inventive abilities of "bricoleurs." (Obviously, I am not talking about specialized composition courses, such as technical writing or proposal writing.) In fact, I completely agree with George Dillon (1981) when he says,

The expository essay as here understood has a rhetorical purpose beyond 'conveying information'; it attempts to convince the reader that its model of experience or the world is valid. It does not seek to engage the reader in a course of action, however, but rather in the process of reflection, and its means of convincing are accordingly limited to the use of evidence [including, from my point of view, the non-logical proofs that I characterize as "appositional"] and logical proof and the posture of openmindedness. These methods are also associated with the liberally educated person, who is meditative, reflective, clear-headed, unbiased, always seeking to understand experience freshly and to find things of interest in the world. (P. 23)

Eureka, the Textbooks

Among textbooks, we can take *Forming, Thinking, Writing: The Composing Imagination,* by Ann E. Berthoff (1978), as the Alpha in regard to heuristics and Young, Becker, and Pike's *Rhetoric: Discovery and Change* (1970) as the Omega.

Berthoff is enormously suspicious of "recipes" such as the tagmemic grid, believing that composition is an organic process which begins with

... meaning, not with thought ("Think of what you want to say ...") or language ("Choose the words which you feel would fit your idea best ..."); we will never get the two together unless we begin with them together. The making of meaning is the work of the active mind, or what used to be called the *imagination*--that power to create, to discover, to respond to form of all kinds. My guiding philosophical principle is that this form-finding and form-creating is a natural activity; the book's central pedagogical principle is that we teach our students *how* to form by teaching them *that* they form. Man is the forming animal, the *animal symbolicum,* as the philosopher Ernst Cassirer puts it. (P. 2)

Berthoff's claim seems to be that in the discovery of meaning, students will find the forms to embody it (provided, I assume that the substratum of competence, pined from reading, is there). We must enthusiastically grant the premise that form follows purpose (see Shuy, 1981), and we know painfully that "dry-run" exercises are the bane of composition classes.

In regard to tagmemic heuristics, I can do no better than quote from and paraphrase a review (1975) that I did of *The Tagmemic Discovery Procedure: an Evaluation of Its Uses in the Teaching of Rhetoric,* by Richard E. Young and Frank M. Koen (1973). (In order to avoid cluttering the text, I will not indicate direct quotes.)

Tagmemic theory postulates that in order to know any "thing" (including abstract concepts), one must understand (1) how it contrasts with everything else in its class, (2) how much it can change and still be itself, and (3) its distribution within the larger system of which it is a part. In other words, one must perceive (1) *contrast,* (2) *variation,* and (3) *distribution.*

Furthermore, any "thing" can be viewed from three perspectives: (1) as an unchanging static entity, (2) as a process, and (3) as a system made up of parts. In other words, borrowing from physics, tagmemicists give us the perspectives of (1) particle, (2) wave, and (3) field.

Finally, a particle, wave, or field can be viewed from the standpoints Of contrast, variation, and distribution. Thus, a nine-item set of topics or, in other words, a heuristic emerges. (For its diagrammatic realization, see table below.)

Table   The Tagmemic Matrix

	Contrast	*Variation*	*Distribution*
Particle	(1) View the unit as an isolated, static entity. What are its contrastive features, i.e., that differentiate it from similar things and serve to identify it?	(4) View the unit as a specific variant form of the concept, i.e., as one among a group of instances that illustrate the concept. What is the range of physical variation of the concept, i.e., how can instances vary without becoming something else?	(7) View the unit as part of a larger context. How is it appropriately or typically classified? What is its typical position in a temporal sequence? In space or geographical array/ In a system of classes
Wave	(2) View the unit as a dynamic object or event. What physical features distinguish it form similar objects or events?	(5) View the unit as a dynamic process. How is it changing?	(8) View the unit as part of a larger dynamic context. How does it interact and merge into its environment? Are its borders clearcut or indeterminate?
Field	(3) View the unit as an abstract multidimensional system. How are the components organized in relation to one another? More specifically, how are they related by class, in class systems, in temporal sequence, and in space?	(6) View the unit as a multidimensional physical system. How do particular instance of the system vary?	(9) View the system as an abstract system within a larger system. What is its position in the larger system? What systematic features and components make it a part of the larger system?

It seems to me that the tagmemic grid is so complex as to be opaque, and I have found it a hindrance in my composition classes. However, it appears obvious to me that questions implied by the perspectives are valuable and, indeed, I have found them to be so. The tagmemic perspectives give students a way to analyze and move toward an understanding of problematic situations. From the grid, I have drawn the following set of questions:

What are the item's FEATURES?

What are the parts of the SYSTEM?

How does the item OPERATE?

What is the DISTRIBUTION of the item--i.e., how does it fit into the larger system(s) of which it is a part?

How does the item CONTRAST with others in its class?

How can the item be CHANGED?

These questions--and their implications and elaborations-- encourage students to "walk around" their subject, viewing it from a variety of angles, and this in itself is a useful function of the heuristic.

In the 1973 study, Young and Koen asked of the procedure, "Does it work?" And the answer to that question:

> The results of the experiments provide clear support for the proposition that strong personal involvement in an intellectual activity and substantial knowledge of the subject tend to improve the quality of what is written. Even though no formal instruction was provided in conventional rhetorical a composition skills (such as usage, sentence and paragraph development, logic, methods of persuasion, and arrangement), English teachers regularly rated final essays more acceptable than initial ones. Students also improved in their ability to analyze problematic situations and state problems; and the results of their explorations of problematic data were more complex and varied; they became more sophisticated in taking hypotheses for adequacy; and they wrote essays that were more understandable and more persuasive at the end of the course.
>
> The experiment, however, did not establish that the improved ability to explore problematic data was directly related to the nine-cell discovery procedure. ... In addition, the tests did not indicate that the theory as presently formulated and the course as it was taught increased students' sensitivity to problematic situations. (Pp. 49-50)

Perkins (1981, pp. 195-96) would agree that there is no hard, fast evidence that heuristics create versatility or originality in thinking.

In rhetorical invention, as in the other departments of our complex art, we have no absolute certainty, but that situation, after all, is not such a disadvantage, for it gives us the freedom to follow our own intuitions and hard-won experiential knowledge, but also the responsibility for knowing what is available, to be sensitively tested in our scene, the composition classroom. Our methods come from our knowledge of the field and its resources and the scholarship and theories behind them, as well as from our own quotidian observant and caring practice with students.

Writing Topics and "Problematization"

I would like to put heuristics into the framework of what Paulo Freire (1982, p. 76) has called "problematization":

Human existence cannot be silent, nor can it be nourished by false words, but only by true words with which men transform the world. To exist, humanly, is to *name* the world, to change it. Once named, the world in its turn appears to the namers as a problem and requires of them a new *naming*. Men are not built in silence, but in word, in work, in action-reflection.

We hear continually--I heard just yesterday--that students do not read widely enough to gain either background or the ability to think critically. Surely students (and most professors, for that matter) do not read extensively or critically, and surely reading is central to a liberal education- -not specialized reading in textbooks or scientific reports, but general reading in books of all kinds, in magazines and newspapers. In our composition classes, we cannot supply the deficit of years, though we can do a great deal to encourage reading and to help students read better. We can help students view their world as a series of problems that invite analysis and discussion, and we can do that with heuristics.

To take a specific example of a problem we all face: We want to judge writing-- especially holistically scored finals--on the basis of both form and content. One way to "control" for content is to assign a group of readings--on atomic power, gun control, capital punishment, legislative reapportionment, entitlements, or whatever--and then gear writing prompts to those topics: "In a brief but carefully thought-out essay, analyze the problem of entitlement and propose a solution." But there is another way, provided students have learned to "problematize" their worlds. Assign a topic that all of them have in common, regardless of reading backgrounds. For example, the university itself is a microcosm of the difficulties of any society, with the super-addition of its own particular quirks: inadequate parking, professors who remain isolated from students, dorms, tuition, course requirements, student voice in university governance, adjusting to academic life. ... None of these is trivial and can result in thoughtful writing if students learn how to recognize and analyze problems.

Obviously, I believe that problematization is the central concern of composition; that being the case, heuristics, properly used, are the most important "methods." After all, Paulo Freire was speaking of peasants just gaining literacy, not of the graduates of Brazil's fancier academies.

Acknowledgments

Grateful acknowledgment is made to the original publishers for permission to reprint the following:

"Brain, Rhetoric, and Style": This essay appeared originally in *Linguistics, Stylistics, and the Teaching of Composition,* ed. Donald A. McQuade (Akron: University of Akron, 1979).

"The Three R's: Reading, Reading, and Rhetoric": This essay appeared originally in *Rhetoric and Change,* ed. William E. Tanner and J. Dean Bishop (Mesquite Tex.: Ide House, 1982). Reprinted by permission.

References

Adams, James L. (1979). *Conceptual Blockbusting: A Guide to Better Ideas*. New York: W.W.Norton.

Benderly, Beryl Lieff (1981). "The Multilingual Mind." *Psychology Today*. (March), 9-12.

Berlin, James A. (1984). *Writing Instruction in Nineteenth-Century American Colleges*. Urbana, Ill.: NCTE.

Berthoff, Ann E.. (1978). *Forming, Thinking, Writing: The Composing Imagination*. Rochelle Park, N.J.: Hayden.

Burke, Kenneth (1969). *A Grammar of Motives*. Berkeley: University of California Press.

------------ (1969). *A Rhetoric of Motives*. Berkeley: The University of California Press.

Christensen, Francis (1967). *Notes Toward a New Rhetoric*. New York: Harper & Row.

Corbett, E.P.J. (1965). *Classical Rhetoric for the Modern Student*. New York: Oxford University Press.

Dillon, George F. (1981). *Constructing Texts: Elements of a theory of Composition and Style*. Bloomington: Indiana University Press.

Emig, Janet (1978). "Hand, Eye, Brain: Some 'Basics' in the Writing Process." Cooper and Odell, Eds. *Research on Composing: Points of Departure*. Urbana, Ill.: NCTE.

Freed, Richard (1981). "Using the Right Brain." *WLA Newsletter*. No. 17 (Spring), 3-4.

Freire, Paulo (1982) [1970]). *Pedagogy of the Oppressed*. Trans. Myra Bergman Ramos. New York: Continuum.

Glassner, Benjamin (1981). "Writing as an Integrator of Hemispheric Function." Kroll and Vann, Eds. *Exploring Speaking/Writing Relationships: Connections and Contrasts*. Urbana, Ill: NCTE.

Hill, Adams Sherman (1897). *The Foundations of Rhetoric* New York: Harper & Brothers.

Hirsch, E.D., Jr. (1977). *The Philosophy of Composition*. Chicago: University of Chicago Press.

Hitchcock, Alfred M. (1923). *Composition and Rhetoric*. New York: Henry Holt.

Irmscher, William (1972). *Holt Guide to English*. New York: Holt, Rinehart and Winston.

Jakobson, Roman (1960). "Linguistics and Poetics." Thomas A. Sebeok, Ed. *Style in Language*. Cambridge, Mass: MIT Press.

Levy, Jerre (1980). "Cerebral Asymmetry and the Psychology of Man." M.C. Wittrock, Ed. *The Brain and Psychology*.

Miner, Earl (1976). "That Literature Is a Kind of Knowledge." *Critical Inquiry*. 2 (Spring), 487-518.

Perkins, D.N. (1981). *The Mind's Best Work*. Cambridge, Mass.: Harvard University Press.

Rohman, D. Gordon and Albert O. Wlecke (1964). *Pre-Writing: The Construction and Application of Models for Concept Formation in Writing*. East Lansing: Michigan State University.

Winterowd, D. Ross (1973). " 'Topics' and Levels in the Composing Process." *College English*. 34:5 (Feb.), 701-09.

---------- (1975). Review of *The Tagmemic Discovery Procedure: An Evaluation of Its Uses in the Teaching of Rhetoric*, by Richard Young and Frank M. Koen. *Philosophy and Rhetoric*. 8:3 (Summer), 183-87.

---------- (1981). *The Contemporary Writer*. Second Edition. New York: Harcourt Brace Jovanovich.

Wittrock, M.C., Ed. (1977). *The Human Brain*. Englewood Cliffs, N.J,: Prentice-Hall.

Young, Richard (1976). "Invention: A Topographical Survey." Gary Tate, Ed. *Teaching Composition: Ten Biographical Essays*. Fort Worth: Texas Christian University.

---------- , Alton L. Becker and Kenneth L. Pike (1970).*Rhetoric: Discovery and Change*. New York: Harcourt Brace Jovanovich.

---------- ,and Frank M. Koen (1973). *The Tagmemic Discovery Procedure: An Evaluation of Its Uses in the Teaching of Rhetoric*. Ann Arbor: University of Michigan.

Analyzing Revision

Lester Faigley and Stephen Witte

Among the activities which are a part of composing, one might think that revision is the easiest to study because it leaves a record. Actually, the surface record belies the complexity of revision. Researchers have sought to understand this complexity in two ways: by examining the effects of revision and by speculating on the causes of revision. The view of revision as a complex activity is recent. For many years teachers saw revision as copy-editing, a tidying-up activity aimed at eliminating surface errors in grammar, punctuation, spelling, and diction. The tidying-up view of revision presupposes the three-stage linear model of composing-consisting of prewriting, writing, and rewriting activities-articulated by Rohman and Wlecke in the mid-60's.[1] Revision was taught as something a writer did after completing a first draft.

Recent research on both the causes and effects of revision has discredited this simple view of composing. Researchers-such as Linda Flower and John R. Hayes[2]--have attempted to study the causes of revision by soliciting verbal protocols that provide a running account of a writer's conscious activities during composing. Evidence from protocols indicates that writers move back and forth among the various activities of composing, and that expert writers frequently review what they have written and make changes while in the midst of generating a text. Similarly, Nancy Sommers' study of the effects of revision strongly suggests that the linear model of composing is overly simplistic, if not wholly inaccurate--incapable of describing the composing processes of either inexperienced or experienced writers.[3]

Sommers also demonstrated that writers of different abilities make different kinds of revisions. She drew distinctions between the revisions of skilled and unskilled writers according to the length of their changes and the type of operation. For the latter Sommers used the same categories--deletion, addition, substitution, and rearrangement-- that Chomsky used to group transformations. Other studies have attempted to gauge the effect of revision changes on the meaning of a text. The National Assessment of Educational Progress in its 1977 survey used subjective categories of meaning such as "organizational," "stylistic," "continuational," and "holistic" to classify revisions.[4] Several literary scholars have made efforts to classify revisions as well. For example,Wallace Hildick described the revision changes of nine well-known writers including Lawrence, Hardy, and James.[5] He posited six categories: (1) Tidying-up Changes ("correcting grammatical lapses," "refining punctuation," p. 13); (2) Roughening-up Changes ("loosening of a speech when it has been made too fluent for the character using it," p. 13); (3) Power Changes ("to achieve greater accuracy of expression..., or to achieve greater force of argument..., or to stamp a deeper impression on the reader's mind," p. 14); (4) Structural Alterations (sweeping changes); (5)

Ideologically Determined Changes (such as Hardy's bowdlerizing changes in serialized versions of his novels); and (6) The Ragbag of Types (miscellaneous). Hildick admits that none of his categories is rigidly exclusive. Neither the National Assessment system nor the Hildick classifications can be applied reliably because most of the categories overlap. They do, nevertheless, show the need for a classification of the effects of revision changes as well as the operations involved.

The purpose of the present study is to present and apply a simple, yet robust, system for analyzing the effects of revision changes on meaning. We do not attempt to propose the definitive methodology for studying revision, only to add a research tool which can be used in combination with other research tools such as protocol analysis. **Part I** describes our taxonomy for analyzing revision. **Part II** reports two studies which used this taxonomy and discusses the implications of these investigations, suggesting directions for further research and pointing to limitations implicit in the concepts and methodology of the two studies reported.

The Influence of Revision on the Meaning of a Text

The taxonomy we developed is based on two distinctions. The first and more important distinction is between revisions that affect the meaning of the text and those that do not. Other students of revision have posited a similar distinction, separating copy-editing adjustments from changes which alter the content.[6] Such separation is not always easy. Changes that affect meaning and changes that do not affect meaning can take the same form. In most cases, for example, capitalization does not change meaning. But some capitalizations, such as the change from *the man is white to the man is White,* can change meaning.

The problem is to sort the changes which affect meaning from those which leave meaning intact. An attempt at a full semantic representation, if it were even possible, would be far too cumbersome.[7] In research on how the content of texts is stored and recalled, psychologists have represented meaning in texts with propositions,[8] units borrowed from formal logic that contain one predicate term (a verb, adjective, adverb, or conjunction) and one or more other concepts related to that predicate.[9] In addition to the problem of representing meaning in the text itself, one faces the problem that speakers and writers rely upon listeners' and readers' abilities to make inferences. Consider the following short text with and without sentence (1A):

   1. I just made it to the station on time.
   1A. I got on the train.
   2. I had to buy my ticket from the conductor.

Suppose sentence (1A) is omitted. If readers know that conductors sell tickets to boarded passengers who have not purchased tickets, then they understand that the narrator of this short text had to get on the train. Absent but understood propositions like sentence (IA) are referred to as "plausible inferences." Some researchers, such as Edward Crothers,[10] include plausible inferences when representing the concepts in a text. Researchers in artificial intelligence, who are trying to get computers to interpret natural language in the ways that humans do, also represent inferences.[11]

Yet we need to think of meaning not only as the concepts in the extant text, but also those concepts which can be reasonably inferred from it. Of course, inferences vary from reader to reader. Great literature admits many possible inferences, and how we should interpret literary works has led to an intense debate among literary critics. Our task here is a great deal more simple than the interpretation of a literary work. We have only to account for those inferences that the writer raises to the surface by adding explicit text or requires by deleting explicit text during revision. Most of these cases are obvious.

Our taxonomy of revision changes is based on *whether new information is brought to the text or whether old information is removed in such a way that it cannot be recovered through drawing inferences.* We call changes that do not bring new information to a text or remove old information *Surface Changes.* Surface Changes are represented on the left branch of Figure 1. *Meaning Changes*, represented on the right branch of Figure 1, involve the adding of new content or the deletion of existing content.

Surface Changes

Under Surface Changes are two subcategories, *Formal Changes* and *Meaning-Preserving Changes.* Formal Changes include most, but not all, conventional copy-editing operations. We divided Formal Changes into changes *in spelling; tense, number, and modality; abbreviations; punctuation; and format.*

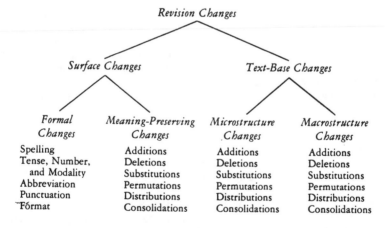

Figure 1. A Taxonomy of Revision Changes

The second subcategory, *Meaning-Preserving Changes,* includes changes that paraphrase" the concepts in the text but do not alter them. *Additions* raise to the surface what can be inferred *(you pay two dollars => you pay a two dollar entrance fee). Deletions* do the opposite so that a reader is forced to infer what had been explicit *(several rustic looking restaurants => several rustic restaurants). Substitutions* trade words or longer units that represent the same concept *(out-of-the-way spots => out-of-*

the-way Places). Permutations involve rearrangements or rearrangements with substitutions *(springtime means to most people => springtime, to most people, means). Distributions* occur when material in one text segment is passed into more than one segment. A change where a writer revises what has been compressed into a single unit so that it falls into more than one unit is a distributional change *(I figured after walking so far the least it could do would be to provide a relaxing dinner since I was hungry. => I figured the least it owed me was a good meal. All that walking made me hungry.). Consolidations* do the opposite. Elements in two or more units are consolidated into one unit *(And there you find Hamilton's Pool. It has cool green water surrounded by 50-foot cliffs and lush vegetation. => And there you find Hamilton's Pool: cool green water surrounded by 50-foot cliffs and lush vegetation).* As the last example suggests, consolidations are the primary revision operation in sentence-combining exercises.

Meaning Changes

Meaning Changes constitute the second important class in our taxonomy. Many Meaning Changes turn out to be of small consequence for the overall text. A phrase is substituted, an example is added, or a sentence is reworked. Other changes have more impact, at times even giving the entire essay a new direction. Hence, a system for classifying revision changes must also distinguish meaning changes which are simple adjustments or elaborations of existing text and changes that make more sweeping alterations.

Our problem was to find some systematic way of differentiating minor and major changes of meaning. We turned to recent work in text linguistics and cognitive psychology that has examined how readers comprehend a text phrase-by-phrase and, at the same time, derive some overall notion of what the text is about, usually spoken of as the *gist* or *topic* of that text. The American psychologist, Walter Kintsch, and the Dutch text linguist, Teun van Dijk, have developed a theoretical model that accounts for how readers process a text.[12] Their model describes meaning at two levels: a *microstructure* level, where all concepts in a text are included (even those that can be inferred), and a *macrostructure* level, which represents the "gist" of the text.[13] A macrostructure can be thought of as a series of labels for sections in a text. Essentially, a macrostructure is a summary of a text. A plot outline is one familiar example of a macrostructure. The difference between a summary and a macrostructure is that, in Kintsch and van Dijk's model, a macrostructure is formally abstracted from the propositions of a text using a series of rules.[14] We find macrostructure theory inadequate for its expressed purpose-- providing a linguistic representation of gist--because it does not accommodate adequately either the reader's prior knowledge or the situational context in interpreting discourse."[15] The gist of a cordial salesman's lead-in ploy is not drawn from his literal remarks. We use our knowledge of the situational context to recognize the purpose underlying the salesman's cordiality.

We do find macrostructure theory useful for distinguishing major and minor revision changes. In our taxonomy, a *Macrostructure Change* is a major revision change. In other words, a *Macrostructure Change* would alter the summary of a text. Below are the first paragraphs from Drafts 1 and 2 of an experienced adult's essay. The change from Draft 1 to Draft 2 illustrates a Macrostructure Change.

Draft 1

It's hard to think about places like Houston, San Antonio, or Dallas without thinking about endlessly sprouting suburbs, Taco Bells, expanding city limits, and mushrooming property values. Growth seems to be overtaking Texas at a breathtaking rate, often at the expense of the central city areas which helped to spawn that growth in the first place. The action often follows the growth outward-industry moves out to be close to the bedroom communities, restaurants and theaters follow on their heels, and before long there is nothing left in the inner city but vacancy signs.

Draft 2

For cities all over America it's a life or death situation, and for many what happens in the 80's will decide their fate. The picture for many is not promising, in the face of massive spending cuts to budgets for social programs. Grants for urban renewal could slow to a trickle or stop. The city governments themselves may be unable to make up the difference and the proposed rebuilding they have planned may become an unfulfilled dream.

Even when considered out of context, the summaries of these two paragraphs are different. The first concerns the decline of inner-cities in Texas; the second concerns the decline of inner-cities across the nation. The second paragraph also considers the role of government assistance in a city survival.

We found, however, that the most reliable way to separate Macro- and Microstructure Changes short of constructing summaries for entire texts is to determine if the concepts involved in a particular change affect the reading of other parts of the text. This particular essay describes the renovation of downtown Austin, a renovation which the writer points out was neither initiated nor supported by city, state, or federal agencies. The entire essay comments on the dilemma raised in the first paragraph. Although the writer never states her conclusion explicitly, clearly she means that cities that have depended on government support for renovation likely will further decay while those that can attract private investment may be able to retain some of their original beauty. That point, strongly enough suggested in Draft 2 to influence a reader's understanding of the rest of the essay, is nowhere even hinted at in Draft 1.

A Microstructure Change, in contrast, is a meaning change that would not affect a summary of a text. For both Micro- and Macrostructure changes, we used the same six operations (addition, deletion, substitution, permutation, distribution, and consolidation) identified under Meaning-Preserving Changes. Unlike Meaning-Preserving Changes, however, Meaning Changes affect the concepts in a text. The following change is an example of a Meaning Change, in this case a Microstructure Addition: *Barton Springs does not fit an outsider's image of Texas. It is an eighth-mile long unchlorinated pool in a natural limestone creekbed => Barton Springs does not fit an outsider's image of Texas. It is an eighth-mile long, unchlorinated pool in a natural limestone creekbed, fed by 27 million gallons of 68-degree water from the Edwards' Aquifer each day.*

Two Studies of Writers Revising

We tested our system until we were satisfied that it could be applied reliably, with two researchers independently reaching over 90% agreement on types of revisions. (Two earlier taxonomies that had additional categories were rejected for lack of reliability.) We then assigned a numerical code to each category to facilitate analysis of revisions. When a revision change spanned more than one sentence, each sentence was analyzed separately. For example, a long macrostructure addition containing seven sentences would have been noted seven times.

We collected examples of revisions from six inexperienced student writers, six advanced student writers, and six expert adult writers. Each student writer was enrolled in a writing class at the University of Texas. The six inexperienced students were recruited from a writing laboratory designed for students deficient in writing skills. The six advanced students were recruited from an elective, upper-division expository writing class, which typically attracts able and motivated students. Expert adults were recruited from professional writers living in Austin. All experts had journalistic experience; three had published fiction.

The procedures for gathering data were similar to those used by Lillian Bridwell.[16] Subjects were tested over a three-day span. On the first day, subjects were presented a writing topic that asked them to describe a place in Austin that an out-of-town audience would not be likely to know about. The writing situation specified that the description would be published in an out-of-town newspaper. Subjects were asked to think about the topic and to make notes if they wished. On day 2, writers wrote an essay on the topic they had been given the previous day. These writing samples were collected and photocopied, and the changes that the writers made while composing were analyzed as Stage I revisions. On day 3, the original first drafts were returned to the writers, who then wrote a second draft. When they had finished, both drafts were collected and analyzed. All changes (identifiable because pens with different color inks were used on different days) on the first draft made on day 3 and all differences between the first and second drafts were analyzed as Stage 2 revisions.[17] In-process revisions on the second draft were analyzed as Stage 3 revisions.

All revisions were- analyzed using the taxonomy described on pages 402-404. Combined results for the major categories appear in Table 1 below.

Table 1 Frequencies of Combined Revision Changes per 1000 Words in Final Drafts for Three Groups of Writers

	Formal Changes	Meaning-Preserving Changes	Micro-Structure Changes	Macro-Structure Changes
Expert Adults	22.3	73.3	29.4	19.6

| Advanced Students | 50.4 | 163.9 | 44.8 | 23. 1 |
| Inexperienced Students | 38.9 | 113.4 | 19.7 | 1.3 |

The results show certain differences in the way the three groups of writers revised their work. The expert adult writers turned out not to be most frequent revisers. The advanced students were the most frequent revisers of the three groups. An analysis of the changes showed that the expert writers made some type of change on the average of 144 times per 1000 words in the final draft, while the inexperienced students made a change 173 times per 1000 words and the advanced students 282 times per 1000 words. More revealing were the kinds of changes the different groups made.

The inexperienced writers' changes were overwhelmingly Surface Changes. Only 12% of the inexperienced writers' revisions were Meaning Changes. The advanced students' and the expert adults' changes, in contrast, were more evenly distributed. About 24% of the advanced students' changes and 34% of the expert adults' changes were Meaning Changes. In some respects, the advanced students revised more like the inexperienced writers, making Surface Changes about twice as often as the expert adults. But in Meaning Changes, the advanced students revised more like the expert adults, especially in Macrostructure Changes, where the frequencies of changes by advanced students (23.1 per 1000 words) and expert adults (19.6 per 1000 words) are similar. Total frequencies of revision operations per 1000 words in the final draft are listed in Table 2.

Besides the differences in frequencies of changes between the essays of the inexperienced students and those of the advanced students and the expert adults, noticeable differences occurred between the groups in the number of revisions made at each stage. Both the expert adults and the advanced students made more revisions of all kinds during the composing of the first draft (Stage 1) than did the inexperienced students. This difference was magnified in Meaning Changes, with the expert adults making on the average 15.4 such changes per 1000 words and the advanced students making 10.4 such changes per 1000 words. These frequencies can be compared with the inexperienced students' average of 3 Meaning Changes per 1000 words. The differences in Stage I revisions are probably attributable to different methods of composing. Flower and Hayes found that experts often stop to reread what they have written, making significant retrospective adjustments as they move forward in writing a text.[18] I Reviewing of texts in progress also helps experts to generate additional content. Inexperienced writers typically do not stop to reread. If inexperienced writers revise during composing, they almost always limit their revision to correcting errors.[19]

Most revisions of all kinds occurred between the first and second drafts (Stage 2). The inexperienced students made predominantly

Table 2 *Total Revision Changes per 1000 Words in Final
Drafts for Three Groups of Writers (Stages 1, 2, and 3)*

	Inexperienced Students	Advanced Students	Expert Adults
I. Surface Changes			
A. Formal Changes			
1. Spelling	22.0	18.7	14.5
2. Tense	4.8	8.8	2.3
3. Abbreviations	3.1	4.7	0
4. Punctuation	9.0	16.4	5.0
5. Paragraph	0	1.3	.5
6. Other Format	0	.5	0
B. Meaning-Preserving Changes			
1. Additions	22.9	20.6	17.9
2. Deletions	33.5	63.2	32.1
3. Substitutions	48.5	59.7	19.1
4. Permutations	4.7	12.0	4.0
5. Distributions	2.5	2.3	0
6. Consolidations	1.3	6.1	.2
II. Meaning Changes			
A. Microstructure Changes			
1. Additions	9.9	21.3	13.9
2. Deletions	4.3	11.2	9.2
3. Substitutions	3.0	5.0	3.7
4. Permutations	.4	3.4	1.7
5. Distributions	2.1	3.5	.7
6. Consolidations	0	.4	.2
B. Macrostructure Changes			
1. Additions	1.3	17.8	12.8
2. Deletions	0	.4	4.5
3. Substitutions	0	0	0
4. Permutations	0	0	1.3
5. Distributions	0	4.9	.2
6. Consolidations	0	0	.8

Surface Changes (98 per 1000 words) at Stage 2, while rarely making Macrostructure Changes (1.3 per 1000 words). Their most frequent single changes were Meaning Preserving Substitutions (32.2 per 1000 words), by and large a substitution of synonyms. Like the inexperienced students, the advanced students made many Surface Changes (101 per 1000 words). Advanced students made frequent Meaning-Preserving Substitutions (29 per 1000 words), as well as frequent Meaning-Preserving Deletions (26.8 per 1000 words). Advanced students also made many Meaning Changes (55.6 per 1000 words) between the first and second drafts. Expert adults, on the other hand, made far fewer Surface Changes between drafts (28.7 per 1000 words), devoting their energies instead to reworking the content of their drafts (16.1 Macrostructure Changes per 1000 words). During and after the writing of the second draft (Stage 3), expert adults and advanced students turned their attention to Surface Changes, cleaning up their manuscripts after they had satisfactorily dealt with their subjects. By this point inexperienced students had largely quit revising.

We are hesitant to draw easy conclusions from these results. Revisions of experienced and inexperienced writers may not be comparable in the ways that our first study suggests. Some expert writers are able to develop a text in their minds and to perform revision operations mentally before committing a text to paper. This ability may account for why the expert adults made far fewer revisions than the advanced students. We decided to do a second study that would perhaps give us a better idea of what revision strategies to teach inexperienced writers. We made copies of the first drafts that three inexperienced writers had written, and we asked the expert adults to revise the three student essays as if they were their own. We then analyzed the changes the experts made, and we compared their changes to those which the inexperienced writers made in their second drafts. Again we found large differences between the revisions of the two groups. Among the skilled adults, 65% of the changes were Macrostructure Changes. In particular, the adults used processes--addition, consolidation, and distribution. They condensed what the students had written and then either elaborated or added information to support the points the students apparently had wanted to make. Below is an example of how an expert rewrote a student draft:

Student Version

Our state capital is a beautiful structure that is very unique. When entering the city of Austin, it is a site that stands out amongst the skyrises that surround it. This building is known for its architecture, the craftsmanship inside the building and the history that it holds.

The architecture of the building is highly ornate and is said to be a duplicate of the State Capital in Washington, D.C. paying special attention to the rotunda ceiling that extends several thousand feet up.

Expert Version

The Capitol of Texas remains the most impressive building in Austin, even though bank skyscrapers and university towers have challenged its one time dominance of the skyline. The Capitol will never again be as prominent as the Nation's Capitol in Washington, where surrounding buildings have been kept in scale, but the richness of the structure itself has not been diminished. It remains a statement of the grandiose vision of the makers of modern Texas.

From a distance the Texas Capitol appears to be little more than another replica of the Nation's Capitol. Only at the edge of the grounds does the grandeur of the building become evident. The Confederate statues along the walk to the front steps mark another time from the age of golden glass banks--a time when Texas was a Southern and not a Sun Belt state, a time when Richard King still ran the King Ranch and Judge Roy Bean was the law west of the Pecos.

The expert writer--a journalist--told us that

> The story lacked information. It needed an angle. State capitols are
> normally uninteresting, so I used the Texas angle. Texans do things differently.
> The original had an organization, but no detail. The writer mentioned history,
> but said nothing about it. I had to work this in.

Other experts made similar comments. All wrote with a detached, yet broad, perspective about the subject the students had selected, and all added their background knowledge, often visual details, about that subject.

Discussion

The results of the two studies of revision tend to support the conclusions of the Sommers' study--that expert writers revise in ways different from inexperienced writers. What the present studies contribute is a method of describing through text analysis what Sommers learned through interviews. As is evident in Sommers'and Bridwell's studies, the only way of quantifying the significance of revision changes up to now has been by the length of change. The method proposed here, we believe, is sounder conceptually than the *ad hoc* methodology used in previous studies of revision changes, indicating that future research in the composing process can make additional applications of current work in text linguistics and text comprehension.

Our results, however, should not be viewed as a mandate to demand that inexperienced writers revise more. We found extreme diversity in the ways expert writers revise. One expert writer in the present study made almost no revisions; another started with an almost stream-of-consciousness text that she then converted to an organized essay in the second draft; another limited his major revisions to a single long insert; and another revised mostly by pruning. To supplement the two studies, we examined the actual revisions of practicing writers of various sorts-writers of fiction, journalists, persons in business and government, and academicians in several disciplines. Again we found considerable variation. For example, we observed a consulting engineer write memos without revising while he was in the process of extensively revising a proposal he had drafted. On another visit we watched him cut and tape, then pencil in headings for an environmental impact statement drafted in sections by several of his associates. Likewise, a colleague who is a fiction writer showed us the manuscript of a novel that he has spent several years revising and manuscripts of published short stories that have minimal revisions after the first paragraph.

The volume and types of revision changes are dependent upon a number of variables besides the skill of the writer. These variables might be called *situational variables* for composing. Included among situational variables are probably the following: the reason why the text is being written, the format, the medium, the genre, the writer's familiarity with the writing task, the writer's familiarity with the subject, the writer's familiarity with the audience, the projected level of formality, and the length of the task and the projected text. So important are these variables that writing skill might be defined in part as the ability to respond to them. If researchers neglect situational variables in studying revision, their results are likely to be skewed. Differences in the difficulty of writing tasks in the 1977 round of the National Assessment of Educational

Progress likely produced the anomalous finding that seventeen-year-olds revise less than thirteen-year-olds.[20]

Successful revision results not from the number of changes a writer makes but from the degree to which revision changes bring a text closer to fitting the demands of the situation. Revisions of inexperienced writers often do not improve their texts. Such writers tend to revise locally, ignoring the situational constraints. Sondra Perl observed that inexperienced writers' revisions often had a negative effect on quality.[21] The major implication of this study, as well as of Sommers' study, for teachers of writing is that revision cannot be separated from other aspects of composing, especially during that period when writers come to grips with the demands of the particular writing situation. Success in revision is intimately tied to a writer's planning and reviewing skills. Inadequate planning will force writers to write several drafts before they discover what it is that they have to say. Inadequate reviewing of extant working drafts often results from poor conception of the audience's needs, which prevents writers from revising their texts to suit their audiences's needs and wishes. Somehow we must teach our students to distance themselves from what they have written, to get them to *see it again,* then revise--much as our expert writers stood back and formed an impression of what they thought an inexperienced writer's text should say, and then realized that impression by substantially altering the original text.

Research will more than likely continue to consider both the causes and effects of revision. One limitation of revision studies has been the small number of subjects included, a limitation necessitated by the complexity of the analyses. In order for researchers on revision to analyze larger samples and, thus, be able to generalize in ways that we could not, better methods of recording revision changes need to be explored. If writers are taught to compose on computers, then complete records of all revisions, including the sequence of changes[22] and length of pauses,[23] can be accumulated and analyzed.

Another limitation in studies of both causes and effects of revision to date has been the artificiality of the writing situation. In the first study reported above, a common topic provided the stimulus for writing. Writers were required to write on consecutive days at specified times in unfamiliar surroundings. Just as in the NAEP study of revision, such artificiality probably influenced not only what the subjects wrote initially, but also the numbers and kinds of revisions they made. A more serious limitation of the present studies is that they, like other effects studies, do not consider the most important question: what causes writers to revise?

Research using protocol analysis tries to address the question of why writers revise. Flower and Hayes' use of thinking-aloud protocols suggests that expert writers plan more extensively and analyze the rhetorical constraints more thoroughly than inexperienced writers.[24] What we learn from protocol analysis, however, is uncertain. Again the writing situation is artificial. Verbal protocols require writers to do two things at once--they must write and they must attempt to verbalize what they are thinking as they pause. Perhaps some subjects can be trained to do both tasks with facility, but many writers find that analyzing orally what they are doing as they write interferes with their normal composing processes, interrupting their trains of thought. Many activities in writing occur simultaneously-from unconscious processes such as ordering the words in a noun phrase to conscious processes ranging from spelling to planning and monitoring.

A lot is going on and not all of it gets verbalized. In addition, what writers can verbalize about their composing processes probably is influenced by the nature of the writing task. Unskilled writers who seem bound by concerns about conventions when arguing for mass transit may show very different concerns when writing to a personal friend. The fact that the writing situation is unnatural forces the investigator to speculate about how to interpret the protocol and how to classify the individual's composing behavior.

Neither experimental studies of the causes nor studies of the effects of revision have been able to answer satisfactorily all the questions that they raise. Perhaps what we need now are more observational studies of writers revising in nonexperimental situations rather than more studies of student writers in contrived situations. In addition to studies of how situational variables influence revision, we need studies of how textual cues lead writers to revise their texts. In short, we need studies that employ more than one methodology, that examine the complexity of revision in a variety of texts across a variety of situations. Only when we understand the multidimensional nature of revision can we better teach revising as a rhetorical concern, bringing inexperienced writers to know revising as something other than a cleansing of errors.

Note on the article's authorship as of 1981. Lester Faigley was teaching courses in discourse analysis and rhetorical theory in the graduate rhetoric program at the University of Texas. Stephen Witte was teaching graduate courses in research design and rhetorical theory at the same university. Both taught undergraduate courses in writing and the teaching of writing. This study was supported in part by the National institute of Education, Grant No. NIE-G-80-0054. The authors thank Margaret Kiersted for her assistance in analyzing revisions, Edward Crothers for his advice on research design, and Maxine Hairston for her comments on an earlier draft of this essay.

NOTES

1. Gordon Rohman and Albert O. Wlecke, *Pre-Writing: The Construction and Application of Models for Concept Formation in Writing,* U.S. Office of Education Cooperative Research Project No. 2174 (East Lansing, Mich.: Michigan State Univ., 1964).
2. For a description of protocol analysis methodology, see "Identifying the Organization of Writing Processes," in *Cognitive Processes in Writing: An Interdisciplinary Approach,* ed. Lee Gregg and Erwin Steinberg (Hillsdale, N.J.: Lawrence Erlbaum, 1980), pp. 3-30.
3. "Revision Strategies of Student Writers and Experienced Adult Writers," *College Composition and Communication,* 31 (December, 1980), 378-388.
4. Rivas, *Write/Rewrite: An Assessment of Revision Skills,* Writing Report No. 05-W-04 (Denver: National Assessment of Educational Progress, 1977).
5. *Word for Word: The Rewriting of Fiction* (London: Faber and Faber, 1965).
6. See, for example, Donald Murray, "Internal Revision: A Process of Discovery," in *Research on Composing: Points of Departure,* ed. Charles Cooper and Lee Odell (Urbana, Ill.: National Council of Teachers of English, 1978), pp. 85-103; Murray distinguishes on the basis of meaning between "internal" and "external" revisions.
7. For some idea of the complexity of a full semantic description, see Robert Montague, *Formal Philosophy,* ed. R.H. Tomason (New Haven, Conn.: Yale University Press, 1974). Even Montague grammar, one of the richest formal systems extant, makes little room for situational determinants of meaning.

8. For examples of research using a propositional analysis of meaning, see Walter Kintsch, *The Representation of Meaning in Memory* (Hillsdale, NJ.: Lawrence Erlbaum, 1974); Carl H. Frederiksen, "Representing Logical and Semantic Structures of Knowledge Acquired from Discourse," *Cognitive Psychology*, 7 July, 1975), 371-458; Bonnie J.F. Meyer, *The Organization of Prose and Its Effect Upon Memory* (Amsterdam: North Holland, 1975).

9. Propositions are usually written with the predicare term first and in capital letters to make clear that they refer to concepts and not words. Concepts are thought of as minimal units of meaning. For example, *Helen likes the car* could be represented as (LIKE, HELEN, CAR).

10. *Paragraph Structure Inference* (Norwood, NJ.: Ablex, 1979).

11. See Roger C. Schank, *Conceptual Information Processing* (New York: American Elsevier, 1975); Roger C. Schank and R.P. Abelson, *Scripts, Plans, Goals, and Understanding: An Inquiry into Human Knowledge Structures* (Hillsdale, NJ.: Lawrence Erlbaum, 1977).

12. "Toward a Model of Text Comprehension and Production," *Psychological Review*, 85 (September, 1978), 363-394. Empirical tests of this model are reported in Walter Kintsch and Douglas Vipond, "Reading Comprehension and Readability in Educational Practice and Psychological Theory," in *Perspectives on Memory Research*, ed. L.G. Nilsson (Hillsdale, NJ.: Lawrence Erlbaum, 1979) pp. 329-365; Douglas Vipond, "Micro- and Macroprocesses in Text Comprehension,"*Journal of Verbal Learning and Verbal Behavior*, 19 (June, 1980), 276-296.

13. Van Dijk's most thorough elaboration of macrostructures is found in *Macrostructures: An Interdisciplinary Study of Global Structures in Discourse, Interaction, and Cognition* (Hillsdale, NJ.: Lawrence Eribaum, 1980).

14. Although macrostructure theory focuses on the text itself, Kintsch and Van Dijk do make some allowances for the reader's prior knowledge of the world of the text. Van Dijk sets out three rules for deriving macrostructures. (See *Macrostructures*, pp. 46-50.) The first and most general rule for forming macrostructures is *deletion*. Readers tend to remember propositions which are repeated later in the text or are important to the interpretation of other propositions. Thus propositions which are not necessary to interpret other propositions or which are only locally relevant are not represented in the macrostructure.

    A second rule is *generalization*, in which a series of particulars can be grouped into a single proposition at a higher level of abstraction. Readers continually generalize from details which they do not normally associate. From the following sequence--

    Jeff brought a model airplane, Erin came with an adventure people set, and Garth carried in an electronic baseball game--

    we might generalize the more abstract proposition *The children brought toys.*

    A third rule is *construction,* in which a series of propositions depicts a conventional action or setting known to us. Consider the following sequence:

    The children watched Ian start to blow out the candles before his mother had finished lighting them. After the candies were relit, everyone cheered when Ian blew them out on the first try and stuck his hand in the cake.

    For this sequence, we could construct the macroproposition, *Someone gave Ian a birthday party.* We make this construction because we recognize conventional elements of a birthday party: a cake, the lighting of candles, the blowing out of candles, and cheering.

15. Jerry L. Morgan and Manfred B. Sellner contend that "van Dijk's approach has the meaning of the whole to be considerably less than the sum of the parts." See "Discourse and Linguistic Theory," in *Theoretical Issues in Reading Comprehension*, eds. Rand J. Spiro, Bertram C. Bruce, and William F. Brewer (Hillsdale, NJ.: Lawrence Eribaum, 1980), p. 195. They argue that the ability to construct a summary presupposes an understanding of that text.

16. "Revising Strategies in Twelfth Grade Students' Transactional Writing," *Research in the Teaching of English*, 14 (October, 1980), 201-203.

17. Bridwell did not directly compare first and second drafts, which may explain why our Stage 2 totals are proportionally much larger than hers. Bridwell's methodology, for example, would show that D.H. Lawrence, who rewrote his novels from the beginning rather than going back through them making changes, was an infrequent reviser.

18. "The Cognition of Discovery: Defining a Rhetorical Problem," *College Composition and Communication*, 31 (February, 1980), 21-32.

19. Sondra Perl, "The Composing Processes of Unskilled College Writers," *Research in the Teaching of English,* 13 (December, 1979), 317-336.
20. See Ellen W. Nold, "Revising," in *Writing: The Nature, Development, and Teaching of Written Composition,* ed. Marcia Farr Whiteman and Joseph Dominic (Hillsdale, NJ.: Lawrence Erlbaum, in press).
21. "Understanding Composing," *College Composition and Communication,* 31 (December, 1980), 363-369.
22. See Stuart K. Card, Thomas P. Moran, and Allen Newell, "Computer Text-Editing: An Information-Processing Analysis of a Routine Cognitive Skill," *Cognitive Psychology,* 12 January, 1980), 32-74.
23. See Ann Matsuhashi, "Pausing and Planning: The Tempo of Written Discourse Production," *Research in the Teaching of English,* 15 (May, 1981), 113-134.
24. "The Cognition of Discovery."

Recognition, Representation, and Revision
Ann E. Berthoff

We should not be surprised that our students so often consider revision as a chance to get "it" right the second time around.[1] Despite recent attempts to differentiate editing and rewriting, most English teachers probably continue to instill the idea that revision is like taking another swing at the ball or shooting again for the basket. The idea of revision as correction is, like readability formulas and sentence combining, consonant with a view of language as, merely, a medium for the communication of our views of a reality *out there:* we have ideas and we put them into language. (Sometimes we might get the wrong slot: try again.) Language is often seen as a window which keeps us from enjoying an immediate vision. The pedagogical corollary is that the best we can do is to teach window washing, trying to keep the view of what is "really there" unobstructed by keeping the prose clean and clear. Revision, in this view, is polishing. I argue in the following that we can learn to teach revision as itself a way of composing if we consider it analogous to acts of mind whereby we make sense of the world.

One rainy afternoon last fall I stopped by to browse among some miscellaneous journals in the gaudy reading room of a graduate school library where, as it turned out, I witnessed a basic writer at work. He sat in a low-slung, purple velour settee, a pad of lined paper on his knee, a nice new yellow pencil and a pack of cigarettes at the ready, and a Dixie Cup of coffee to hand. He seemed prepared for the labors of composition. He would write a sentence or two, light a cigarette, read what he had written, sip his coffee, extinguish the cigarette--and the two sentences. He had pretty much worn out the eraser by the time I left. (That would be an interesting research index: How long does the eraser last, if it is not bitten off in momentary despair?) My eyes glazed over more quickly than usual as I leafed through *Research in the Teaching of English* because my mind was otherwise engaged in formulating what I would have said to this earnest graduate student, if I had had the nerve. Something like this:

> You need to get some writing down on paper and to keep it there long enough
> so that you can give yourself the treat of rewriting. What you need is a
> ballpoint pen so you can't erase and some cheap paper so you can deliberately
> use a lot of it--and one very expensive sheet of creamy foolscap for your
> inventory of glosses: it's a sensuous pleasure to write on a beautiful surface after

First published in *Journal of Basic Writing,* 3 (Fall-Winter, 1981). Reprinted in *A Sourcebook for Basic Writing Teachers,* ed. Theresa Enos (New York: Random House, 1987).

you've been scratching away on canary pads. But wait a minute! Where are your notes to yourself? Where are your lists? Where are your points of departure? Where are your leads? Where is your lexicon? Where are your quoted passages? Where is your chaos? Nothing comes of nothing! Here you are in this spaceship pod of a chair, this womb, with essentials like coffee and cigarettes, but without the essential essential--language! How can you know what you think until you hear what you say? see what you've written?

I think it is instructive to consider how the "writing behaviors" of this graduate student resemble those of our basic writers. There is, of course, a difference: whereas the graduate cannot get beyond the compulsive readjustment of the (doubtless) insubstantial and formless generalization he has begun with, our students hate even to start--for a dozen reasons which have been carefully formulated and studied in recent years--and once they do have something down, they are loath to touch it: those few words are hard-won and therefore precious, not to be tampered with. The graduate destroys by restatement because he does not know how to get the dialectic going; the undergraduate cannot conceive of adjustment or development because his fragile construct might collapse. But insofar as neither knows how to make language serve the active mind, they both are basic writers: they do not understand rewriting because they do not understand how writing gets written in the first place.

My tendentious claim is that the same is often true also of their teachers: revision is poorly taught, or is not taught at all, because composition teachers and composition textbook authors often do not know how writing gets written. Without a substantial understanding of composing as a dialectical process in which the *what* and the *how* continually inform one another--a nonlinear process motivated by both feedback and what I.A. Richards calls "feedforward"--there will be no way for teachers to differentiate between revision and editing, no way to teach revision not as a definite phase, a penultimate stage, but as a dimension of composing. Revision is, indeed, reseeing and it goes on continually in the composing process.

There is, of course, a great deal of talk currently about "the composing process," but there are very few pedagogies which are consonant with the kind of process composing actually is. I have elsewhere discussed the reasons for this state of affairs: current rhetorical theory has provided little guidance for our classroom practice because it has no philosophically sound way of accounting for how words work. There is no understanding in current rhetorical theory that in composing everything has to happen at once or it does not happen at all. If there is not something to think about, if there are not ideas to think *with*, if language is not in action, if the mind is not actively engaged, no meanings can be made. The pedagogical challenge is to help students take advantage of *allatonceness*, to see it as a resource, not the mother of dilemmas.

The linear sequence by which "the composing process" is commonly represented--prewriting, writing, rewriting--is antithetical to the "audit of meaning," I.A. Richards' term for dialectic. Instead of allatonceness, it suggests that there is a nonreversible order, a sequence of activities which unfold in a predetermined manner. The interrelationships of the triad are obscure; the notion, for instance, that pre and re have anything to do with one another, logically or psychologically, seems unheard of. If prewriting is, in many instances, presented as a matter of amassing the slottables, rewriting is considered a matter of checking out what has been slotted. "Think of what you want to say" in prewriting is matched by such instructions as these for rewriting: "Go back over what you have written. Are there any unnecessary words? Does everything you say refer to your thesis? Is your main point at the end of the paragraph? Are they any mechanical errors?" These questions are only transformations of the old imperatives: "Do not use unnecessary words. Assure that all statements support your thesis. Avoid mechanical errors." Get law and order. Plant a tree. Love your mother. People who have done a lot of writing themselves frequently consider it a self-evidently sensible thing to teach the use of this kind of checklist to inexperienced writers. What they leave out of account is that the experienced writer has criteria which are brought into play by asking such questions: that's what it means to have "experience."

I think it is fair to say that the linear model of composing as prewriting, writing, rewriting fosters a pedagogy of exhortation. Now, if we are to undertake to teach composing as a dialectical process of which revision is not a stage but a dimension, how can we prevent what was earlier described, the write--erase--write again--erase it all syndrome? The short answer is, as I have noted, to teach students to take advantage of the allatonceness of composing, to assure that they continually rediscover how forming, thinking, and writing can be simultaneous and correlative activities. Beginning writers need the experience of seeing how it is that consciousness of the *what* leads to understanding the *how*. This is what Paulo Freire means by "conscientization," the chief principle of his "pedagogy of knowing." If a pedagogy of knowing is to be the successor to the pedagogy of exhortation, we will need as models of knowing those acts of mind which are logically and psychologically analogous to writing, namely, perception and concept formation.

Taking perception as a model for writing lets us exploit the ancient wisdom that seeing and knowing are radically alike. Our word *idea* derives from the Greek *oida,* which meant both *I have seen* and *I know.* The eye is not a passive recorder; Ruskin's notion of "the innocent eye" has been superseded by that of "the intelligent eye."[2] When we see, we compose. Rudolf Arnheim lists as the operations involved in visual perception the following: "Active exploration, selection, grasping of essentials, simplification, abstraction, analysis and synthesis, completion, correction, comparison, problem-solving, as well as combining, separating, putting in context" (*Visual* 13). Is there any aspect of the composing process not represented in that list?

From Arnheim, E.H. Gombrich, R.L. Gregory, and other philosophers and scientists, we can learn that perception involves matching and reordering, from the molecular level on up: *Vision* is through and through a matter of *revision.* Indeed, seeing is actually contingent on reseeing. To clarify this fascinating fact, I have students read Owen Barfield's explanation of how it is that cognition depends on recognition. He asks the reader to suppose that

he is standing in the midst of a normal and familiar environment ... when suddenly he is deprived by some supernatural stroke of every vestige of memory--and not only of memory, but also of all those assimilated, forgotten experiences which comprise his power of recognition. He is asked to assume that, in spite of this, he still retains the full measure of his cognitive faculty as an adult. It will appear, I think, that for the first few moments his consciousness--if it can bear that name--will be deprived not merely of all thought, but even of all perception. It is not merely that he will be unable to realize that that square, red and white object is a "house" ...; he will not even be able to see it *as* a square, red and white object (*Reclaiming* 39-40).

Seeing the point, my students speak of "Barfield's meaningless man." We can make meaning because we see in terms of what we have seen. Without remembered forms to see *with*, we would not see at all. Seeing is thus the primal analogizing in which thinking has its origin.

Now these philosophical principles of perception--seeing is knowing, seeing is contingent on reseeing, the intelligent eye forms by analogizing--provide the foundation for a pedagogy of knowing. How can we use what we can learn about perception in order to make observation not a preliminary exercise but a model of the composing process?

The allatonceness of composing is well represented by looking and writing in tandem. Since learning to record observations has a self-evident usefulness for everybody from nuclear physicists to nurses, from parents to doctors, and since observing our observations *requires* language, assignments which involve looking and looking again can rationally involve writing and writing again. Exercises which make recording and commenting correlative and virtually simultaneous have an authenticity which is unusual in composition assignments. One procedure which helps writers enact revision as a mode of composing is what I call a dialectical notebook: notes, lists, statements, critical responses, queries of all sorts are written on one side; notes on these notes, responses to these responses are written on the facing page. The inner dialogue which is thinking is thus represented as a dialectic, the beginning of thinking about thinking. This double-entry journal encourages a habit which is of immediate usefulness, since this format is the best there is for taking notes on lectures and reading. And it is easily adapted to what Dixie Goswami calls a "speculative draft," a procedure for writing papers which allows students to take advantage of allatonceness by keeping notes and queries, formulations and reformulations in continual dialogue on facing pages.

The dialectical notebook teaches the value of keeping things tentative. Without that sense, the allatonceness of composing is dangerous knowledge that can cause a severe case of writer's block. Unless students prove to themselves the usefulness of tentativeness, no amount of exhortation will persuade them to forego "closure," in the current jargon. The willingness to generate chaos; patience in testing a formulation against the record; careful comparing of proto-statements and half-statements, completed statements and restatements: these are all expressions of what Keats famously called "negative capability," the capacity to remain in doubt. The story is told of a professor of internal medicine who brought home to his students the value of this attitude in diagnosis with the slogan: "Don't just DO something: Stand there!"

Along with the value of tentativeness, practice in observation teaches the importance of perspective and context, which become ideas to think *with* as students practice observing natural objects, for instance, and observing their observations. A shell or pebble on the beach has one kind of appearance; if you bring it home, it has another. Such facts call for recognition, formulation, and articulation. In the practice of looking and looking again, of writing and writing again, as students learn to compare kinds of appearances, they are also learning that perception depends on presuppositions, remembrances, anticipations, purposes, and so on. In my own teaching, I hand out weeds and grasses, seeds and bones because natural forms are themselves compositions, pedagogically useful emblems of historical process. Friends and colleagues have occasionally argued that nature is an alien point of departure and that such an exercise as Ira Shor's examination of the contents of a wastebasket is more likely to engage the attention of basic writers. Detective work or archaeology is certainly as useful a metaphor for interpretation as nature study: the point is to make the transformation of the familiar to the strange and the strange to the familiar an exemplification of what goes on in all interpretation; to foreground the process of "reading," of construing, of making sense of whatever is under observation, from different perspectives, in different contexts.

Freire shows us how. The peasants in his culture circles, who are learning *how* they make meaning and *that* they make meaning simultaneously with learning to recognize words and sounds, study pictures depicting familiar scenes, reading them as texts, translating and interpreting them, and interpreting their interpretations in dialogue. What Freire calls "problematizing the existential situation" is a critical act of mind by which historical contexts for objects and pictures are developed: careful observation of what is depicted works together with the interpretation of its significance. Perception thus provides the point of departure for a pedagogy of knowing because it is through and through conceptual.

Problematic symbols and problem-posing pictures at one end; organic structures in the middle; at the other end, abstract designs and diagrams which we can ask students to observe, translating in the process from pictorial to verbal language. I.A. Richards, in a valuable essay called "Learning and Looking," suggests just how challenging that translation can be *(Design)*. He is ostensibly discussing the problems of literacy training in societies in which depiction is not thought of as representational, but in the course of demonstrating how "reading" certain diagrams exercises the translation-transformation capacity necessary for handling the graphic code, he does much more. For one thing, he shows how comparing depends on the principle of opposition, which is essential to all critical inquiry into "what varies with what while the rest is treated as remaining constant." Even more important, he provides demonstrations of how perspective and context function heuristically. Careful looking and experimental translation teach the observer to use oppositions to limit the range of choices. Just as learning to keep things tentative is an all-important support structure for the concept of the allatonceness of composing, so learning the use of limits is essential if beginning writers are to understand that composing necessarily involves choosing. Limits are their means of defining and controlling choices; unless we teach the function of limits, no amount of exhortation will persuade our students to tolerate the risks which revision entails.

By keeping looking and writing together, we can teach revision as analogous to recognition in perception. If we can keep thinking and writing together, our students can learn how revision is analogous to the representation which language makes possible. Language has, of course, an indicative function, but it is its power to represent our interpretations of experience which is vital for a pedagogy of knowing. No thinking--no composing- -could happen if we had no means of stabilizing images of what we have seen, of recalling them as forms to think about and to think *with.* Language is our means of *re*presenting images as forms: *forming* is our means of seeing relationships from one or another perspective and in different contexts.

Writing teachers have not, generally speaking, taken advantage of this power of language and mind--it was once called *imagination*--because linguistics, as institutionalized by current rhetorical theory, has no way of accounting for it. The conventional notion of thinking finds no room for the dialectic which language makes possible. It is based, rather, on the dichotomy of induction/deduction: either, it is thought, we go from "the data" to one or another principle, or we go from "high level abstractions" to the substantiating particulars. If teachers want to benefit from the fact that everything that happens when we think is analogous to what we do when we compose, they will need to form the concept of forming.

The logical ground for the analogy of thinking and writing is *forming*--seeing relationships, recognizing and representing them. Understanding that principle can show us how to start with thinking and writing together, and if we start with them together we will be more likely to keep them together. The way to bridge from so-called personal writing to so-called expository writing, from creative to critical writing, and, I will argue, from writing to rewriting is not to allow a separation in the first place. I want to concentrate now on one particular implication for classroom practice and course design of the premise that thinking and writing involve us in *seeing relationships:* how that can help us to teach revision not as a definite phase but as a dimension of the composing process.

From the idea that composing is a matter of seeing relationships, we might profitably conclude that at the pedagogical center of any composition course there should be not the grammatical unit of the sentence but the rhetorical unit of the paragraph.[3] Sentences depend on how they relate to other sentences; it is therefore easier to construe several sentences than it is one. The writer as reviser is a writer reading. Reading a paragraph, he has many points of entry; if he does not see a relationship as he starts to read, he might catch hold of another as he goes on. He can then reread and apprehend the earlier sentence. Because it articulates a structure of relationships, the paragraph provides a more appropriate focus for learning revision than the single sentence does. Apprehending the logical and rhetorical relationships of sentences in a paragraph is analogous to perception and concept formation in a way that apprehending those relationships articulated according to grammatical conventions *within* the sentence is not. That is why Gertrude Stein is right: "So paragraphing is a thing that anyone is enjoying and sentences are less fascinating."

Seeing relationships, as an idea to think with, can help offset the effects of certain theories of learning which, taking motor activity as the model, lead to the idea that because we must walk before we can run, we must therefore study sentences before paragraphs. Surely first things come first, but wherever language is concerned that will always mean that complexity comes before the allegedly simple. That is because meanings are not elements but relationships. It is by virtue of its complexity that the paragraph is simpler to take hold of than the sentence. This kind of paradox is central to the pedagogy of knowing. I do not mean that we ignore sentence structure when we teach revision. My point is that although errors are best identified in isolation, sentences are best revised in context, in the relational terms which the paragraph provides or which the would-be paragraph can be brought to the point of supplying. We are taking advantage of the allatonceness of making meaning when we teach our students to compose paragraphs in the course of revising sentences.

Along with the dialectical notebook, "glossing" paragraphs can raise consciousness of the interdependence of saying and intending. I ask students to summarize their paragraphs in oppositional form, to represent in a double phrase in the margin what is being set over against what. Thus identified, the logical structure of the paragraph can be used as an Archimedean point from which to survey the individual sentences. If it is impossible to formulate a gloss, that will tell a student more than exhortatory comments on incoherence ever could. Or it may be that in the process of glossing the student will express a hitherto unspoken intention which the paragraph can use. In that case, the gloss can be revised in sentence form and incorporated. Invention of needed sentences is contingent on recognizing the need, in my opinion, that recognition is inspired not by asking empty questions about what the audience needs to know but by seeing what the paragraph needs to say. To discover logical and rhetorical needs is to discover purpose, a process which is at once more complex and more manageable than trying to ascertain audience needs directly. They, of course, must be hypothesized and considered in conjunction, dialectically, with purposes. But to instruct the student to determine "the audience's needs" is frequently only an updated version of asking him to ask himself "What am I trying to say?" That is not, I think, a heuristically useful inquiry.

A way to encourage students to ask what a paragraph needs- -what their argument or explanation or description or narrative needs--is to have them read their own paragraphs (a day or so after they have been written) a sentence at a time with the remaining sentences covered, anticipating at each period what the next sentence will be, will do, by writing one in its place. The writer can do this on his own, of course, but it is best done in conference or in company with other readers, dialogue being the best model of dialectic there is. The newly framed sentence can then be compared with the original sentence, of which it may, of course, be a replica: having two ways of saying to work with, or one way twice, is important in the practice of revision. The choice can be made, then, of which serves better in answering the perhaps newly felt need, but nothing should be thrown away, since the paragraph might well require the old original sentence in a new setting.

Developing a sense of rhetorical and logical form is in large part a matter of anticipating what comes next, of knowing what is needed, recognizing its emergence. That is not a "skill" but a power of mind, and it is exactly comparable to recognition in perception and representation with language. We do not need to teach this power, but we should assure that it is exercised. These simple techniques of paragraph review can serve that purpose because they keep the dialectic of intending and forming lively. Glossing and anticipating can help students see to it that the "what I mean" does not remain an amorphous, ghostly nonpresence but is embodied over and over again. To find out if you have said what you meant, you have to know what you mean and the way to determine that is to say "it" again.

Only when a paragraph has been reviewed in the light of its gloss, the various sentences abandoned or rewritten, restored, and reordered according to emerging criteria, is it time to work on sentence correction. Error identification is often tantamount to error correction and, as I have noted, that is best carried out if the sentence can be "heard" in isolation from its support system, the context which makes meaning rather than grammatical structure predominate. The procedure I recommend is to read the paragraph backwards aloud, sentence by sentence--an old proofreader's trick. If the student stumbles or hesitates, that is a sign of recognition and actual rewriting can begin. Nothing will come of this or any other such procedure, of course, if the student cannot recognize a faulty sentence when he hears one. By assuring that there are occasions for reading good prose closely, carefully, and frequently aloud, we can help our students to develop an "ear" for syntax, like an "ear" for music, to expect the way a sentence will go or can go so that when it goes awry, they can hear the error. The remedy for a deficient "ear" is hearing good prose, and that means that student writing will not be the exclusive "text" in a well-designed composition course.

When it is a simple matter of agreement, pronoun reference, tense consistency, or punctuation (in some cases), grammatical instruction can be useful. But sentences which fail because of pleonasm, faulty parallelism, misused idiom, or mixed constructions are, generally speaking, a different matter. They will yield to our grammatical analysis or the student's, but that analysis will serve no heuristic function.

Take, for instance, the following sentences:

The elemental beach and the music of the sea was more preferable than that other summer beach.
North Carolina is a state where the long straight roads that lead to small quiet places has an unusually loud bunch of inhabitants.
I have always seen that as a silver lining behind the cloud.
Teachers judge the quality of the student's performance much like that of the farmer's grading his beef.

In my opinion, the best way to work with sentences like these is for everybody in a small group, or for both student and tutor in conference, to revise the sentence by means of composing several interpretive paraphrases, using the parent paragraph is a sounding board. Restating, representing is a way to recognize intention: interpreting by means of paraphrase, rather than tinkering with the incorrect sentence as it stands, allows a student to call upon the resources he has for making meaning which are independent of any explicit knowledge of grammatical laws. I do not mean that rhetorical and logical forms are simply "generated": written discourse is not natural in the way that speech, in a social setting, is. I have no faith that well-formed intentions will surface from the deep if only grammarians will step aside. Returning to intention is a hard journey, but it is profitable because of what can be learned on the way about the making of meaning.

Syntactical structures are linguistic forms which find conceptual forms: making them accessible to our students is one of our chief duties. Kenneth Koch's experiments are important to us all because they remind us of the value of teaching syntactical structures as generative forms rather than as slots to be filled or inert elements to be combined. We can learn from Koch and others how to make syntax itself a heuristic. The procedure I have found most useful is called "persona paraphrase," in which a specific passage is selected, illustrating a particular kind of structure. Students then copy its structure, phrase by phrase, sentence by sentence, substituting completely different subject matter.[4] Kenneth Burke's conception of recalcitrance explains the principle on which persona paraphrase is based: "A statement is an attitude rephrased in accordance with the strategy of revision made necessary by the recalcitrance of the materials employed for embodying this attitude" (*Permanence 255*). Insofar as it recognizes the dialectics of recalcitrance, the paradox that complexity is simple, the fact that concept formation is dynamic, the fact that saying and intending inform one another--insofar as persona paraphrase is a technique which can teach revision as a mode of composing, it is the antithesis of sentence combining. This is not surprising. It presupposes a philosophy of language entirely foreign to the conceptions which underlie the manipulations of sentence combining.

Revising at this level in these ways means slowing things down: allatonceness always does. Composing a persona paraphrase can take a full hour; composing interpretive paraphrases for a single conceptually faulty sentence can take up the entire class or conference time. It is time well spent, but there is a very difficult pedagogical challenge in seeing to it that this necessarily slow, deliberate pace is not the only one at which the composition course moves. Others have probably long since discovered the paradox I have been slow to come to, namely, that allatonceness requires a double track, if not a triple focus. Students should work independently on a long-term project for which the dialectical notebook is the enabling means of making meaning; they should continually be revising paragraphs with their fellow students; every day, in class or out, they should focus on the analysis and correction of a single sentence. The difference between the 101 section for basic writers, the noncredit course required of graduate students, and the Continuing Education workshops in writing should be a matter not of which elements are included but only of the ratios among them and the pace at which the entire course proceeds.

If we reject the linear model of composing and the pedagogy it legitimates-- teaching the allegedly first things first; subskills before skills; the *know how* before the *know what;* walking (sentences) before running (paragraphs)--we will be free to invent courses which are consonant with the idea of the composing process as a continuum of forming. I have been claiming that recognition and representation, as the central operations of perception and concept formation, provide the models of forming which can help us teach revision as a way of composing.

NOTES

1. This finding is reported by Susan V. Wall and Anthony R. Petrosky in "Freshman Writers and Revision: Results from a Survey," *Journal of Basic Writing, 3* (Fall-Winter 1981).

2. Richard Coe brought my attention to the fascinating book with this title by R.L. Gregory. Coe's textbook, *Form and Substance* (New York: Wiley, 1981), is one of the few which present perception as profoundly conceptual, as an act of mind as well as of brain.

3. I agree with those who argue that the paragraph is a rhetorical convention and that a single sentence may constitute a paragraph. See "The Logic and Rhetoric of Paragraphs," *Forming/Thinking/Writing* 215ff. For the time being, I use the term to mean a sentence sequence which displays logical coherence.

4. Phyllis Brooks, "Mimesis: Grammar and the Echoing Voice," *College English,* 35 (November 1973), 161-68. As Brooks notes, persona paraphrase is highly adaptable. I have described certain uses which my students have made of it in *Forming/Thinking/Writing* 211-15.

B. Selected Bibliography

Pre-Writing Processes

Belanoff, Pat, Peter Elbow, and Sheryl I. Fontaine, eds. *Nothing New Begins with N: New Investigations of Freewriting.* Carbondale: Southern Illinois UP, 1991

Corbett, Edward P.J. *Classical Rhetoric for the Modern Student.* 3rd ed. New York: Oxford UP, 1990.

Crowley, Sharon. *The Methodical Memory: Invention in cCrrent-Traditional Rhetoric.* Carbondale: Southern Illinois UP, 1990.

Fulwiler, Toby. *The Journal Book.* Portsmouth, NH: Boynton/Cook, 1987.

Harrington, David V., et al. "A Critical Survey of Resources for Teaching Rhetorical Invention: A Review-Essay." *College English* 40 (1979): 641-61.

Kneupper, Charles W. "Revising the Tagmemic Heuristic: Theoretical and Pedagogical Considerations." *CCC* 31 (1980): 160-68.

LeFevre, Karen Burke. *Invention as a Social Act.* Carbondale: Southern Illinois UP, 1987.

Murray, Donald M. "Write Before Writing." *CCC* 29 (1978): 375-82

Rohman, D. Gordon. "Pre-Writing: The State of Discovery in the Writing Process." *CCC* 16 (1965): 106-12.

Rose, Mike. *Writer's Block: The Cognitive Dimension.* Carbondale: Southern Illinois UP, 1984.

Composing Processes

Berthoff, Ann E. *Forming/Thinking/Writing: The Composing Imagination.* 2nd ed.Portsmouth, NH: Boynton/Cook, 1988.

Bizzell, Patricia. "Composing Processes: An Overview." *The Teaching of Writing.* Eighty-fifth Yearbook of the National Society for the Study of Education, Part 2. Ed. Anthony R. Petrosky and David Bartholomae. Chicago: National Society for the Study of Education, 1986. 49-70.

Cooper, Marilyn M. "Unhappy Consciousness in First-Year English: How to Figure Things Out for Yourself." *Writing as Social Action*. Marilyn M. Cooper and Michael Holzman. Portsmouth, NH: Boynton/Cook, 1987. 28-60.

Faigley, Lester. "Competing Theories of Process: A Critique and a Proposal." *CE* 48 (1986): 527-542.

Elbow, Peter. *Writing with Power: Techniques for Mastering the Writing Process*. New York: Oxford UP, 1981.

Flower, Linda, and John R. Hayes. "A Cognitive Process Theory of Writing." *CCC* 32 (1981): 365-87.

Flower, Linda, and John R. Hayes. "Problem-Solving Strategies and the Writing Process." *CE* 39 (1977): 442-48.

Knoblauch, C.H. "Intentionality in the Writing Process: A Case Study." *CCC* 31 (1980): 153-59.

Lindemann, Erika. *A Rhetoric for Writing Teachers*. 3d ed. New York: Oxford UP, 1995.

MacKenzie, Nancy. "Teaching the Composing Process: A Three-Part Project." *The Writing Instructor* 1 (1982): 103-111.

Revising Processes

Brannon, Lil, Melinda Knight, and Vera Neverow-Turk. *Writers Writing*. Upper Montclair, NJ: Boynton/Cook, 1982.

Butturf, Douglas R., and Nancy L. Sommers. "Placing Revision in a Reinvented Rhetorical Tradition." *Reinventing the Rhetorical Tradition*. Eds. Avia Freedman and Ian Pringle. Conway: L & S Books, 1980. 99-104.

Elbow, Peter. *Writing with Power: Techniques for Mastering the Writing Process*. New York: Oxford UP, 1981.

Faigley, Lester, and Stephen Witte. "Analyzing Revision," *CCC* 32 (1981): 400-414.

Harris, Muriel. "Composing Behaviors of One- and Multi-Draft Writers." *CE* 51 (1989): 174-91.

Laib, Nevin. "Conciseness and Amplification." *CCC* 41 (1990): 443-58.

Murray, Donald. "Teaching the Motivating Force of Revision." *Learning by Teaching.* Upper Montclair, NJ: Boynton/Cook, 1983.

Schwartz, Mimi. "Revision Profiles: Patterns and Implications." *CE* 45 (1983): 549-58.

Sommers, Nancy. "Revision Strategies of Student Writers and Experienced Adult Writers." *College Composition and Communication* 31 (1980): 376-388.

Wall, Susan V. "In the Writer's Eye: Learning to Teach the Rereading/Revising Process," *English Education* 14 (Feb. 1982).

Wall, Susan V. "Revision in a Rhetorical Context: Case Studies of First Year College Writers." diss., U. of Pittsburgh, 1982, 48-118.

Wall, Susan V. "The Languages of the Text: What Even Good Students Need to Know about Re-Writing." *Journal of Advanced Composition* 7.1 (1987): 31-40.

Williams, Joseph. *Style: Ten Lessons in Clarity and Grace*, 2nd ed. Glenview: Scott Foresman, 1985.

C. Form and Organization --LargerElements

As Richard M. Coe writes in the first piece in this section, "An Apology for Form; or, Who Took the Form Out of Process?" (originally published in *College English* 49 [1987]: 13-28), the writing process movement has not been entirely comfortable with the teaching of form. Coe, in fact, claims that it is more precise to say that process-oriented pedagogies arose in opposition to formalist pedagogy instead of product-centered pedagogy. This formalist writing instruction has taught students the modes of discourse (narration, description, exposition, and argumentation) and the patterns of exposition (primarily comparison/contrast, division and classification, process, cause and effect, definition, exemplification), has treated coherence and paragraphing in formalist terms, and has stressed style and correctness, all without regard to students' composing processes and in isolation of the audience, purpose, situation, and invention. Sentences and paragraphs were regarded as building blocks for the essay, and students often received instruction in writing sentences and paragraphs as preparation for essay- writing. Process-oriented instruction now typically teaches students the larger matters of form--organization, coherence, and paragraphing--in the context of a entire written work and as part of revising.

Coe finds this treatment of form inadequate, arguing that composition is "a forming process." Drawing on linguistic theory and information theory, Coe advocates a renewed emphasis on form, but states that this instruction should occur as part of a process pedagogy that ties form to considerations of purpose, invention, audience, and rhetorical situation, and that views forms as strategies for generating, revising, and communicating meaning. Rejecting the metaphor of form as a "container" of content and the romantic conception that "form grows organically to fit the shape of the subject matter," Coe shows that forms are heuristic, that they provide writers with "structured searches" for exploring their subjects. Forms do not exist in isolation but are "socially shared," reflecting communities' ways of knowing and communicating that writers need to learn.

Betty Bamberg also turns to linguistics to provide a better understanding of coherence in "What Makes a Text Coherent?" (first published in *College Composition and Communication* 34 [1983]: 417-29). Bamberg calls for a redefinition of coherence in writing because traditional instruction has confused coherence, which deals with a reader's experience of a text, with cohesion, which is a system of textual cues like transitional expressions, repetition of key words, and use of pronouns that connect the parts of a text. While these cohesive ties contribute to the coherence of a text, Bamberg states, "Meaning and coherence are not inscribed in the text, . . . but arise from readers' efforts to construct meaning and to integrate the details in the text into a coherent whole." Writers cannot achieve coherence solely by manipulating transitions, pronouns, and key words, for coherence cannot be separated from the knowledge and expectations readers bring to a text and the purposes the writer has in composing the text. Readers continually guess at a text's overall meaning, purpose, and structure as they read, and writers achieve coherence, not just by providing cohesive ties such as transitional expectations, by helping readers in their predictions, with passages that orient audience expectations and provide a context for what the writer has to say, as well as with effective decisions about organization.

Michael G. Moran's "The English Paragraph," an essay taken from *Research in*

Composition and Rhetoric: A Bibliographic Sourcebook, edited by Moran and Ronald F. Lunsford (Westport, CT: Greenwood, 1984), surveys past and present literature on the paragraph and its instruction. Early in the essay, Moran states that theories of the paragraph normally fall into two groups, "that the paragraph is a unit . . . that possesses an internal structure that can be described using a finite set of rules" and "that the paragraph is a stretch of discourse that owes its existence to the larger requirements of a whole piece of prose" and "does not exist as a separate unity but as a flexible and convenient method of marking some stage in a larger organic process." Since the beginning of English composition instruction, teaching has usually reflected models of the paragraph as a unit, based on nineteenth-century theories that originated the concepts of the topic sentence, unity, coherence, development, and patterns of paragraph exposition. This theory came under attack in the 1960s, Moran writes, and composition scholars then began developing theories that better describe the form and function of the paragraph, although versions of nineteenth-century paragraph theory still dominate first-year writing instruction. Moran describes the central theories of the paragraph that composition scholars have developed since the 1960s. Some, like Francis Christensen's generative theory of the paragraph, which views the paragraph as a "macrosentence" in which the first sentence acts like a base clause modified by subsequent sentences, are new formalist theories that consciously join form with invention, teaching paragraph patterns to help students generate subject matter in their writing. Other theories, like that of Paul C. Rodgers, Jr., treat a writer's paragraphing decisions rhetorically, in the context of the whole text, considering the logical, psychological, rhythmical, tonal, and other purposes of the writer. Moran ends his essay with an overview of important articles and textbooks since the 1950s on methods for teaching paragraph writing.

All three selections reveal the influence not only of process pedagogies in the teaching of form but much of the interdisciplinary nature of composition studies. Present theories and pedagogies on organization, coherence, and paragraphing are informed by such diverse fields as linguistics, cognitive theories on reading, information theory, and literary theory. Most of our concepts of form conceive it as a heuristic that generates subject matter for the writer, not something separate from content, and tie decisions on form closely to considerations of audience and situation.

An Apology for Form; or,
Who Took the Form Out of the Process?
Richard M. Coe

> Form ... is an arousing and fulfillment of desires. A work has form in so far as
> one part of it leads a reader to anticipate another part, to be gratified by the
> sequence.
>
> (Burke, *Counter-Statement* 124)

> Desire is the presence of an *absence.*
>
> (Kojeve 134)

> Translated into terms of the composition class, "form" becomes "organization"
> and brings with it ... the most dismal stuff that students and teachers must deal
> with. And yet, the concept of form in discourse is utterly fascinating, for it
> concerns the way in which the mind perceives infinitely complex relationships.
> The way, indeed, in which the mind constructs discourse.
>
> (Winterowd 163)

I. History, Politics, and Theory

At this point in the history of our profession, the conflicts within the fold of the faithful
(i.e., among adherents of "the process approach" to teaching composition) are far more
significant than the opposition between process and "product" approaches. Which
process emphasis one chooses matters a great deal, not only to the type of success
students may achieve but also to such relationships as those between writing and
humanistic education, between writers as individuals and writing as process. Certain
conceptions of process (and of the relationship between form and process) prevent us
from realizing the full potential of process approaches to composition.

Historically, the process approach must be understood as antithesis.   At the
Dartmouth Conference and elsewhere, practitioners such as John Dixon, D. Gordon
Rohman, Ken Macrorie, Stephen Tchudi, Donald Graves, Donald Murray, et al. spoke
and wrote from their own experiences, but also in response to a traditional way of
teaching writing--proffering an antidote, if you will, to the inadequacies of that
traditional approach. Their emphases, as always in an antithetical situation, were
defined to some significant extent by what they were opposing. To reach a clearer
understanding of writing as process, we must sublate (i.e., simultaneously transcend and
conserve) this antithesis.

Before distinguishing types of process approaches, it is important to clarify the
distinction between process writing and what preceded it. These days, it has become

commonplace to juxtapose process writing with a so-called "product approach." Rather than defining what the traditional approach is, this inadequate and derogatory title shifts our attention to what it is not (i.e., not process). Properly termed, what the past two decades saw was a conflict between a (traditional) *formal* approach and a (renewed) *process* approach. To sublate the antithesis and avoid the simplistic choice, we must clarify the relationship between form and process, define the place of forms in the process.

Although it dabbled occasionally (and inaccurately) in process--what else is outlining?--the traditional formal approach essentially taught good form. It answered, formally, the question, "What is good writing?" Because it radically dichotomized form from "content," its answer emphasized structure: sentence structure, paragraph structure, essay structure, even the proper structures for term papers, business letters, resumes--all that Winterowd calls "dismal stuff." If the proper forms were defined, they could be described and exemplified for students. After students wrote, they could be shown where their writing failed to match the ideal forms. And then, the formalists hoped, students would correct their writing to create a better match.

Unfortunately, most students failed to do this because the formalists told them only *what* to do, not also *how* to do it. Until a few decades ago, however, this was not a major social problem because such students also failed to stay in school. Although the data vary from country to country and region to region, we may safely say that only after World War II do even half the students who start grade one complete high school. But then radical changes in the nature of work and other social realities led to declining drop-out rates and increasing postsecondary enrollment, creating a need for a pedagogy that would work with students who used to disappear before senior high school--and thus forming a historical opening for process approaches (Coe, "Literacy `Crises'"). For any process approach, by definition, concerns itself with one or more of the *hows* formalists traditionally ignore: how writers create; how writers think, feel, and verbalize to enable writing; how writers learn while writing; how writing communicates with readers; and *how* social processes and contexts influence the shaping and interpreting of texts.[1]

There is not one process approach; there are many. All share an emphasis on process, and any process approach inevitably involves intervening in the creative process, if only by recontextualizing it. But writing comprises many processes, and the strongest pedagogical conflict is between those who emphasize writing as a learning process and those who emphasize writing as a communicative process (see Fig. 1; cf. Perelman 471-72, Faigley 527-28).

Those concerned with process writing as a means of learning tend to emphasize underlying mental processes and techniques for destructuring invention, for enabling

---

[1] . There is, of course, a sense in which this distinction between mental and social processes is false, for our minds are themselves social as well as individual. The metaphor that equates mind with brain misleads us into locating our minds "in" our heads; but while the brain is a crucial locus of mind, we would avoid many errors if we made a radical epistemological shift and began thinking of our minds as open systems, as structures and flows of information that pass through our brains. Cf. Bateson (esp. 478-88 and 494-505). Burke makes a similar point when he locates motives.

unconscious processes (e.g., freewriting). Those concerned with writing as a process with worldly uses tend to emphasize communicative process and techniques for structuring invention, for enabling conscious planning (e.g., heuristics, nutshelling). Although there are certainly senses in which both emphases deal with writing as social, these are very different senses, and the treatment of form also differs radically between these two emphases, which I shall call Expressionist and New Rhetorical.[2]

Behind the traditional conception of form lies a long-dead metaphor--one so dead we fail to notice it--inherited from such conservative neo-Classicists as Samuel Johnson. In this metaphor, form is a *container* to be filled (hence the term *content*). If the metaphor is to make sense, our conception of the matter with which we fill forms must be sufficiently "liquid" (i.e., independent of form) to accept the out-lines imposed by the shape of the form. This is not Cicero's conception of form, but it is Samuel Johnson's, which is why he can speak of language as a dress thought puts on. For neo-Classicists, ideas exist first; then we dress them in (socially conventional) words and forms. (It is highly significant that most New Critics, neo-Romantics when they deal with literature, adopt this neo-Classical conception of form when they must teach composition.)

Although advocates of Expressionist process writing are radical neo-Romantics, and thus more consistent with what was and probably still is the majority approach to literature, they continue to operate in terms of a form/content dichotomy. For them, however, form grows organically to fit the shape of the subject matter. Thus there is little need to teach form except as an afterthought (along with punctuation) late in both the teaching and writing processes. Thus the Expressionist process approach and the traditional formal approach are indeed opposites: where the traditional approach ignores

---

[2]   2. In evoking this antithesis, I use Berlin's terms, in part because I think they are significantly accurate, in part to avoid a proliferation of terminologies. My point, however, does not depend upon his analysis. Indeed, I disagree with parts of Berlin's analysis and recognize that any analysis of this nature reduces the complex variety of what is actually happening--that is how it achieves clarity and defines the core of the issue. But I think it is fair to assert that the two major influences on classroom practice, at least in North America, were the traditional formal approach and the Expressionist process approach.

The traditional formal approach avoided questions of substance by defining "content" as outside the field of composition, i.e., either as unteachable art (as in "inspiration") or as the proper concern of other disciplines ("content" courses, as contrasted with "skills" courses). The Expressionist process approach, taking its cue from the derivation of *education* (to lead out, to draw forth), also avoided questions of substance but by placing "content" within students; this process approach begins by removing constraints, creating contexts and processes through which students can express themselves, can articulate (hence, on another level, discover) what *they* want to say, can *ex-press* what is presumably already "inside" them.

The differences in the ways the two process approaches deal with the social aspect of process writing is consistent with their respective conceptions of form. The New Rhetorical treatment of form is radically distinct from either the traditional formal approach or the Expressionist process approach.

content to teach form, Expressionist process writing enables content, allowing form to develop organically. Interestingly, Ken Macrorie's pragmatic description of "good form" represents the same stylistic values (and often the same particulars) as does Strunk and White's; but *Telling Writing* presents them as secondary, to be dealt with during revision, while in *The Elements of Style* they are virtually the whole ball of wax. And the very act of enabling content, of encouraging student writers to write about what concerns them, does create the potential of writing as a liberating *social* act of self-discovery (cf. Schultz).

Figure 1. The Process Approach

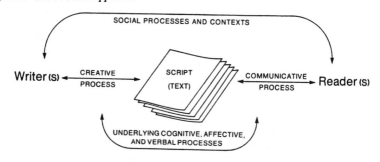

The teaching process involves *intervening* in the various
processes surrounding and underlying the writing

In *The Philosophy of Rhetoric*, I.A. Richards urges us to "avoid some traditional mistakes--among them the use of bad analogies which tie us up if we take them too seriously." Some of these bad analogies, Richards asserts,

> are notorious; for example, *the opposition between form and content.* ... These are wretchedly inconvenient metaphors. So is that other which makes language a dress which thought puts on. We shall do better to think of meaning as though it were a plant that has grown--not a can that has been filled or a lump of clay that has been molded. (12, emphasis added)

Richards reminds us that implicit in the form/content opposition is the "dead" neo-Classical metaphor which makes form a container. If form is like a container, then form and "content" are relatively independent: a can hold peas (or marbles) quite as well as beans, and pouring your peas (or marbles) from one can to another does not affect their substance. Like clay, "content" is malleable, capable of adapting to any mold without changing its essential nature.

These metaphors are "inconvenient," Richards argues, because they lead us to misconceive the relation of form to (what we should *not* call) "content." There is no meaning without form: information is *formed* matter (which becomes meaningful in relation to contexts). When you trans*form* a message into a new form, as when you translate a poem, you have re*form*ulated it, thus to some extent changing the meaning. Information is made by putting data (i.e., subject matter) *in formation*, by forming. What neo-Classical formalists called "content" is unknowable in its formlessness; it becomes substantive and knowable only when formed. (And this formed matter becomes meaning-full only when someone relates it to some context--but that is another issue.)

Figure 2. *Matter to Meaning*

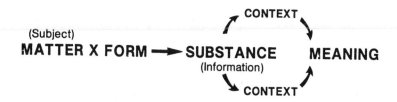

Richards' assertion, perhaps controversial when made in 1936, is now thoroughly confirmed by research in cognitive psychology, information theory, and other such disciplines. As Richards argued, perception itself is humanly impossible until sensory input has been formed (i.e., coded, juxtaposed with mental schema that allow us to perceive pattern in the thousands of "bits" of input that would otherwise overwhelm our mental capacities). As the information theorists would have it:

Noise x Code → Information

Broadly, then, we can define form in terms of its function in a process of forming. This definition is purposively tautological: whatever is used to inform--to impose pattern on noise, cosmos on chaos--is form. Even when we define form narrowly (as rhetorical forms, patterns of development, and so on), we should retain this process conception of form, which reminds us of function.

In composition, as elsewhere, the formalists promulgated a falsely static sense of form. They ignored, rather than refuted, Richards. Meanwhile, the conception we need to sublate the static form/content dichotomy awaited us in the New Rhetoric: the theory we find in Richards and, especially, Kenneth Burke; later from practitioners such as Francis Christensen and Ann Berthoff come practical applications to teaching composition.

Frank D'Angelo summarized the concept this way in *A Conceptual Theory of Rhetoric*:

> Following Aristotle's system I take form to be closely related to the formal principle, i.e., one of the causes of a mode of being which produces discourse. ... Patterns of development are not only organizational, they ... also ... serve a heuristic function. ... They are ... dynamic organizational processes, symbolic manifestations of underlying mental processes, and not merely conventional static patterns. (56-57)

In this conception form is both generative and constraining--or, better said, generative because constraining. Form is empty, an absence. But this emptiness has shape (i.e., form). In human beings, at least, this emptiness creates a desire to find what might fill it--which is at least part of what Burke means in "Definition of Man" when he wryly defines us as "rotten with perfection" (*Language* 16 ff.).

Another aspect of Burke's point--Burke's significant points are never singular-- reminds me of Donald Murray (the writer, *not* the theoretician of writing) describing invention as knowing how to sit waiting under the lightning. Murray recounted how various wordings of a particular subject struck him until, recognizing the last as a poem, he wrote it out ("Talking to Yourself"; cf. Murray's essay in Waldrep's collection).

I take his report of the process as exceptionally significant because it sublates his own theory. Somehow, Murray recognized a particular set of words *as a poem*. His selection of this version as poem was also, inevitably, a rejection/deflection of other versions (as non-poem or, at least, as inferior poem). And his recognition could only have occurred because Murray had within his mind a schema for poem, an abstract (i.e., empty) formal idea of *poem*--a "perfection" through which Murray is "rotten," far beyond his willingness to admit, *with the social.* For since this poem was later recognized by an editor (hence published) and by readers, I take it that Murray's schema of poem is shared, not idiosyncratic.

In short, we have here a shared form "provided by language," a cultural form, a social structure enabling the creative process. That Murray, like many writers, finds it useful to ignore the place of cultural/social structures in his writing process is neither here nor there--it certainly does not imply that teachers of writing should ignore the impact of such structures on the creative process.

Form, in its emptiness, is heuristic, for it guides a structured search. Faced with the emptiness of a form, a *human* being seeks matter to fill it. Form becomes, therefore, a motive for generating information. Like any heuristic, it motivates a search for information of a certain type: when the searchers can anticipate what shape of stuff they seek, generation is less free, but much more efficient; by constraining the search, form directs attention. (Heuristics, in this sense, are distinct from unstructuring discovery techniques such as freewriting.)

Consider, for example, the form we entitle "the five-paragraph essay." In my more cynical moments, I suspect that the better part of several generations of students have been socialized to believe that, at least in school, there are three reasons for (and/or three examples of) anything. Although the five-paragraph essay originates as an exercise in using the Classical *proposition + partition* to structure an essay, and although there is no reason whatsoever why it should not sometimes contain two or four or more body paragraphs, students who have memorized the form almost inevitably generate three.

In my less cynical moments, I recognize the good in this: left on their own, many of these same students would discover only one reason or example. Thus even this static school form has some liberal value. My main point here, however, is that the form, *because it contains three **empty** slots,* motivates students to continue inventing until they have discovered subject matter to fill three slots. (For a broader critique of formal tyranny in school essays, see Fort.)

In this respect, any form is like the forms we are often served by various bureaucracies (e.g., income tax forms). They move us to consider certain types of things, to search for particular information and, generally, to find something (if only "N/A") to fill every slot. And the other side of this mundane example is the sense in which all heuristics, not just the tagmemic grid but also the Pentad and the journalists' 5Ws, are empty forms whose shaped emptinesses motivate writers to generate appropriate information.

Rhetorical structures are in this sense the social memory of standard responses to particular types of rhetorical situations and subject matter.[3] Like language, form is thus social. One function of discourse communities is to provide, prescribe, and prefer forms. Learning conventional forms, often by a tacit process of "indwelling," is a way of learning a community's discourse, gaining access, communicating with that community. For a form implies a strategy of response, an attitude, a way of sorting factors, sizing up situations. If a text, as Burke would have it, dances an attitude, then forms are attitudes frozen in synchronicity. Insofar as a form is socially shared, adopting the form involves adopting, at least to some extent, the community's attitude, abiding by its expectations.

Readers who make up the community use these same forms to focus their attention, to anticipate as they approach and move through a text, as they use the text to reinvent meanings. Recognizing forms--both of the whole text (sonnet, editorial, term paper) and of parts within the text (definition, example, instructions)--is an important aspect of reading. Readers' abilities to recognize--even (or perhaps especially) subliminally--various kinds of formal patterns of development allow them to "process" text (i.e., to understand it) efficiently. Those who fail to recognize forms, perhaps because they are from another culture or subculture, not part of the community, often misinterpret function, hence meaning.

Writers' abilities to use formal patterns particular readers will recognize allow them to communicate accurately and effectively. In general, communication is most likely to succeed, to generate understanding rather than misunderstanding, when writer(s) and reader(s) know and use the same forms.[4] (For writers, "use" may mean reproducing or *varying* the form; in either case, recognition enables reading.)

---

3. Cf. Burke's assertion that "critical and imaginative works are answers to questions posed by situation in which they arose," that we should think of "any work of critical or imaginative cast" as "the adopting of various strategies for the encompassing of situations. These strategies size up the situations, name their structure and outstanding ingredients, and name them in a way that contains an attitude towards them. ... The symbolic act is the *dancing of an attitude"* (*Philosophy* 3, 8-9). The point I am making about rhetorical forms is Burke's point generalized--as the forms are generalized texts. Forms are synchronic structures that function as generalized memories of (diachronic) processes. For an application this conception of form to the interpretation of literature (and architecture), see Wayne's *Penshurst.*

4. De Beaugrande coins the term "frame defense" to argue that a text may be "rejected or simply not understood" if it conflicts with a reader's informational or situational frame (168). Hypothetically, I would apply this notion to formal frames as well. Cf. Kinsch's argument that readers structure information within a knowledge

Conventional forms, as they function in both creative and communicative processes, are a major part of what makes those processes social. And, to continue along these Burkean lines, inasmuch as an attitude is an incipient action, i.e., a potential action waiting for an activating situation, so forms are suasive, rhetorical insofar as by shaping our attitudes they guide our responses to situations.

Thus an example somewhat more interesting than the five-paragraph essay or a bureaucratic form is the form that allows us to "know" there are two sides to a question or issue even before we know what the question or issue is. The apparent motive behind this form is usually to get someone who is seeing only one side to look for another. In that sense, this is a generative form. Perhaps because it fits so neatly with binary dualism and other reductionist tendencies in modern Western culture, however, it is also a constraining form that allows us to feel fulfilled after we have discovered only two sides: how else can we explain several decades during which otherwise intelligent Westerners looked at the Middle East and saw *only* two sides? And, worse, this form becomes the basis of Golden Mean dualism, which allows us to know that both extremes are wrong and the liberal middle correct even before we know what the issue is. (What is the Golden Mean in the conflict between rapist and victim?)

As this example indicates, form is cultural, not neutral. The sense in which conventional forms are culture-bound is most apparent; but other sorts of forms, such as those discussed by D'Angelo (*Conceptual Theory* 38-60) or those Burke calls progressive and repetitive (*Counter-Statement* 124-25), vary more from culture to culture than most of us realize.

A form may be generative insofar as it motivates a search for more information; but any form also biases the direction of the searching and constrains against the discovery of information that does not fit the form. A particular message may be very difficult (if not impossible) to communicate within the parameters of a conventional form. Literary history is filled with examples of writers who needed to invent new forms to communicate new messages. More mundanely, certain messages are hard to squeeze into a business letter, for example, because they exceed the maximum effective length of that form (i.e., two typewritten pages). A pedagogically significant example is the standard formal technique for achieving focus, which often constrains against what a student writer has set out to say (Coe, "If Not to Narrow"). Form can, in this sense, be ideological: when a particular form constrains against the communication of a message contrary to the interests of some power elite, it serves an ideological function. Insofar as form guides function, formal values may carry implicit moral/political values.

As this series of examples indicates, the nature of form is variable. If you accept the notion of form I am putting forth, one implication is that we need to study form--and forming--much more carefully and in many more contexts than we have: form as organic, as construct; as flexible, as rigid; as generative, as constraint; as an instrument of creation and meaning; as the social penetrating the personal. In order to emphasize the essential nature of form, I have in this essay been conflating distinctions that would

---

frame they bring to the text and Goffman's notion of "primary frames" (21-39). Burke, of course, has made various comparable analyses earlier, although without using the same terminology.

distinguish various types of forms. For the unity is logically prior to the partition. That unity grasped, however, we do need better insights into the various functions of distinct formal principles. And while remembering Burke's warning "not to confine the explanation [of form] to *one* principle, but to formulate sufficient principles to make an explanation possible" (*Counter-Statement* 129), we could certainly do worse than to start from his discussion of progressive (syllogistic and qualitative), repetitive, conventional, and minor or incidental form.

Even without awaiting further study, we can draw certain implications from the general thesis argued here. As humanists, we should be able to explain (especially to our students) the relation of forms to functions. As rhetoricians, we should explicitly invent forms to meet new needs, new functions, as Young, Becker, and Pike formally invented Rogerian persuasion. As writing teachers we need a more articulated understanding than do writers of how form functions in the writing process.

That brings me to "Monday morning."

II. Monday Morning

If you agree with the New Rhetorical conception of form asserted here, what should you do on Monday morning?

1. You should help students learn those forms socially necessary for effective communication within the society in which they live. (This is comparable to teaching them Standard English so that they have functional access to professional jobs, power, etc.)

2. .You should help them learn--and invent--forms that allow them to understand and communicate what they want to understand and communicate, what it is in their interests to understand and communicate.

3. You should help students grasp this New Rhetorical conception of form and learn how to think critically about form--but, let me add immediately, not by pontificating about form; rather by creating processes that allow them to experience both the constraining and generative powers of forms.

Learning socially significant forms--and understanding how they function, how to use them appropriately--is a key to success (sometimes even to survival) in a discourse community. This is perhaps particularly so in schools, for schools serve in part to teach such forms, or at least to weed out those who do not know them. As Frances Christie argues,

> Those who fail in schools are those who fail to master the genres of schooling: the ways of structuring and of dealing with experience which schools value in varying ways (24; cf. Heath).

So it matters that we continue to teach the basic forms which constitute a condition of access to professional discourse, and hence to professional communities, in modern societies. But it also matters that we discuss these forms, as any others, in terms of their functions in various writing processes (cf. Figure 1 above): how they serve (or limit) the creative process, how they enable (or disable) communication, how they structure what happens in our minds, how they mesh with social processes.

Like other rhetorical factors, form should be taught in context, in terms of appropriateness and effectiveness. When teaching such standard forms as the thesis paragraph (i.e., thesis statement + partition used to prefigure the argument), it matters that we explain the importance of this form in academic (and other professional) discourse, make clear why it predominates in certain types of discourse (academic, scientific, professional--and textbooks). We should validate (and limit) this form by showing that it makes a certain type of critical reading easier because proofs can be evaluated more easily if readers know in advance what they purportedly prove, because information can be taken in more efficiently if one knows in advance the outline of what is to be learned. In this way, we should put whatever forms we teach in functional rhetorical context.

Figure 3. Basic Patterns of Arrangement

	SYNCHRONIC PATTERNS	PROGRESSIVE PATTERNS
REPORT PATTERNS	Description	Narration
EXPLANATORY PATTERNS	Comparison/contrast Classification and division Definition Analogy and exemplification	Process-analysis Causal explanation Logical progression

Though we might wish to emphasize patterns relevant to our students' educational, professional and humane purposes, we can begin with the standard formal *patterns of development,* largely on the hypothesis that they correspond with basic patterns of thought (cf. D'Angelo, *Conceptual Theory* 28-29, 42-47, 53-59; Berthoff 38-45). The main innovation is to treat the formal patterns as representing mental functions and to place them functionally within the creative process.

I start with narration and description, modes in which the structure of the text is ordinarily shaped to a significant extent by the chronology of the story being narrated or the arrangement of what is being described. Studies in contrastive rhetoric demonstrate that even narrative and description are not simple reflections of reality; on the contrary, they vary significantly from one culture to another. (To cite just one example, place is very important in the stories of aboriginal Australians, but it is stated near the end; when those stories are translated for Anglo Australians, the translators generally move the statement of place to the beginning, where English narrative form demands it.) There is, nonetheless, a sense in which the arrangements of narrative and description are shaped by the structure of their subject matter to a greater extent than are the arrangements of more abstract modes. The cognitive task of arrangement is, therefore, easier in these modes, and so I do start with them.

Thence I follow traditional pedagogy to comparison/contrast, the thought structure of which may be represented by the grid in Figure 4. Obviously, this structure focuses attention, hence invention, toward a particular task (i.e., toward comparing and contrasting). Students instructed to compare and contrast generate different substance than would students instructed to, say, describe and exemplify. Thus teaching this pattern of development teaches a heuristic technique; already the formalists' static conception of form is sublated. (Is not the grid in Figure 4 just as much a heuristic as the tagmemic grid?)

Figure 4. Comparison/Contrast.

	Subject A	Subject B
Characteristic 1:		
Characteristic 2:		
Characteristic 3:		
Characteristic 4:		
Characteristic 5:		
Characteristic 6:		
. . .		
Characteristic N:		

But there are further implications because two distinct rhetorical forms can be used to communicate comparison/contrast. In the half-and-half format, composition moves vertically down the grid: Subject A is described first, then Subject B is compared and contrasted. In the alternating characteristics format, composition moves horizontally: each characteristic of Subject A is compared and/or contrasted with Subject B before the next characteristic is raised.

How boring! No, because even in a case such as this the choice of rhetorical format may significantly affect the substance of what gets invented. Ask a writer who has used the half-and-half format to reformulate using the alternating characteristics format, and the message will sometimes change. First, the close juxtaposition of each comparison/contrast point often leads writers to notice that they have left something out. Second, and more significantly, when the rhetorical format forces close juxtaposition, writers sometimes decide that an example, or even the point, is not so strong as they thought. For an instance of what happened to one student's literary critical essay when she was assigned to reformulate it in this way, (see Coe, *Form* 238-41).

A more interesting exercise of the same type involves the juxtaposition of two rhetorical forms that serve the same general purpose. For instance, one can juxtapose Classical and Rogerian persuasion. It quickly grows obvious to students that the choice of a form for persuasion affects both tone and substance. I effect the juxtaposition this way:

1. First, I ask students to pair themselves with someone with whom they can agree on a thesis for a persuasive writing. Each pair must submit a single thesis statement.

2. Working in pairs, using Aristotle's *topoi,* brainstorming, and whatever other invention techniques they wish, each pair of students invents as many arguments as they can in support of their chosen thesis.

3. One student of each pair elects to try the Classical form, the other to try the Rogerian form. Each chooses an appropriate audience, i.e., a group of potential readers who would (a) initially disagree with the thesis, and (b) effectively be addressed by whichever form that student has elected. (Note that the exercise is inevitably artificial here: in real world writing situations, writers generally know the audience first, choose an appropriate form second--and the nature of the audience is usually an important factor in the invention of arguments.)

4. Each student submits a brief audience analysis, outlining the relevant knowledge, beliefs, and vested interests of the chosen audience. On the basis of this audience analysis, each selects arguments from those the pair has invented, adds any others that might be suggested by the nature of the audience, and writes a persuasion using the elected format.

5. The persuasions are read and criticized (in terms of how well they are likely to persuade the chosen audiences). They are then revised.

6. To discover how audience and form have influenced the tone and substance, we do comparison/contrast of persuasions written from the same corpus of invented arguments to support the same thesis.

Quite a number of birds get hit by this one assignment: learning to work with another writer, at least through the stage of invention; developing the ability to empathize with and analyze an audience; learning two rhetorical forms for organizing persuasion; learning something about the relationship between audience and rhetorical structure; developing some control of tone and understanding of the relationship between audience and tone; and learning something, hands on, about the relationship between form and substance.

It is important that students understand composition *as a forming process.* As Ann Berthoff argues,

> Composing is like an organic process, not an assembly line on which some prefabricated parts are fitted together. However, plants and animals don't just "grow" mystically, developing from seed to flower and fully framed creatures, without plan or guidance or system. All organic processes are forms in action: the task of the composer is to find the forms that find forms; the structures that guide and encourage growth; the limits by means of which development can be shaped. [This] method of composing ... is a way of making meanings by using the forms provided by language to re-present the relationships we see. (153)

The curriculum and pedagogy championed by Berthoff exemplifies this emphasis. For pedagogical examples, see *forming/thinking/writing* (50-62, on classifying, and 94-100, on defining); cf. Berthoff, "The Intelligent Eye and the Thinking Hand," in Hays et al.

In North America, at least, Francis Christensen is the best-known early proponent of teaching what I call *generative form.* First on the level of the sentence, then on the level of the paragraph, and posthumously (through his followers) on the level of the whole piece of writing, Christensen taught form as "generative rhetoric." If one teaches students the form of the cumulative sentence, replete with "loose" or free modifiers, he argued, the students will generate the material to fill "empty" modifier slots in their sentences. Thus their writing will acquire what Christensen termed "texture": details, examples, reasons, qualifiers, etc. Comparable lessons on the paragraph level will motivate them to generate that form of texture writing teachers hake traditionally called good or full "development." (For pedagogical examples and detailed discussion, see Christensen's articles on generative rhetoric and his *Rhetoric Program,* the cited articles by Grady, D'Angelo, Nold and Davis, and Shaughnessy's chapter, "Beyond the Sentence," in *Errors and Expectations.*)

Taking this lesson one step further, I will argue that a new form often must be created in order to express a radically new idea--and that knowing a form with which an idea can be articulated improves the likelihood of thinking that idea. Teaching a new form is a pedagogy often used to encourage a new *form of discourse.* Before reading Richards, I used to call this, "New Forms for New Content." Oppressed social groups often find it necessary to invent new forms because the socially dominant forms will not readily carry their ideas. Several examples of this kind of formal invention can be found in the work of feminists.

There is, for instance, the formula for constructive criticism, synthesized by U.S. feminists from humanistic psychology and Mao Zedung's essay on criticism/self-criticism, that I find tremendously useful in my composition classes. The formula, simply, is:

When you _____, I feel/think _____, so I wish you would _____ instead.

When you tell me my writing is "incoherent, ungrammatical and confused," *I feel* stupid, discouraged, and angry, *so I wish you would* make more specific and constructive criticisms *instead.*

This formula has two virtues: (a) it encourages constructive criticism (rather than blaming criticism) by helping to keep criticism specific, making it clear that a particular action (not the whole person) is being criticized, focusing attention on the effect of the criticized action and forcing the critic to indicate what can be done about the criticism; and (b) by providing an appropriate structure, the formula makes it easier for people to express criticisms. Indeed, if one looks at feminist assertiveness training, one sees that providing appropriate forms is one of the most important techniques for enabling a new kind of communication.

This same principle can be applied to teaching the standard rhetorical patterns of development. I have done so frequently, especially when asserting that the traditional cause-to-effect pattern should be complemented with instruction in causal explanation by constraints. Explanation by constraints focuses more attention on context as a possible locus of cause and motive, thus improving students' ability to think and communicate about organized complexity (e.g., about human motives, human societies, ecosystems).[55] A similar argument can be made that while the standard forms of Western thought are effective for thinking about stasis and essences, teaching the form of reasoning and communication embodied by the Hegelian/Marxist dialectic (or even the Taoist/Zen Buddhist dialectic) helps people think and communicate more effectively about process and change.

Though the kind of instruction I am describing is in a significant sense a formal and sublates certain aspects of traditional formal curricula, it is worlds (or, more accurately, levels) away from traditional static formalism. For it places form in the context of various processes: creative, communicative, mental, social, and learning. Thus formalism is not rejected, but subordinated to process. And we create a kind of process approach that encompasses and transforms formalism, rather than simply opposing it.

---

[5]   5. The essence of this argument is that the cause-to-effect pattern of development taught in traditional composition courses overestimates the extent to which occurrences are explainable as the result of prior events that actively "caused" them and underestimates the sense in which certain types of occurrences are better explained as responses or adaptations to contexts. The theory of evolution is an excellent example of an idea invented because its inventor stopped tooking for "causes" and started looking at contexts. The increasing tendency in various practical and academic disciplines to discuss causation in terms of "parameters:" "restraints" and "constraints"indicates increasing awareness that contextual factors are crucial for explaining events and decisions shaped by organized complexity. Contextual factors are qualitatively different from mechanistic causes, but it is difficult to emphasize, communicate or even think about that qualitative difference while using the cause-to-effect pattern of development. See especially Coe "Closed System Composition," "Rhetoric 2001," and "Causation" in *Form and Substance* (300-20). CE Bateson (399-410), the discussion of scenic factors in Burke'S *Grammar* (esp., xv-vii, 3-7, 127-70), and of order and hierarchy in Burke's *Rhetoric* (Part III).

What I am advocating is that we teach this New Rhetorical kind of process writing. That in part through theory, but mostly through hands-on practice, we help our students develop an awareness of form as simultaneously constraining and generative that will empower them to understand, use, and even invent new forms for new purposes.

Note on the article's authorship as of 1987. Richard M. Coe, author of the innovative text, *Form and Substance,* was teaching at Simon Fraser University. He was also currently working on the "grammar" of passages and the rhetoric of form.

WORKS CITED

Bateson, Gregory. *Steps to an Ecology of Mind.* New York: Ballantine, 1972.

Berlin, James A. "Contemporary Composition: The Major Pedagogical Theories." *College English* 44 (1982): 765-77.

Berthoff, Ann E. *forming/thinking/writing.* Rochelle Park, NJ: Hayden, 1978.

Burke, Kenneth. *Counter-Statement.* 1931. Berkeley: U of California P, 1968.

_____. *A Grammar of Motives.* 1945. Berkeley: U of California P, 1969.

_____. *Language as Symbolic Action.* Berkeley: U of California P, 1966.

_____. *A Rhetoric of Motives.* 1950. Berkeley: U of California P, 1969.

_____. *The Philosophy of Literary Form.* 1941. New York: Vintage, 1957.

Christensen, Francis. *The Christensen Rhetoric Program.* New York: Harper, 1966.

_____. "A Generative Rhetoric of the Paragraph." *College Composition and Communication* 16 (1965): 144-56.

_____. "A Generative Rhetoric of the Sentence." *College Composition and Communication* 14 (1963): 155-61.

Christie, Frances. "Language and Schooling." *Language, Schooling and Society.* Ed. Stephen Tchudi. Upper Montclair, NJ: Boynton, 1985. 21-40.

Coe, Richard M. "Closed System Composition." *ETC., A Review of General Semantics* 32 (1975): 403-12.

_____. *Form and Substance.* New York: Wiley: Scott, 1981.

"If Not to Narrow, Then How to Focus." *College Composition and Communication* 32 (1981): 272-77.

_____. "Literacy 'Crises': A Systemic Analysis." *Humanities in Society* 4 (1981): 363-78.

_____. Rhetoric 2001. " *Freshman English News* 3.1 (1974): 1-13.

D'Angelo, Frank. *A Conceptual Theory of Rhetoric.* Cambridge, MA: Winthrop, 1975.

_____. "A Generative Rhetoric of the Essay." *College Composition and Communincation* 25 (1974): 388-96.

De Beaugrande, Robert. *Text, Discourse, and Process: Toward a Multidisciplinary Science of Texts.* Norwood, NJ: Ablex, 1980.

Faigley, Lester. "Competing Theories of Process: A Critique and a Proposal." *College English* 48 (1986): 527-42.

Fort, Keith. "Form, Authority, and the Critical Essay." *College English 33* (1971): 629-39.

Goffman, Erving. *Frame Analysis.* New York: Harper, 1974.

Grady, Michael. "A Conceptual Rhetoric of the Composition." *College Composition and Communication* 22 (1971): 348-54.

_____. "On Teaching Christensen Rhetoric." *English Journal* 61 (1972): 859 +.

Hays, Janice N., et al., eds. *The Writer's Mind: Writing as a Mode of Thinking.* Urbana: NCTE, 1983.

Heath, Shirley Brice. *Way with Words: Language, Life, and Work in Communities and Classrooms.* Cambridge, Cambridge UP, 1983.

Kinsch, Walter. "On Modeling Comprehension." *Literacy, Society, and Schooling.* Ed. Suzanne de Castell, Allan Luke, and Kieran Egan. Cambridge, UK: Cambridge UP, 1986.

Kojeve, Alexandre. *Introduction to the Reading of Hegel.* Tran. J.H. Nichols, Jr. New York: Basic, 1969.

Macrorie, Ken. *Telling Writing.* 3rd ed. Rochelle Park, NJ: Hayden, 1980.

Murray, Donald M. "Talking to Yourself: The Reason Writers Write." Opening Sess. Wyoming Conference on Freshman and Sophomore English. Laramie, 24 June 1985.

Nold, Ellen W., and Brent E. Davis. "The Discourse Matrix." *College Composition and Communication* 31 (1980): 141-52.

178   Form and Organization -- Larger Elements

Perelman, Les. "The Context of Classroom Writing," *College English* 48 (1986): 471-79.

Richards, I.A. *The Philosophy of Rhetoric.* London: Oxford, 1936.

Shaughnessy, Mina. *Errors and Expectations.* New York: Oxford, 1977.

Shultz, John. "Story Workshop." *Research on Composing.* Ed. Charles Cooper and Lee Odell. Urbana: NCTE, 1978. 151-87.

Strunk, William, and E.B. White. *The Elements of Style.* New York: Macmillan, 1959.

Waldrep, Tom, ed. *Writers on Writing.* New York: Random, 1985.

Wayne, Don E. *Penshurst: The Semiotics of Place and the Poetics of History.* Madison: U of Wisconsin P, 1984.

Winterowd, W. Ross, ed. *Contemporary Rhetoric.* New York: Harcourt, 1975.

Young, Richard, Alton Becker, and Kenneth Pike. *Rhetoric: Discovery and Change.* New York: Harcourt, 1970.

What Makes a Text Coherent?

Betty Bamberg

Pedagogical interest in coherence has its roots in the nineteenth century, its probable beginnings in Alexander Bain's first rule of the paragraph: "The bearing of each sentence upon what precedes shall be explicit and unmistakable."[1] By the end of the nineteenth century coherence, along with unity and emphasis, was an established canon of paragraph structure. The view of coherence in some of today's popular composition texts still closely resembles Bain's original formulation. For example, McCrimmon's *Writing With a Purpose,* one of the most widely used freshman composition texts, defines coherence as follows:

> A paragraph is coherent when the reader can move easily from one sentence to the next and read the paragraph as an integrated whole, rather than a series of separate sentences.

McCrimmon then advises writers to make paragraphs coherent by weaving sentences together with "such connective devices as pronouns, repetitive structures, contrast, and transitional markers.[2]

Coherence is generally accepted as a *sine qua non* in written discourse; writing that lacks coherence will almost certainly fail to communicate its intended message to a reader. Even though most composition texts and rhetorics have routinely included a section on coherence, interest in this topic has intensified during the last five years. In part, this increased interest grows out of linguistic research, which has evolved from a focus on the sentence to a consideration of "texts," or extended sections of discourse. But the interest also arises from the renewed emphasis on writing instruction and the recognition, in writing instruction, that many problems in writing require attention at the level of the whole discourse rather than at the level of the word of sentence.

In 1975, as we began to see other evidence of a decline in students' writing skills, the National Assessment of Educational Progress (NAEP) reported that the average level of performance on one of their writing tasks had decreased significantly between 1969 and 1974. Students had been asked to write an impromptu essay describingsomething they knew about "so that it could be recognized by someone who has read your description." NAEP's preliminary analysis of these essays concluded that lack of coherence contributed substantially to the lower scores received by the 1974 essays.[3] Although NAEP's analysis of these essays identified coherence as a major problem, it could offer no guidelines for writing instruction because the essays had not been analyzed to determine what difficulties in the texts might be described as "lack of coherence." To identify these difficulties, I recently read over 800 essays written by thirteen- and seventeen-year-olds for the 1974 Assessment. I was particularly interested in the essays written by seventeen-year-olds because their writing was likely to be close to the level of writing of freshman composition students.

Betty Bamberg. "What Makes a Text Coherent?" *College Composition and Communication,* December 1983. Copyright © 1983 by the National Council of Teachers of English. Reprinted with permission.

interested in the essays written by seventeen-year-olds because their writing was likely to be close to the level of writing of freshman composition students. My first reading of the essays made clear that the traditional view of coherence derived from Bain was too limited to account for the coherence problems I found. This traditional view treats coherence as a phenomenon somewhat similar to what many linguists and rhetoricians now call cohesion. In *Cohesion in English,* Halliday and Hasan define "cohesion" as a relationship between two textual elements in which one is interpreted by the other. For example, in the sentence "He said so," "He" and "so" presuppose something that has gone before. We cannot interpret this sentence (as opposed to decoding it) unless we can relate "He" and "so" to words in a preceding sentence. Such relationships between words create cohesive "ties" and allow us to differentiate sentences that constitute a "text" from sequences of unrelated sentences. Halliday and Hasan define a text as "a semantic unit: a unit not of form but of meaning..." that "may be anything from a single proverb to a whole play."[4]

However, this view of "cohesion" differs from the traditional concept of coherence as presented by Bain. His formulation of "coherence" stressed between-sentence connections that created tightly-structured, autonomous paragraphs which were then linked together into a larger text by transitions. As discussed by Halliday and Hasan, however, "cohesive" ties often connect adjacent sentences (or more precisely, adjacent T-units), but they may also connect "remote" rather than "immediate" sections of text. In a "remote" tie, the cohesive elements are separated by at least one t-unit and may extend across paragraph boundaries. "Cohesion," therefore, describes a linguistic system that extends through the text and binds together larger chunks of discourse, in addition to forming smaller discourse units.

Research and theory in discourse analysis now view cohesive ties as part of what makes a text coherent; however, these ties are not, by themselves, sufficient to create coherent text. After analyzing cohesive ties in student essays, Steven Witte and Lester Faigley differentiated between cohesion and coherence, concluding that "coherence defines those underlying semantic relations that allow a text to be understood and used" and "coherence conditions are governed by the writer's purpose, the audience's knowledge and expectations, and the information to be conveyed."[5] The text linguist T.A. van Dijk points out that cohesive ties create only "local" coherence (his term for cohesion) and are unable by themselves to create discourse-level or "global" coherence.[6] He illustrates the difference between local and global coherence in the following example:

> I bought this typewriter in New York. New York is a large city in the USA. Large cities often have serious financial problems....

Although this passage contains lexical cohesive ties--repetitions of "New York" and "large city"--readers will not consider the text as a whole to be coherent unless they can discover a broader topic that incorporates buying typewriters, large cities, and financial problems. Van Dijk further notes that essays, in addition to being unified around a theme or topic, must have an overall form or structure if readers are to find them coherent over the whole discourse.[7]

Research on artificial intelligence has found that we rely heavily on conventional structures of knowledge known as scripts, frames, or schema to organize experience and knowledge so that we can understand it.[8] A script may prescribe a sequence of actions to be followed in a particular situation. For example, in a restaurant we expect to order food from a menu, to be served by a waitress or waiter, and to pay for our meal after eating it. However, the restaurant script will vary, depending upon the type of restaurant we select. Buying a hamburger at MacDonald's follows a script different from ordering a meal at Howard Johnson's, and both differ from the script prescribed at Chasen's or Le Pavillon. Textual information also follows conventional patterns. Labov found that oral narratives could be divided into five parts: abstract, orientation, complication, resolution, and coda. More recently, a number of discourse theorists have constructed "story grammars" that describe narrative structure.[9] Scientific reports also have a predictable structure: they begin with an abstract and are then divided into introduction, method, results, and discussion. Form is more fluid in expository essays, but certain methods of development--classification, comparison/contrast--tend to provide familiar structures. Despite their different forms, all schema serve the same function: they help readers anticipate upcoming textual information, thereby enabling them to reduce and organize the text into an understandable and coherent whole.

The complexity of any inquiry into the sources of coherence is further increased by recent research on reading and on discourse comprehension, which shows that the reading process "constructs" a text and that the reader's prior knowledge--both conscious and tacit--affects the understanding of a text.[10] Meaning and coherence are not inscribed in the text, this research shows, but arise from readers' efforts to construct meaning and to integrate the details in the text into a coherent whole. Although readers are guided by textual cues, they also draw on their own knowledge and expectations to bridge gaps and to fill in assumed information. Louise Phelps argues that failures in coherence occur either because writers undercue- -provide too few cues for readers to let them perceive the relationships between parts of a text or because they miscue- -give conflicting or misleading cues.[11]

The interaction between text and reader and its effect on judgments about coherence can best be understood in the context of psycholinguistic reading theory. To comprehend a text, fluent readers do not read word for word, but, in what Kenneth Goodman has called a "psycholinguistic guessing game," predict meanings from graphic, semantic, and syntactic cues, sampling only enough of the text to confirm their predictions. They predict meaning from nonvisual information--their prior knowledge and expectations--as well as from the letters on the page.[12] For example, tacit knowledge of the English language (acceptable letter combinations and their relative frequency of occurrence, along with syntactic rules) helps readers predict the meanings of individual words by limiting the possible choices of meaning[13] Similarly, a knowledge of discourse conventions helps readers predict meaning and structure. Preschool children have learned that "once upon a time" signals the beginning of a story, and experienced readers of research reports are able to read an abstract and then turn to sections of interest, perhaps skipping the review of research or description of methodology and going directly to the results and discussion.

While reading, readers draw on their tacit knowledge at the level of the sentence and of the whole discourse by using a "top-down," "bottom-up" strategy. That is, as they process individual words and sentences at the beginning of a text, they attempt to form an overall conception of the structure and meaning of the whole text into which they can fit the information that follows.[14] This anticipation of structure and meaning, m turn, directs their guesses about individual words and phrases. Clearly stated topic sentences, an obvious organizational pattern, statements of topic and purpose, and headings which indicate divisions of the text--these are all cues that facilitate a reader's integration of details in a text into a coherent whole. When such cues are missing, readers may be unable to make this integration.

Theoretical discussions of coherence--whether of sentences or of a whole discourse--usually analyze hypothetical texts constructed to highlight the principles being considered. Although useful for theoretical discussions, these passages do not resemble the writing of our students, nor do they help us discover which coherence conditions students have the most difficulty meeting. Examining the presence or absence of coherence in student texts such as those written for the National Assessment can not only give us insights into students' difficulties in producing coherent texts, but can suggest ways for us to intervene productively in students' writing processes to help them write more coherently.

I had initially intended to compare a coherent and incoherent essays using ratings from the National Assessment analysis. The original NAEP analysis consisted of two parts; a holistic general impression score and a detailed description of specific features (particularly grammatical and mechanical errors) known as the "mechanics" scoring. Coherence ratings were given during the mechanics scoring; raters evaluated the coherence of each paragraph according to a set of criteria provided. In a preliminary analysis, I discovered that NAEP's rubric and scoring procedures for coherence rendered many of the coherence ratings invalid. To begin with, the analysts rated the coherence of individual paragraphs, so essay- or discourse-level coherence was not rated unless an essay consisted of a single paragraph. In addition, the coherence scoring guide did not include all coherence features, omitting particularly any consideration of overall structure or form, a feature often critical for coherence through the whole essay, and the guide also confounded coherence with paragraph development.[15] To overcome the limitations of NAEP's mechanics analysis. I developed a new rubric that assessed coherence at both the local (or sentence) and global (or discourse) levels. The rubric asked raters to focus on all textual features that affect coherence and to assign a holistic score for the entire essay, ignoring paragraph indentations and development. Results from these holistic ratings were then used to separate coherent from incoherent essays."[16]

The coherence scale I used to rescore the NAEP essays has the strengths as well as the weaknesses of other holistic scales. Although it reliably rank orders writing according to a set of criteria, it does not identify which features are present or missing in particular essays.[17] To identify specific features that result in perceived incoherence, I analyzed the coherence features in a subset of essays, looking for the presence or absence of linguistic features or rhetorical structures specified in the rubric. Not surprisingly, essays with coherence scores in the lower half lacked coherence between sentences and through the whole discourse:

He had huge body frame that obtain shock, bumps, cuts, but it is also in some ways powerful, smart, graceful like a dancer; quick on his feet, speed like lightning, a eye for direction and a mind that keep saying push on and fear of anybody. Hand that slap feet that are step, leg that are broken, arm that bend, and a head that get push in the ground, but into all of those thing a person that is determine to push on because glory is at the end.[18]

The perceived absence of local coherence in the essay above is due primarily to mechanical and grammatical errors, a type of miscue not usually considered in theoretical discussions of coherence. However, such errors do interfere with a reader's attempt to construct a text and integrate details into a coherent whole. The writer of the essay above left out thirteen inflectional endings, including five "ed" past tense verb endings, two third-person singular "s" verb endings, and eight noun plural "s" inflections. The writer also omitted words, ("had huge body frame," "fear of anybody") and used other unexpected words and phrases--"obtain shocks," "eye for direction," "into all of those." To process the text, readers must backtrack and reread to fill in missing words and grammatical inflections. Not only do the errors interfere with the processing of sentences, but readers' focus on individual words and letters distracts their attention from global cues.

However, editing the essay above to eliminate grammatical and mechanical errors would not make it coherent. The essay above illustrates a problem common even among 17-year-old writers: the writer failed to identify the topic--to tell the reader who or what the essay is about. Readers can infer that the essay is describing a large man ("he," "huge body frame") and find enough details to form some impressions of the man's physical and mental qualities, but they cannot identify him. The description suggests a fighter, but is it a particular fighter--Muhammed Ali or the hero of *Rocky* is it someone known only to the writer? Writers of incoherent essays often failed to identify their topic even though the instructions for the writing task reminded them to "name what you are describing." These writers apparently assumed that readers shared the information they possessed and that the topic was, therefore, "given" information.[19] Their descriptive details enabled readers to infer a superordinate term-man, building, monument, etc.--but not to identify the topic unless it was a very familiar object or place (i.e., the Statue of Liberty).

Writers of essays with clear topic statements, on the other hand, regarded the topic as new information that should be stated at the beginning of the essay. The most skillful writers not only identified their topic but provided an introduction that oriented the reader to the situation and placed the subject in context by identifying time, place, and circumstance.[20]

When you cross the Golden Gate Bridge from San Francisco to Sausalito, on your right you see an ominous object in the middle of the bay. It's an island called Alcatraz. Water smashes up against the rocks and gulls fly over this godforsaken, lonely, deserted prison. There are many buildings which now lay crumbling to ruins. A lone water tower juts up from the rest of the building. Once the buildings were white but now only gray buildings sun cracked remain.

It sits out in the middle of the San Francisco Bay by itself crying for it has been the ruin of many men. It was almost unescapable until it was shut down. The Indians took it over and much of it was burned and devastated in the early seventies. The only way to reach it was by small boat. No one was permitted on it unless given special governmental permission. In August 1974 it was opened to the public.

The description of Alcatraz begins successfully because the writer establishes the setting (San Francisco Bay) and the tone ("ominous object") in addition to identifying the topic. More often, writers announced the topic, but expected the reader to fill in the context:

I am describing an ancient Egyptian statue of the goddess Bastet. The statue is made of bronze, and is extremely old, dating back to perhaps 1087 b.c. The figure of Bastet is slender, with fine contours of the body. The goddess is cat-headed, with large erect ears and slanting eyes. She is wearing a tight-fitting sheath-like garment, which emphasizes her graceful female body and noble carriage. At her feet are several tiny bronze kittens.

The writer of the essay above clearly identifies her topic, even emphasizes it by setting it off as a paragraph, but fails to create a context for the description. A reader must draw on his world knowledge--ancient statues are usually viewed in museums- -to construct the context. Whether readers can construct a context will, of course, depend upon their background and their prior knowledge as well as on the information provided by the writer.

The "describe" topic tended to elicit from writers a list of attributes, a more difficult organizational structure for readers to process and recall than structures such as comparison, problem-solution, or cause-effect.[21] When writers failed to arrange these details according to an overall plan, readers often had difficulty integrating the details into a coherent whole. Writers of coherent essays used several different ordering plans to create a global structure. One effective arrangement orders descriptive details according to a plan of movement such as general to particular, whole to part, and container to contained.[22] The essay on Alcatraz begins with such a strategy: the writer first gives general statements describing the whole complex ("This godforsaken, lonely, deserted prison"), then moves to particular details describing parts of the prison ("buildings crumbling to ruins," "a lone water tower"). He does not sustain this order through the essay, however, and the last section simply lists events that occurred after the prison was closed. The writer who described Bastet arranges her description more effectively by sustaining the whole-to-part, general-to-particular plan throughout the essay and by arranging particular details describing the statue in a spatial order from top to bottom. The reader thus sees Bastet much as he might if standing before a glass case in a museum--first the whole statue, then her "cat's head," her "graceful female body," and finally the "tiny bronze kittens" at her feet.

The "riddle" structure was another plan used--with surprising frequency and varying success.[23] In "riddle" essays, the writer deliberately withheld the identity of the subject, listed attributes that would let the reader "guess" the subject, and optionally revealed the "answer" in the final sentence. Generally, riddle essays were judged coherent when the writer finally identified the topic or included enough description details to enable the reader to infer the subject. The most successful riddle essays did both, the final identification confirming the reader's guess.

Other writers organized descriptive details in the form of a "tour." In these essays the writer seemed to be taking the reader on a guided tour of the place being described, a strategy that transformed spatial information into a chronologically organized narrative.[24] In the essay below, the writer first created a context for the reader by narrating the events leading up to a family visit to Pala Dura Canyon and the initial stage of the trip. She began her tour as her family's car entered the canyon:

> As we entered the entrance gates of Pala Dura we could gaze down and look at the tall trees and cliffs which were much lower than we were. The narrow paved road was built on the side of a mountain and the far side was protected by guard railings. Many signs were up warning tourists not to park on this road because of the possibility of falling rocks. As we continued on down the road our ears soon became stopped up because of the rapid decrease in altitude. When we finally reached the bottom of the canyon, we could look up and see what we had seen coming down.

By carefully signalling each stage of the tour through the canyon--"As we entered the entrance gates"; "As we continued on down the road"; "When we finally reached the bottom of the canyon" The writer recreated the visit for readers, thereby providing a narrative sequence into which descriptive details could be woven.

The whole-to-part, riddle, and tour plans used to arrange descriptive details share a common feature: they are structures of knowledge familiar in our experience and are thus ready accessible to both writers and readers. The whole-to-part, general-to-particular and spatial orders reflect the way we normally perceive places or objects--first grasping the gestalt, then observing particulars, usually in a systematic spatial order. Riddles and tours, both part of the typical elementary school child's world, are well practiced and familiar patterns by age seventeen. Writers who failed to draw on these or other ordering strategies produced essays that were essentially lists of unordered details:

> It is a exciting place with characters such as Mickey Mouse or Donald Duck running around.
>
> The rides are fun, but the lines can become quite long. The rides all seem to be real. And in the president's Hall of Fame, the presidents actually breathe. When Lincoln is giving a speeches, two other president's turn toward each other and start whispering.
>
> The grounds are always clean. There are boys and girls who go around with a tray on a handle and brooms and pick up everything even cigerate butts.
>
> When you first go in, you buy a book of tickets. And when you ride something, you give them a ticket. Also, when you leave your motel, you ride on a monorail.
>
> The motels are nice. They both have heated pools and you can rent boats (peddle) and ride in the lagoon.
>
> The experience is well worth your time and your money. But it is better to go during school, so it won't be as crowded.

Although many readers can probably infer that the essay above is describing Disneyland, they will find no structure to help them organize the details. Even though each paragraph indentation signals a different set of descriptive details (the rides, the grounds, the motels, etc.), the details follow no logical, spatial, or temporal order. Placing them in separate paragraphs gives readers little help in integrating them into a coherent whole.

The failure of 17-year-olds to achieve coherence because of incomplete announcement of the topic, failure to establish a context, and/or selection of an inadequate organizational plan may seem surprising, particularly since the topic makes relatively low-level cognitive demands.[25] Essays on more complex topics often lack global or overall coherence because writers have not yet discovered the main point they wish to make about their subject or have not yet fully understood the relationships among their ideas. In most of the essays in this study, however, writers simply failed to give readers necessary information about the topic or to organize the details adequately.

Writers (students and others) may have difficulties in focusing on topic and selecting a plan of organization, or in creating a context for their readers, because they continue to struggle with the production of words and sentences. Fear of error can halt the flow of discourse and cripple a writer's attempts to project and sustain plans.[26] However, many essays lacking discourse-level coherence were not particularly error-ridden. (See, for example, the essay above that describes Disneyland.) These essays fit Linda Flower's description of "writer-based" prose: retaining an egocentric focus, ordering ideas with a narrative framework or merely listing them randomly in survey form, and relying on general "code" words or phrases that draw their meaning from the writer's individual experience and are, therefore, not accessible to readers. Flower views the composing of "writer-based" prose as a functional strategy because it allows writers to avoid overloading the short term memory, lets them concentrate on retrieving information from memory, and postpones the task of forming complex concepts or considering the reader's needs. Flower argues that "writer-based" prose should be seen as a "half-way place," writing that can later be transformed into reader-based prose that takes into account the reader's needs and purpose in reading.[27] Accordingly, impromptu essays such as these should be regarded as first drafts, not as the best writing that students can produce.

Nevertheless, the writing elicited by the topic illustrates a full range of writing skills among 17-year-olds. The better writers were able to take the reader's perspective from the beginning and produced well-structured, coherent essays. This ability seems to be a consequence of both the writer's skill and experience and the relative lack of difficulty in the writing task. Based on the holistic ratings of coherence, the percentage of students able to write coherent or partially coherent first drafts on this topic increased from 39% to 51% between ages 13 and 17, a reflection of the writers' developing control over written discourse. However, some writers of coherent first drafts on this topic would almost certainly be unable to duplicate their success if given a conceptually more demanding topic. The National Assessment's first analysis of mechanics found that essays written in 1974 contained fewer coherent paragraphs than those written in 1969,[28] and some "back-to-the-basics" critics interpreted these results as further justification for more instruction in grammar and in production of correct sentences. But another look at the failures of coherence in these essays indicates that the most serious coherence problems occurred over the whole discourse.

The difficulties students experienced in writing coherent essays for the National Assessment give us a starting point for identifying ways in which we can intervene in students' composing processes to help them produce more coherent texts. Essays that have only local coherence problems can often be improved by careful editing or proofreading--adding words and phrases to make relationships between sentences more explicit or correcting mechanical errors that interfere with the reading process. However, essays that are incoherent overall almost always require major restructuring and rewriting to provide the unity, organization, and identification of context needed by a reader.

Writers cannot always take the reader's perspective during their initial planning and drafting, but they can revise their first efforts into coherent texts if they know what makes a text coherent and know how to revise so that a text meets those conditions for coherence. However, research on revision indicates that most student writers do not revise effectively. They revise primarily sentences or words, making minor adjustments that are largely cosmetic or have a minimal effect on the text. Others, especially weaker writers, edit their work prematurely and are unable to sustain their focus on a topic or maintain a plan of organization. Only a few seem able to make the substantive changes that would convert writer-based to reader-based prose.[29]

If producing writer-based prose is to be for students a functional goal of composing, we must be able to teach them to revise effectively. Finding effective teaching strategies, however, is not easy. Peer group reading of essays in progress, one of the most frequently recommended techniques derived from research on the writing process, promotes effective revision by helping students internalize the needs of readers. It not only gives them responses to their writing from a real audience, but also makes them aware of the needs of that audience as readers when they respond to essays written by their fellow students. Peer readers are particularly good at pointing out places where more detail or information is needed in order to orient readers or to fill in gaps in the text, where terms are unclear, where connections between sentences need to be more explicit, and where digressions or shifts of topic occur. But although peer readers can often identify poor organization as a problem, they are less often able to propose a plan or overall design that will eliminate the difficulty.

Both composition teachers and textbook writers recognize the importance of organization. But, like peer readers, both groups are often unable to help students find satisfactory designs for their essays. Perhaps the best known attempt to propose an essay structure which students can start with has resulted in the Procrustean formula for the five-paragraph essay, a prescription rightly rejected as too rigid and limiting. Nevertheless, the most successful NAEP essays were those in which writers projected and sustained an overall design--such as the whole-to-part and tour plans--that controlled the entire essay. But even though these plans successfully organize descriptive details, they are likely to have limited applicability to other types of writing. They could not, for example, serve as adequate designs for the more analytic expository and persuasive discourse commonly demanded by universities and businesses. Moreover, the NAEP essays were quite short, and longer essays attempting more complex tasks may need to draw at various times on several different plans to organize their information.

Writers need to learn practical and flexible strategies that will help them organize the information in their essays--even when these are fairly short--and to learn ways to help readers remain aware of these plans.[30]

When we look at coherence in its broadest sense, we become aware that almost any feature--whether seen locally or over the whole discourse--has the potential to affect a reader's ability to integrate details of a text into a coherent whole. But although effective writing will be coherent at both levels, attention to overall coherence must precede most concerns about local coherence. First drafts are likely to have global or overall coherence only when the writing task is routine or when it makes relatively low-level cognitive demands. Our goal as writing teachers must be to create a classroom setting that enables students to understand what makes a text coherent and to teach them ways of revising their writing to meet those conditions.

Note on the article's authorship as of 1983: Betty Bamberg served as Director of the USC/California Writing Project and Programs for Freshman Writing. She has published essays in *Research in the Teaching of English, College English, and California English.* The work reported in this essay is part of a larger study on coherence in the writing of thirteen- and seventeen-year-olds, funded by the NCTE Research Foundation.

NOTES

1. Bain's six paragraph rules first appeared in the 1866 edition of *English Composition and Rhetoric,* a manual designed for his classes at the University of Aberdeen. All six rules, adapted from the 1866 and 1887 editions, are restated in Ned A. Shearer, "Alexander Bain and the Genesis of Paragraph Theory," *Quarterly Journal of Speech,* 58 (December, 1972), 413. For a discussion of these rules and the development of paragraph theory in the second half of the nineteenth century, see Paul C. Rodgers, Jr., "Alexander Bain and the Rise of the Organic *Paragraph,"Quarterly Journal of Speech,* 51 (December, 1965), 399-408.
2. *Writing With a Purpose, Short Edition* (Boston: Houghton Mifflin Company, 1980), pp. 104-110.
3. National Assessment of Educational Progress, *Writing Mechanics 1969-1974,* Writing Report No. 05-W-01. (Washington, D.C.; U.S. Government Printing Office, 1975).
4. *Cohesion in English* (London: Longman, 1976), pp. 1-30.
5. "Coherence, Cohesion, and Writing Quality," *College Composition and Communication, 32* (May, 1981), 189-204.
6. See van Dijk's discussion in *Macrostructures* (Hillsdale, NJ: Lawrence Erlbaum Associates, 1980), pp. 32-46. Local coherence differs from cohesion in that, for local coherence, logical relationships between sentences need not be explicitly stated. In this essay, I am using Van Dijk's more inclusive term "local coherence" rather than Halliday and Hasan's term "cohesion."
7. Teun A. van Dijk, *Text and Context: Explorations in the Semantics and Pragmatics of Discourse* (London: Longmans, 1977). p. 149.
8. Roger Schank and Robert Abelson, *Scripts, Plans, Goals and Understanding,* (Hillsdale, NJ: Lawrence Erlbaum Associates, 1977).
9. "The Transformation of Experience in Narrative Syntax," *Language in the Inner City: Studies in the Black English Vernacular* (Philadelphia: University of Pennsylvania Press, 1972), pp. 354-396. One of the earliest and best known story grammars is David Rumelhart, "Notes on a Schema for Stories," in D. Bobrow and A. Collins, ed., *Representation and Understanding* (New York: Academic Press, 1975), pp. 237-272. For a recent summary of this research see Teun A. van Dijk, "Story Comprehension: An Introduction," *Poetics 9* (June, 1980), 1-21.
10. Marcel Just and Patricia Carpenter, eds., *Cognitive Processes in Comprehension (Hillsdale,* NJ.: Lawrence Erlbaum Assoc., 1977).
11. "Rethinking Coherence: A Conceptual Analysis and Its Implications for Teaching Practice," in Marilyn Sternglass and Douglas Buttruff, ed., *Building the Bridge Between Reading and Writing,* (Conway, AR: L&S Books, in press).

12. "Reading: A Psycholinguistic Guessing Game," in Doris V. Gunderson, ed., *Language and Reading* (Washington, D.C.: Center for Applied Linguistics, 1970), pp. 107-119.

13. Frank Smith, *Understanding Reading* (New York: Holt, Rinehart & Winston, 1971).

14. Marilyn Adams and Allan Collins, "A Schema-Theoretic View of Reading," in Roy O.Freedle, ed., *New Directions in Discourse Processing, Vol. 2* (Norwood, NJ: Ablex Publishing Co., 1979), pp. 1-21.

15. In the "1974 Mechanics Scoring Guide" (mimeo, 12 pp., n.d.), paragraph coherence was defined as "the interconnectedness among sentences and among the ideas of those sentences." The scoring guide listed four major ways of achieving coherence: (1) consistency in time, voice, person, number, subject; (2) clear pronoun reference; (3) use of transitional markers; and (4) use of rhetorical strategies such as lexical repetition, parallel structure, antithesis. Paragraphs were both coherent and developed if, in addition to meeting the above criteria, they had an expressed or implied topic sentence that "identifies and limits the central area of concern in the paragraph" with each subsequent sentence adding to or explaining something about the main idea in an orderly manner. Paragraphs which were "neither coherent nor developed" according to the criteria above, along with most one-sentence paragraphs, were grouped into a category labeled "Paragraph Used." This amorphous term allowed NAEP to group together paragraphs that lacked coherence and paragraphs in which the indentation was essentially a graphic device. The number of paragraphs in this last category was used by the National Assessment to estimate the level of coherence in National Assessment essays. A short form of the scoring guide may be found in *Writing Mechanics 1969-1974*, 1975.

16. Essays meeting the following criteria were rated "fully coherent" (4) on the four point holistic coherence rubric: writer identifies the topic; writer does not shift topics or digress; writer orients the reader by describing the context or situation; writer organizes details according to a discernible plan that is sustained throughout the essay; writer skillfully uses cohesive ties such as lexical cohesion, conjunction, reference, etc. to link sentences and/or paragraphs together; writer often concludes with a statement that gives the reader a definite sense of closure; writer makes few or no grammatical and/or mechanical errors that interrupt the discourse flow or the reading process. Essays that were partially coherent (3) met enough of the criteria above so that a reader could make at least a partial integration of the text. Essays were rated incoherent (2) when some of the following prevented a reader from integrating the text into a coherent whole: writer does not identify the topic and the reader would be unlikely to infer or guess the topic from the details provided; writer shifts topics or digresses frequently from the topic; writer assumes the reader shares his/her context and provides little or no orientation; writer has no organizational plan in most of the text and frequently relies on listing; writer uses few cohesive ties such as lexical cohesion, conjunction, reference, etc. to link sentences and/or paragraphs together; writer creates no sense of closure; writer makes numerous mechanical and/or grammatical errors, resulting in interruption of the reading process and a rough or irregular discourse flow. Essays receiving the lowest score (1) were literally incomprehensible because missing or misleading cues prevented readers from making sense of the text. Inter-rater reliability on the holistic rescoring was .85. Although the holistic scores and original NAEP coherence ratings overlapped, almost 40% of the 17-year-olds' essays containing one or more paragraphs not given a "coherent" rating by NAEP were reclassified as coherent by the holistic scoring. Most of these essays contain brief one- or two-sentence paragraphs that were on the topic and fit into the overall organization of the essay but were excluded from NAEP's "coherent" paragraph category because of their brevity.

17. For a discussion of holistic and other types of evaluation scales, see Lee Odell and Charles Cooper, "Procedures for Evaluating Writing: Assumptions and Needed Research," *College English*, 42 (September, 1980), 35-43.

18. This and all subsequent essays used as examples were written by 17-year-olds for the 1974 National Assessment. Essays are transcribed exactly, including all grammatical and mechanical errors. Essays from the *Writing Mechanics Analysis* are available on computer tape from the Education Commission of the States, Suite 700, 1860 Lincoln Street; Denver, Colorado 80203.

19. Herbert Clark and Susan Haviland, "Comprehension and the Given-New Contract," in Roy O.Freedle, ed., *Discourse Production and Comprehension, Vol. 1* (Norwood, NJ: Ablex Publishing Co., 1977), pp. 1-39.

20. Teun A. van Dijk discusses state descriptions (descriptions of places or static objects) and the importance of creating a context in *Macrostructures*, p. 35.

21. Bonnie J. Meyer, "What is Remembered From Prose: A Function of Passage Structure," in Roy O. Freedle, Ed., *Discourse Production and Comprehension, Vol. 1* (Norwood, NJ: Ablex Publishing Co., 1977), pp. 307-336.

22. Van Dijk, *Macrostructures*, p. 35.

23. Colleen Aycock and Kevin O'Connor, two graduate students at the University of Southern California, first identified the riddle plan in these essays.

24. My use of this term is taken from a study by Charlotte Linde and William Labov, "Spatial Networks as a Site for the Study of Language and Thought," *Language*, 51 (December, 1975), 924-939. Almost all (97%) of the New Yorkers asked to describe the layout of their apartment used a tour plan. Readers of transcribed

apartment tours often found them confusing and hard to follow, perhaps because of the complex spacial relationships. In the NAEP essays the tour plan was usually an effective organizational structure.

25. In *The Development of Writing Abilities (11-18)*, (London: MacMillan Education Ltd., 1975), James Britton divides transactional writing into seven categories according to level of abstraction. Within his divisions, most of the "describe" essays would be classified at the second level, report, and a few at the next level up, generalized narrative.

26. Mina Shaughnessy, *Errors and Expectations* (New York: Oxford University Press, 1977) and Sondra Perl, "The Composing Processes of Unskilled College Writers," *Research in the Teaching of English*, 13 (December, 1979), 317-336, document this phenomenon from different perspectives.

27. "Writer-Based Prose, A Cognitive Basis for Problems in Writing," *College English*, 41 (September, 1979), 19-37.

28. *Writing Mechanics Report*, 1975.

29. For research on students' revision strategies see Richard Beach, "Self-Evaluation Strategies of Extensive Revisers and Nonrevisers," *College Composition and Communication*, 27 (May, 1976), 160-164; Nancy Sommers, "Revision Strategies of Student Writers and Experienced Adult Writers," *Cothgo Composition, and Communication* 31 (December, 1980), 378-388; and Lillian Bridwell, "Revising Strategies in Twelfth Grade Students' Transactional Writing," *Research in the Teaching of English*, 14 (October, 1980), 197-222.

30. In "Toward a Linear Rhetoric of the Essay," *College Composition and Communication* (May, 1971), 140-146, Richard Larson illustrates a method of essay analysis that focuses on writers' purposes as a way of perceiving their organizational plans. He suggests that this procedure may help students construct plans for their own writing. In a recent paper "Pragmatics of Form: In This Paper I Will Assert, Dispute, Confirm, Recount, and Recommend, presented at the Conference on College Composition and Communication, Dallas, March 1981, Marilyn Cooper links a writer's purposes to specific speech acts and discusses the conditions for their successful performance. She argues that a writees illocutionary intentions can be used to create a pragmatic form--that is, form conceived as a series of purposes to be achieved rather than simply a series of topics to be discussed.

The English Paragraph
Michael G. Moran

The word *paragraph* is derived from two Greek words, *para* meaning "beside," and *graph,* meaning "to write." In ancient Greek, the word means "to write beside," which gives a sense of the original concept of paragraphing: as ancient manuscripts show, scribes marked important passages with a marginal symbol to draw attention to their significance or to indicate some sort of break or shift. As E.G. Turner noted in *Greek Manuscripts of the Ancient World* (1971), the *paragraphus* appears in most ancient Greek manuscripts, and it serves a variety of functions and takes a variety of forms. It is used to separate verse from prose, to mark a change in speaker, to mark the end of a section of poetry, or to mark divisions within verse. Just as it serves many functions, the *paragraphus* took a myriad of forms, there being no single character to represent it in ancient manuscripts. In its earliest form it appeared as a single horizontal stroke, often with a dot over it. Edwin Herbert Lewis in *The History of the English Paragraph* (1894) traced the development of these marginal marks from the earliest to the modem reference mark ( ), which evolved, he speculated, from the Latin *P.* By the fifteenth century, however, the modern method of indenting the first sentence was fairly well established in English printing and prose.

Although the concept of the paragraph is ancient, scholars continue to debate its nature and function. Two major views have frequently appeared in various forms. One argues that the paragraph is a unit--either logical, rhetorical, linguistic, psychological, or a combination of them--that possesses an internal structure that can be described using a finite set of rules. The other view argues that the paragraph is a stretch of discourse that owes its existence to the larger requirements of the whole piece of prose. In this view, the paragraph does not exist as a separate entity but as a flexible and convenient method of marking some stage in a larger organic process. These two views appear in various forms throughout all periods of scholarly debate, although recently several scholars have attempted to synthesize the two. As of this writing, only two major bibliographies on the paragraph are in print. The first is Richard L. Larson's "Structure and Form in Non-Fiction Discourse" (1976), which reviews much of the important current theoretical work. The second, which is more extensive but only lightly annotated, is James P. Bennett and colleagues' "Paragraph" (1977). This list is concerned mostly with literary stylistics, although it does cite many sources for the teacher and researcher of composition.

Nineteenth-Century Paragraph Theory

Although the two early grammarians Lindley Murray, in *An English Grammar* (1808), and Joseph Angus, in *Handbook of the English Tongue* (1862), sketch rules of

Michael G. Moran. "The English Paragraph" from *Research in Composition and Rhetoric: A Bibliographic Sourcebook,* edited by Michael G. Moran and Ronald F. Lunsford, reprinted with permission of Greenwood Publishing Group, Inc., Westport, CT. Copyright © 1984 by Michael G. Moran and Ronald F. Lunsford.

paragraphing, the first rhetorician to discuss the device in detail is Alexander Bain in *English Composition and Rhetoric* (1867). He was the first to define the concept: "The division of discourse next higher than the sentence is the Paragraph: which is a collection of sentences with unity of purpose" (p. 142). This purpose, he noted, is to exhaust a particular subject, not to serve a communicative function.

Bain was also the first rhetorician to establish a set of rules for effective paragraphing. First, "the bearing of each sentence upon what precedes shall be explicit and unmistakable" (p. 142). Under this, he discussed a number of conjunctions and connectives that maintain coherence. Second, sentences illustrating or restating the same idea should be in the same, parallel structure. Third, the opening sentence should generally establish clearly the paragraph's subject. Fourth, each paragraph should "be consecutive, or free from dislocation" as dictated by the essay as a whole. Fifth, the paragraph should be unified and have a definite purpose that allows for no digressions. Sixth, the paragraph should maintain the proper relationship between ordinate and subordinate parts, to give it focus.

Contemporary writers have debated the validity of Bain's work. Paul C. Rodgers, Jr., in "Alexander Bain and the Rise of the Organic Paragraph" (1965), attacked Bain's notion of the topic sentence and his view that the paragraph is a logical unit. Rodgers argued that the rules grow from Bain's interest in logic and that writers do not always structure paragraphs that are logical units exhausting a single subject. Ned A. Shearer, however, in "Alexander Bain and the Genesis of Paragraph Theory" (1972), defended Bain by claiming that he was not the first to discuss the topic sentence and other paragraph rules (Murray and Angus preceded him) and that Bain's six rules grew not out of his study of logic but out of his interest in association psychology. Furthermore, the rules are consistent, useful, and psychologically valid.

Although Bain had introduced the concept, John G.R. McElroy introduced the term *topic sentence* to paragraph theory in *The Structure of English Prose* (1885). He was also the first to claim that the paragraph is "a whole composition in miniature," an assertion that continues to appear in modern textbooks (p. 196). Another early writer who made new observations is John Earle. In his *English Prose* (1890), he observed that the paragraph developed in part because of the shortness of English sentences. More prescriptively, he introduced the still common assertion that a paragraph must consist of at least three sentences.

After Bain, the most influential--and most idiosyncratic--of the early theorists is Barrett Wendell. In his *English Composition* (1891), originally a set of popular lectures delivered at the Lowell Institute, he stated the sentence-paragraph analogy that Bain had implied: "A Paragraph is to a sentence what a sentence is to a word" (p. 119). Even though this greatly simplifies the complexity of paragraph structure, the idea continues to influence current paragraph pedagogy. Wendell also applied the same three principles--unity, mass, and coherence--to the sentence, the paragraph, and the essay, although the principles function differently in each. He claimed that paragraphs, unlike sentences, are the results of *prevision,* not revision, a view that most contemporary rhetoricians concerned with the writing process reject.

Wendell's major contribution to paragraph theory is his concept of mass, one of his three principles. *Mass* is concerned with where, physically, in the paragraph significant ideas appear. He noted that the opening sentence is not the only place for important ideas, since the eye tends to fall on the end as well as the beginning of a passage. Furthermore, as a rule of thumb, writers should give more physical space to principal rather than to subordinate ideas. Thus the concern becomes one of number of words and amount of space on the page rather than one of syntactic relationship alone.

Another early theorist who contributed to paragraph theory is John F. Genung. In his *Practical Elements of Rhetoric* (1892), he was one of the first to argue that the paragraph functions as a unit of invention, and he developed a heuristic of the paragraph. This consists of three functions that the writer can use to develop a subject: definition of the subject, establishment of the subject, and application of the subject. Under each function, Genung listed several strategies that the writer can combine in many ways. In his revision of *Elements* entitled *The Working Principles of Rhetoric* (1900), he fell under the influence of other theorists who argue for the tight sentence-paragraph analogy. He consequently did not develop his insight into the paragraph as a unit of invention any further. Instead, he viewed it as a stage of style, thus making his revised book more concerned with the mechanics of paragraphing.

Genung's second major contribution was to classify paragraph types. He discussed four: the *propositional,* which begins with an assertion that other sentences must prove; the *amplifying,* which has an implied assertion and is most often found in description and narration; the *preliminary,* which presents the general theme of a piece; and the *transitional,* which connects two larger pieces of discourse.

The first book devoted entirely to the paragraph is Fred N. Scott and Joseph V. Denney's textbook *Paragraph Writing* (3rd ed., 1893), which went through several editions. It is important for two major reasons. First, it establishes a method of teaching writing based on the progression from paragraphs to entire themes that is designed to help the weak writer. Second, it announces a theoretical position that views the paragraph as an organic unit within a larger piece of discourse.

Scott and Denney, observing that newspaper editorials of the time often consisted of a single paragraph, defined the *isolated paragraph,* which functions as an essay in miniature. They based their pedagogy, therefore, on the belief that students can be taught to write single paragraphs in order to learn principles that they can apply to entire compositions. To achieve this, they teach five laws, four of which grow out of Bain's work: unity, selection, sequence, and variety. The fifth idea, that of *proportion,* possesses two qualities. First, a paragraph must develop its subject fully enough to exhaust its purpose and idea. Thus there can be no single rule for paragraph length since this is tied to the breadth of the idea and the author's purpose in developing it. Second, details should be developed according to their relationship to the main idea. Subordinate ideas therefore cannot be developed as extensively as main ideas.

More important than the pedagogy, *Paragraph Writing* contains a significant theoretical discussion. Although the authors teach the isolated paragraph using modifications of Bain's rules, they defined the paragraph in relationship to the entire essay. They argued that the paragraph performs functions analogous to those of the composition, but the paragraph can be neither arbitrary nor accidental since it performs a given function within the organic essay, which is the record of the writer's movement of thought toward an achievable goal. Thinking, however, progresses in stages, or *stadia,* and paragraphs are articulations of thought within these arenas. Essays can be paragraphed in a number of ways, since one paragraph can contain several stadia or a stadium can be divided into several paragraphs, depending on the purpose of the writer and the needs of the reader. By emphasizing the dynamic nature of the paragraph, Scott and Denney escaped from the mechanistic, prescriptive approaches that mark most nineteenth-century discussions.

The only book-length, scholarly discussion of the paragraph is Edwin Herbert Lewis's *History of the English Paragraph* (1894). Although dated, this work remains the most important single study of the subject and continues to influence current scholarship. Lewis discussed the paragraph as (1) a marginal character in ancient manuscripts used to mark significant passages; (2) a similar character placed within a text; (3) a division of discourse marked either by a symbol or an indentation; and (4) a rhetorical unit possessing an organic internal arrangement.

Although the book contains the only detailed discussion of ancient paragraph marks (an area needing further study), Lewis's most important contributions are his discussions of paragraph rhetoric. Building on L.A. Sherman's *Analytics of Literature* (1893), Lewis argued that there is a relationship between sentence length and paragraph rhetoric. By studying selected paragraphs from the earliest writers to his contemporaries, he discovered that the average number of words was doubled since Ascham. He attributed this to the decline of the long, Latin sentence that led to shorter sentences requiring other methods such as the paragraph to maintain cohesion and unity. He also noted that even early English writers thought in units larger than the sentence. They used the paragraph because they thought in larger, nebulous stages before thinking more accurately in short, precise steps. He was contemporary in his thinking, because he rejected the pedagogical school of theorists who viewed the paragraph as a group of related sentences. Instead, he argued that it is a logical or rhetorical stadium that performs a function within the whole composition. By rejecting logical structure as the only principle, he allowed for other reasons for paragraphing, including rhetorical and artistic concerns.

Lewis's study is marred by poor research methodology. His conclusions are based on simple word and sentence counts of randomly selected prose from a few English writers also randomly selected. Lewis, however, pointed the way for more focused and controlled work.

After the turn of the century, the paragraph receives little attention, although several articles appear that either support or modify earlier theory. L.W. Crawford, Jr., in "Paragraphs as Trains" (1912) and J.M. Grainger in "Paragraphs as Trains--The Caboose" (1913) discussed the importance of the topic sentence as controlling element. Herbert Winslow Smith argued in "Concerning Organization of Paragraphs" (1920) that students need work on topic sentences and logical development to help them think straight. Leon Mones, however, in "Teaching the Paragraph" (1921) argued that Bain and his followers teach only rules, not habits of writing. To counter this, Mones proposed a process-oriented pedagogy. Charles E. Whitmore in "A Doctrine of the Paragraph" (1923) also questioned key ideas about paragraphs including the notions of the topic sentence and logical development. He noted that all paragraphs do not have topic sentences; only expository and argumentative ones generally do. All paragraphs do, however, have *motive,* a unifying end or purpose, that may or may not be stated. Whitmore also questioned the concept of logical development and made a useful distinction between *support* and *development.* Many paragraphs have *support,* which consists of details or illustrations that make the motive concrete. Only paragraphs of a more logical kind possess *development*. In them, the writer must plan strategies--such as definition, enforcement, and other essentially logical processes to develop the motive. Finally, H.B. Lathrop in "Unity, Coherence, and Emphasis" (1918) attacked the three principles of sound paragraphing that grew out of Bain's and Wendell's work. In agreement with Scott and Denney and Lewis, Lathrop viewed the composition as a process of moving to an end. Coherence and emphasis, he argued, are actually parts of unity, the primary quality that good paragraphs and essays must possess, because a process is unified inasmuch as connections between parts are clear and the parts each receive proper emphasis.

A good evaluation of the early theorists is Virginia M. Burke's "Paragraph" (1968). She was critical of Bain and Wendell for being rule bound, but she found the ideas of Scott, Denney, Lewis, and Lathrop sounder since they recognized composition as a process. She also correctly noted that the early theories failed because they did not account for the complex semantic and syntactic relationships that function within and between paragraphs. Burke also edited *The Paragraph in Context* (1969), which contains selections from the work of Sherman, Lewis, Scott and Denny, and Lathrop as well as several essays by current theorists. Her introduction to the volume puts the nineteenth-century work in social and intellectual contexts.

Contemporary Paragraph Theory

Relatively little scholarship on the paragraph appeared during the first half of this century. Although virtually every textbook and handbook published covered the paragraph, little new information appeared. In 1958, the Conference on College Composition and Communication (CCCC) report "The Rhetoric of the Paragraph" (1958) concluded that new theories of the paragraph were needed. Several years later, the work of Francis Christensen, Alton Becker, and Paul C. Rodgers, Jr., appeared. This led to the NCTE monograph *The Sentence and the Paragraph* (1963), edited by Christensen, that reprints the most important articles on the paragraph as well as the "Symposium on the Paragraph" (1963) in which these three theorists and several others commented on one another's work.

In Christensen's "Generative Rhetoric of the Paragraph," which appears in his *Notes Toward a New Rhetoric* (1978), he developed a theory of the paragraph based on a structural analogy between the paragraph and the cumulative sentence: the top sentence of a paragraph is equivalent to the base clause of a cumulative sentence, and the supporting sentences are equivalent to the free modifiers of the sentence. He viewed the paragraph as a "macrosentence" or a "metasentence" and analyzed the paragraph's structure using the same techniques developed to describe the cumulative sentence: its levels of generality, direction of modification or movement, and its density of texture. Instead of being a logical unit, the Christensen paragraph is a sequence of sentences related by coordination- -sentences that are structured alike and on the same level of generality--and subordination--sentences structured differently and on different, lower levels of generality. This theory is generative in that it can help students intuit these hierarchical relationships between sentences and assist them in making appropriate leaps of thought and corresponding syntactic connections between sentences. In "A New

Approach to Freshman Composition" (1972), Charles A. Bond reported on an experiment suggesting that this rhetoric is more effective than a traditional course, and Michael Grady in "On Teaching Christensen Rhetoric" (1972) reported similar positive results and gave some helpful advice on using it.

Several theorists have qualified, modified, or expanded Christensen's work. David H. Karrfalt's papers question the concept of levels of generality. in the "Symposium on the Paragraph" (1963) he distinguished between *vertical structures* (modification and coordination) and *horizontal structures* (predication and complementation) of sentences and paragraphs, and he criticized Christensen for being concerned only with the vertical. He noted that parts of a sentence other than sentence modifiers, such as predication and complementation, may be more important than the modifiers themselves; he thus questioned the singular importance of the cumulative sentence. Likewise, paragraphs do not always have a vertical structure. Many have horizontal ones in which each sentence adds to the previous one without being subordinate to it. Karrfalt continued Christensen's analogy between the sentence and the paragraph, suggesting however that horizontal structuring is analogous to the relationship between the predicate and its subject, not the modifier and its head word. In a later article, "The Generation of Paragraphs and Larger Units" (1968), Karrfalt summed up his theory, demonstrating his essential relationship to Christensen, by arguing for three, not two, dimensions of generality: *coordination,* sentences at the same level of generality; *subordination,* those at a different level; and *completion,* those at a higher level of abstraction. This work suggests that some paragraphs advance in a series of ideas horizontally rather than develop and explore a single idea vertically. In a third essay, "Some Comments on the Principle of Rhythm in a Generative Rhetoric" (1969), Karrfalt argued that the concept of rhythm, working in conjunction with the concept of structure, helps students construct sound paragraphs.

Richard L. Larson also expanded on Christensen's paragraph theory in "Sentences in Action" (1967) by arguing that coordinate and subordinate relationships are not the only ones that function in prose. Each sentence acts to accomplish a particular task in conjunction with other sentences, and he presented a list of 17 roles that sentences can play in paragraphs.

Another theorist who has advanced Christensen's work is Willis L. Pitkin, Jr. In "Discourse Blocs" (1969), he argued that all language is hierarchically organized. He applied this concept to the sentence, the paragraph, and larger units of discourse. In place of the sentence and paragraph, he used the more general term *discourse bloc* to emphasize that the writer must establish junctures between blocs to maintain coherence. These blocs, functioning as a series of hierarchical units embedded in or added to larger blocs to form a continuum, should be discovered by their function in the overall discourse. This rhetorical emphasis is a departure from Christensen's theory, which is primarily concerned with structural relationships. Pitkin followed Karrfalt by recognizing the horizontal as well as vertical relationships between discourse blocs, but be attempted to clarify the exact nature of the relationships by emphasizing the function of each. In place of Christensen's coordination, he proposed *horizontal relation,* which includes simple coordination and Karrfalt's complementation, when two blocs are meaningful in terms of their own relationship (such as cause-effect). Instead of Christensen's subordination, Pitkin proposed *vertical relation,* including subordination, which is the logical movement from genus to species, and *superordination* (similar to Karrfalt's completion), from species to genus. He made an attempt, therefore, to avoid Christensen's problem of levels of generality by making the vertical relationships logical categories of inclusiveness so that smaller blocs are contained within larger ones, although he used the term *embedded,* which is confusing given its grammatical associations.

In a later article, "Hierarchies and the Discourse Hierarchy" (1977a), Pitkin attempted to clarify the essential ambiguity in the term *hierarchy* as applied to his own and Christensen's theories. He isolated three distinct uses of the term. The first refers to *grammatical or structural rank,* the traditional hierarchies of structuralism that range from the smallest elements of discourse to the largest ones. The second use of the term refers to *levels of semantic generality,* Christensen's concept, and this use also fails to recognize the operational nature of discourse, capturing only one relationship, that of specific-general, important in the encoding and decoding of discourse. The third and most appropriate use of the term *hierarchy* is *levels of functional inclusiveness,* an idea that grows out of his earlier notion of discourse blocs. Smaller blocs are included within larger ones, but the relationships are not logical or structural. In fact, structure and function are often at odds, and this creates a tension between the two. The same morpheme, for instance, can have one structural form but an entirely different hierarchical function, so analysis of the same unit will differ greatly depending on whether the analysis is structural or functional. This principle is important in teaching, since it suggests that structure cannot be taught separately from function. In a third article, "X/Y" (1977b), Pitkin developed in more detail some of the possible operational binary relationships that exist between functional units of discourse.

Several theorists have tried to apply Christensen's paragraph theory to the entire essay. Michael Grady in "A Conceptual Rhetoric of the Composition" (1971) discussed a method of teaching the freshman paper as a structure with an introductory sequence analogous to the top sentence, a series of body paragraphs related to it by coordination and subordination, and a concluding sequence that reiterates main ideas. Frank D'Angelo in "Arrangement" (1975) took a different approach by viewing the essay as a macroparagraph just as Christensen saw the paragraph as a macrosentence. The sentences within the essay are related to each other by coordination and subordination. Richard L. Larson in "Toward a Linear Rhetoric of the Essay" (1971) developed the notion of *linear analysis,* defined as a series of steps taken in a temporal sequence to reach a goal or conclusion, that complements Christensen's hierarchical model. The concept combines invention with arrangement, emphasizing the writer's need to identify the audience, the goal in writing, and the steps needed to achieve that end.

Some work has been done to develop pedagogies based on the Christensen paragraph. The most thorough treatment is Francis Christensen and Bonniejean Christensen's *New Rhetoric* (1976), which explains in detail Christensen's sentence and paragraph principles. R. Craig Hogan in "Self-Instructional Units Based on the Christensen Method" (1977) reported on a method of teaching Christensen rhetoric of the paragraph using short, self-instructional units that simplify the terminology. Stanley Archer in "Christensen's Rhetoric of the Paragraph Revisited" (1977) discusses how he applied the theory in the classroom.

For recent criticisms of Christensen's theory, see Joseph Williams's "Nuclear Structures of Discourse" (1981) and Rick Eden and Ruth Mitchell's "Paragraphing for the Reader" (1986).

The second major theorist is Alton L. Becker, whose interest in the paragraph grows in part out of Kenneth Pike's application of tagmemic theory in two early articles, "A Linguistic Contribution to Composition" (1964b) and "Beyond the Sentence" (1964a). The second paper is useful because it outlines how tagmemic theory can analyze larger linguistic structures.

In "A Tagmemic Approach to Paragraph Analysis" (1965), Becker established his basic theory, the fundamental notion of which is the *tagmeme*. This is both a grammatical slot and a slot filler, a composite of form and function. Expository paragraphs (the only kind he discussed) can be viewed as having slots and forms to fill them, and Becker isolated several major patterns common to many expository paragraphs. The first is the T (Topic) R (Restriction) I (Illustration) form. This type shares obvious similarities to the Christensen paragraph since the R slot is usually a statement of lower generality than the T slot. The second pattern, P (Problem) S (Solution), often follows the form of question-answer (QA). The S slot, however, often follows the TRI form, which can be embedded in it. One of the powerful components of Becker's theory is the notion that various operations can be performed on these basic patterns to make them flexible. These operations include deletion, reordering, addition, and combination. They offer teachers a potentially powerful instructional device: instruction can begin with the most common patterns and advance through various permutations.

There are, however, a limited number of formal signs that mark internal tagmemic structures of paragraphs despite the wide variation of slot orderings. The simplest of them, according to Becker, is the graphic marker *indentation,* a convention that signals the reader that the unit possesses internal structure. Two types of lexical markers also operate: (1) *equivalence classes,* commonly known as key terms with their synonyms and pronouns repeated throughout the structure; and (2) *lexical transitions,* transition words and phrases marking semantic concord. Changes in either of these marker systems often signal the beginning of a new slot. in "The Role of Lexical and Grammatical Cues in Paragraph Recognition" (1966), Richard Young and Becker reported an experiment that suggests readers can recognize these signs when reading paragraphs with their content words changed to nonsense syllables. Young, Becker, and Kenneth Pike, in Chapter 15 of *Rhetoric* (1970), emphasized even more the importance of chains of lexical items that run through sentences and bind them together into coherent and unified paragraphs. In Chapter 14 of the text, they developed a method of analyzing paragraphs that emphasize invention more than Becker's earlier articles do. They introduced the idea of the *plot,* a conventional sequence of slots that creates a structural framework for the paragraph. The TRI and PS slots are two of the most common, generalized plot structures for expository paragraphs, but the writer can invent others. The writer's job is to reveal the plot structure clearly to the reader and to insure that the plot conveys a sense of closure and completion after the topic sentence arouses reader expectation.

Becker also explored the paragraph as a psychological and grammatical unit, and this has led to experiments of interest to the composition teacher. The first, conducted by Frank Koen, Young, and Becker, "The Psychological Reality of the Paragraph" (1969), attempts to determine (1) the degree of agreement between subjects identifying paragraph boundaries in unindented prose passages; (2) the number of cues to paragraph structure that are formal; (3) the role semantic cues play in determining the structure; and (4) the role that age and experience play in the development of paragraph sense. The experimenters used ten prose passages of various modes and changed the content words into nonsense paralogs. In general, they found a high degree of interjudge agreement in the marking of paragraph breaks in the English passages, in the nonsense passages, and between the two. This suggests "that the paragraph is a psychologically real unit" (p. 52). Furthermore, they found that the youngest subjects, third graders, often placed the markers in mid-sentence, suggesting that these youngsters have not yet learned, either through direct teaching or through their reading, the concept of the paragraph. This experiment has been extended by Betty Cain in "Discourse Competence in Nonsense Paralogs" (1973).

Other scholars have used tagmemic theory to analyze extended discourse. Victor J. Vitanza in "A Tagmemic Heuristic for the Whole Composition" (1979) applied Becker's tagmemic slots TRI, PS, and QA to the essay. This system, he maintained, helps students generate entire compositions as well as the paragraphs within them. For an extensive application of tagmemic theory to Philippine languages, see Robert E. Longacre's *Discourse, Paragraph, and Sentence Structures in Selected Philippine Languages* (1968).

The third major contemporary theorist is Paul C. Rodgers, Jr. who, as I mentioned earlier, attacked Bain's rule-bound theory of the paragraph. instead of viewing the paragraph as an isolated unit, Rodgers argued in "A Discourse-Centered Rhetoric of the Paragraph" (1966) that paragraphs are actually not always logical breaks within a piece of discourse. To replace the paragraph as a basic unit of writing, he returned to the idea of the *stadium of discourse* introduced in the nineteenth century. This unit is a logical whole that is often a paragraph but not always. This, he claimed, represents the actual practice of modern writers, who indent their prose for a number of reasons other than for logical breaks. These reasons include structural, physical, rhythmical, formal, tonal, and rhetorical considerations. A stadium can be divided into several paragraphs or a single paragraph can include several stadia. Like Scott and Denney and Lewis of the nineteenth century, he viewed discourse as an organic process and allowed writers considerable flexibility when marking paragraph breaks.

Rodgers developed his theory more fully in "The Stadium of Discourse" (1967), in which he explored its rhetorical orientation in more detail. To determine the function of the paragraph, the reader must ask why it was written, what purpose the writer was trying to fulfill. The stadium usually has a topic sentence, but it is offered for its own sake, its own intrinsic value, not because it is attached to a paragraph, and the rest of the stadium justifies, clarifies, or emphasizes the major sentence--but not necessarily in a single paragraph. Paragraph structure, Rodgers argued, is an ineffable quality, "the web of argument, the pattern of thought flow, the system of alliances and tensions among associated statements" (p. 178).

Recent evidence supports Rodgers's contention that contemporary writers do not use topic sentences in all paragraphs. In "The Frequency and Placement of Topic Sentences in Expository Prose" (1974), Richard Braddock analyzed the paragraphs of 25 essays in major popular magazines published from 1964 to 1965 by breaking them down into T-units, identifying the topic sentences, and determining their forms. He discovered four major kinds of topic sentences plus two extra-paragraph types: (1) the *simple* topic sentence that is stated in one T-unit; (2) the *delayed-completion* topic sentence that begins in one T-unit and ends in a later one; (3) the *assembled* topic sentence found by combining phrases scattered throughout the paragraph; (4) the *inferred* topic sentence implied by the author; (5) the *major* topic sentence that controls a number of paragraphs; and (6) the *subtopic* sentence that states part of the main idea of a previous paragraph. Braddock found that only 45 percent of all topic sentences are simple, and almost as many, 39 percent, are assembled. The more text that a topic sentence controls, however, the more likely it is to be simple. Most topic sentences are implicit (55 percent), compared with 44 percent that are explicit. As for placement, only 13 percent of expository prose paragraphs begin with a topic sentence. Arther A. Stern in "When Is a Paragraph?" (1976) reported that students, when asked to mark paragraph breaks in passages, invariably place the breaks in different but equally justifiable places. This supports Braddock's findings that not all paragraphs begin with a simple topic sentence.

The theoretical work of Christensen, Becker, and Rodgers has not always been received enthusiastically. In "Further Comments on the Paragraph" (1966), Leo Rockas argued that these theories ask the wrong questions because they assume that paragraphs exist. A better approach, he argued, is to examine how sentences are connected in discourse, an argument he returned to in "The Rhetoric of Doodle" (1978). In "Response to Leo Rockas' `Further Comments on the Paragraph'" (1967), Christensen answered these objections by noting that the basic unit of narration is the sentence, but the basic unit of exposition is the paragraph. In "The Persistent Ptolemy and the Paradox of the Paragraph" (1968), Rockas, in the manner of Sterne, poked fun at theorists for arguing over the nature of paragraphing, which is an art, not a science. Textbook and handbook authors have often ignored current work on the paragraph as J. Karl Nicholas showed in "Handbooks and Horsesense" (1973), an article in which he examined several popular texts for the influence of contemporary paragraph theory.

Although Christensen, Becker, and Rodgers have been the most influential theorists, other scholars have also written important essays on the subject. Herbert Read in *English Prose Style* (1952) rejected many traditional ideas about paragraphs, particularly the notion that they are logical structures. He viewed them as devices of punctuation that offer readers a breathing space. Paragraphs also help writers explore their subjects until relevant ideas are exhausted and therefore represent a psychological process of exploring all facets of a thought. One of Read's most innovative ideas is that paragraphs possess rhythmical unity, the paragraph in fact being the "first complete unit of prose rhythm" (p. 59). Rhythm, however, has less to do with words than with thoughts, so the paragraph became for Read the shape of thought, a gestalt that possesses its own unity and hierarchical organization. Paul Franklin Baum, in ... *the other harmony of prose* ... (1952) objected to Read's "mystical" notions and analyzed several paragraphs closely to show that rhythm is not always associated with their thought patterns in obvious ways.

Other contemporary theorists have been concerned about paragraph form. Josephine Miles in "What We Compose" (1963) suggested a tripartite system of function classes that help students compose meaningful sentences, paragraphs, and essays. The first is *assertive*, a subject and its predicate; the second is *development*, the addition of modification; and the third is *connective*, the use of prepositions, conjunctions, and other connectives. Robert Gorrell in "Not by Nature" (1966) developed another approach by discussing three other principles: addition, continuity, and selection. By *addition* he meant those techniques- -predication, linkage, coordination, and subordination--by which writers add comments to topics in both sentences and paragraphs. By *continuity* he meant that every unit of coherent discourse must establish a kind of contract between reader and writer. The paragraph must establish a commitment to what follows it and function as a response to what precedes it. Finally, by *selection* he meant that writers must select from a limited set of discourse alternatives for each slot. Gorrell briefly discussed these concepts in the context of our need for a new rhetoric in "Very Like a Whale" (1965). Edna L. Furness in "New Dimensions in Paragraph Instruction" (1968) also proposed a new view of paragraph form based on structural and strategic sentences.

In "Aesthetic Form in Familiar Essays" (1971), Howard C. Brashers explained a series of organizational categories that apply to familiar essays that are artistically rather than logically organized. He viewed form as being comprised of the interaction of two principles, design and pattern. *Design,* which contributes variety to familiar prose, consists of four principles: contrast, gradation, theme and variation, and restraint. These principles are associated with structures of thought as well as paragraph organization. Of less importance to paragraph theory are Brasher's concepts of *pattern,* which are larger methods of organizing discourse into wholes. These concepts are linear, radical-circular, and mytho-literary. Although of limited use for teaching argument and exposition, this system can explain the organization of artistic, non-logical paragraphs and essays. Another writer who addressed this question is William F. Irmscher. In *Teaching Expository Writing* (1979), he used the theories of artist Ben Shahn to discuss "the shape of content," arguing that in any writing, content comes first and then is shaped into appropriate form, not vice versa. He discussed "outer shape" and "inner parts." The *outer shape* sets the limits of the piece and the *inner parts,* which directly concern matters of paragraphing, determine the ways that discourse is made coherent and unified.

Richard Warner in "Teaching the Paragraph as a Structural Unit" (1979) used linguistic principles to teach paragraph structure by developing a set of generative-transformational, as well as rhetorical, rules to generate paragraphs, which he argued are recognizable units of linguistic structure. The *generative rules* consist of three sentence functions that can produce analytic paragraph structures. These rules are topic (T), limitor (L), and developer (D). Transformational rules can then delete and rearrange these functions, changing TLD structures to DLT, for instance. The third set of rules, the *rhetorical,* motivates the transformations. Another linguistic discussion of form is Jay Kyle Perrin's "Subject Isn't What It Seems" (1972) in which she noted that the main subject of a paragraph--generally the subject of the topic sentence--performs various grammatical functions in the body sentences.

A new, promising direction in paragraph research makes use of information from psycho-linguistic, linguistic, and reading research. Rick Eden and Ruth Mitchell's "Paragraphing for the Reader" (in press) used this research to develop a theory of paragraphing based on the premise that writers do not need to learn common paragraph patterns; instead, they need to learn how to use paragraph conventions to affect the reader's perception of prose discourse.

This view finds support in the empirical research in reading theory. Bonnie J.F. Meyer's work, reported in her "What Is Recalled After Hearing a Passage?" (1973), coauthored with G.W. McConkie, and in her *Organization of Prose and its Effect on Memory* (1975), explored the effect of content structure of a paragraph on a reader's memory. Using Joseph E. Grime's *Tread of Discourse* (1975) as a theoretical base, she designed experiments suggesting that superordinate semantic content placed high in the content structure tended to be recalled more readily than subordinate information low in the structure. This phenomenon, known as top-down processing, suggests that readers need an abstract statement to orient them before they can make sense of following details. Perry Thorndyke in "Cognitive Structures in Comprehension and Memory of Narrative Discourse" (1977) and J.D. Bransford and M.K. Johnson in "Considerations of Some Problems of Comprehension" (1973) also explored this question.

Although Robert de Beaugrande's experiments reported in "Psychology and Composition" (1979) do not support this position, most work by reading specialists does. James Coomber in "Perceiving the Structure of Written Materials" (1975) reported that students cannot write paragraphs because they cannot read to distinguish main from subordinate material. William Wensch in the review article "What Reading Research Tells Us about Writing" (1979) argued that reading research supports the importance of traditional principles of paragraphing such as the beginning topic sentence. David E. Kieras in "Good and Bad Structure in Simple Paragraphs" (1978) found that subjects had more difficulty processing and remembering paragraphs that did not conform to the conventions of coherent development and opening topic sentences.

Studies also suggest that organization, context, and reader experience and belief-structures affect text processing. L.T. Frase in "Paragraph Organization of Written Materials" (1969) reported on an experiment suggesting that organizing sentence sequences so that they follow the conceptual structure inherent in the material facilitates learning. Marcie Waller and F.L. Durley in "The Influence of Context on the Auditory Comprehension of Paragraphs by Aphasic Subjects" (1978) found that establishing a verbal context for subjects before they read the paragraphs significantly improved recall. Richard C. Anderson and colleagues in "Frameworks for Comprehending Discourse" (1977) questioned the predominant belief that meaning resides in language and that readers merely need linguistic skills to process it. The authors demonstrated that readers interpret an ambiguous paragraph according to their knowledge of the world and their analysis of the paragraph's context. For writers, this suggests that paragraphs cannot be seen apart from the beliefs and general background and expectations of those reading them. Douglas Sjogren and W. Timpson in "Frameworks for Comprehending Discourse" (1979) replicated Anderson's study and reached similar conclusions.

Work in the area of readability also supports the need for traditionally sound paragraphing. In *The Philosophy of Composition* (1977), E.D. Hirsch, Jr., argued that psycho-linguistic research suggests that traditional techniques of paragraphing assist the memory and help maintain attention. Jack Selzer in "Another Look at Paragraphs in Technical Writing" (1980) questioned the validity of readability formulas that do not take the paragraph into consideration. Current work in rhetoric, linguistics, and cognitive psychology shows that meaning grows from the relationship between the parts of the paragraph, not just from the length of words and sentences. In "Readability of Expository Paragraphs with Identical or Related Sentence Topics" (1979), William J. Vande Kopple reported experimental findings about the relationship between readability and paragraphs. He demonstrated that most readers consider paragraphs more readable that present older material in the topic position and newer material in the predicate position that naturally receives more stress. This is known as the "Functional Sentence Perspective" (FSP). The most readable paragraph, he concluded, is the one that repeats the topic idea at the beginning of each sentence. In another study, "Readability of a Rhetorically Linked Expository Paragraph" (1980), Vande Kopple tested a second type of paragraph. This one links all of its sentences together by having new information in the stressed position of one sentence carry over to the non-stressed, topic position of the following one. Readers judged this paragraph more readable than a paragraph arranged in the opposite manner. Vande Kopple discussed the pedagogical implications of FSP in "Functional Sentence Perspective, Composition, and Reading" (1982). A.S. Fishman in "The Effect of Anaphoric References and Noun Phrase Organizers on Paragraph Comprehension" (1978) found that general nouns introduced in the topic sentences of paragraphs help readers organize and remember what they read. This "noun phrase organizer" names a category and is frequently repeated throughout the paragraph, and this leads to superior recall.

Coherence is another traditional principle of sound paragraphing that has received support from recent scholarship. The seminal work in the area is M.A.K. Halliday and R. Hasan's *Cohesion in English* (1976), which exhaustively explores the major cohesive devices of English. The study identifies cohesion as one of the most important qualities of a text, which is a semantic unit possessing *texture,* a rich interconnection between its parts. Halliday and Hasan discussed five devices that English uses to achieve coherence: reference, substitution, ellipses, conjunction, and lexical cohesion.

Although Halliday and Hasan's work has been widely read by composition specialists, the work of Edward J. Crothers, whose *Paragraph Inference Structures* (1979) extends Halliday and Hasan's *Cohesion in English* (1976), is not as well known. Unlike Halliday and Hasan, who are concerned mostly with syntactic and semantic relationships within a text, Crothers argued that cohesion also depends on psychological and logical patterns that are extra-linguistic. These patterns he called "inferences." Unstated assumptions, *inferences* are propositions not manifested in the text but assumed by it. Inferences contribute to cohesion by connecting statements much as mortar connects bricks.

Other theorists also discuss the importance of coherence in paragraphing. E.K. Lybbert and D.W. Cummings in "On Repetition and Coherence" (1969) argued that unity and coherence are two independent variables. Unity grows from the selection of related material, and coherence grows from fitting together parts to form a whole. Anita Brostoff in "Coherence" (1981) developed a program for teaching the concept based on the work of Piaget, Christensen, Hayakawa, Burke, and Young, Becker, and Pike. Dennis J. Packard in "From Logic to Composition and Reading" (1976) presented a method of using logic to help students achieve and maintain coherence in paragraphs. Stephen P. Witte and Lester Faigley in "Coherence, Cohesion, and Writing Quality"

(1981) argued that coherence and cohesion are essential qualities found in good paragraphs. They analyzed high- and low-rated essays using Halliday and Hasan's classification and found that the better essays were richer in their use of cohesive devices. They attributed this to better writers possessing skills of invention that allow them to elaborate and extend concepts. Although cohesion is important, they concluded that coherence, the way a text fits into a larger world situation, may be even more so.

Although much of the research cited on the last few pages supports the importance of traditional paragraphing, not all scholars believe that form in the traditional sense is important to teach. Thomas W. Wilcox in "Composition Where None Is Apparent" (1965) argued that available rhetorics of the paragraph do not reflect the sense of formlessness found in serious contemporary literature. If teachers recognize that our best writers break all conventions to express their world views, why do they continue to insist that their students write unified paragraphs? Winston Weathers in "Grammars of Style" (1976) offered an alternative to traditional grammar and rhetoric in the form of *Grammar B,* which includes, among other innovations, the *crot,* which is a short, impressionistic alternative to the paragraph. In this essay and in his *Alternative Style* (1980), Weathers maintained that students should be exposed to Grammar B because it is as effective as the traditional Grammar A. Furthermore, it has a long list of practitioners, including Sterne, Whitman, Joyce, and the New Journalists. Jane R. Walpole in "Rhetorical Form" (1979) suggested that the crot has advantages over the traditional paragraph because it is more flexible and expressive.

Teaching the Paragraph

Although most of the theory discussed so far has implications for teaching, some articles have been written on the paragraph that are primarily pedagogical in intent. They include exercises, assignments, and textbooks. As would be expected, much of this material is designed for the basic writing classroom or can be used to meet the needs of basic writers.

Relatively little work has been done on teaching elementary students to paragraph. Jo Tagliente in "The Edible Paragraph" (1973) taught paragraph structure to young students by comparing it to a Dagwood sandwich, and Don M. Wolfe in "Crucial First Assignment" (1970) argued that young students should be introduced to the paragraph by means of a simple description assignment. R.W. Reising in "Turning the Corner" (1970) compared the walls of the classroom to the paragraphs of an essay. Turning corners while walking around the room is analogous to a writer's thinking while paragraphing each major unit of an essay. In the seminal article "Nobody Writes a Paragraph" (1972), O.S. Trosky and C.C. Wood described a method to teach young children that paragraphs are parts of larger discourse. The method grows out of research on brainstorming and problem-solving, and it requires students to complete the following five steps: (1) list ideas about a subject; (2) group them appropriately; (3) name each group to show how the ideas fit together; (4) number the ideas in each group systematically; and (5) write about the ideas of each group to form connected paragraphs. In a second article, "Paragraph Writing" (1975), Trosky and Wood described a method to help students group the ideas and name the groups more effectively. Finally, James Charnock in "Paragraphing Made Simple" (1978) discussed how to teach students to list information under a topic, organize it into categories, rank it in order of importance, and fashion paragraphs first in oral and then in written form. Even less work has been done on teaching junior and senior high school students to paragraph. Ruth M. Barns in "Try Paragraph Writing" (1956) reported a step-by-step method for moving students from discussing a model paragraph to writing one of their own. Joseph P. Fotos in "Teaching the Paragraph in Junior High School" (1966) described a technique for evaluating student paragraphs by having the class develop its own criterion that the teacher can gradually expand. Finally, Leo M. Schell in "Paragraph Composition" (1969) explained a systematic procedure for teaching high school students by beginning with a topic sentence and working sentence by sentence to the conclusion.

More work has been done on teaching basic writers to paragraph. Harvey S. Wiener in "The Single Narrative Paragraph and College Remediation" (1972) argued that basic writers should be taught to write short narrative paragraphs rather than the more difficult expository ones, because the first, being short and personal, allows students to concentrate on structural elements. After mastering the narrative paragraph, students can then learn to write short expository pieces. Writing for teachers of English. as a second language, Michael Donley in "The Paragraph in Advanced Composition" (1976) suggested a series of exercises that use paragraph models heuristically to teach students the role that reader expectation plays in paragraph development. He gives students parts of paragraphs--the topic sentence, for instance--and asks them to predict how the rest of the structure will unfold. William Jones in "A Little Pen and Pencil Magic" (1977) reported on a method for helping basic writers to fill out sparse, poorly developed paragraphs by adding sentences between sentences of the original. Dean R. Baldwin in "Introducing Rhetoric in Remedial Writing Courses" (1978) required his basic writers to answer questions on Pre-writing Sheets about the audience and the purpose of each paragraph. Linda Feldmeir in "Teaching Paragraph Coherence" (1979) taught coherence by giving basic writers a topic sentence followed by a series of related sentences that need to be reconstructed to form a paragraph. Finally, Beverly D. Stratton, John Charlton-Seifert, and Maurice G. Williams in "Reading and Writing Shapes" (1980) taught basic writers paragraph organization by showing geometric shapes to reinforce five general patterns of development.

Some work has also been done on teaching freshman writers to paragraph. Hermann C. Bowersox in "The Idea of the Freshman Composition Course" (1955) discussed a technique to make students more aware of paragraph rhetoric. After they analyzed the rhetorical strategies of paragraphs, he had students make grammatical and structural changes in particular sentences and then discuss the effects on the paragraph as a whole. Donald Cunningham in "Analyzing Paragraph Structure" (1971) explained a system to teach students three types of functional sentences operating in many paragraphs: topic, explanatory, and exemplification. Norma J. Engberg in "Pumpkin-Head Paragraphs" (1974) described how to teach style by preventing students with a short paragraph comprised only of simple sentences and having the class make and discuss a number of changes in sentence structure and diction. Carol Cohan in "Writing Effective Paragraphs" (1976) taught paragraphs by emphasizing that topic sentences must pose questions for the body sentences to answer. John H. Clarke in "Generating Paragraphs in a Four-Part Formula" (1978) taught his students to structure paragraphs according to four slots, each with its own question: (1) *leader* (What's true?); (2) *qualifier* (Why is it true); (3) *example* (Where or when with details?); and (4) *interpretation* (So what?). Finally, Laurie G. Kirszner in "Supporting Topic Sentences" (1978) described how to teach concrete support by providing groups of students with topic sentences that they can develop.

One method of teaching the paragraph that has received considerable attention is imitation, one of the oldest methods of writing instruction. It includes a cluster of techniques such as copying a passage, substituting new content while following the original's syntax and organization, paraphrasing the original, and loosely using it as a model. James W. Ney in "On Not Practicing Errors" (1963) based his entire semester on close imitation. Until mid-semester, he had his students imitate sentences; then he had them imitate paragraphs. C.D. Rogers in "The Sedulous but Successful Ape" (1967) described a similar program. J.F. McCampbell in "Using Models for Improving Composition" (1966) argued that imitation of paragraphs helps remedial students internalize syntactic structures, larger organizational patterns, and other structural conventions. Also working with basic writers, Phyllis Brooks in "Mimesis" (1973) argued that *persona paraphrase*, a form of imitation, helps basic writers develop mature voices when writing. Frank D'Angelo in "Imitation and Style" (1973) noted that imitating a paragraph allows students to participate in archetypal forms. Like invention, imitation is generative, but it has the advantage of helping students develop sophisticated styles relatively quickly. D.G. Kehl in "Composition and the Mimetic Mode" (1975) articulated a broad system of invention based on imitation and Christensen paragraph theory. Finally, several textbooks use imitation to teach paragraph structure including Edward P.J. Corbett's *Classical Rhetoric for the Modern Student* (1971), which discusses the importance of imitation in classical rhetoric; M.E. Whitten's *Creative Pattern Practice* (1966); Winston Weathers and Otis Winchester's *Copy and Compose* (1969), a text devoted entirely to imitating models; and Frank D'Angelo's *Process and Thought in Composition* (1980).

Another method that has received considerable attention is the scrambled-sentence approach. James Stronks in "Coherence in the Paragraph" (1976) described an exercise in which students receive a scrambled paragraph that they must reconstruct and then compare with the original version. Suzanne F. Kistler in "Scrambling the Unscramblable" (1978) worked first with scrambled professional models and then turned to scrambled student models to help students find weaknesses in coherence. Michael G. Moran in "An Inductive Method of Teaching the Paragraph" (1981) described a learning game that has student groups compete to reconstruct scrambled paragraphs. Finally, Peter M. Schiff in "Problem Solving and the Composition Model" (1978) lent credence to the method by reporting experimental results suggesting that students taught to manipulate sentence strips of model paragraphs write statistically superior paragraphs compared to those in a control group. The problem-solving process, he concluded, leads to improvement.

Relatively little work has been done on opening and closing paragraphs. In "An Effective Opening" (1969), Thomas Stanko described how he gave his students the first sentence of professional openings and asked them to generate the rest of the paragraph. Lila Chaplin in "On Improving Opening Paragraphs" (1967) listed numerous effective techniques to begin essays. They include things such as beginning with a question, a quotation, or an anecdote. Robert M. Gassen in "A Sense of Audience and Commitment" (1975) described how he taught students that openings must interest the reader and express the writer's enthusiasm for the subject. Robert L. Baker in "Twelve Ways to End Your Article Gracefully" (1982) discussed effective ways to conclude popular essays.

Since almost every textbook and handbook published contains a section on paragraphing, I cannot discuss all of them. This is no great loss since most books approach paragraphing by means of the modes or patterns of discourse, a method that has been questioned by the work of Richard A. Meade and W. Geiger Ellis. In their "Paragraph Development in the Modern Age of Rhetoric" (1970), they described a study in which they examined 300 paragraphs from contemporary periodicals and found that more than half (56 percent) were not developed using a traditional pattern. Most were developed using additional comment, reasons, examples, or a combination of these three patterns. In "The Use in Writing of Textbook Methods of Paragraph Development" (1971), Meade and Ellis presented the statistics of the study and concluded that instruction should focus on methods of development other than the traditional. Because of this, I will cite only textbooks that take novel approaches to paragraphing.

Chapter 4 of W. Ross Winterowd's *Contemporary Writer* (1976) not only reflects many of the findings from current paragraph research, but it also introduces several new, useful concepts. Winterowd assumed that conscious and unconscious imitation of models helps students develop as writers, so he provided numerous samples of interesting, well-written paragraphs throughout the chapter. He also discussed non-traditional methods of development such as the tagmemic slots, examples, images, facts, analogy, and others. Perhaps his most innovative idea is that of distance. Paragraphs fall along a spectrum from a private, intimate vision using intuitive methods of development to an impersonal presentation using formal chains of logic.

Other rhetorics with interesting sections on the paragraph include William F. Irmscher's *Holt Guide to English* (1981), which discusses nine function slots similar to tagmemic slots (TRIAC-SELD); Donald Daiker, Andrew Kerek, and Max Morenberg's *Writer's Options* (1982), which in Units 11-13 uses sentence- combining to teach principles of paragraphing; and Frederick Crews's *Random House Handbook* (1980), which discusses the development of direct, turnabout, and climactic paragraphs. In *Writing* (1984) Charles Bridges and Ronald Lunsford introduced a paragraphing scheme based on Kenneth Burke's Logological Analysis.

Several textbooks, many of them geared to freshmen and basic writers, treat the paragraph as the major unit of discourse. I will cite only two of them. The best remains John B. Lord's *Paragraph* (1964). This book views the paragraph as both a unit of structure and style, and Lord intelligently discussed questions of organization, development, movement, diction, rhythm, and tone. Less innovative but also good is Helen Mills's *Commanding Paragraphs* (1981), which is the best book available for teaching traditional paragraph theory. It also has an excellent instructor's manual with suggestions for using the text in various classroom contexts.

REFERENCES

Anderson, Richard C., et al. "Frameworks for Comprehending Discourse." *Am Educ Res J*, 14 (1977), 367-81.

Angus, Joseph. *Hand-Book of the English Tongue*. London: Religious Tract Society, 1862.

208   Form and Organization -- Larger Elements

Archer, Stanley. "Christensen's Rhetoric of the Paragraph Revisited." *Ex E,* 21 (1977), 22-27.

Bain, Alexander. *English Composition and Rhetoric: A Manual.* New York: Appleton, 1867.

Baker, Robert L. "Twelve Ways to End Your Article Gracefully." *Writer's Digest,* Oct. 1982, pp. 30-33.

Baldwin, Dean R. "Introducing Rhetoric in Remedial Writing Courses. " *CCC,* 29 (1978), 392-94.

Barns, Ruth M. "Try Paragraph Writing." *EJ,* 45 (1956), 412-14.

Baum, Paul Franklin. *... the other harmony of prose ...* Durham, N.C.: Duke University Press, 1952, pp. 61-74.

Becker, Alton L. "A Tagmemic Approach to Paragraph Analysis." *CCC,* 16 (1965), 237-42.

Bennett, James, et al. "The Paragraph: An Annotated Bibliography." *Style,* 11 (1977), 107-18.

Bond, Charles A. "A New Approach to Freshman Composition: A Trial of the Christensen Method." *CE,* 33 (1972), 623-27.

Bowersox, Hermann C. "The Idea of the Freshman Composition Course--A Polemical Discussion." *CCC,* 6 (1955), 38-44.

Braddock, Richard. "The Frequency and Placement of Topic Sentences in Expository Prose." *RTE,* 8 (1974), 287-302.

Bransford, J.D., and M.K. Johnson. "Consideration of Some Problems of Comprehension." In *Visual Information Processing.* Ed. W.D. Chase. New York: Academic, 1973.

Brashers, Howard C. "Aesthetic Form in Familiar Essays." *CCC,* 22 (1971), 147-55.

Bridges, Charles W., and Ronald Lunsford. *Writing: Discovering Form and Meaning.* San Francisco: Wadsworth, 1984.

Brooks, Phyllis. "Mimesis: Grammar and the Echoing Voice." *CE,* 35 (1973), 161-68.

Brostoff, Anita. "Coherence: `Next to' Is Not `Connected to.'" *CCC,* 32 (1981), 278-94.

Burke, Virginia. "The Paragraph: Dancer in Chains." In *Rhetoric: Theories for Applications.* Ed. Robert Gorrell. Champaign, Ill.: NCTE, 1968. Shortened version: "Continuity of the Paragraph." In *Prose Style: A Historical Approach Through Studies.* Ed. James R. Bennett. San Francisco: Chandler, 1971, pp. 18-23.

_____, ed. *The Paragraph in Context.* Indianapolis: Bobbs-Merrill, 1969.

Cain, Betty. "Discourse Competence in Nonsense Paralogs." *CCC,* 24 (1973), 171-81.

Chaplin, Lila. "On Improving Opening Paragraphs." *CCC,* 18 (1967), 53-56.

Charnock, James. "Paragraphing Made Simple." *Teacher,* Jan. 1978, p. 90.

Christensen, Francis. "Response to Leo Rockas' `Further Comments on the Paragraph.'" *CCC,* 18 (1967), 186-88.

_____. "A Generative Rhetoric of the Paragraph. " In *Notes Toward a New Rhetoric.* 2nd ed. New York: Harper, Row, 1978, pp. 74-103.

_____, ed. *The Sentence and the Paragraph.* Champaign, Ill.: NCTE, 1963.

_____, and Bonniejean Christensen. *A New Rhetoric.* New York: Harper, Row, 1976, pp. 83-192.

Clark, John R. "Paragraphs for Freshmen." *CE,* 32 (1970), 66-72.

Clarke, John H. "Generating Paragraphs in a Four-Part Formula." *Ex E,* 23 (1978), 28-30.

Cohan, Carol. "Writing Effective Paragraphs." *CCC,* 27 (1976), 363-65.

Coomber, James W. "Teaching Organizational Skills in Reading and Writing." *Minn Engl J,* 9 (1973), 37-41.

_____. "Perceiving the Structure of Written Materials." *RTE,* 9 (1975), 263-66.

Corbett, Edward P.J. *Classical Rhetoric for the Modern Student.* 2nd ed. New York: Oxford University Press, 1971, pp. 496-538.

Crawford, L.W., Jr. "Paragraphs as Trains." *EJ,* 10 (1912), 644.

Crews, Frederick. *The Random House Handbook.* 3rd ed. New York: Random House, 1980, pp. 90-124.

Crothers, Edward J. *Paragraph Inference Structures.* Norwood, N.J.: Albex, 1979.

Cunningham, Donald. "Analyzing Paragraph Structure." *Elem Eng,* 16 (1971), 8-9. Also in *Writing Exercises from Exercise Exchange.* Ed. Littleton Long. Urbana, Ill.: NCTE, 1976, pp. 45-47.

Daiker, Donald, Andrew Kerek, and Max Morenberg. *The Writer's Options.* 2nd ed. New York: Harper, Row, 1982.

D'Angelo, Frank. "Imitation and Style." *CCC,* 24 (1973), 283-90.

_____. "A Generative Rhetoric of the Essay." *CCC,* 25 (1974), 388-96.

_____. "Arrangement." In *A Conceptual Theory of Rhetoric.* Cambridge, Mass.: Winthrop, 1975.

_____. *Process and Thought in Composition.* 2nd ed. Cambridge, Mass.: Winthrop, 1980, pp. 317-74, 425-58.

de Beaugrande, Robert. "Generative Stylistics: Between Grammar and Rhetoric." *CCC,* 28 (1977), 240-46.

_____. "Psychology and Composition. " *CCC,* 30 (1979), 50-53.

Donley, Michael. "The Paragraph in Advanced Composition: A Heuristic Approach." *Engl Lang Teach J.* 30 (1976), 224-35.

Earle, John. *English Prose.* New York: Putnam's, 1890.

Eden, Rick, and Ruth Mitchell. "Paragraphing for the Reader." *CCC,* 37 (1986): 416-30, 441.

Engberg, Norma J. "Pumpkin-Head Paragraphs." *FEN,* 3 (1974), 15-17.

Feldmeir, Linda. "Teaching Paragraph Coherence." *Ex E,* 24 (1979), 41-44.
Fishman, A.S. "The Effect of Anaphoric References and Noun Phrase Organizers on Paragraph Comprehension." *J Read Behav,* 10 (1978), 159-69.
Fotos, Joseph P. "Teaching the Paragraph in the Junior High School." *EJ,* 55 (1966), 1071-72.
Frase, L.T. "Paragraph Organization of Written Materials: The Influences of Conceptual Clustering Upon the Level and Organization of Recall." *Educ Psychol,* 60 (1969), 394-401.
Furness, Edna L. "New Dimensions in Paragraph Instruction." *Education,* 89 (1968), 105-10.
Gassen, Robert M. "A Sense of Audience and Commitment: An Approach to Teaching the Introductory Paragraph." *JETT,* 8 (1975), 25-27.
Genung, John F. *The Practical Elements of Rhetoric: With Illustrative Examples.* Boston: Ginn. 1892, pp. 193-214.
_____. *The Working Principles of Rhetoric: Examined in Their Literary Relations and Illustrated with Examples.* Boston: Ginn, 1900, pp. 356-83.
Gorrell, Robert. "Very Like a Whale--A Report on Rhetoric." *CCC,* 16 (1965), 138-43.
_____. "Not by Nature: Approaches to Rhetoric." *EJ* 55 (1966), 49, 409-16.
Grady, Michael. "A Conceptual Rhetoric of the Composition." *CCC,* 22 (1971), 348-54.
_____. "On Teaching Christensen Rhetoric." *EJ,* 61 (1972), 77, 859-73.
Grainger, J.M. "'Paragraphs as Trains'--The Caboose." *EJ,* 2 (1913), 126.
Grimes, Joseph E. *The Thread of Discourse.* The Hague: Mouton, 1975.
Gruber, William E. "'Servile Copying' and the Teaching of English Composition." *CE,* 39 (1977), 491-97.
Halliday, M.A.K., and Ruqaiya Hasan. *Cohesion in English.* London: Ungman, 1976.
Hirsch, E.D., Jr. *The Philosophy of Composition.* Chicago: University of Chicago Press, 1977.
Hogan, R. Craig. "Self-Instructional Units Based on the Christensen Method." *CCC,* 28 (1977), 275-77.
Irmscher, William F. *Teaching Expository Writing.* New York: Holt, Rinehart, Winston, 1979, pp. 94-106.
_____. *The Holt Guide to English.* 3rd ed. New York: Holt, Rinehart, Winston, 1981, pp. 79-84.
Jones, William. "A Little Pen and Pencil Magic: Adapting an English-as-a-Second-Language Technique for Native Speakers of English." *Ex E,* 22 (1977), 21-26.
Karrfalt, David H. "Symposium on the Paragraph." In *The Sentence and the Paragraph.* Ed. Francis Christensen, Champaign, Ill.: NCTE,. 1963, pp. 71-76.
_____. "The Generation of Paragraphs and Larger Units." *CCC,* 19 (1968), 211-17.
_____. "Some Comments on the Principle of Rhythm in a Generative Rhetoric." *JETT,* (1969), 4-15.
Kehl, D.G. "Composition and the Mimetic Mode: Imitation and Exertitiatio." In *Linguistics, Stylistics, and the Teaching of Composition.* Ed. Donald McQuade. Akron, Ohio: University of Akron, 1975, pp. 135-42.
Kieras, David E. "Good Structure and Bad Structure in Simple Paragraphs: Effects on Apparent Theme, Reading Time, and Recall." *J Verb Learn Verb Behav,* 17 (1978), 13-28.
Kirszner, Laurie G. "Supporting Topic Sentences: An Exercise for Composition Courses. *Ex E,* 22 (1978), 3-7.
Kistler, Suzanne F. "Scrambling the Unscramblable: Coherence in the Classroom." *CCC,* 29 (1978), 198-200.
Koen, Frank, Richard Young, and Alton Becker. "The Psychological Reality of the Paragraph," *Stud Lang & Lang Behav,* 3 (1967), Part 1, 526-38.
_____. "The Psychological Reality of the Paragraph." *Stud Lang & Lang Behav,* 4 (1968), Part II, 482-98.
_____. "The Psychological Reality of the Paragraph." *J Vrb Learn Verb Behav,* 8 (1969), 49-53.
Larson, Richard B. "Back to the Board." *CCC,* 29 (1978), 292-94.
Larson, Richard L. "Sentences in Action: A Technique for Analyzing Paragraphs." *CCC,* 18 (1967), 16-22.
_____. "Toward a Linear Rhetoric of the Essay." *CCC,* 22 (1971), 140-46.
_____. "Structure and Form in Non-Fiction Discourse." In *Teaching Composition: 10 Bibliographic Essays.* Ed. Gary Tate. Fort Worth: Texas Christian University Press, 1976, pp. 45-72.
Lathrop, H.B. "Unity, Coherence, and Emphasis." University of Wisconsin Studies in Language and Literature, No. 2. Madison: University of Wisconsin, 1918, pp. 77-98.
Lewis, Edwin Herbert. *The History of the English Paragraph.* Chicago, 1894; rpt. New York: AMS, 1970.
Longacre, Robert E. *Discourse, Paragraph, and Sentence Structure in Selected Philippine Languages.* Part II, Santa Ana, Calif.: Summer Institute of Linguistics, 1968, pp. 53-192.
Lord, John B. *The Paragraph: Structure and Style.* New York: Holt, Rinehart, Winston, 1964.
Lybbert, E.K., and D.W. Cummings. "On Repetition and Coherence." *CCC,* 20 (1969), 35-38.
McCampbell, J.F. "Using Models for Improving Composition." *EJ,* 55 (1966), 772-76.
McElroy, John G.R. *The Structure of English Prose: A Manual of Composition and Rhetoric.* New York: Armstrong, 1885.
Meade, Richard A., and W.G. Ellis. "Paragraph Development in the Modern Age of Rhetoric." *EJ,* 59 (1970), 219-26; rpt. in *Rhetoric and Composition: A Sourcebook for Teachers.* Ed. Richard L. Graves. Rochelle Park, N.J.: Hayden, 1978, pp. 193-200.

210   Form and Organization -- Larger Elements

_____. "The Use in Writing of Textbook Methods of Paragraph Development." *J Educ Res,* 65 (1971), 74-76.

Meyer, Bonnie J.F. *The Organization of Prose and Its Effects on Memory.* Amsterdam: North-Holland, 1975.

_____, and George W. McConkie. "What is Recalled After Hearing a Passage?" *J Edu Psychol,* 65 (1973), 109-17.

Miles, Josephine. "What We Compose." *CCC,* 14 (1963), 146-54; rpt. in *Rhetoric and Composition,* Ed. Richard L. Graves. Rochelle Park, N.J.: Hayden, 1978, pp. 183-92.

Mills, Helen. *Commanding Paragraphs.* 2nd ed. Glenview, Ill.: Scott, Foresman, 1981.

Mones, Leon. "Teaching the Paragraph." *EJ,* 10 (1921), 456-60.

Moran, Michael G. "An Inductive Method of Teaching the Paragraph: The Paragraph Game." *NOTE,* 9 (1981), 12-14.

Murray, Lindley. *An English Grammar.* Vol. 1. York: Wilson, 1808, pp. 296-99.

Ney, James W. "On Not Practicing Errors." *CCC,* 14 (1963), 102-6.

Nicholas, J. Karl. "Handbooks and Horsesense." *FEN,* 2 (1973), 3-4.

Packard, Dennis J. "From Logic to Composition and Reading." *CCC,* 27 (1976), 366-72.

Perrin, Jay Kyle. "The Subject Isn't What It Seems." *EJ,* 61 (1972), 1334-37.

Pike, Kenneth. "Beyond the Sentence." *CCC,* 15 (1964a), 129-35.

_____. "A Linguistic Contribution to Composition." *CCC,* 15 (1964b), 82-88.

Pincas, A. "Writing in Paragraphs." *Eng Lang Teach J,* 24 (1970), 182-85.

Pitkin, Willis L., Jr. "Discourse Blocs." *CCC,* 20 (1969), 138-48.

_____. "Hierarchies and the Discourse Hierarchy." *CE,* 38 (1977a), 648-59.

_____. "X/Y: Some Basic Strategies of Discourse." *CE* 38 (1977b), 660-72.

Read, Herbert. *English Prose Style.* New York: Pantheon, 1952, pp. 52-65.

Reising, R.W. "Turning the Corner: A Strategy for Teaching Paragaphing." *PJE,* 47 (1970), 308-9.

"The Rhetoric of the Paragraph: Principles and Practices." Report on *CCC* Workshop. *CCC,* 9 (1958), 191-92.

Rockas, Leo. "Further Comments on the Paragraph." *CCC,* 17 (1966), 148-51.

_____. "The Persistent Ptolemy and the Paradox of the Paragraph." *CCC,* 19 (1968), 135-37.

_____. "The Rhetoric of Doodle." *CE,* 40 (1978), 139-40.

Rodgers, Paul C., Jr. "Alexander Bain and the Rise of the Organic Paragraph." *QJS,* 51 (1965), 399-408.

_____. "A Discourse-Centered Rhetoric of the Paragraph." *CCC,* 17 (1966), 2-11.

_____. "The Stadium of Discourse." *CCC,* 18 (1967), 178-85.

Rogers C.D. "The Sedulous but Successful Ape." *EJ,* 56 (1967), 1309-11.

Sauer, Edwin H. "The Cooperation Correction of Paragraphs." In *Essays on the Teaching of English.* Ed. E.J. Gordon and E.S. Noyes. New York: Appleton: Century-Crofts, 1960, pp. 138-49.

Schell, Leo M. "Paragraph Composition: A Suggested Sequential Outline." *Education,* 90 (1969), 158-60.

Schiff, Peter M. "Problem Solving and the Composition Model: Reorganization, Manipulation, Analysis." *RTE,* 12 (1978), pp. 203-10.

Scott, Fred N., and Joseph V. Denney. *Paragraph Writing: A Rhetoric for Colleges.* 3rd ed. Boston: Allyn, Bacon, 1893.

Selzer, Jack. "Another Look at Paragraphs in Technical Writing." *J Tech Writ Comm,* 10 (1980), 293-301.

Shearer, Ned. A. "Alexander Bain and the Genesis of Paragraph Theory.'" *QJS,* 58 (1972), 408-17.

Sherman, L.A. *Analytics of Literature: A Manual for the Objective Study of English Prose and Poetry.* Boston: Ginn, 1983.

Sjogren, Douglas, and W. Timpson. "Frameworks for Comprehending Discourse: A Replication Study." *Am Educ Res J,* 16 (1979), 341-46.

Smith, Herbert Winslow. "Concerning Organization in Paragraphs." *EJ,* 9 (1920), 390-400.

Stanko, Thomas. "An Effective Opening." *CCC,* 20 (1969), 233-37.

Stern, Arthur A. "When Is a Paragraph?" *CE,* 27 (1976), 253-57.

Stratton, Beverly D., John Charlton-Seifert, and Maurice G. Williams. "Reading and Writing Shapes." *J Dev Rem Educ,* 3 (1980), 21-22.

Stronks, James. "Coherence in the Paragraph." In *Writing Exercises from Exercise Exchange.* Ed. Littleton Long. Urbana, Ill.: *NCTE,* 1976, pp. 48-51.

Tagliente, Jo. "The Edible Paragraph--Dagwood's Sandwich." *Elem Eng,* 50 (1973), 954-58.

Thaddeus, Janice. "Imitation and independence." *Teachers and Writers Magazine,* 12 (1981), 2-6.

Thompson, C.J. "Thought-Building in the Paragraph." *EJ,* 5 (1916), 610-19.

Thorndyke, Perry. "Cognitive Structures in Comprehension and Memory of Narrative Discourse." *Cog Psychol,* 9 (1977), 77-110.

Trotsky, O.S., and C.C. Wood. "Nobody Writes a Paragraph." *Elem Eng,* 49 (1972), 372-75.

_____. "Paragraph Writing: A Second Look." *Elem Eng,* 52 (1975), 197-200, 238.

Turner, E.G. *Greek Manuscripts of the Ancient World.* Princeton, N.J.: Princeton University Press, 1971, pp. 9-17.

Vande Kopple, William J. "Readability of Expository Paragraphs with Identical or Related Sentence Topics." *Psychol Rep*, 45 (1979), 947-52.

_____. "Readability of a Rhetorically Linked Expository Paragraph." *Perc Motor Skills*, 51 (1980), 245-46.

_____. "Functional Sentence Perspective, Composition, and Readings," *CCC*, 33 (1982), 50-63.

Vitanza, Victor J. "A Tagmemic Heuristic for the Whole Composition." *CCC*, 30 (1979), 270-74.

Waller, Marcie R., and F.L. Durley. "The Influence of Context on the Auditory Comprehension of Paragraphs by Aphasic Subjects." *J Speech Hear Res*, 21 (1978), 732-45.

Walpole, Jane R. "Rhetorical Form: A Crockful of Crols." *FEN*, 8 (1979), 1-2.

Warner, Richard. "Teaching the Paragraph as a Structural Unit." *CCC*, 30 (1979), 152-55.

Weathers, Winston. "Grammars of Style: New Options for Composition." *FEN*, 4 (1976), 4-12.

_____. *An Alternative Style: Options for Composition*. Montclair, N.J.: Boynton/Cook, 1980.

_____, and Otis Winchester. *Copy and Compose: A Guide to Prose Style*. Englewood Cliffs, N.J.: Prentice-Hall, 1969.

Wendell, Barrett. *English Composition*. New York: Ungar, 1963. First published as *Eight Lectures*, 1891.

Wensch, William. "What Reading Research Tells Us about Writing." 1979. ERIC ED 178 956.

Whitmore, Charles E. "A Doctrine of the Paragraph." *EJ*, 12 (1923), 605-10.

Whitten, M.E. *Creative Pattern Practice: A New Approach to Writing*. New York: Harcourt, Brace, World, 1966, pp. 187-200.

Wiener, Harvey S. "The Single Narrative Paragraph and College Remediation." *CE*, 33 (1972), 660-69.

Wilson, Thomas W. "Composition Where None is Apparent: Contemporary Literature and the Course of Writing." *CCC*, 16 (1965), 70-75.

Williams, Joseph. "Nuclear Structures of Discourse." In *Selected Papers from the 1981 Texas Writing Research Conference*. Ed. Maxine C. Hairston and Cynthia L. Selfe. Austin: Texas Writing Research Group, 1981, pp. 165-89.

Winterowd, W. Ross. "The Grammar of Coherence." *CE*, 31 (1970), 828-35.

_____. *The Contemporary Writer*. New York: Holt, Rinehart, Winston, 1976, pp. 110-35.

Witte, Stephen P., and Lester Faigley. "Coherence, Cohesion, and Writing Quality." *CCC*, 32 (1981), 189-206.

Wolfe, D.M. "Crucial First Assignment: Describing a Room." *Elem Eng*, 47 (1970), 784-86.

Young, Richard E., and Alton Becker. "The Role of Lexical and Grammatical Cues in Paragraph Recognitions." *Stud Lang & Lang Behav*, 2 (1966), 1-6.

_____, Alton Becker, and Kenneth Pike. *Rhetoric: Discovery and Change*. New York: Harcourt, Brace, Jovanovich. 1970.

C. Selected Bibliography

Braddock, Richard. "The Frequency and Placement of Topic Sentences in Expository Prose." *Research in the Teaching of English* 8 (1974): 287 - 302.

Christensen, Francis. *Notes Toward a New Rhetoric.* New York: Harper & Row, 1967.

Coe, Richard M. "If Not to Narrow, Then How to Focus: Two Techniques for Focusing." *CCC* 32 (1981): 272-77.

--------------. *Toward a Grammar of Passages.* Carbondale, IL: Southern Illinois UP, 1988.

D'Angelo, Frank. *A Conceptual Theory of Rhetoric.* Cambridge: Winthrop, 1975.

-------------. "The Topic Sentence Revisited." *CCC* 37 (1986): 431-41.

-------------. "Topoi and Form in Composition." *The Territory of Language: Linguistics, Stylistics, and the Teaching of Composition.* Ed. Donald A. McQuade. Carbondale, IL: Southern Illinois UP, 1986.

Markels, Robin Bell. *A New Perspective on Cohesion in Expository Paragraphs.* Carbondale: Southern Illinois UP, 1984.

Moran, Michael G. "The English Paragraph." *Research in Rhetoric and Composition: A Bibliographic Sourcebook.* Eds. Michael G. Moran and Ronald F. Lunsford. Westport: Greenwood, 1984. 425-50.

Perl, Sondra. "Understanding Composing." *CCC* 31 (1980): 363-69.

Podis, JoAnne M., and Leonard M. Podis. "Identifying and Teaching Rhetorical Plans for Arrangement." *CCC* 41 (1990): 430-42.

Podis, Leonard A. "Teaching Arrangement: Defining a More Practical Approach." *CCC* 31 (1980): 197-204.

Popken, Randell L. "A Study of Topic Sentence Use in Academic Writing." *Written Communication* 4 (1987): 209-28.

-------------. *The Sentence and the Paragraph.* Urbana IL: NCTE, 1963.

Smith, Rochelle. "Paragraphing for Coherence: Writing as Implied Dialogue." *CE* 46 (1984): 8-21.

Stotsky, Sandra. "Types of Lexical Cohesion in Expository Academic Discourse." *CCC* 34 (1983): 430-46.

Wilcox, Lance. "Time Lines in the Composing of Narratives: A Graphic Aid to Organization." *The Writing Instructor* 6 (1987): 162-73.

Vande Kopple, William J. "Something Old, Something New: Functional Sentence Perspective." *Research in the Teaching of English* 17 (1983): 85-99.

Williams, Joseph. *Style: Ten Lessons in Clarity and Grace*, 2nd ed. Glenview: Scott Foresman, 1985.

Witte, Stephen P., and Lester Faigley. "Coherence, Cohesion, and Writing Quality." *CCC* 32 (1981): 189-204.

D. Style--Writing Sentences

Style is a troublesome subject for writing instructors, especially in first-year composition classes. In "Teaching Style," the first piece in this section, Edward P. J. Corbett writes that writing instructors seldom discuss style at all. There usually isn't time.

Theophrastus, an ancient Greek rhetorician who studied with Aristotle, identified four virtues of style: ornamentation, appropriateness, clarity, and correctness. The Stoics later added a fifth virtue, brevity. Using these classifications, it is easy to identify the stylistic priorities of modern composition teaching. It has emphasized correctness, followed by clarity and conciseness, usually concentrating on students' errors and problems with clarity and "awkwardness." And it has neglected instruction of figures of speech and of appropriateness to audience and situation. Those priorities are changing, however. Study after study has shown that traditional lectures and exercises on grammar do not reduce the number of errors in student writing significantly, as Patrick Hartwell discusses here in "Grammar, Grammars, and the Teaching of Grammar." Sociolinguistic studies of standard English and of other English dialects have challenged our assumptions of correctness and "good English," as reflected in the Conference of College Composition and Communication statement *Students' Right to Their Own Language*. Teachers such as Ken Macrorie, Peter Elbow, and Donald Murray and feminist scholars such as the authors of *Women's Ways of Knowing* advocate instruction that values personal voice and individual style. Renewed attention to audience and rhetorical situation and the writing across the curriculum movement have made appropriateness an important concern once again.

The four articles in this section offer suggestions for teaching style, usage, and editing effectively. In "Teaching Style" (originally published in *The Territory of Language: Linguistics, Stylistics, and the Teaching of Composition*, ed. Donald A. McQuade [Carbondale: Southern Illinois UP, 1986]), Edward P. J. Corbett describes pedagogies from the past and present in which students learn about stylistic techniques and choices by analyzing the writings of published authors and develop their styles with a range of imitation exercises. Corbett argues that close analysis of another's style teaches students to use language self-consciously as readers and writers and provides them with a vocabulary to help them analyze their sentences and make informed stylistic decisions. Although he realizes that his regimen of analysis and imitation exercises from classical rhetoric and from recent works on style may be impractical in many classrooms, Corbett believes that they will enrich the styles of students who practice them as well as their appreciation of how others use language.

In "Sentence Combining in the Teaching of the Writing Process" (originally published in ***Sentence Combining: A Rhetorical Perspective*, edited by Donald A. Daiker, Andrew Kerek, and Max Morenberg**. Carbondale: Southern Illinois University Press, 1986), Richard Gebhardt discusses an important pedagogy for improving students' style developed in the 1970s. In sentence combining, students build complex sentences from short sentences, using specific syntactic structures such as relative clauses. Sentence combining exercises often require students to do more than create isolated sentences, to build a paragraph or brief essay from a number of short sentences. Although most studies of sentence combining have shown that students' writing usually improves with this pedagogy, sentence combining has drawn criticism, Gebhardt   writes, because the exercises do not work with students' own sentences, and this seems to conflict with process pedagogies.   Gebhardt disagrees with this assessment and describes how   sentence combining can be integrated into a process-oriented composition course.

The next two pieces address what Patrick Hartwell calls "the   grammar issue." Decades of studies that question the value of teaching formal grammar have not settled the issue of how to   teach students to edit their writing to avoid violations of the conventions of standard American English.   In "Grammar, Grammars,   and the Teaching of Grammar" (originally published in *College   English* 47 [1985]: 105-27), Hartwell reviews this debate but   hopes to inform our understanding of error with linguistic theory and research.   Hartwell argues that we need to recognize that most errors are not "conceptual errors" that will disappear with the study of formal rules. Most errors are "performance errors" that can stem from any of a number of causes.

Following the implications of Hartwell's article, Muriel   Harris and Katherine E. Rowan develop ways of improving students'   editing in "Explaining Grammatical Concepts" (originally   published in *Journal of Basic Writing* 6 [Fall 1989]: 21-41). They present editing as an activity of detection, diagnosis, and   revision that involves critical thinking, not as a simple one- step process.   Instead of the traditional lectures and grammar   drills, Harris and Rowan argue for teaching grammatical concepts only when they can help students understand a problem that they are contending with.   Such instruction should focus on the   elements of the concept that are crucial for understanding and   correcting the error and should present the student with a range of examples.   Conferences with students should help students form questions that build on their innate knowledge of their language to guide their editing.

Whatever time we decide to devote to the teaching of style, we should remember that when we teach style and usage, we are   dealing with matters of thought and identity. Language is not just a conduit through which we transmit our thoughts to each other. It's the stuff we think with.   Our styles reflect our gender, our ethnicities, our class, our professions, and our avocations, the ways we see the world.   They are closely linked to who we are and who we might become, as individuals, as members of our various communities, and as participants in academic life.

Teaching Style

Edward P.J. Corbett

If your educational experience in any way resembled mine, you have been uncertain about what style is. *Style* was a familiar enough word for you, but your concept of style was probably vague. You sensed that certain authors had a distinctive style, but you were not quite sure what it meant to say that an author "has style" and even less sure about what made a style distinctive. In reading a piece of prose, you experienced an undeniable effect, but you could not designate just what it was in that collection of sentences that caused that effect. Consequently, you still may not know how to analyze style or how to talk about it in any meaningful way.

Style may be a vague concept to us because our own teachers spent little or no time talking about style. They may have used such general terms as "lucid," "elegant," "labored," "Latinate," "turgid," or "flowing" in commenting on an author's style, but they never bothered to analyze the features or the constituents of the styles that bore those epithets. Those were largely impressionistic labels, and if we too regarded a certain authors style as, say, "turgid"--whatever *that* was--then we agreed with our teacher's classification of the style. But if we felt that this same author had a "lilting style" we knew no way of describing a "lilting style" or no way of refuting our teacher's judgment. So we dutifully copied down in out notebooks the appropriate epithets for each author we read and discussed in class, and we delighted in moving on to talk about more determinable matters, like the content or the structure of the piece of literature. If we listed ourselves as members of that post-World War II generation of students who regularly practiced the Brooks and Warren method of close analysis, we could talk about the linguistic features of a poem with great specificity. Yet we may well have been stymied when we wanted to talk about the linguistic features of a prose text.

If you could put these questions concerning style (what is it? what effects does it produce in a reader? what does one look for in studying it?) to a Renaissance schoolboy, he could give you satisfactory answers. His education was predominantly language-oriented. From the beginning to the end of the school day, he was steeped in words--English words, Latin words, sometimes even Greek words. He had to recite the grammatical rules that he had memorized the night before; he had to paraphrase sentences; he had to translate Latin sentences into English sentences or English sentences into Latin sentences; he had to be able to write original sentences according to a prescribed pattern; he had to paraphrase sentences in a variety of ways; he had to be able to recognize, classify, and define the schemes and tropes in a passage being studied (and there were more than a hundred of those listed in the Renaissance rhetoric texts). T.W. Baldwin's *William Shakespere's Small Latine & Lesse Greeke*, or Sister Miriam Joseph's Shakespeare's *Use of the Arts of Language*, or Donald L. Clark's *John Milton at St. Paul's School* will give you a generous sense of the language-arts regimen that the Tudor school boy was subjected to in the grammar schools.[1]   If we required of our students what Renaissance schoolmasters demanded of theirs, we would no doubt face a general revolt.

This rigorous regimen, however, produced students who really learned grammar and rhetoric and who knew not only the meaning of style but also the procedures for analyzing someone else's style and improving their own. They could tell you that style represented the choices that an author made from the lexical and syntactical resources of the language. Style represented a curious blend of the idiosyncratic and the conventional. The more idiosyncratic a style, the more distinctive it became; the more conventional, the more bland it likely became--although not necessarily less serviceable for being bland. In one sense, then, "Style was the man," because it represented the characteristic way in which a person expressed his or her thoughts and feelings.

For that reason, everyone can be said to "have a style." But some styles are more pleasing, more distinctive, more effective than others. Some writers can command several styles--a range of styles into which they can readily shift as the subject matter, the occasion, or the audience necessitates. There are high styles and low styles and middle styles. In his book *The Five CLocks,* Martin Joos compares these various styles to what he calls the five registers--the frozen, the formal, the consultative, the casual, and the intimate.[2] Joos also notes that sophisticated language-users can shift into and out of these registers as the occasion demands. Some people do not command the full range of styles or registers, simply because they have not yet acquired the full repertory of diction and syntax needed for stylistic versatility. As the philosophers would say, they have the command *potentially* but not *actually.* Our task as teachers is to turn the *potency* into *act.*

If we as teachers want to engage our students in the study of style, the first point that needs to be made is that the circumstances in which we teach may not allow us to deal with style at all. Many of us teach in a curriculum so crowded that there simply is not enough time to deal adequately with style. And the study of style does take time. The Renaissance schoolmaster had the same group of pupils for the full academic year, often had them six days a week for six to eight hours a day. That generous allotment of time allowed for relentless recitation, rigorous drill, and reinforcing repetition. And the curriculum then was not as cluttered as it is now. If you cannot devote at least two weeks to the study of style, either in a concentrated period or in scattered sessions throughout the semester, you had better not deal with style at all.

The relative sophistication of your students in language matters may also determine whether you can deal with style in the classroom. I can imagine some teachers saying, "Good heavens, I have all I can do just to get my students to the point where they can consistently write sentences that parse. My students have to learn how to walk before I can teach them how to run." There is no question that a minimal grammatical competence is a *sine qua non* for stylistic studies. If style represents the choices one makes from the available grammatical options, then students must have at least a basic awareness of what the grammatical options are if they are to profit from stylistic studies. But a deficiency in conscious knowledge of grammar is not an insuperable disqualification for studying style. Many students can learn their grammar while studying style. I have found that students are invariably fascinated by style--not only because it offers something new and different but also because it provides an element of fun in changing words and shifting parts. And in such a positive and creative atmosphere, students may well be more inclined to develop an interest in grammar or at least to absorb grammar subconsciously.

Studying style in English courses can have two focuses or objectives: to learn either how to analyze someone else's style or how to improve our own. These two objectives are ancillary rather than countervailing. As teachers, we can pursue either or both, but we should determine our main objective for the course at the outset. Learning how to analyze someone else's style belongs primarily to the literature class; learning how to improve one's own style belongs primarily to the composition class. But there is no reason why both kinds of learning cannot take place in both classes. In fact, learning how to analyze someone else's style in the composition class is almost a necessary prelude for learning how to improve one's own style. By analyzing an accomplished writer's style, we can recognize the marks of effective style, and then we can begin, either consciously or unconsciously, to incorporate some of those features into our own style. The process works in reverse too. By deliberately working on our own style to refine it, we learn what to look for in analyzing someone else's style.

Studying style begins with some awareness of what we should look at or look for. In the chapter on style in my *Classical Rhetoric for the Modern Student* and in my "A Method of Analyzing Prose Style, with a Demonstration Analysis of Swift's `A Modest Proposal,'" I outline the features that can be observed and analyzed.[3] I divide these features into four main categories: diction, sentence patterns, figures of speech, and paragraphing. But my designating those main categories may not be very helpful to you. What about diction? What about sentence patterns? Just what aspects of diction and sentence patterns are significant?

Let me be a little more specific here. A writer's choice of words contributes to the effects that style has on readers. If we think about it for a moment, we must acknowledge that choosing a big word or a little word, a general word or a specific word, an abstract word or a concrete word does make a difference in what the text conveys to us either explicitly or implicitly. And when we observe that certain kinds of words are recurrent, when we observe that sets of words exemplify certain motifs, these words become even more significant because of what they tell us about an author's characteristic way of saying things. A writer's working vocabulary--the stock of words that a writer actually uses in a piece of writing rather than the words that he or she can recognize in someone else's writing--reflects the range of a writer's knowledge and interests. The larger one's working vocabulary, the more likely it is that one can choose precise diction. Shakespeare's working vocabulary of over 21,000 words was an extraordinary lexicon--and not only for his time.

The study of the lexical element of style involves fewer objectively observable items than the study of any other stylistic element. By the term "objectively observable item," I mean an item which can be definitely classified by observation rather than by judgment. For instance, one can decide whether a particular word is monosyllabic or polysyllabic by simply looking at the word. The decision, however, about whether a word is abstract or concrete, general or specific, often involves a judgment, because those dichotomies are more relative than absolute. Consider, for example, a sentence like "The wealthy Texan owned huge herds of cattle." Is the word *cattle* general or specific? It is more specific than *livestock* but less specific than *steers*. Because of the relativity of the general-specific dichotomy, the classifier has to make an arbitrary judgment about the word *cattle* in this particular context. In this respect, it is worth remembering that any tabulating of percentages of words in a text according to whether the words are abstract or concrete, general or specific, formal or informal, denotative or connotative is likely to be somewhat less than precise, simply because in many instances the yes-no decision represents someone's arbitrary judgment.

When we move on to study collocations of words in sentences, we find not only more objectively observable items but more significant features of writing habits. Most of the stylistic features of sentences are objectively observable items: length of sentences (in number of words); grammatical types of sentences (simple, compound, complex, compound-complex); rhetorical types of sentences (loose, periodic, balanced, antithetical); functional types of sentences (statement, question, command, exclamation); types and frequency of sentence-openers; methods and location of expansions in sentences; amount of embedding. Analysis and classification of features like those tell us a great deal about the level of a writer's "syntactic fluency."

Syntactic patterns also tell us something about the way a writer structures his or her thoughts, about a writer's "epistemic orientation," to use Richard Ohmann's term.[4] The frequent occurrence, for instance, of balanced or antithetical patterns in Dr. Johnson's sentences suggests that he tended to structure his thinking in terms of parallel or opposing dichotomies. The many levels of subordination in John Henry Newman's prose suggests that he tended to see things in terms of hierarchies. The stringing together of independent clauses in Hemingway's prose, often with redundant use of coordinating conjunctions, indicates that Hemingway tended to view the phenomenal world as a flux of discrete, coordinate elements. Henry James's heavy use of parenthetical elements reflects a mind disposed to meticulous qualifications. And so on.

The gathering of data about syntactic patterns involves a lot of tedious counting and tabulating. Data of that sort were not previously available because the counting and measuring had to be done by hand and took hours and weeks. When Edwin Lewis and L.A. Sherwin did their studies in the 1890s of sentence and paragraph length in the works of several British writers, they did all their counting by hand.[5] Today, the computer facilitates such tedious data-gathering, and as a result, stylistic studies of large corpuses of prose and poetry have proliferated.

Collecting data--once tedious and time-consuming--still must be done. We are much more impressed when someone pronounces that a certain writer strings together unusually long sentences and supports that claim with the empirically derived evidence that the writer's average sentence length is 37.8 words. And we are further impressed by the disclosure that 18 percent of that writer's sentences are ten or more words longer than that average.

How much of a corpus has to be studied before valid generalizations can be made about someone's style? I have told undergraduate students studying style--either their own or some professional writer's--that they must analyze somewhere between 1000 and 1500 words of a piece of prose. That is not very much really at most four double-spaced typescript pages, maybe two pages of printed text. But it is substantial enough to allow for some valid inferences to be drawn. Students writing a dissertation or a scholarly article on someone's prose style should be reminded not only that they would have to study a much larger corpus but also that they would have to study several specimens of a writer's prose, pieces written at different periods and on different subject matters for different audiences. As in any inductive study, the larger and the more representative the sampling, the safer the conclusions will be.

The gathering of data is a necessary stage but should not be the stopping point. Necessary as the gathering of the data is, what one does with the data matters more. Data--even raw statistical data--can convey some illuminating information. But often the full or the most salient significance of the data depends upon interpretation. The act of interpretation calls upon all of one's intellectual and imaginative powers; it requires that one shift from the role of a mere counter to the role of a critic.

Critical interpretation demands that one be able to detect the relevance or the relationship of the data to the exigencies of the rhetorical situation--to the occasion, purpose, subject matter, audience, or author of the discourse. We may find, for instance, that in a particular discourse, the author used an unusually high percentage of interrogative sentences--let us say 18 percent, almost one out of every five sentences. Why? A question like that poses a real challenge for the critic. The critic may find the answer by relating the statistical fact to the nature of the subject matter that the author addressed. The writer may have been writing on a subject about which he was uncertain. He was exploring the subject, probing for answers. So he frequently resorted to questions, knowing that sometimes asking the right questions can be as illuminating as proposing hesitant answers. Or the critic might relate the statistical fact to the disposition of the audience for this piece of discourse. The author, let us say, knew that his audience harbored a certain hostility to the position he was espousing. He knew that he could exacerbate that hostility if he were dogmatic in his pronouncements. So he decided that it would be a prudent strategy to soften his assertiveness by frequently resorting to the tentativeness of questions. But looking closely at his questions might reveal, for example, that many of them are framed as rhetorical questions in which the writer has subtly implied the answers he wants to elicit from his audience.

That kind of interpretation, that kind of relating of fact to function, may be beyond the capacity of some students in basic writing courses. After all, that kind of interpretation requires a great deal of linguistic and rhetorical sophistication. Some students may not be mature enough to make such connections and to come forth with anything more than the most superficial interpretation. But the present incapacity of some students for such critical insights is not the issue. They have learned something valuable about the text simply from gathering the data. They have learned something too from the mere *attempt* to interpret the data. Inadequate as their interpretation may be, they have grown a few inches in the attempt.

In addition to diction and syntax, there are other aspects of style that we might have our students look at: the incidence of figures of speech, the rhythms of sentences, the manner of paragraphing.

A figure of speech may be defined as any artful deviation from the ordinary way of speaking or writing. The classical rhetoricians commonly divided the *figura* into two main groups: schemes and tropes. A scheme involves a deliberate deviation from the ordinary pattern or arrangement of words. In addition to common patterns like parallelism and antithesis, schemes include such artistic patterns as the inversion of the natural or normal word order (*anastrophe),* deliberate omission of the normally expected conjunctions in a series of related words, phrases, or clauses (*asyndeton),* repetition of the same word or group of words at the beginning of successive clauses (*anaphora*), repetition of initial consonants in two or more adjacent words (*alliteration*), and reversal of the grammatical structures in successive clauses (*chiasmus* or *crisscross*). Tropes, the second main kind of figurative language, are deliberate deviations from the ordinary *meaning* of words and include such familiar figures as metaphor, simile, hyperbole, synecdoche, metonymy, oxymoron, and irony.

In the schools of rhetoric, pupils were expected to be able to identity, define, and illustrate the figures they encountered in the texts they read and to be able to invent similar figures. Their task was complicated by the fact that the number of schemes and tropes had proliferated enormously. *Rhetorica ad Herennium,* an influential Roman rhetoric text, listed 65 figures; the 1577 edition of Henry Peacham's *The Garden of Eloquence* identified 184. Undoubtedly, the proliferation of the figures resulted from overly subtle anatomizing, but amazingly, once students were made aware of the many kinds of artful deviations from the normal meanings or arrangements or words, they readily found the figures in the prose and poetry they read. In the second edition of my *Classical Rhetoric for the Modern Student,* more than half of the schemes and tropes illustrated there were supplied to me by two classes of freshman students who, over a six-week period, searched for examples in their reading. They found a surprising number of examples in magazine advertisements and television commercials. Once students become familiar with a wide range of schemes and tropes, they find them everywhere, even where authors were not conscious that they were creating figures.

What should teachers encourage students to look for when studying the figures, and what does the occurrence of figures tell them about an author's style? First of all, we ought to ask them simply to look for the schemes and tropes. When they find them, they ought to identify and tabulate them and perhaps draw up some statistical information about them. If there are many schemes and tropes, they can begin to classify them into groups or clusters. A particular author, let us say, uses mainly schemes of repetition. Most of this author's metaphors are based on agricultural analogies. Certain patterns or motifs begin to emerge that tell students something about a particular author's mind-set. The presence--or the absence--of figures tells students something about the texture and flavor of an author's prose.

In the modern classroom, teachers rarely, if ever, consider prose rhythms, but our forebears in Greek and Latin schools regularly engaged their pupils in analyzing and composing various prose rhythms. The Greeks and the Romans, of course, had developed elaborate prosodies for their synthetic languages, and since a good deal of their formal communication took place in the oral medium, they were much more conscious than we of the sounds and rhythms of words when they composed their orations. We have only to read sections of Cicero's rhetoric texts or his orations to find out the careful attention this rhetorician gave to the composition of euphonious prose.

English-speaking people probably lost their ear for verbal rhythms when written or printed documents superseded oral discourse as the primary mode of communication. In the late eighteenth century, the elocutionary movement in England, fostered by former actors like Thomas Sheridan, tried to revive interest in the sounds of prose.[6] Although English teachers continued to teach students how to scan lines of poetry, they began to lose all interest in the aural dimensions of prose early in the twentieth century, along about 1915, when teachers of speech formally divorced themselves from the National Council of Teachers of English and formed their own speech association. But at a time when the aural element has become dominant again and music is the favorite medium of young people, perhaps we should revive the study of prose rhythms in the classroom. Litterateurs like George Saintsbury have shown us that there is an elaborate prosody for scanning prose, rhythms,[7] but I would not recommend that we spend valuable time in the classroom exploring the technicalities of that system. If we would revive the practice of reading prose aloud, we might be able to cultivate our students'ears for the harmonies of prose. In the February 1977 issue of *College Composition and Communication,* Thomas Kane published an engaging article about what teachers might do in the classroom to cultivate a sense for the ring and rhythm of well-constructed sentences.[8] Prose, of course, is most often read silently, but curiously enough, euphonious sentences somehow disclose their meanings more easily than awkwardly constructed sentences do, even when read silently. Rhythm is a neglected area of stylistic study, but the classical rhetoricians were right when they preached that the harmonies of prose did make a positive contribution to the conveyance of a message.

For the classical rhetoricians, stylistic study rarely extended beyond the limits of the sentence. Maybe the reason for that neglect was that the concept of paragraphing had not yet developed, even in their writing system. The typographical device of paragraphing was largely the invention of printers, and it was not until the late nineteenth century that a systematic rhetoric of the paragraph was developed by Alexander Bain.[9] Recently, however, such rhetoricians as Francis Christensen, Alton Becker, Paul C. Rodgers, and Frank D'Angelo have convinced us that there is such a thing as a "style" of paragraphing.[10]

What should teachers and students look for in studying the "style" of paragraphing? They can, for example, examine the length of paragraphs, measured in number of words or sentences per paragraph. Information about the average length of paragraphs reveals whether an author tends to break up the discourse into small units or into large units and whether an author tends to develop topics elaborately or minimally. Teachers and students can also note whether an author uses explicit topic sentences and where those topic sentences are placed in the paragraph. Moreover, they can observe the coherence devices that an author uses to articulate sequences of sentences within and between paragraphs. Using Francis Christensen's system, they can diagram the levels of coordination and subordination in paragraphs. They can also catalogue the methods of development that an author uses. Indeed, the kinds of choices that an author makes in composing a paragraph are comparable to, if not identical with, the kinds of choices an author makes in composing a sentence. There is, then, a style of paragraphing.

Each aspect that teachers and students can look at when studying someone else's style can be applied to studying specimens of their own prose. And I would strongly urge teachers to analyze their own style. They can take a paper of 1000 to 1500 words that they wrote for one of their college classes or a paper that they have published and subject it to some of the kinds of counting and measuring that I outlined. They will find the investigation fascinating, and they will discover some surprising features about their style--some felicitous characteristics and some regrettable mannerisms.

Improving our students' analytical skills is a proper concern of English teachers, but improving our students' synthetical skills should be our main concern as teachers of composition. And let me suggest, although in the broadest terms, the kinds of exercises that can help our students refine their style and enhance their stylistic virtuosity.

In my own rhetoric texts, I have suggested a number of imitative exercises that have proven fruitful for me and for my students. Let me just mention those exercises, without elaborating on them. (1) Simply copying verbatim admired passages of prose. (2) Copying a passage but changing one element in it- -for instance, changing all the past-tense verbs to present-tense verbs. (3) Composing a sentence on the pattern of a sentence written by some admired author. (4) Taking a sentence that someone else has written and seeing in how many different ways one can say essentially what the model sentence says. (5) Taking a group of isolated kernel sentences and combining them into a single sentence.

You can get more details about these exercises by consulting the chapters on style in my two rhetoric texts, in Francis Christensen's article "A Generative Rhetoric of the Sentence," in the two NCTE monographs on sentence-combining by John Mellon and Frank O'Hare, in Walker Gibson's *Tough, Sweet, and Stuffy,* in Winston Weathers and Otis Winchester's *Copy and Compose,* in Joseph Williams' *Style: Ten Lessons in Clarity and Grace,* or in Thomas Whissen's *A Way With Words.*[11]

Perhaps the classroom practices I have suggested here are wholly impracticable for your situation. With all the requirements--and time constraints--of a composition course, the study of style may be more than you can handle. Or some of your students may be so minimally literate that engaging them in any of the analyses or exercises I have proposed would prove futile. But even if your students are not ready to engage in stylistic studies, you can do so yourself. Such a regimen promises to help you grow immeasurably in your awareness of the remarkable richness and variety of our language and in your resourcefulness as a teacher of language, literature, and composition.

NOTES

1.   T.W. Baldwin, *William Shakespere's Small Latine Lesse Greeke,* 2 vols. (Urbana, IL: Univ. of Illinois Pr., 1944); Sister Miriam Joseph, *Shakespeare's Use of the Arts of Language* (New York: Columbia Univ. Pr., 1947); Donald L. Clark, *John Milton at St. Paul's School: A Study of Ancient Rhetoric in Renaissance Education* (New York: Columbia Univ. Pr., 1948).

2.   Martin Joos, *The Five Clocks* (New York: Harcourt, Brace, and World, Harbinger Books, 1962), p. 11.

3.   Edward P.J. Corbett, "Style," in *Classical Rhetoric for the Modern Student,* 2d ed. (New York: Oxford Univ. Pr., 1971), pp. 414-593; Edward P.J. Corbett, "A Method of Analyzing Prose Style, with a Demonstration Analysis of Swifts *A Modest Proposal,*" in *The Writing Teacher's Sourcebook,* ed. Gary Tate and Edward P.J. Corbett (New York: Oxford Univ. Pr., 1981), pp. 333-52.

4.   Richard Ohmann, *Shaw, the Style and the Man* (Middletown, CT. Wesleyan Univ. Pr., 1962).

5.   Edwin H. Lewis, *History of the English Paragraph* (Chicago: Univ. of Chicago Pr., 1894); L.A. Sherman, *Some Observations upon Sentence Length in English Prose* (Lincoln, NB: Univ. of Nebraska Pr., 1892).

6.   See Wilbur Samuel Howell, "The British Elocutionary Movement," in his *Eighteenth-Century British Logic and Rhetoric* (Princeton, NJ: Princeton Univ. Pr., 1971), pp. 145-256.

7.   George Saintsbury, *A History of Prose Rhythm* (London, 1912; re-issued Bloomington, IN: Indiana Univ. Pr., 1965).

8. Thomas S. Kane, "'The Shape and Ring of Sentences,'" *College Composition and Communication,* 28 (February 1977), 38-42.
9. Paul C. Rodgers, Jr., "Alexander Bain and the Rise of the Organic Paragraph," *Quarterly Journal of Speech,* 50 (December 1965), 399-408.
10. Francis Christensen, "A Generative Rhetoric of the Paragraph," in his *Notes Toward a New Rhetoric* (New York: Harper and Row, 1967), pp. 74-103; Alton L. Becker, "A Tagmemic Approach to Paragraph Analysis," *College Composition and Communication* 16 (December 1965), 237-42; Paul C. Rodgers, Jr., "A Discourse-Centered Rhetoric of the Paragraph," *College Composition and Communication,* 17 (February 1966), 2-11; Frank D'Angelo, "Style as structure," *Style,* 8 (Spring 1974), 322-64.
11. Edward P. J. Corbett, "Style," in *Classical Rhetoric,* pp. 414-593; Edward P.J. Corbett, "Expressing What You Have Discovered, Selected, and Arranged," in *The Little Rhetoric and Handbook,* 2d ed. (Glenview, IL: Scott, Foresman, 1982), pp. 70-120; Francis Christensen, "A Generative Rhetoric of the Sentence," in his *Notes Toward a New Rhetoric* pp. 23-44; John C. Mellon, *Transformational Sentence Combining: A Method for Enhancing the Development of Syntactic Fluency* (Urbana, IL: National Council of Teachers of English, 1969); Frank O'Hare, *Sentence Combining: Improving Student Writing Without Formal Grammar Instruction* (Urbana, IL: National Council of Teachers of English, 1973); Walker Gibson, *Tough, Sweet, and Stuffy* (Bloomington, IN: Indiana Univ. Pr., 1966); Winston Weathers and Otis Winchester, *Copy and Compose: A Guide to Prose Style* (Englewood Cliffs, NJ: Prentice-Hall, 1969); Joseph Williams, *Style: Ten Lessons in Clarity and Grace,* 2d ed. (Glenview, IL: Scott, Foresman, 1984); Thomas Whissen, *A Way with Words: A Guide for Writers* (New York: Oxford Univ. Pr., 1982).

ADDITIONAL READINGS

Those interested in pursuing the study of style may consult the following selected readings, as well all the books and articles cited in the notes.

Bennett, James R., et al. "The Paragraph: An Annotated Bibliography." *Style,* II (Spring 1972), 107-18.
Corbett, Edward P.J. "Approaches to the Study of Style." *Teaching Composition: 10 Bibliographical Essays.* Ed. Gary Tate. Fort Worth: Texas Christian University Press, 1976, pp. 73-109.
Corbett, Edward P.J. "Ventures in Style." *Reinventing the Rhetorical Tradition.* Ed. Aviva Freedman and Ian Pringle. Ottawa, Ontario: Canadian Council of Teachers of English, 1980, pp. 79-87.
Davidson, Donald. "Grammar and Rhetoric: The Teacher's Problem." *Quarterly Journal of Speech,* 39 (December 1953), 425-36.
Fleishauer, John. "Teaching Prose Style Analysis: One Method." *Style,* 9 (Winter 1975), 92-102.
Graves, Richard. "A Primer for Teaching Style." *College Composition and Communication* 25 (May 1974), 186-90.
Love, Glen A., and Michael Payne. eds. *Contemporary Essays on Style: Rhetoric, Linguistics, and Criticism.* Glenview, IL: Scott, Foresman, 1969.
Milic, Louis T. "Theories of Style and Their Implications for the Teaching of Composition." *College Composition and Communication,* 16 (May 1965), 66-69, 126.
Milic, Louis T. *Style and Stylistics: An Analytical Bibliography.* New York: Free Press, 1967. Since 1967, the journal *Style* has been publishing the annual bibliographies on style and also several special bibliographies on style.
Price, Marian. "Recent Work in Paragraph Analysis: A Bibliography." *Rhetoric Society Quarterly,* 12 (Spring 1982), 127-31.
Secor, Marie J. "The Legacy of Nineteenth-Century Style Theory. " *Rhetoric Society Quarterly,* 12 (Spring 1982), 76-94.
Vitanza, Victor J. "A Comprehensive Survey of Course Offerings in the Study of Literary Style in American Colleges and Universities." *Style,* 12 (Fall 1978), 342-82.
Weathers, Winston. "Teaching Style: A Possible Anatomy." *College Composition and Communication,* 21 (May 1970), 144-149.
Weaver, Richard M. "Some Rhetorical Aspects of Grammatical Categories." In his *The Ethics of Rhetoric.* Chicago: Henry Regnery, 1953, pp. 115-127.

Sentence Combining in the
Teaching of the Writing Process
Richard Gebhardt

For some years I have argued that the writing process should be the center of the composition curriculum.[1] I used to resist sentence combining, which in its early manifestations seemed little more than the manipulation of prepackaged written products. This did not prevent my using sentence combining to get at specific instructional goals, such as helping writers develop a broader repertoire of sentence structures and an intuitive feel for grammar. But since I had reservations about how well such instructional approaches actually fit into the process-centered class, I worried that I might be contributing to a sort of schizophrenia in students in my classes or in the teachers working within the writing program I administered.

Over the past few years, I have had a change of mind about the place of sentence combining in process-centered composition classes. This change occurred as I realized that the writing process is different from what I once thought--something I will discuss later. Even before this change I discovered, as have so many teachers in the past few years, that sentence combining can work very effectively to help students explore their topics and revise their drafts. More recently, I have come to speculate on connections that sentence combining may have to the actual processes of writing-- speculations that will make up the bulk of this paper.

As that last sentence suggests, I see "writing process" to be something far different than it is described in most texts and courses. When I speak of exploring a topic or revising a draft, for example, I am not talking about the writing process at all, but about activities (like pre-writing, writing, and rewriting) that seem suspiciously neat divisions in a phenomenon research has shown to be far more complex and interconnected. Such stages along the route to a completed "writing project" *are* useful organizers within composition classes.

For instance, soon after students receive an assignment they face the problem of making a start--an exploration of the topic, a generation of material to use in an essay. As the following student example suggests, sentence combining can work effectively at this early point in the writing process.

Solar Fire

"Solar Fire" is a painting of outer-space using relatively few colours. The combinations of red, yellow, black, and white are used to create some really nice shades of colour.   The picture consists of planets with light radiating from them, into a black void filled with stars. The light coming from the planets gets brighter and brighter until finally it ends in the black void, giving a very startling effect.

The painting reminds me of excitement and mystery, the colours are so realistic you could reach out and grab ahold of them. At the same time, the painting reminds me of solitude and tranquility with the planets and stars being the only thing in the universe. It gives you a feeling of "too far away to touch" and "too close to not be aware of." It looks like outer-space with all its mysteries which is full of solar fire filling all humans as a result of too much heat burning their bodies.

Very well painted, it was a good idea which was unique looking with the dark colour setting off the bright colours and vice-versa. The picture shows man very small compared to outerspace. This is not only in terms of size but also because of the fact that man has to rely on technology, where space is self-sufficient.

First Exploration: Student-Formulated Kernels

The picture is red.
The picture is yellow.
The picture is black.
The picture is white.

There are stars in the picture.
There are planets in the picture.
The radiating light expands into a black void.
The black void has stars in it.

The picture reminds me of outer space.
The outer space is full of solar fire.
The solar fire would kill all humans.
The killing would be a result of too much heat.
The heat would burn their body.
The picture reminds me of solitude.
The only thing in the universe.
It is too far to touch.

It is too close to not be aware of
It reminds me of tranquility.
It reminds me of excitement.
The excitement is a result of the bright colours.

It is very well painted.
It was a good idea.
The idea was unique looking.
The dark color sets off the bright colors.

The bright colors set off the dark color.

The picture shows man compared to outer space.
Man looks small in the comparison.
Space takes care of itself without help.
Man needs help of technology he thinks.

Second Exploration: Combining Student Sentences

The picture is red, yellow, black, and white.

In the picture there are stars in a black void and planets with light radiating from them into the void.

The picture reminds me of outer space which is full of solar fire killing all humans as a result of too much heat.

The bright colors makes this picture exciting, but at the same time it reminds me of solitude and tranquility, with it being the only thing in the universe too far to touch and too close to not be aware of.

Very well painted, it was a good idea which was unique looking with the dark color setting off the bright colors and the bright colors setting off the dark color.

The picture shows man compared to outer space which makes man look small because of the fact that space takes care of itself without help whereas man thinks he needs the help of technology.

"Solar Fire" is a the first draft of a descriptive essay about an abstract painting. It was done by a developmental student coerced into the college's gallery by my assignment to study one of the paintings on exhibit and to write about it. What that assignment might have brought forth without the use of sentence combining as exploration and generating strategy I would prefer not to think about. But the student was used to combining kernels from his work with William Strong's *Sentence Combining: A Composing Book*.[2] And he responded fairly well to directions to make up at least two dozen kernel sentences of description and reaction; to try to arrange them into five or six clusters that looked like an exercise in the text book; to combine the clusters; and then to write a few paragraphs using as much of the earlier work as he wanted.

Much later along the path to a completed writing project, students operate with the conscious motive of revising their drafts. As the second student example suggests, sentence combining also can offer students useful strategies for this revision. The first paragraph is part of a first-draft description a developmental student wrote about the time he competed in a state high-school wrestling tournament. Since we had been working with sentence-combining exercises, my marginal comment--"try to combine sentences here in different ways so that they are not so choppy"--prompted improvement in readability and "flow" in the second paragraph.

Show Down

There I was with a capacity croud observing me. The atmosphere was very tense to me. I couldn't believe all the people. And the noise they possessed. The 101 weight class was up. I had at least one hour to wait before I wrestled. My weight was one forty one; which at the time was the most competitive in the state that year. With my luck I had to wrestle the best kid in the states that year. His name was Tim C_____. He was a returning state champ, and also the most valuable wrestler that year. I was so nervous that I actually started sweating, and felt butterflies go through me. At the point that I almost threw up. My Father kept giving me a pep talk, but it didn't work, my nerves were shot.

Revision

A tense atmosphere filled Jadwyn Gym, with 7500 people observing the state wrestling tournament. I couldn't believe the noise and the people the gym possessed. The 101 weight class was up, and I had at least an hour to wait until I wrestled. My class was 141, which at the time was the most competitive class in the state.

I knew I had to wrestle Tim C_____, a returning state champ who had been the most valuable wrestler the year before. I was so nervous that I started sweating and felt butterflies go through me to the point that I almost threw up. My father kept giving me a pep talk. But it didn't work, because my nerves were shot.

I do not claim that "Solar Fire" and "Show Down" show as much improvement as we would like to see in student work. (They do not even show as much improvement as these two students ultimately made in their papers.) My point is simply that, by working with sentence combining, students can learn approaches that help them explore their own topics, generate their own sentences, revise their own prose. In saying that, however, I am not really saying much about the way that sentence combining may relate to the processes of writing. In the rest of this paper, I will deal with relationships between sentence combining and the real writing processes.

Some definitions are in order here. By "writing process" I do not mean any sequence of stages. "Stages"--such as generating material, drafting for a purpose and audience, and revising--play an important role in writing, in that they are intentions or motives that direct how a writer manifests the processes of writing at a given point in a writing project. But as I suggest in "Process and Intention: A Bridge from Theory to Classroom,"[3] generating, drafting, and revising--or any neat set of stages- -are not themselves the processes of writing. Instead, the real writing processes are the complex and interacting operations of the hands, brain, and eyes of a human writer. Donald Murray offered a dynamic illustration of these processes at work in his address at this conference (chap. 13). And I have suggested their complexity in figure 14.1.

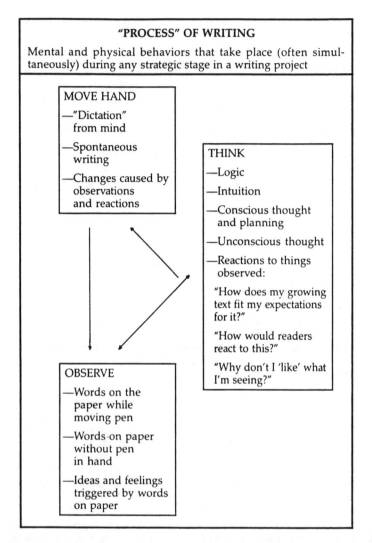

Figure 14.1. "Processes" of writing. Reprinted from Gebhardt, "Process and Intention: A Bridge from Theory to Classroom," The Writing Instructor, 1 (1982), 141.

"Thinking," "Moving Hands," and "Observing" seems to me a far more adequate summation of the writing process than generating, drafting, and revising. In the remainder of this paper, I will discuss--and occasionally speculate on--ways that sentence combining relates to the actual processes of writing.

To begin with, it is obvious that sentence combining bears a strong relationship to the interconnected operations of hands, brain, and eyes. Here is a simple combining exercise:

1. Sentence combining is a teaching strategy.
2. The teaching strategy has been widely studied.

Sentence combining is a teaching strategy that has been widely studied.

To do even that simple combining, a person must do many things. First, he or she must read analytically and actively, with the brain making judgments about the points of similarity and difference in the two kernel sentences, about which verb logically needs to be retained as the core of the combined sentence, about which elements of the sentences are redundant enough that one can be turned into a pronoun for compression without losing clarity, etc. Then, of course, the hand (or hands if the person is using a word processor or typewriter) go to work trying to create a new sentence consistent with the earlier judgments. And, even as words appear before the writer's eyes, the mind continues to make judgments and perhaps offer midcourse corrections in the direction the words seem to be taking.

Those interconnecting operations are--in microcosm--the same sort of things that go on when we read as part of our preparation for writing, and then move on to drafting our own articles. During the research we do for an article, we would need to make judgments about the reading, to look for key ideas and points of similarity or contrast, to simplify many pages into manageable concepts. And, as our ideas about the concepts begin to work their way out in words on paper, their course is monitored and, when necessary, periodically adjusted by our minds.

Such a coordinated operation of hands, brain, and eyes is, I believe, the essence of the writing process--with the further specification that what I am glibly calling "the brain" is a hugely complex array of operations that are logical, intuitive, conscious, unconscious, and reflective of a person's knowledge, values, biases, etc. In "Writing as a Mode of Learning" and "Hand, Eye, Brain,"[4] Janet Emig shows that these three forces interact powerfully in writing, each exercising an influence on the other. And some of the most important composition researchers have illustrated how this interaction takes place, though without using such physiological terms.

In Linda Flower and John Hayes's "A Cognitive Process Theory of Writing,"[5] for instance, "the text produced so far" is an important force in composing, a situation that could only occur if there were a visual link between paper and brain. Flower and Hayes also hypothesize the existence of a "monitor" or "writing strategist which determines when the writer moves from one process to another,"[6] and this clearly implies the role of an active, judging brain during composing. Similarly, Nancy I. Sommers's work on revision is based on the visual monitoring of a developing text by a brain that contains a conceptual formulation of where the writing should be going. Thus, Sommers describes revision as a process "in which writers recognize and resolve dissonance ... between what a text does and what the writer thinks it should do, between the product and the conception."[7] Sondra Perl, to use just one more example, also shows that writers face a complex task of text-production, text-observation, and text-modification as they work. In "Understanding Composing", Perl describes writing as growing from two simultaneous forces.[8] First, there is "retrospective structuring," in which writers check the words going down on paper against a "felt sense" they have of what they want to write. And there is "projective structuring," in which they test, against the needs they presume their readers will have, their intentions for a piece of writing and the shape the writing is taking on the page. Words on paper tested against mentally held assumptions--those seem to be the ideas behind Perl's terms, with the requirement of the eye as the link that makes the testing possible. This is clearer, when Perl describes how judgments accompany word formation during composition:

> Once a felt sense forms, we match words to it. As we begin to describe it, we get to see what is there for us. We get to see what we think, what we know....
> If the process is working, we begin to move along, sometimes quickly. Other times, we need to return to the beginning, to reread, to see if we captured what we meant to say. Sometimes after rereading we move on again, picking up speed. Other times by rereading we realize we've gone off the track, that what we've written doesn't quite "say it," and we need to reassess. Sometimes the words are wrong and we need to change them. Other times we need to go back to the topic, to call up the sense it initially evoked to see where and how our words led us astray. Sometimes in rereading we discover that the topic is "wrong," that the direction we discovered in writing is where we really want to go.[9]

This is quite a barrage of activities to manage--moving pen in response to some general sense of where writing should be headed, observing as the words go down, thinking about the words, testing them against intentions, determining where words or intentions need to be modified, and modifying the text were necessary. Donald Murray's introspective paper (chap. 13) illustrates this barrage, and also the fact that experienced, fluent writers can manage it. But less experienced writers--and here I turn to a second point--have difficulty juggling all these balls at once.

For some students the problems begin with words and sentences, so that they are hardly able to monitor and control what they are writing. Mina Shaughnessy points to this problem when she notes that basic writers often have difficulty managing the coordinating and subordinating consolidations so important in complex ideas because "these operations require a memory for written words and grammatical structures that the inexperienced writer may not have," and because the writer does not "easily recall what he has written once his hand has moved on to another part of the sentence. ..."[10]

For other students, the problem seems more a matter of cognitive overload that results, on the one hand, from the complexity of composing I have been discussing, and, on the other hand, from limitations in cognitive ability or reading skills such as Andrea Lunsford considers in "Cognitive Development and the Basic Writer" and Marilyn Sternglass discusses in "Sentence Combining and the Reading of Sentences."[11] Having to do so much at once, that is, may outstrip the generalizing powers or overload the short-term memory of students so that they rely on limited and unlimited writing strategies. Inexperienced readers, Sternglass writes, "have difficulty holding syntactic patterns and meanings in their memories long enough to be able to link them up correctly within the sentences they are working with."[12] The reason is that weak readers, focusing on one word at a time, "quickly exceed the limitations of short-term memory in building a relationship among items in any sentence that has more than five to seven words."[13]

Since reading--the visual link in the hands-brain-eyes triumvirate--is central to writing, Sternglass's observations would seem applicable to the problems many students have with writing. If they are unable to follow the sweep of meaning in written material because they read one word at a time, one wonders whether they are able to comprehend and monitor the sweep of meaning that must go down on paper during writing.

But Sternglass's observations about the limitations of short-term memory have an even broader application to the composing problems of inexperienced writers. Remembering the intended direction for a paper places a load on the memory. Noting the key ideas of paragraph after paragraph, to test them against the intended direction, makes more demands on short-term memory. Forming a tentative judgment on the text-- like "This may be a better idea than the one I started with"--and holding it for later verification or dismissal add another load. Remembering that verbs are being used in the present tense, that the subject of a long sentence is singular, that you are trying to avoid contractions--such textual constraints further load the short-term memory. And so does every "new" fact and every concept with which a writer is not familiar. The net result, of course, is that a writer may have a great deal of difficulty composing effectively. And he or she may take destructive defensive actions, such as giving up on trying to keep track of overall intentions and trying to keep the text developing in the direction of those intentions.

Sentence combining, to turn to my third point, can give composition teachers a way to address the overload that many students face when they begin to write. For sentence combining is a way to give students controlled practice with the simultaneous operations of hands, brain, and eyes.

The key words in that last sentence are "controlled" and "eyes." That is, sentence combining focuses attention on a writing task more immediately manageable than, say, writing a ten-page paper. And it does so in a way that requires more concentrated attention to words on paper than most students give to their own words as they write. Speaking at the First Miami Conference on Sentence Combining and the Teaching of Writing, James L. Kinneavy asked whether the key to sentence combining's instructional success isn't simply that it requires writing. It might be asked, he said, "if the writing improvement may not simply come from a disciplined writing practice, rather than from sentence combining as such," and whether the careful reading of kernel sentences" rather than the sentence combining itself is what "causes the improvement in reading ability.[14] For some students, I believe, the answer to Kinneavy's questions probably is "yes." But for students who suffer from the reading limitations or cognitive overloads discussed earlier, the answer probably is "no." For these students, the procedure of sentence combining clearly seems valuable, and can be a potent teaching device in courses that stress the processes of writing.

To begin with, the kernel sentences give writers a "content" for the writing exercise, removing a major factor from competition for the short-term memory so that students can concentrate attention on testing text against intentions, modifying the developing text, and the like. On the other hand, overt signals or implicit textual clues within strings of kernels can provide a syntactic or logical "form," a fact that relieves another pressure on short-term memory. Whichever way you look at it, the benefit seems the same: students can learn to monitor words during writing, less burdened of the cognitive demands that can interfere with effective drafting.

Sentence combining gives structure to what a student must do. By being definite--twenty-three kernels to be combined in a given exercise, for instance--a sentence-combining assignment can protect inexperienced students from the stress they may feel at an openended paper assignment. At the same time, the definite structure of a sentence-combining exercise can prevent students from doing as little writing as they may be inclined to do in response to a more open assignment.

Sentence combining also lets teachers structure exercises- -moving from the brief and simple, to longer and more complex--so that we can help students build up their capacities to handle the simultaneous demands of producing, reading, judging, and modifying words. And sentence combining also gives us a way to help students understand and develop control over important grammatical structures at the same time as they are expanding their confidence with the writing processes of hands, brain, and eyes.

Finally, there is at least one more way that sentence combining may assist in the teaching of writing process: it can help students develop the ability to combine many facts, and details into fewer generalizations, with a resultant reduction in the cognitive overload. In sentence combining, Marilyn Sternglass writes, students "can build meaningful groups of words into phrases and clauses and treat the meaning extracted from each group as one `chunk,'" so that the student can "hold a number of these `chunks' in short-term memory and build the conceptual bridges among them that are necessary for reading comprehension."[15] This capacity to build conceptual bridges by chunking information is also crucial to efficient handling of the constant flow of details and ideas with which a writer must cope during composition. Sentence combining seems to help students learn skills and habits of abstracting and generalizing, of isolating meaning in kernels, deducing logical connections between kernels, and of compressing and blending meaning and logic from several kernels into a more compact unit with the same meaning. And it seems quite reasonable to me that students who have developed such abilities within the controlled setting of sentence combining win be able, later, to cope better with the complexity of composition when they face more open writing tasks.

NOTES

1. See Richard Gebhardt, "The Writing Process: Core of the Writing Program." *Freshman English News,* 9 (Spring 1980), 19-22

2. William Strong, *Sentence Combining: A Composing Book* (New York: Random House, 1973).

3. Richard Gebhardt, "Process and Intention: A Bridge from Theory to Classroom," *The Writing Instructor,* 1 (1982), 135-45.

4. Janet Emig, "Writing as a Mode of Learning," *CCC,* 28 (1977), 122-28, and "Hand, Eye, and Brain," in *Research on Composing: Points of Departure,* ed. Charles R. Cooper and Lee Odell (Urbana, IL: NCTE, 1978).

5. Linda Flower and John Hayes, "A Cognitive Process Theory of Writing," *CCC,* 32 (1981).

6. Flower and Hayes, p. 374.

7. Nancy I. Sommers, "Revision Strategies of Student Writers and Experienced Writers," *English Language Arts Bulletin*, 20 (1980), 12.

8. Sondra Perl, "Understanding Composing," *CCC*, 31 (1980).

9. Perl, p. 367.

10. Mina Shaughnessy, *Errors and Expectations* (New York: Oxford Univ.Pr., 1977), p.59.

11. Andrea Lunsford, "Cognitive Development and the Basic Writer," *CE*, 41 (1979), 39-46; and Marilyn Sternglass, "Sentence Combining and the Reading of Sentences," *CCC*, 31 (1980), 325-29.

12. Sternglass, p. 325.

13. Sternglass, p. 326.

14. James L. Kinneavy, "Sentence Combining in a Comprehensive Language Framework," in *Sentence Combining and the Teaching of Writing*, ed. Donald A. Daiker, Andrew Kerek, and Max Morenberg (Conway, AK: L & S Books, 1979), pp. 69-71.

15. Sternglass, p. 326.

Grammar, Grammars, and the Teaching of Grammar

Patrick Hartwell

For me the grammar issue was settled at least twenty years ago with the conclusion offered by Richard Braddock, Richard Lloyd-Jones, and Lowell Schoer in 1963.

> In view of the widespread agreement of research studies based upon many types of students and teachers, the conclusion can be stated in strong and unqualified terms: the teaching of formal grammar has a negligible or, because it usually displaces some instruction and practice in composition, even a harmful effect on improvement in writing.[1]

Indeed, I would agree with Janet Emig that the grammar issue is a prime example of "magical thinking": the assumption that students will learn only what we teach and only because we teach.[2]

But the grammar issue, as we will see, is a complicated one. And, perhaps surprisingly, it remains controversial, with the regular appearance of papers defending the teaching of formal grammar or attacking it.[3] Thus Janice Neuleib, writing on "The Relation of Formal Grammar to Composition" in *College Composition and Communication* (23 [1977], 247-50), is tempted "to sputter on paper" at reading the quotation above (p. 248), and Martha Kolln, writing in the same journal three years later ("Closing the Books on Alchemy," *CCC,* 32 [1981], 139-51), labels people like me "alchemists" for our perverse beliefs. Neuleib reviews five experimental studies, most of them concluding that formal grammar instruction has no effect on the quality of students' writing nor on their ability to avoid error. Yet she renders in effect a Scots verdict of "Not proven" and calls for more research on the issue. Similarly, Kolln reviews six experimental studies that arrive at similar conclusions, only one of them overlapping with the studies cited by Neuleib. She calls for more careful definition of the word *grammar*--her definition being "the internalized system that native speakers of a language share" (p. 140)--and she concludes with a stirring call to place grammar instruction at the center of the composition curriculum: "our goal should be to help students understand the system they know unconsciously as native speakers, to teach them the necessary categories and labels that will enable them to think about and talk about their language" (p. 150). Certainly our textbooks and our pedagogies--though they vary widely in what they see as "necessary categories and labels"--continue to emphasize mastery of formal grammar, and popular discussions of a presumed literacy crisis are almost unanimous in their call for a renewed emphasis on the teaching of formal grammar, seen as basic for success in writing.[4]

Patrick Hartwell. "Grammar, Grammars, and the Teaching of Grammar," *College English,* February 1985. Copyright © 1985 by the National Council of Teachers of English. Reprinted with permission.

An Instructive Example

It is worth noting at the outset that both sides in this dispute- -the grammarians and the anti-grammarians--articulate the issue in the same positivistic terms: what does experimental research tell us about the value of teaching formal grammar? But seventy-five years of experimental research has for all practical purposes told us nothing. The two sides are unable to agree on how to interpret such research. Studies are interpreted in terms of one's prior assumptions about the value of teaching grammar: their results seem not to change those assumptions. Thus the basis of the discussion, a basis shared by Kolln and Neuleib and by Braddock and his colleagues--"what does educational research tell us?"seems designed to perpetuate, not to resolve, the issue. A single example will be instructive. In 1976 and then at greater length in 1979, W.B. Elley, I.H. Barham, H. Lamb, and M. Wyllie reported on a three-year experiment in New Zealand, comparing the relative effectiveness at the high school level of instruction in transformational grammar, instruction in traditional grammar, and no grammar instruction.[5] They concluded that the formal study of grammar, whether transformational or traditional, improved neither writing quality nor control over surface correctness.

> After two years, no differences were detected in writing performance or language competence; after three years small differences appeared in some minor conventions favoring the TG [transformational grammar) group, but these were more than offset by the less positive attitudes they showed towards their English studies. (p. 18)

Anthony Petroskey, in a review of research ("Grammar Instruction: What We Know," *English Journal,* 66, No. 9 [1977], 86-88), agreed with this conclusion, finding the study to be carefully designed, "representative of the best kind of educational research" (p. 86), its validity "unquestionable" (p. 88). Yet Janice Neuleib in her essay found the same conclusions to be "startling" and questioned whether the findings could be generalized beyond the target population, New Zealand high school students. Martha Kolln, when her attention is drawn to the study ("Reply to Ron Shook," *CCC, 32* [1981], 139-151), thinks the whole experiment "suspicious." And John Mellon has been willing to use the study to defend the teaching of grammar; the study of Elley and his colleagues, he has argued, shows that teaching grammar does no harm.[6]

It would seem unlikely, therefore, that further experimental research, in and of itself, will resolve the grammar issue. Any experimental design can be nitpicked, any experimental population can be criticized, and any experimental conclusion can be questioned or, more often, ignored. In fact, it may well be that the grammar question is not open to resolution by experimental research, that, as Noam Chomsky has argued in *Reflections on Language* (New York: Pantheon, 1975), criticizing the trivialization of human learning by behavioral psychologists, is simply misdefined.

> There will be "good experiments" only in domains that lie outside the organism's cognitive capacity. For example, there will be no "good experiments" in the study of human learning.
>
> This discipline ... will, of necessity, avoid those domains in which an organism is specially designed to acquire rich cognitive structures that enter

into its life in an intimate fashion. The discipline will be of virtually no intellectual interest, it seems to me, since it is restricting itself in principle to those questions that are guaranteed to tell us little about the nature of organisms. (p. 36)

Asking the Right Questions

As a result, though I will look briefly at the tradition of experimental research, my primary goal in this essay is to articulate the grammar issue in different and, I would hope, more productive terms. Specifically, I want to ask four questions:

1.   Why is the grammar issue so important? Why has it been the dominant focus of composition research for the last seventy-five years?

2.   What definitions of the word *grammar* are needed to articulate the grammar issue intelligibly?

3.   What do findings in cognate disciplines suggest about the value of formal grammar instruction?

4.   What is our theory of language, and what does it predict about the value of formal grammar instruction? (This question--"what does our theory of language predict?"--seems a much more powerful question than "what does educational research tell us?")

In exploring these questions I will attempt to be fully explicit about issues, terms, and assumptions. I hope that both proponents and opponents of formal grammar instruction would agree that these are useful as shared points of reference: care in definition, full examination of the evidence, reference to relevant work in cognate disciplines, and explicit analysis of the theoretical bases of the issue.

But even with that gesture of harmony it will be difficult to articulate the issue in a balanced way, one that will be acceptable to both sides. After all, we are dealing with a professional dispute in which one side accuses the other of "magical thinking," and in turn that side responds by charging the other as "alchemists." Thus we might suspect that the grammar issue is itself embedded in larger models "of the transmission of literacy, part of quite different assumptions about the teaching of composition.

Those of us who dismiss the teaching of formal grammar have a model of composition instruction that makes the grammar issue "uninteresting" in a scientific sense. Our model predicts a rich and complex interaction of learner and environment in mastering literacy, an interaction that has little to do with sequences of skills instruction as such. Those who defend the teaching of grammar, tend to have a model of composition instruction that is rigidly skills-centered and rigidly sequential: the formal teaching of grammar, as the first step in that sequence, is the cornerstone or linchpin. Grammar teaching is thus supremely interesting, naturally a dominant focus for educational research. The controversy over the value of grammar instruction, then, is inseparable from two other issues: the issues of sequence in the teaching of composition and of the role of the composition teacher. Consider, for example, the force of these two issues in Janice Neuleib's conclusion: after calling for yet more experimental research on the value of teaching grammar, she ends with an absolute (and unsupported) claim about sequences and teacher roles in composition.

We do know, however, that some things must be taught at different levels. Insistence on adherence to usage norms by composition teachers does improve usage. Students can learn to organize their papers if teachers do not accept papers that are disorganized. Perhaps composition teachers can teach those two abilities before they begin the more difficult tasks of developing syntactic sophistication and a winning style. ("The Relation of Formal Grammar to Composition," p. 250)

(One might want to ask, in passing, whether "usage norms" exist in the monolithic fashion the phrase suggests and whether refusing to accept disorganized papers is our best available pedagogy for teaching arrangement.)[7]

But I want to focus on the notion of sequence that makes the grammar issue so important: first grammar, then usage, then some absolute model of organization, all controlled by the teacher at the center of the learning process, with other matters, those of rhetorical weight--"syntactic sophistication and a winning style"--pushed off to the future. It is not surprising that we call each other names: those of us who question the value of teaching grammar are in fact shaking the whole elaborate edifice of traditional composition instruction.

The Five Meanings of "Grammar"

Given its centrality to a well-established way of teaching composition, I need to so about the business of defining grammar rather carefully, particularly in view of Kolln's criticism of the lack of care in earlier discussions. Therefore I will build upon a seminal discussion of the word *grammar* offered a generation ago, in 1954, by W. Nelson Francis, often excerpted as "The Three Meanings of Grammar."[8] It is Worth reprinting at length, if only to re-establish it as a reference point for future discussions.

The first thing we mean by "grammar" is "the set of formal patterns in which the words of a language are arranged in order to convey larger meanings." It is not necessary that we be able to discuss these patterns self-consciously in order to be able to use them. In fact, all speakers of a language above the age of five or six know how to use its complex forms of organization with considerable skill; in this sense of the word--call it "Grammar 1"--they are thoroughly familiar with its grammar.

The second meaning of "grammar"--call it "Grammar 2"- -is "the branch of linguistic science which is concerned with the description, analysis, and formulization of formal language patterns." Just as gravity was in full operation before Newton's apple fell, so grammar in the first sense was in full operation before anyone formulated the first rule that began the history of grammar as a study.

The third sense in which people use the word "grammar" is "linguistic etiquette." This we may call "Grammar 3." The word in this sense is often coupled with a derogatory adjective: we say that the expression "he ain't here" is "bad grammar." ...

As has already been suggested, much confusion arises from mixing these meanings. One hears a good deal of criticism of teachers of English couched in such terms as "they don't teach grammar any more." Criticism of this sort is based on the wholly unproven assumption that teaching Grammar 2 will improve the student's proficiency in Grammar 1 or improve his manners in Grammar 3. Actually, the form of Grammar 2 which is usually taught is a very inaccurate and misleading analysis of the facts of Grammar 1; and it therefore is of highly questionable value in improving a person's ability to handle the structural patterns of his language. (pp. 300-301)

Francis' Grammar 3 is, of course, not grammar at all, but usage. One would like to assume that Joseph Williams' recent discussion of usage ("The Phenomenology of Error," *CCC,* 32 (1981), 152-168), along with his references, has placed those shibboleths in a proper perspective. But I doubt it, and I suspect that popular discussions of the grammar issue will be as flawed by the intrusion of usage issues as past discussions have been. At any rate I will make only passing reference to Grammar 3-- usage- -naively assuming that this issue has been discussed elsewhere and that my readers are familiar with those discussions.

We need also to make further discriminations about Francis' Grammar 2, given that the purpose of his 1954 article was to substitute for one form of Grammar 2, that "inaccurate and misleading" form "which is usually taught," another form, that of American structuralist grammar. Here we can make use of a still earlier discussion, one going back to the days when *PMLA* was willing to publish articles on rhetoric and linguistics, to a 1927 article by Charles Carpenter Fries, "The Rules of the Common School Grammars" (42 [1927], 221-237). Fries there distinguished between the scientific tradition of language study (to which we will now delimit Francis' Grammar 2, scientific grammar) and the separate tradition of "the common school grammars," developed unscientifically, largely based on two inadequate principles- -appeals to "logical principles," like "two negatives make a positive," and analogy to Latin grammar; thus, Charlton Laird's characterization, "the grammar of Latin, ingeniously warped to suggest English" (*Language in America* [New York: World, 1970], p. 294). There is, of course, a direct link between the "common school grammars" that Fries criticized in 1927 and the grammar-based texts of today, and thus it seems wise, as Karl W. Dykema suggests ("Where Our Grammar Came From," *CE,* 22 (1961), 455-465), to separate Grammar 2, "scientific grammar," from Grammar 4, "school grammar," the latter meaning, quite literally, "the grammars used in the schools."

Further, since Martha Kolln points to the adaptation of Christensen's sentence rhetoric in a recent sentence-combining text as an example of the proper emphasis on "grammar" ("Closing the Books on Alchemy," p. 140), it is worth separating out, as still another meaning of *grammar,* Grammar 5, "stylistic grammar," defined as "grammatical terms used in the interest of teaching prose style." And, since stylistic grammars abound, with widely variant terms and emphases, we might appropriately speak parenthetically of specific forms of Grammar 5--Grammar 5 (Lanham); Grammar 5 (Strunk and

White); Grammar 5 (Williams, Style); even Grammar 5 (Christensen, as adapted by Daiker, Kerek, and Morenberg).[9]

The Grammar in Our Heads

With these definitions in mind, let us return to Francis' Grammar 1, admirably defined by Kolln as "the internalized system of rules that speakers of a language share" ("Closing the Books on Alchemy," p. 140), or, to put it more simply, the grammar in our heads. Three features of Grammar 1 need to be stressed: first, its special status as an "internalized system of rules," as tacit and unconscious knowledge; second, the abstract, even counterintuitive, nature of these rules, insofar as we are able to approximate them indirectly as Grammar 2 statements; and third, the way in which the form of one's Grammar 1 seems profoundly affected by the acquisition of literacy. This sort of review is designed to firm up our theory of language, so that we can ask what it predicts about the value of teaching formal grammar.

A simple thought experiment will isolate the special status of Grammar 1 knowledge. I have asked members of a number of different groups--from sixth graders to college freshmen to high-school teachers--to give me the rule for ordering adjectives of nationality, age, and number in English. The response is always the same: "We don't know the rule." Yet when I ask these groups to perform an active language task, they show productive control over the rule they have denied knowing. I ask them to arrange the following words in a natural order:

French   the   young   girls   four

I have never seen a native speaker of English who did not immediately produce the natural order, "the four young French girls." The rule is that in English the order of adjectives is first, number, second, age, and third, nationality. Native speakers can create analogous phrases using the rule--"the seventy-three aged Scandinavian lechers"; and the drive for meaning is so great that they will create contexts to make sense out of violations of the rule, as in foregrounding for emphasis: "I want to talk to the French four young girls." (I immediately envision a large room, perhaps a banquet hall, filled with tables at which are seated groups of four young girls, each group of a different nationality.) So Grammar 1 is eminently usable knowledge--the way we make our life through language--but it is not accessible knowledge; in a profound sense, we do not know that we have it. Thus neurolinguist Z.N. Pylyshyn speaks of Grammar 1 as "autonomous," separate from common-sense reasoning, and as "cognitively impenetrable," not available for direct examination.[10] In philosophy and linguistics, the distinction is made between formal, conscious, "knowing about" knowledge (like Grammar 2 knowledge) and tacit, unconscious, "knowing how" knowledge (like Grammar 1 knowledge). The importance of this distinction for the teaching of composition--it provides a powerful theoretical justification for mistrusting the ability of Grammar 2 (or Grammar 4) knowledge to affect Grammar 1 performance--was pointed out in this journal by Martin Steinmann, Jr., in 1966 ("Rhetorical Research," *CE,* 27 [1966], 278-285).

Further, the more we learn about Grammar 1--and most linguists would agree that we know surprisingly little about it- -the more abstract and implicit it seems. This abstractness can be illustrated with an experiment, devised by Lise Menn and reported by Morris Halle, about our rule for forming plurals in speech. It is obvious that we do indeed have a "rule" for forming plurals, for we do not memorize the plural of each noun separately. You will demonstrate productive control over that rule by forming the spoken plurals of the nonsense words below:

thole   flitch   plast

Halle offers two ways of formalizing a Grammar 2 equivalent of this Grammar 1 ability. One form of the rule is the following, stated in terms of speech sounds:

a. If the noun ends in /s z s z c j/, add /Iz
b. otherwise, if the noun ends in /p t k f O/, add /s/;
c. otherwise, add /z/.[11]

This rule comes close to what we literate adults consider to be an adequate rule for plurals in writing, like the rules, for example, taken from a recent "common school grammar," Eric Gould's *Reading into Writing: A Rhetoric, Reader, and Handbook* (Boston: Houghton Mifflin, 1983):

Plurals can be tricky. If you are unsure of a plural, then check it in the dictionary.
The general rules are
Add *s* to the singular: *girls, tables*
Add *es* to nouns ending in *ch, sh, x or s: churches, boxes, wishes*
Add *es* to nouns ending in *y* and preceded by a vowel once you have changed *y* to *i: monies, companies.* (p. 666)

(But note the persistent inadequacy of such Grammar 4 rules: here, as I read it, the rule is inadequate to explain the plurals of *ray* and *tray,* even to explain the collective noun *monies,* not a plural at all, formed from the mass noun *money* and offered as an example.) A second form of the rule would make use of much more abstract entities, sound features:

a.   If the noun ends with a sound that is [coronal, strident], add /Iz/;
b.   otherwise, if the noun ends with a sound that is [non-voiced), add /s/;
c.   otherwise, add /z/.

(The notion of "sound features" is itself rather abstract, perhaps new to readers not trained in linguistics. But such readers should be able to recognize that the spoken plurals of *lip* and *duck,* the sound [s], differ from the spoken plurals *sea* and *gnu,* the sound [z], only in that the sounds of the latter are "voiced"--one's vocal cords vibrate-- while the sounds of the former are "non-voiced.")

To test the psychologically operative rule, the Grammar 1 rule, native speakers of English were asked to form the plural of the last name of the composer Johann Sebastian *Bach,* a sound [x], unique in American (though not in Scottish English. If speakers follow the first rule above, using word endings, they would reject a) and b), then apply c), producing the plural as /baxz/, with word-final /z/. (If writers were to follow the rule of the common school grammar, they would produce the written plural *Baches,* apparently, given the form of the rule, on analogy with *churches.)* If speakers follow the second rule, they would have to analyze the sound [x] as [non-labial, non-coronal, dorsal, non-voiced, and nonstrident], producing the plural as /baxs/. with word-final /s/. Native speakers of American English overwhelmingly produce the plural as /baxs/. They use knowledge that Halle characterizes as "unlearned and untaught" (p. 140).

Now such a conclusion is counterintuitive--certainly it departs maximally from Grammar 4 rules for forming plurals. It seems that native speakers of English behave as if they have productive control, as Grammar 1 knowledge, of abstract sound features (± coronal, ± strident, and so on) which are available as conscious, Grammar 2 knowledge only to trained linguists--and, indeed, formally available only within the last hundred years or so. ("Behave as if," in that last sentence, is a necessary hedge, to underscore the difficulty of "knowing about" Grammar 1.)

Moreover, as the example of plural rules suggests, the form of the Grammar 1 in the heads of literate adults seems profoundly affected by the acquisition of literacy. Obviously, literate adults have access to different morphological codes: the abstract print -*s* underlying the predictable /s/ and /z/ plurals, the abstract print -*ed* underlying the spoken past tense markers /t/, as in "walked," /ed/, as in "surrounded," /d/, as in "scored," and the symbol /O/ for no surface realization, its in the relaxed standard pronunciation of "I walked to the store." Literate adults also have access to distinctions preserved only in the code of print (for example, the distinction between "a good Ku" and "a good sailor" that Mark Aranoff points out in "An English Spelling Convention," *Linguistic Inquiry,* 9 [1978], 299-303). More significantly, Irene Moscowitz speculates that the ability of third graders to form abstract nouns on analogy with pairs like *divine::divinity* and *serene::serenity,* where the spoken vowel changes but the spelling preserves meaning, is a factor of knowing how to read. Carol Chomsky finds a three-stage developmental sequence in the grammatical performance of seven-year-olds, related to measures of kind and variety of reading; and Rita S. Brause finds a nine-stage developmental sequence in the ability to understand semantic ambiguity, extending from fourth graders to graduate students.[12] John Mills and Gordon Hemsley find that level of education, and presumably level of literacy, influence judgments of grammaticality, concluding that literacy changes the deep structure of one's internal grammar; Jean Whyte finds that oral language functions develop differently in readers and non-readers; José Morais, Jésus Alegria, and Paul Bertelson find that illiterate adults are unable to add or delete sounds at the beginning of nonsense words, suggesting that awareness of speech as a series of phones is provided by learning to read an alphabetic code. Two experiments--one conducted by Charles A. Ferguson, the other by Mary E. Hamilton and David Barton--find that adults' ability to recognize segmentation in speech is related to degree of literacy, not to amount of schooling or general ability.[13]

It is worth noting that none of these investigators would suggest that the developmental sequences they have uncovered be isolated and taught as discrete skills. They are natural concomitants of literacy, and they seem best characterized not as isolated rules but as developing schemata, broad strategies for approaching written language.

Grammar 2

We can, of course, attempt to approximate the rules or schemata of Grammar 1 by writing fully explicit descriptions that model the competence of a native speaker. Such rules, like the rules for pluralizing nouns or ordering adjectives discussed above, are the goal of the science of linguistics, that is, Grammar 2. There are a number of scientific grammars--an older structuralist model and several versions within a generative-transformational paradigm, not to mention isolated schools like tagmemic grammar, Montague grammar, and the like. In fact, we cannot think of Grammar 2 as a stable entity, for its form changes with each new issue of each linguistics journal, as new "rules of grammar" are proposed and debated. Thus Grammar 2, though of great theoretical interest to the composition teacher, is of little practical use in the classroom, as Constance Weaver has pointed out (*Grammar for Teachers* [Urbana, Ill.: NCTE, 1979], pp. 3-6). Indeed Grammar 2 is a scientific model of Grammar 1, not a description of it, so that questions of psychological reality, while important, are less important than other, more theoretical factors, such as the elegance of formulation or the global power of rules. We might, for example, wish to replace the rule for ordering adjectives of age, number and nationality cited above with a more general rule- -what linguists call a "fuzzy" rule--that adjectives in English are ordered by their abstract quality of "nouniness": adjectives that are very much like nouns, like *French* or *Scandinavian,* come physically closer to nouns than do adjectives that are less "nouny," like *four* or *aged.* But our motivation for accepting the broader rule would be its global power, not its psychological reality.[14]

I try to consider a hostile reader, one committed to the teaching of grammar and I try to think of ways to hammer in the central point of this distinction, that the rules of Grammar 2 are simply unconnected to productive control over Grammar 1. I can argue from authority: Noam Chomsky has touched on this point whenever he has concerned himself with the implications of linguistics for language teaching, and years ago transformationalist Mark Lester stated unequivocally, "there simply appears to be no correlation between a writer's study of language and his ability to write."[15] I can cite analogies offered by others: Francis Christensen's analogy in an essay originally published in 1962 that formal grammar study would be "to invite a centipede to attend to the sequence of his legs in motion,"[16] or James Britton's analogy, offered informally after a conference presentation, that grammar study would be like forcing starving people to master the use of a knife and fork before allowing them to eat. I can offer analogies of my own, contemplating the wisdom of asking a pool player to master the physics of momentum before taking up a cue or of making a prospective driver get a degree in automotive engineering before engaging the clutch. I consider a hypothetical argument, that if Grammar 2 knowledge affected Grammar 1 performance, then linguists would be our best writers. (I can certify that they are, on the whole, not.) Such a position, after all, is only in accord with other domains of science: the formula for catching a fly ball in baseball ("Playing It by Ear," *Scientific American,* 248, No. 4 [1983], 76) is of such complexity that it is beyond my understanding--and, I would suspect, that of many workaday centerfielders. But perhaps I can best hammer in this claim--that Grammar 2 knowledge has no effect on Grammar 1 performance--by offering a demonstration.

The diagram on the next page is an attempt by Thomas N. Huckin and Leslie A. Olsen (*English for Science and Technology* [New York: McGraw-Hill, 1983]) to offer, for students of English as a second language, a fully explicit formulation of what is, for native speakers, a trivial rule of the language--the choice of definite article, indefinite article, or no definite article. There are obvious limits to such a formulation, for article choice in English is less a matter of rule than of idiom ("I went to college" versus "I went to a university" versus British "I went to university"), real-world knowledge (using indefinite "I went into a house" instantiates definite "I looked at the ceiling," and indefinite "I visited a university" instantiates definite "I talked with the professors"), and stylistic choice (the last sentence above might alternatively end with "the choice of the definite article, the indefinite article, or no article").

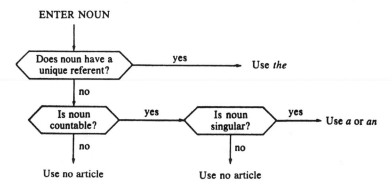

ENTER NOUN

Does noun have a unique referent? — yes → Use *the*

no

Is noun countable? — yes → Is noun singular? — yes → Use *a* or *an*

no — Use no article

no — Use no article

Huckin and Olsen invite non-native speakers to use the rule consciously to justify article choice in technical prose, such as the passage below from P.F. Brandwein (*Matter: An Earth Science* [New York: Harcourt Brace Jovanovich, 1975]). I invite you to spend a couple of minutes doing the same thing, with the understanding that this exercise is a test case: you are using a very explicit rule to justify a fairly straightforward issue of grammatical choice.

Imagine a cannon on top of _____ highest mountain on Earth. It is firing _____ cannonballs horizontally. _____ first cannonball fired follows its path. As _____ cannonball moves, _____ gravity pulls it down, and it soon hits _____ ground. Now _____ velocity with which each succeeding cannonball is fired is increased. Thus, _____ cannonball goes farther each time. Cannonball 2 goes farther than _____ cannonball 1 although each is being pulled by _____ gravity toward the earth all _____ time. _____ last cannonball is fired with such tremendous velocity that it goes completely around _____ earth. It returns to _____ mountaintop and continues around the earth again and again. _____ cannonball's inertia causes it to continue in motion indefinitely in _____ orbit around earth. In such a situation, we could consider _____ cannonball to be _____ artificial satellite, just like _____ weather satellites launched by _____ U.S. Weather Service. (p. 209)

Most native speakers of English who have attempted this exercise report a great deal of frustration, a curious sense of working against, rather than with, the rule. The rule, however valuable it may be for non-native speakers, is, for the most part, simply unusable for native speakers of the language.

Cognate Areas of Research

We can corroborate this demonstration by turning to research in two cognate areas, studies of the induction of rules of artificial languages and studies of the role of formal rules in second language acquisition. Psychologists have studied the ability of subjects to learn artificial languages, usually constructed of nonsense syllables or letter strings. Such languages can be described by phrase structure rules:

$$S => VX$$
$$X => MX$$

More clearly, they can be presented as flow diagrams, as below:

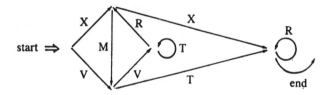

This diagram produces "sentences" like the following:

VVTRXRR.	XMVTTRX.	XXRR.
XMVRMT.	VVTTRMT.	XMTRRR.

The following "sentences" would be "ungrammatical" in this language:

*VMXTT.   *RTXVVT.   *TRVXXVVM.

Arthur S. Reber, in a classic 1967 experiment, demonstrated that mere exposure to grammatical sentences produced tacit learning: subjects who copied several grammatical sentences performed far above chance in judging the grammaticality of other letter strings. Further experiments have shown that providing subjects with formal rules--

giving them the flow diagram above, for example--remarkably degrades performance: subjects given the "rules of the language" do much less well in acquiring the rules than do subjects not given the rules. Indeed, even telling subjects that they are to induce the rules of an artificial language degrades performance. Such laboratory experiments are admittedly contrived, but they confirm predictions that our theory of language would make about the value of formal rules in language learning.[17]

The thrust of recent research in second language learning similarly works to constrain the value of formal grammar rules. The most explicit statement of the value of formal rules is that of Stephen D. Krashen's monitor model.[18] Krashen divides second language mastery into *acquisition*--tacit, informal mastery, akin to first language acquisition--and formal learning--conscious application of Grammar 2 rules, which he calls "monitoring" output. In another essay Krashen uses his model to predict a highly individual use of the monitor and a highly constrained role for formal rules:

> Some adults (and very few children) are able to use conscious rules to increase the grammatical accuracy of their output, and even for these people, very strict conditions need to be met before the conscious grammar can be applied.[19]

In *Principles and Practice in Second Language Acquisition* (New York: Pergamon, 1982) Krashen outlines these conditions by means of a series of concentric circles, beginning with a large circle denoting the rules of English and a smaller circle denoting the subset of those rules described by formal linguists (adding that most linguists would protest that the size of this circle is much too large):

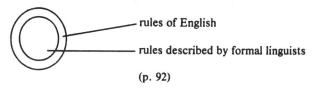

rules of English

rules described by formal linguists

(p. 92)

Krashen then adds smaller circles, as shown below--a subset of the rules described by formal linguists that would be known to applied linguists, a subset of those rules that would be available to the best teachers, and then a subset of those rules that teachers might choose to present to second language learners:

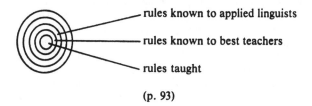

rules known to applied linguists

rules known to best teachers

rules taught

(p. 93)

Of course, as Krashen notes, not all the rules taught will be learned, and not all those learned will be available, as what he calls "mental baggage" (p. 94), for conscious use. An experiment by Ellen Bialystock, asking English speakers learning French to judge the grammaticality of taped sentences, complicates this issue, for reaction time data suggest that learners first make an intuitive judgment of grammaticality, using implicit or Grammar 1 knowledge, and only then search for formal explanations, using explicit or Grammar 2 knowledge.[20] This distinction would suggest that Grammar 2 knowledge is of use to second language learners only after the principle has already been mastered as tacit grammar 1 knowledge. In the terms of Krashen's model, learning never becomes acquisition (*Principles*, p. 86).

An ingenious experiment by Herbert W. Seliger complicates the issue yet further ("On the Nature and Function of Language Rules in Language Learning," *TESOL Quarterly*, 13 [1979], 359-369). Seliger asked native and non-native speakers of English to orally identify pictures of objects (e.g., "an apple," "a pear, "a book," "an umbrella"), noting whether they used the correct form of the indefinite articles *a* and *an*. He then asked each speaker to state the rule for choosing between *a* and *an*. He found no correlation between the ability to state the rule and the ability to apply it correctly, either with native or non-native speakers. Indeed, three of four adult non-native speakers in his sample produced a correct form of the rule, but they did not apply it in speaking. A strong conclusion from this experiment would be that formal rules of grammar seem to have no value whatsoever. Seliger, however, suggests a more paradoxical interpretation. Rules are of no use, he agrees, but some people think they are, and for these people, assuming that they have internalized the rules, even inadequate rules are of heuristic value, for they allow them to access the internal rules they actually use.

The Incantations of the "Common School Grammars"

Such a paradox may explain the fascination we have as teachers with "rules of grammar" of the Grammar 4 variety, the "rules" of the "common school grammars." Again and again such rules are inadequate to the facts of written language; you will recall that we have known this since Francis' 1927 study. R. Scott Baldwin and James M. Coady, studying how readers respond to punctuation signals ("Psycholinguistic Approaches to a Theory of Punctuation," *Journal of Reading Behavior*, 10 [1978], 363-83), conclude that conventional rules of punctuation are "a complete sham" (p. 375). My own favorite is the Grammar 4 rule for showing possession, always expressed in terms of adding -'s or -s' to nouns, while our internal grammar, if you think about it, adds possession to noun phrases, albeit under severe stylistic constraints: "the horses of the Queen of England" are "the Queen of England's horses" and "the feathers of the duck over there" are "the duck over there's feathers." Suzette Haden Elgin refers to the "rules" of Grammar 4 as "incantations" (*Never Mind the Trees*, p. 9: see footnote 3).

It may simply be that as hyperliterate adults we are conscious of "using rules" when we are in fact doing something else, something far more complex, accessing tacit heuristics honed by print literacy itself. We can clarify this notion by reaching for an acronym coined by technical writers to explain the readability of complex prose--COIK: "clear only if known." The rules of Grammar 4--no, we can at this point be more honest--the incantations of Grammar 4 are COIK. If you know how to signal possession in the code of print, then the advice to add - *'s* to nouns makes perfect sense, just as the collective noun *monies* is a fine example of changing -*y* to -*i* and adding -es to form the plural. But if you have not grasped, tacitly, the abstract representation of possession in print, such incantations can only be opaque.

Worse yet, the advice given in "the common school grammars" is unconnected with anything remotely resembling literate adult behavior. Consider, as an example, the rule for not writing a sentence fragment as the rule is described in the best-selling college grammar text, John C. Hodges and Mary S. Whitten's, *Harbrace College Handbook,* 9th ed. (New York: Harcourt Brace Jovanovich, 1982). In order to get to the advice, "as a rule, do not write a sentence fragment" (p. 25), the student must master the following learning tasks:

> Recognizing verbs.
> Recognizing subjects and verbs.
> Recognizing all parts of speech. (*Harbrace* lists eight.)
> Recognizing phrases and subordinate clauses. *(Harbrace* lists six types of
> phrases, and it offers incomplete lists of eight relative pronouns and
> eighteen subordinating conjunctions.)
> Recognizing main clauses and types of sentences.

These learning tasks completed, the student is given the rule above, offered a page of exceptions, and then given the following advice (or is it an incantation?):

> Before handing in a composition, ... proofread each word group
> written as a sentence. Test each one for completeness. First, be sure that it has
> at least one subject and one predicate. Next, be sure that the word group is not a
> dependent clause beginning with a subordinating conjunction or a relative
> clause. (p. 27)

The school grammar approach defines a sentence fragment as a conceptual error--as not having conscious knowledge of the school grammar definition of *sentence.* It demands heavy emphasis on rote memory, and it asks students to behave in ways patently removed from the behaviors of mature writers. (I have never in my life tested a sentence for completeness, and I am a better writer--and probably a better person--as a consequence.) It may be, of course, that some developing writers, at some points in their development, may benefit from such advice--or, more to the point, may think that they benefit--but, as Thomas Friedman points out in "Teaching Error, Nurturing Confusion" (*CE,* 45 [1983], 390-399), our theory of language tells us that such advice is, at the best, COIK. As the Maine joke has it, about a tourist asking directions from a farmer, " you can't get there from here."

Redefining Error
In the specific case of sentence fragments, Mina P. Shaughnessy (*Errors and Expectations* [New York: Oxford University Press, 1977]) argues that such errors are not conceptual failures at all, but performance errors--mistakes in punctuation. Muriel Harris' error counts support this view ("Mending the Fragmented Free Modifier," *CCC*, 32 [1981], 175-182). Case studies show example after example of errors that occur *because of* instruction--one thinks, for example, of David Bartholmae's student explaining that he added an *-s* to *children* "because it's a plural" ("The Study of Error." *CCC*, 31 [1980], 262). Surveys, such as that by Muriel Harris ("Contradictory Perceptions of the Rules of Writing." *CCC*, 30 [1979], 218-220), and our own observations suggest that students consistently misunderstand such Grammar 4 explanations (COIK, you will recall). For example, from Patrick Hartwell and Robert H. Bentley and from Mike Rose, we have two separate anecdotal accounts of students, cited for punctuating a *because*-clause as a sentence, who have decided to avoid using *because*. More generally, Collette A. Daiute's analysis of errors made by college students shows that errors tend to appear at clause boundaries, suggesting short-term memory load and not conceptual deficiency as a cause of error.[21]

Thus, if we think seriously about error and its relationship to the worship of formal grammar study, we need to attempt some massive dislocation of our traditional thinking, to shuck off our hyperliterate perception of the value of formal rules, and to regain the confidence in the tacit power of unconscious knowledge that our theory of language gives us. Most students, reading their writing aloud, will correct in essence all errors of spelling, grammar, and, by intonation, punctuation, but usually without noticing that what they read departs from what they wrote.[22] And Richard H. Haswell ("Minimal Marking," *CE*, 45 [1983], 600-604) notes that his students correct 61.1% of their errors when they are identified with a simple mark in the margin rather than by error type. Such findings suggest that we need to redefine error, to see it not as a cognitive or linguistic problem, a problem of not knowing a "rule of grammar" (whatever that may mean), but rather, following the insight of Robert J. Bracewell ("Writing as a Cognitive Activity," *Visible Language*, 14 [1980], 400-422), as a problem of metacognition and metalinguistic awareness, a matter of accessing knowledges that, to be of any use, learners must have already internalized by means of exposure to the code. (Usage issues--Grammar 3--probably represent a different order of problem. Both Joseph Emonds and Jeffrey Jochnowitz establish that the usage issues we worry most about are linguistically unnatural, departures from the grammar in our heads.)[23]

The notion of metalinguistic awareness seems crucial. The sentence below, created by Douglas R. Hofstadter ("Metamagical Themas," *Scientific American*, 235, No. 1 [1981], 22-32), is offered to clarify that notion; you are invited to examine it for a moment or two before continuing.

Their is four errors in this sentence. Can you find them?

Three errors announce themselves plainly enough, the misspellings of *there* and *sentence* and the use of *is* instead of *are*. (And, just to illustrate the perils of hyperliteracy, let it be noted that, through three years of drafts, I referred to the choice of *is* and *are* as a matter of "subject-verb agreement.") The fourth error resists detection, until one assesses the truth value of the sentence itself--the fourth error is that there are not four errors, only three. Such a sentence (Hofstadter calls it a "self-referencing sentence") asks you to look at it in two ways, simultaneously as statement and as linguistic artifact--in other words, to exercise metalinguistic awareness.

A broad range of cross-cultural studies suggest that metalinguistic awareness is a defining feature of print literacy. Thus Sylvia Scribner and Michael Cole working with the triliterate Vai of Liberia (variously literate in English, through schooling; in Arabic, for religious purposes; and in an indigenous Vai script, used for personal affairs), find that metalinguistic awareness, broadly conceived, is the only cognitive skill underlying each of the three literacies. The one statistically significant skill shared by literate Vai was the recognition of word boundaries. Moreover, literate Vai tended to answer "yes" when asked (in Vai), "Can you call the sun the moon and the moon the sun?" while illiterate Vai tended to have grave doubts about such metalinguistic play. And in the United States Henry and Lila R. Gleitman report quite different responses by clerical workers and PhD candidates asked to interpret nonsense compounds like "house-bird glass": clerical workers focused on meaning and plausibility (for example, "a house-bird made of glass"), while PhD candidates focused on syntax (for example, "a very small drinking cup for canaries" or "a glass that protects house-birds").[24] More general research findings suggest a clear relationship between measures of metalinguistic awareness and measures of literacy level.[25] William Labov, speculating on literacy acquisition in inner-city ghettoes, contrasts "stimulus-bound" and "language-bound" individuals, suggesting that the latter seem to master literacy more easily.[26] The analysis here suggests that the causal relationship works the other way, that it is the mastery of written language that increases one's awareness of language as language.

This analysis has two implications. First, it makes the question of socially nonstandard dialects, always implicit in discussions of teaching formal grammar, into a non-issue.[27] Native speakers of English, regardless of dialect, show tacit mastery of the conventions of Standard English, and that mastery seems to transfer into abstract orthographic knowledge through interaction with print.[28] Developing writers show the same patterning of errors, regardless of dialect.[29] Studies of reading and of writing suggest that surface features of spoken dialect are simply irrelevant to mastering print literacy.[30] Print is a complex cultural code--or better yet, a system of codes--and my bet is that, regardless of instruction, one masters those codes from the top down, from pragmatic questions of voice, tone, audience, register, and rhetorical strategy, not from the bottom up, from grammar to usage to fixed forms of organization.

Second, this analysis forces us to posit multiple literacies, used for multiple purposes, rather than a single static literacy, engraved in "rules of grammar." These multiple literacies are evident in cross-cultural studies.[31] They are equally evident when we inquire into the uses of literacy in American communities.[32] Further, given that students, at all levels, show widely variant interactions with print literacy, there would seem to be little to do with grammar--with Grammar 3 or with Grammar 4--that we could isolate as a basis for formal instruction.[33]

Grammar 5: Stylistic Grammar
Similarly, when we turn to Grammar 5, "grammatical terms used in the interest of teaching prose style," so central to Martha Kolln's argument for teaching formal grammar, we find that the grammar issue is simply beside the point. There are two fully-articulated positions about "stylistic grammar," which I will label "romantic" and "classic," following Richard Lloyd-Jones and Richard E. Young.[34] The romantic position is that stylistic grammars, though perhaps useful for teachers, have little place in the teaching of composition, for students must struggle with and through language toward meaning. This position rests on a theory of language ultimately philosophical rather than linguistic (witness, for example, the contempt for linguists in Ann Berthoff's *The Making of Meaning: Metaphors, Models, and Maxims for Writing Teachers* [Montclair, N.J.: Boynton/Cook, 1981]); it is articulated as a theory of style by Donald A. Murray and, in somewhat different grounds (that stylistic grammars encourage overuse of the monitor), by Ian Pringle. The classic position, on the other hand, is that we can find ways to offer developing writers helpful suggestions about prose style, suggestions such as Francis Christensen's emphasis on the cumulative sentence, developed by observing the practice of skilled writers, and Joseph Williams' advice about predication, developed by psycholinguistic studies of comprehension.[35] James A. Berlin's recent survey of composition theory (*CE,* 45 [1982], 765-777) probably understates the gulf between these two positions and the radically different conceptions of language that underlie them, but it does establish that they share an overriding assumption in common: that one learns to control the language of print by manipulating language in meaningful contexts, not by learning about language in isolation, as by the study of formal grammar. Thus even classic theorists, who choose to present a vocabulary of style to students, do so only as a vehicle for encouraging productive control of communicative structures.

We might put the matter in the following terms. Writers need to develop skills at two levels. One, broadly rhetorical, involves communication in meaningful contexts (the strategies, registers, and procedures of discourse across a range of modes, audiences, contexts, and purposes). The other, broadly metalinguistic rather than linguistic, involves active manipulation of language with conscious attention to surface form. This second level may be developed tacitly, as a natural adjunct to developing rhetorical competencies--I take this to be the position of romantic theorists. It may be developed formally, by manipulating language for stylistic effect, and such manipulation may involve, for pedagogical continuity, a vocabulary of style. But it is primarily developed by any kind of language activity that enhances the awareness of language as language.[36] David T. Hakes, summarizing the research on metalinguistic awareness, notes how far we are from understanding this process:

> the optimal conditions for becoming metalinguistically competent involve growing up in a literate environment with adult models who are themselves metalinguistically competent and who foster the growth of that competence in a variety of ways as yet little understood. ("The Development of Metalinguistic Abilities," p. 205: see footnote 25)

Such a model places language, at all levels, at the center of the curriculum, but not as "necessary categories and labels" (Kolln, "Closing the Books on Alchemy." p. 150), but as literal stuff, verbal clay, to be molded and probed, shaped and reshaped, and, above all, enjoyed.

The Tradition of Experimental Research

Thus, when we turn back to experimental research on the value of formal grammar instruction, we do so with firm predictions given us by our theory of language. Our theory would predict that formal grammar instruction, whether instruction in scientific grammar or instruction in "the common school grammar," would have little to do with control over surface correctness nor with quality of writing. It would predict that any form of active involvement with language would be preferable to instruction in rules or definitions (or incantations). In essence, this is what the research tells us. In 1893, the Committee of Ten (*Report of the Committee of Ten on Secondary School Studies* [Washington, D.C.: U.S. Government Printing Office, 1893]) put grammar at the center of the English curriculum, and its report established the rigidly sequential mode of instruction common for the last century. But the committee explicitly noted that grammar instruction did not aid correctness, arguing instead that it improved the ability to think logically (an argument developed from the role of the "grammarian" in the classical rhetorical tradition, essentially a teacher of literature--see, for example, the etymology of *grammar* in the *Oxford English Dictionary*).

But Franklin S. Hoyt, in a 1906 experiment, found no relationship between the study of grammar and the ability to think logically; his research led him to conclude what I am constrained to argue more than seventy-five years later, that there is no "relationship between a knowledge of technical grammar and the ability to use English and to interpret language" ("The Place of Grammar in the Elementary Curriculum." *Teachers College Record,* 7 [1906], 483-484). Later studies, through the 1920s, focused on the relationship of knowledge of grammar and ability to recognize error; experiments reported by James Boraas in 1917 and by William Asker in 1923 are typical of those that reported no correlation. In the 1930s, with the development of the functional grammar movement, it was common to compare the study of formal grammar with one form or another of active manipulation of language; experiments by I.O. Ash in 1935 and Ellen Frogner in 1939 are typical of studies showing the superiority of active involvement with language.[37] In a 1959 article, "Grammar in Language Teaching" (*Elementary English,* 36 [1959], 412-421), John J. DeBoer noted the consistency of these findings.

> The impressive fact is ... that in all these studies, carried out in places and at times far removed from each other, often by highly experienced and disinterested investigators, the results have been consistently negative so far as the value of grammar in the improvement of language expression is concerned. (p. 417)

In 1960 Ingrid M. Strom, reviewing more than fifty experimental studies, came to a similarly strong and unqualified conclusion:

> direct methods of instruction, focusing on writing activities and the structuring of ideas, are more efficient in teaching sentence structure, usage, punctuation,

and other related factors than are such methods as nomenclature drill, diagramming, and rote memorization of grammatical rules.[38]

In 1963 two research reviews appeared, one by Braddock, Lloyd-Jones, and Schorer, cited at the beginning of this paper, and one by Henry C. Meckel, whose conclusions, though more guarded, are in essential agreement.[39] In 1969 J. Stephen Sherwin devoted one-fourth of his *Four Problems in Teaching English: A Critique of Research* (Scranton, Penn.: International Textbook, 1969) to the grammar issue, concluding that "instruction in formal grammar is an ineffective way to help students achieve proficiency in writing" (p. 135). Some early experiments in sentence combining, such as those by Donald R. Bateman and Frank J. Zidonnis and by John C. Mellon, showed improvement in measures of syntactic complexity with instruction in transformational grammar keyed to sentence combining practice. But a later study by Frank O'Hare achieved the same gains with no grammar instruction, suggesting to Sandra L. Stotsky and to Richard Van de Veghe that active manipulation of language, not the grammar unit, explained the earlier results.[40] More recent summaries of research--by Elizabeth I. Haynes, Hillary Taylor Holbrook, and Marcia Farr Whiteman--support similar conclusions. Indirect evidence for this position is provided by surveys reported by Betty Bamberg in 1978 and 1981, showing that time spent in grammar instruction in high school is the least important factor, of eight factors examined, in separating regular from remedial writers at the college level.[41]

More generally, Patrick Scott and Bruce Castner, in "Reference Sources for Composition Research: A Practical Survey" (*CE*, 45 [1983]" 756-768), note that much current research is not informed by an awareness of the past. Put simply, we are constrained to reinvent the wheel. My concern here has been with a far more serious problem: that too often the wheel we reinvent is square.

It is, after all, a question of power. Janet Emig, developing a consensus from composition research, and Aaron S. Carton and Lawrence V. Castiglione, developing the implications of language theory for education, come to the same conclusion: that the thrust of current research and theory is to take power from the teacher and to give that power to the learner.[42] At no point in the English curriculum is the question of power more blatantly posed than in the issue of formal grammar instruction. It is time that we, as teachers, formulate theories of language and literacy and let those theories guide our teaching, and it is time that we, as researchers, move on to more interesting areas of inquiry.

Note an the article's authorship as of 1985. Patrick Hartwell, Professor of English at Indiana University of Pennsylvania, is the co-author, with Robert H. Bentley, of *Open to Language: A New College Rhetoric* (Oxford University Press, 1982).

Professor Hartwell wishes to thank Wayne Edkin, Camden (New York) Public Schools; Michael Marler, Brigham Young University-Hawaii; and Ron Shook, Utah State University, for discussing these issues with him, and particularly to thank his colleague Dan J. Tannacito for references and discussion.

NOTES

1. *Research in Written Composition* (Urbana, Ill.: National Council of Teachers of English, 1963), pp. 37-38.

2. "Non-magical Thinking: Presenting Writing Developmentally in Schools," in *Writing Process, Development and Communication*, Vol. II of *Writing: The Nature, Development and Teaching of Written Communication*, ed. Charles H. Frederiksen and Joseph F. Dominic (Hillsdale, N.J.: Lawrence Erlbaum. 1980). pp. 21-30.

3. For arguments in favor of formal grammar teaching, see Patrick F. Basset, "Grammar--Can We Afford Not to Teach It?" *NASSP Bulletin*, 64, No. 10 (1980), 55-63; Mary Epes, et al., "The COMP-LAB Project: Assessing the Effectiveness of a Laboratory- Centered Basic Writing Course on the College Level" (Jamaica, N.Y.: York College, CUNY, 1979) ERIC 194 908; June B. Evans, "The Analogous Ounce: The Analgesic for Relief," *English Journal*, 70, No. 2 (1981), 38-39; Sydney Greenbaum. "What Is Grammar and Why Teach It?" (a paper presented at the meeting of the National Council of Teachers of English, Boston, Nov. 1982) ERIC 222 917; Marjorie Smelstor, *A Guide to the Role of Grammar in Teaching Writing* (Madison: University of Wisconsin School of Education, 1978) ERIC 176 323; and A.M. Tibbetts, *Working Papers: A Teacher's Observations on Composition* (Glenview, Ill.: Scott, Foresman, 1982).

   For attacks on formal grammar teaching, see Harvey A. Daniels, *Famous Last Words: The American Language Crisis Reconsidered* (Carbondale: Southern Illinois University Press, 1983); Suzette Haden Elgin, *Never Mind the Trees: What the English Teacher Really Needs to Know about Linguistics* (Berkeley: University of California College of Education, Bay Area Writing Project Occasional Paper No. 2. 1980) ERIC 198 536; Mike Rose, "Remedial Writing Courses: A Critique and a Proposal." *College English*, 45 (1983), 109-128; and Ron Shook, "Response to Martha Kolln." *College Composition and Communication*, 34 (1983), 491-495.

4. See, for example, Clifton Fadiman and James Howard, *Empty Pages: A Search for Writing Competence in School and Society* (Belmont, Cal.: Fearon Pitman, 1979); Edwin Newman, *A Civil Tongue* (Indianapolis, Ind.: Bobbs-Merrill, 1976); and *Strictly Speaking* (New York: Warner Books, 1974): John Simons, *Paradigms Lost* (New York: Clarkson N. Potter. 1980); A.M. Tibbets and Charlene Tibbets, *What's Happening to American English?* (New York: Scribner's, 1978); and "Why Johnny Can't Write," *Newsweek*, 8 Dec. 1975. pp. 58-63.

5. "The Role of Grammar in a Secondary School English Curriculum." *Research in the Teaching of English*, 10 (1976). 5-21; *The Role of Grammar in a Secondary School Curriculum* (Wellington: New Zealand Council of Teachers of English, 1979).

6. "A Taxonomy of Compositional Competencies," in *Perspectives on Literacy*, ed. Richard Beach and P. David Pearson (Minneapolis: University of Minnesota College of Education, 1979). pp. 247-272.

7. On usage norms, see Edward Finegan. *Attitudes toward English Usage: The History of a War of Words* (New York: Teachers College Press. 1980), and Jim Quinn, *American Tongue in Cheek: A Populist Guide to Language* (New York: Pantheon, 1980); on arrangement, see Patrick Hartwell, "Teaching Arrangement: A Pedagogy," *CE*, 40 (1979). 548-554.

8. "Revolution in Grammar," *Quarterly Journal of Speech*, 40 (1954), 299-312.

9. Richard A. Lanham. *Revising Prose* (New York: Scribner's, 1979); William Strunk and E.B. White. *The Elements of Style*, 3rd ed. (New York: Macmillan, 1979); Joseph Williams, *Style: Ten Lessons in Clarity and Grace* (Glenview, Ill.: Scott, Foresman, 1981). Christensen, "A Generative Rhetoric of the Sentence." *CCC*, 14 (1963). 155-161; Donald A. Daiker, Andrew Kerek, and Max Morenberg, *The Writer's Options: Combining to Composing*. 2nd ed. (New York: Harper & Row, 1982).

10. "A Psychological Approach," in *Psychobiology of Language*, ed. M. Studdert-Kennedy (Cambridge, Mass.: MIT Press, 1983). pp. 16-19. See also Noam Chomsky, "Language and Unconscious Knowledge." in

254   Style -- Writing Sentences

Psychoanalysis and Language: Psychiatry and the Humanities, Vol. III, ed. H. Smith (New Haven, Conn.: Yale University Press, 1978), pp. 3-44.

11. Morris Halle, "Knowledge Unlearned and Untaught: What Speakers Know about the Sounds of Their Language," in *Linguistic Theory and Psychological Reality,* ed. Halle, Joan Bresnan, and George A. Miller (Cambridge. Mass.: MIT Press, 1978), pp. 135-140

12. Moscowitz, "On the Status of Vowel Shift in English," in *Cognitive Development and the Acquisition of Language,* ed. T.E. Moore (New York: Academic Press. 1973). pp. 223-60; Chomsky, "Stages in Language Development and Reading Exposure," *Harvard Educational Review,* 42 (1972), 1-33; and Brause, "Developmental Aspects of the Ability to Understand Semantic Ambiguity, with Implications for Teachers," *RTE,* 11 (1977), 39-48.

13. Mills and Hemsley, "The Effect of Levels of Education on Judgments of Grammatical Acceptability." *Language and Speech,* 19 (1976). 324-342; Whyte, "Levels of Language Competence and Reading Ability: An Exploratory Investigation," *Journal of Research in Reading, 5* (1982). 123-132; Morais, et al., "Does Awareness of Speech as a Series of Phones Arise Spontaneously?" *Cognition,* 7 (1979). 323-331; Ferguson, *Cognitive Effects of Literacy: Linguistic Awareness in Adult Non-readers* (Washington, D.C.: National Institute of Education Final Report. 1981) ERIC 222 857; Hamilton and Barton, "A Word Is a Word: Metalinguistic Skills in Adults of Varying Literacy Levels" (Stanford, Cal.: Stanford University Department of Linguistics, 1980) ERIC 222 859.

14. On the question of the psychological reality of Grammar 2 descriptions, see Maria Black and Shulamith Chiat, "Psycholinguistics without `Psychological Reality'," *Linguistics,* 19 (1981), 37-61; Joan Bresnan, ed., *The Mental Representation of Grammatical Relations* (Cambridge, Mass.: MIT Press, 1982); and Michael H. Long, "Inside the `Black Box': Methodological Issues in Classroom Research on Language Learning," *Language Learning,* 30 (1980), 1-42.

15. Chomsky. "The Current Scene in Linguistics." *College English,* 27 (1966). 587-595; and "Linguistic Theory." in *Language Teaching: Broader Contexts.* ed. Robert C. Meade, Jr. (New York: Modern Language Association, 1966), pp. 43-49; Mark Lester, "The Value of Transformational Grammar in Teaching Composition," *CCC,* 16 (1967), 228.

16. Christensen, "Between Two Worlds." in *Notes toward a New Rhetoric: Nine Essays for Teachers,* rev. ed., ed. Bonniejean Christensen (New York: Harper & Row, 1978). pp. 1-22.

17. Reber, "Implicit Learning of Artificial Grammars," *Journal of Verbal Learning and Verbal Behavior,* 6 (1967), 855- 863; "Implicit Learning of Synthetic Languages: The Role of Instructional Set," *Journal of Experimental Psychology: Human Learning and Memory.* 2 (1976), 889-94; and Reber, Saul M. Kassin, Selma Lewis, and Gary Cantor. "On the Relationship Between Implicit and Explicit Modes in the Learning of a Complex Rule Structure." *Journal of Experimental Psychology: Human Learning and Memory,* 6 (1980), 492-502.

18. "Individual Variation in the Use of the Monitor," in *Principles of Second Language Learning,* ed. W. Richie (New York: Academic Press, 1978), pp. 175-185.

19. "Applications of Psycholinguistic Research to the Classroom." in *Practical Applications of Research in Foreign Language Teaching,* ed. D.J. James (Lincolnwood, Ill.: National Textbook, 1963). p. 61.

20. "Some Evidence for the Integrity and Interaction of Two Knowledge Sources," in *New Dimensions in Second Language Acquisition Research,* ed. Roger W. Andersen (Rowley, Mass.: Newbury House, 1981), pp. 62-74.

21. Hartwell and Bentley, *Some Suggestions for Using Open to Language* (New York: Oxford University Press, 1982), p. 73; Rose *Writer's Block: The Cognitive Dimension* (Carbondale: Southern Illinois University Press, 1983), p. 99; Daiute, "Psycholinguistic Foundations of the Writing Process," *RTE,* 15 (1981), 5-22.

22. See Bartholmae, "The Study of Error"; Patrick Hartwell, "The Writing Center and the Paradoxes of Written-Down Speech," in *Writing Centers: Theory and Administration,* ed. Gary Olson (Urbana, Ill.: NCTE, 1984).

pp. 48-61; and Sondra Perl, "A Look at Basic Writers in the Process of Composing," in *Basic Writing: A Collection of Essays for Teachers, Researchers, and Administrators* (Urbana, Ill.: NCTE, 1980), pp. 13-32.

23. Emonds, *Adjacency in Grammar: The Theory of Language-Particular Rules* (New York: Academic, 1983); and Jochnowitz, "Everybody Likes Pizza, Doesn't He or She?" *American Speech,* 57 (1982). 198-203.

24. Scribner and Cole. *Psychology of Literacy* (Cambridge, Mass.: Harvard University Press, 1981); Gleitman and Gleitman, "Language Use and Language Judgment," in *Individual Differences in Language Ability and Language Behavior,* ed. Charles J. Fillmore, Daniel Kemper, and William S.Y. Wang (New York: Academic Press, 1979), pp. 103-126.

25. There are several recent reviews of this developing body of research in psychology and child development: Irene Athey, "Language Development Factors Related to Reading Development," *Journal of Educational Research,* 76 (1983). 197-203; James Flood and Paula Menyuk, "Metalinguistic Development and Reading/Writing Achievement." *Claremont Reading Conference Yearbook,* 46 (1982), 122-132; and the following four essays: David T. Hakes, "The Development of Metalinguistic Abilities: What Develops?," pp. 162-210; Stan A. Kuczaj, II, and Brooke Harbaugh, "What Children Think about the Speaking Capabilities of Other Persons and Things," pp. 211-227: Karen Saywitz and Louise Cherry Wilkinson, "Age-Related Differences in Metalinguistic Awareness," pp. 229-250; and Harriet Salatas Waters and Virginia S. Tinsley, "The Development of Verbal Self-Regulation: Relationships between Language, Cognition, and Behavior," pp. 251-277; all in *Language, Thought, and Culture,* Vol. II of *Language Development,* ed. Stan Kuczaj, Jr. (Hillsdale, N.J.: Lawrence Erlbaum, 1982). See also Joanne R. Nurss, "Research in Review: Linguistic Awareness and Learning to Read," *Young Children,* 35. No. 3 [1980], 57-66.

26. "Competing Value Systems in Inner City Schools," in *Children in and Out of School: Ethnography and Education,* ed. Perry Gilmore and Allan A. Glatthorn (Washington, D.C.: Center for Applied Linguistics, 1982), pp. 148-171; and "Locating the Frontier between Social and Psychological Factors in Linguistic Structure," in *Individual Differences in Language Ability and Language Behavior,* ed. Fillmore, Kemper, and Wang, pp. 327-340.

27. See, for example, Thomas Farrell, "IQ and Standard English," *CCC,* 34 (1983), 470-484; and the responses by Karen L. Greenberg and Patrick Hartwell, *CCC,* in press.

28. Jane W. Torrey, "Teaching Standard English to Speakers of Other Dialects," in *Applications of Linguistics: Selected Papers of the Second International Conference of Applied Linguistics,* ed. G.E. Perren and J.L.M. Trim (Cambridge, Mass.: Cambridge University Press, 1971), pp. 423-428, James W. Beers and Edmund H. Henderson, "A Study of the Developing Orthographic Concepts among First Graders," *RTE,* 11 (1977), 133-148.

29. See the error counts of Samuel A. Kirschner and G. Howard Poteet, "Non-Standard English Usage in the Writing of Black, White, and Hispanic Remedial English Students in an Urban Community College," *RTE,* 7 (1973), 351-355; and Marilyn Sternglass, "Close Similarities in Dialect Features of Black and White College Students in Remedial Composition Classes." *TESOL Quarterly,* 8 (1974), 271-283.

30. For reading, see the massive study by Kenneth S. Goodman and Yetta M. Goodman, *Reading of American Children whose Language Is a Stable Rural Dialect of English or a Language other than English* (Washington, D.C.: National Institute of Education Final Report, 1978) ERIC 175 754; and the overview by Rudine Sims, "Dialect and Reading: Toward Redefining the Issues," in *Reader Meets Author/Bridging the Gap: A Psycholinguistic and Sociolinguistic Approach,* ed. Judith A. Langer and M. Tricia Smith-Burke (Newark, Del.: International Reading Association, 1982), pp. 222-232. For writing, see Patrick Hartwell, "Dialect Interference in Writing: A Critical View," *RTE,* 14 (1980), 101-118; and the anthology edited by Barry M. Kroll and Roberta J. Vann, *Exploring Speaking-Writing Relationships: Connections and Contrasts* (Urbana, Ill.: NCTE, 1981).

31. See, for example, Eric A. Havelock, *The Literary Revolution in Greece and its Cultural Consequences* (Princeton, N.J.: Princeton University Press. 1982); Lesley Milroy on literacy in Dublin, *Language and Social Networks* (Oxford: Basil Blackwell, 1980); Ron Scollon and Suzanne B.K. Scollon on literacy in central Alaska, *Interethnic Communication: An Athabascan Case* (Austin, Tex.: Southwest Educational Development Laboratory Working Papers in Sociolinguistics, No. 59. 1979) ERIC 175 276; and Scribner and Cole on literacy in Liberia, *Psychology of Literacy* (see footnote 24).

32. See, for example, the anthology edited by Deborah Tannen, *Spoken and Written Language: Exploring Orality and Literacy* (Norwood, N.J.: Ablex, 1982); and Shirley Brice Heath's continuing work: "Protean Shapes in Literacy Events: Ever-Shifting Oral and Literate Traditions," in *Spoken and Written Language*, pp. 91-117. *Ways with Words: Language, Life and Work in Communities and Classrooms* (New York: Cambridge University Press, 1983); and "What No Bedtime Story Means," *Language in Society*, 11 (1982), 49-76.

33. For studies at the elementary level, see Dell H. Hymes, et al., eds., *Ethnographic Monitoring of Children's Acquisition of Reading/Language Arts Skills in and Out of the Classroom* (Washington, D.C.: National Institute of Education Final Report, 1981) ERIC 208 096. For studies at the secondary level, see James L. Collins and Michael M. Williamson, "Spoken Language and Semantic Abbreviation in Writing," *RTE*, 15 (1981), 23-36. And for studies at the college level, see Patrick Hartwell and Gene LoPresti, "Sentence Combining as Kid-Watching," in *Sentence Combining: Toward a Rhetorical Perspective*, ed. Donald A. Daiker, Andrew Kerek, and Max Morenberg (Carbondale: Southern Illinois University Press, in press).

34. Lloyd-Jones. "Romantic Revels--I Am Not You." *CCC*, 23 (1972). 251-271: and Young, Concepts of Art and the Teaching of Writing," in *The Rhetorical Tradition and Modern Writing*, ed. James J. Murphy (New York: Modern Language Association, 1982), pp. 130-141.

35. For the romantic position, see Ann E. Berthoff, "Tolstoy, Vygotsky, and the Making of Meaning," *CCC*, 29 (1978). 249-255, Kenneth Dowst, "The Epistemic Approach." in *Eight Approaches to Teaching Composition*, ed. Timothy Donovan and Ben G. McClellan (Urbana, Ill.: NCTE, 1980), pp. 65-85; Peter Elbow, "The Challenge for Sentence Combining"; and Donald Murray, "Following Language toward Meaning," both in *Sentence Combining: Toward a Rhetorical Perspective* (in press; see footnote 33); and Ian Pringle, "Why Teach Style? A Review-Essay," *CC*, 34 (1983), 91-98.
    For the classic position, see Christensen's "A Generative Rhetoric of the Sentence"; and Joseph Williams' "Defining Complexity." *CE*, 41 (1979), 595-609, and his *Style: Ten Lessons in Clarity and Grace* (see footnote 9).

36. Courtney B. Cazden and David K. Dickinson. "Language and Education: Standardization versus Cultural Pluralism," in *Language in the USA*, ed. Charles A. Ferguson and Shirley Brice Heath (New York: Cambridge University Press, 1981). pp. 446-468; and Carol Chomsky. "Developing Facility with Language Structure." in *Discovering Language with Children*, ed. Gay Su Pinnell (Urbana, Ill.: NCTE, 1980). pp. 56-59.

37. Boraas, "Formal English Grammar and the Practical Mastery of English." Diss. University of Illinois, 1917: Asker, "Does Knowledge of Grammar Function?" *School and Society*, 17 (27 January 1923). 109-111; Ash, "An Experimental Evaluation of the Stylistic Approach in Teaching Composition in the Junior High School." *Journal of Experimental Education*. 4 (1935), 54-62; and Frogner, "A Study of the Relative Efficacy of a Grammatical and a Thought Approach to the Improvement of Sentence Structure in Grades Nine and Eleven," *School Review*, 47 (1939). 663-675.

38. "Research on Grammar and Usage and its Implications for Teaching Writing," *Bulletin of the School of Education*, Indiana University, 36 (1960), pp. 13-14.

39. Meckel, "Research on Teaching Composition and Literature," in *Handbook of Research on Teaching*, ed. N.L. Gage (Chicago: Rand McNally, 1963), pp. 966-1006.

40. Bateman and Zidonis, *The Effect of a Study of Transformational Grammar on the Writing of Ninth and Tenth Graders* (Urbana, Ill.: NCTE, 1966); Mellon, *Transformational Sentence Combining: A Method for*

Enhancing the Development of Fluency in English Composition (Urbana, Ill.: NCTE. 1969); O'Hare, *Sentence-Combining: Improving Student Writing without Formal Grammar Instruction* (Urbana, Ill.: NCTE, 1971); Stoisky, "Sentence-Combining as a Curricular Activity: Its Effect on Written Language Development." *RTE,* 9 (1975), 30-72; and Van de Veghe, "Research in Written Composition: Fifteen Years of Investigation," ERIC 157 095.

41. Haynes, "Using Research in Preparing to Teach Writing," *English Journal, 69*, No. 1 (1978), 82-88; Holbrook, "ERIC/RCS Report: Whither (Wither) Grammar," *Language Arts, 60* (1983), 259-263; Whiteman, "What We Can Learn from Writing Research," *Theory into Practice, 19* (1980), 150-156; Bamberg, "Composition in the Secondary English Curriculum: Some Current Trends and Directions for the Eighties," *RTE, 15* (1981), 257-266; and "Composition Instruction Does Make a Difference: A Comparison of the High School Preparation of College Freshmen in Regular and Remedial English Classes," *RTE, 12* (1978), 47-59.

42. Emig, "Inquiry Paradigms and Writing." *CCC, 33* (1982), 64-75; Carton and Castiglione, "Educational Linguistics: Defining the Domain." in *Psycholinguistic Research: Implications and Applications,* ed. Doris Aaronson and Robert W. Rieber (Hillsdale, N.J.: Lawrence Erlbaum, 1979), pp. 497-520.

Emplaining Grammatical Concepts

Muriel Harris and Katherine E. Rowan

Although editing for grammatical correctness rightly begins when composing is basically complete, editing is--at least for unpracticed writers--almost as demanding as composing. Editing for grammatical errors is not a one-step process, but a complete series of steps which involve detecting a problem (finding a mistake), diagnosing the error (figuring out what's wrong), and rewriting (composing a more acceptable version). Skilled writers don't always consciously need to move through all of these steps, but most students do. As writing lab instructors, we are acutely aware of situations when students are able to detect sentence-level problems but have few clues for resolving them. "That sentence isn't right--should I take it out?" a student will mumble as we sit with them. "This needs something, but I don't know what," another will say. Or, "I know I should be checking for commas, so maybe I should put some in this sentence." Anxiety, frustration, and even anger surface as they flail around knowing that something should be done--if they only knew what.

Certainly no one needs prescriptive grammar to generate grammatically complete oral sentences: everyone masters this mysterious skill before the age of four. And as those opposed to the teaching of grammar are quick to point out, many people can rely on their competence as native speakers to "sense" a fragment or agreement error and correct it without resorting to conscious knowledge of grammar. But this detection skill does little or nothing to help many students edit their papers. Admittedly, these students don't need to be able to spout grammatical *terminology* (e.g., "That's a participial phrase"). But they do need to understand fundamental grammatical *concepts* so that they can successfully edit their writing. And grammatical concepts, effectively taught, can be learned. However, despite the hype of textbook salesmen, the glossy packages of supplements, and the stacks of free review copies of books that inundate our mailboxes, it is not particularly obvious *how* grammatical concepts can best be learned. As Patrick Hartwell notes, many tried-and-true explanations of grammar are COIK-- clear only if known (119).

Hartwell has identified a core issue: too much of what passes for explanation of grammar may be perfectly clear to the teacher or textbook writer but leaves the student groping for help. To address this problem, we draw on concept learning research, a field which identifies the reasons why students generally have difficulties learning concepts and which offers tested strategies for overcoming these problems. Support for this approach comes from recent reviews of research on the teaching of grammar (Hillocks 140) and in the field of concept learning. What concept learning research offers is not some heretofore unknown approach or miracle cure but an affirmation of the need to combine a variety of interlocking strategies for success. Any standard textbook will illustrate some of these strategies or partial use of some approaches, but concept learning research emphasizes the need for thoroughness in our presentations. As we shall point out, using a few misleading examples to support a flawed explanation can cause confusion or misperceptions that may thwart a student's attempts to edit for years to come.

The term "concept," as used here and in concept learning research, refers to those mental abstractions that represent a class (or set) of entities which share certain essential characteristics. The names of these concepts (for example, the terminology traditionally used in grammar instruction) are merely conveniences for communicating about the concept. Although terminology can facilitate talking about grammatical concepts, a focus on learning terminology may cause problems because learners can mistakenly think that knowing the name means knowing all the critical features of the concept. Being able to identify ten (or two hundred) restrictive clauses in no way ensures that the student knows all the critical features of the concept. The broad definition of concepts helps us to see that concept learning principles are meant for all disciplines. While some of the research in concept learning is conducted with lessons in other fields, many projects include instruction in grammatical and poetic concepts, which researchers have successfully taught to students in junior high through college. These studies are not often cited in composition research, perhaps because the work appears in journals that composition teachers don't normally think of as being in their domain, e.g., *Educational Technology and Communication Journal, The Journal of Educational Psychology,* and *Review of Educational Research.*[1] Our purpose in this essay is to show how insights and strategies from concept learning literature can make the teaching of grammatical concepts efficient and effective. Throughout, we use instruction in the grammatically complete sentence as an example of how the principles of concept learning can facilitate understanding of grammatical concepts.[2] We've chosen sentence completeness because it is one of the writer's basic tools for clear, correct writing. In addition, a shaky concept of the sentence can inhibit writers from composing sentences they might otherwise construct. In a study of sentence errors, Dona Kagan describes the fragment as "among the most prevalent and irremediable errors" found in student writing (127).

Research in concept learning shows that a basic criterion for good explanations of difficult ideas is that they address students' most frequent misunderstandings. Hence, to identify our students' notions of the complete sentence, we first examined and categorized fragments that they wrote. We then altered a student essay slightly so that each of these characteristic fragments was represented (see Appendix A). To see what information students call upon while editing for fragments, we asked 179 students to identify each of thirty items in the essay as either a sentence or a fragment and to explain, in writing, why they made each choice. The students were enrolled in nine classes at our university, classes ranging from freshman composition to advanced writing, business writing, technical writing, and journalism. This gave us a sample of students about half of whom were juniors or seniors who had completed one or more college writing courses and another half of whom were completing their first semester of freshman composition. The tabulations of the students' responses (Table 1) show that while no item was correctly identified by all the respondents, some were more confusing to them than others.[3]

More important for our purposes than the matter of correct identifications are the reasons the students offered for their decisions. These responses open a window into student conceptions--and misconceptions--of the sentence. We use examples of these student responses to illustrate what concept learning researchers have identified as problems in learning concepts in nearly any field. After describing each problem, we offer strategies from concept learning research which overcome the particular difficulty.

These strategies, as we illustrate, are found to some degree in contemporary grammar textbooks and programmed learning guides. However, concept learning research has shown that no one of these strategies can be truly effective if used alone. Instead, concept learning strategies are interlocking and reinforcing and achieve their purpose only in combination. In short, partial explanations, examples, and practice too often produce, at best, partial learning.

Learning Concepts: Key Difficulties and Effective Strategies in Overcoming Them

1. Recalling Background Knowledge

Evidence of the Difficulty:

The work of learning theorists like Robert Gagne shows that learning a new concept usually involves building on other, more basic, concepts. If these other concepts are not familiar to a student, any explanation of the new concept can be a classic case of COIK, clear only if known. This is obvious to a teacher trying to explain the sentence to students who lack knowledge of subjects and predicates. To understand the concept of subjects, students have to know not only what nouns and pronouns are but, ultimately, phrases and clauses too, since all can exist as subjects. They may have some partial knowledge of these concepts, but it is necessary that at some point they have access to complete knowledge of all forms that can act as subjects. Otherwise, as we saw among the students we studied, the inability to consistently recognize subjects and predicates causes frequent errors in distinguishing sentences from fragments. For example, some of the students who identified the complete sentences #22, 23, and 27 in the test essay (Appendix A) as fragments did so because they said that there was no subject, an indication that the pronouns in these sentences weren't recognized as subjects. Even more confusion appears to exist for the student who identified a fragment (#16) as a sentence because it contains a verb, "perfect," and a noun, "his." Other students labeled item #19 as a fragment, saying "it has no subject or verb." (It has both, though in dependent clauses.)

Students also revealed their difficulties in distinguishing dependent from independent clauses. As a typical example, one student incorrectly identified item #4 as a fragment "because each clause cannot stand by itself," and another student incorrectly labeled item #13 as a fragment "because it is a prepositional phrase." This small, but representative sampling of the students' comments could be extended, but it is clear that these students' background knowledge is inadequate and that there is no point in expecting them to understand a definition of a fragment which assumes an understanding of the subject, verb, phrase, and clause.

Strategy for Overcoming the Difficulty.

Meeting this difficulty by providing background knowledge may seem to lead to an endless regression, but this is not the case. In their studies of concept learning, Tennyson and his associates have demonstrated the effectiveness of presenting background information at the point that the student seems to need help (Tennyson and

Cocchiarella 62-63). For example, this technique is used to teach the sentence in the opening pages or "frames" of Joseph Blumenthal's *English 2200, 2600,* and *3200,* a venerable and widely used--but not unflawed--series of self-instructional texts.[4] Included in Blumenthal's definition of a complete sentence are the concepts of subject and predicate which are defined as the "naming" and "telling" parts of the sentence. Practice is then offered for identifying the "naming" and "telling" parts of several sentences. In Lynn Quitman Troyka's *Simon and Schuster Handbook for Writers,* the sentence fragment is also defined and illustrated. Then, as the definition is extended, the concept of "verb" is introduced, explained, and illustrated, and the subject is explained next. Then, with this background information provided, the handbook explains dependent and independent clauses, beginning with an explanation of subordinating conjunctions (260-263). Thus at each step, background information is provided as needed.

2. Controlling *All* the Critical Features of a Concept

Evidence of the Difficulty:

Another problem faced by students learning new concepts is that of internalizing all the concept's critical (or essential) attributes, that is, of building a mental representation which includes every one of these necessary attributes. In the classic view of concept learning, recognizing a list of critical features was viewed as sufficient. But research on applied problems of concept learning has shown that people learn concepts by forming a mental prototype, that is, a clear case or best example (Reitman and Bower; Tennyson, Chao, and Youngers; Tennyson, Youngers, and Suebsonthi). In learning a specific concept, the more of its critical features our prototype includes, the fuller and more complete our grasp of this concept is. Nevertheless, what we store in memory is not a list of a concept's critical features but a prototype, an abstraction derived from *examples* of the concept that we've encountered.

The chief difficulty in forming a prototype is that of identifying the particular cluster of attributes which are truly critical and of distinguishing this cluster from the variable attributes, those that can and do occasionally or frequently appear, but aren't necessary. We can thus mistakenly include in the cluster of critical features attributes that are really only variables or omit a critical feature because we wrongly think it is a variable. For example, we can understand the source of confusion experienced by the child who, watching a kilted Scottish bagpiper in full regalia, says, "Why does that lady have a beard?" Skirts may be most frequently associated with women, but it is not a critical attribute of skirts that they be worn only by women. Assuming a variable to be a critical attribute is also a common source of humor, particularly with stereotypes: "Why did Adam remain happy when he left the Garden of Eden?" "Because he *still* had no mother-in-law." Unpleasantness, despite the vast repertoire of jokes on the subject, is a variable, not a critical attribute of mothers-in-law.

In our study we noticed numerous problems in students' prototypes of sentences which resulted from their confusion or misperceptions about critical and variable features. For example, in our pilot work, Teresa told us that the sentence, "John went to the store," was not a complete thought because it did not say what John bought at the store. For Teresa, the semantic feature "fully informative" was a critical attribute of all sentences rather than a variable attribute. (Sentences in context in paragraphs are not always fully informative.) Thus, we found students labeling as fragments complete sentences such as items #26, 27, and 30 because these items contained references to previous sentences by means of pronouns such as "he" and "that" and were therefore somehow "incomplete." Transition words (at the beginning of items #7, 13, and 15) and the phrase "on the other hand" in item #9 also provoked this sense of incompleteness. Among the students who said that the transitional phrase "to sum up" (item #25) marked a sentence as a fragment, one explained that it was incomplete by noting "To sum up what?" To prove the point that "first" (items #7 and 15) causes incompleteness, one student wrote. "What's second?" Another student wrote, "If there's a first, there needs to be a second thought to complete the sentence." These misperceptions raise the question of whether some students avoid the connectives we encourage for coherence because they see these as making a word group not "able to stand alone" (another commonly used definition of the sentence that students were unable to operationalize successfully). The conjunctions "and" and "but" are also definitely forbidden as sentence openers in the minds of many students. They noted that "and" as the first word of item #18 and "but" as the first word of item #26 identified these sentences as fragments. Said one student, "After putting in a subject and verb I allow a sentence to do almost anything it wants except begin with a conjunction." This misconception is most probably due to advice that students mistakenly store as a fixed rule.

The problem of viewing variable attributes of sentences as critical caused other difficulties as well. For example, sentence length, a variable attribute, exists as a critical attribute in the minds of those students who incorrectly labeled items #5 and 21 as fragments with explanations such as "it's too short" and a lengthy fragment (#28) as a sentence with explanations such as "it has enough words." The criterion of word length was given for other items as well. (Kagan's study documents the same misconception, that complete sentences need to exceed a certain number of words.) This raises the question of whether some students don't vary the word length of their sentences because they fear violating some rule they think applies to complete sentences. We found internal punctuation within the sentence included in many students' concepts of the sentence as well. For example, students incorrectly said that items #2 and 9 were fragments because of internal punctuation problems. Item #1 was incorrectly identified as a fragment because of "missing punctuation before the quote," item #12 was incorrectly marked as a fragment because "it needs punctuation after `patience,'" and item #26 was also incorrectly identified as a fragment because "it needs commas." For other students, usage errors caused a word group to be a fragment. Thus, for item #22, a reason given by several students for incorrectly identifying it as a fragment was their discomfort with the phrase "fast and easy." Another student noted that item #27 (a sentence) was a fragment because "something is wrong with `both very much.'"

In all this confusion we can see either ignorance of what constitutes the critical features of a sentence or elaborate but dysfunctional representations of the sentence. As Shaughnessy has argued, the problem is not that students are novices with a "lack" of knowledge but rather that from their bits of knowledge, they have constructed some elaborate, convoluted, and misleading conceptions. Kagan reaches a similar conclusion when she notes that "poor writers may simply have misperceived examples of written language and thus have abstracted incorrect rules regarding the structure of complete sentences" (127). Behind many of the students' comments in the responses we read, we heard echoes of familiar, overly brief, incomplete definitions such as "a sentence is a group of words with a subject and a verb," "a sentence tells who and what," "a sentence expresses a complete thought." Such inadequate definitions, accompanied by a few examples carefully chosen to support the definitions, leave students thinking they understand what a sentence is. However, such definitions also leave students without any way to think about sentences where the "who" or "what" is less than obvious (as in the sentence, "What she did to him is wrong") or about sentences which make sense only in context of other sentences (e.g., "They did it again"). The problem here is that students mistakenly apply the notion of "completeness" to the semantic meaning of the sentence and think that sentences must be fully informative. However, in realty, many grammatically complete sentences are not fully informative or "complete thoughts" outside the context of other surrounding sentences. In many of the mistaken student responses in our study, we observed a great deal of confusion when the students used semantic completeness as a test for a sentence rather than grammatical completeness. The weakness of the "tells who or what" definition is particularly evident in the frequency with which it turned up in student responses as justification for incorrectly identifying dependent clauses as complete sentences.

Strategy for Overcoming the Difficulty:

In the discussion of student perceptions--and misperceptions--of the sentence, we noted that definitions help students mentally represent the critical attributes of a concept. Evidence for the usefulness of definitions comes from C.S. Dunn's study of six methods of teaching science concepts. She found that the least effective was a "discovery" approach in which students were not given definitions. Instead, they were asked to discern the critical attributes of a concept from a set of diverse examples. Since the purpose of a definition is to highlight the critical attributes of a concept, the definition should contain a list of these critical features with each feature graphically highlighted.

Along with definitions, clear, typical, and varied examples also help students to master a concept's critical attributes. Grammar handbooks, intended primarily to be used as references rather than as programs of instruction, do not generally have space to include all the typical examples that are needed, but they often have quite adequate definitions. For example, the definition in Troyka's handbook is helpful in that it includes, among several definitions from various perspectives, a grammatical one: "Grammatically, a sentence contains an independent clause, a group of words that can stand alone as an independent unit" (154). Troyka then goes on to discuss the structure of a sentence and also presents a range of clear, typical examples. Initially, there are also five examples of fragments. The first three are phrasal fragments (no verb, no subject, no verb or subject) which, as we and Kagan found in our studies, students are most likely to recognize. The last two are clausal fragments (dependent clause and a subject with a dependent clause), the ones which students have more trouble recognizing and are more likely to produce (Harris). The discussion in Troyka's book then builds up to more complex examples of typical fragments. Other widely used handbooks such as the *Harbrace College Handbook* or the *Random House Handbook* tend to have a more limited number and range of examples, and the difficulty of attempting a brief, easily grasped (but incomplete) definition can be seen in the popular workbook. *Grassroots.* Here students are told: "For a sentence to be complete, it must contain a *who* or *what* word." Further down the page in *Grassroots,* the subject is defined as the "*who* or *what* word" (4), thus failing to distinguish subjects from objects. Such a definition can create further confusion in that it does not allow for subjects which consist of more than one word. In sum, then, good definitions list all of the critical features of a concept and are accompanied by a range of clear, typical examples.

3. Recognizing New Instances of a Concept

Evidence of the Difficulty:

Another problem in learning a concept, as suggested in the examples cited above, is that of recognizing newly encountered instances of the concept. In fact, researchers such as Homa, Sterling, and Trepel; and Tennyson, Chao, and Youngers say that this is one of the most frequent problems learners have. Certainly it is familiar to teachers: students can recite a definition of a sentence, but they have difficulty identifying now examples of sentences or fragments, or examples in unfamiliar contexts. People struggle to recognize concepts in context because, first, some of the guises or forms in which a concept appears are easier to spot than others and, second, to identify a new instance of a concept one must recognize all of its critical attributes. For example, some of the students who incorrectly tabeled items #18 and 26 as fragments did so because they noted that these items "lacked verbs." What they did not recognize were verbs which are manifested in contractions ("he's" and "that's"). However, other examples of fragments were easy for students in our study to recognize. For example, most students recognized short, phrasal fragments such as those in items #6, 11, 16, and 29. But a dependent clause (in item #19) was harder to recognize. Kagan also found that students had difficulty recognizing as fragments verbs followed by various structures, particularly objects modified by prepositional phrases. From the perspective of concept learning research, then, some students either may not understand all of the forms in which subjects and predicates can appear, or they may not understand that fragments can be either phrases or dependent clauses.

Strategy for Overcoming the Difficulty:

To help students recognize new instances of a concept, it is particularly important to use examples, more examples, and even more examples if possible, though they have to be carefully constructed and ordered. As already noted, we need to start with clear, typical cases that accompany definitions so that students can form and encode a prototype in memory. After that, students need an extended presentation of various kinds of examples, displayed in matched sets and discussed in easy-to-difficult order. The sets of examples should illustrate a wide range of critical and variable attributes. Highlighting for visual emphasis, particularly in explaining the examples, is very helpful.

- **Matched Sets.** Examples should be in matched sets of examples and nonexamples to help students discriminate between critical and variable features. Examples and nonexamples are matched when all the irrelevant or variable attributes of the set are as similar as possible. For example, because students may have trouble realizing that some contractions may include verbs, matched sets of examples and nonexamples could be used to illustrate this fact:

  Concept: verb in a contraction

  > *Matched sets:*
  > Example: She *is* lovely.
  > Example: She'*s* lovely.
  > Nonexample: She lovely.
  >
  > Example: When cotton shirts are old, they *are* more comfortable.
  > Example: When cotton shirts are old, they'*re* more comfortable.
  > Nonexample: When cotton shirts are old, they more comfortable.
  >
  > *Explanation:* Some verb forms can be present in contractions. In the matched sets above, the word groups that can stand alone as sentences (examples) contain complete verbs. The nonexamples lack verbs.

The use of nonexamples may seem to contradict a currently popular approach, offering instruction which is described as "nonerror based." The assumption in nonerror based instruction is that students should avoid seeing examples of errors. However, a number of studies indicate the power of the nonexample in effective concept formation (Markle and Tiemann; Tennyson 1973; Tennyson and Park; Tennyson, Woolley, and Merrill).

For example, since some students think that a pronoun cannot be the subject of a sentence (perhaps because a pronoun as the subject would cause the sentence to be less than fully informative), an effective sequence of instruction would present a sentence with a pronoun as a subject and an accompanying fragment with the same pronoun as a subject. An explanation of the pair would point out that both the sentence and the fragment have a pronoun as a subject. (Putting the sentence in the context of other sentences would help the student see that sentences refer to each other.) This kind of matching is helpful because the purpose of the nonexample is to have students see that a variable feature is indeed irrelevant.

Because the irrelevant or variable features to present are those likely to cause confusion, we can look at our students' writing to determine which variable attributes to illustrate. For example, since 20% of the students we studied labeled sentence #8 (a fragment containing a subject with a lengthy dependent clause modifying it) as a complete sentence, the following example/nonexample pair might be presented and discussed:

Six of the players who had poor grades on their mid-semester exams *are sitting* on the bench.

(This is an example of a sentence because it has a subject, "six," with a lengthy word group describing it and then the verb "are sitting" which tells what the six are doing.)

Six of the players who had poor grades on their mid-semester exams.

(This is not a sentence because it has a subject, "six," with a word group describing it but no verb. The word group after the subject describes only the subject.)

Given the confusions about sentence length that we found, another matched pair should contain only a few words while a third should be lengthy to emphasize that length is not a critical feature of the sentence.

The English 2200, 2600, 3200 books make considerable use of this kind of matching. When these texts offer examples of new concepts, the examples are usually paired with matched nonexamples. For instance, in *3200,* Blumenthal offers the following advice and matched sets:

Remember, too, that the length of a word group has nothing to do with its being a sentence or not. Two words may form a sentence provided that they are a subject and verb and make sense by themselves.

a. (The) *Neighbors objected*   b. The *neighbors.*
Which is a complete sentence?--

(33, frame 1367)

To further show that length is a variable and irrelevant feature of sentences, Blumenthal offers another matched set:

[a.] The *neighbors,* who were annoyed by Joanne's practicing her trombone at all hours of the day and night, (37, frame 1369) [versus]
[b.] The *neighbors,* who were annoyed by Joanne's practicing her trombone at all hours of the day and night, *complained.* (41, frame 1371)

By using these and many more matched sets, Blumenthal illustrates the irrelevance of length as a feature of sentences and highlights the critical importance of subjects and verbs.

- **Easy-to-difficult order.** Researchers have also found that students benefit when matched pairs are discussed in "easy-to-difficult" order. Easy examples have variable attributes that students make fewer mistakes with, and the progression should be to variable attributes that are more and more likely to cause students difficulties. To determine whether examples and nonexamples are easy or difficult, instructors can examine students' own writing or give diagnostic tests. In their work, Tennyson, Woolley, and Merrill found that when students are exposed only to easy items, they either fail to recognize all of the critical attributes of a concept, or they fail to recognize the full range of guises in which these attributes may appear. (Of course, this range will vary as students mature and become more proficient writers.)

- **Divergence between sets.** There should also be divergence between sets of examples. This helps students in discriminating a variety of apparent from real instances of a concept when they encounter new examples. Thus, for instance, when teaching sentences, we would include some matched sets of sentences/fragments beginning with the conjunctions, transitional words, and phrases that too many students think indicate fragments and other sets without such beginnings. Students would see, for example, both a sentence and a fragment starting with "but" and another matched set lacking this initial term. Other variable attributes would also be drawn from the lists of problems and confusions students have.

- **Highlighting.** Another characteristic that increases the effectiveness of presentations, particularly in discussing examples, is the use of "attribute isolation," that is, the use of typographical or graphic highlighting such as underlining, italics, and/or white space to call attention to the critical features of a concept (Tennyson "Pictorial Support"). A text that uses attribute isolation particularly effectively is Troyka's handbook which, in the discussion of fragments, uses boldface lettering, shaded boxes, contrasting colors of print (red and black), and generous use of white space to highlight important points. In the classroom, with homegrown materials, we are not likely to have at our disposal such elegant type features, but we can make use of underlining, circling, arrows, and white space.

Accompanying the examples should be explanations, to call attention to the various critical features that we want students to notice. For the sentence, we might present examples and nonexamples and note: "This is an example of a sentence because it has both a subject and a predicate, which constitute an independent clause," or "This is not an example of a sentence because it has only a dependent clause." These examples and accompanying explanations ("expository presentations") perform a necessary and important function in concept learning, for it is here that students see what Tennyson and Cocchiarella call the "dimensionality or richness of the conceptual knowledge" (61). Presenting only simple sentences with clear subjects and predicates sidesteps all the elaborations and variety of real sentences (and fragments) that occur when students actually write.

For examples of good expository presentations in current texts, see the discussion of fragments in the *Harbrace College Handbook*--which uses matched sets, divergence across sets, and some highlighting--or Troyka's extended expository presentation on fragments (260-64) which makes good use of nonexamples in matched sets, divergence across sets, easy-to-difficult order, and highlighting. Although

Grassroots has very short expository presentations or discussions of concepts, it does illustrate the use of practice exercises in easy-to-difficult order and uses some highlighting to emphasize key words. An example of a presentation which omits nonexamples, matched sets, divergence across sets, and easy-to-difficult ordering can be seen in the *Random House Handbook.*

4. Discriminating Apparent from Real Instances of a Concept

Evidence of the Difficulty:

A fourth aspect of learning difficult concepts is that of discriminating apparent from real instances of the concept's application. Students develop this discriminatory ability only with time, practice, and feedback (Dunn). In our study, we did not explore the history of our subjects' attempts to master the sentence-fragment distinction; however, the study does show that even as juniors and seniors, many students had fuzzy notions of the sentence which did little to help them master this distinction. Those who reported using the "complete thought" definition often seemed to use this in some vague semantic sense. Those who used the "who or what does the action" criterion failed to understand that their notion of the sentence did not include predication. For example, one student incorrectly identified item #24 as a sentence because it "gives who or what." Perhaps such students have inaccurate notions because they never practiced the sentence-fragment distinction in a context where they received continual feedback which explained why their answers were correct or incorrect.

Strategy for Overcoming the Difficulty:
To distinguish between apparent and real instances of a concept, students continually need reminders about the features that are truly critical to it. Tennyson and his associates found that students are more likely to classify concepts correctly and recall them better when they not only have a chance to read expository presentations of examples but also have the chance to work through "inquisitory practice sessions" (Dunn; Tennyson, Chao, and Youngers). These are exercises in which students are presented with new examples and nonexamples and are asked to identify them by working through a list of questions. After they give both correct and incorrect answers, students receive feedback which reminds them of the basis on which they should have made their identification (i.e., whether or not a given item had or didn't have all critical attributes of the concept). By working through these questions (which ask students to think about a concept's critical attributes) and by receiving feedback (which discusses the presence or absence of a given critical attribute in a particular item), students gradually learn to look for these critical attributes on their own. For an example of inquisitory practice, see Figure 1.
Similar strategies can be seen elsewhere in Troyka's handbook where, for example, at the beginning of the first exercise on fragments, students are told: "Check each word group according to the Test for Sentence Completeness on p. 261" (264). Students have to flip back and forth between the test and the exercises, but they are reminded of how they should proceed in determining whether or not a word group is a sentence or a fragment. *Grassroots* does not phrase the critical attributes of fragments as

Inquisitory Practice

<u>Concept</u>: Fragment

<u>Definition</u>: A fragment is one word or a group of words that cannot pass Troyka's Test for Sentence Completeness

[Troyka's] Test for Sentence Completeness
1. Is there a verb? If no, there is a sentence fragment.
2. Is there a subject? If no, there is a sentence fragment.
3. Do the subject and verb start with a subordinating word—and lack an independent clause to complete the thought? If yes, there is a sentence fragment. (Troyka 261)

Applying the Test—1

Directions: Identify all the sentence fragments incorrectly punctuated as sentences in the passage below. To do so, examine each numbered item by asking the three questions in Troyka's test.

The Change in Our Family

(1) When I was sixteen. (2) My father died. (3) Our family, my mom, me, and my two sisters, struggled to make ends meet. (4) We decided to move to an apartment because we couldn't afford our house any more. (5) The apartment, a big adjustment for us all. (6) For we had always seen ourselves as middle class. (7) The move made us wonder if we still were. (8) We have adjusted over the years and learned to be more realistic, I think. (9) It's not been easy. (10) But maybe we're a more honest family now.

Applying the Test—2

Directions: Using Troyka's Test to guide your decisions, punctuate the following passage.

Passage: To celebrate the opening of his theater   the owner decided to give a television set   to the person holding the lucky ticket when the number was called   seventy-two people flocked to the box office   each having the lucky number   the printer had made a slight mistake. (Blumenthal 71, frame 1386)

Figure 1. "Applying the Test" exercises are examples of inquisitory practice. The first exercise (#1) should be easier than the second (#2) because it requires students to make fewer decisions. The second exercise is more difficult but more realistic, requiring students to detect, diagnose, and edit.

questions, but it does remind students of at least some of these critical attributes by beginning an exercise with the following instructions: "All of the following are *fragments;* they lack either a subject or a verb or both. Add either a subject or verb or both in order to make the fragments into sentences"ᴸ-(17). Unfortunately, this fails to help students whose fragments are primarily dependent clauses, but it is more helpful than the instructions in the *Harbrace College Handbook,* which tells students: "Eliminate each fragment below by including it in the adjacent sentence or by making it into a sentence" (29).

Tennyson, Chao, and Youngers have demonstrated the importance of providing students with both expository presentations and inquisitory practice in a study which contrasted three learning situations. In the first, students were given only an expository presentation with examples. In the second, they were given only the inquisitory practice, while in the third, they were given both. The students in all three situations were able to recall the concept's critical attributes and some examples. However, the students who worked through both the expository presentation and the inquisitory practice had significantly higher scores than the other two groups in identifying new examples of the concept in context and in discriminating between instances of the concept and entities that appeared to be instances. In Dunn's replication of this study, once again it was the combination of explanations of matched examples and nonexamples and inquisitory practice that increased performance in every aspect of concept attainment.

Conclusion

In all of the information that concept learning research has to offer, one point stands out: students do not learn difficult concepts when presented with any single technique. What works is a *combination* of techniques:

- Providing background information when and where it is needed
- Offering definitions that list critical attributes and that are not overly simple or misleading
- Using a wide array of examples and nonexamples, chosen to reflect students' actual difficulties, and discussing the examples
- Including practice sessions, with feedback, that help students turn a concept's critical attributes into questions they ask themselves.

As we have seen, some of these principles are at work in our textbooks, but not as consistently or thoroughly as concept learning research would urge. But we can keep these guidelines in mind when choosing workbooks and textbooks and when offering instruction--both in classrooms and in tutoring sessions. And we can supplement, where necessary, adequate but not entirely complete textbook assignments and computer-assisted instruction. (However, spending time on uprooting misconceptions caused by inept textbooks is, like swatting mosquitoes, a frustrating, unending task.) The use of concept learning strategies is not the only way into better explanation of grammatical concepts, but it is a way, one based on sound principles and extensive research. It may appear to involve a great deal of effort, but if our students have convoluted, erroneous concepts that have to be untangled or corrected, we can't give short shrift and expect good results. They come to our classes with the capacity to detect some editing problems. They should leave with their detection, diagnosis, and revision skills enhanced.

Item #	No. (and %) identifying it as a sentence	No. (and %) identifying it as a fragment
1 (sentence)	161 (90%)	17 (9%)
2 (sentence)	144 (89%)	31 (17%)
3 (fragment)	3 (2%)	175 (98%)
4 (sentence)	161 (90%)	17 (9%)
5 (sentence)	165 (92%)	13 (7%)
6 (fragment)	4 (2%)	175 (98%)
7 (sentence)	153 (85%)	24 (13%)
8 (fragment)	36 (20%)	140 (78%)
9 (sentence)	168 (94%)	10 (6%)
10 (sentence)	175 (98%)	3 (2%)
11 (fragment)	4 (2%)	172 (96%)
12 (sentence)	162 (91%)	15 (8%)
13 (sentence)	98 (55%)	79 (44%)
14 (sentence)	174 (97%)	4 (2%)
15 (sentence)	160 (89%)	18 (10%)
16 (fragment)	9 (5%)	168 (94%)
17 (sentence)	164 (92%)	12 (7%)
18 (sentence)	60 (34%)	114 (64%)
19 (fragment)	23 (13%)	152 (85%)
20 (fragment)	75 (42%)	97 (54%)
21 (sentence)	167 (93%)	5 (3%)
22 (sentence)	148 (83%)	25 (14%)
23 (sentence)	156 (87%)	17 (9%)
24 (fragment)	14 (8%)	157 (88%)
25 (sentence)	144 (80%)	28 (16%)
26 (sentence)	54 (30%)	114 (64%)
27 (sentence)	154 (86%)	15 (8%)
28 (fragment)	21 (12%)	150 (84%)
29 (fragment)	3 (2%)	167 (93%)
30 (sentence)	154 (86%)	14 (8%)

Table 1. Tabulation of student responses to the test essay. (Number of students = 179. Because of some omitted responses, totals are not always 100%.)

Appendix A
(included here is the essay that students in our study were given. They were asked to identify each sentence as either a sentence or a fragment and to explain their responses.)

My Brothers

(1) The phrase I heard only too often when I was younger was `You're too little to play.' (2) Whatever my older brothers did I wanted to do, wherever they went I wanted to go. (3) Pat being two years older than myself and allowed to hang out with Randy, being four years older. (4) Since there was such a difference in age. I developed different and unique relationships with each.

(5) My brothers have clashing identities. (6) Total opposites of each other. (7)First, Pat is the kind of brother you see on television. (8) The kind that would help you with your homework and your problems. (9) Randy, on the other hand, isn't the smartest brother in the world but, he's been around and knows a lot. (10) The best summary of Randy is that he's the Mr. Hyde of Pat. (11) Not exactly bad, though a lot different. (12) He has no patience especially when he gets angry. (13) Then he goes on apologizing for days.

(14) There are traits in both of my brothers that I dislike. (15) First, Pat is too perfect. (16) Much too perfect for his own good. (17) The biggest annoyance is that he gets great grades. (18) And he's also nice to people that bother him. (19) Because he thinks it's important to be polite. (20) Not to mention his mannerisms are good at all times. (21) Randy likes to move around a lot. (22) He gets bored with a job fast and easy. (23) He just can't stay in the office very much. (24) Which makes him a very good salesman.

(25) To sum up, we have our differences. (26) But that's just like any other family. (27) I still like them both very much. (28) Any differences that I may have because of age or size which wasn't resolved or will be through time. (29) For a final note to this assignment. (30) I would never say any of this to their faces, just on paper.

Note on the article's authorship as of 1989. Muriel Harris, as associate professor of English, Purdue University, and director of the Writing Lab, edited the *Writing Lab Newsletter*, authored two textbooks, and was currently completing a brief grammar handbook (published by Prentice-Hall). Her interest in individualized instruction, the theory and practice of writing centers, and the tutorial teaching of writing is reflected in her numerous journal articles *(e.g. College English, College Composition and Communication, Journal of Basic Writing, Written Communication, English Journal, Writing Center Journal,* and *Teaching One-to-One: The Writing Conference (NCTE).*

Katherine E. Rowan, as assistant professor of communication, Purdue University, was teaching journalistic writing. She conducted research on the development of written communication skills, particularly the skills associated with explaining difficult ideas. Her work has appeared in *Written Communication, Journalism Educator,* and the *Journal of Technical Writing and Communication.*

Notes

[1] In such journals one can find the work of Robert Tennyson and his associates, e.g., Johansen and Tennyson; Merrill and Tennyson; Tennyson, Welsh, Christensen, and Hajovy; and Tennyson, Woolley, and Merrill. An accessible summary for teachers of this work is M. David Merrill and Robert Tennyson's *Teaching Concepts: An Instructional Design Guide.* Reviews of more recent research in concept learning can be found in an article by Tennyson and Park and another by Tennyson and Cocchiarella.

[2] We should note that the "grammar" being referred to here is that set of school grammar conventions labeled "grammar 4" by Patrick Hartwell, to distinguish it from other grammars, such as the descriptive grammar of linguists, stylistic grammar, or the internal grammar which guides all of our language use.

[3] While it was not our purpose to look for developmental gains as students progress through writing courses, we should note here that the students in the upper level writing courses did not perform appreciably better than the freshmen in distinguishing complete sentences from fragments.

[4] The books we use as examples in this paper are among those frequently used to teach grammar at the college level, according to sales information from major publishers.

Works Cited

Blumenthal, Joseph C. *English 3200: A Programmed Course in Grammar and Usage,* 3rd ed. New York: Harcourt, 1981.

Crews, Frederick and Ann Jessie Van Sant. *The Random House Handbook,* 4th ed. New York: Random, 1984.

Dunn, C.S. "The Influence of Instructional Methods on Concept Learning." *Science Education* 67 (October 1983): 647-56.

Fawcett, Susan and Alvin Sandberg. *Grassroots: The Writer's Workbook,* 3rd ed. Boston: Houghton, 1987.

Gagne, Robert. *Essentials of Learning for Instruction.* Hinsdale, IL: Dryden, 1974.

Harris, Muriel. "Mending the Fragmented Free Modifier." *College Composition and Communication* 32 (May 1981): 175-82.

Hartwell, Patrick. "Grammar, Grammars, and the Teaching of Grammar." *College English* 47 (February 1985): 105-27.

Hillocks, George Jr. *Research on Written Composition: New Directions for Teaching.* Urbana, IL: ERIC Clearinghouse on Reading and Communication Skills, 1986.

Hodges, John C., Mary E. Whitten, with Suzanne S. Webb. *Harbrace College Handbook,* 10th ed. New York: Harcourt, 1986.

Homa, D., S. Sterling, and L. Trepel. "Limitations of Exemplar-Based Generalizations and the Abstraction of Categorical Information." *Journal of Experimental Psychology: Human Learning and Memory* 7(November 1981): 418-39.

Johansen, Keith J. and Robert D. Tennyson. "Effects of Adaptive Advisement on Perception in Learner-Controlled, Computer-Based Instruction Using a Rule-Learning Task." *Educational Communication and Technology Journal* 31 (Winter 1983): 226-36.

Kagan, D.M. "Run-on and Fragment Sentences: An Error Analysis." *Research in the Teaching of English* 14 (May 1980): 127-38.

Markle, S.M. and P.W. Tiemann. "Some Principles of Instructional Design at Higher Cognitive Levels." *Control of Human Behavior.* Eds. R. Ulrich, T. Stocknik, and J. Mabry. Vol. III. Glenview, IL: Scott, 1974.

Merrill, M. David and Robert D. Tennyson. *Teaching Concepts: An Instructional Design Guide.* Englewood Cliffs, NJ: Educational Technology Publications, 1977.

Reitman, J.S. and G.H. Bower. "Structure and Later Recognition of Exemplars of Concepts." *Cognitive Psychology* 4 (March 1973): 194-206.

Tennyson, Robert D. "Effect of Negative Instances in Concept Acquisition Using a Verbal-Learning Task." *Journal of Educational Psychology* 64 (April 1973): 247-60.

_____. "Pictorial Support and Specific Instructions as Design Variables for Children's Concept and Rule Learning." *Educational Communication and Technology* 26 (Winter 1978): 291-99.

Tennyson, Robert D., J.N. Chao, and J. Youngers. "Concept Learning Effectiveness Using Prototype and Skill Development Presentation Forms." *Journal of Educational Psychology* 73 (June 1981): 326-34.

Tennyson, Robert D. and Martin J. Cocchiarella. "An Empirically Based Instructional Design Theory for Teaching Concepts." *Review of Educational Research* 56 (Spring 1986): 40-71.

Tennyson, Robert D. and O. Park. "The Teaching of Concepts: A Review of Instructional Design Literature." *Review of Educational Research 50* (Spring 1980): 55-70.

Tennyson, Robert D., M.W. Steve, and R.C. Boutwell. "Instance Sequence and Analysis of Instance Attribute Representation in Concept Acquisition." *Journal of Educational Psychology* 67 (December 1975): 821-27.

Tennyson, Robert D., James C. Welsh, Dean L. Christensen, and Halyna Hajovy. "Interactive Effect of Information Structure, Sequence of Information, and Process Learning Time on Rule Learning Using Computer-Based Instruction." *Educational Communication and Technology Journal* 33 (Fall 1985): 213-23.

Tennyson, Robert D., F.R. Woolley, and M. David Merrill. "Exemplar and Nonexemplar Variables Which Produce Correct Concept Classification Behavior and Specified Classification Errors." *Journal of Educational Psychology* 63 (April 1972): 144-52.

Tennyson, Robert D., J. Youngers. and P. Suebsonthi. "Acquisition of Mathematical Concepts by Children Using Prototype and Skill Development Presentation Forms." *Journal of Educational Psychology* 75 (April 1983): 280-91.

Troyka, Lynn Quitman. *Simon and Schuster Handbook for Writers.* Englewood Cliffs, NJ: Prentice. 1987.

D. Selected Bibliography

Allen, Robert L. *English Grammars and English Grammar.* New York: Charles Scribner's Sons, 1972.

Bartholomae, David. "The Study of Error." *CCC.* 31 (1980): 253-69.

Brown, J.I., and T.E. Pearsall. *Better Spelling: Fourteen Steps to Spelling Improvement.* Lexington, MA: D.C. Heath, 1985.

Dobie, A.B. "Orthographical Theory and Practice, or How to Teach Spelling." *Journal of Basic Writing* 5 (1986): 41-48.

Elbow, Peter. "The Challenge for Sentence Combining." *Sentence Combining: A rhetorical Perspective.* Ed. Don Daiker, Andrew Kerek, and Max Morenberg. Carbondale: Southern Illinois UP, 1985, 232-45.

Grubgeld, E. "Helping the Problem Speller without Suppressing the Writer." *English Journal* 75 (1986): 58-61.

Hairston, Maxine. "Not All Errors Are Created Equal: Nonacademic Readers in the Professions Respond to Lapses in Usage." *CE* 43 (1981): 794-806.

Harris, Jeannette. "Proofreading: A Reading/Writing Skill." *CCC* 38 (1987): 464-66.

Hartwell, Patrick. "Grammar, Grammars, and the Teaching of Grammar." *CE* 47.2 (1985): 105-127.

Laib, Nevin. "Conciseness and Amplification." *CCC* 41 (1990): 443-58.

Lees, Elaine O. "Proofreading as Reading, Errors as Embarrassments." *A Sourcebook for Basic Writing Teachers.* Ed. Theresa Enos. New York: Random, 1987. 216-30.

Noguchi, Rei R. *Grammar and the Teaching of English: Limits and Possibilities.* Urbana, IL: NCTE, 1991.

Quirk, Randolph, Sidney Greenbaum, Geoffrey Leech, and Jan Svartvik. *A Comprehensive Grammar of the English Language.* New York: Longman, Inc. 1985.

Richard, Jack C. ed., *Error Analysis: Perspectives on Second Language Acquisition.* London: Longman, 1977.

Shaughnessy, Mina. *Errors and Expectations: A Guide for the Teacher of Basic Writing.* New York: Oxford UP, 1977.

Sloan, G. "The Subversive Effects of an Oral Culture on Student Writing." *CCC* 30 (1979): 156-60.

Students' Right to Their Own Language, CCC 25. Urbana: NCTE, 1974.

Williams, Joseph M. "The Phenomenology of Error." *CCC* 32 (1981): 152-68.

Williams, Joseph. *Style: Ten Lessons in Clarity and Grace,* 2nd ed. Glenview: Scott Foresman, 1985.

E. Critical Thinking, Reading, and Writing

A college writing course should teach students to think critically. That may seem like an uncontroversial position to take, especially if you reject mechanistic approaches to teaching writing that limit instruction mainly to mastery of the five- paragraph and clear, error-free sentences. But such a position presents composition teachers with a number of difficulties. For one thing, how should we define critical thinking? Should we teach problem-solving, or should we try to teach students to pose problems themselves as well? Should we teach students Aristotelian logic or Stephen Toulmin's logical system? Or should we teach students the limits of traditional logic and reason and instead instruct them in the analytical methods of cultural studies or feminism? Should we begin teaching the methodologies of different academic disciplines in first-year writing courses? Or should we attempt to implement something like Paulo Freire's radical conception of "critical literacy"?

The articles here and in the section on argumentation that follows, as well as the suggestions for further reading, discuss a number of productive ways for defining and teaching critical thinking in a writing course. In this section, the articles focus on linking critical reading and writing. Composition teachers sometimes resist assigning students to write about texts written by others. The central texts of a writing course should be the writings of the students. When a composition course deals heavily with texts written by published authors, classtime often is dominated by discussion of these works, and the students' writing is neglected. Many teachers also find that writing courses offer a valuable opportunity for students to examine their lives and beliefs in serious ways and that students usually produce their best and most motivated writing when they write from personal experience.

However, in "A Relationship Between Reading and Writing: The Conversational Model" (first published in *College English* 41 [1980]: 656-61 and later included in his book *Constructing Experience*, Carbondale: Southern Illinois UP, 1994), Charles Bazerman opposes confining student writing only to personal experience in composition courses. "Each piece of writing," he states, is "a contribution to an ongoing written conversation," a conversation that requires the writer to read and consider what others have said earlier and to develop a response that considers the situation and purposes behind others' statements. In order to prepare students for writing in their major disciplines and in other personal and public forums, Bazerman argues, "we must cultivate various techniques of absorbing, reformulating, commenting on, and using reading." He proposes a multi-stage pedagogy that teaches students to comprehend texts, then to respond to them, to evaluate them, and finally to define issues and informed positions in their reading and writing.

In "Five Ways of Interpreting a Text," a chapter of the book *The Elements of Critical Reading* (Boston: Allyn & Bacon, 1991), John Peters describes five perspectives for reading and analyzing texts "that apply across the disciplines and that form the basis of even specialized critical discussions." The five perspectives are the social perspective (which considers a text's relation to culture), the emotional or psychological perspective (which examines the emotional appeals and conflicts of a text), the rhetorical perspective (which focuses on a work's form and style), the logical perspective (which analyzes the reasoning of a work), and the ethical perspective (which examines the moral and political values discussed and implied in a text). Peters provides a brief set of questions to help students apply each interpretive strategy and illustrates each analysis with close readings of Abraham Lincoln's Gettysburg Address, Joan Didion's "On Going Home," and Lewis Thomas' "Making Science Work." Margaret Kantz argues for teaching critical reading strategies for the research paper in "Helping Students Use Textual Sources Persuasively" (first published in *College English* 52 [1990]: 74-91). Normally, she writes, students treat their sources as repositories of facts and read them mainly to glean information to plug into their research papers. Their stance as readers grants sources an almost unassailable authority and makes it difficult for students to write argumentative research papers instead of papers that merely report and synthesize information. Kantz proposes that students learn to read all texts as arguments based on claims, which students can and should examine and challenge, and that students employ a problem-solving approach to writing a research paper.

Bazerman, Peters, and Kantz treat reading and writing as parallel processes in which students construct meaning with language. As recent literary theories and cognitive research on reading argue, readers compose meanings just as writers do, planning, drafting, and revising to form interpretations and evaluations of a text. The movement to integrate reading and writing in composition courses has developed out of a recognition that reading and writing are closely linked meaning-making activities.

A Relationship Between Reading and Writing: The Conversational Model

Charles Bazerman

The connection between what a person reads and what that person then writes seems so obvious as to be truistic. And current research and theory about writing have been content to leave the relationship as a truism, making no serious attempt to define either mechanisms or consequences of the interplay between reading and writing. The lack of attention to this essential bond of literacy results in part from the many disciplinary divorces in language studies over the last half century: *Speech* has moved out taking *rhetoric* with it; *linguistics* has staked a claim to all skilled language behavior but has attended mostly to spoken language; *sociology* and *anthropology* have offered more satisfactory lodgings for the study of the social context and meaning of literacy; and *English* has gladly rid itself of basic *reading* to concern itself purely with the higher reading of *literary criticism*. Writing in its three incarnations as basic composition, creative writing, and the vestigial advanced exposition, remains an unappreciated houseguest of *literature*. All these splits have made it difficult for those of us interested in writing to conceive of writing in terms broad enough to make essential connections: our accommodation has been to focus on the individual writer alone with the blank piece of paper and to ignore the many contexts in which the writing takes place. This essay will review developments in composition in light of this difficulty, propose a remedy in the form of a conversational model for the interplay of reading and writing, and then explore the implications of the model for teaching.

One of the older views, with ancient antecedents, held that a neophyte writer was an apprentice to a tradition, a tradition the writer became acquainted with through reading. The beginning student studied rules and practiced set forms derived from the best of previous writing; analysis and imitation of revered texts was the core of more advanced study of writing. The way to good writing was to mold oneself into the contours of prior greatness. Although current composition theory largely rejects this tradition/apprentice model as stultifying, teachers of other academic disciplines still find the model attractive, because writing in content disciplines requires mastery of disciplinary literature. The accumulated knowledge and accepted forms of writing circumscribe what and how a student may write in disciplines such as history, biology, and philosophy.

Recent work in composition has chosen instead to emphasize the writer's original voice, which has its source in an independent self. The model of the individual writer shaping thought through language informs recent investigations into the composing process, growth of syntactic maturity, and the source of error. We have aided the student in the struggle to express the self by revealing the logic of syntax, by asking for experiential and personal writing, and by offering techniques for prewriting and invention to help the student get closer to the wellsprings of thought that lie inside. Even traditional rhetoric finds its new justification in the reflection of organic psychological realities. By establishing the importance of the voice of the writer and the authority of personal perception, we have learned to give weight to what the student wants to say, to be patient with the complex process of writing, to offer sympathetic advice on *how* to rather than *what not to,* and to help the student discover the personal motivations to learn to write.

Yet the close observation of the plight of the individual writer has led us to remember that writing is not contained entirely in the envelope of experience, native thought, and personal motivation to communicate. Communication presupposes an audience, and deference to that audience has led to a revived concern for the forms of what is now called standard written English. E.D. Hirsch, in *The Philosophy of Composition,* locates the entire philosophy in readability; that is, concern for the audience. We have also noticed that most writing our students do during college is in the context of their academic studies; interest in writing across the curriculum has been the result. In the most thoughtful study coming out of this approach, *The Development of Writing Abilities* (11-18), James Britton and his colleagues begin to notice that students use readings, but in personal and original ways, in order to write for their academic courses. "Source-book material may be used in various ways involving different levels of activity by the writer" (23).

We may begin to understand those "various ways" and "different levels of activity" Britton refers to if we consider each piece of writing as a contribution to an ongoing, written conversation. Conversation requires absorption of what prior speakers have said, consideration of how earlier comments relate to the responder's thoughts, and a response framed to the situation and the responder's purposes. Until a final statement is made or participants disengage themselves, the process of response continues. The immediacy of spoken conversation does, I must admit, differ significantly from the reflectiveness of written conversation, but the differences more illuminate the special character of writing than diminish the force of the model. Speech melody, gestural communication, rapidly shifting dynamics, and immediate validation on one side are set against explicitness, development, complexity, contemplation, and revision on the other. The written conversation also may bring together a more diffuse range of participants than the spoken one, although the example of an exchange of office memos or the closed circle represented in professional journals indicate that such is not always the case. Further, in spoken conversation the makers of previous comments are more likely to be the auditors of the response. But again the counterexamples of the teacher who turns one student's question into the occasion for a lecture to the entire class, or the printed back and forth of a literary war, suggest that this distinction should not be oversimplified.

The conversational model points up the fact that writing occurs within the context of previous writing and advances the total sum of the discourse. Earlier comments provide subjects at issue, factual content, ideas to work with, and models of discourse appropriate to the subject. Later comments build on what came before and may, therefore, go farther. Later comments also define themselves against the earlier, even as they dispute particulars, redefine issues, add new material, or otherwise shift the discussion.

If as teachers of writing we want to prepare our students to enter into the written interchanges of their chosen disciplines and the various discussions of personal and public interest, we must cultivate various techniques of absorbing, reformulating, commenting on, and using reading. In the tradition/apprentice model, such skills were fostered only implicitly under the umbrella assignment of the research paper, but they were not given explicit, careful attention. Only access to the tradition (information gathering) and acknowledgement of the tradition (documentation) were the foci of instruction. In the newer model of the voice of the individual self, assignments such as the research paper are superfluous, remaining only as vestiges of former syllabi or as the penance imposed on a service department. The model of the conversation, however, suggests a full curriculum of skills and stages in the process of relating new comments to previously written materials. The following partial catalog of stages, skills, and assignments points toward the kinds of issues that might be addressed in writing courses. The suggestions are in the form of a framework rather than of specific lessons in order to leave each teacher free to interpret the consequences of the model through the matrix of individual thoughts, experiences, and teaching styles. Similarly, the teacher will need to interpret the model through those conversations that are most familiar and important to students. Given the diversity of existing written conversations and the variety of individual responses, it is not profitable to prescribe a single course for everyone.

Intelligent response begins with *accurate understanding of prior comments,* not just of the facts and ideas stated, but of what the other writer was trying to achieve. A potential respondent needs to know not just the claims a writer was making but also whether the writer was trying to call established beliefs into question or simply add some detail to generally agreed-upon ideas. The respondent needs to be able to tell whether a prior statement was attempting to arouse emotions or to call forth dispassionate judgment. The more we understand of the dynamics as well as the content of a conversation, the more we have to respond to. Vague understanding is more than careless; it is soporific. Particular writing assignments can help students become more perceptive readers and can help break down the tendency toward vague inarticulateness resulting from purely private reading. Paraphrase encourages precise understanding of individual terms and statements; the act of translating thoughts from one set of words to another makes the student consider exactly what was said and what was not. Summary reveals the structure of arguments and the continuity of thought; the student must ferret out the important claims and those elements that unify the entire piece of writing. Both paraphrase and summary will also be useful skills when in the course of making original arguments, the student will have to refer to the thoughts of others with some accuracy and efficiency. Finally, having students analyze the technique of writing in relation to the writing's apparent purpose will make students sensitive to the ways writing can create effects that go beyond the overt content. Analysis of propaganda and advertising will provide the extreme and easy cases, but analysis of more subtle designs, such as that of legal arguments or of reports of biological research, will more fully reveal the purposive nature of writing.

The next stage, *reacting to reading,* gives students a sense of their own opinions and identity defined against the reading material. As they try to reconcile what they read with what they already think, students begin to explore their assumptions and frameworks of thought. At first their responses may be uninformed, either fending off the new material or acquiescing totally to what appears to be the indisputable authority of the printed word. But with time and opportunities to articulate their changing responses, students can become more comfortable with the questions raised by their reading; they enter into a more dialectical relationship with those who have written before. Prior assimilated reading becomes grist for processing new reading. Three kinds of exercise encourage the development of more extensive and thoughtful reactions: marginal comments on reading, reading journals, and informal reaction essays. From early in the semester, teachers should encourage students to record their thoughts about the reading in marginal notes. The teacher must be careful to distinguish this kind of reaction annotation from the more familiar study-skills kind of content annotation, perhaps by suggesting that content annotations go on the inside margin and reactions go on the wider outside margins. This reaction in the margins increases the student's awareness of moment-by-moment responses to individual statements and examples. Reading journals written after each day's reading give the student additional room to explore the immediate responses at greater length and to develop larger themes. Again the teacher must insist on the distinction between content summaries and reactions, no matter how tentative the latter may at first be. Finally, the informal response essay allows the student to develop a single reaction at length, perhaps drawing on a number of related, more immediate responses. Here the teacher should make sure that the response maintains contact with issues growing out of the reading and does not become purely a rhapsody on a personal theme unrelated to the reading. For all three types of assignment, the teacher can refer the student to previously held opinions, experiences, observations, and other readings as starting points for reactions. As students become more sensitive to their responses to reading, they will spontaneously recognize likely starting points.

Developing reactions leads to more formal *evaluation of reading,* measuring what a book or article actually accomplishes compared to its apparent ambitions, compared to reality, and compared to other books. The evaluative review, if treated as more than just a notice covered with a thin wash of reaction, is an effective exercise, for it requires the student both to represent and to assess the claims of the book or article. The reader's reaction to the book is also significant to the evaluation, for if the reader finds him- or herself laughing when he or she should be nodding in assent, the book has failed to meet at least some of its purposes. Another kind of evaluative essay measures the claims of the reading against observable reality. The data the student compares to the book's claims may be from prior experience, new observations, formal data gathering using social science techniques, or technical experiments. Here the teacher may discuss the variety of purposes, criteria, and techniques of data gathering in different academic disciplines as well as other human endeavors. Finally, students may be asked to compare the claims and evidence of a number of different sources. In this kind of exercise, the students have to judge whether there is agreement, disagreement, or merely discussion of different ideas; then students must identify on what level the agreement or disagreement occurs, whether of simple fact, interpretation, idea, or underlying approach; and finally, they must determine how the agreements can be fitted together and the disagreements reconciled or adjudicated. Conflicts cannot, of course, always be resolved, but students become aware of the difficulties of evaluation. Comparison of matched selections, reports requiring synthesis, reviews of literature, and annotated bibliographies are all assignments compatible with this last purpose. Reviews of literature and annotated bibliographies also give the student a coherent picture of how previous comments add up in pursuit of common issues.

Students can then begin to define those *issues* they wish to pursue and to develop *informed views* on those issues. Two kinds of exercise, definitions of problem areas and research proposals, require the students to identify some issue he or she would like to know more about, to assemble the prior statements relevant to the issue, and to indicate the limitations of those sources. The proposal requires the further task of planning how the gap of knowledge in the literature can be overcome. Problem definition and proposals are early stages of the familiar assignment of the research paper. Also familiar is the teacher's disappointment upon receiving a derivative research report instead of an original, informed view in the form of a research essay. The use of preparatory assignments--not just the proposal, but also progress reports, reflections on the evidence, hypothesis testing, and idea sketches--will help remind the student of the original goal of the work while encouraging creative and detailed use of the source material. Prior instruction in the skills discussed above will also insure that the student knows how to use reading to form independent attitudes toward the sources and so facilitate the development of original theses. Other, more specific exercises that set the conditions for the development of informed views involve setting factual and theoretical sources against each other. Three case studies can be compared to elicit general patterns, or one writer's theories can be measured against another's factual material. These two assignments are, in fact, forms of critical analysis using a coherent set of categories derived from a theoretical standpoint to sort out specifics. Such exercises show the student the many uses of source material beyond simple citation of authority in support of predetermined opinion.

The independent, critical standpoint the student develops with respect to reading other people's works can also help the student frame and revise his or her own writing to be a purposeful and appropriate contribution to an ongoing conversation. Consideration of the relationship to previous statements will help the student decide what techniques are likely to serve new purposes. Will a redefinition of basic concepts, the introduction of a new concept, or the close analysis of a case study best resolve confusion? Or perhaps only a head-on, persuasive argument will serve. Further, knowledge of the literature likely to have been read by an audience helps a writer determine what needs to be explained at length and what issues need to be addressed.

The model of written conversation even transforms the technical skills of reference and citation. The variety of uses to be made of quotation, the options for referring to others' ideas and information (e.g., quotation, paraphrase, summary, name only), and the techniques of introducing and discussing source materials are the tools that allow the accurate but pointed connection of one's argument to earlier statements. The mechanics of documentation more than being an exercise in intellectual etiquette, become the means of indicating the full range of comments to which the new essay is responding.

When we ask students to write purely from their selves, we may tap only those prior conversations that they are still engaged in and so limit the extent and variety of their thinking and writing. We can use reading to present new conversational

284   Critical Thinking, Reading, and Writing

opportunities that draw the students into wider public, professional, and academic communities. Thus, the students will learn to write within the heavily literate contexts they will meet in college and later life. Whether writing tasks are explicitly embedded in prior written material--a review of literature, a research paper, or a legal brief--or whether they are only implicitly related to the thought and writing of others, as in critical analyses or matters of public debate, if students are not taught the skills of creating new statements through evaluating, assimilating, and responding to the prior statements of the written conversation, we offer them the meager choice of being parrots of authority or raconteurs stocked with anecdotes for every occasion. Only a fortunate few will learn to enter the community of the literate on their own.

Works Cited

Hirsch, E.D., Jr. (1977). *The Philosophy of Composition.* Chicago: University of Chicago Press.

Britton, James T., Martin N. Burgess, A. Mcleod, and H. Rosen. *The Development of Writing Abilities (11-18)*

(London: Macmillan   Education,   1975).

Five Ways of Interpreting a Text
John Peters

Interpretation can be frustrating if you don't know where to begin. Suppose you're in a classroom or other meeting place where a text is being discussed. Maybe the target is an essay or a chapter or a formal report of some kind. Though you've read the material as closely as others have, you feel awkward talking about it. You remember most of what you have read, but when it comes to commenting on its meaning or importance, you don't know where to start. You hear other people saying things, and you know you're expected to say something too. All of a sudden, the professor or discussion leader turns to you and asks, "What's your view?"

Silence descends. Faces stare at you. After catching your breath, you stammer a few words as chill perspiration bedews your forehead. Then the discussion moves on to someone else while you sit frozen, trying to recall what you said. You hope it sounded reasonable, but you're not sure. Could it be that you didn't have a "view" at all?

Nonsense! You probably had plenty of views, but you weren't used to organizing or expressing them effectively. What you lacked was a means of approach that would allow you to bring your ideas together.

In this chapter we review five ways of approaching a text of any kind. These are ways that apply across the disciplines and that form the basis of even specialized critical discussions. Even though we shall be reviewing them here in brief and somewhat simplified terms, you'll find that they can be adapted easily to more advanced circumstances, depending on your needs and interests.

NOTE [from the author's "Preface":] This is a book about reading and elementary criticism. It is addressed to college undergraduates who must learn traditional ways of analyzing, discussing, and evaluating what they are assigned to read. In a wider sense, however, this book is for anyone--in college or out--who must read often and who is in some doubt as to what "critical reading" means.

[From the introduction to Chapter 2 :]: .... In order to demonstrate the five critical perspectives, we shall need to refer often to ... three sample texts ... as models for practice. Besides, those three texts--Lincoln's Gettysburg Address, Joan Didion's "On Going Home," and Lewis Thomas's "Making Science Work"--are good examples of the kinds of writing which college students and other critical readers nowadays find themselves interpreting. Those three texts represent respectively the "classic" document of historic reputation, the contemporary personal memoir, and the expository or argumentative essay. The skills you develop in discussing those kinds of texts will help prepare you for future critical reading across the disciplines.

From *The Elements of Critical Reading,* John Peters, (California State University, Northridge CA), Chapter 4. New York: Macmillan, 1991. Copyright ©1991 by Macmillan College Publishing Company. Reprinted by permission of Prentice-Hall, Inc.

THE SOCIAL PERSPECTIVE

Using the social perspective means discussing the text in relation to society. Just about everything you read has some social relevance. Invitations, legal contracts, letters, and advertising are obvious examples. In the case of essays, nonfiction books, and other demanding texts, you can begin to take a social perspective by answering a few key questions:

What Social Concerns Does the Text Reveal?

One way to answer this question is simply to think about what general function or usefulness the text may have. Magazine articles, for example, may be reporting on new trends, showing people how to do things, or giving opinions on subjects of popular interest. On the other hand, some texts have less obvious social relevance. A mathematics textbook may not reveal social concerns directly; but if you consider how necessary applied math is to technology we use, the social significance of polynomials or differential equations should be evident. Thinking about how a text is used by others is one way to discover its relation to society.

Another way of answering the question is to think about any problems or conflicts that the text may address. Because all writing involves contrast, you can reexamine a given text's contrasts to see if any of them is social in nature. Ordinary reading material may present obvious social contrasts, as when a magazine ad tries to convince you of the difference between the wise people who own a given product and the fools who don't. But in longer texts, the social contrasts may have to do with anything from family tensions to class conflict, generation gaps, professional rivalries, political differences, or even war.

If you have read the three sample texts reprinted in the Appendix, try to summarize the social issues raised within each. You may discover that in Lincoln's Gettysburg Address the most obvious social conflict is the Civil War, for as Lincoln reminds his audience: "We are met on a great battle-field of that war." But other social concerns are detectable as well. One student summarized them this way:

> The author is also concerned about the continuing struggle for equality and the preservation of our nation, which is "dedicated to the proposition that all men are created equal."

The question of whether a government "of the people" will survive or perish is certainly a social issue, and so is the issue of slavery--a matter not directly discussed in the speech itself but implied by the allusion to the Civil War.

As for the other two models in the Appendix, you may find that Joan Didion's essay reveals social concerns having to do with family identity and the meaning of "home," while Lewis Thomas's essay focuses on the social uncertainties brought about by twentieth-century science. Is the American family what it used to be? Is technology our friend or our enemy? These are matters which Didion and Thomas address respectively. The social perspective allows you to focus on those issues as you discuss their essays.

Not everyone will agree on exactly how a text's social concerns should be summarized. But to make the effort is to begin using the social perspective as an approach to the text. When you've discovered what you believe are the key social issues, you can move on to another question that the social perspective calls for:

How Does the Text Relate to the Past?

In considering whatever social concerns a text reveals, you might ask how the text relates to the times during which it was written. Newspaper articles are an obvious example of how nonfiction depends on the world around it. In the case of books, essays, and other less "news"-oriented texts, the relation of text to history may be more subtle. Yet most writing does reflect the author's awareness of his or her times. Scientific writing, for example, may not always seem concerned with the society around it, but the scientist's findings will be influenced by the current state of research in his or her century. More personal writing, such as memoirs and autobiographies, often comments on social trends that the author has witnessed.

Consider again the three texts in the Appendix. Joan Didion's "On Going Home" is a product of the 1960s. The author takes her times into account by speculating on whether she is a member of "the last generation to carry the burden of 'home,' to find in family life the source of all tension and drama" (par. 2). Lewis Thomas, whose essay appeared in the early 1980s, also takes history into account by surveying the past 300 years of science in contrast to the rapid developments of the past half century (par. 2). And, of course, we can't overlook Abraham Lincoln's famous allusions to historical events as he saw them in 1863: the founding of the nation "four score and seven years ago"; the battle at Gettysburg; and the unresolved fate of the nation during the Civil War. If you ask yourself whether a given text has something to say about the times before or during which it was written, the answer will often be *yes*--maybe even *a great deal!*

There is still another question you can ask from a social perspective, and it is this:

How Does the Text Relate to Right Now?

Important as it is to consider how a text relates to the past, even more important may be how it relates to the present. If you've just read this morning's newspaper, the relation between the text and "right now" may seem obvious. In college, however, much of what you read may have been written months, years--even centuries ago. For that reason you should be ready to ask whether social concerns raised by a text still affect us.

This question may cause you to emphasize matters that earlier audiences might have found less central to the text. For example, the crowd listening to Lincoln's 1863 speech probably felt that the key concern was whether the Civil War could be won by the Union forces. Today we know the answer to *that* question, and so we may choose to focus on broader concerns raised by the speech, such as freedom and the aims of government. Is the Gettysburg Address still relevant to American society in the late twentieth century? Here is what one student said:

I find this speech very moving. The racial issue was a powerful and destructive force then--it still is. As a nation, we've come a long way. As a world, we have so far to go in matters of race, religion, and gender. For our nation, it seems the march was openly begun with this war, with this speech.

If you agree that Lincoln's words still challenge us to preserve democracy, you'll have a basis for discussing how this old text addresses the present.

What about works of more recent vintage, such as essays or books written within the past few decades? Here the question may be whether the social concerns raised by the text still reflect current behavior or practice in matters of custom, social activity, fashion, science, business, or whatever the subject may be. You may have to do some sifting to decide what still applies. In the case of Lewis Thomas's essay, you might be aware that scientific funding from business and government has increased since the essay was written, but still find timely the author's point about the continuing need for basic research. And in considering Joan Didion's "On Going Home," you might find the allusion to a girl dancing topless on crystal a bit dated; nevertheless, you could still find the author's uncertainty about the meaning of "home" relevant to the 1990s.

Summary

Discussing things from a social perspective allows us to view a text in relation to the world around it. By focusing on a text's social concerns as they apply to both the past and "right now," we may find that we already have plenty to say. But there are at least four other useful ways of approaching what we've read.

THE EMOTIONAL PERSPECTIVE

A second way of looking at a text is from a psychological viewpoint, or what we might simply call the emotional perspective. Though some texts seem emotionless (a legal contract, for example), most writing appeals to human feelings in one way or another. Focusing on a text from an emotional perspective can reveal new areas for interpretive discussion.

Does the Text Contain Objects of Emotion?

First, look for objects that the text invests with strong emotional significance. In the bible, for example, such objects include the apple that tempts Adam, the Ark of the Covenant, and the Cross in the New Testament. While poetry and other kinds of imaginative literature are usually rich in emotive symbols, even nonfiction will sometimes display objects of emotion to signify moods or attitudes within the text.

In Joan Didion's "On Going Home," we come across several such objects: the contents of a drawer (par. 3), the telephone (par. 4), the vandalized cemetery (par. 4), and the sundress from Madeira (final par.). In context, those objects become associated with moods of nostalgia, uncertainty, dread, and hope--or, at least, those are general terms that might be used to describe their effects on the author. We can see that Didion is using those objects as symbols to intensify the emotional dynamics of her very personal essay. Consider also this from paragraph 3: "Paralyzed by the neurotic lassitude engendered by meeting one's past at every turn, around every corner, inside every cupboard, I go aimlessly from room to room." This eerie and rather discomforting sentence suggests that the ordinary objects in the house are for Didion more than mere objects of sentiment. They become associated with a "lassitude" that slows her down as she moves among them.

The more impersonal the writing, the fewer objects of emotion we might expect to find. However, if you look closely at Lewis Thomas's "Making Science Work," you'll notice how the author describes scientific discoveries as moments of "surprise" final par.). Also, early in the essay he calls attention to the hostile emotions of those who distrust science itself:

> Voices have been raised in protest since the beginning, rising in pitch and violence in the nineteenth century during the early stages of the industrial revolution, summoning urgent crowds into the streets. ...

Here the author deliberately uses emotion-charged terms--"protest," "violence," "urgent crowds"--to characterize science's detractors as being like an angry mob. Fair or not, this characterization dramatizes the contrast Thomas wants to draw between his opponents and scientists like himself.

Finally, consider the Gettysburg Address. Here Lincoln underscores the solemnity of the occasion by alluding to a single object--the battlefield. It has become "a final resting place for those who here gave their lives." For Lincoln the field is a symbol of sacrifice, but also, he tells us, a point of departure from which the living can take "increased devotion."

Naming and discussing the objects of emotion found in a text should help you to develop an interpretive analysis. But there is more to the emotional perspective than identifying a few key objects and the moods associated with them. Often there are several contrasting emotions to deal with, and for that reason we should pay attention to any emotional conflicts within the text.

Do You Find Evidence of Conflicting Emotions?

Since contrast is necessary to the structure of any text, we may well find that part of the contrast is emotional. In the Biblical story of Eden, for example, the apple may at first seem to signify temptation. But once Adam has sinned, the emotional picture grows very complicated. If we study the Eden story from an emotional perspective, we find many conflicts being raised: desire versus loyalty, pleasure versus pain, innocence versus guilt, and so forth. By recognizing those emotional contrasts we can learn something about the emotional *range* of the text.

When Abraham Lincoln tells his Gettysburg audience that "in a larger sense, we can not dedicate--we can not consecrate--we can not hallow--this ground," he is introducing an emotional conflict of sorts. The respect for the dead soldiers is so profound that the mourners are incapable of enacting that respect merely by dedicating the cemetery. The soldiers have already consecrated the ground "above our poor power," as Lincoln puts it. He then *resolves* that emotional conflict by turning from the dedication of the cemetery to a greater alternative: the dedication of ourselves: "It is rather for us to be here dedicated to the great task remaining before us. ..." In other words, we must turn from mourning to a spirit of new commitment. Lincoln's appeal to his audience thus moves from one emotional plane to another, challenging the audience to share in a transition from sadness to hope.

Sometimes the emotional conflicts within a text are left unresolved. In "Making Science Work," Thomas contrasts the "surprise" of pure scientific discovery with the desire of society for predictable technological advances. The author cannot tell us where this conflict of interests will lead, exactly, but he does assure us that the surprises won't stop coming: "... we will not be able to call the shots in advance" (final par.). Similarly, in "On Going Home," Joan Didion describes emotional tensions between her husband and her family, between her two senses of "home," and between one generation and another. But she does not tell us how those tensions will be resolved.

It's important to realize that many texts do leave emotional conflicts unresolved, sometimes because they must. A text isn't a failure or poorly written just because it doesn't offer a solution to every problem it poses. Emotional conflict within writing is known as *irony* (a literary term for the balancing of opposites), and many fine works are full of emotional ironies. We can't as readers be expected to resolve all of those ironies any more than we can expect the author to do it for us, but we can share the author's awareness of conflict and thereby move closer to a sympathetic understanding of the text.

What Is the Tone of the Author?

The word tone refers to the attitude of the author toward the subject he or she is writing about. Even when particular objects in the text become associated with particular emotions, and even when the text contains emotional conflicts, we may find that the overall work takes on a tone which we may infer as characteristic of the author. Thus, for example, we might say that Lincoln has a "solemn" tone throughout the Gettysburg Address, that Joan Didion writes "wistfully" about her family home, or that Lewis Thomas's writing conveys a tone that is serious but lively.

Characterizing tone is bound to be a subjective exercise on the part of the reader. That is because we infer tone from our personal responses to the subject matter of the text. Also, when we describe tone we allow ourselves to generalize about what are really many separate aspects of the writing: content, diction, prose style, and so forth. But even though describing the author's tone may be risky, no discussion of a text from an emotional perspective can be complete without our taking the chance. For of all the emotions that may be present in the text, it is the author's own that are likely to affect us most.

Summary

The emotional perspective considers whatever objects of emotion may be present, any emotional conflicts that may arise within the text, and finally the author's overall tone.

It's important to remember that sometimes the emotions of a text vary, and that we cannot always expect emotional conflicts to be neatly resolved.

THE RHETORICAL PERSPECTIVE

Rhetorical analysis takes as its focus the form and style of the writing. Here, rather than concerning yourself with the social any emotional issues that might be raised, you give your attention to *how* a text is constructed. If you want to learn to write well, you can benefit from applying the rhetorical perspective. That is because rhetoric has to do with skills employed by writers to achieve desired effects. By looking carefully at the form and style of particular texts, you can discover ways to advance your own writing skills. In fact, you will find yourself appreciating more fully the *art* of writing.

Here are some questions you can ask to begin using the rhetorical perspective:

How Can the Text's Form Be Described?

Describing form means recognizing categories to which the text may belong. For example, you can begin by asking yourself whether the text is nonfiction or imaginative literature. If you know it's nonfiction, go on to categorize it by *genre*. Is it an essay, a speech, a biography, an editorial, a technical operations manual, or what? If it is a work of imagination, is it poetry, drama, or prose fiction? More specifically, is it a lyric poem, an epic, a short story, a novel, a tragedy, a comedy, or what? If you are in doubt as to the definitions of the various genres and subgenres, you can consult a handbook of literary terms for help. To know why a text belongs to a particular category, you need first to know how that category is defined.

The term *essay,* for example, denotes a short, nonfictional prose work that comments on some aspect of reality. As a form, the essay goes back at least as far as the sixteenth-century *essais* of Michel de Montaigne. That French author asked himself, "What do I know?" His many essays become answers to that question, commenting on subjects from war and politics to religion and literature. Today the essay is a popular means of exploring what *we* know about the various disciplines and experiences that affect our lives. In general, we come upon two kinds of essays: those that are *personal,* involving reminiscences about the author's own past; and those that are *impersonal,* containing little or no reference to the author's private life.

Joan Didion's "On Going Home" is an example of a personal essay, while Lewis Thomas's "Making Science Work" is an impersonal one--at least in terms of its subject matter. We find that Didion's essay refers often to her family, her home(s), her special memories, and her own identity in relation to what she has witnessed. By contrast, Lewis Thomas's essay tells us nothing about the author's private life; instead, the focus is on a public controversy having to do with science and technology. What Thomas writes does of course reflect his personal views and judgment, but his own personality is not the focal point of the essay.

Another subgenre of nonfiction is the speech, or what is more precisely called *oration.* Speeches, too, can be either personal or impersonal, though the historic ones tend to be the latter. Lincoln's Gettysburg Address is not about Lincoln himself, after all, but about the future of the nation. If you look up a definition of *oratory* in a handbook or encyclopedia, you'll find that a classical oration contains three parts: an *exordium*, which appeals to the traditions or customs of the audience; an *argument*, which sets forth the main message and offers reasons for agreeing with the speaker; and a *peroration*, or summing up, that heightens or message. The Gettysburg Address is an unusually short oration, but it does contain all three parts if you look closely. The first sentence invokes the nation's past; the rest, except for the last sentence, argues on behalf of renewed dedication to national principles; and the last sentence serves as the peroration. In other words, this very short speech does follow the form of classical oratory.

Once you've identified the overall form of a text--as being a personal essay, a classic oration, or whatever--you are ready to go on with a more detailed analysis of the text's rhetoric.

Which Rhetorical Modes Do You Find in the Text?

We use the term *rhetorical modes* to describe methods of organizing writing to serve particular functions. Those functions may include describing, narrating, defining, comparing, contrasting, classifying, illustrating, summarizing, as well as persuading. All texts make use of at least some rhetorical modes, and the text's overall form may determine the kinds being used.

The kinds of rhetorical modes found in an essay, for example, may depend on whether that essay is personal or impersonal. Because Joan Didion's "On Going Home" is a personal essay, we might expect to find modes that help make her personal experience vivid. Those modes include *description* and *narration*. Describing means providing sense impressions having to do with sight, sound, taste, touch, and/or scent. Narrating means telling about a sequence of events. We find that both of those modes are used throughout Didion's essay:

> ... I drive across the river to a family graveyard. It has been vandalized since my last visit and the monuments are broken, overturned in the dry grass. Because I once saw a rattlesnake in the grass I stay in the car and listen to a country-and-Western station. Later I drive with my father to a ranch he has in the foothills.

Notice that the quoted passage contains both descriptive images (the broken monuments, the dry grass, etc.) and narrative (visiting the cemetery, listening to the radio, etc.). Personal writing often blends description and narration artfully so that the reader can experience an event and at the same time become aware of the setting. Precise narrative-descriptive detailing is almost a necessity in personal essays, though other rhetorical modes may be present as well.

On the other hand, impersonal essays tend to employ rhetorical modes suited to research reporting. Those include *definition, summary, classification, illustration, process analysis,* and *comparison/contrast* (see the Glossary for further explanations of those terms). In Lewis Thomas's "Making Science Work," for example, we find *summary* occurring in the essay's opening sentence: "For about three centuries we have been doing science, trying science out, using science for the construction of what we call modern civilization." Elsewhere, Thomas makes use of *classification* when he reviews scientific developments in fields from biology to social science (pars. 4-11), and again when he discusses the types of institutions that support basic research (pars. 12-16). This sort of formal distinguishing among types or categories is characteristic of impersonal essays, or what we call expository prose. The aim is to expose differences and distinctions that help explain a problem and/or point to its possible solution.

If you look carefully at Lincoln's Gettysburg Address, you may find the chief rhetorical modes to be contrast (i.e., between past and present), definition (i.e., the greater meaning of *dedicate),* and summary (i.e., of the events leading up to the dedication ceremony). You may find others, too.

By identifying which rhetorical modes appear in a text, you can reveal what functions the text is performing. That is true not only of essays but of all kinds of writing. In analyzing fiction, for example, you'll probably find plenty of narration and description, just as you will in personal essays, for the aim of fiction is to bring you close to the lives of imaginary characters. Business documents, textbooks, and other kinds of expository nonfiction may be given to other modes, especially classification, definition, process analysis, and summary.

How Can the Author's Style Be Described?

As E.B. White once pointed out, style is always something of a mystery: "Who can confidently say what ignites a certain combination of words, causing them to explode in the mind?" We can analyze the grammar of a text's sentences for clues, and we can talk about the "tone" of the author's voice. But style, like personality, is likely to remain more than the sum of its parts. Our efforts to describe an author's style probably won't succeed completely. But that doesn't mean we shouldn't try.

A graceful prose style often reflects a writer's keen awareness of grammar. Smooth parallel structures--known as parallelism or coordination--are often regarded as virtues of style, whereas misplaced modifiers, mixed metaphors, and verbosity are usually seen as flaws. (See the Glossary for more about those terms.) Analyzing the grammar of sentences can teach you a great deal about what works and what doesn't.

Some prose styles can be described as highly "formal." That is, they're marked by evenly balanced sentence structures resembling the fine cadences of classical music. The Gettysburg Address has that kind of polished formality. Consider this sentence: "The world will little note, nor long remember, what we say here, but it can never forget what they did here." Obviously, we *do* remember what Lincoln said here, partly because he said it so well. The sentence shows fine coordination as he balances the rise and fall of clauses on either side of the conjunction *but.* The verb phrases are parallel in form (i.e., "little note"--"long remember"--"never forget"). Furthermore, the repeating of the word "here," which otherwise might seem verbose, works like a resounding chord because of the rhythmic spacing.

Less formal styles are often called "conversational" because they come closer to the varied rhythms and loose structure of everyday speech. That doesn't mean, however, that an informal style isn't carefully done. Consider this passage from Lewis Thomas's "Making Science Work":

We will solve our energy problems by the use of science, and in no other way. The sun is there, to be sure, ready for tapping, but we cannot sit back in the lounges of political lobbies and make guesses and wishes; it will take years, probably many years, of research. Meanwhile, there are other possibilities needing deeper exploration.

Here, as in conversation, the language moves forward unevenly. The lengths of the three sentences vary, and within those sentences some clauses are much shorter than others. There is a sort of stop-and-go urgency that gives emphasis to certain terms. Notice how Thomas writes "it will take years, probably many years, of research." The double stress on *years* seems deliberate, but also a bit hesitant. We seem to be hearing someone thinking aloud, letting his style reflect the natural course of his reasoning.

Often you'll find that a prose style falls somewhere between the high formality of Lincoln and the more conversational quality of Thomas. If you consider Joan Didion's style, for example, you'll find her a bit closer to Lincoln when it comes to balanced phrases within sentences, but much closer to Thomas when it comes to varying the lengths of sentences themselves. Notice how her essay ends:

> I would like to give her more. I would like to promise her that she will grow up with a sense of her cousins and of rivers and of her great-grandmother's teacups, would like to pledge her a picnic on a river with fried chicken and her hair uncombed, would like to give her *home* for her birthday, but we live differently now and I can promise her nothing like that. I give her a xylophone and a sundress from Madeira, and promise to tell her a funny story.

If you're tempted to say that the personal subject matter and the pronoun "I" make this style less formal than Lewis Thomas's, look again. The long sentence is far more oratorical than conversational, building rhythmically on a series of parallel phrases. But you'd be right in saying that, like Thomas, Didion sharply varies the sentence lengths and thereby brings her prose style closer to the normal pacing of everyday speech.

Let's say that you've now looked at the form, rhetorical modes, and style of the text. There is still another matter to consider when you are using the rhetorical perspective:

What About Ambiguity?

As philosophers from Francis Bacon to Jacques Derrida have reminded us, language is ambiguous. The same word or term can be understood to mean different things to different readers or listeners. The word "pride," for example, suggests healthy self-respect to some persons, but to others it connotes the sin of overestimating what we deserve. Thus saying that someone is a "proud person" could be taken as a compliment or a rebuke, depending on the intent of the speaker and on the understanding of the audience. Dictionaries can supply us with general definitions, called *denotations*. But each reader also interprets terms according to personal *connotations*--meaning his or her own previous experiences with those terms. As the semanticist S.I. Hayakawa once pointed out, if we hear the phrase "Bessie the cow," we are all likely to think of different cows. The full implications of this problem are far reaching. If all language is potentially ambiguous, no two readers will read a text in quite the same way, and even the same reader may read a text differently on different occasions.

If you accept the notion that any word may be ambiguous, finding ambiguities in texts should be fairly simple. All you have to do is point to any line and say, "This can be read in different ways." You'd be right. But as a practical matter, we can't pause to challenge every word or term we read. What we need to look for are those words whose ambiguity raises serious questions about the meaning of the whole text.

In considering this problem we should first distinguish between ordinary--or "bad"--ambiguity that results from stylistic faults, and a literary--or "good"--kind that enhances the quality of the text. Ambiguity of the ordinary "bad" kind can be caused by mixed metaphors, misplaced modifiers, equivocation, imprecise translation from a foreign language, or by verbosity (refer to listings in the Glossary). Ambiguity of the literary or "good" kind is another matter. Here the reader's uncertainty as to the meaning isn't caused by poor writing but, on the contrary, by the ability of the author to heighten or intensify words in a way that creates new levels of possible meaning for them.

One way to find these "good" ambiguities is to look for terms that the author stresses as being hard to define. Sometimes a text will begin to raise questions about its own key words. Consider, for example, this passage from Joan Didion's "On Going Home":

> I am home for my daughter's first birthday. By "home" I do not mean the house in Los Angeles where my husband and I and the baby live, but the place where my family is, in the Central Valley of California. It is a vital although troublesome distinction.

Here the author gives us two connotations for the word "home." She tells us that she will be using the second one--home as the place where her family is--in this essay. But she also says that the distinction between the two senses of "home" is troublesome. Later in the essay, we find that Didion is still uncertain as to what "home" means:

> Sometimes I think that those of us who are now in our thirties were born into the last generation to carry the burden of "home," to find in family life the source of all tension and drama. ... The question of whether or not you could go home again was a very real part of the sentimental and largely literary baggage with which we left home in the fifties; I suspect that it is irrelevant to the children born of the fragmentation after World War II.

In this second passage, the author no longer uses "home" to stand for her childhood house in the Central Valley of California. Now she associates the word with abstract ideas such as "burden" and the "tension and drama" of family life. But Didion cannot be sure that this wider, more abstract meaning still holds true for a post-World War II generation. Thus the meaning of "home" remains a problem throughout the essay. The author may be saying that one's sense of "home" depends on one's age and viewpoint, but that the ultimate meaning may be undecidable. In any case, we need to recognize that special ambiguity of the word "home" in this essay, for the difficulty of knowing what "home" means is largely what the essay itself is about.

The two other texts reprinted in the Appendix also raise questions about some of their own key terms. Lewis Thomas's essay is largely concerned with what "science" has come to mean in the modern world. He admits that part of the meaning remains unclear:

Illumination is the product sought, but it comes in small bits, only from time to time, not ever in broad, bright flashes of public comprehension, and there can be no promise that we will ever emerge from the great depths of the mystery of being.

Science may not be only a matter of proving things, Thomas suggests, but also of living with uncertainty. As one example of that uncertainty, he points to the word "cell":

For a while things seemed simple and clear; the cell was a neat little machine, a mechanical device ready for taking to pieces and reassembling, like a tiny watch. But just in the last few years it has become almost imponderably complex, filled with strange parts whose functions are beyond today's imagining.

Here, Thomas shows us that a scientific term like "cell" can be as ambiguous as an everyday term like "home." But by facing up to that ambiguity, the essayist can address not only the question of what the word has meant--but also the question of what it is coming to mean. The reader is invited to wonder right along with the author.

Consider, finally, the Gettysburg Address. Here the word "dedicate" is surely a key term. In one sense, the dedication of the cemetery is a social ritual for which the audience has gathered. But Lincoln quickly challenges that ordinary sense of "dedicate." In a larger sense, he says, "We can not dedicate ... this ground." The brave soldiers, he reminds us, have already done so. Setting aside the dedicating of the cemetery, therefore, Lincoln instead uses "dedicate" in other contexts: for example, being "dedicated to the proposition that all men are created equal," and being a "nation ... " so dedicated." If we look carefully at Lincoln's repeated use of "dedicate" within the speech, we realize that he is doing more than just reviewing familiar connotations of the word. He is creating new meaning:

It is rather for us to be here dedicated to the great task remaining before us-- that from these honored dead we take increased devotion to that cause for which they here gave the last full measure of devotion--that we here highly resolve that ... this nation, under God, shall have a new birth of freedom--and that, government of the people, by the people, for the people, shall not perish from the earth.

Here Lincoln has given new meaning to the word "dedicate." That new meaning inspires a commitment to ideals that transcend the hour of mournful commemoration. Being dedicated in the newer sense is a matter of "increased devotion." But the full sense of what Lincoln means by "dedicate" may be indefinable--a sublime ambiguity. For it remains a word among others, and those other words--"unfinished work," "task remaining," "new birth of freedom"--all point to an uncertain future when the present act of dedication must be fulfilled.

Ambiguity is thus an important issue in rhetorical analysis. Sometimes the question of what a text means comes down to the question of what a particular word means. If that word is important within the text but treated by the author as having different connotations, chances are that deciding what that word means is a challenge that the text itself is facing.

Summary

The rhetorical perspective allows us to discuss a text's form, its rhetorical modes, its style, and its words. Once we have considered those matters, we should have a pretty fair idea
of how the text is constructed.

THE LOGICAL PERSPECTIVE

The logical perspective takes into account the reasoning used by an author to reach a conclusion. Sometimes that reasoning can be very complicated, as in, say, a treatise on physics or a detailed legal brief. At other times, logic may seem to have been suspended altogether, as in a fairy tale where things happen by magic. But in the course of reading standard nonfictional material, you'll need to look carefully at the text's logic as a basis for deciding whether or not you agree with the views expressed. Here are some questions you might ask.

What Debatable Issue Is Raised by the Text?

A debatable issue is one that allows for controversy. It is a problem whose solution has not been agreed upon by everyone before the text was written. Sometimes a text will raise several such issues, though all of them will usually cluster around a central problem.

What is at issue in the Gettysburg Address? Lincoln puts it very succinctly: "Now we are engaged in a great civil war, testing whether that nation, or any nation so conceived, and so dedicated, can long endure." For the audience listening at Gettysburg in 1863, the question of whether the United States could survive as a nation was surely an unresolved issue. The war was not yet won, nor was its outcome in sight. Many believed that the Union forces would prevail, but half of America was still in rebellion. How could the Union hope to win? Lincoln raises precisely that question.

Or consider Joan Didion's "On Going Home." Hers is a personal essay, not a work of formal argumentation. But Didion does raise a controversial issue when she speculates on whether she is part of "the last generation to carry the burden of 'home,' to find in family life the source of all tension and drama." At issue here is whether American values changed after World War II in such a way that the "tension and drama" of family life lost much of its former importance. Obviously, not everyone would agree that such a change occurred. The issue is open for debate, as Didion recognizes.

Consider also Lewis Thomas's essay. Here the author is addressing a general readership concerned about the future of science. The author raises a controversial issue early in the essay:

> Three hundred years seems a long time for testing a new approach to human interliving, long enough to settle back for critical appraisal of the scientific method, maybe even long enough to vote on whether to go on with it or not. There is an argument. Voices have been raised in protest since the beginning. ... Give it back, say some of the voices, it doesn't really work. ...

The scientists disagree, of course, partly out of occupational bias, but also from a different way of viewing the course and progress of science in the past fifty years.

The issue, then, is whether science does "really work." Thomas reminds us that while some people fear and distrust science, others--scientists themselves--have a different view. As readers we infer that the essay will go on to explore this controversy in more detail, and of course it does so.

What Conclusions Does the Text Reach?

After discovering what issues have been raised, you want to know what conclusions the text reaches about those issues. Logical thinking about a matter of controversy often results in a stated position which the audience is invited to share. To analyze the reasoning by which that conclusion is reached, you might begin by identifying the conclusion itself.

If the main issue raised by the Gettysburg Address is whether a "nation ... so dedicated" can long endure, the main conclusion is that survival depends on the dedication of the living to the "unfinished work" of the past. Lincoln encourages his audience to share the belief that further sacrifice to preserve "government of the people, by the people, for the people" is necessary.

And if the main issue in Didion's "On Going Home" is whether the meaning of "home" changed following World War II, the conclusion seems to be that the meaning did indeed change. At the end of the essay, the author wants to give her daughter "home" in the sense of family picnics by the river, but instead she gives her a sundress from Madeira and a promise to tell a funny story. The symbolism here may suggest that in the author's view commercialism and the promise of "fun" have become substitutes for the "tension and drama" of family life.

In the case of Thomas's essay, the issue--whether or not science works--is one upon which the author has strong opinions. The major conclusion is perhaps found in this passage:

Science is useful, indispensable sometimes, but whenever it moves forward it does so by producing a surprise; you cannot specify the surprise you'd like.

Technology should be watched closely, monitored, criticized, even voted in or out by the electorate, but science itself must be given its head if we want it to work.

Much of Thomas's essay argues that while we may distrust technology, or applied science, we should recognize that basic scientific inquiry "works" if given the freedom to produce its surprises. The key to workable science, in the author's view, is respect for the difference between science and technology.

Does the Text Contain Sufficient Evidence?

Once you've identified issues and conclusions, you need to analyze the reasoning by which conclusions are reached. In effect, you now become a bit like a jury weighing the evidence.

When you ask whether a text contains "sufficient evidence," you are really asking whether that text gives convincing reasons to show why its conclusion is valid. To answer that question, you need to take another look at the reasoning. In general, there are two possible kinds of reasons any text can offer you: those based on deduction and those based on induction. Most texts of any length offer you both kinds, though one kind may predominate. Again, let's consider the three texts in the Appendix as examples.

The Gettysburg Address, like many speeches, is primarily a work of *deductive reasoning.* Lincoln's argument for continuing the Civil War is based on general principles, and his conclusion follows from the application of those principles to the issue at hand. In effect, he reasons that only the living can complete the "unfinished work" of democracy, that "we" are the living, and that therefore only we can complete the task begun by our founding fathers. If you sketched out this line of reasoning in the form of a syllogism, it would look like this:

Major premise: Only the living can save democracy.
Minor premise: We are the living.
Conclusion: Only we can save democracy.

Of course, Lincoln doesn't use quite those terms. But if you infer his reasoning from the speech, you can see that his argument for dedicating ourselves to the task ahead rests on the major premise that responsibility falls on the living.

The two other model texts rely mainly on *inductive* evidence to support their conclusions. Reasoning by induction means drawing conclusions from the observation of facts or data. Such reasoning is at the heart of most scientific writing. But it also shows up in more personal writing when an author sets out to interpret his or her own experience.

Joan Didion's "On Going Home" is packed with inductive evidence to show that times have changed--and with them the meaning of "home." Her writing concentrates on precise factual details: the contents of a drawer, the vandalized cemetery, the image of a girl dancing in a San Francisco bar, the telephone calling Didion back to another city, the fried-chicken picnics she remembers versus the xylophone and sundress she buys for her daughter. Contrasts between past and present occur even in the conversation she holds with her great-aunts, who no longer know where she lives. All of the essay's details contribute to a sense of loss, a hypothesis about the "fragmentation" after World War II.

It may be easy to see the validity of that hypothesis as a applied to the author's own circumstances, which are after all the subject matter of the essay. But it may be wrong to go further and say that the text contains sufficient evidence to justify a general conclusion about society as a whole. After all, Didion is reasoning from a range of facts bearing on her own family; she can only wonder whether she is a member of the last generation to carry the "burden" of home. The reader, in turn, must decide on the basis of his or her own experience whether the speculation about society rings true.

Lewis Thomas's essay is also in large part a work of inductive reasoning, though the scope of that reasoning is more impersonal. To support his hypothesis about the need for science, Thomas surveys history and specifies facts about the challenges ahead. He also comments on the various fields of science- -biology, aerospace, earth science, astronomy, and so on--and suggests how each is facing new horizons. He summarizes the inductive evidence by saying this:

The doing of science on a scale appropriate to the problems at hand was launched only in the twentieth century and has been moving into high gear only within the last fifty years. We have not lacked explanations at any time in our recorded history, but now we must live and think with the new habit of requiring reproducible observations and solid facts for the explanations.

If you find the inductive reasoning in this essay convincing, you'll probably agree that we must now live with the habit of requiring "reproducible observations"--in other words, with the habit of science.

Thomas also argues that science must remain independent of technology in order to succeed. That argument may be more deductive than inductive, for it rests on the assumption that all scientific progress occurs as "surprise" and that "basic, undifferentiated science" is what make surprise possible. Your acceptance or rejection of that line of reasoning will probably determine whether you agree that science and technology are as different as this essay concludes.

However well reasoned the argument of a text may be, almost any conclusion remains open to question or future debate. That is because logic alone cannot account for everything. Deductive reasoning depends on premises that in turn depend on the author's personal beliefs. Inductive reasoning depends on the ability of a hypothesis to apply in all future cases. Because deductive premises are "givens" based on faith, and because inductive hypotheses can be overturned by future exceptions to the rule, argument remains a process in which opposing views are always possible.

Does the Text Take Opposing Arguments into Account?

In formal debate of the kind practiced by lawyers and college forensic teams, taking opposing views into account is always important. Often one side will summarize the opponents' reasoning, then attack it for containing errors or omissions. *Fallacies* are formal charges made against an opponent's reasoning; they include question begging, hasty generalization, stereotyping, and so on. (See the Glossary for a more complete list.) Making fallacy charges against someone else's argument is a bit like throwing punches in a boxing match, and usually there is plenty of punching from both sides.

However, most argumentative texts that you read are not structured like formal debates. There is no rule which says that an author must take into account every possible counterargument and refute it. Consequently, you may find that the attention paid to an opposing view is a minor or even nonexistent part of the text. Nevertheless, it's a good idea to search for any places where the author does allude to opposing views, for those places may give you clues as to which other lines of reasoning you might investigate on your own.

The Gettysburg Address is one example of an argument that does *not* take opposing views into account, at least not directly. Many readers have noticed how Lincoln avoids any mention of the Confederacy or of the South's argument for fighting the Civil War. One reason may be that the occasion did not call for it; another may be that Lincoln hoped to include opponents in his appeal for a "new birth of freedom." Because he does not attack Confederate logic in this speech, we can only wonder if Lincoln has his opponents in mind when he appeals to national idealism.

Texts that contain narrative writing will sometimes bring in opposing views by telling about persons who disagree--either with the author or with each other. In "On Going Home," Joan Didion presents her husband as an outsider who doesn't share her understanding of her family's home:

> Nor does he understand that when we talk about sale- leasebacks and right-of-way condemnations we are talking in code about the things we like best, the yellow fields and the cottonwoods and the rivers rising and falling and the mountain roads closing when the heavy snow comes in. We miss each other's points, have another drink and regard the fire. My brother refers to my husband, in his presence, as "Joan's husband." Marriage is the classic betrayal.

Like the reader, the author's husband hasn't shared all of her childhood experiences, and his more distant and sometimes uncomprehending view of her family home is perhaps closer to the reader's own perspective. He serves as a foil to the nostalgia that Didion feels, and his presence in the essay reminds us that there are other ways of looking at what "home" means. Late in the essay when he telephones to suggest that she "get out, drive to San Francisco or Berkeley," we are hearing a call to another way of life, a renewed involvement in the larger world beyond the family of one's childhood.

When it comes to exploring opposing views, impersonal expository essays are more likely to approximate the structure of formal debate. In Lewis Thomas's "Making Science Work," for example, the second and third paragraphs present two contrasting views of science: the first being the view that science "doesn't really work," and the second being the view of scientists who "disagree."

Though Thomas remains on the side of the scientists throughout the essay, he is careful to acknowledge the evidence cited by his opponents. At several points he draws attention to the problems and dangers that science has brought. He reminds us of the "radioactivity from the stored, stacked bombs or from leaking, flawed power plants, acid rain, pesticides, leached soil, depleted ozone, and increased carbon dioxide in the outer atmosphere." He also acknowledges that "[u]ncertainty, disillusion, and despair are prices to be paid for living in an age of science." By naming the drawbacks cited by his opponents, Thomas forces us to see the issue from two sides. He also helps his own cause by making his argument appear more objective than it otherwise might seem.

Besides introducing views opposed to his own on the question of whether science whether science works, "Thomas also summarizes disagreements between business and the academic community:

Each side maintains adversarial and largely bogus images of the other, money-makers on one side and impractical academics on the other. Meanwhile, our competitors ... have long since found effective ways to link industrial research to government and academic science, and they may be outclassing this country before long.

Here the author does not join one side or the other, but attacks them both. By saying that each side maintains "largely bogus images of the other," Thomas in effect charges both with the fallacy of stereotyping. He also causes the reader to wonder if reasoning on the basis of "bogus images" may prove costly to the nation's future.

Summary

Taking opposing views into account thus adds new dimensions to an author's argument. As a reader, you can study those opposing views for leads to other arguments that lie beyond the scope of the essay or book you may be reading. But remember that logical analysis is first a matter of studying the author's own argument: its issues, conclusions, and reasons offered as evidence.

THE ETHICAL PERSPECTIVE

You may feel that an interpretation should be over once the social, emotional, rhetorical, and logical factors have been taken into account. But there is one more important perspective to consider, especially if the text discusses or depicts human behavior. You should not overlook the question of moral values, or what might be called the ethics of the text.

Morality is a touchy subject to discuss. For that reason it is important to respect certain ground rules as you approach the whole matter. One is that you not attempt to impose your own moral values on the text. In other words, you shouldn't try to "read into" a text values that are not actually there. It is also important to remember that some authors do not advocate particular ethical positions but instead try to be objective or "unbiased" reporters. With those ground rules in mind, you should be ready to make use of the ethical perspective. Here are some questions to ask:

What Is the Highest Good Envisioned by the Text?

In moral philosophy the *summum bonum*--the highest good--is the ultimate ideal toward which ethical behavior is directed. Precisely what that ideal is can vary from person to person. However, the history of ethics suggests that duty, happiness, and perfection are among the most widespread concepts of the highest good. You might therefore begin by asking whether a text seems to aim at one of those three ideals, while keeping in mind that it may not.

Duty is an ancient and important ideal. When Moses carried the Ten Commandments down from the mountain, he may have brought with him the ethics of obedience. We find duty idealized by Socrates and the Greek stoics, by many religions, and by military codes throughout history. For the philosopher Immanuel Kant (1724-

1804), duty is a matter of intuitive conduct. According to Kant's belief, you should "act only on that principle which you can at the same time will to be a universal law." This axiom, called the "categorical imperative," suggests that the individual should recognize intuitively what ought to be done--and then do it. Many philosophers have agreed that conscience is the basis for duty and that each person's struggle to obey the dictates of conscience leads to the highest good.

If we consider the Gettysburg Address, for example, it is easy to see that Lincoln is stressing the importance of duty. As one student put it,

> Lincoln states that the people must "resolve" to continue to fight the war for freedom. Using the word resolve imparts a sense of duty. By his ending statement--"and that, government ... shall not perish from the earth"--he implies that if people do not continue this fight, the government which they created will not last.

Though Lincoln does not use the word "duty" as such, he admonishes his audience to be "dedicated to the unfinished work" and to preserve a government formed "of the people, by the people, for the people." Since duty may be defined as fulfilling one's sense of moral obligation to a cause, the Gettysburg Address is above all an appeal to conscience and a call to duty.

Happiness as the highest good is also an ancient ideal. The ethics of happiness (also called *eudaemonistic* ethics) dates back at least as far as Aristotle. Though there have been many disputes over what "happiness" may mean in particular circumstances, we may in general say that acts or ideas are aimed at happiness if their end result would bring pleasure or a sense of well-being. In our own time, many kinds of popular texts seem aimed at happiness. Travel magazines, self-help books, and light fiction may be obvious examples, though sometimes very serious literature also has happiness as a chief concern. In some cases, an author may reveal his or her longing for happiness by depicting its absence.

Throughout her essay "On Going Home," Joan Didion alludes to moments of past happiness and reveals her desire to pass on to her daughter the pleasures of family life. "I would like to promise her that she will grow up with a sense of her cousins and of rivers and of her great-grandmother's teacups. ..." The regret that she can promise her daughter "nothing like that" suggests how deeply the author is aware of lost happiness. In an ideal world based on this essay's nostalgic vision, the highest good might be a perfect "home" that can be passed on from generation to generation. That such a home may now be out of reach does not prevent its remaining an ideal in this essay.

Perfection as the highest good is an ideal often associated with scientific progress. Philosophers such as Condorcet (1743-1794) and Auguste Comte (1798-1857) teach that whereas happiness may be an elusive goal, we can at least contribute to social and scientific progress and thereby help create a future perfection. Texts that report on ways to improve existing knowledge are thus often aimed at perfection as an ideal.

Thomas's "Making Science Work" might be viewed as such a text. The opening paragraphs of the essay suggest that science is flawed but "just at its beginning." Give science more time, Thomas urges. Give it time to perfect itself:

> What lies ahead, or what *can* lie ahead if the efforts in basic research are continued, is much more than the conquest of human disease or the

amplification of agricultural technology or the cultivation of nutrients in the sea. As we learn more about the fundamental processes of living things in general we will learn more about ourselves, including perhaps the ways in which our brains, unmatched by any other neural structures on the planet, achieve the earth's awareness of itself. It may be too much to say that we will become wise through such endeavors, but we can at least come into possession of a level of information upon which a new kind of wisdom might be based.

Like many scientists before him, Thomas looks toward a future in which new discoveries, new capabilities, and ultimately new wisdom can be realized. The price for that future may be living with uncertainty, but we can dream of a time when our work will have paid off. Rather like Lincoln in the Gettysburg Address, Thomas asks us to consider our unfinished work. But whereas Lincoln reminds us of our national heritage in order to call us to duty, Thomas reminds us of our present ignorance in order to make us desire a perfected wisdom. "It is a gamble to bet on science for moving ahead," Thomas tells us, but in his view science is now the only game in town."

Though duty, happiness, and perfection may not encompass all possible ideas of the highest good, they do often serve as signposts marking the main ethical routes along which many texts are moving. Even so, in looking closely at the ethics of a text we need also to consider specific convictions.

What Ethical Convictions Does the Text Reveal?

If we know which highest good the text seems aimed at, we can then ask what convictions are involved in the pursuit of that ideal. An ethical conviction is a belief about the rightness or wrongness of a particular way of behaving. There are many kinds of ethical convictions, but among the major categories are those which we may respectively call altruistic, egoistic, and political.

Altruistic convictions hold that the best way to do one's duty, achieve happiness, or reach perfection is by selfless commitment. That commitment may be to other people or to a cause deemed greater than oneself. Altruists in history include St. Paul, Joan of Arc, Mahatma Gandhi, and others who gave themselves wholly to the causes in which they believed. When Abraham Lincoln in the Gettysburg Address challenges us to be "here dedicated to the great task remaining," he is expressing an altruistic conviction. If we are to fulfill our duty to the nation, Lincoln tells his audience, we must give ourselves to the cause of preserving democracy.

Egoistic convictions have in common the belief that the highest good can be achieved through self-fulfillment of the individual. *Egoism,* or the concern with one's own destiny, should not be confused with *egotism,* or mere selfishness. An "egotistical" conviction may have to do simply with one's self-importance, but an egoistic conviction has to do with how one can best come to terms with oneself. "The good or ill of man lies within his own will," said the Greek philosopher Epictetus. And according to Henry David Thoreau, "What a man thinks of himself, that it is which determines, or rather indicates, his fate."

Because personal essays, letters, and other autobiographical texts tend to focus on the author's life they can be expected to reveal some egoistic convictions. In Joan Didion's "On Going Home," for example, the author is concerned with her own identity in relation to her family and with how to face the changes in her life. Although she has an altruistic desire to give her daughter the same forms of happiness she herself experienced as a child, she comes to terms with the fact that present realities force her to behave differently. Perhaps it is just as well, Didion says, "that I can offer her little of that life." She will try instead to bring her daughter happiness in other ways, dependent on the newer circumstances of a postwar generation.

Political convictions relate the highest good to the welfare of the community. Such convictions range widely over the various ideologies that make up partisan politics and contrasting systems of government: Republicanism, Liberalism, Socialism, Monarchism, and so on. Obviously, the convictions of those political philosophies will vary with regard to specific issues. But you should at least recognize political convictions when you see them. They are different from egoistic convictions insofar as the latter stress the self working alone to fulfill ideals, whereas political convictions focus on group relations as the key to ethical behavior.

In "Making Science Work," Lewis Thomas states a political conviction when he calls for a closer partnership between industry and academic institutions:

> There needs to be much more of this kind of partnership. The nation's future may well depend on whether we can set up within the private sector a new system for collaborative research. Although there are some promising partnership ventures now in operation, they are few in number; within industry the tendency remains to concentrate on applied research and development, excluding any consideration of basic science. The academic community tends, for its part, to stay out of fields closely related to the development of new products.

Here we have a political statement that can't be neatly labeled "Democrat" or "Republican," liberal or conservative, but it is political nonetheless. Thomas is saying that if we are to perfect our science, we need closer relations between two sectors of the economy. Such closer relations might not have much to do with the politics of government, but they would have plenty to do with the politics of industry and with the academic politics of institutions. Moreover, if you were to disagree with Thomas on this matter, you would quickly find yourself involved in a controversy that could only be described as political.

Summary

The ethical perspective leads us to consider a text on the basis of ideals and convictions. Often a book or essay may present several ideals and many separate convictions. In some cases the author may boldly stress his or her own; in other cases ethical implications may be subtle. But even when the text does not seem to make an issue of ethics, the reader should search for whatever ideals may be implied--and whatever ethical convictions may be apparent.

REVIEW OF QUESTIONS TO ASK

The Social Perspective

>   What social concerns does the text reveal?

>   How does the text relate to the past?

>   How does the text relate to right now?

The Emotional Perspective

>   Does the text contain objects of emotion?

>   Are there emotional conflicts?

>   What is the tone of the text?

The Rhetorical Perspective

>   How can the form be described?

>   Which rhetorical modes do you find?

>   How can the author's style be described?

>   What about ambiguity?

The Logical Perspective

>   What debatable issue is raised?

>   What conclusions are reached?

>   Is there sufficient evidence?

>   Does the text take opposition into account?

The Ethical Perspective

What "highest good" does the text envision?

What ethical convictions are revealed?

Helping Students Use
Textual Sources Persuasively

Margaret Kantz

Although the researched essay as a topic has been much written about, it has been little studied. In the introduction to their bibliography, Ford, Rees, and Ward point out that most of the over 200 articles about researched essays published in professional journals in the last half century describe classroom methods. "Few," they say, "are of a theoretical nature or based on research, and almost none cites even one other work on the subject" (2). Given Ford and Perry's finding that 84% of freshman composition programs and 40% of advanced composition programs included instruction in writing research papers, more theoretical work seems needed. We need a theory-based explanation, one grounded in the findings of the published research on the nature and reasons for our students' problems with writing persuasive researched papers. To understand how to teach students to write such papers, we also need a better understanding of the demands of synthesis tasks.

As an example for discussing this complex topic, I have used a typical college sophomore. This student is a composite derived from published research, from my own memories of being a student, and from students whom I have taught at an open admissions community college and at both public and private universities. I have also used a few examples taken from my own students, all of whom share many of Shirley's traits. Shirley, first of all, is intelligent and well-motivated. She is a native speaker of English. She has no extraordinary knowledge deficits or emotional problems. She comes from a home where education is valued, and her parents do reading and writing tasks at home and at their jobs. Shirley has certain skills. When she entered first grade, she knew how to listen to and tell stories, and she soon became proficient at reading stories and at writing narratives. During her academic life, Shirley has learned such studying skills as finding the main idea and remembering facts. In terms of the relevant research, Shirley can read and summarize source texts accurately (cf. Spivey; Winograd). She can select material that is relevant for her purpose in writing (Hayes, Waterman, and Robinson; Langer). She can make connections between the available information and her purpose for writing, including the needs of her readers when the audience is specified (Atlas). She can make original connections among ideas (Brown and Day; Langer). She can create an appropriate, audience-based structure for her paper (Spivey), take notes and use them effectively while composing her paper (Kennedy), and she can present information clearly and smoothly (Spivey), without relying on the phrasing of the original sources (Atlas; Winograd). Shirley is, in my experience, a typical college student with an average academic preparation.

Although Shirley seems to have everything going for her, she experiences difficulty with assignments that require her to write original papers based on textual sources. In particular, Shirley is having difficulty in her sophomore-level writing class. Shirley, who likes English history, decided to write about the Battle of Agincourt (this part of Shirley's story is biographical). She found half a dozen histories that described the circumstances of the battle in a few pages each. Although the topic was unfamiliar, the sources agreed on many of the facts. Shirley collated these facts into her own version, noting but not discussing discrepant details, borrowing what she assumed to be her sources' purpose of retelling the story, and modelling the narrative structure of her paper on that of her sources. Since the only comments Shirley could think of would be to agree or disagree with her sources, who had told her everything she knew about the Battle of Agincourt, she did not comment on the material; instead, she concentrated on telling the story clearly and more completely than her sources had done. She was surprised when her paper received a grade of C-. (Page 1 of Shirley's paper is given as Appendix A.)

Although Shirley is a hypothetical student whose case is based on a real event, her difficulties are typical of undergraduates at both private and public colleges and universities. In a recent class of Intermediate Composition in which the students were instructed to create an argument using at least four textual sources that took differing points of view, one student, who analyzed the coverage of a recent championship football game, ranked her source articles in order from those whose approach she most approved to those she least approved. Another student analyzed various approaches taken by the media to the Kent State shootings in 1970, and was surprised and disappointed to find that all of the sources seemed slanted, either by the perspective of the reporter or by that of the people interviewed. Both students did not understand why their instructor said that their papers lacked a genuine argument.

The task of writing researched papers that express original arguments presents many difficulties. Besides the obvious problems of citation format and coordination of source materials with the emerging written product, writing a synthesis can vary in difficulty according to the number and length of the sources, the abstractness or familiarity of the topic, the uses that the writer must make of the material, the degree and quality of original thought required, and the extent to which the sources will supply the structure and purpose of the new paper. It is usually easier to write a paper that uses all of only one short source on a familiar topic than to write a paper that selects material from many long sources on a topic that one must learn as one reads and writes. It is easier to quote than to paraphrase, and it is easier to build the paraphrases, without comment or with random comments, into a description of what one found than it is to use them as evidence in an original argument. It is easier to use whatever one likes, or everything one finds, than to formally select, evaluate, and interpret material. It is easier to use the structure and purpose of a source as the basis for one's paper than it is to create a structure or an original purpose. A writing-from-sources task can be as simple as collating a body of facts from a few short texts on familiar topic into a new text that reproduces the structure, tone, and purpose of the originals, but it can also involve applying concepts from one area to an original problem in a different area, a task that involves learning the relationships among materials as a paper is created that may refer to its sources without resembling them.

Moreover, a given task can be interpreted as requiring an easy method, a difficult method, or any of a hundred intermediate methods. In this context, Flower has observed, "The different ways in which students [represent] a `standard' reading-to-write task to themselves lead to markedly different goals and strategies as well as different organizing plans" ("Role" iii).

To write a synthesis, Shirley may or may not need to quote, summarize, or select material from her sources; to evaluate the sources for bias, accuracy, or completeness; to develop original ideas; or to persuade a reader. How well she performs any of these tasks--and whether she thinks to perform these tasks- - depends on how she reads the texts and on how she interprets the assignment. Shirley's representation of the task, which in this case was easier than her teacher had in mind, depends on the goals that she sets for herself. The goals that she sets depend on her awareness of the possibilities and her confidence in her writing skills.

Feeling unhappy about her grade, Shirley consulted her friend Alice. Alice, who is an expert, looked at the task in a completely different way and used strategies for thinking about it that were quite different from Shirley's.

"Who were your sources?" asked Alice. "Winston Churchill, right? A French couple and a few others. And they didn't agree about the details, such as the sizes of the armies. Didn't you wonder why?"

"No," said Shirley. "I thought the history books would know the truth. When they disagreed, I figured that they were wrong on those points. I didn't want to have anything in my paper that was wrong."

"But Shirley," said Alice, "you could have thought about why a book entitled *A History of France* might present a different view of the battle than a book subtitled *A History of British Progress.* You could have asked if the English and French writers wanted to make a point about the history of their countries and looked to see if the factual differences suggested anything. You could even have talked about Shakespeare's *Henry V,* which I know you've read--about how he presents the battle, or about how the King Henry in the play differs from the Henrys in your other books. You would have had an angle, a problem. Dr. Boyer would have loved it."

Alice's representation of the task would have required Shirley to formally select and evaluate her material and to use it as proof in an original argument. Alice was suggesting that Shirley invent an original problem and purpose for her paper and create an original structure for her argument. Alice's task is much more sophisticated than Shirley's. Shirley replied, "That would take me a year to do! Besides, Henry was a real person. I don't want to make up things about him."

"Well," said Alice "You're dealing with facts, so there aren't too many choices. If you want to say something original you either have to talk about the sources or talk about the material. What could you say about the material? Your paper told about all the reasons King Henry wasn't expected to win the battle. Could you have argued that he should have lost because he took too many chances?"

"Gee," said Shirley, "That's awesome. I wish I'd thought of it."

This version of the task would allow Shirley to keep the narrative structure of her paper but would give her an original argument and purpose. To write the argument, Shirley would have only to rephrase the events of the story to take an opposite approach from that of her English sources, emphasizing what she perceived as Henry's mistakes and inserting comments to explain why his decisions were mistakes--an easy argument to write. She could also, if she wished, write a conclusion that criticized the cheerleading tone of her British sources.

As this anecdote makes clear, a given topic can be treated in more or less sophisticated ways--and sophisticated goals, such as inventing an original purpose and evaluating sources, can be achieved in relatively simple versions of a task. Students have many options as to how they can fulfill even a specific task (cf. Jeffery). Even children can decide whether to process a text deeply or not, and purpose in reading affects processing and monitoring of comprehension (Brown). Pichert has shown that reading purpose affects judgments about what is important or unimportant in a narrative text, and other research tells us that attitudes toward the author and content of a text affect comprehension (Asche; Hinze; Shedd; Goldman).

One implication of this story is that the instructor gave a weak assignment and an ineffective critique of the draft (her only comment referred to Shirley's footnoting technique, cf. Appendix A). The available research suggests that if Dr. Boyer had set Shirley a specific rhetorical problem such as having her report on her material to the class and then testing them on it, and if she had commented on the content of Shirley's paper during the drafts, Shirley might well have come up with a paper that did more than repeat its source material (Nelson and Hayes). My teaching experience supports this research finding. If Dr. Boyer had told Shirley from the outset that she was expected to say something original and that she should examine her sources as she read them for discrepant facts, conflicts, or other interesting material, Shirley might have tried to write an original argument (Kantz, "Originality"). And if Dr. Boyer had suggested that Shirley use her notes to comment on her sources and make plans for using the notes, Shirley might have written a better paper than she did (Kantz, "Relationship").

Even if given specific directions to create an original argument, Shirley might have had difficulty with the task. Her difficulty could come from any of three causes: 1) Many students like Shirley misunderstand sources because they read them as stories. 2) Many students expect their sources to tell the truth; hence, they equate persuasive writing in this context with making things up. 3) Many students do not understand that facts are a kind of claim and are often used persuasively in so-called objective writing to create an impression. Students need to read source texts as arguments and to think about the rhetorical contexts in which they were written rather than to read them merely as a set of facts to be learned. Writing an original persuasive argument based on sources requires students to apply material to a problem or to use it to answer a question, rather than simply to repeat it or evaluate it. These three problems deserve a separate discussion.

Because historical texts often have a chronological structure, students believe that historians tell stories and that renarrating the battle cast them as a historian. Because her sources emphasized the completeness of the victory/defeat and its decisive importance in the history of warfare, Shirley thought that making these same points in her paper completed her job. Her job as a reader was thus to learn the story, i.e., so that she could pass a test on it. (cf. Vipond and Hunt's argument that generic expectations affect reading behavior. Vipond and Hunt would describe Shirley's reading as story-driven rather than point-driven). Students commonly misread texts as narratives. When students refer to a textbook as "the story," they are telling us that they read for plot and character, regardless of whether their texts are organized as narratives. One reason

Shirley loves history is that when she reads it she can combine her story-reading strategies with her studying strategies. Students like Shirley may need to learn to apply basic organizing patterns, such as cause-effect and general-to-specific, to their texts. If, however, Dr. Boyer asks Shirley to respond to her sources in a way that is not compatible with Shirley's understanding of what such sources do, Shirley will have trouble doing the assignment. Professors may have to do some preparatory teaching about why certain kinds of texts have certain characteristics and what kinds of problems writers must solve as they design text for a particular audience. They may even have to teach a model for the kind of writing they expect.

The version of Shirley's problem, which Flower calls "writer-based prose," occurs when Shirley organizes what should be an expository analysis as a narrative, especially when she writes a narrative about how she did her research. Students frequently use time-based organizing patterns, regardless of the task, even when such patterns conflict with what they are trying to say and even when they know how to use more sophisticated strategies. Apparently such common narrative transitional devices such as "the first point" and "the next point" offer a reassuringly familiar pattern for organizing unfamiliar material. The common strategy of beginning paragraphs with such phrases as "my first source," meaning that it was the first source that the writer found in the library or the first one read, appears to combine a story-of-my-research structure with a knowledge-telling strategy (Bereiter and Scardamalia, *Psychology*). Even when students understand that the assignment asks for more than the fill-in-the-blanks, show-me-you've-read-the-material approach described by Schwegler and Shamoon, they cling to narrative structuring devices. A rank ordering of sources, as with Mary's analysis of the football game coverage with the sources listed in an order of ascending disapproval, represents a step away from storytelling and toward synthesizing because it embodies a persuasive evaluation.

In addition to reading texts as stories, students expect factual texts to tell them "the truth" because they have learned to see texts statically, as descriptions of truths, instead of as arguments. Shirley did not understand that nonfiction texts exist as arguments in rhetorical contexts. "After all," she reasoned, "how can one argue about the date of a battle or the sizes of armies?" Churchill, however, described the battle in much more detail than Shirley's other sources, apparently because he wished to persuade his readers to take pride in England's tradition of military achievement. Guizot and Guizot de Witt, on the other hand, said very little about the battle (beyond describing it as "a monotonous and lamentable repetition of the disasters of Crecy and Poitiers" [397]) because they saw the British invasion as a sneaky way to take advantage of a feud among the various branches of the French royal family. Shirley's story/study skills might not have allowed her to recognize such arguments, especially because Dr. Boyer did not teach her to look for them.

When I have asked students to choose a topic and find three or more sources on it that disagree, I am repeatedly asked, "How can sources disagree in different ways? After all, there's only pro and con." Students expect textbooks and other authoritative sources either to tell them the truth (i.e. facts) or to express an opinion with which they may agree or disagree. Mary's treatment of the football coverage reflects this belief, as does Charlie's surprise when he found that even his most comprehensive sources on the Kent State killings omitted certain facts, such as interviews with National Guardsmen.

Students' desire for truth leads them to use a collating approach whenever possible, as Shirley did (cf. Appendix A), because students believe that the truth will include all of the facts and will reconcile all conflicts. (This belief may be another manifestation of the knowledge-telling strategy [Bereiter and Scardamalia, *Psychology]* in which students write down everything they can think of about a topic.) When conflicts' cannot be reconciled and the topic does not admit a pro or con stance, students may not know what to say. They may omit the material altogether, include it without comment, as Shirley did, or jumble it together without any plan for building an argument.

The skills that Shirley has practiced for most of her academic career--finding the main idea and learning content- -allow her to agree or disagree. She needs a technique for reading texts in ways that give her something more to say, a technique for constructing more complex representations of texts that allow room for more sophisticated writing goals. She also needs strategies for analyzing her reading that allow her to build original arguments.

One way to help students like Shirley is to teach the concept of rhetorical situation. A convenient tool for thinking about this concept is Kinneavy's triangular diagram of the rhetorical situation. Kinneavy, analyzing Aristotle's description of rhetoric, posits that every communicative situation has three parts: a speaker/writer (the Encoder), an audience (the Decoder), and a topic (Reality) (19). Although all discourse involves all three aspects of communication, a given type of discourse may pertain more to a particular point of the triangle than to the others, e.g., a diary entry may exist primarily to express the thoughts of the writer (the Encoder); an advertisement may exist primarily to persuade a reader (the Decoder). Following Kinneavy, I posit particular goals for each corner of the triangle. Thus, the primary goal of a writer doing writer-based discourse such as a diary might be originality and self-expression; primary goals for reader-based discourse such as advertising might be persuasion; primary goals for topic-based discourse such as a researched essay might be accuracy, completeness, and mastery of subject matter. Since all three aspects of the rhetorical situation are present and active in any communicative situation, a primarily referential text such as Churchill's *The Birth of Britain* may have a persuasive purpose and may depend for some of its credibility on readers' familiarity with the author. The term "rhetorical reading," then (cf. Haas and Flower), means teaching students to read a text as a message sent by someone to somebody for a reason. Shirley, Mary, and Charlie are probably practiced users of rhetorical persuasion in non-academic contexts. They may never have learned to apply this thinking in a conscious and deliberate way to academic tasks (cf. Kroll).

The concept of rhetorical situation offers insight into the nature of students' representations of a writing task. The operative goals in Shirley's and Alice's approaches to the term paper look quite different when mapped onto the points on the triangle. If we think of Shirley and Alice as Encoders, the topic as Reality, and Dr. Boyer as the Decoder, we can see that for Shirley, being an Encoder means trying to be credible; her relationship to the topic (Reality) involves a goal of using all of the subject matter; and her relationship to the Decoder involves an implied goal of telling a complete story to a reader whom Shirley thinks of as an examiner--to use the classic phrase from the famous book by Britton et al.--i.e., a reader who wants to know if Shirley can pass an exam on the subject of the Battle of Agincourt. For Alice, however, being an Encoder means having a goal of saying something new; the topic (Reality) is a resource to be used; and the Decoder is someone who must be persuaded that Alice's ideas have merit. Varying task representations do not change the dimensions of the rhetorical situation: the Encoder, Decoder and Reality are always present. But the way a writer represents the task to herself does affect the ways that she thinks about those dimensions--and whether she thinks about them at all.

In the context of a research assignment, rhetorical skills can be used to read the sources as well as to design the paper. Although teachers have probably always known that expert readers use such strategies, the concept of rhetorical reading is new to the literature. Haas and Flower have shown that expert readers use rhetorical strategies "to account for author's purpose, context, and effect on audience ... to recreate or infer the rhetorical situation of the text" (176; cf. also Bazerman). These strategies, used in addition to formulating main points and paraphrasing content, helped the readers to understand a text more completely and more quickly than did readers who concentrated exclusively on content. As Haas and Flower point out, teaching students to read rhetorically is difficult. They suggest that appropriate pedagogy might include "direct instruction ... modeling, and ... encouraging students to become contributing and committed members of rhetorical communities" (182). One early step might be to teach students a set of heuristics based on the three aspects of the communicative triangle. Using such questions could help students set goals for their reading.

In this version of Kinneavy's triangle, the Encoder is the writer of the source text, the Decoder is the student reader, and Reality is the subject matter. Readers may consider only one point of the triangle at a time, asking such questions as "Who are you (i.e., the author/Encoder)?" or "What are the important features of this text?" They may consider two aspects of the rhetorical situation in a single question, e.g., "Am I in your intended (primary) audience?"; "What do I think about this topic?"; "What context affected your ideas and presentation?" Other questions would involve all three points of the triangle, e.g., "What are you saying to help me with the problem you assume I have?" or "What textual devices have you used to manipulate my response?" Asking such questions gives students a way of formulating goals relating to purpose as well as content.

If Shirley, for example, had asked a Decoder-to-Encoder question--such as "Am I in your intended audience?"--she might have realized that Churchill and the Guizots were writing for specific audiences. If she had asked a Decoder-to-Reality question-- such as "What context affected your ideas and presentation?"--she might not have ignored Churchill's remark, "All these names [Amiens, Boves, Bethencourt] are well known to our generation" (403). As it was, she missed Churchill's signal that he was writing to survivors of the First World War, who had vainly hoped that it would be war to end all wars. If Shirley had used an Encoder-Decoder-Reality question--such as "What are you saying to help me with the problem you assume I have?"--she might have understood that the authors of her sources were writing to different readers for different reasons. This understanding might have given her something to say. When I gave Shirley's source texts to freshmen students, asked them to use the material in an original argument, and taught them this heuristic for rhetorical reading, I received, for example, papers that warned undergraduates about national pride as a source of authorial bias in history texts.

A factual topic such as the Battle of Agincourt presents special problems because of the seemingly intransigent nature of facts. Like many people, Shirley believes that you can either agree or disagree with issues and opinions, but you can only accept the so-called facts. She believes that facts are what you learn from textbooks, opinions are what you have about clothes, and arguments are what you have with your mother when you want to stay out late at night. Shirley is not in a position to disagree with the facts about the battle (e.g., "No, I think the French won"), and a rhetorical analysis may seem at first to offer minimal rewards (e.g., "According to the Arab, Jewish, and Chinese calendars the date was really ...").

Alice, who thinks rhetorically, understands that both facts and opinions are essentially the same kind of statement: they are claims. Alice understands that the only essential difference between a fact and an opinion is how they are received by an audience. (This discussion is derived from Toulmin's model of an argument as consisting of claims proved with data and backed by ethical claims called warrants. According to Toulmin, any aspect of an argument may be questioned by the audience and must then be supported with further argument.) In a rhetorical argument, a fact is a claim that an audience will accept as being true without requiring proof, although they may ask for an explanation. An opinion is a claim that an audience will not accept as true without proof, and which, after the proof is given, the audience may well decide has only a limited truth, i.e., it's true in this case but not in other cases. An audience may also decide that even though a fact is unassailable, the interpretation or use of the fact is open to debate.

For example, Shirley's sources gave different numbers for the size of the British army at Agincourt; these numbers, which must have been estimates, were claims masquerading as facts. Shirley did not understand this. She thought that disagreement signified error, whereas it probably signified rhetorical purpose. The probable reason that the Guizots give a relatively large estimate for the English army and do not mention the size of the French army is so that their French readers would find the British victory easier to accept. Likewise, Churchill's relatively small estimate for the size of the English army and his high estimate for the French army magnify the brilliance of the English victory. Before Shirley could create an argument about the Battle of Agincourt, she needed to understand that, even in her history textbooks, the so-called facts are claims that may or may not be supported, claims made by writers who work in a certain political climate for a particular audience. She may, of course, never learn this truth unless Dr. Boyer teaches her rhetorical theory and uses the research paper as a chance for Shirley to practice rhetorical problem-solving.

For most of her academic life, Shirley has done school tasks that require her to find main ideas and important facts; success in these tasks usually hinges on agreeing with the teacher about what the text says. Such study skills form an essential basis for doing reading-to-write tasks. Obviously a student can only use sources to build an argument if she can first read the sources accurately (cf. Brown and Palincsar; Luftig; Short and Ryan). However, synthesizing tasks often require that readers not accept the authors' ideas. Baker and Brown have pointed out that people misread texts when they blindly accept an author's ideas instead of considering a divergent interpretation. Yet if we want students to learn to build original arguments from texts, we must teach them the skills needed to create divergent interpretations. We must teach them to think about facts and opinions as claims that are made by writers to particular readers for particular reasons in particular historical contexts.

Reading sources rhetorically gives students a powerful tool for creating a persuasive analysis. Although no research exists as yet to suggest that teaching students to read rhetorically will improve their writing, I have seen its effect in successive drafts of students' papers. As mentioned earlier, rhetorical reading allowed a student to move from simply summarizing and evaluating her sources on local coverage of the championship football game to constructing a rationale for articles that covered the fans rather than the game. Rhetorical analysis enabled another student to move from summarizing his sources to understanding why each report about the Kent State shootings necessarily expressed a bias of some kind.

As these examples suggest, however, rhetorical reading is not a magical technique for producing sophisticated arguments. Even when students read their sources rhetorically, they tend merely to report the results of this analysis in their essays. Such writing appears to be a college-level version of the knowledge-telling strategy described by Bereiter and Scardamalia *(Psychology)* and may be, as they suggest, the product of years of exposure to pedagogical practices that enshrine the acquisition and expression of information without a context or purpose.

To move students beyond merely reporting the content and rhetorical orientation of their source texts, I have taught them the concept of the rhetorical gap and some simple heuristic questions for thinking about gaps. Gaps were first described by Iser as unsaid material that a reader must supply to/infer from a text. McCormick expanded the concept to include gaps between the text and the reader; such gaps could involve discrepancies of values, social conventions, language, or any other matter that readers must consider. If we apply the concept of gaps to Kinneavy's triangle, we see that in reading, for example, a gap may occur between the Encoder-Decoder corners when the reader is not a member of the author's intended audience. Shirley fell into such a gap. Another gap can occur between the Decoder-Reality corners when a reader disagrees with or does not understand the text. A third gap can occur between the Encoder-Reality points of the triangle if the writer has misrepresented or misunderstood the material. The benefit of teaching this concept is that when a student thinks about a writer's rhetorical stance, she may ask "Why does he think that way?" When a student encounters a gap, she may ask, "What effect does it have on the success of this communication?" The answers to both questions give students original material for their papers.

Shirley, for example, did not know that Churchill began writing *The Birth Of Britain* during the 1930s, when Hitler was rearming Germany and when the British government and most of Churchill's readers ardently favored disarmament. Had she understood the rhetorical orientation of the book, which was published eleven years after the end of World War II, she might have argued that Churchill's evocation of past military glories would have been inflammatory in the 1930s but was highly acceptable twenty years later. A gap between the reader and the text (Decoder-Reality) might stimulate a reader to investigate whether or not she is the only person having this problem; a gap between other readers and the sources may motivate an adaptation or explanation of the material to a particular audience. Shirley might have adapted the

Guizots' perspective on the French civil war for American readers. A gap between the author and the material (Encoder-Reality) might motivate a refutation.

To discover gaps, students may need to learn heuristics for setting rhetorical writing goals. That is, they may need to learn to think of the paper, not as a rehash of the available material, but as an opportunity to teach someone, to solve someone's problem, or to answer someone's question. The most salient questions for reading source texts may be "Who are you (the original audience of Decoders)?"; "What is your question or problem with this topic?"; and "How have I (the Encoder) used these materials to answer your question or solve your problem?" More simply, these questions may be learned as "Why," "How," and "So what?" When Shirley learns to read sources as telling not the eternal truth but a truth to a particular audience and when she learns to think of texts as existing to solve problems, she will find it easier to think of things to say.

For example, a sophomore at a private university was struggling with an assignment that required her to analyze an issue and express an opinion on it, using two conflicting source texts, an interview, and personal material as sources. Using rhetorical reading strategies, this girl discovered a gap between Alfred Marbaise, a high school principal who advocates mandatory drug testing of all high school students, and students like those he would be testing:

> Marbaise, who was a lieutenant in the U.S. Marines over thirty years ago ... makes it very obvious that he cannot and will not tolerate any form of drug abuse in his school. For example, in paragraph seven he claims "When students become involved in illegal activity, whether they realize it or not, they are violating other students ... then I become very, very concerned ... and I will not tolerate that."
>
> Because Marbaise has not been in school for nearly forty years himself, he does not take into consideration the reasons why kids actually use drugs. Today the social environment is so drastically different that Marbaise cannot understand a kid's morality, and that is why he writes from such a fatherly but distant point of view.

The second paragraph answers the So what? question, i.e., "Why does it matter that Marbaise seems by his age and background to be fatherly and distant?" Unless the writer/reader thinks to ask this question, she will have difficulty writing a coherent evaluation of Marbaise's argument.

The relative success of some students in finding original things to say about their topics can help us to understand the perennial problem of plagiarism. Some plagiarism derives, I think, from a weak, nonrhetorical task representation. If students believe they are supposed to reproduce source material in their papers, or if they know they are supposed to say something original but have no rhetorical problem to solve and no knowledge of how to find problems that they can discuss in their sources, it becomes difficult for them to avoid plagiarizing. The common student decision to buy a paper when writing the assignment seems a meaningless fill-in-the-blanks activity (cf. Schwegler and Shamoon) becomes easily understandable. Because rhetorical reading leads to discoveries about the text, students who use it may take more interest in their research papers. Let us now assume that Shirley understands the importance of creating an original argument, knows how to read analytically, and has found things to say about the Battle of Agincourt. Are her troubles over? Will she now create that A paper that she yearns to write? Probably not. Despite her best intentions, Shirley will probably write another narrative/paraphrase of her sources. Why? Because by now, the assignment asks her to do far more than she can handle in a single draft. Shirley's task representation is now so rich, her set of goals so many, that she may be unable to juggle them all simultaneously. Moreover, the reading technique requires students to discover content worth writing about and a rhetorical purpose for writing; the uncertainty of managing such a discovery task when a grade is at stake may be too much for Shirley.

Difficult tasks may be difficult in either (or both of) two ways. First, they may require students to do a familiar subtask, such as reading sources, at a higher level of difficulty, e.g., longer sources, more sources, a more difficult topic. Second, they may require students to do new subtasks, such as building notes into an original argument. Such tasks may require task management skills, especially planning, that students have never developed and do not know how to attempt. The insecurity that results from trying a complex new task in a high-stakes situation is increased when students are asked to discover a problem worth writing about because such tasks send students out on a treasure hunt with no guarantee that the treasure exists, that they will recognize it when they find it, or that when they find it they will be able to build it into a coherent argument. The paper on Marbaise quoted above earned a grade of D because the writer could not use her rhetorical insights to build an argument presented in a logical order. Although she asked the logical question about the implications of Marbaise's persona, she did not follow through by evaluating the gaps in his perspective that might affect the probable success of his program.

A skillful student using the summarize-the-main-ideas approach can set her writing goals and even plan (i.e., outline) a paper before she reads the sources. The rhetorical reading strategy, by contrast, requires writers to discover what is worth writing about and to decide how to say it as or after they read their sources. The strategy requires writers to change their content goals and to adjust their writing plans as their understanding of the topic develops. It requires writers, in Flower's term, to "construct" their purposes for writing as well as the content for their paper (for a description of constructive planning, see Flower, Schriver, Carey, Haas, and Hayes). In Flower's words, writers who construct a purpose, as opposed to writers who bring a predetermined purpose to a task, "create a web of purposes ... set goals, toss up possibilities ... create a multi-dimensional network of information ... a web of purpose ... a bubbling stew of various mental representations" (531-32). The complex indeterminacy of such a task may pose an intimidating challenge to students who have spent their lives summarizing main ideas and reporting facts.

Shirley may respond to the challenge by concentrating her energies on a familiar subtask, e.g., repeating material about the Battle of Agincourt, at the expense of struggling with an unfamiliar subtask such as creating an original argument. She may even deliberately simplify the task by representing it to herself as calling only for something that she knows how to do, expecting that Dr. Boyer will accept the paper as close enough to the original instructions. My students do this frequently. When students decide to write a report of their reading, they can at least be certain that they will find material to write about.

Because of the limits of attentional memory, not to mention those caused by inexperience, writers can handle only so many task demands at a time. Thus, papers produced by seemingly inadequate task representations may well be essentially rough drafts. What looks like a bad paper may well be a preliminary step, a way of meeting certain task demands in order to create a basis for thinking about new ones. My students consistently report that they need to marshal all of their ideas and text knowledge and get that material down on the page (i.e., tell their knowledge) before they can think about developing an argument (i.e., transform their knowledge). If Shirley's problem is that she has shelved certain task demands in favor of others, Dr. Boyer needs only to point out what Shirley should do to bring the paper into conformity with the assignment and offer Shirley a chance to revise.

The problems of cognitive overload and inexperience in handling complex writing tasks can create a tremendous hurdle for students because so many of them believe that they should be able to write their paper in a single draft. Some students think that if they can't do the paper in one draft that means that something is wrong with them as writers, or with the assignment, or with us for giving the assignment. Often, such students will react to their drafts with anger and despair, throwing away perfectly usable rough drafts and then coming to us and saying that they can't do the assignment.

The student's first draft about drug testing told her knowledge about her sources' opinions on mandatory drug testing. Her second draft contained the rhetorical analysis quoted above, but presented the material in a scrambled order and did not build the analysis into an argument. Only in a third draft was this student able to make her point:

> Not once does Marbaise consider any of the psychological reasons why kids turn away from reality. He fails to realize that drug testing will not answer their questions, ease their frustrations, or respond to their cries for attention, but will merely further alienate himself and other authorities from helping kids deal with their real problems.

This comment represents Terri's answer to the heuristic "So what? Why does the source's position matter?" If we pace our assignments to allow for our students' thoughts to develop, we can do a great deal to build their confidence in their writing (Terri raised her D+ to an A). If we treat the researched essay as a sequence of assignments instead of as a one-shot paper with a single due date, we can teach our students to build on their drafts, to use what they can do easily as a bridge to what we want them to learn to do. In this way, we can improve our students' writing habits. More importantly, however, we can help our students to see themselves as capable writers and as active, able, problem-solvers. Most importantly, we can use the sequence of drafts to demand that our students demonstrate increasingly sophisticated kinds of analytic and rhetorical proficiency.

Rhetorical reading and writing heuristics can help students to represent tasks in rich and interesting ways. They can help students to set up complex goal structures (Bereiter and Scardamalia, "Conversation"). They offer students many ways to think about their reading and writing texts. These tools, in other words, encourage students to work creatively.

And after all, creativity is what research should be about. If Shirley writes a creative paper, she has found a constructive solution that is new to her and which other people can use, a solution to a problem that she and other people share. Creativity is an inherently rhetorical quality. If we think of it as thought leading to solutions to problems and of problems as embodied in questions that people ask about situations, the researched essay offers infinite possibilities. Viewed in this way, a creative idea answers a question that the audience or any single reader wants answered. The question could be, "Why did Henry V win the battle of Agincourt?" or, "How can student readers protect themselves against nationalistic bias when they study history?" or any of a thousand other questions. If we teach our Shirleys to see themselves as scholars who work to find answers to problem questions, and if we teach them to set reading and writing goals for themselves that will allow them to think constructively, we will be doing the most exciting work that teachers can do, nurturing creativity.

Note on the article's authorship as of 1990.   Margaret Kantz was assistant professor of English at Central Missouri State University. She has presented papers at CCCC and published on composing processes in researched student papers.

Appendix A: Page 1 of Shirley's paper

The battle of Agincourt ranks as one of England's greatest military triumphs. It was the most brilliant victory of the Middle Ages, bar none. It was fought on October 25, 1414, against the French near the French village of Agincourt.

Henry V had claimed the crown of France and had invaded France with an army estimated at anywhere ~~between~~ *from* 10,000[1] ~~and~~ *to* 45,000 men[2]. During the seige of Marfleur dysentery had taken (1/3) of them[3], his food supplies had been depleted[4], and the fall rains had begun. In addition the French had assembled a huge army and were marching toward him. Henry decided to march to Calais, where his ships were to await him[5]. He intended to cross the River Somme at the ford of Blanchetaque[6], but, falsely informed that the ford was guarded[7], he was forced to follow the flooded Somme up toward its source. The French army was shadowing him on his right. Remembering the slaughters of Crecy and Poictiers, the French constable, Charles d'Albret, hesitated to fight[8], but when Henry forded the Somme just above Amiens[9] and was just

---

1. Carl Stephinson, Medieval History, p. 529.

2. (Guizot, Monsieur and Guizot, Madame) World's Best Histories-France, Volume II, p. 211.

3. Cyrid E. Robinson, England-A History of British Progress, p. 145.

4. Ibid.

5. Winston Churchill, A History of the English-Speaking Peoples, Volume I: The Birth of Britain, p. 403.

6. Ibid.

7. Ibid.

8. Robinson, p. 145.

9. Churchill, p. 403.

you footnote material that does not need to be footnoted.

Works Cited

Asch, Solomon. *Social Psychology*. New York: Prentice, 1952.

Atlas, Marshall. *Expert-Novice Differences in the Writing Process*. Paper presented at the American Educational Research Association, 1979. ERIC ED 107 769.

Baker, Louise, and Ann L. Brown. "Metacognitive Skills and Reading." *Handbook of Reading Research*. Eds. P. David Person, Rebecca Barr, Michael L. Kamil, and Peter Mosenthal. New York: Longman, 1984.

Bazerman, Charles. "Physicists Reading Physics: Schema-Laden Purposes and Purpose-Laden Schema." *Written Communication* 2.1 (1985): 3-24.

Bereiter, Carl, and Marlene Scardamalia. "From Conversation to Composition: The Role of Instruction in a Developmental Process." *Advances in Instructional Psychology*. Ed. R. Glaser. Vol. 2. Hillsdale, NJ: Lawrence Erlbaum Associates, 1982. 1-64.

_____. *The Psychology of Written Composition*. Hillsdale, NJ: Lawrence Erlbaum Associates, 1987.

Briscoe, Terri. "To test or not to test." Unpublished essay. Texas Christian University, 1989.

Britton James, Tony Burgess, Nancy Martin, Alex McLeod, and Harold Rosen. *The Development of Writing Abilities (11-18)*. Houndmills Basingstoke Hampshire: Macmillan Education Ltd., 1975.

Brown, Ann L. "Theories of Memory and the Problem of Development: Activity, Growth, and Knowledge." *Levels of Processing in Memory*. Eds. Laird S. Cermak and Fergus I.M. Craik. Hillsdale, NJ: Laurence Erlbaum Associates, 1979. 225-258.

_____, Joseph C. Campione, and L.R. Barclay. *Training Self-Checking Routines for Estimating Test Readiness: Generalizations from List Learning to Prose Recall*. Unpublished manuscript. University of Illinois, 1978.

_____ and Jeanne Day. "Macrorules for Summarizing Texts: The Development of Expertise." *Journal of Verbal Learning and Verbal Behavior* 22.1 (1983): 1-14.

_____ and Annmarie S. Palincsar. *Reciprocal Teaching of Comprehension Strategies: A Natural History of One Program for Enhancing Learning*. Technical Report #334. Urbana, IL: Center for the Study of Reading, 1985.

Churchill, Winston S. *The Birth of Britain*. New York: Dodd, 1956. Vol. I of *A History of the English-Speaking Peoples*. 4 vols. 1956-58.

Flower, Linda. "The Construction of Purpose in Writing and Reading. *College English 50.5* (1988): 528-550.

_____. *The Role of Task Representation in Reading to Write*. Berkeley, CA: Center for the Study of Writing, U of California at Berkeley and Carnegie Mellon. Technical Report, 1987.

_____. "Writer-Based Prose: A Cognitive Basis for Problems in Writing." *College English* 41 (1979): 19-37.

Flower, Linda, Karen Schriver, Linda Carey, Christina Haas, and John R. Hayes. *Planning in Writing: A Theory of the Cognitive Press*. Berkeley, CA: Center for the Study of Writing, U of California at Berkeley and Carnegie Mellon. Technical Report, 1988.

Ford, James E., and Dennis R. Perry. "Research Paper Instruction in the Undergraduate Writing Program." *College English* 44 (1982): 825-31.

Ford, James E., Sharla Rees, and David L. Ward. *Teaching the Research Paper: Comprehensive Bibliography of Periodical Sources*, 1980. ERIC ED 197 363.

Goldman, Susan R. "Knowledge Systems for Realistic Goals. *Discourse Processes 5* (1982): 279-303.

Guizot and Guizot de Witt. *The History of France from Earliest Times to 1848*. Trans. R. Black. Vol. 2. Philadelphia: John Wanamaker (n.d.).

Haas, Christina, and Linda Flower. "Rhetorical Reading Strategies and the Construction of Meaning." *College Composition and Communication* 39 (1988): 167-84.

Hayes, John R., D.A. Waterman, and C.S. Robinson. "Identifying the Relevant Aspects of a Problem Text." *Cognitive Science*, 1 (1977): 297-313.

Hinze, Helen K. "The Individual's Word Associations and His Interpretation of Prose Paragraphs." *Journal of General Psychology* 64 (1961): 193-203.

Iser, Wolfgang. *The act of reading: A theory of aesthetic response*. Baltimore: The Johns Hopkins UP, 1978.

Jeffery, Christopher. "Teachers' and Students' Perceptions of the Writing Process." *Research in the Teaching of English* 15 (1981): 215-228.

Kantz, Margaret. *Originality and Completeness: What Do We Value in Papers Written from Sources?* Conference on College Composition and Communication. St. Louis, MO, 1988.

_____. *The Relationship Between Reading and Planning Strategies and Success in Synthesizing: It's What You Do with Them that Counts*. Technical report in preparation. Pittsburgh: Center for the Study of Writing, 1988.

E. Selected Bibliography

Integrating Reading, Thinking, Writing

Bartholomae, David. 'Wanderings, Misreadings, Miswritings, Misunderstandings." *Only Connect: Uniting Reading and Writing.* Ed. Thomas Newkirk. Upper Montclair, NJ: Boynton/Cook, 1986. 89-118.

Berthoff, Ann E. "Reading the World ... Reading the Word"; Paulo Freire's Pedagogy of Knowing." *Only Connect: Uniting Reading and Writing.* Ed. Thomas Newkirk. Upper Montclair, NJ: Boynton/Cook, 1986. 119-130.

Brookfield, Stephen D. *Developing Critical Thinkers.* San Francisco: Jossey-Bass, 1987.

Browne, Neil M., and Stuart M. Keeley. *Asking the Right Questions.* 2nd ed. Englewood Cliffs, NJ: Prentice-Hall, 1986.

Elbow, Peter. *Writing Without Teachers.* New York: Oxford, 1973.

Golub, Jeff, and the NCTE Committee on Classroom Practices, eds. *Activities to Promote Critical Thinking.* Urbana, IL: NCTE, 1986.

Goodman, K. and Y. Goodman. "Reading and Writing Relationships: Pragmatic Functions." *Language Arts* 60 (1983): 590-599.

Kurfiss, Joanne G. *Critical Thinking: Theory, Research, and Possibilities.* ASHE-ERIC Higher Education Report No. 2. Washington, DC: Association for the Study of Higher Education, 1988.

Marzano, Robert J., et al. *Dimensions of Thinking: A Framework for Curriculum and Instruction.* Alexandria, VA: ACSD, 1988.

Meyers, Chet. *Teaching Students to Think Critically.* San Francisco: Jossey-Bass, 1986.

Newkirk, Thomas, ed. *Only Connect: Uniting Reading and Writing.* Upper Montclair, NJ: Boynton/Cook, 1986.

Smith, Frank. "Reading Like a Writer." *Language Arts* 60 (1983): 558-567.

Collected Readings on Connecting Reading, Thinking, and Writing

Bazerman, Charles, and David R. Russell, eds. *Landmark Essays on Writing Across the Curriculum.* Davis, CA: Hermagoras, 1995. Thaiss, Christopher, ed. *Writing to Learn: Essays and Reflections on Writing Across the Curriculum.* San Francisco: Jossey-Bass, 1983.

Fulwiler, Toby, and Art Young, eds. *Language Connections: Writing and Reading Across the Curriculum.* Urbana, IL: NCTE, 1982.

Meyers, Chet. *Teaching Students to Think Critically: A Guide for Teachers in All Disciplines.* San Francisco: Jossey-Bass, 1986.

Young, Art, and Toby Fulwiler, eds. *Writing Across the Disciplines: Research into Practice.* Upper Montclair, NJ: Boynton/Cook, 1986.

Writing Research Papers

Gibaldi, Joseph. *The MLA Style Manual* 4th Edition. New York: MLA, 1995.

Bizzell, Patricia, and Bruce Heerzberg. "Research as a Social Act." *The Clearing House* 60 (1987): 303-06.

CBE Style Manual, 5th ed. Bethesda, MD: CBE, 1983.

Coon, Anne C. "Using Ethical Questions to Develop Autonomy in Student Researchers." *CCC* 40 (1989): 85-89.

Dellinger, Dixie G. "Alternatives to Clip and Stitch: Real Research and Writing in the Classroom." *English Journal* 78 (1989): 31-38.

Ford, James E. "The Research Loop: Helping Students Find Periodical Sources." *CCC* 37 (1986): 223-27.

Fulkerson, Richard. "Oh, What a Cite! A Teaching Tip to Help Students Document Researched Papers Accurately." *The Writing Instructor* 7 (1988): 167-72.

Kantz, Margaret. "Helping Students Use Textual Sources Persuasively." *CE* 52 (1990): 74-91.

Kroll, Barry M. "How College Freshmen View Plagiarism." *Written Communication* 5 (1988): 203-21.

Lutzker, Marilyn. *Research Projects for College Students: What to Write Across the Curriculum.* Westport, CT: Greenwood, 1988.

McCartney, Robert. "The Cumulative Research Paper." *Teaching English in the Two-Year College* 12 (1985): 198-202.

Publication Manual (of the American Psychological Association). 3rd ed. Washington, DC: APA, 1983.

Schmersahl, Carmen B. "Teaching Library Research: Process, Not Product." *Journal of Teaching Writing* 6 (1987): 231-38.

Strickland, James. "The Research Sequence: What to Do Before the Term Paper." *CCC* 37 (1986): 233-36.

Wells, Dorothy. "An Account of the Complex Causes of Unintentional Plagiarism in College Writing." *Writing Program Administration* 16.3 (1993): 59-71.

Whitaker, Elaine E. "A Pedagogy to Address Plagiarism." *CCC* 44.4 (1993): 509-514.

Williams, Nancy. "Research as a Process: A Transactional Approach." *Journal of Teaching Writing* 7 (1988): 193-204.

F. Argumentation

Argumentation is the capstone of many writing courses and often the focus of entire courses. This reflects the importance of argumentation in academic and public discourse. By teaching argumentation, we encourage students to analyze people's arguments and to examine their own beliefs critically and hope to provide students with the means for advocating informed positions in public forums.

Teaching students to write arguments traditionally has involved lectures and exercises on formal logic and logical fallacies. Instruction in formal logic, however, does not necessarily translate into instruction on how to write effective arguments, as Jeanne Fahnestock and Marie Secor explain in the first piece in this section. And instruction that focuses on avoiding logical fallacies may make students aware of potential problems in their writing but provides little guidance on how to build effective arguments, just as instruction that stresses avoiding sentence errors does not provide students tools for composing effective sentences. The three articles in this section each explain a different model for teaching argumentation in a writing class.

In "Teaching Argument: A Theory of Types" (originally published in *College Composition and Communication* 34 [1983]: 20- 30), Jeanne Fahnestock and Marie Secor give a brief overview of three basic approaches to teaching argumentation: logical/analytical (teaching argument by teaching students the principles of formal logic), content/problem-solving (teaching argument simply by having students write arguments that develop out of assigned readings or case studies), and rhetorical/ generative (teaching argument by teaching invention). Arguing that a rhetorical/generative pedagogy is the most effective approach, Fahnestock and Secor explain that there are four types of propositions for arguments, each answering a different question: categorical propositions ("What is this thing?"), causal statements ("What caused it or what effects does it have?"), evaluations ("Is is good or bad?"), and proposals ("What should be done about it?"). Fahnestock and Secor explain the invention process and structure for each type of argument as well as the problems students often have with each type.

In "Teaching Argument: An Introduction to the Toulmin Model" (first published in *College Composition and Communication* 29 [1978]: 237-41), Charles W. Kneupper provides a clear, brief explanation of the model of argumentation that Stephen Toulmin develops in his book *The Uses of Argument*. Toulmin proposes that an argument has three basic parts--a claim, the conclusion or thesis of the argument; data or evidence; and a warrant, a general principle, often unstated, that connects the data to the claim. More complicated arguments include other elements, a qualifier for the claim, reservations that spell out restrictions to the warrant, and backing to support the warrant. Kneupper believes that the Toulmin model is a simpler and more powerful model than formal logic for teaching students to analyze and compose arguments.

John T. Gage proposes that instructors teach students Aristotle's concept of the enthymeme for argumentation in "Teaching the Enthymeme: Invention and Arrangement" (first published in *Rhetoric Review* 2 [1983]: 38-50). Aristotle called the enthymeme a "rhetorical syllogism." Gage interprets Aristotle to mean that, unlike deducation in formal logic, the enthymeme provides writers with a logic that takes readers and rhetorical context into consideration. The enthymeme, Gage explains, provides students not only with a heuristic for logical analysis of a position but also with a heuristic for analyzing audience and situation and with a structure for a persuasive paper. Employing the enthymeme guides the writer to to discover the questions about a subject that concern an audience and the assumptions that the writer and audience hold in common.

The models for argumentation described in these three articles do not exhaust the models available to composition students. Models of argumentation based on the writings of psychotherapist Carl Rogers and on feminist theory, for example, ask writers to take less adversarial stances in their arguments and to come to decisions through a process of collaboration and negotiation with others.

Teaching Argument: A Theory of Types

Jeanne Fahnestock and Marie Secor

The climax of many composition courses is the argumentative essay, the last, longest, and most difficult assignment. An effective written argument requires all the expository skills the students have learned, and, even more, asks for a voice of authority and certainty that is often quite new to them. Aware of the difficulty and importance of argument, many composition programs are devoting more time to it, even an entire second course. At Penn State, for example, the second of our required composition courses is devoted entirely to written argument, out of our conviction that written argument brings together all other writing skills and prepares students for the kinds of writing tasks demanded in college courses and careers.

We know what we want our students to do by the end of our second course: write clear, orderly, convincing arguments which show respect for evidence, build in refutation, and accommodate their audience. The question is, how do we get them to do it? What is the wisest sequence of assignments? What and how much ancillary material should be brought in? The composition teacher setting up a course in argument has three basic approaches to choose from: the logical/ analytic, the content/problem-solving, and the rhetorical/generative. All of these approaches teach the student something about argument, but each has problems. Our purpose here is to defend the rhetorical/generative approach as the one which reaches its goal most directly and most reliably.

The teacher who uses the logical/analytic approach in effect takes the logic book and its terminology into the classroom and introduces students to the square of opposition, the syllogisms categorical and hypothetical, the enthymeme, the fallacies, induction and deduction. It has not been demonstrated, however, that formal logic carries over into written argument. Formal logic, as Chaim Perelman and Stephen Toulmin have pointed out, is simply not the same as the logic of discourse;[1] students who become adept at manipulating fact statements in and out of syllogisms and Venn diagrams still may not have any idea how to construct a written argument on their own.

Another supposed borrowing from logic is the distinction between induction and deduction as forms of reasoning and therefore as distinct forms of written argument. Induction and deduction are sometimes seen to be as different as up and down, induction reaching a generalization from particulars and deduction affirming a particular from a generalization. Actually the exact distinction between the two is a matter of some controversy. In his *Introduction to Logic* Irving M. Copi defines the two not as complementary forms of reasoning, but as reasoning toward a certain conclusion (deduction) and reasoning toward a probable conclusion (induction).[2] And Karl Popper in *Conjectures and Refutations* obliterates the distinction by showing that induction, as traditionally defined, is not valid.

But in fact the belief that we can start with pure observations alone, without anything in the nature of a theory, is absurd; as may be illustrated by the story of the man who dedicated his life to natural science, wrote down everything he could observe, and bequeathed his priceless collection of observations to the Royal Society to be used as inductive evidence. This story should show us that though beetles may profitably be collected, observations may not.

Twenty-five years ago I tried to bring home the same point to a group of physics students in Vienna by beginning a lecture with the following instructions: `Take pencil and paper; carefully observe, and write down what you have observed!' They asked, of course, *what* I wanted them to observe. Clearly the instruction, `Observe!' is absurd. ... Observation is always selective. It needs a chosen object, a definite task, an interest, a point of view, a problem. And its description presupposes a descriptive language, with property words; it presupposes similarity of classification, which in its turn presupposes interests, points of view and problems.[3]

Thus according to Popper, the observations that supposedly lead to a conclusion are, in fact, controlled by a prior conclusion. There is no pure form of reasoning which goes "example + example = conclusion," as it is represented in many rhetorics. We cannot reason "x chow is vicious + y chow is vicious = z chow is vicious = most chows are vicious" unless we assume "Chows x, y and z are typical chows." The conclusion of a so-called inductive argument depends not on the number of examples but on their typicality. The reasoning in such an argument does not leap from particular to general but proceeds from an assumption of typicality and particular evidence (in this case three examples of vicious chows) to a conclusion. This process is not essentially different from deduction. Students are misled if they think their minds work in two gears, inductive forward and deductive reverse, or if they believe it is possible to argue purely from evidence without assumptions. But students who recognize the necessity for typical evidence can fruitfully consider whether their audience will accept their evidence as representative or whether they must explicitly argue that it is.

Another continually attractive if indirect way of teaching argument in the composition classroom is the content/problem-solving approach, which assumes that students will absorb the principles and methods of written argument simply by doing it. In such content-based courses, which may use a case book (now rare) or a group of related readings or even the lectures and readings of another course, the instructor may not even define the writing as argument. Instead, students write papers with "theses" which grow naturally out of their readings or are suggested by the instructor. Another variety of this approach is the problem-solving method, as in *Cases for Composition* (by John P. Field and Robert H. Weiss, Boston: Little, Brown & Co., 1979), which frames assignments not only by specifying topics but also by defining rhetorical situations. Students write their way out of problems, arguing in letters, memos, reports, and brief articles.

The content/problem-solving approach effectively approximates real-life writing situations which supply both purpose and content. Moreover, a course that teaches writing this way is attractive because the instructor can present for discussion a coherent body of material from philosophy, sociology, psychology or even literature; if such a course works well, invention is not a problem because students are directly stimulated by the content, and they do practice writing arguments. And at best students may learn a method of problem-solving which they can apply to other writing situations when their instructor is no longer suggesting topics nor the controlled reading stimulating invention. However, the content in such courses tends to crowd out the writing instruction or, increasingly, it is given away to the real experts in other departments and the composition teacher reduced to an overseer of the revision process, a police officer with a red pencil.

The composition course which does not organize itself around a body of content can take what we will call the "rhetorical/generative" approach and explicitly teach invention. Now the composition course devoted entirely to argument can turn to the classical sources which are still the only scheme of invention purely for argument. These sources (definition, comparison, cause and effect, and authority) do help students find premises for the proposals and evaluations they usually come up with when left on their own to generate theses for arguments. But the sources are less help when we ask students to take one step further back and support the very premises which the sources have generated. If, for example, the student wants to argue that "the federal government should not subsidize the airlines," thinking about definition might yield a premise like "because airline subsidies are a form of socialism," and thinking about cause and effect might yield a premise like "because once an industry is subsidized, the quality of its service deteriorates." But how is either of these premises to be supported? How does one actually argue for a categorization such as the first or a cause and effect relationship such as the second? To tell the student to continually reapply the four sources is rather discouraging advice. Thus while the classical sources are powerful aids to invention in the large-scale arguments that evaluations and proposals require, they do not help students construct smaller-scale supporting arguments.

It is possible to give students more specific aid in inventing arguments if we begin by distinguishing the basic types of arguments and the structures characteristic of each. We derived this approach when confronted by the variety of propositions our students volunteered as subjects for argument. After collecting scores of these, we found they could be sorted into four main groups answering the questions 1. "What is this thing?" 2. "What caused it or what effects does it have?" 3. "Is it good or bad?" and 4. "What should be done about it?" Propositions which answer these questions are, respectively, categorical propositions, causal statements, evaluations, and proposals. The thesis of any argument falls into one of these categories. The first two, which correspond to the classical sources of definition and cause and effect, demand their own forms of argument with distinctive structures. Arguments for the third and fourth, evaluations and proposals, combine the other two. If we take students through these four types of argument, from the simpler categorical proposition to the complex proposal, we have a coherent rationale for organizing a course in argument.

Any statement about the nature of things fixed in some moment of time can be cast as what logicians call a categorical proposition (CP), a sentence which places its subject in the category of its predicate. The pure form of a CP is

Subject	*Linking Verb*	*Predicate*
All art	is	an illusion
Caligula	was	a spoiled brat
Ballet dancers	are	really athletes

Statements about the nature of things do not always come in such neat packages, but even a proposition without a linking verb, like "Some dinosaurs cared for their young," is still a CP which could be recast into pure form, "Some dinosaurs were caring parents."

Whenever a CP is the thesis of an argument, it makes certain structural demands. Since supporting a CP is always a matter of showing that the subject belongs in the category of or has the attributes of the predicate, that predicate must be defined whenever its meaning cannot be assumed, and evidence or examples must be given to link the subject up with that predicate. The arguer for a CP, then, works under two constraints: the definition of the predicate must be acceptable to the audience and the evidence or examples about the subject must be convincing and verifiable. We can see these two constraints operating on the arguer constructing support for a CP like "America is a class society." For most audiences, the definition of "class society" cannot be assumed. If our arguer defined a "class society" as one in which people live in different sized towns, he or she could produce plenty of evidence that Americans do indeed live in towns small, medium, and large, but "class society" has been defined in what speakers of English would intuitively recognize as a completely unacceptable way. It may be a vague term, but there are some meanings it cannot have. On the other extreme, the writer could define "class society" more acceptably as "a society structured into clearly defined ranks, from peasantry to nobility," but where could he or she find the non-metaphoric American duke or serf? Obviously, the arguer must construct a definition which is acceptable to its audience while it fits real evidence.

But suppose a student writes a brief argument supporting a CP like "My roommate is generous." He or she will bypass definition and go straight to examples of the roommate's generosity: the lending of money, clothes, shampoo, and time. The student can go right to such evidence because he or she has a clear definition of "generous" in mind and cannot imagine any audience having a different one. Still a definition of "generous," whether or not articulated in the argument, controls the choice of examples. It was not the roommate's behavior which led to the label "generous," but a definition of "generous" which led to the categorization of the behavior. Because we tend to forget the controlling power of definition, we delude ourselves into thinking that the examples come first and lead inductively to the thesis when in fact the process goes the other way.

Once the student understands that definition and specific evidence are the structural requirements of a CP argument, several organizational options become available. The controlling definition can sit at the beginning of the argument, can emerge at the end, or can have its elements dispersed.[4] In this last option, the definition of the predicate is broken down into components, each supported, with appropriate evidence. Take a CP like "Wilkle Collins's *Armadale* is a sensation novel." An arguer for this proposition might specify a multi-part definition of "sensation novel" which would supply the whole structure of the paper: "a sensation novel is characterized by its ominous setting, grotesque characters, suspenseful plot, and concern with the occult." Each of the elements from this definition becomes the predicate of its own CP (again requiring definition where necessary) and the topic sentence of its own paragraph." e.g. *"Armadale* has grotesque characters," "Collins dabbles in the occult in *Armadale.* "

Once students have learned the fundamentals of the CP argument, they have the tools to support a comparison or a contrast as well. An arguer for a single comparison, "Kissinger is like Metternich," for instance, finds one or more traits that the two subjects have in common. "Both Kissinger and Metternich had no chauvinistic pride." This is simply a CP with a compound subject which can be divided into two simple CPs ("Kissinger had no chauvinistic pride," "Metternich had no chauvinistic pride"), each supported, as much as the audience requires, by definition and evidence.

A second type of proposition needs quite a different kind of argument. An assertion of cause and effect adds the dimension of time and is therefore not supported with definition but with another kind of ruling assumption, that of *agency,* a basic belief about what can cause what. Just as users of the same language share a set of definitions, so do people in the same culture share many causal assumptions. We have a common-sense understanding, for instance, of such natural agencies as light, heat and gravity, as well as many accepted human agencies whose operation we believe in as readily as we believe in the operation of physical law. Philosophers, psychologists, anthropologists and social scientists debate about what to call these agencies- -motives, instincts, or learned patterns of behavior. But we recognize a believable appeal to the way human nature works, just as we recognize an appeal to the way physical nature works; we no more accept happiness as a motive for murder than we would accept the power of rocks to fly.

Definition and agency, then, are the warrants (to use Toulmin's term) behind the two basic kinds of arguments.[5] If we make a claim about the nature of things (a CP), we rely on an assumption about the nature of things, a definition. If we make a claim about causal relations, we rely on an assumption about what can cause what, an agency. And whether or not we articulate agency in a causal argument depends largely on audience. For example, if we argue that a significant cause of teenage vandalism is violence on TV, the agency between these two is imitation. Since most audiences will readily accept imitation as a human motive, we would not have to stop and argue for it. But if we claimed that wearing a mouth plate can improve athletic performance (*Sports Illustrated,* 2 June 1980), we will certainly have to explain agency. (The article did.)

Students have two problems with causal argument. First, they need help thinking up the possible causes of an event. Students tend to overlook the complex interaction of factors, conditions, and influences that yield an effect; they will seize on one cause without understanding how that cause works in connection with others. We have to teach them to think backwards along the paths of known causal agencies, and we can help them do this by introducing the existing terminology of causality. Causes can be identified as necessary and sufficient, as remote and proximate, or as conditions and influences acted on by a precipitating cause. Or sometimes any linear model of causality is a falsification and we have to look at causes and effects as reciprocal, as acting on each other; inflation urges pay raises and higher wages fuel inflation. And, oddly enough, students have to consider what was missing when they think about causes, for an event can take place because a blocking cause was absent. Finally, whenever people are involved in a consideration of causes, the question of responsibility arises. We look for whoever acted or failed to act, or at the person in charge, as causes (usually with the ribbon of praise or the stigma of blame in our hands). In the aftermath of the Three Mile Island reactor breakdown, for instance, the operators in the control room, the engineers who designed the reactor, and even the Nuclear Regulatory Commission officials whose safety regulations controlled its operation were all considered in varying degrees as causes of the accident. Students who are familiar with these possible frames or sets of causes, from necessary cause to responsible cause, can put together models of how causes interacted to bring about the effect they are interested in.

Convincing an audience that a particular cause did in fact operate is the second problem students need help with. The writer of a causal argument can choose from several tactics for presenting evidence that two events are connected as cause and effect. A remote cause, for instance, can be linked to an effect by a chain of causes. NASA provides us with a good example of this technique in their argument claiming that sunspots caused Skylab's fall. Sunspots are storms on the sun which hurl streams of electromagnetic particles into space; these streams, the solar wind, heat up the earth's outer atmosphere. The heated atmosphere expands into Skylab's orbit, increasing the drag on the craft; the craft therefore slows down and falls. Identifying such a chain of causes in effect replaces an implausible leap from cause to effect, a leap an audience is not prepared to take, with a series of small steps they are willing to follow.

Although proximity in time is by itself insufficient evidence of a causal relationship (indeed this is the *post hoc* fallacy), nevertheless, in the presence of plausible agency, time sequence is another tactic for supporting a causal assertion. So is causal analogy, a parallel case of cause and effect; we believe for instance that saccharin or red dye no. 2 causes cancer in humans because it causes cancer in animals. And in the case of a causal generalization such as "Jogging increases self-confidence," a series of individual cases, so long as agency is plausible (and in this instance a definition of self-confidence established), will lend support.

John Stuart Mill's four methods for discovering causes are also powerful aids to invention in causal argument. If the student can find at least two significantly parallel cases, one in which an effect occurred and one in which it didn't, the *single difference* between them can be convincingly nominated as a cause. Or if the same effect occurs several times, any *common factor* in the antecedent events is possibly a cause; this was the method of the health officials searching for the cause of Legionnaire's disease. Another method, that of *concomitant variation,* is the favorite of the social scientist who looks for influences and contributing factors; when two trends vary proportionately, when the hours of TV watching increase over a decade as SAT scores decline, a causal relationship is suggested, especially when a plausible agency can be constructed between the two. Mill's fourth method, *elimination,* is the ruling-out of all but one possible sufficient cause. It is the favorite of Sherlock Holmes and other detectives faced with a limited number of possible causes.

The student who uses one of Mill's methods can construct a convincing causal argument by repeating the process in writing. Take our sample proposition, "Violence on TV encourages teenage vandalism." Support may come from concomitant variation if we can document an increase in TV violence and a corresponding increase in vandalism perpetrated by teenagers. (The propositions that teenage vandalism exists and has increased along with TV violence can be supported with CP arguments, which the student knows by now require careful definition. What, for instance, precisely constitutes "violence" on TV?) And since this causal claim is a generalization, it could also be supported by citing specific acts of violence clearly inspired by similar acts on TV.

Arguments for CPs and causal statements are the two basic types. Once students have learned to construct these simpler arguments they can combine them into the more complex arguments required for evaluations and proposals. An evaluation is a proposition which makes a value judgment: e.g. "The San Diego Padres are a bad team," *"Jane Eyre* is a great novel," "The open classroom is a poor learning environment." We have to encourage our students to see such propositions as genuinely arguable, as claims which an audience can be convinced of and not merely as occasions for the expression of personal taste. The key is, once again, finding and, when necessary, articulating and defending the sharable assumptions or criteria on which the evaluation is made. Just as the CP argument rests on definition and the causal on agency, so do all evaluations rest ultimately on criteria or assumptions of value.

Students can be taught to construct evaluations by first learning to distinguish the various subjects of evaluations. We evaluate objects both natural and man-made, including the practical and the aesthetic. We also judge people, both in roles and as whole human beings, and we evaluate actions, events, policies, decisions and even abstractions such as lifestyles and institutions which are made up of people, things and actions. Constructing a good evaluation argument is a matter of finding acceptable criteria appropriate to the subject. Our students are already familiar with the typical standards behind the "consumer" evaluations of practical objects. They are far less familiar with the formal criteria used or implied in aesthetic judgments. Most challenging of all are the evaluations of people, actions, and events which require the application of ethical criteria. Students must be encouraged to see that arguing about ethics is not the exclusive province of religion or law, but that we all have beliefs about what is right, proper, or of value which an arguer can appeal to in an evaluation.

In form, an evaluation proposition looks exactly like a CP and, overall, the argument is carried on like a CP argument. Our example above places *Jane Eyre* in the class "great novel." An arguer for this proposition must construct a plausible "definition" or set of criteria for "great novel" which fits the evidence from the book. But the criteria or standard of an evaluation can easily include good or bad consequences as well as qualities, and thus evaluations often require causal arguments showing that the subject does indeed produce this or that effect. If we want to argue, for example, that it was right to bring the Shah to the U.S. for medical treatment, we could do so by classifying that decision as an humanitarian one in a CP argument; or we could argue that the decision was wrong by exploring its consequences in a causal argument. (Of course, whether a consequence can be labeled good or bad gets us right back to ethical assumptions which must be either appealed to or defended, depending on one's audience. Evaluations can lead us into an infinite regress unless we stop eventually on an appeal to shared values.)

The fourth and final type of proposition is the proposal, the call to action. The specific proposal which recommends an exact course of action requires a special combination of smaller CP and causal arguments. We can imagine this argument's structure as something like an hour glass, preliminary arguments funneling in from the top, proposal statement at the neck, and supporting arguments expanding to the base.

We can see how that structure works if we imagine ourselves carrying through an argument for a proposal such as, "Wolves should be reestablished in the forests of northern Pennsylvania and a stiff fine levied for killing them." No one will feel a desire to take action on this proposal unless first convinced that some problem exists which needs this solution; that is the work of the preliminary arguments. An opening CP argument establishes the existence of a situation, in this case the absence or extreme rarity of wolves in certain areas. But an audience may agree that a situation exists yet not perceive it as a problem; it may take a further causal argument to trace the bad consequences (i.e. deer herds are out of control) or show the ethical wrongness of the situation (i.e. a species has been removed from its rightful habitat). These opening parts amount to a negative evaluation. Another preliminary step might be a causal argument singling out the dominant reason for the problem, for ideally the proposal should remove or block this cause or causes, rather than simply patch up the effect alone. If wolves have become nearly extinct in northern Pennsylvania because of unrestricted hunting, then a ban on hunting wolves ought to take care of that.

After the specific proposal is disclosed, it can be supported with another series of CP and causal arguments. The proposal will lead to good consequences (the causal: deer population will be controlled), and it will be ethically right (CP: the balance of nature will be as it ought to be). And most important, the proposal is feasible; the time, money, and people are available (CP), and the steps to its achievement are all planned out (causal).

Just how much of this full proposal outline is actually needed for the writer to make a convincing recommendation depends entirely on audience and situation. A problem may be so pressing that preliminary arguments can be dispensed with entirely; after the last flood, the people of Johnstown did not have to be convinced they had a problem. And not every call to action requires a full proposal argument. One which ends with an unspecified plea, "We really ought to do something about this," is actually a negative evaluation. Such a vague call to awareness is really a coda resting on the widely-held assumption that if something is wrong it ought to be corrected.

In addition to dealing with the four types of arguments we have described, any course in argument must treat the two elements common to all arguments: accommodation and refutation. Consideration of audience (accommodation) and consideration of potential or actual opposition (refutation) inform all argument, affecting invention, arrangement, and style. Where do they sensibly come in a course? The only answer is first, last, and all the way through, worked into every discussion of every type of argument.

Once students have learned the necessary structures of CP and causal arguments and learned how these types combine in support of evaluations and proposals, they have not only the help they need for constructing arguments but tools for the critical analysis of argumentative discourse as well. They can recognize what type of proposition an argument is trying to support, identify the necessary structural elements both explicit and implied and, considering the argument's audience, determine whether all was skillfully done. We might illustrate how this process works by taking a brief look at James Madison's *Federalist* No. 10, reprinted in Corbett's *Classical Rhetoric for the Modern Student* and followed by a careful analysis of its logical elements and the arguments from the sources (2nd edition, New York: Oxford University Press, 1971, pp. 239-256). Madison's argument is an all but perfectly symmetrical full proposal with preliminary arguments (pars. 1-13), explicit proposal (par. 14), and supporting arguments (pars. 15-23). Given his audience and purpose, Madison needs no lengthy demonstration of the existence of a problem; he has only to appeal to "the evidence of known facts." He turns quickly, therefore, to a causal analysis of the problem and finds it in "faction," rooted in the corrupt nature of man. The ethical problem facing his audience is that of preserving two self-evident goods, the control of faction and some form of popular government. The solution which will bridle the effects (for the causes, as he cogently argues, are untouchable) is the federal union, which Madison then goes on to support by tracing the good consequences that will flow from it. Its feasibility has of course been argued elsewhere. Such an analysis is possible to the student who recognizes types of arguments and can thus identify the necessary structural elements in a given argument and even come to a satisfying understanding of why they are where they are.

The approach to argument we have outlined, then, makes it possible to teach argument coherently while avoiding some of the pitfalls of existing approaches. We can avoid extensive and unnecessary diversions into formal logic while keeping to the principles of sound reasoning. And the overall method of building from simple, basic types of argument to types requiring a combination of steps gives the student transferable structures which are suitable for any subject but are not so automatic as to preclude the student from doing his or her own thinking.

Note on the article's authorship as of 1983: *Jeanne Fahnestock* served as Assistant Professor of English at the University of Maryland. Her doctorate is from the University of London; her current interests included theories of coherence in the paragraph. An article by her on the paragraph was ready to appear in *CCC* late in 1983 or early in 1984. *Marie Secor* served as Assistant Professor of English at Penn State University. Her doctorate is from Brown University. She was currently working on the idea of "eloquence." Fahnestock and Secor collaborated on the text, A *Rhetoric of Argument* (1981).

Notes

1. Chaim Perelman and L. Olbrechts-Tyteca, *The New Rhetoric: A Treatise on Argument* (Notre Dame, IN: University of Notre Dame Press, 1969), pp. 1-4; Stephen Toulmin, *The Uses of Argument* (Cambridge, England: Cambridge University Press, 1958), p. 146.

2. Irving M. Copi, *Introduction to Logic*, 5th ed. (New York: Macmillan, 1978), pp. 23-26.

3. Karl Popper, *Conjectures and Refutations: The Growth of Scientific Knowledge* (New York: Harper & Row, 1963), pp. 46-47.

4. Here perhaps is the only legitimate use of the terms "inductive" and "deductive" in written argument. They can be used to describe the organization of arguments, the deductive setting out the thesis at the beginning and the inductive disclosing it at the end.

5. Stephen Toulmin, finding the syllogism ambiguous, created a new pattern for analyzing arguments. In his terminology, a "claim" is supported by "data" linked to the claim by a "warrant." Warrants are "inference licenses," "the general hypothetical statements which can act as bridges between the data and the claim" (Toulmin, p. 98). Warrants often require backing themselves. They are not always interchangeable with the minor premise of a syllogism, which may be either a warrant or its backing.

Teaching Argument:
An Introduction to the Toulmin Model

Charles W. Kneupper

Because of its complexity, argument is probably the most difficult form of discourse to teach. Composition teachers receive little help from most standard texts. A survey of composition texts reveals at best an abbreviated treatment of argument. The most commonly used approach to teaching argument is instruction in fallacies. This is a negative approach to argument (it tells students what not to do), and used alone, it fails to provide a positive sense of the necessary constituents of argument. Some teachers of composition attempt to provide a more direct approach through instruction in syllogistic reasoning. Yet many complaints are voiced against this approach, in part because of its burdensome complexity but more importantly because logically valid syllogistic arguments are rarely found in rhetorical discourse. Rhetoric deals in probabilities and relies on inductive modes or generalizations based on inductive processes.[1]

Difficulties with syllogistic logic and its usefulness as a heuristic device for the invention of rhetorical argument are shared by Speech and English. Recently, speech instruction has largely abandoned the syllogistic paradigm, and most recent texts in public speaking, argumentation, and persuasion are now using a model of argument developed by the philosopher, Stephen Toulmin.[2] This essay is intended to explain the Toulmin model of argument and to suggest its utility as a teaching tool.

I

Stephen Toulmin, in *The Uses of Argument* (Cambridge: Cambridge University Press, 1969), indicates that "the science of logic has throughout its history tended to develop in a direction leading away ... from practical questions about the manner in which we have occasion to handle and criticize arguments in different fields, and towards a condition of complete autonomy, in which logic becomes a theoretical study of its own" (p. 4). Toulmin is critical of the disjuncture of formal logic and the practical concerns of "real life" rhetorical argument. In the context of a general theory of argument, his model attempts to provide a working logic. In its simplest form, the model contains three elements:

DATA_____**So,** CLAIM

|

|

Since,

WARRANT

An *explicitly* developed argument must exhibit these three elements. The *claim* is the conclusion of the argument and the point at issue in a controversy. The *data* is evidence for the claim. The *Warrant* provides the link which shows the relation between data and claim. Toulmin provides the following example of an argument of this structure:

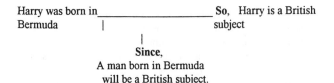

Harry was born in_____ **So,**   Harry is a British
Bermuda | subject
                     |
                  Since,
            A man born in Bermuda
            will be a British subject.

Arguments are not always explicitly developed in rhetorical discourse. Warrants, in particular, are frequently implicit. Yet in controversial arguments, implicit warrants are likely to be challenged to become explicit and to be defended.

Because of this likely challenge and the probabilistic nature of rhetorical arguments, Toulmin found it necessary to develop a more complex model. Erwin P. Bettinghaus provides a useful schematic of the fully-developed model[3] (see Figure A.): The three additional elements in this model are *qualifier, reservation,* and *backing.* The *qualifier* is usually an acknowledgment of the probabilistic nature of the claim, the *reservation* specifies conditions in which the warrant does not apply, the *backing* supports or justifies the warrant.

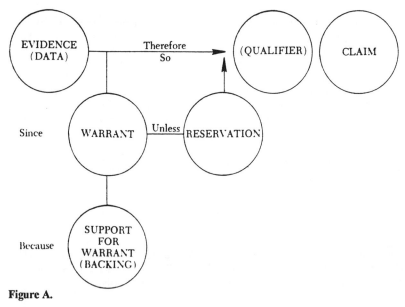

Figure A.

To illustrate this more complex form in a non-diagrammatic way, I have modified an argument from Brockreide and Ehninger:[4]

> (DATA) The historical consensus of opinion is that an unstable balance of power led to World War I. (DATA) World leaders today recognize that nuclear weapons are creating an imbalance of power. (CLAIM) Therefore, nuclear weapons development (QUALIFIER) might lead to World War III, (WARRANT) since the imbalance resulting from continued development would be essentially similar to the power imbalance prior to World War I. (BACKING) Both imbalances were characterized by an arms race and dynamic power blocks. (RESERVATION) Our only hope is that fear of a nuclear war will be an effective deterrent.

Although the substance of the argument is debatable (rhetorical arguments usually are), the important point is that by explicitly following the model, a qualified and supported argument results. Because the functional elements of the Toulmin model are present in the explicit argument, the imputed relation between claim and evidence can be more easily grasped and more specifically criticized.

In a more extended argumentative essay, a chain of arguments might have been developed. Several paragraphs might be used to argue the accuracy of the data through historical evidence and the use of authoritative opinion to establish the "factualness" of the data. More detailed enumeration of the similarities between the current situation and those preceding World War I could be developed to strengthen the backing. A coherent essay could result from the development of each functional element of the Toulmin model in the kernel argument and from tying the interrelated claims together in a conclusion.[5]

II

Besides providing a more understandable model of argument than syllogistic logic and a useful heuristic for developing an argumentative essay, the Toulmin model is also useful in discourse analysis and in teaching the "logical" outline. The diagram can be profitably applied to many speeches and essays, and the examination of implicit missing elements can be especially interesting.

To illustrate the potential usefulness of the Toulmin model in discourse analysis, I will apply the model to the first paragraph of Thoreau's "Civil Disobedience." For ease of reference, each sentence of the paragraph will be numbered.

> 1. I heartily accept the motto, "That government is best which governs least"; and I should like to see it acted up to more rapidly and systematically.
>
> 2. Carried out, it finally amounts to this, which also I believe, "That government is best which governs not at all"; and when men are prepared for it that will be the kind of government they will have.
>
> 3. Government is at best but an expedient; but most governments are usually, and all governments are sometimes, inexpedient.

4. The objections which have been brought against a standing army, and they are many and weighty, and deserve to prevail, may also at last be brought against a standing government.
5. The standing army is only an arm of the standing government.
6. The government itself, which is only the mode which the people have chosen to execute their will, is equally liable to be abused and perverted before the people can let through it.
7. Witness the present Mexican War, the work of a comparatively few individuals using the standing government as their tool; for, in the outset, the people would not have consented to this measure.

In analyzing this paragraph as an argument, one looks for its structure in terms of the way in which the functional elements of the Toulmin model are related--i.e. one is looking for *claim, warrant, data*, etc. and how they are related. I am going to diagram a simplified form of Thoreau's argument. (Sentence numbers in which the functional elements of the Toulmin model are apparent in the paragraph from Thoreau will be placed in parentheses below the statement.)

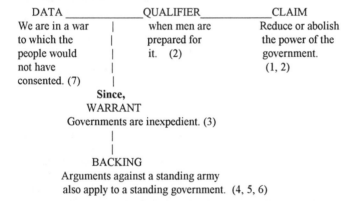

DATA	QUALIFIER	CLAIM
We are in a war	when men are	Reduce or abolish
to which the	prepared for	the power of the
people would	it. (2)	government.
not have		(1, 2)
consented. (7)		

Since,
WARRANT
Governments are inexpedient. (3)

BACKING
Arguments against a standing army
also apply to a standing government. (4, 5, 6)

One interesting observation about this argument is that there is no reservation. For Thoreau, the warrant is absolute, and less government or no government is only a matter of waiting until the time "men are
prepared for it."

The Toulmin model treats the overall functional relations of the claim and provides insight into the structure of the argument. The model requires a holistic approach, which forces the analyst to determine the claim and then how other material in the discourse is utilized to develop and support that claim.

Another use for the model as a teaching tool is its application to the "logical" outline. The application is very simple. It amounts to giving students the following instructions after they have been taught the model: (1) Roman-numeral levels should function as claims; (2) Capital-letter levels should function as warrants; (3) Arabic-numeral levels should function as data or backing. An outline structured in this pattern would look something like this:

CLAIM	I. A national program of health care should be adopted.
WARRANT	A. A national program is necessary to deal with the magnitude of the problem.
DATA	1. Millions of people cannot afford health care.
DATA	2. States, localities, and charities cannot afford to provide for so many people.
WARRANT	B. A national program is a moral imperative.
DATA	1. The results of inadequate health care are unnecessary death and suffering for millions.
BACKING	2. Failing to act to correct this problem when we are capable of doing so leaves us morally responsible.
BACKING	3. Do unto others as you would have them do you.

When such a procedure is followed by students, it does not guarantee that they will produce satisfactory arguments. It may be that they do not provide sufficient data, that the warrant fails to adequately link the data to the claim, that the claim is too general and needs greater qualification, etc. But the important point is that *how they are arguing will be clearer.* The outline helps the student see relationships between parts of the argument and helps the teacher to criticize the argument more specifically.

University of Texas at San Antonio

Endnotes

[1]   See Charles W. Kneupper, "Rhetoric and Probability Theory," *Central States Speech Journal,* 24 (Winter, 1973), 288-296.

[2] See for instance, Donald Byker and Loren J. Anderson, *Communication as Identification* (New York: Harper and Row, 1975); John J. Makay *Speaking With an Audience* (New York: Thomas Crowell, 1977); Gordon Zimmerman *et al., Speech Communication* (New York: West, 1977); Gerald Miller, *Perspectives on Argumentation* (Chicago: Scott, Foresman, 1966); Richard D. Rieke and Malcolm O. Sillars, *Argumentation and the Decision Making Process* (New York: John Wiley and Sons, 1975).

[3] Erwin P. Bettinghaus, "Structure and Argument," *Perspectives on Argument,* ed. Gerald Miller (Chicago: Scott, Foresman, 1966), p. 148.

[4]   Wayne Brockriede and Douglas Ehringer, "Toulmin on Argument: An Interpretation and Application," *Quarterly Journal of Speech,* 46 (February, 1960), 49.

[5] See Rieke and Sillars, pp. 87-88 for a discussion and a schematic display of chained arguments.

Teaching the Enthymeme:
Invention and Arrangement
John T. Gage

Elsewhere, I have recommended that the enthymeme be taught as a way to bridge the gap that sometimes exists between invention and arrangement. The invention of a single enthymeme which provides the structural framework for a whole essay can encourage an organic sense of structure and at the same time involve students in a process of thinking through their own ideas in relation to the conclusions and reasons of a real audience. My recommendation has come, however, at the ends of essays which have criticized some other teaching methods for depending on a formulaic sense of structure and encouraging students to neglect to test their ideas against the reasons and conclusions of others.[1] Thus, I have not yet given an adequate account of how the enthymeme might perform the functions for which I have recommended it. I want, therefore, to be practical here, to describe how I think the enthymeme can be taught as an invention strategy leading to the control of structural choices. If, in this practical rationale for teaching the enthymeme, I also engage in some theory and polemics, the reason is this: The method I will describe is classical in origin, but its contemporary use can solve problems that seem to me to be created by more modern teaching methods. As such problems arise in relation to the enthymeme, I will discuss them briefly.

Misinterpretation of the role of the enthymeme in Aristotle's *Rhetoric* has led to its neglect in recent composition theory, and this may be the result of Aristotle's own use of the term in two senses. Most descriptions of the enthymeme found in composition texts--when it is mentioned at all--depend on one of Aristotle's meanings, but ignore another, more basic, one. The enthymeme is usually considered to be a logical strategic device at the sentence level, or any truncated syllogism, As such, it would be expected to appear in students' writing only here and there, if at all, and only when students are writing in a logical"mode." What such a definition ignores, however, is Aristotle's statement that the enthymeme is the "body" of all artistic rhetorical proof, inductive as well as deductive, *ethos* and *pathos* as well as *logos*. He used the enthymeme in this sense to emphasize that considerations about every aspect of rhetorical decisions are enthymematic. If the enthymeme is not merely any shortened syllogism, but a syllogistic relationship with probable premises contributed or derived from the audience, then the conditions which apply to forming a strategic enthymeme at the sentence level also apply to other rhetorical choices: How is what I *do* say to make my point dependent on my unstated assumption of what my audience already knows or thinks? In Aristotle's view, it seems that all choices, including stylistic ones, must be based on a determination of what shared grounds exist for choosing some unshared thing to say that will have the potential to lead to new shared understanding.[2] This dynamic is represented in the structure of the enthymeme, which derives its function from the relationship between a

John T. Gage. "Teaching the Enthymeme: Invention and Arrangement," *Rhetoric Review*, Vol. 2, No. 1, September 1983. Reprinted with permission.

writer's intended conclusions and an audience's pre-existing assumptions. As such, the enthymeme can stand for the rhetorical conditions underlying all compositional decisions. Aristotle's description of arrangement is also enthymematic in this sense. Instead of prescribing the traditional divisions of an oration, which he calls "absurd," Aristotle says that all one need know is the question and the grounds for proving one's answer to it. In so saying, Aristotle implied, I think, that the structures of whole arguments can be seen to derive from a single enthymeme, one which produces both the essential logic of any argument as well as its essential structure.

Thus, from this more basic sense of enthymeme in Aristotle's treatise, we can derive invention procedures which aim at constructing the underlying enthymeme of a whole essay and which, once created, can provide terms to be used in arranging the parts of a composition strategically.[3] Those parts and their order cannot be known in advance of working out the enthymematic relation between one's own ideas and the assumptions held by one's audience--provided structure is perceived as deriving from one's ideas rather than as an *a priori* formula independent of them. No *a priori* structural formula, such as the five-part oration or the five-paragraph essay--or others presently in use-- can have this necessary connection to the specific logic of one's ideas or the specific assumptions of one's audience. Such structural paradigms are indifferent to whether the ideas that fill them out are chosen for their credibility or otherwise tested against other available arguments, whether, in short, they are good or bad ideas. The practical use of the enthymeme that I will describe requires that the question of the quality of one's ideas and reasons be addressed throughout the invention and arrangement process. The enthymeme provides a basis for ensuring that quality of thought be measured by the potential assent of an audience understood to have equally good reasons for initially not accepting what a writer wishes to conclude. The enthymeme which students write as a first step in composing is intended to put their conclusions into a logical relation with ideas which a dissenting audience contributes as assumptions.

The enthymeme can constitute a guide to such thinking if its parts derive from the essential variables of any rhetorical situation.

1. questions at issue,
2. probable answers to those questions, or stances taken,
3. potential strategies for leading to those answers, and
4. assumptions which make the strategies work.

Among these variables, answers (2) and strategies (3) are what the *writer* is able to choose, on the basis of questions (1) and assumptions (4) shared by or derived from the writer's *audience*. (See fig. 1.) A student writer's rhetorical situation will be incomplete without all of these variables. The question at issue is defined by students' presence in a situation of disagreement which motivates the need to assert and defend their thoughts. It cannot therefore be a student's own invention, strictly speaking, but is discovered because it is the mutual invention of that student and his or her own audience. If all agree on some issue, that issue is not likely to recommend itself as a subject worth writing about. I should say here, then, that I am talking about a real audience in which students find themselves in real situations of disagreement. The process of enthymematic invention begins when students discuss ideas on which they can take stances and be confronted by questions that, to them, need answers.

The student's first compositional task, therefore, is to move from a discussion which has provoked disagreement to the formulation of a specific answer to a specific question at issue which that discussion has revealed. In discussions with a real audience, no matter what form they take, many potential issues arise, many potential answers are considered, and many potential reasons are offered to support them. From this intractable array, students should be encouraged to work toward finding an assertion which seems to need saying because articulate members of the class have demonstrated that they think otherwise. This assertion will become the first part of an enthymeme. All of the mental stages that will hereafter go into making a useful, structural enthymeme will be based on an inquiry into the student's own assertion as it conflicts with or is supported by known ideas from that student's audience--those members of the class who discussed the issue and held different stances.

Needless to say, in the process of coming up with one enthymeme which represents a whole argument which can be made for that audience, every element of the enthymeme itself is subject to adjustment, including the conclusion. The aim of composing the enthymeme is to encourage students to question their own positions until they can state them in such a way that they are no longer the pre-conditioned, unexamined responses with which they may have begun the discussions. The positions which students must take--if an enthymeme is to result--are such that they know they can defend to an audience that can be assumed to have good reasons of its own for answering the same question differently. They cannot be the conventional, or "knee jerk," positions that students typically take when asked for "argumentative" writing and that often lead to illogical and undeveloped tirades. The object henceforth is for the student to *earn* his or her assertion.

The student's next task is to complete the enthymeme by adding a premise, or "because clause," to the assertion. The assertion will represent the student's thesis. The because clause will represent the strategy, developed out of many potential strategies, which can form the basis of leading to that thesis most persuasively. By persuasively, however, I do not mean that the student is thinking about bullying or tricking the reader into a conclusion, but is thinking about how to earn that conclusion on the basis of understandings which are shared by the reader. So, in constructing the enthymeme, students are asked to write a syllogistic statement which relates two ideas and in so doing moves from an implied premise that is shared with the audience (the assumption) to a previously unshared conclusion. It is on the basis of this "essential deduction" that the specific strategy represented by the because clause is decided upon. (See fig. 1.)

Coming up with an enthymeme that creates this kind of logical connection to the audience will be the hardest part of the student's task because, afterward, the composition of the paper itself will be guided by a process of thought that is already familiar and will hold few surprises. The enthymeme, then, cannot be seen as an end in itself; it must be evaluated according to the coherence of the paper it is capable of generating. The following diagram is intended to illustrate the relations between the elements of a student's rhetorical situation, the enthymeme which results from it and the structure of the whole composition which results from the enthymeme.

Figure 1

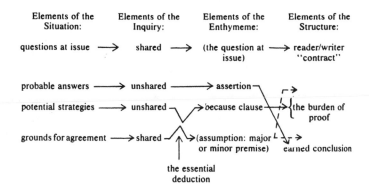

| Elements of the Situation: | Elements of the Inquiry: | Elements of the Enthymeme: | Elements of the Structure: |

The enthymeme stands in the middle of a process that begins with concern for a problem confronted in discussion and ends with the assertion of an earned conclusion to that problem at the end of a structurally coherent paper. I will describe the structural considerations in more detail shortly. Here I wish only to make the point that the enthymeme, consisting of an assertion and a because clause but implying a question at issue and an assumption, can be evaluated for its effectiveness from either direction: as an adequate response to the student's rhetorical situation and as a potential structure for generating an extended discussion in writing. Redrafting the enthymeme until it provides both of these functions is necessary, and this process can be aided by constantly applying certain criteria to trial efforts. Following discussions of issues and the students' initial efforts to respond to them with enthymemes, class time should be devoted to analyzing proposed enthymemes with their criteria as a guide, and rewriting the enthymemes accordingly.

First, the enthymeme must consist of two complete, declarative sentences, one of which is stated as the reason for the other. The assertion, as I have said, represents the thesis of the paper, although the nature of that assertion will invariably change from its first form as the student probes deeper. The assertion will always imply the question at issue to which it is an answer. The next criterion, therefore, is whether that question is in fact at issue. The assertion cannot propose to answer a question which the class (as the student's audience) did not discuss, even though they may have discussed the *subject* of the question. Nor can the assertion propose to answer a question which the class answered with one unanimous "yes" or "no." It must address, in other words, a real "stasis."[4] This criterion would rule out many of the theses that a student might *want* to argue but which would not result in the *need* to control the structural features of the argument. If no one shares the question, who cares how we get to the answer? Most of the theses that students argue when they are presented with predetermined structural paradigms, I'm afraid, would not pass this test because, in such cases, the actual intention of the writing is to practice using a paradigm, rather than to earn a conclusion that needs earning.

Next, in order for the student to know the shared ground on which the logic of the enthymeme is built, the relations of the two parts of the enthymeme must be tested against the implied syllogism they create. Any relation between an assertion and a premise will imply a linking proposition, the logical assumption that makes the assertion "follow" from the stated premise. It is the implied premise which makes the enthymeme logical.[5] It must be assumable on the part of the writer's audience, and to test this the student writer must be able to get it out in the open for examination. This requires knowing how a syllogism works and how to reconstruct, from any two stated propositions of a syllogism, the third unstated one. Syllogisms about Socrates illustrate this process as easily as statements such as this: "I know that Mary's lamb was at the opera last night, *because* I saw Mary there." The stated reason, of course, will seem logical only to those who already hold the (in this case obvious) unstated assumption. Student enthymemes will not be as simple as any concerning Mary or Socrates, but the principle of reconstructing the missing premise will be the same.

In order for this reconstruction to be possible, the assertion and the because clause must share one of the terms predicated by the assertion, even though those terms may be worded differently. (See fig. 3.) The implicit assumption always states the relationship between the predicated terms of the enthymeme that are not shared by the assertion and the because clause. Once it can be reconstructed as the assumption on which this particular logic depends, the question is whether the audience can be expected to agree to it without argument. This will depend entirely on the student's knowledge of the audience; it is not the student's prerogative to invent what is or isn't assumable independent of what others have said on the same issue. If students find that they cannot ground what they originally intend to argue in a shared assumption, it might not be only the because clause that needs adjustment but the assertion itself. In such fashion, students are encouraged to discover that they must alter their positions under the pressure to find sharable reasons for what they believe. It is for this reason, I think, that Aristotle called rhetoric the counterpart of dialectic: its aim is the discovery of possible knowledge, not the use of knowledge for purposes of manipulation.[6]

Perceiving these logical relations is more difficult when the enthymeme is crowded with too many of the things that students might have to say about their ideas. Another criterion, therefore, is to make sure that the enthymeme is as precise as possible, which means that it should not contain all of the possible qualifications, explanations, examples, definitions, and so forth that will no doubt find their place in the paper itself. The logical relations in an enthymeme will stand out if the statements are reduced to their fundamentals. Thus, the nouns should be precise and unambiguous. Imprecise terms in an enthymeme will not have been deliberated carefully by the student, and will lead to roadblocks in the paper when an assertion is suddenly made that has not been thought through to its consequences.

The verbs which predicate the terms of the two statements in the enthymeme are equally important and will make the difference between a structure which moves forward by logical stages and one which ends up repeating itself.[7] It is the predication in the enthymeme, more than its subject, that will determine the structural necessities of the composition. The verbs will also determine whether the enthymeme is sufficiently "narrow." As Josephine Miles has written, the "first need ... is to talk about ideas as sentences, that is, predicating the subject, saying something about something, establishing relations. ... There is no such thing as too large or unwieldy a subject; what the student wants to say about it is what needs estimation."[8] The enthymeme serves its generative function best if the verbs are transitive and dynamic. In the case of copulative verbs, the unshared terms too often produce a definition as the assumption, in which case the underlying syllogism will actually have two terms instead of three and the paper will end up going in circles. Intransitive verbs will provide no third term for the logic at all, and the student's composition will quickly run out of logical direction and resort to cataloging examples.

One final criterion for evaluating a useful enthymeme has to do with the nature of the question at issue and the kind of assertion that is constructed to argue it. We might, for the sake of simplicity, say that one can argue:

> questions of value--is it good?
> questions of policy--should it be done?
> questions of fact--what is true about it?

The answers to these questions will frequently depend on each other. If I want to argue a policy, for instance, I must already have answered, or assume the answer to, a question of value. The because clause of a "should" assertion will nearly always be a statement of fact or consequence, and the policy follows gratuitously from it on the assumption that "We should do whatever the factual condition is that doing it will lead to," on the further assumption that this condition is good. In such a case, the argument would depend on the quality of my reasons for saying that the factual condition would result, yet I would not have included that reasoning in the enthymeme. To ensure that students take their reasoning far enough back to establish real rather than gratuitous grounds, they should address the question of fact that the other questions come down to. By conflating the assertion and the because clause, or by making the because clause the assertion and looking for a new strategy, students may have to push an initial enthymeme backwards any number of times. Policy and value statements sometimes work quite well. It is a matter of judgment, but it is generally most productive for students to revise their logic toward the facts and consequences of the issue and let the values and policies speak for themselves, as they always will. I should say here that by "statement of fact" I do not mean to imply a distinction between fact and opinion. By "fact" here I mean whatever is said to be the case and can be supported by answers to the question "What makes it true?" Thus, the assertion "Television viewing habits are responsible for declining literacy" is a statement of fact, even though it is also an opinion and only as good as the evidence that will be claimed to support it. It can be distinguished from assertions such as "Television viewing is bad for children," or "Television should be abolished," which are statements of value and policy, respectively, and much less likely to lead to workable enthymemes, and to structurally coherent compositions.

Figure 2 CRITERIA FOR A STRUCTURAL ENTHYMEME

1. It has two parts, each of which is a declarative sentence: an *assertion* and a *because clause*.
2. The assertion proposes the *thesis* of the paper. It answers a *question at issue* for the audience.
3. The assertion and the *because clause* must share one predicated term. the relation between the unshared terms will provide the *assumption* on which the logic depends.
4. The implied assertion must be agreeable to the same audience who does not initially share the assertion.
5. The noun phrase should be precise and unambiguous. The grammatical; relations should be direct.
6. The verbs should be transitive and dynamic.
7. The assertion should, ordinarily, answer a question of fact or consequence, rather than a question of value or policy.

The enthymeme which fulfills all of these criteria will have been written after considerable thought about possible reasons and assumptions, and the student will have already considered valuable elements of an essay and rejected useless ones. In making such discriminations possible, no *a priori* formula can substitute, I think, for the pressure of having to find a conclusion and to earn it. Going from the enthymeme to the structure of the paper is now a matter of perceiving the structural implications of the terms in the enthymeme, and ordering them accordingly. The resulting paper will have an essentially deductive structure, but any number of amplifications, inductions, examples, citations, analogies, definitions or refutations may find a necessary place in the developing logic of that central deduction. The point of having labored over the construction of an enthymeme that satisfies the formal and rhetorical criteria we have placed on it, is so that the composition can be guided by the logical steps that are necessary and sufficient to lead up to an earned conclusion. Here again I must interject a quarrel with some methods of teaching invention and arrangement. Having discovered a thesis by various means, students are invariably told that it should be stated in the first paragraph. If many of them cannot thereafter control the structural relations and transitions in the rest of the paper, *control* them, that is, without falling back on some arbitrary paradigm, this advice may very well be the reason. Having stated their thesis at the beginning, they have no sense of destination against which to test the relevance and the order of each new thing they say. Once the thesis is stated, the pressure to earn it is off, and most students, without the artificial aid of a paradigm, will immediately digress or repeat themselves. The remedy is quite simple: save the thesis until you have earned it; consider the paper as developing by logical steps progressively *toward* it. When the thesis *can* be asserted, the paper is over. This sense of structure allows the introduction of the paper to function as a "reader/writer contract," by discussing the need for answering the question and thereby creating the particular kinds of expectations that the argument will fulfill.

Figure 3 FROM ENTHYMEME TO STRUCTURE

Enthymeme
Recognizing the right to refuse allegiance to the authority of the law will not lead to anarchy because the decision to disobey those laws which violate individual conscience will be made by each individual out of disrespect for different laws.

Analysis

Recognizing the right to refuse allegiance to the authority of the law.	will not lead to	anarchy
(A)		**(B)**
	because	
(A)		**(C)**
the decision to disobey laws which violate individual conscience	will be made	by each individual out of disrespect for different laws.

(Assumption) Anarchy **(B)** exists when many people choose collectively to disobey all laws (not C).

- - - - - - - - - -

Structure

	It is said that recognizing Thoreau's "right	**question**
A --> B	to refuse" cannot be tolerated because it will	**at**
	lead to anarchy, or a lawless society.	**issue**

A	This right applies to individuals who choose to disobey a law because it violates individual conscience.	
	If conscience is individual and not collective, this choice will be made by different people according to their own perception of justice.	} } } **burden**
A -->C {		} **of**
	Such acts of civil disobedience, then, will be directed by different people toward different laws.	} **proof** } }
	In a society in which different people choose	}
C . . .	to disobey different laws, the majority will still be obeying the majority of laws.	} **assumption**
	But "anarchy" means a lawless society, and	
B --> C	implies that many people will choose collectively to disobey all laws.	**conclusion** **(thesis)**

Moving from an enthymeme to a structure is not simply a matter of stating and elaborating each of the three propositions of the implied syllogism. It is a matter of recreating the relationships which hold the logic of the enthymeme together. Thus, students should consider the argument as progressing from term to term in the enthymeme according to the predications it asserts. There is no prescribed order in which the terms must be taken up; every enthymeme will suggest a different dynamic of ideas. But students who have worked through to a satisfactory enthymeme will perceive these relationships, better than they will do if told by some formula how the parts must be arranged independent of the ideas.

[Figure 3 above] illustrates how an enthymeme can be analyzed for the purpose of discovering the essential structure of the paper it is intended to generate. The predicated terms, marked A, B, and C, are the elements of the logic, and the structure which results is no more than the reassembly of these terms into a developing order. The result is an outline, but it is an outline of *ideas* and not an outline of subjects. Once a student has been able to think through all the parts of an enthymeme, the structure will develop as a natural consequence of it--even though working out the details will require perceiving its connections intuitively: no prescribed order of relating A, B, and C will suffice. Every enthymeme will imply its own structure of ideas. Writing the complete paper, then, is a matter of sticking to this plan, developing these ideas, and adding definitions, explanations, examples, quotations, and refutations as the need for them arises. Whatever the students might wish to say ought to "belong" somewhere in this structure. The structure is available to use as a guide and as a test for digressions: if each new part of the paper does not advance us toward the conclusion by this strategy, it does not belong in *this* essay.

The example above assumes, of course, that the rhetorical criteria for the enthymeme have been met. It cannot be judged a good or bad enthymeme apart from the particular rhetorical situation that prompted it. The class, as audience, has discussed the issue and come up with different stances, one of which has provided this student with her own position: someone has argued that civil disobedience cannot be tolerated because it will lead to anarchy in society. In wanting to defend civil disobedience, this student has had to discover a position and a strategy that will meet that audience half way considering what its reasons have been. Her paper does not pretend to take on the entire issue of civil disobedience, but tries to do justice to some small part of that issue which she can discuss rationally with that audience. Her paper will not be the end of the matter, for her or for her readers, but it is an attempt to think clearly and directly about it, rather than to remain content with the muddled thoughts that always attend real questions in dispute. The example illustrates also that in attempting to find the right structure for a paper, the student must continue to rethink the logic of the enthymeme: in the fifth statement of this "outline," this student faces the problem of justifying a controversial statement, the probability of which is necessary to her logic.The enthymeme, treated as a logical and rhetorical roadmap, is not intended to solve all of the problems of thoughtful writing, but, in part, to disclose some of those problems to students who would otherwise skip over them mentally, as we all do. When the logic is on paper, in this manipulable form, the problems come to our attention and we thereby learn, I hope, that thinking is not a rule bound enterprise but an open and imaginative one.

This method, as you have gathered, is anti-formulaic, even though the enthymeme itself is a form. It is a form of thought, however, and not a form of composition; it does not appear in the paper at all, as such. The actual structure of the paper cannot be prescribed in advance but must develop out of the logical necessities of the particular ideas measured against the ideas of a particular audience.

In Plato's *Phaedrus,* Socrates notes that Lysias' speech begins with its conclusion, and he asks whether Lysias has "a really congent reason for stating his second point in the second place" or whether instead he "swam (on his back!) upstream against the current of his own discourse." Socrates asks instead for an organic arrangement between the parts of a composition- -not "boldly setting down whatever happened to come into his head." This sense of structure seems to require two considerations, for Plato: first, it follows from a careful examination of one's knowledge to decide whether it is warranted. The second consideration is whether the purpose of the composition is, like Lysias' speech, to make an unwarranted idea go over with an audience who is a passive receptacle, or whether, as in the case of the dialectical rhetoric of Plato and Aristotle, one's ideas develop in relation to an active audience with whom one attempts to discover shared grounds for new knowledge that cannot be learned in any other way. The enthymeme, as I have tried to illustrate, can answer at least some of Plato's objections to sophistic rhetoric.

We must recognize, however, that the enthymeme can also be reduced to an empty formulaic exercise, just as can all other methods that may have been created to meet these same ideals. The enthymeme was used by Aristotle to address the human problem that truth is not available to us about all of the questions we deliberate, and it represented the dynamics of the search for real knowledge that can be shared without the systematic perfection of pure reason. With that in mind, the enthymeme can be a constant adventure for students and for teachers, both of whom must, in using it, acknowledge the uncertainty it entails. The knowledge that it requires us to search out is of the contingent, probable sort. Perhaps this means that by such a method we are also chancing to teach students something about what knowledge is: not a thing that is always necessarily all true or all false, or for which easy means of knowing can be counted on, but more, as Wayne Booth has said, a matter of degrees of conviction measured against the quality of the reasons that ask for assent.[9]

Note on the article's authorship as of   1978:   John Gage was teaching English and directing the composition program at the University of Oregon. He had currently published *In the Arresting Eye: The Rhetoric of Imagism,* as well as a number of articles on rhetoric and composition.

Notes

1. See, e.g., "Towards an Epistemology of Composition," *Journal of Advanced Composition* 2 (1982), 1-10; "Freshman English: in Whose Service?", *College English 44* (September, 1982), 15-20.
2. For a discussion of the enthymeme from this perspective, in relation to the whole of Aristotle's philosophy of rhetoric, see William A. Grimaldi, S.J., *Studies in the Philosophy of Aristotle's Rhetoric* (Wiesbaden: Franz Steiner Verlag, 1972), esp. chapter 2.
3. To my knowledge, the first use of the enthymeme as the structural basis for whole compositions was developed for the composition program of the Rhetoric Department, University of California at Berkeley, and subsequently made available in the textbook *The Craft of Writing* by William J. Brandt, et al. (Englewood Cliffs, N.J.: Prentice-Hall, 1969). I am indebted to my mentors and colleagues in this program for prompting many of my thoughts in this essay.
4. See my "On the Difference Between Invention and Pre-Writing." *Freshman English News* 10 (Fall, 1981), 4-14.

5. "Assumption," as used here, may be either the major or the minor premise of the reconstructed syllogism, whichever is not stated in the enthymeme itself it is related to what Stephen Toulmin has called the "backing." See his *The Uses of Argument* (Cambridge: Cambridge University Press, 1958), esp. pp. 94-107.

6. See Grimaldi, chapter 1.

7. See Lawrence D. Green, "Enthymemic Invention and Structural Predication," *College English* 41 (February, 1980), 623-34. Green's sophisticated discussion of this method goes beyond my general purpose here; my essay could well be regarded as an introduction to his.

8. Josephine Miles, *Working Out ideas: Predication and Other Uses of Language* (Berkeley: Bay Area Writing Project Curriculum Publication #5, 1979), 14-16.

9. See esp., "The Uncritical American: or, Nobody's From Missouri Any More," *Now Don't Try to Reason With Me: Essays and Ironies for a Credulous Age* (Chicago: University of Chicago Press, 1970), 63-75.

Selected Bibliography

Writing Arguments

Ede, Lisa S., and Andrea Lunsford. "On Distinctions between Classical and Modern Rhetoric." *Essays on Classical Rhetoric and Modern Discourse.* Eds. Robert J. Connors, Lisa S. Ede, and Andrea A. Lunsford. Carbondale, IL: Southern Illinois UP, 1984. 37-49.

Fulkerson, Richard. "Technical Logic, Comp-Logic, and the Teaching of Writing." *CCC* 39 (1988): 436-52.

Levin, Gerald. "On Freshman Composition and Logical Thinking." *CCC* 28 (1977): 359-64.

Porter, Jeffrey. "The Reasonable Reader: Knowledge and Inquiry in Freshman English." *CE* 49 (1987): 332-44.

Rapkins, Angela A. "The Uses of Logic in the College Freshman English Classroom." *Activities to Promote Critical Thinking: Classroom Practices in Teaching English.* Urbana, IL: NCTE, 1986.

Rottenberg, Annette. *Elements of Argument.* 2d ed. Boston: Bedford, 1988.

Secor, Marie J. "Recent Research in Argumentation Theory." *Technical Writing Teacher* 14 (1987): 337-54.

Toulmin, Stephen. *The Uses of Argument.* New York: Cambridge UP, 1964.

Writing About Literature

Atkins, C. Douglas, and Michael L. Johnson, eds. *Writing and Reading Differently: Deconstruction and the Teaching of Composition and Literature.* Lawrence: UP of Kansas, 1985.

Clifford, John, ed. *The Experience of Reading: Louise Rosenblatt and Reader-Response Theory.* Portsmouth, NH: Boynton/Cook, 1991.

Eagleton, Terry. *Literary Theory: An Introduction.* Minneapolis: U Minnesota P, 1983.

Farrell, Edmund J., and James R. Squire, eds. *Transactions with Literature: A Fifty-Year Perspective.* Urbana, IL: NCTE, 1990.

Horner, Winifred Bryan, ed. *Composition and Literature: Bridging the Gap.* Chicago: U of Chicago P, 1983.

Kermode, Frank. *The Genesis of Secrecy: On the Interpretation of Narrative.* Cambridge: Harvard UP, 1979.

Kroll, Barry M. *Teaching Hearts and Minds: College Students Reflect on the Vietnam War in Literature.* Carbondale: Southern Illinois UP, 1992.

Lindemann, Erika. "Freshman Composition: No Place for Literature." *CE* 55.3 (1993): 311-316.

Lynn, Steven. "A Passage Into Critical Theory." *CE* 52 (1990): 258-71.

Morgan, Dan. "Connecting Literature to Students' Lives." *CE* 55.5 (1993): 491-500.

Scholes, Robert. *Textual Power: Literary Theory and the Teaching of English.* New Haven: Yale UP, 1985.

Tate, Gary. "A Place for Literature in Freshman Composition." *CE* 55.3 (1993): 317-321.

G. Designing, Responding to, and Evaluating Writing Assignments

Composition classes are largely structured by the writing the instructor assigns to students, and much of the instructor's teaching, especially in a process-oriented class, consists of commenting on and evaluating what students have written in response to these assignments. The purposes, designs, and sequence of assignments and the teacher's comments on and evaluations of students' writing reflect and communicate the goals, priorities, and theories that inform the class. Assigning, responding, and evaluating are closely intertwined activities, as any teacher who has tried to comment on and grade papers written for an assignment that didn't work can tell you. The five pieces in this section show that there is no one procedure for designing and sequencing assignments and no one right way of responding to and evaluating student writing. These articles provide guidelines and options for assigning, responding, and evaluating as well as theories and questions for analyzing our goals and purposes, our students, and our teaching situations in order to develop sound and effective practices.

The first selection, "Creating Effective Writing Assignments," a chapter from the book *Scenarios for Teaching Writing: Contexts for Discussion and Reflective Practice* by Chris M. Anson, Joan Graham, David A. Jolliffe, Nancy S. Shapiro, and Carolyn H. Smith (Urbana, IL: NCTE, 1993), instead of providing suggestions for designing assignments, attempts to help teachers come to their own decisions by analyzing case studies based on real incidents. Instead of discussing theories and teaching practices, the authors describe several scenarios dealing with designing and sequencing assignments and ask readers questions about them. These scenarios raise issues about assignments' purposes and appropriateness for different students; the content, structure, and style of assignment sheets; the use of assigned readings in conjunction with assignments; responding to unexpected student interpretations of and confusions about assignments; and sequencing assignments to achieve help students achieve the goals of the course.

"Assigning and Evaluating Transactional Writing" by Toby Fulwiler and Robert Jones (originally published in *Language Connections: Writing and Reading Across the Curriculum*, edited by Fulwiler and Art Young, Urbana, IL: NCTE, 1982) discusses designing and evaluating informative and persuasive writing assignments. Fulwiler and Jones explain that some of the causes of poor student writing are poorly designed writing assignments, assignments that are vague, dull, badly planned or sequenced, or based on wrong assumptions about students' knowledge, as well as responses to student writing that do not clearly direct and encourage students to improve their writing. Fulwiler and Jones argue that teachers need to put effort into planning writing assignments, and they provide questions and suggestions to help teachers create and evaluate assignments and essay exams. Fulwiler and Jones also advocate process-oriented responses and evaluations that focus on how each text addresses its intended audiences and purposes, and they list practical suggestions to guide comments and evaluations.

Leonard A. Podis and Joanne M. Podis describe and illustrate a process-oriented approach to responding to student writing based on the principles of error analysis in "Improving Our Responses to Student Writing: A Process-Oriented

Approach" (originally published in *Rhetoric Review* 5 [1986]: 90-98). Instead of product-centered comments that judge student papers against an "Ideal Text" in the instructor's head, Podis and Podis argue that teachers should engage in a close reading of a student's text to try to understand the student's intentions and mental processes. Problems in a paper normally signal difficulties that the student has had working through his or her "process of discovery" or in "negotiating a particular rhetorical situation."

In "Ranking, Evaluating, and Liking: Sorting Out Three Forms of Judgment" (originally published in *College English* 55 [1993]: 187-206), Peter Elbow takes on the subject of grading. Elbow opposes grading or ranking individual papers because the process is unreliable and uncommunicative and students become more concerned about grades. Elbow describes several ways in which teachers can fulfill institutional demands for a course grade that avoid grading individual papers and instead encourage evaluation, "looking hard and thoughtfully at a piece of writing in order to make distinctions as to the quality of different features or dimensions." These include portfolios, analytic grids for evaluation, and contract grading. Elbow also makes a strong argument that students benefit when the teacher provides "evaluation-free zones" in a class, opportunities to write without evaluation such as freewriting.

Creating Effective
Writing Assignments

Chris Anson, Joan Graham, David A. Joliffe,
Nancy S. Shapiro, and Carolyn H. Smith

When we think of designing a writing course, we think primarily of how we will engage our students in meaningful writing projects. Of all the cliches in the business, "Students learn to write by writing" stands out as one of the oldest and truest. What we tell students (lectures) and what we have them read may prepare them for writing, but only by writing do they become more competent and mature as writers. What will we have them write? Does it matter how we extend "assisted invitations" to write? Does it matter how we order our assignments which ones we start with, which ones come later? And if those things matter, are there any guidelines that help us generate engaging, interesting writing assignments?

This chapter presents scenarios drawn from the experiences of typical college writing teachers. The first scenario, a set of three brief case studies, deals with what we might call the microlevel of assignment making: What does a good individual assignment sheet look like? What type of genre or written output should you look for? The second scenario addresses a pedagogical issue: What should you do when your expectations as a teacher do not match the reality of your class? The third scenario presents a number of assignment ideas, but asks a more global question: How would you sequence these assignments? What principles of learning or cognitive development might help guide a sequence? What are the "cognitive aims" of different assignments are some more complex than others? Can we apply any hierarchies to assignment sequencing? And the fourth scenario tests our limits for what counts as an "appropriate" response to a writing assignment.

Articulating Writing Assignments: The Peer Teacher Team

Brian Jackson, Margo Brown, and Linda Barton are three writing instructors at a large university. Brian and Margo are first-year teaching assistants (TAs), and Linda has been around the English department for several years as a graduate student. Because of their similar teaching schedules, these three have been assigned to the same peer teacher team (one of the support structures the university sets up for instructors). The team members are expected to meet regularly to discuss their writing and reading assignments, student papers, and any other issues or topics that grow out of their teaching experiences.

Early in the semester they settle into a routine where each one takes a turn presenting a draft of an assignment at successive weekly meetings. The group critiques an assignment, and then the author revises it on the basis of insights gained from the group's discussion.

As you read through these case studies, you will come to see how teachers in the same program can approach similar types of assignments with different theoretical assumptions and different expectations of their students. As you work through the questions developed around the individual assignments, do not hesitate to move between and among the three, comparing and contrasting the language, style, focus, and purposes of the assignments.

For the purposes of this discussion, you can assume that when the teachers refer to a common text (for example, Freire), they engaged the class in some related discussion and informal prewriting leading up to these assignment sheets.

Bring It Back: A Narrative Assignment

Brian Jackson came to graduate school after teaching for three years in a high school and working part-time at a local newspaper. He was more mature than most of the new graduate students and had some practical teaching experience to draw on as he faced his first introductory freshman writing class. Yet, while his high school teaching experience may have given him more "presence" in the classroom those first few weeks, he felt quite unprepared to create the type of writing assignments that had been introduced in his new-TA orientation.

Brian was used to giving assignments drawn from readings in a required American literature high school textbook, the kind that asked students to analyze characters, identify themes, and relate one work to another. But throughout his weeklong TA orientation, the directors of the writing program emphasized writing in an academic context. They spoke of freshmen joining the "academic discourse community" (whatever that meant). During orientation, Brian learned that writing assignments should be designed to encourage "critical thinking and reflection at the college level." The directors identified three elements of a successful college writing assignment:

1. Specify the content.
2. Suggest or identify some prewriting stimuli.
3. Give the assignment some rhetorical context--that is, give the students an audience and purpose to write for.

After a week and a half of classes, Brian tried conscientiously to follow his directors in setting up his first writing assignment. Brian's assignment appears below.

Narrative Assignment

Narratives tell stories. In this assignment you will tell the story of a significant educational experience you have had. What is a "significant educational experience," you ask? Any event which enlarges or alters your thinking could be considered an educational experience.

In a recent interview with *Omni* magazine, Paulo Freire, whom you've all read, relates a "significant educational experience" he had as a young boy. He explains the influence of his mother on his early education: "I had been taught by my mother, a woman with the rigid ethics of a devout Catholic." Then he relays this autobiographical story:

> One day my brothers and I caught a neighbor's chicken that had wandered into our yard. We killed it. My mother heard the chicken's cries and came running. I expected her to punish us, give the chicken back to the neighbor, and ask him to forgive us. But she picked it up, went to the kitchen, and we ate it. A beautiful lunch! She was very realistic. I forgot the incident until much later, after she died. But I've often wondered what sort of turmoil she went through as she stood there looking at the dead chicken, then at us, deciding if she should return it or feed us. (pp. 74, 78-79, 94)

Imagine the young boy's shock at his devout Catholic mother's behavior. Stealing is a sin, but they were starving, and a mother has an obligation to her children...

Before slaying the chicken, the eleven-year-old Freire saw the world, and perhaps particularly his mother, as two-dimensional, black and white, right and wrong. However, after his mother's reaction, he begins to see that life is not as simple as an immature Catholic perspective may want to frame it.

If Freire were writing this assignment, he would emphasize a particular aspect of this day in his telling of the story. For example, he may want to emphasize his surprise and bewilderment regarding his mother's reaction. Or he may wish to emphasize how he really feared his mother, but feared his brothers more, and therefore went along with something he thought they would be punished for.

Whichever aspect he chooses to describe, however, would not be the point of the narrative. The reason for story is to tell how he learned from the event. The emphasized aspect dramatizes the educational process as it occurs and brings the narrative to life. For us to see how Freire learned from the experience, though, we need to know how he thought before the incident, and how he thinks afterwards. Be sure to include such information in your own narratives.

Remember: Write your name and any other pertinent information (i.e., the date, the class) in the upper right corner of the first page; center the title, and put one staple through the upper left corner of the pages. You may want to put your last name alongside the page numbers of pages 2, 3, etc. The narrative is due at the beginning of class on Wednesday, October 3.

ISSUES FOR DISCUSSION

- If you were a student in Brian's class, what would you think of this as the first assignment? Can you think of an incident that you would write about? Is there anything in this assignment that could help a student decide on a topic? Was the Freire anecdote helpful?

- To what extent does the assignment encourage college-level critical thinking? To what extent does the assignment reflect the three elements of a successful writing assignment outlined above?

- Brian offers this written rationale for his first writing assignment in the course:

> I'm assigning such an essay at the start of the semester, and thus at the start of my students' college experience (they are all first-year frosh, seventeen to eighteen years old), with the goal of getting them to be more self-conscious of their education. I think many students come to college with the high school schedule and routine still well entrenched in their minds. Time outside of class becomes "free" time in which you don't talk about "school." I hope that this assignment may begin to break down some of those mental corridors established by high school modular scheduling. I am curious to see how many of them will write of events that happened outside of school, which they later saw as significant because of some discussion or activity in school. Then, perhaps, they could see how "school" is related to the "real world" The goal is to have the students rethink how events that stand out in their memory because of their significance may be formidable educational experiences.

What do you think of Brian's rationale?

- Margo read Brian's assignment and just shook her head. "Come on, Brian!" she chided. "You know that when you ask them to write about what they learned from some experience, you'll just get that trite garbage, like `I learned a lot' or `I really grew up.' You've got to do better than that if you want anything original."

Do you agree with Margo?

- Linda had a different objection. "These kids aren't ready for Freire haven't you figured that out yet? You've got to teach them to walk before they can run. If you ask them to do too much--like where you ask them to reflect on `how they learned from an event, how they think about it differently before and afterwards'--I bet you won't even get a decent narrative, let alone a thoughtful essay."

What do you think of Linda's comments?

- Would you use this assignment or an assignment like it?

Fight It Out: An Argumentative Assignment

Unlike Brian, Margo Brown has no prior classroom experience. A new twenty-two-year-old graduate student working for a master's degree in fine arts (creative writing), she worries about presenting herself as confident and knowledgeable about composition. As a poet, she intuitively speaks and writes in metaphors, and her images are often quite striking. She wants her students to come to appreciate the beauty and power of language, but she clearly understands that the freshman writing class is not the place to offer creative writing instruction. She is committed to helping her students excel in the academy by learning effective strategies for academic writing.

In presenting her second assignment to her peer team, she was quick to point out how her ideas about getting students to think about academic writing differed from Brian's. Her argumentative assignment follows.

The Argument Paper

We have been studying strategies that different writers use when they write argumentative essays. For this assignment, you will be taking a position on a controversial topic and applying the strategies that we have discussed. Today's newspapers are filled with hotly debated issues: Should condoms be distributed in high schools? Should euthanasia be legal? Should mass murderers be able to plead temporary insanity? Should addictive drugs be legalized? Should health care workers be tested for AIDS? Obviously, you can think of many more.

As you plan your position paper, imagine an audience that holds the diametrically opposite viewpoint. To argue forcefully, you must marshal your facts, organize them strategically in a way that outmaneuvers your opponent, and anticipate the potential objections from your readers. The more ammunition you have in the way of facts and rhetorical strategies, the more effective you will be. If you can find out your opponent's positions and usual lines of argument, you will be in a position to discredit and shoot down these objections before they can be raised.

Your weapons include definition, analogy, example, comparison and contrast--in fact, all the rhetorical strategies we have been discussing in class. Imagine that the context for your argument is a letter to the editor of the college newspaper or your local, hometown newspaper. You begin with credibility as a member of the community you are addressing. Remember that your purpose is to destroy the advocates of the other position with the logic of your own position. You are not required to do research for this paper, but you may want to arm yourself with a few facts from reliable sources.

Due: Oct. 14
Length: 3-5 pages

ISSUES FOR DISCUSSION

* Is this an appropriate early assignment for a freshman writing class?

* What topics would you expect students to write about for this paper? Where should they go for information?

- How well do you think Margo addressed all three necessary aspects of the assignment: content, stimuli, and rhetorical situation?

- When asked about her rationale, Margo wrote:

> The purpose of this assignment was to get my students to flex their rhetorical muscles. I realize that argument is one of the more difficult rhetorical modes, but I also think it is the most stimulating. I want my students to write because they care deeply about something. I believe that the best writing comes from that emotional involvement. The more they practice integrating the rhetorical strategies in their writing, the more fluent they will become.
>
> I try to emphasize that writing is not merely a record of events or a transcription of thoughts-instead, it constitutes an epistemological process that would be non-existent without the written word. I address the idea of audience by giving them concrete situations that they could actually imagine themselves in.

- Brian liked the rhetorical context that Margo provided for this assignment, but he was worried. "Aren't you afraid that your students will just fill up pages with rant?" he asked.
  "Is that so bad?" Margo wanted to know. "At least they'll be practicing rhetoric." Do you agree with Margo or Brian? Why?
- Linda liked Margo's assignment a lot, too. "My only concern is that you don't tell them how to do this," she offered. "Don't you leave yourself open to lots of questions about sources and topics and things like that? Do you think they'll take your suggestions as the best ideas?" Do you agree with Linda?
- Would you use this assignment or an assignment like it? Why or why not?

Look It Up: A Research Paper Assignment

At the other end of the spectrum from Brian and Margo is Linda Barton, an advanced graduate student who is in the last stages of writing her dissertation and spends a lot of time in the library. Because her fellowship has expired, she petitioned to teach a section of freshman writing as an instructor. She also teaches part-time at a local community college. As she plans her courses, Linda recalls her previous teachers who emphasized library research as a tool for succeeding in college. She wants to equip her students with those same kinds of skills. The research paper assignment reprinted below came toward the end of her course.

The Research Paper: Assignment Sheet

Due: Dec. 7
Length: 3-4 typed pages

First. Decide on a topic. (We'll do some brainstorming in class-you can also locate some worthwhile political topics by reading the newspaper.) Be sure to try to pick a topic you're interested in.

Second. Go to the campus library and find the New York Times and Washington Post indexes. Find your topic in the indexes and read their summaries of the articles' contents. Write down any titles, dates, etc. of the ones that look as if they'd have information that would help in your research, either those that seem to specifically relate to your topic, those that may have good detailed information, or those that would provide helpful background information you (as an expert) would need to know in order to write authoritatively. Find the microfilm of the New York Times and the Washington Post; then find and read the articles you're looking for. Take notes as you read. Perhaps photocopy some of the more important articles. **Be sure to record all bibliographic information.**

Third. Go to the Reader's Guide and see if any magazine articles were written on your subject. Find a few by (first) finding out if the university (or your local library) owns issues of that magazine, and (second) find its location in the library (one of several possible places). (At any point in this [some-times frustrating] process you start to go crazy, ask the librarians for help--that's what they're there for.) Read some of the articles, take notes, possibly photocopy a few articles.

Next. Continue to fill in gaps, and begin to write. What I am looking for is an essay, that is, paragraphs that are unified, filled with facts (quotes, statistics, incidents, examples, details, names, etc.) that support their paragraph's clear, well thought out topic sentence. In turn, each paragraph's topic sentence should address the paper's thesis--and the thesis will itself be the answer to the question asked either by you or chosen by you from those on the "Suggested Research Topics" page. **Remember: This paper must have a thesis.**

Finally. Finish your research. Write your paper. Revise it as much as it needs in order to be clear, tight, convincing, and obviously the best paper you've written in here so far. Proof it carefully. Make sure your paper's documentation is clear and accurate. **Plagiarism is serious--whether intentional or not.**

- DO NOT use articles or sources more than three years old.
- DO NOT wait until the last minute to begin your library research.
- All papers must be typed, double-spaced, with 1-inch margins on all sides.
- Use MLA style for citations and works cited.

ISSUES FOR DISCUSSION

- How would you respond to this assignment if you were one of Linda's students?

- How well has Linda incorporated the three essentials (content, stimuli, and rhetorical context) in her assignment?

- What kind of papers do you expect that Linda will receive on the basis of these instructions?

- At this point in the peer-group discussions, Brian begins to express doubts about the purpose of assignments. "I'm worried that my first assignment was so wishy-washy," he commented. "Linda's looks so much more straightforward and easier to follow."

    Margo, on the other hand, expressed veiled contempt for Linda's assignment: "It looks like a cookbook variety assignment" she muttered. "Anybody could teach writing if this is all you have to do." How do you react to Brian's and Margo's comments?

- Linda reflects on her assignment:

    I believe that writing assignments should offer students as much concrete support as possible. In this assignment I really did not concern myself too much with the topic of their paper--it was the process that I was especially interested in. I think students appreciate explicit directions--exactly what to do, and what not to do should be spelled out. That way, students won't have to guess what the teacher wants. I constructed this assignment to be free from the diversionary, mysterious chitchat that I've seen in some assignments.

What do you think of Linda's rationale?

- Would you use this assignment or one like it? Why or why not?

- Look at the differences in tone among the three assignment sheets. What effect do you think tone will have on the students' responses to these assignments?

- Which tone do you like most of the three? Why?

Todd's Assignment Backfires

Todd Froelich was teaching his first section of basic English, a course designed for inexperienced student writers who need to prepare for the university's general introductory writing course. Todd had taught the general introductory course four times, and he had enjoyed having students read professional texts about contemporary social and political issues, discuss the issues in class, and then write essays in response to rather open-ended prompts. He found that the students really became engaged in discussing topics like race, gender roles, environmental ethics, and the like. Moreover, after considerable experimentation with the wording of writing assignments, he determined that the students actually wrote much better if the assignment did not guide them too much--if it did not prescribe exactly who the audience of their text was supposed to be, what its primary purpose was, what format the essay should take, how long it should be, and so on. As the students wrote their essays and conferred with Todd and their peers about drafts, these issues would get fleshed out in discussion.

While preparing his first major assignment for basic English, Todd assumed that the same strategy would work well with the inexperienced student writers. If anything, he thought, these students might be even more comfortable, and therefore more successful, if he were not too directive--if he did not seem to be taking too much initiative for making decisions about audience, purpose, genre, stance, and so on away from the students. They need to succeed as writers, Todd thought, and this leeway will allow them to do so.

His plan for the first week of class, containing three sessions, was fairly straightforward. On the first day, as usual, he would introduce policies and principles and go over the syllabus. He assigned the students to read a brief, humorous piece, "I Want a Wife:' by Judy Syfers, for the next session. They spent the hour discussing the main idea of the essay, the structure and diction, and the character of the speaker. At the end of class that day, Todd handed out the following writing assignment:

> If you feel that traditional gender roles are disappearing from present-day society, discuss those influences that are responsible for weakening them.

He told the students to work on a draft of an essay responding to this assignment and to bring their drafts to class for the final session of week one. At that session, Todd explained, the students would trade papers with a classmate and discuss ways to revise their drafts into more polished essays.

At the next class session, much to Todd's surprise, only four of the fifteen students had written any kind of draft in response to the assignment. Three others had written down a few notes about the topic, but nothing they could share with a peer reader. Eight of the fifteen came to class empty-handed.

Todd was flabbergasted. "Why didn't you write anything?" he asked, trying to keep his cool. Nobody said a word. "Okay," he said, "Let's write your questions about this assignment on the board and talk about them." Finally, one student spoke up: "Were we supposed to use the story we read for class when we wrote this theme?" Once the ice was broken, two other students raised their hands quickly. "What's an influence?" one young woman asked. "How do we discuss something in an essay?" a young man blurted out. "Don't you have to have at least two people to have a discussion? And there's only one person writing an essay, right?"

Todd realized that he needed to rethink his pedagogical approach.

ISSUES FOR DISCUSSION

• How should Todd respond to each of the questions the students put to him on the last day of the first week's classes?

For different kinds of students-basic, general, or honors students how much guidance should a writing assignment provide about the following features:
    The need to conduct research?

The potential use of readings?
The intellectual tasks called for?
The genre?
The length?
The audience?
The purpose?
Any other features?

A Sequence of Dilemmas

Greg Holsebach, a first-year teaching assistant who was planning his freshman writing syllabus, was very concerned about offering his students good writing assignments. As part of his planning, he talked to several experienced teachers and asked them to provide model or sample assignments. He was so impressed by several of them that he decided the best way to structure his own course was to ask his students to write essays based on five of the best assignments he collected. His problem, though, was that he was not sure how to sequence the assignments in a way that would work to increase his students' competence little by little. He was afraid of overwhelming the students with too many cognitive demands, inadvertently exacerbating the writer's block of already anxious freshmen.

Greg identified five related cognitive aims-goals he hoped the students would achieve through writing activities in the course:

1. Appreciate what they already know about a subject.
2. Discover new knowledge and new ways of thinking about a subject.
3. Reflect on their changing ideas.
4. Anticipate and accommodate readers' needs.
5. Take a critical perspective on their own writing.

Greg knew that it is a lot easier to list goals or objectives for a course than it is to accomplish them in a term, but he felt that if he were careful about sequencing his assignments and provided enough support at each level, students would be able to use these strategies to continue to improve their thinking and writing throughout their undergraduate careers.

After considerable deliberation, Greg decided on a sequence for the five major assignments in his course. To solicit one more reaction to his plan, he showed the assignments, in the sequence he intended to give them, to Louise Roth, his faculty adviser. Here are the five assignments in the order Greg intended to give them:

Assignments[1]
1. After reading Alfred Kazin's essay "The Kitchen," think about the kitchen you grew up in. Can you recall details that led to a dominant impression? Quite possibly many of the individual memories clash--you will remember both happy and sad times, bustling activity and quiet times. Begin by searching your memory for many details of the kitchen, including people and events associated with that space. Then try to distill a single impression, and select from your long list those elements that would recreate the impression for a reader.

2. Watch two episodes of a popular TV series ("Cosby," "Roseanne" "Family Ties," etc.) and take notes on the depiction of social class on TV. You may pay attention to living conditions, jobs, speech patterns, possessions, leisure activities, etc. Hint: you might want to think about what is not included in the show (are poor people represented? people from different cultures?). What assumptions are being made by the producers? Write a critique for your local newspaper about how social class is portrayed on television.

3. Write an extended definition of a significant term from your major or from an area that you know reasonably well. Your audience is the general public, and your purpose is to clarify the meaning of a term your audience may not have heard of or may have misconceptions about.

4. Read the Time magazine article on "The Simple Life: Rejecting the Rat Race, Americans Get Back to Basics" (April 8, 1991, pp. 58-63). First, write a summary of the article, identifying the main points of the argument. What is the author trying to demonstrate or prove? What kind of evidence does the author use? Second, interview three people (preferably of different generations or different backgrounds) about their reactions to the thesis presented by this article. You can summarize it for them briefly, then ask if they agree with the thesis. Third, referring to the original article and the notes you took from your interviews, formulate your own analysis of this thesis. Does a trend really exist, or is the author or editor forcing the issue? Write your response as a letter to the editor of Time.

5. After reading two opposing articles on affirmative action (one pro and one con), ask students to write a letter to the editor of the college newspaper, supporting or criticizing the current affirmative action policies of their university.

The next day after showing his mentor the assignments in his proposed sequence, Greg found this note from her in his mailbox:

Greg:
Your assignments all look interesting as isolated exercises, but for the life of me, I can't see what principle unifies them so that collectively they could constitute a legitimate writing course. What reason do students have for proceeding from one assignment to the next? What kinds of inquiry are they going to be engaging in for the entire term? How will that inquiry develop? How will your assignments support the process of inquiry? Here's a suggestion: Rather than having students write in response to all five of these assignments, why not select just one and really ask students to "unpack" it in several smaller assignments. For example, you could break up the assignment, using the eries of questions James Moffett sets out in Teaching the Universe of Discourse: What is happening? (Drama) What happened? (Narration) What happens? (Generalization) What might happen if? (Argument). Or you could develop a sequence of assignments

based on James Kinneavy's major aims, explained in <u>A Theory of Discourse:</u> expressive writing, referential writing (informative, exploratory, and demonstrative), and persuasive writing. You could even adopt some form of the "modes" or methods of exposition: description, narration, definition, comparison, classification, and so on. If the assignments are so subdivided, your students could work very hard on one--or maybe two--of them during the course. I think you'll find that the students will learn a lot more both about how to write effectively and about how writing fosters learning. I'd be happy to discuss your syllabus in greater detail at your convenience.

Best,   Louise

ISSUES FOR DISCUSSION

- What do you think of Greg's initial plan to ask his colleagues to give him successful sample or model writing assignments from their classes? What are the benefits and the problems in this practice?

- What do you think about the advice Louise Roth offers Greg? What suggestions would you give him as he plans his syllabus? How would you explain your rationale for sequencing?

- If you were to use any of the five assignments Greg chose, would you want to modify them in terms of audience, purpose, or complexity?

Personal Porn

Chris Eastman has been teaching composition as a part-time (adjunct) faculty member at a large university for almost six years. His teaching method includes peer-revision conferences, which take place each time his students have written a full rough draft of an assignment. During the week of conferences, Chris cancels two regular class sessions and meets, one at a time, with each group of four students, usually in the cafeteria of the university student union. His conference style is facilitative: he prefers to listen to the group discuss each other's drafts and to chime in when he thinks the discussion is going astray or when he wants to add an important point. His small-group conferences are quite successful; students like their informal feel and say they get a lot of good feedback from their peers.

Chris always begins his courses with a personal narrative assignment. He believes that narrative helps students to think about their writing processes, and he likes the way he can rely on memories as occasions for introducing methods for discovering ideas, elaborating or exploring them, and then articulating them in vivid, stylish prose.

This time around, however, he wanted to try something new. He knew that model readings used for imitation have been out of fashion for some time in composition, and he knew that such modeling cannot be solidly supported theoretically. But something about using model readings kept tugging at him; he liked the way the students could *see* an author's use of personal memories and experiences as they thought about writing their own narratives. He decided to experiment a little, recasting his usual narrative assignment as follows:

First Assignment: Personal Narrative

For this first assignment, please select a reading by a professional author that you would like to model your own narrative on. You are free to choose whomever you like-- select a reading you've seen before, or else "read around" a little until you find something appealing. Your "professional" narrative may even be a piece of fiction, as long as there is a narrator who is describing a specific experience that happened to him or her.

In your own narrative, be sure to follow our in-class techniques for elaborating specific events and memories. Use especially the technique of taking generalized events and then listing specific features beneath them to embellish your memories. Try to feel the event or action; try to see it; try to hear it; try to re-create and reexperience it. The life of a narrative is in detail-- don't forget the cardinal rule of showing, not telling.

Please bring four extra copies of your rough draft on Friday.

On Friday morning, Chris devoted a few minutes at the end of his class session to what he calls the "paper shuffle," when each group trades drafts. In the midst of the paper shuffle, he handed out his peer-revision guide, a list of ten questions focusing on the characteristics of good narratives. The students were to fill these guides out for each of their peers' papers so that each writer would receive fully articulated commentary from three other readers.

On Tuesday morning, Chris got to the student union cafeteria twenty minutes before his first conference group was scheduled to meet. He liked waiting until shortly before the group meeting to read quickly through each batch of four papers, because without much time for reflection he would be less likely to dominate the discussion.

As he glanced at the names on the drafts, Chris remembered that this was his "loose ends" group, formed last because of the students' extremely tight schedules (8:00 a.m. being the only time when they all could meet). Chris knew that this group in particular would need some special attention, first because there was a gender imbalance (three men plus himself, and only one woman), and second because the students' personal profiles showed that the three men were all from rural settings and seemed rather young and naive (none, for example, had visited a large city more than once or twice), while Anna Piel, the woman in the group, had lived all her life in the city and was worldly-wise and street-smart. Chris's quick reading of the papers written by the young men confirmed his expectations: John Campa's paper was a bland account of his grandmother's death, loosely modeled on a story by a writer Chris did not recognize. Keith Jackson's paper was an equally sophomoric description of a summer job he took in high school as a roofer, modeled on a fragment from Studs Terkel's book *Working*. And Richard Wilson's paper told of an expedition he and three friends made into a national park on a cold weekend when they had a hard time lighting a fire, Jack London's famous story being the authorial model.

Then Chris turned to Anna's draft, which began like this:

I was living in a house with three guys and two girls in the summer of my third year after high school. We were all doing acid [LSD] and smoking dope until

our brains were nowhere, and this is a story about how I was introduced to
group sex and learned to go down on men and women at the same time. At first
going down on women and guys together was scary but then it started to blow
my mind.

After reading this paragraph, Chris felt mixed emotions. He was taken aback by
Anna's forthrightness, but he was eager, in an almost voyeuristic way, to read on. At the
same time, he was concerned that Anna had taken too many liberties with his
assignment. He also wondered how the three shy young men would respond. Flipping to
the end of Anna's long paper, he discovered a photocopied page, stapled to the draft,
from one of Henry Miller's novels. It was a vivid account of the narrator's experience
soliciting and then engaging in sex with a prostitute in Paris.

Returning to Anna's draft, Chris was shocked to find, as he read on, that she
had described not one but six different sexual encounters with men and women,
sometimes alone, sometimes in groups, in detail that would make the most explicit
pornographic magazines sound like *Winnie-the-Pooh*. Anna had apparently used all the
brainstorming and detail-enhancing techniques to elaborate her experiences with the
most vivid minutiae of sound, smell, sight, taste, and touch. While Chris thought
himself a fairly experienced reader who had, in his thirty-four years, seen more than a
few genres of text, Anna's draft was so explicit that he found himself instinctively
leaning over it a little and checking around to see if anyone else was nearby. By the time
he had finished the draft, he felt completely conflicted-aroused by Anna's erotic
descriptions, amazed by her meticulous detail, thoroughly engaged in her unusual story,
guilty that he had succumbed in this way, worried about his teacherly role, and utterly
confused about how to respond.

A few minutes after Chris had skimmed through to the end of Anna's paper, the
group members began to arrive, first John and Rich, then Anna, who dropped her books
confidently on the table, and finally Keith, flustered from catching a late bus. When
everyone had gotten something from the cafeteria line and sat down to discuss the
papers, Chris noticed that the three men were making little eye contact with him, with
each other, or with Anna. They seemed to be waiting for Chris to say something, and it
was clear that Anna's paper had created some tension in the group. Anna, for her part,
seemed in high spirits and had displayed the papers and revision guides around her in
anticipation of a lively and fruitful discussion.

Still dazed, Chris looked tentatively around the table. "Okay," he asked, "who
wants to begin?"

ISSUES FOR DISCUSSION

- If you were Chris, how would you respond to Anna's paper in light of the
  assignment? Is Anna "wrong" to describe an unusual sexual experience? If Anna
  has, in fact, demonstrated all of Chris's criteria for successful narratives, including
  expertly elaborated descriptions, does Chris have a right to criticize her choice of
  "event" to practice these techniques?

• If you were to use Chris's assignment, would you want to forestall a paper like Anna's? Could you do that by modifying the assignment in terms of audience or purpose?

Chris did not expect Anna's paper; as an audience (and creator of the assignment), he has certain expectations about what is appropriate to write about in his class. But teachers often refer to the entire class as the "audience" for students' writing. Imagine that Chris runs the group conference and the three young men confess that they loved Anna's story and were attracted to her vivid details. Whose "criteria" for appropriate writing should be privileged under these circumstances: the students' or Chris's? Why? How could your answer to this question be made clearer to students in Chris's assignment?

• In his assignment, should Chris have specified the ways that the readings ought to be taken as models, perhaps asking students to practice using his guide by identifying "characteristics of good narratives" in the models they chose? Anna apparently used the professional reading she chose as a model for her *subject*. Is it appropriate to use professional readings as subject models?

• Highly constraining assignments can avoid unwelcome responses but may also stifle creativity. Is it more important to invite students to take risks and be imaginative or to keep them reigned in? Why?

• On the basis of your discussions of the scenarios in this chapter, construct a list of do's and don'ts for creating effective writing assignments. Afterwards, compare lists with a colleague or a group of colleagues. What similarities do you notice? What differences?

Note

1. A version of assignments 1 and 2 appears in *Constellations: A Contextual Reader for Writers,* edited by John Schilb, Elizabeth Flynn, and John Clifford (New York: HarperCollins, 1992), 159, 477.

Assigning and Evaluating
Transactional Writing

Toby Fulwiler and Robert Jones

Transactional writing is writing to get things done, to inform or persuade a particular audience to understand or do something. This most common category of school writing is also most commonly demanded in the world of work--in corporations, industries, and bureaucracies. In school such writing is exemplified by book reviews, term papers, laboratory reports, research projects, masters proposals, and doctoral dissertations; outside school, such writing takes the form of letters, memos, abstracts, summaries, proposals, reports, and planning documents of all kinds. Students who practice transactional forms of writing in their classroom will have lots of opportunities to practice it on their jobs. It is important, therefore, that students learn to do it well--clearly, correctly, concisely, coherently, and carefully.

We believe that all classroom teachers are, to some extent, language teachers. They all play a role in how students view writing; they play this role subtly when they make writing assignments and more obviously when they evaluate those assignments. How teachers assign and respond to transactional writing has a lot to do with whether or not students value it and how well they learn to produce it. Consider, for example, the following situations:

A paper is written as extra credit in a geography class; it is due at the end of the semester and has as its subject "The Forests of North America." The paper is mechanically competent (spelling and punctuation are fine), but the five pages of writing are unfocused, generalized, and superficial.

A take-home examination in history is handed in after being assigned the previous day. The paper has numerous spelling mistakes, misused commas, and a few fragment sentences. The answers, while not wrong, are general and wordy.

A technical report is turned in by a sophomore enrolled in a chemistry class; it is her first such report, and much of the information is presented incorrectly: the conclusion is at the end; the "discussion" is written in first person; no "abstract," "table of contents," nor "sub-headings" is provided.

For instructors under time and workload constraints, the easiest response to each "poor paper" is a low grade. However, while `D' and `F' are easy and common responses, they are not necessarily effective in changing behavior, nor really efficient--if succeeding papers show no improvement.

Grading poor writing has about the same effect as grading poor test answers; it measures the specific performance, but does not result in improved learning. Since writing is a skill which takes a long time to master fully, simply assigning low grades cannot be very effective writing pedagogy. Instructors who want to be more helpful in their responses to poor writing might begin by asking themselves questions about each writing assignment. The preceding three examples suggest some possible lines of inquiry.

The geography instructor might ask: (a) Did I ask the student to explore his topic with me in advance? (b) Did I (or anyone else) see or critique a first draft? (c) Did I ask for a first draft? (d) Have I explored the nature of library research with my class or this student? (e) What options have I left for the student, now that the semester is over?

The history professor might ask: (a) How long did the student spend writing this paper? (b) Are the mistakes due to ignorance or carelessness? (c) How many spelling mistakes, such as "thier" and "hisory," are really typos? (d) Is my best response an "F," a conference, or a request for revision? (e) Do I want to "test" the student's knowledge, "teach" academic discipline, or "motivate" the student to learn more history?

The chemistry teacher might ask: (a) Does this student know how science reports differ from history term papers? (b) Did I explain the requirements for this report orally or in writing? (c) Do my students know the logic behind scientific reporting? (d) Is the first person always forbidden in report writing? (e) Is my best response a low grade, a conference with the individual, or a conversation with the whole class?

Serious instructors *do* ask questions about the causes of poor student writing. They do not often find simple answers, though, because writing and the teaching of writing involve complicated processes. Teachers interested in better student writing must begin with questions such as these: What do I want my students to learn? How can I prepare my students to write better? How should I evaluate a piece of writing?

The following sections are intended to show how these questions might be answered.

Writing and Learning

We are all familiar with student writing problems, problems due to poor composing skills, insufficient knowledge, immature thinking, and lack of interest--to name a few. But what about the problems caused by teachers? Is it possible that some of the problems are teacher-centered rather than student-centered? We're thinking here about vague or poorly explained directions on a writing assignment; exam questions which make false assumptions about what students know or should know; assignments which do not challenge students and are perceived as dull, repetitious, or tedious; incomplete or harmful responses by teachers to student writing; and poor planning, timing, or sequencing of assignments. These are but some of the ways that teachers, without malice and with good intentions, may affect the quality of student writing by poor assignments and ill-considered response to that writing.

Teachers often spend days in preparation and even weeks (or units) talking about, demonstrating, and explaining information to students; the same teachers, however, may not spend much time thinking about how writing can assist in both the learning and evaluating of that information. For example, one social studies teacher told me that she made "essay question" assignments when she didn't have time to compose a good objective test. This is not necessarily a poor or lazy decision on the teacher's part- - depending, of course, on class context, among other things. In fact, the decision to ask for a long student answer from a brief teacher question seems to be a simple time trade-off when compared to a short student answer in response to a long teacher question. The objective test, so long in the making, is short in correcting; the essay test, short in the making, will be longer in correcting. But, of course, this decision involves something more complex than merely juggling time.

Asking for the student's answer *in writing* should be an important pedagogical decision, not simply a trade-off in time. In the objective test the teacher does most of the careful conceptual work, thinking through how best to create choices and how to word those choices. In the essay test, the situation is reversed, with the student being asked both to make choices and to choose the words. To *compose* something is a more demanding task--coordinating knowledge with both logic and rhetoric--for the student than simply *deciding* (or guessing at) something. Asking for a piece of writing involves students more profoundly in the learning process; they must demonstrate not only "knowledge" but also the ability to organize and explain that knowledge.

The teacher who asks "What do I want students to learn" will assign writing that is most likely to generate a specific form of learning. For example, different question types call for different kinds of responses. If we ask the "date" on which the Vietnam War started, the answer ought to be a matter of simple *recall*--something learned somewhere and now recalled. If we ask for a list of the chief "causes" of the war, recall is involved but also some choices and some *analysis* ("This cause is more important than that cause"). Third, if we ask about the relationship between the war and the women's movement, a great deal of information must be *synthesized* to arrive at a coherent, believable answer. Finally, if we ask whether it was right or wrong that America became involved in Vietnam, a judgment based on some standard or other is called for.

These four different test objectives--recall, analysis, synthesis, judgment-- suggest in concrete terms the manner in which the teacher's question determines the kind of thinking students must do. If it is important that social studies students learn to analyze, then teacher questions ought to reflect that; if humanities students must learn to express and defend value judgments, their teachers may aid that process by asking judgmental questions. Only in the area of simple recall would the essay seem to have little advantage over the short answer.

Preparing Assignments

Most teachers realize through personal experience that most acts of writing represent stages in a larger process: that is, whether the writing is an answer to an essay question, a preliminary draft of a formal paper, or a response to a class question, it represents only one point along a continuum. The poet William Wordsworth said that poetry is the "spontaneous overflow of emotion recollected in tranquility," but he still revised some of his poems dozens of times. Though we cannot ask for twelve revisions of a piece of student writing, we can learn an important principle from Wordsworth's practice: Any act of writing involves a multistage process of thinking, rethinking, writing, rewriting, and editing. We can and should provide an academic environment where students see this clearly.

General principles for making good assignments evolve directly from understanding the *process* of composition--what happens when human beings put words on paper. While each specific assignment depends on course content, teacher personality, student skills, and everybody's time and energy, teachers who keep the writing process in mind will help their students learn to write better.

When we stop to think about it, we quickly realize that the act of writing is complicated, certainly more involved than simply putting down on paper what's already in the writer's head. We seldom begin writing with well-formed sentences and paragraphs in our heads already. To understand the word "process" as applied to writing, it is only necessary to think through all the thoughts and activities associated with our own formal writing activities: we need to have (1) a purpose for writing in mind and (2) an audience to write to. We further need to (3) find an idea, (4) refine and incubate that idea, (5) write it down in words, (6) organize and reshape it, (7) try it out on a trial audience and receive feedback, which often necessitates (8) rewriting or revising that idea, (9) editing, and finally (10) proofreading- -then sometimes starting all over again because new information now modifies our prior assumptions. Of course, the writing process is not "Ten Steps" as this list implies, nor is it sequential and orderly, but these hypothetical steps do indicate some of the factors common to school writing tasks.

Teachers aware of the composing process use this knowledge in making, intervening in, and evaluating writing assignments. Consider the following suggestions:

1. Find out in advance how much students know and don't know about the kind of writing you are asking for. Do they know what a research paper is and how it differs from a book report or personal opinion paper? Discuss these differences.

2. Lead up to assignments with deliberate invention techniques, including oral brainstorming, free writing, and journal writing. Most of us who have graduated from college have learned, often the hard way, to write notes to ourselves, outline, and talk with others to get our writing started in the right direction; we can teach our students to use these techniques to start their writing assignments.

3. Try to stimulate personal involvement between writer and writing assignments. This can be done not only by giving a variety of choices in topics but also by engaging students in dialogues about potential topics and asking them to keep journals--dialogues with themselves--about what is important to them and what not.

4. Create class contexts for writing assignments so that the topic grows from a prepared culture. For example, bring in outside speakers on the topic, take context-producing field trips, assign and discuss relevant readings, and engage in a lot of clarifying class discussion.

5. Pose problems to the class--or ask the class to help pose problems. Use the blackboard or overhead projector liberally in this process so that problems in need

of written solution are visually clear and precise. Ask students to consider papers as "solutions" to these problems. This approach exemplifies what a "thesis" is and how it may be supported or proven.

6. Assign several short papers during the term rather than one long one at the end. You can find out an enormous amount about the students' grasp of conventions and organizing abilities in a two-page paper (300-500 words); assigning it means you will have more time to respond to each paper and to make suggestions that can be followed up in the next assignment.

7. Ask for multiple drafts of papers, if you have the chance--even short two-page papers become more effective learning projects when students are asked to (or allowed to) revise them according to specific critical suggestions.

8. Explain what you expect from each writing assignment in advance and evaluate accordingly. If you are concerned that students do a particular kind of research on an assignment, how well they report and explain that research ought to be the primary trait determining the students' grades. In an assignment meant to be carried through several drafts, the teacher can sequence these expectations: first draft is most concerned with organizing and structuring an idea; second draft is more concerned with use of supporting examples, and so on. Students should always understand clearly what is expected of them.

9. Show students models of student-written papers. This will give them a concrete sense of how the assignment might be fulfilled. Some teachers create files of good samples from previous classes; others use published examples; a very few show their own writing about the assignment to students. Models give students confidence that the assignment *can* be done because it *has* been done and show them that there might be several solutions to the writing problem.

10. If you get bored by sameness and dullness when reading a pile of student papers, make it clear when making an assignment that students who take some risks to be original will be rewarded--or at least not penalized. Some students will not trust you the first time on this, but passing out samples of successful "risk" papers may encourage the cautious to try new things.

    This discussion has been concerned primarily with formal writing assignments which students do outside of class. While the manner in which the teacher structures the assignment plays a significant role in how well the student handles the assignment, the students' responsibility is considerable; we expect their papers to display an organized knowledge of the topic in clear, concise, correct, and coherent prose. We must modify those expectations when we ask students to write in class.

Essay Tests

The essay examination is a common way to use writing in liberal arts classrooms. It provides teachers with a means of checking the student's knowledge and ideas while also determining whether the student can express them in a well organized manner. Though essay answers are usually first draft efforts, we often treat them otherwise. Professional writers do not expect correct error-free writing on first drafts. Neither should we. Essay examinations can be a sound educational tool, but, like more formal assignments the students must be prepared to take them.

Teachers can provide students with the opportunity to practice answering the questions and establish models and standards by which the writer's work will be evaluated. We would not expect the piano student to perform and be evaluated without practice and a chance to hear the piece played correctly. Yet many of us simply assume that our students know intuitively how to write clear answers to complex questions.

The following suggestions, based on work with teachers in various disciplines, are designed to help students understand better what is expected on essay examinations.

Sample question. Provide a few minutes of class time occasionally to write an answer to a sample essay question. If the essay examinations you give are based on class discussions, this practice can match the overall goals for any given course. For example, an ecology class may have been discussing the conflict of pollution and progress in a town which suffers from acute unemployment. Asking the student to take a few minutes to organize in writing the particulars of each position not only helps them clarify their perceptions of the conflict, but also helps them master the facts involved. Do they recall what studies have shown? Are they arguing from the facts rather than from the situation or *ad hominum?*

Peer groups. Ask students to share practice essay questions either in pairs or in small groups of three or four. Pairing and grouping of students encourages active learning. Too often lecture and textbook are our students' only access to information. When students can share ideas in small discussion groups, they are often more willing to inform, persuade, and challenge each other than they would be before an entire class.

Homework. Give a question as homework and then briefly go over the answers, making few comments. Without actually grading the paper, you can in a nonthreatening way simply acknowledge that a student has completed an assignment. You need not stress the same types of comments on each set of papers. Tell the students one time that you're looking closely at organization, another time that you are concerned with sentence construction. Over time the students will receive much needed practice in writing, which subtly enhances grammatical and mechanical competence as well as composition proficiency.

Model answers. Write an answer to a sample question before asking the students to answer it and share your effort with the class. Students are fond of this practice for several reasons. First, they see that you are willing to do the assignments that you require of them. Second, they get an idea of how a professional responds to this type of assignment; thus, they follow a model which demonstrates the fusing of both information and acceptable form. Third, they have a chance to critique the teacher's work, while the teacher has the advantage of seeing the assignment from the student's perspective. (Was the question clear? How hard was it for you to answer? Did you spend longer writing the answer than you expected?) In short, taking the role of the writer benefits both teacher and student.

Student samples. Show samples of student writing which exemplify strengths and weaknesses. Especially when viewed on an overhead or opaque projector, these papers provide a strong focus for comments from students and teacher. Moreover, you can clearly label strengths and note such problems as redundant words or ideas. Overhead projection of sample papers saves time because you don't have to create and pass out dittoed papers.

Expectations. Discuss with the students how different questions call for different kinds of reasoning; point out that "what" and "when" questions usually demand recall, while "how" and "why" questions usually demand more complicated types of thinking--analysis, synthesis, or judgment. Clarify to both your students and yourself what you want when you ask students to "discuss" or "explain"--each of these directions can be ambiguous.

The essay examination is a good means of testing students' knowledge, but without adequate preparation it can also be a source of frustration to both teacher and student. As the student becomes better prepared to write a soundly developed, clearly written answer, that frustration lessens. One last caution: No matter how much we prepare our students to write sound answers to essay questions, those answers will seldom match the quality of ones on which the students can spend more time revising and editing. The essay question asks for certain reasoning and writing skills; but it does not provide writers with a chance to demonstrate their comprehensive writing abilities as do more formal writing assignments.

Preparing students to write better by attending to the writing process both in class and out goes a long way toward improving student writing. However, viewing writing as a "process" also modifies some traditional notions of evaluation. In the final section of this chapter we consider a variety of evaluative responses.

Evaluating Student Writing

Like "assignment making," the concept of "evaluation" makes a different kind of sense when placed in the context of writing as a process. just as writing makes more sense when conceived with a variety of *audiences* in mind, from oneself through peers and the distant public, so too does evaluation make more sense when related to the various audiences that a piece of writing might have.

1. Students can learn certain response techniques to evaluate their own writing. (Teacher provided guide sheets, regularly required revision, etc.)

2. Students can learn to respond in nonthreatening, nonjudgmental ways to each other's writing. ("I was interested in this ... I want more information on that.")

3. Teachers can explore nongraded responses to help students through different phases of the writing process. ("Can you elaborate on your argument on page two?")

4. Students can write for real public audiences and receive "evaluation" through an editor's acceptance or rejection. (Letters to the editor, essays in a school publication, professional newsletters, etc.)

Another way of looking at responses to writing, again suggested by a study of the whole composing process, is to consider what function, exactly, a piece of writing is meant to serve. Depending on what assignment a teacher makes, evaluation might take one form rather than another. For example, a teacher who asks for a research project due late in the term may incorporate evaluative responses at various steps along the way, as different aspects of research are undertaken by the students: library search techniques, information categorizing, documenting procedures, presentation of evidence, and so on. Each step in the process may suggest one critical intervention rather than another, including, for example, self-paced library worksheets, teacher review of research proposals, and peer critique of rough drafts. Or, by contrast, a teacher response to pieces of writing produced by an examination situation might require (traditionally) a single grade marked on the paper or (experimentally) a request for individual or collaborative revision and resubmission. In other words, a writing task suggests evaluative response.

The two major determiners that shape a piece of writing, audience and function, should determine the response to that piece of writing. Teachers who are aware of other parts of the composing process can also discover other appropriate points of intervention. At the conceptual stage, for example, large group brainstorming and small group critiques can help individual student writers get started. At the terminal stage of "proofreading," paired paper exchanges immediately prior to paper submission can help students eliminate annoying small errors. This helps (speeds) teacher reading and also teaches a valuable real-life writing technique, sharing a piece of writing with a colleague or spouse before sending it to a professional editor.

At the Michigan Tech writing workshops we commonly discuss principles of response and evaluation which teachers should keep in mind as they comment on and grade student papers. The following list of guidelines is the result of a discussion among a group of college teachers representing different disciplines across the campus:

1. Give positive feedback wherever possible. Even the most error-filled paper usually has something redeeming about it, a place where the writer, once encouraged, can get a new start. None of us feels like reworking a piece when nothing good is said about it.

2. Do not grade early drafts of a writing assignment. Putting a grade on a paper you want students to keep working on shuts down the incentive to revise; they read that shorthand evaluation ("D") rather than your written words. Grading something suggests finality and almost guarantees that the learning process, in this situation, has stopped.

3. Respond with specific suggestions for improvement wherever you can. "AWK" or "OUCH!" or "YUK" go only so far in telling the student what to do to make it better.

4. Create simple guidelines or self-critique sheets to help students respond more critically to their own writing--this may save you time in the long run if they become adept at catching some of their own errors. Such sheets might ask, for

example: What is your point? What is your pattern of organization? Have you supported all generalizations with specific examples? Do you avoid wordy construction, repetitious phrases, and clichés? Have you proofread for errors in spelling, punctuation, or typing?

5. Plan personal conferences for difficult or sensitive problems. In some cases, no amount of written commentary will bridge the gap between you and a misunderstanding student. The personal conference creates a human dimension to evaluation that writing cannot duplicate.

6. Give students some responsibility for evaluating each other's work; remember that each writer also benefits from becoming a critic and editor. (Guideline sheets similar to those in no. 4 work for pairs and small groups too.)

7. Don't separate form from content. Most writing is all of a piece; when a proposition is awkwardly stated it is often poorly understood. Consider the written expression as an integral part of the mental process; that way students will learn how the real world will, in fact, respond to them. (Consider also the appearance of a piece of writing as, to some extent, analogous to that which the writer personally presents to the world: sloppy and smudged or careful and clear?)

This chapter suggests that there is an important relationship between what we know about the composing process and (1) what we ask for on writing assignments, (2) how we prepare students to write our assignments, and (3) how we evaluate the writing that results. We feel confident that teachers who explore these relationships and translate them into solid pedagogical strategies will help their students write better formal papers and, at the same time, increase their students' abilities to reason and understand.

Improving Our Responses to Student Writing: A Process-Oriented Approach

Leonard A. and Joanne M. Podis

"Awk!" "Frag." "Unity?" "Coh." Such are the response symbols on which composition instructors have traditionally been reared. Of course many writing teachers have come to reject such responses and the evaluative approach to commentary they bespeak, viewing them as useless (Knoblauch and Brannon, "Teacher Commentary" 285-88), if not downright harmful (Hartwell 9). In recent years a significant number of instructors have adopted more thoughtful, enlightened attitudes in commenting on student writing, in some cases not merely eschewing the strictly evaluative response, but going so far as to "deconstruct" drafts in order to perceive student intentions so that these may be "mapped onto later drafts" (Comprone). It is just such a "deconstructionist" approach that we would like to set forth in this essay, although our method rather than consciously drawing on post-modernist literary theory, emphasize the attitude of the error analyst in responding to writing (Shaughnessy; Kroll and Schafer; Bartholomae). We hope the essay will also constitute a step toward taxonomizing some of the more process-oriented responses to student writing.

A brief survey of recent literature on responding to student writing indicate that the dominant model for instructors' comments is still the traditional evaluative response. In their first of several statements on the subject, for example Knoblauch and Brannon reported that product-centered, judgmental response have overwhelmingly remained the norm; they noted, "Our assumption has been that evaluating the product of composing is equivalent to intervening in the process" ("Teacher Commentary" 288). Even less flattering to our profession was Nancy Sommers' "Responding to Student Writing"(148-56). In the responses of the instructors whose work she studied, Sommers found "hostility and meanspiritedness" (149). Moreover, she judged most comments to be confusing to students because they failed to differentiate between low-level an high-level textual problems. In a follow-up to their earlier article, Brannon and Knoblauch concluded that instructors tended in their responses to appropriate students' texts, devaluing them in relation to some "Ideal Text" the instructor had in mind ("On Students' Rights" 158-59). Knoblauch and Brannon's most recent treatment of the subject discusses at length the type of "facilitative commentary" that might profitably replace the traditional evaluative response (*Rhetorical Traditions* 126-30). They appear to endorse Sommer's belief that "We need to develop an appropriate level of response for commenting on a first draft ..." (155).

In our approach, instructors encourage student potential by identifying draft weaknesses and interpreting them in the light of recent findings about the composing

Leonard A. Podis and Joanne M. Podis. "Improving Our Responses to Student Writing: A Process-Oriented Approach," *Rhetoric Review*, Vol. 5, No. 1, Fall 1986, pp. 90-98. Reprinted with permission.

process. Specifically, we propose that, by analogy to the work of those who practice error analysis, writing instructors routinely undertake close readings of student drafts in order to pinpoint rhetorical or structural problems that might signal legitimate intentions rather than simple failure or inadequacy. Although draft weaknesses are not technically "errors" in the same sense as syntactic or grammatical problems, we believe that the *attitude* involved in error analysis--the desire to comprehend the mental process that underlies some evidence of difficulty in creating a discourse--is appropriate in reading and responding to the writing of learners. We have recognized that many textual weaknesses represent useful stages in the writer's composing process. Such an approach seems particularly valid in light of the work of process advocates and researchers, who tell us that normal composing often includes the production of incomplete or flawed drafts (Murray; Hairston 85-86). Our method, then, calls for instructors to approach draft difficulties as potential keys to understanding student writers' intentions, and in some cases as keys to helping the writers better define their intentions in their own minds.

We have chosen three examples to illustrate our method and to provide the beginnings of a taxonomy for this kind of response. In addition, in our conclusion we briefly identify several more kinds of draft weaknesses and suggest appropriate responses. Each of the three main examples was selected because we believed it represented some issue that teachers of writing may face while responding to student drafts and because we were successful in guiding revision by first identifying a draft weakness and then interpreting it as resulting from a healthy difficulty in composing. In each case we explain what the initial problem was, how we interpreted it as signifying a potentially legitimate difficulty in composing, how we responded, and what happened in subsequent revisions.

Our first example begins with a paragraph written in a basic writing course, addressing the topic of "an unreasonable assignment made at school or work." We can see that the student began with the intention of discussing unreasonable math assignments but then moved away from that idea:

> I had a math teacher in junior high named Mr. Douglas that I thought gave a lot of homework. Maybe it was because I didn't like math that much. I feel as you get older you start to realize that you have to have some sort of responsibility. In a way I think homework is a form of responsibility. In my first year of high school I hardly ever did any homework and barely passed. In my junior year I did a little better because I started realizing that homework was important. At the end of my junior year I told myself that I was going to put homework first on my priority list as far as school work went. I never really had an unreasonable assignment made at school. I think I was blessed will some good teachers in my first 12 years of school.

If we evaluate this paragraph according to traditional standards, we must judge it as disorganized and uncertain in focus, particularly in relation to the assignment it was addressing. It is the type of writing that can all to easily lead a composition instructor to resort to the "mean-spirited" marginal comments that Nancy Sommers found so prevalent in her study. However, a closer look at the paragraph's major flaws shows that the rambling organization and uncertain focus, while they make for a weak text, do appear to be leading the student to some kind of understanding about his school career. Starting with sentence three, we can detect a group of sentences that apparently leads the writer toward the realization that his attitude about assignments changed. Sensing this possibility, the instructor decided not to concentrate on the paragraph's weakness as a sign of failure, but rather as a potential reflection of a healthy difficulty in composing, as the messy residue that can accompany writing as discovery. In so doing, the instructor decided against urging the student to revise in order to create her own "Ideal Text"--one that would discuss "an unreasonable assignment made at school." Instead, she responded by noting that the paragraph suggested the student had learned something important about assignments while in school, and that the writing seemed to be helping him to discover what it was he had learned.

The instructor's response, then, was not a negative evaluation of the paragraph but an assurance to the student that the paragraph was indeed a good way to have *begun* his composing, though it was not necessarily a good finished product. Instead of strongly criticizing the paragraph, she conveyed a positive message about it and emphasized the new awareness the student had reached through the act of writing it. She concluded by asking the student to revise. The following is his second draft:

> I guess I never really had an unreasonable assignment made at school, although sometimes they seemed unreasonable to me. In junior high school I did think my ninth-grade math teacher gave an awful lot of homework, but maybe it was because I didn't like math that much and didn't understand the importance of school work. Over the years I realized that homework is important and should be put on the priority list as far as school goes. It's no coincidence that I started getting better grades once I changed my attitude. Now that I'm older I can look back and say none of my assignments was unreasonable. They helped teach me a sense of responsibility.

The second version is better organized and has a clearer focus. It could, of course, be improved further. However, it shows that the student, having been encouraged to view his original paragraph as a promising draft rather than a flawed text, has begun to understand how he can improve both his writing and his awareness of the process that effective writers often follow.

Our second example focuses on another common student text weakness, plot summary in the critical essay on literature. It can perhaps be most usefully understood as a manifestation of what Linda Flower and John Hayes call "writer-based" prose, prose which uses patterns borrowed, in the case of plot summary, "from a structure inherent in the material the writers examined" (459).

This student's initial text was laden with sections in which she retold parts of Faulkner's "The Bear," adding few interpretive remarks and seemingly allowing the story to speak for itself. In this case the instructor's initial response was more traditional. He had disparaged the paper as a poor critical essay that substituted plot summary for interpretation.

Bringing her marked paper with her to her conference, the student expressed her frustration with comments in the margin about the need to avoid summarizing the plot. That advice, she said, is what her English teachers had always given her, but she couldn't understand how it was possible to do what they told her to. How, she asked, could she write any generalizations about the story when she didn't know what they were until she worked through some of the important parts of the plot on paper? Her method had been to choose instinctively the events she felt to be important and to let her discussion of them lead her to an understanding of them. By writing down exactly what happened, in the order it happened, she clarified, even discovered, the meaning of the material. What she had not realized was that her weak "finished papers" might be legitimate discovery drafts. For her, the chief effect of the instructor's plot-summary comment was to make her doubt the value of the *way she was composing* as much as the text she composed.

Reconsidering her paper, the instructor attempted to understand how its chief weakness might reflect some legitimate problem of composing. For this writer, it occurred to him, retelling the plot was apparently a necessary stage in invention. Thus she was perplexed by responses that criticized her own approach and enjoined her to "put generalizations first" She apparently needed a response that initially *valued* her plot summarizing as a useful drafting technique,but then recommend a revision in which the plot summary, having served its heuristic purpose, would be condensed or eliminated to create a more presentable finished paper.

In her revision she was in fact able to pare down her retelling of the story and to add more interpretive generalizations about the importance of the episodes she did discuss. The problem finally did not rest in her inability to interpret the story or to express herself. It rested in her inability to function well within the traditional single-submission, evaluative-response system, for given only one chance at drafting, she had an inability to distinguish between the written record of an invention technique and an acceptable finished text.

Writer-based prose such as plot summary may be a natural stage in the process of learning to write more effectively, but both students and instructors need to be aware of this before students can improve. Moreover, the nature of the instructor's response is often crucial in determining whether a student such as the one just discussed will come to recognize the distinction between a discovery draft and a completed paper.

Our final extended example is somewhat similar to the first one we discussed in that the student apparently failed to do the assignment requested of her. But the reasons in this instance were much different. In such a case we've found it's important for the instructor to tailor a response by first attempting to determine the writer's intentions. Whether the assignment is completed unsatisfactorily because of an honest misunderstanding, because of ineptitude, or because of chicanery, for instance, should make a big difference in the instructors response to it. In our example the instructor learned that the student's first draft signified her attempt to negotiate a rhetorical situation complicated enough that she could not accomplish her aim without some further guidance.

The following paragraph is the introduction to a four-page draft in which the student apparently failed to respond adequately to the assignment her women's studies instructor had given her. She was to interview an older working woman and then write an essay analyzing the pressures that woman had faced during her career, The opening paragraph reflects the content or the draft:

> Mrs. Thelma Morton Arnold has worked for Oberlin College for thirty years. In December of 1981, she was promoted from the position of dormitory custodian to that of supervisor of dorm custodians on the north end of campus. Last week, Mrs. Arnold talked with me about her life.

Essentially, the paper that followed was a straight biography of Mrs. Arnold with no apparent analysis of any pressures she had encountered. Significantly, there were passages in the draft that could be construed as bearing on career pressures, but the writer herself didn't seem to recognize their relevance. The instructor noted these points in his initial response.

In conference, the student confided that she in fact knew her draft had evaded the issue. Apparently she had avoided explicitly analyzing the pressures in Mrs. Arnold's career because she had promised to let Mrs. Arnold read the paper that would result from the interview. Mrs. Arnold was such a trusting, pleasant woman that the student could not bring herself to do what she regarded as a "cold, clinical analysis" of her life. She was so uncomfortable with this notion, in fact, that she was willing to accept a low grade in her women's studies course to avoid displeasing Mrs. Arnold and embarrassing herself.

In this case the student had written the paper mainly to one audience--Mrs. Arnold--because she assumed that writing more to her other audience--her women's studies instructor--would ruin the paper for Mrs. Arnold. Her composition instructor attempted to convince her that it was possible for her to juggle the expectations and demands of both audiences, to please both Mrs. Arnold and the women's studies instructor. If she could see herself at some point in the role of the *lab-coated clinician*. but at other points in the role of, say, the *main speaker at a testimonial dinner* for Mrs. Arnold, she might be able to satisfy both audiences. Here is the opening paragraph of her revision:

> Mrs. Thelma Morton Arnold has worked for Oberlin College for thirty years. In December of 1981, she was promoted from the position of dormitory custodian to that of supervisor of dorm custodians on the north end of campus. As a black working woman, she has faced discriminatory pressures in choosing her occupation, as well as in her attempts to earn promotions and equal pay. She has fought to overcome these pressures and gain just treatment for herself and others.

While the first two sentences of this paragraph are the same as in the earlier version, the third sentence of the earlier version--"Last week, Mrs. Arnold talked with me about her life"- -has been replaced with two sentences, each of which represents a nod toward one of the two competing audiences. Sentence three of the new version is aimed at the instructor, for it encapsulates the analysis of pressures which is to come in the paper. Sentence four, on the other hand, prefigures the tone of praise which will also characterize the paper to come.

Having conferred with her composition instructor, the student was able to revise in such a way that her dilemma was solved. Her first draft represented her view of a problem which she was unsure of handling. In one sense her attempt reflected a genuine strength: She had chosen a single audience toward which to write, a legitimate intention underlying the weakness in her draft. To make the most helpful response in this instance, the instructor needed to recognize another facet of the composing process, one also stressed by proponents of the new pedagogy: that writing does in fact occur in the context of a rhetorical situation.

In our examples we have examined three types of draft weaknesses: uncertainty of focus, plot summary in the critical essay, and lack of attention to some aspect of the assignment. In all cases, the weaknesses in the initial drafts resulted either from difficulties related to writing as a process of discovery, or from an inability to negotiate a particular rhetorical situation. In each instance we were able to respond most helpfully to our students by interpreting their difficulties as evidence of legitimate attempts to deal with the complexities of composing.

We want to suggest some other possible situations in which our approach would help students revise their work. For example, the student narrative, whether written about historical events for a history class or about personal experiences for a composition class, will often feature an over abundance of short, simple sentences and a lack of subordination and complicating modification. Rather than simply indicating a weak style or even an inability to interpret the material, such writing often stems from the student's respect for reporting the verifiable facts related to a given event. In other words, some students produce flat, deadpan narratives, not because of limited verbal ability or inadequate analytic powers, but because they believe they are doing the right thing in producing what they consider to be a camera-copy of reality. Probably the most helpful response in such a case is to correct the students view of the purpose of such writing, to clarify what the audience's demands and expectations really are, as opposed to what the student supposes them to be.

Similarly, consider the case of the student paper which is written in overblown generalities and which makes use of pompous academese. Typical responses to such writing urge the use of more concrete details and specific examples, which is certainly fine advice. Yet the most effective response may be the one which recognizes that the student's writing has resulted from a belief that his or her audience values overblown generalities, and which then attempts to clarify the student's picture of the audience.

The often artificial nature of the classroom setting may also create difficulties in students whose concern for the form of an assignment may override any considerations of what they actually have to say. They then produce writing which employs the required "comparison-contrast" or "descriptive" modes, as the case may be, but which is woefully inadequate in terms of content and style. We have found that by discussing with students their motivations for choosing, for example, a given pattern of development, we can determine whether students made their selections after following sound invention strategies, or whether they selected on the basis of pressure to turn in papers which fit the required form. If the latter is true, then an effective revision may result after the student is counseled to follow better heuristics for invention.

Digressions are another common text weakness, the exploration of which may lead to an improved product. In our experience digressions sometimes signal that a writer's thinking has moved in a potentially more interesting or valuable direction. Discussing with students the way in which writing can encourage thinking, and suggesting that perhaps that is why a particular digression occurred, may lead them to realize that they are just beginning the writing process for a paper they assumed was completed. In short, the apparent digression may actually represent a fruitful line of inquiry stimulated by the composing process itself. We have seen many cases where students have successfully revised their work by refocusing it on ideas initially thought to be "digressions."

Finally, students who produce drafts with repetitive ideas couched in somewhat different terms have generally been criticized for producing texts weak in both structure and content. But is their repetition always the sign of a tenuous grasp of exposition and a paucity of ideas, or might it reflect a more positive attempt to try out different ways of saying something in an effort to achieve greater clarity or effect? Might not a repetitive discourse sometimes reflect a healthy attempt to achieve a fuller command of style and substance?

Certainly for some instructors this method of interpreting draft difficulties in order to understand the mental processes that gave rise to a writer's problems is not completely new. Particularly those instructors who teach process-oriented courses featuring multiple drafts and revisions may already be reading and responding to drafts in ways similar to those we have recommended. Still, the findings of Sommers and Brannon and Knoblauch suggest that our profession as a whole is far from adopting such "facilitative" approaches to commentary. We believe that, with further attempts to identify and codify various categories of draft weaknesses matched with the kind of comments we have recommended above, our profession can make successful inroads against the domain of the evaluative response.

Note on the article's authorship as of 1986: Leonard A. Podis was directing the Expository Writing Program at Oberlin College. JoAnne M. Podis was serving as Provost, Dean of Instruction, and Professor of English at Dyke College. They have, singly or in collaboration, authored numerous pieces in the areas of rhetoric, language, and literature, including *Writing: Invention, Form, and Style* (Scott, Foresman 1984) and articles in journals including *College Composition and Communication, Style, Studies in Short Fiction,* and *Theater Annual.* They had recently they been serving as consultants for new programs in writing across the curriculum. They were also (perhaps not surprisingly) planning to begin a study of collaborative authorship.

Works Cited

Bartholomae, David. "The Study of Error." *CCC* 31 (1980): 253-69

Brannon. Lil, and C.H. Knoblauch. "On Students' Rights to Their Own Texts: A Model of Teacher Response." *CCC* 33 (1982) 157- 66.

Comprone, Joseph J. "Recent Literary and Composition Theory: Readerly and Writerly Texts." Presented at the Conference on College Composition and Communication, Minneapolis, 21 March 1985.

Flower Linda, and John Hayes. "Problem-Solving Strategies and the Writing Process." *CE* 39 (1977): 449-61.

388   Designing, Responding to, Evaluating Writing Assignments

Hairston, Maxine. "The Winds of Change: Thomas Kuhn and the Revolution in the Teaching of writing." *CCC* 33 (1982): 76- 78.

Hartwell, Patrick. "Paradoxes and Problems: The Value of Traditional Textbook Rules." *Pennsylvania Writing Project Newsletter 3* (1983): 7-9.

Knoblauch, C.H., and Lil Brannon. "Teacher Commentary on Student Writing: The State of the Art." *Rhetoric and Composition: A Sourcebook for Teachers and Writers.* Ed. Richard L. Graves 2nd ed. Upper Montclair, NJ: Boynton/Cook, 1984: 285-91.

_____. *Rhetorical Traditions and the Teaching of Writing.* Upper Montclair, NJ: Boynton/Cook, 1984

Kroll, Barry M., and John C. Schafer. "Error Analysis and the Teaching of Composition." *CCC* 29 (1978): 243-48

Murray, Donald C. "Internal Revision: A Process of Discovery." *Research on Composing: Points of Departure.* Ed. Charles R. Cooper and Lee Odell. Urbana, IL: NCTE, 1978.

Shaughnessy, Mina. Errors and Expectations. New York: Oxford UP, 1977.

Sommers, Nancy. "Responding to Student Writing." CCC 33 (1982): 148-56.

Ranking, Evaluating, and Liking:
Sorting Out Three Forms of Judgment
Peter Elbow

This essay is my attempt to sort out different acts we call assessment--some different ways in which we express or frame our judgments of value. I have been working on this tangle not just because it is interesting and important in itself but because assessment tends so much to drive and control *teaching*. Much of what we do in the classroom is determined by the assessment structures we work under.

Assessment is a large and technical area and I'm not a professional. But my main premise or subtext in this essay is that we nonprofessionals can and should work on it because professionals have not reached definitive conclusions about the problem of how to assess writing (or anything else, I'd say). Also, decisions about assessment are often made by people even less professional than we, namely legislators. Pat Belanoff and I realized that the field of assessment was open when we saw the harmful effects of a writing proficiency exam at Stony Brook and worked out a collaborative portfolio assessment system in its place (Belanoff and Elbow; Elbow and Belanoff). Professionals keep changing their minds about large-scale testing and assessment. And as for classroom grading, psychometricians provide little support or defense of it.

THE PROBLEMS WITH RANKING AND THE BENEFITS OF EVALUATING

By ranking I mean the act of summing up one's judgment of a performance or person into a single, holistic number or score. We rank every time we give a grade or holistic score. Ranking implies a single scale or continuum or dimension along which all performances are hung.

By evaluating I mean the act of expressing one's judgment of a performance or person by pointing out the strengths and weaknesses of different features or dimensions. We evaluate every time we write a comment on a paper or have an conversation about its value. Evaluation implies the recognition of different criteria or dimensions--and by implication different contexts and audiences for the same performance. Evaluation requires going *beyond* a first response that may be nothing but a kind of ranking ("I like it" or "This is better than that"), and instead looking carefully enough at the performance or person to make distinctions between parts or features or criteria.

It's obvious, thus, that I am troubled by ranking. But I will resist any temptation to argue that we can get rid of all ranking--or even should. Instead I will try to show how we can have *less* ranking and *more* evaluation in its place.

I see three distinct problems with ranking: it is inaccurate or unreliable; it gives no substantive feedback; and it is harmful to the atmosphere for teaching and learning.

(1) First the unreliability. To rank reliably means to give a fair number, to find the single quantitative score that readers will agree on. But readers don't agree. This is not news--this unavailability of agreement. We have long seen it on many fronts. For example, research in evaluation has shown many times that if we give a paper to a set of readers, those readers tend to give it the full range of grades (Diederich). I've recently come across new research to this effect--new to me because it was published in 1912. The investigators carefully showed how high school English teachers gave different grades to the same paper. In response to criticism that this was a local problem in English, they went on the next year to discover an even greater variation among grades given by high school geometry teachers and history teachers to papers in their subjects. (See the summary of Daniel Starch and Edward Elliott's 1913 *School Review* articles in Kirschenbaum, Simon, and Napier 258-59.)

We know the same thing from literary criticism and theory. If the best critics can't agree about what a text means, how can we be surprised that they disagree even more about the quality or value of texts? And we know that nothing in literary or philosophical theory gives us any agreed-upon rules for settling such disputes.

Students have shown us the same inconsistency with their own controlled experiments of handing the same paper to different teachers and getting different grades. This helps explain why we hate it so when students ask us their favorite question, "What do you want for an A?": it rubs our noses in the unreliability of our grades.

Of course champions of holistic scoring argue that they get *can* get agreement among readers--and they often do (White). But they get that agreement by "training" the readers before and during the scoring sessions. What "training" means is getting those scorers to stop reading the way they normally read--getting them to stop using the conflicting criteria and standards they normally use outside the scoring sessions. (In an impressive and powerful book, Barbara Herrnstein Smith argues that whenever we have widespread inter-reader reliability, we have reason to suspect that difference has been suppressed and homogeneity imposed--almost always at the expense of certain groups.) In short, the reliability in holistic scoring is not a measure of how texts are valued by real readers in natural settings, but only of how they are valued in artificial settings with imposed agreements.

Defenders of holistic scoring might reply (as one anonymous reviewer did), that holistic scores are not perfect or absolutely objective readings but just "judgments that most readers will agree are the appropriate ones given the purpose of the assessment and the system of communication." But I have been in and even conducted enough holistic scoring sessions to know that even that degree of agreement doesn't occur unless "purpose" and "appropriateness" are defined to mean acceptance of the single set of standards imposed on that session. We know too much about the differences among readers and the highly variable nature of the reading process. Supposing we get readings only from academics, or only from people in English, or only from respected critics, or only from respected writing programs, or only from feminists, or only from sound readers of my tribe (white, male, middle-class, full professors between the ages of fifty and sixty). We *still* don't get agreement. We can sometimes get agreement among readers from some subset, a particular community that has developed a strong set of common values, perhaps one English department or *one* writing program. But what is the value of such a rare agreement? It tells us nothing about how readers from other English departments or writing programs will judge- -much less how readers from other domains will judge.

(From the opposite ideological direction, some skeptics might object to my skeptical train of thought: "So what else is new?" they might reply. "Of *course* my grades are biased, `interested' or `situated'--always partial to my interests or the values of my community or culture. There's no other possibility." But how can people consent to give grades if they feel that way? A single teacher's grade for a student is liable to have substantial consequences--for example on eligibility for a scholarship or a job or entrance into professional school. In grading, surely we must not take anything less than genuine fairness as our goal.)

It won't be long before we see these issues argued in a court of law, when a student who has been disqualified from playing on a team or rejected from a professional school sues, charging that the basis for his plight--teacher grades--is not reliable. I wonder if lawyers will be able to make our grades stick.

(2) Ranking or grading is woefully uncommunicative. Grades and holistic scores are nothing but points on a continuum from "yea" to "boo"--with no information or clues about the criteria behind these noises. They are 100 percent evaluation and 0 percent description or information. They quantify the degree of approval or disapproval in readers but tell nothing at all about what the readers actually approve or disapprove of. They say nothing that couldn't be said with gold stars or black marks or smiley-faces. Of course our first reactions are often nothing but global holistic feelings of approval or disapproval, but we need a system for communicating our judgments that nudges us to move beyond these holistic feelings and to articulate the basis of our feeling--a process that often leads us to change our feeling. (Holistic scoring sessions sometimes use rubrics that explain the criteria--though these are rarely passed along to students--and even in these situations, the rubrics fail to fit many papers.) As C.S. Lewis says, "People are obviously far more anxious to express their approval and disapproval of things than to describe them" (7).

(3) Ranking leads students to get so hung up on these oversimple quantitative verdicts that they care more about scores than about learning--more about the grade we put on the paper than about the comment we have written on it. Have you noticed how grading often forces us to write comments to justify our grades?--and how these are often not the comment we would make if we were just trying to help the student write better? ("Just try writing several favorable comments on a paper and then giving it a grade of D" [Diederich 21].)

Grades and holistic scores give too much encouragement to those students who score high--making them too apt to think they are already fine--and too little encouragement to those students who do badly. Unsuccessful students often come to doubt their intelligence. But oddly enough, many "A" students also end up doubting their true ability and feeling like frauds--because they have sold out on their own judgment and simply given teachers whatever yields an A. They have too often been rewarded for what they don't really believe in. (Notice that there's more cheating by students who get high grades than by those who get low ones. There would be less incentive to cheat if there were no ranking.)

We might be tempted to put up with the inaccuracy or unfairness of grades if they gave good diagnostic feedback or helped the learning climate; or we might put up with the damage they do to the learning climate if they gave a fair or reliable measure of how skilled or knowledgeable students are. But since they fail dismally on both counts, we are faced with the striking question of why grading has persisted so long.

There must be many reasons. It is obviously easier and quicker to express a global feeling with a single number than to figure out what the strengths and weaknesses are and what one's criteria are. (Though I'm heartened to discover, as I pursue this issue, how troubled teachers are by grading and how difficult they find it.) But perhaps more important, we see around us a deep *hunger to rank*--to create pecking orders: to see who we can look down on and who we must look up to, or in the military metaphor, who we can kick and who we must salute. Psychologists tell us that this taste for pecking orders or ranking is associated with the authoritarian personality. We see this hunger graphically in the case of IQ scores. It is plain that IQ scoring does not represent a commitment to looking carefully at people's intelligence; when we do that, we see different and frequently uncorrelated *kinds* or *dimensions* of intelligence (Gardner). The persistent use of IQ scores represents the hunger to have a number so that everyone can have a rank. ("Ten!" mutter the guys when they see a pretty woman.)

Because ranking or grading has caused so much discomfort to so many students and teachers, I think we see a lot of confusion about the process. It is hard to think clearly about something that has given so many of us such anxiety and distress. The most notable confusion I notice is the tendency to think that if we renounce ranking or grading, we are renouncing the very possibility of judgment and discrimination--that we are embracing the idea that there is no way to distinguish or talk about the difference between what works well and what works badly.

So the most important point, then, is that *I am not arguing against judgment or evaluation.* I'm just arguing against that crude, oversimple way of *representing* judgment--distorting it, really--into a single number, which means ranking people and performances along a single continuum.

In fact I am arguing *for evaluation.* Evaluation means looking hard and thoughtfully at a piece of writing in order to make distinctions as to the quality of different features or dimensions. For example, the process of evaluation permits us to make the following kinds of statements about a piece of writing:

- The thinking and ideas seem interesting and creative.

- The overall structure or sequence seems confusing.

- The writing is perfectly clear at the level of individual sentences and even paragraphs. There is an odd, angry tone of voice that seems unrelated or inappropriate to what the writer is saying.

- Yet this same voice is strong and memorable and makes one listen even if one is irritated.

- There are a fair number of mistakes in grammar or spelling: more than "a sprinkling" but less than "riddled with."

To rank, on the other hand, is to be forced to translate those discriminations into a single number. What grade or holistic score do these judgments add up to? It's likely, by the way, that more readers would agree with those separate, "analytic" statements than would agree on a holistic score.

I've conducted many assessment sessions where we were not trying to impose a set of standards but rather to find out how experienced teachers read and evaluate, and I've had many opportunities to see that good readers give grades or scores right down through the range of possibilities. Of course good readers sometimes agree--especially on papers that are strikingly good or bad or conventional, but I think I see difference more frequently than agreement when readers really speak up.

The process of evaluation, because it invites us to articulate our criteria and to make distinctions among parts or features or dimensions of a performance, thereby invites us further to acknowledge the main fact about evaluation: that different readers have different priorities, values, and standards.

The conclusion I am drawing, then, in this first train of thought is that we should do less ranking and more evaluation. Instead of using grades or holistic scores-- single number verdicts that try to sum up complex performances along only one scale-- we should give some kind of written or spoken evaluation that discriminates among criteria and dimensions of the writing- -and if possible that takes account of the complex context for writing: who the writer is, what the writer's audience and goals are, who we are as readers and how we read, and how we might differ in our reading from other readers the writer might be addressing.

But how can we put this principle into practice? The pressure for ranking seems implacable. Evaluation takes more time, effort, and money. It seems as though we couldn't get along without scores on writing exams. Most teachers are obliged to give grades at the end of each course. And many students--given that they have become conditioned or even addicted to ranking over the years and must continue to inhabit a ranking culture in most of their courses--will object if we don't put grades on papers. Some students, in the absence of that crude gold star or black mark, may not try hard enough (though how hard is "enough"- -and is it really our job to stimulate motivation artificially with grades--and is grading the best source of motivation?).

It is important to note that there are certain schools and colleges that do *not* use single-number grades or scores, and they function successfully. I taught for nine years at Evergreen State College, which uses only written evaluations. This system works fine, even down to getting students accepted into high quality graduate and professional schools.

Nevertheless we have an intractable dilemma: that grading is unfair and counterproductive but that students and institutions tend to want grades. In the face of this dilemma there is a need for creativity and pragmatism. Here are some ways in which I and others use *less ranking* and *more evaluation* in teaching--and they suggest some adjustments in how we score large-scale assessments. What follows is an assortment of experimental compromises- -sometimes crude, seldom ideal or utopian-- but they help.

(a) Portfolios. Just because conventional institutions oblige us to turn in a single quantitative course grade at the end of every marking period, it doesn't follow that we need to grade individual papers. Course grades are more trustworthy and less damaging because they are based on so many performances over so many weeks. By avoiding frequent ranking or grading, we make it *somewhat* less likely for students to become addicted to oversimple numerical rankings--to think that evaluation always translates into a simple number--in short, to mistake ranking for evaluation. (I'm not trying to defend conventional course grades since they are still uncommunicative and they still feed the hunger for ranking.) Portfolios permit me to refrain from grading individual papers and limit myself to writerly evaluative comments--and help students see this as a positive rather than a negative thing, a chance to be graded on a body of their best work that can be judged more fairly. Portfolios have many other advantages as well. They are particularly valuable as occasions for asking students to write extensive and thoughtful explorations of their own strengths and weaknesses.

A midsemester portfolio is usually an informal affair, but it is a good occasion for giving anxious students a ballpark estimate of how well they are doing in the course so far. I find it helpful to tell students that I'm perfectly willing to tell them my best estimate of their course grade--but only if they come to me in conference and only during the second half of the semester. This serves somewhat to quiet their anxiety while they go through seven weeks of drying out from grades. By midsemester, most of them have come to enjoy not getting those numbers and thus being able to think better about more writerly comments from me and their classmates.

Portfolios are now used extensively and productively in larger assessments, and there is constant experimentation with new applications (Belanoff and Dickson; *Portfolio Assessment Newsletter, Portfolio News).*

(b) Another useful option is to make a strategic retreat from a wholly negative position. That is, I sometimes do a *bit* of ranking even on individual papers, using two "bottom-line" grades: H and U for "Honors" and "Unsatisfactory." I tell students that these translate to about A or A- and D or F. This practice may seem theoretically inconsistent with all the arguments I've just made, but (at the moment, anyway) I justify it for the following reasons.

First, I sympathize with a *part* of the students' anxiety about not getting grades: their fear that they might be failing and not know about it--or doing an excellent job and not get any recognition. Second, I'm not giving *many* grades; only a small proportion of papers get these H's or U's. The system creates a "non-bottom-line" or "non-quantified" atmosphere. Third, these holistic judgments about best and worst do not seem as arbitrary and questionable as most grades. There is usually a *bit* more agreement among readers about the best and worst papers. What seems most dubious is the process of trying to rank that whole middle range of papers--papers that have a mixture of better and worse qualities so that the numerical grade depends enormously on a reader's priorities or mood or temperament. My willingness to give these few grades goes a long way toward helping my students forgo most bottom-line grading.

I'm not trying to pretend that these minimal "grades" are truly reliable. But they represent a very small amount of ranking. Yes, someone could insist that I'm really ranking every single paper (and indeed if it seemed politically necessary, I could put an OK or S [for satisfactory] on all those middle range papers and brag, "Yes, I grade everything.") But the fact is that I am doing *much less sorting* since I don't have to sort them into five or even twelve piles. Thus there is a huge reduction in the total amount of unreliability I produce.

(It might seem that if I use only these few minimal grades I have no good way for figuring out a final grade for the course- -since that requires a more fine-grained set of ranks. But I don't find that to be the case. For I also give these some minimal grades to the many other important parts of my course such as attendance, meeting deadlines, peer responding, and journal writing. If I want a mathematically computed grade on a scale of six or A through E, I can easily compute it when I have such a large number of grades to work from--even though they are only along a three-point scale.)

This same practice of crude or minimal ranking is a big help on larger assessments outside classrooms, and needs to be applied to the process of assessment in general. There are two important principles to emphasize. On the one hand we must be prudent or accommodating enough to admit that despite all the arguments against ranking, there *are* situations when we need that bottom-line verdict along one scale: which student has not done satisfactory work and should be denied credit for the course? which student gets the scholarship? which candidate to hire or fire? We often operate with scarce resources. But on the other hand we must be bold enough to insist that we do far more ranking than is really needed. We can get along not only with fewer occasions for assessment but also with fewer gradations in scoring. If we decide what the *real* bottom-line is on a given occasion--perhaps just "failing" or perhaps "honors" too--then the reading of papers or portfolios is enormously quick and cheap. It leaves time and money for evaluation--perhaps for analytic scoring or some comment.

At Stony Brook we worked out a portfolio system where multiple readers had only to make a binary decision: acceptable or not. Then individual teachers could decide the actual course grade and give comments for their own students--so long as those students passed in the eyes of an independent rater (Elbow and Belanoff, Belanoff and Elbow). The best way to begin to wean our society from its addiction to ranking may be to permit a tiny bit of it (which also means less unreliability)--rather than trying to go "cold turkey."

(c) Sometimes I use an analytic grid for evaluating and commenting on student papers. An example is given in Figure 1.

I often vary the criteria in my grid (e.g. "connecting with readers" or "investment") depending on the assignment or the point in the semester.

Strong OK Weak

			CONTENT, INSIGHTS, THINKING, GRAPPLING WITH TOPIC
			GENUINE REVISION, SUBSTANTIVE CHANGES, NOT JUST EDITING
			ORGANIZATION, STRUCTURE, GUIDING THE READER
			LANGUAGE: SYNTAX, SENTENCES, WORDING, VOICE
			MECHANICS: SPELLING, GRAMMAR, PUNCTUATION, PROOFREADING
			OVERALL [Note: this is not a sum of the other scores.]

Figure 1.

Grids are a way I can satisfy the students' hunger for ranking but still not give in to conventional grades on individual papers. Sometimes I provide nothing but a grid (especially on final drafts), and this is a very quick way to provide a response. Or on midprocess drafts I sometimes use a grid in addition to a comment: a more readerly comment that often doesn't so much tell them what's wrong or right or how to improve things but rather tries to give them an account of what is *happening to me* as I read their words. I think this kind of comment is really the most useful thing of all for students, but it frustrates some students for a while. The grid can help these students feel less anxious and thus pay better attention to my comment.

I find grids extremely helpful at the end of the semester for telling students their strengths and weaknesses in the course--or what they've done well and not so well. Besides categories like the ones above, I use categories like these: "skill in giving feedback to others," "ability to meet deadlines," "effort," and "improvement." This practice makes my final grade much more communicative.

(d) I also help make up for the absence of ranking--gold stars and black marks-- by having students share their writing with each other a great deal both orally and through frequent publication in class magazines. Also, where possible, I try to get students to give or send writing to audiences outside the class. At the University of Massachusetts at Amherst, freshmen pay a ten dollar lab fee for the writing course, and every teacher publishes four or five class magazines of final drafts a semester. The effects are striking. Sharing, peer feedback, and publication give the best reward and motivation for writing, namely, getting your words out to many readers.

(e) I sometimes use a kind of modified *contract grading*. That is, at the start of the course I pass out a long list of all the things that I most want students to do--the concrete activities that I think most lead to learning--and I promise students that if they do them *all* they are guaranteed a certain final grade. Currently, I say it's a B--it could be lower or higher. My list includes these items: not missing more than a week's worth of classes; not having more than one late major assignment; *substantive* revising on all major revisions; good copy editing on all final revisions; good effort on peer feedback work; keeping up the journal; and substantial effort and investment on each draft.

I like the way this system changes the "bottom-line" for a course: the intersection where my authority crosses their self-interest. I can tell them, "You have to work very hard in this course, but you can stop worrying about grades." The crux is no longer that commodity I've always hated and never trusted: a numerical ranking of the quality of their writing along a single continuum. Instead the crux becomes what I care about most: the *concrete behaviors* that I most want students to engage in because they produce more learning and help me teach better. Admittedly, effort and investment are not concrete observable behaviors, but they are no harder to judge than overall quality of writing. And since I care about effort and investment, I don't mind the few arguments I get into about them; they seem fruitful. ("Let's try and figure out why it looked to me as though you didn't put any effort in here.") In contrast, I hate discussions about grades on a paper and find such arguments fruitless. Besides, I'm not making fine distinctions about effort and investment--just letting a bell go off when they fall palpably low.

It's crucial to note that I am not fighting evaluation with this system. I am just fighting ranking or grading. I still write evaluative comments and often use an evaluative grid to tell my students what I see as strengths and weaknesses in their papers. My goal is not to get rid of evaluation but in fact to emphasize it, enhance it. I'm trying to get students to listen *better* to my evaluations--by uncoupling them from a grade. In effect, I'm doing this because I'm so fed up with students *following* or *obeying* my evaluations too blindly--making whatever changes my comments suggest but doing it for the sake of a grade; not really taking the time to make up their own minds about whether they think my judgments or suggestions really make sense to them. The worst part of grades is that they make students obey us without carefully thinking about the merits of what we say. I love the situation this system so often puts students in: I make a criticism or suggestion about their paper, but it doesn't matter to their grade whether they go along with me or not (so long as they genuinely revise in some fashion). They have to think; to decide.

Admittedly this system is crude and impure. Some of the really skilled students who are used to getting A's and desperate to get one in this course remain unhelpfully hung up about getting those A's on their papers. But a good number of these students discover that they can't get them, and they soon settle down to accepting a B and having less anxiety and more of a learning voyage.

THE LIMITATIONS OF EVALUATION AND THE BENEFITS OF EVALUATION-FREE ZONES

Everything I've said so far has been in praise of evaluation as a substitute for ranking. But I need to turn a corner here and speak about the *limits* or *problems* of evaluation. Evaluating may be better than ranking, but it still carries some of the same problems. That is, even though I've praised evaluation for inviting us to acknowledge that readers and contexts are different, nevertheless the very word *evaluation* tends to imply fairness or reliability or getting beyond personal or subjective preferences. Also, of course, evaluation takes a lot more time and work. To rank you just have to put down a number; holistic scoring of exams is cheaper than analytic scoring.

Most important of all, evaluation harms the climate for learning and teaching-- or rather *too much* evaluation has this effect. That is, if we evaluate *everything* students write, they tend to remain tangled up in the assumption that their whole job in school is to give teachers "what they want." Constant evaluation makes students worry more about psyching out the teacher than about what they are really learning. Students fall into a kind of defensive or on-guard stance toward the teacher: a desire to hide what they don't understand and try to impress. This stance gets in the way of learning. (Think of the patient trying to hide symptoms from the doctor.) Most of all, constant evaluation by someone in authority makes students reluctant to take the risks that are needed for good learning--to try out hunches and trust their own judgment. Face it: if our goal is to get students to exercise their own judgment, that means exercising an immature and undeveloped judgment and making choices that are obviously wrong to us.

We see around us a widespread hunger to be evaluated that is often just as strong as the hunger to rank. Countless conditions make many of us walk around in the world wanting to ask others (especially those in authority), "How am I doing, did I do OK?" I don't think the hunger to be evaluated is as harmful as the hunger to rank, but it can get in the way of learning. For I find that the greatest and most powerful breakthroughs in learning occur when I can get myself and others to *put aside* this nagging, self-doubting question ("How am I doing? How am I doing?")--and instead to take some chances, trust our instincts or hungers. When everything is evaluated, everything counts. Often the most powerful arena for deep learning is a kind of "time out" zone from the pressures of normal evaluated reality: make-believe, play, dreams--in effect, the Shakespearian forest.

In my attempts to get away from too much evaluation (not from all evaluation, just from too much of it), I have drifted into a set of teaching practices which now feel to me like the *best* part of my teaching. I realize now what I've been unconsciously doing for a number of years: creating "evaluation-free zones."

(a) The paradigm evaluation-free zone is the ten minute, nonstop freewrite. When I get students to freewrite, I am using my authority to create unusual conditions in order to contradict or interrupt our pervasive habit of always evaluating our writing. What is essential here are the two central features of freewriting: that it be private (thus I don't collect it or have students share it with anyone else); and that it be nonstop (thus there isn't time for planning, and control is usually diminished). Students quickly catch on and enter into the spirit. At the end of the course, they often tell me that freewriting is the most useful thing I've taught them (see Belanoff, Elbow, and Fontaine).

(b) A larger evaluation-free zone is the single unevaluated assignment--what people sometimes call the "quickwrite" or sketch. This is a piece of writing that I ask students to do- -either in class or for homework--without any or much revising. It is meant to be low stakes writing. There is a bit of pressure, nevertheless, since I usually ask them to share it with others and *I* usually collect it and read it. But I don't write any comments at all--except perhaps to put straight lines along some passages I like or to write a phrase of appreciation at the end. And I ask students to refrain from giving evaluative feedback to each other--and instead just to say "thank you" or mention a couple of phrases or ideas that stick in mind. (However, this writing-without-feedback can be a good occasion for students to discuss the *topic* they have written about--and thus serve as an excellent kick-off for discussions of what I am teaching.)

(c) These experiments have led me to my next and largest evaluation-free zone--what I sometimes call a "jump start" for my whole course. For the last few semesters I've been devoting the first three weeks *entirely* to the two evaluation-free activities I've just described: freewriting (and also more leisurely private writing in a journal) and quickwrites or sketches. Since the stakes are low and I'm not asking for much revising, I ask for *much more* writing homework per week than usual. And every day we write in class: various exercises or games. The emphasis is on getting rolling, getting fluent, taking risks. And every day all students read out loud something they've written--sometimes a short passage even to the whole class. So despite the absence of feedback, it is a very audience-filled and sociable three weeks.

At first I only dared do this for two weeks, but when I discovered how fast the writing improves, how good it is for building community, and what a pleasure this period is for me, I went to three weeks. I'm curious to try an experiment with teaching a whole course this way. I wonder, that is, whether all that evaluation we work so hard to give really does any more good than the constant writing and sharing (Zak).

I need to pause here to address an obvious rejoinder: "But withholding evaluation is not normal!" Indeed, it is *not* normal- -certainly not normal in school. We normally tend to emphasize evaluations--even bottom-line ranking kinds of evaluations. But I resist the argument that if it's not normal we shouldn't do it.

The best argument for evaluation-free zones is from experience. If you try them, I suspect you'll discover that they are satisfying and bring out good writing. Students have a better time writing these unevaluated pieces; they enjoy hearing and appreciating these pieces when they don't have to evaluate. And I have a much better time when I engage in this astonishing activity: reading student work when I don't have to evaluate and respond. And yet the writing improves. I see students investing and risking more, writing more fluently, and using livelier, more interesting voices. This writing gives me and them a higher standard of clarity and voice for when we move on to more careful and revised writing tasks that involve more intellectual pushing- -tasks that sometimes make their writing go tangled or sodden.

THE BENEFITS AND FEASIBILITY OF LIKING

Liking and disliking seem like unpromising topics in an exploration of assessment, They seem to represent the worst kind of subjectivity, the merest accident of personal taste. But I've recently come to think that the phenomenon of liking is perhaps the most important evaluative response for writers and teachers to think about. In effect, I'm turning another corner in my argument. In the first section I argued against ranking--with evaluating being the solution. Next I argued not *against* evaluating--but for no-evaluation zones in *addition* to evaluating. Now I will argue neither against evaluating nor against no-evaluation zones, but for something very different in addition, or perhaps underneath, as a foundation: liking.

Let me start with the germ story. I was in a workshop and we were going around the circle with everyone telling a piece of good news about their writing in the last six months. It got to Wendy Bishop, a good poet (who has also written two good books about the teaching of writing), and she said, "In the last six months, I've learned to *like* everything I write." Our jaws dropped; we were startled--in a way scandalized. But I've been chewing on her words ever since, and they have led me into a retelling of the story of how people learn to write better.

The old story goes like this: We write something. We read it over and we say, "This is terrible. I *hate* it. I've got to work on it and improve it." And we do, and it gets better, and this happens again and again, and before long we have become a wonderful writer. But that's not really what happens. Yes, we vow to work on it--but we don't. And next time we have the impulse to write, we're just a *bit* less likely to start.

What really happens when people learn to write better is more like this: We write something. We read it over and we say, "This is terrible. ... But I *like* it. Damn it, I'm going to get it good enough so that others will like it too." And this time we don't just put it in a drawer, we actually work hard on it. And we try it out on other people too--not just to get feedback and advice but, perhaps more important, to find someone else who will like it.

Notice the two stories here--two hypotheses. (a) "First you improve the faults and then you like it." (b) "First you like it and then you improve faults." The second story may sound odd when stated so baldly, but really it's common sense. Only if we like something will we get involved enough to work and struggle with it. Only if we like what we write will we write again and again by choice--which is the only way we get better.

This hypothesis sheds light on the process of how people get to be published writers. Conventional wisdom assumes a Darwinian model: poor writers are unread; then they get better, as a result, they get a wider audience; finally they turn into Norman Mailer. But now I'd say the process is more complicated. People who get better and get published really tend to be driven by how much *they* care about their writing. Yes, they have a small audience at first--after all, they're not very good. But they try reader after reader until finally they can find people who like and appreciate their writing. I certainly did this. If someone doesn't like her writing enough to be pushy and hungry about finding a few people who also like it, she probably won't get better.

It may sound so far as though all the effort and drive comes from the lonely driven writer--and sometimes it does (Norman Mailer is no joke). But, often enough, readers play the crucially active role in this story of how writers get better. That is, the way writers *learn* to like their writing is by the grace of having a reader or two who likes it--even though it's not good. Having at least a few appreciative readers is probably indispensable to getting better.

When I apply this story to our situation as teachers I come up with this interesting hypothesis: *good writing teachers like student writing* (and like students). I think I see this borne out--and it is really nothing but common sense. Teachers who hate student writing and hate students are grouchy all the time. How could we stand our work and do a decent job if we hated their writing? Good teachers see what is only *potentially* good, they get a kick out of mere possibility--and they encourage it. When I manage to do this, I teach well.

Thus, I've begun to notice a turning point in my courses- -two or three weeks into the semester: "Am I going to like these folks or is this going to be a battle, a struggle?" When I like them everything seems to go better--and it seems to me they learn more by the end. When I don't and we stay tangled up in struggle, we all suffer-- and they seem to learn less.

So what am I saying? That we should like bad writing? How can we see all the weaknesses and criticize student writing if we just like it? But here's the interesting point: if I *like* someone's writing it's *easier* to criticize it.

I first noticed this when I was trying to gather essays for the book on freewriting that Pat Belanoff and Sheryl Fontaine and I edited. I would read an essay someone had written, I would want it for the book, but I had some serious criticism. I'd get excited and write, "I really like this, and I hope we can use it in our book, but you've got to get rid of this and change that, and I got really mad at this other thing." I usually find it hard to criticize, but I began to notice that I was a much more critical and pushy reader when I liked something. It's even fun to criticize in those conditions.

It's the same with student writing. If I like a piece, I don't have to pussyfoot around with my criticism. It's when I don't like their writing that I find myself tiptoeing: trying to soften my criticism, trying to find something nice to say--and usually sounding fake, often unclear. I see the same thing with my own writing. If I like it, I can criticize it better. I have faith that there'll still be something good left, even if I train my full critical guns on it.

In short--and to highlight how this section relates to the other two sections of this essay--liking is not same as ranking or evaluating. Naturally, people get them mixed up: when they like something, they assume it's good; when they hate it, they assume it's bad. But it's helpful to uncouple the two domains and realize that it makes perfectly good sense to say, "This is terrible, but I like it." Or, "This is good, but I hate it." In short, I am not arguing here *against* criticizing or evaluating. I'm merely arguing *for* liking.

Let me sum up my clump of hypotheses so far:

- It's not improvement that leads to liking, but rather liking that leads to improvement.

- It's the mark of good writers to like their writing.

- Liking is not the same as evaluating. We can often criticize something better when we like it.

- We learn to like our writing when we have a respected reader who likes it.

- Therefore, it's the mark of good teachers to like students and their writing.

If this set of hypotheses is true, what practical consequences follow from it? How can we be better at liking? It feels as though we have no choice--as though liking and not-liking just happen to us. I don't really understand this business. I'd love to hear discussion about the mystery of liking--the phenomenology of liking. I sense it's some kind of putting oneself out--or holding oneself open--but I can't see it clearly. I have a hunch, however, that we're not so helpless about liking as we tend to feel.

For in fact I can suggest some practical concrete activities that I have found fairly reliable at increasing the chances of liking student writing:

(a) I ask for lots of private writing and merely shared writing, that is, writing that I don't read at all, and writing that I read but don't comment on, This makes me more cheerful because it's so much easier. Students get *better* without me. Having to evaluate writing--especially bad writing--makes me more likely to hate it. This throws light on grading: it's hard to like something if we know we have to give it a D.

(b) I have students share lots of writing with each other- -and after a while respond to each other. It's easier to like their writing when I don't feel myself as the only reader and judge. And so it helps to build community in general: it takes pressure off me. Thus I try to use peer groups not only for feedback, but for other activities too, such as collaborative writing, brainstorming, putting class magazines together, and working out other decisions.

(c) I increase the chances of my liking their writing when I get better at finding what *is* good--or *potentially* good--and learn to praise it. This is a skill. It requires a good eye, a good nose. We tend--especially in the academic world--to assume that a good eye or fine discrimination means criticizing. Academics are sometimes proud of their tendency to be bothered by what is bad. Thus I find I am sometimes looked down on as dumb and undiscriminating: "He likes bad writing. He must have no taste, no discrimination." But I've finally become angry rather than defensive. It's an act of discrimination to see what's good in bad writing. Maybe, in fact, this is the secret of the mystery of liking: to be able to see potential goodness underneath badness.

Put it this way. We tend to stereotype liking as a "soft" and sentimental activity. Mr. Rogers is our model. Fine. There's nothing wrong with softness and sentiment--and I love Mr. Rogers. But liking can also be hard-assed. Let me suggest an alternative to Mr. Rogers: B.F. Skinner. Skinner taught pigeons to play ping-pong. How did he do it? Not by moaning, "Pigeon standards are failing. The pigeons they send us these days are no good. When I was a pigeon ..." He did it by a careful, disciplined method that involved close analytic observation. He put pigeons on a ping-pong table with a ball, and every time a pigeon turned his head 30 degrees toward the ball, he gave a reward (see my "Danger of Softness").

What would this approach require in the teaching of writing? It's very simple ... but not easy. Imagine that we want to teach students an ability they badly lack, for example how to organize their writing or how to make their sentences clearer. Skinner's insight is that we get nowhere in this task by just telling them how much they lack this skill: "It's disorganized. Organize it!" "It's unclear. Make it clear!"

No, what we must learn to do is to read closely and carefully enough to show the student little bits of *proto*-organization or *sort of* clarity in what they've already written. We don't have to pretend the writing is wonderful. We could even say, "This is a terrible paper and the worst part about it is the lack of organization. But I will teach you how to organize. Look here at this little organizational move you made in this sentence. Read it out loud and try to feel how it pulls together this stuff here and distinguishes it from that stuff there. Try to remember what it felt like writing that sentence-- creating that piece of organization. Do it some more." Notice how much more helpful it is if we can say, "Do *more* of what you've done here," than if we say, "Do something *different* from anything you've done in the whole paper."

When academics criticize behaviorism as crude it often means that they aren't willing to do the close careful reading of student writing that is required. They'd rather give a cursory reading and turn up their nose and give a low grade and complain about failing standards. No one has undermined behaviorism's main principle of learning: that reward produces learning more effectively than punishment.

(d) I improve my chances of liking student writing when I take steps to get to know them a bit as people. I do this partly through the assignments I give. That is, I always ask them to write a letter or two to me and to each other (for example about their history with writing). I base at least a couple of assignments on their own experiences, memories, or histories. And I make sure some of the assignments are free choice pieces--which also helps me know them.

In addition, I make sure to have at least three conferences with each student each semester--the first one very early. I often call off some classes in order to keep conferences from being too onerous (insisting nevertheless that students meet with their partner or small group when class is called off. Some teachers have mini-conferences with students during class--while students are engaged in writing or peer group meetings. I've found that when I deal only with my classes as a whole--as a large group-- I sometimes experience them as a herd or lump--as stereotyped "adolescents"; I fail to experience them as individuals. For me, personally, this is disastrous since it often leads me to experience them as that scary tribe that I felt rejected by when *I* was an eighteen-year-old--and thus, at times, as "the enemy." But when I sit down with them face to face, they are not so stereotyped or alien or threatening--they are just eighteen-year-olds.

Getting a glimpse of them as individual people is particularly helpful in cases where their writing is not just bad, but somehow offensive--perhaps violent or cruelly racist or homophobic or sexist--or frighteningly vacuous, When I know them just a bit I can often see behind their awful attitude to the person and the life situation that spawned it, and not hate their writing so much. When I know students I can see that they are smart behind that dumb behavior; they are doing the best they can behind that bad behavior. Conditions are keeping them from acting decently; something is holding them back.

(e) It's odd, but the more I let myself show, the easier it is to like them and their writing. I need to share some of my own writing--show some of my own feelings. I need to write the letter to them that they write to me--about my past experiences and what I want and don't want to happen.

(f) It helps to work on my own writing--and work on learning to *like* it. Teachers who are most critical and sour about student writing are often having trouble with their own writing. They are bitter or unforgiving or hurting toward their own work. (I think I've noticed that failed PhDs are often the most severe and difficult with students.) When we are stuck or sour in our own writing, what helps us most is to find spaces free from evaluation such as those provided by freewriting and journal writing. Also, activities like reading out loud and finding a supportive reader or two. I would insist, then, that if only for the sake of our teaching, we need to learn to be charitable and to like our own writing.

A final word. I fear that this sermon about liking might seem an invitation to guilt. There is enough pressure on us as teachers that we don't need someone coming along and calling us inadequate if we don't *like* our students and their writing. That is, even though I think I am right to make this foray into the realm of feeling, I also acknowledge that it is dangerous--and paradoxical. It strikes me that we also need to have permission to hate the dirty bastards and their stupid writing.

After all, the conditions under which they go to school bring out some awful behavior on their part, and the conditions under which we teach sometimes make it difficult for us to like them and their writing. Writing wasn't meant to be read in stacks of twenty-five, fifty, or seventy-five. And we are handicapped as teachers when students are in our classes against their will. (Thus high school teachers have the worst problem here, since their students tend to be the most sour and resentful about school.)

Indeed, one of the best aids to liking students and their writing is to be somewhat charitable toward ourselves about the opposite feelings that we inevitably have. I used to think it was terrible for teachers to tell those sarcastic stories and hostile jokes about their students: "teacher room talk." But now I've come to think that people who spend their lives teaching *need* an arena to let off this unhappy steam. And certainly it's better to vent this sarcasm and hostility with our buddies than on the students themselves. The question, then, becomes this: do we help this behavior function as a venting so that we can move past it and not be trapped in our inevitable resentment of students? Or do we tell these stories and jokes as a way of staying stuck in the hurt, hostile, or bitter feelings--year after year--as so many sad teachers do?

In short I'm not trying to invite guilt, I'm trying to invite hope. I'm trying to suggest that if we do a sophisticated analysis of the difference between liking and evaluating, we will see that it's possible (if not always easy) to like students and their writing--without having to give up our intelligence, sophistication, or judgment.

Let me sum up the points I'm trying to make about ranking, evaluating, and liking:

- Let's do as little ranking and grading as we can. They are never fair and they undermine learning and teaching.

- Let's use evaluation instead--a more careful, more discriminating, fairer mode of assessment.

- But because evaluating is harder than ranking, and because too much evaluating also undermines learning, let's establish small but important evaluation-free zones.

- And underneath it all--suffusing the whole evaluative enterprise--let's learn to be better likers: liking our own and our students' writing, and realizing that liking need not get in the way of clear-eyed evaluation.

Noptes on the article's authorship as of 1993: Peter Elbow was serving as Professor of English at the University of Massachusetts at Amherst. He has written books about writing and *Oppositions in Chaucer* and, *What Is English?* He has taught at diverse institutions and directed the writing program at SUNY-Stony Brook.

WORKS CITED

Diederich, Paul. *Measuring Growth in English*. Urbana: NCTE, 1974.
Belanoff, Pat, and Peter Elbow. "Using Portfolios to Increase Collaboration and Community in a Writing Program." *WPA: Journal of Writing Program Administration* 9.3 (Spring 1986): 27-40. (Also in *Portfolios: Process and Product*. Ed. Pat Belanoff and Marcia Dickson. Portsmouth, NH: Boynton/Cook-Heinemann, 1991.)
Belanoff, Pat, Peter Elbow, and Sheryl Fontaine, eds. *Nothing Begins with N: New Investigations of Freewriting*. Carbondale: Southern Illinois UP, 1991.
Bishop, Wendy. *Something Old, Something New: College Writing Teachers and Classroom Change*. Carbondale: Southern Illinois UP, 1990.
_____. *Released into Language: Options for Teaching Creative Writing*. Urbana: NCTE, 1990.
Elbow, Peter. "The Danger of Softness." *What Is English?* New York: MLA, 1990. 197-210.
Elbow, Peter, and Pat Belanoff. "State University of New York: Portfolio-Based Evaluation Program." *New Methods in College Writing Programs: Theory into Practice*. Ed. Paul Connolly and Teresa Vilardi. New York: MLA, 1986. 95-105. (Also in *Portfolios: Process and Product*. Ed. Pat Belanoff and Marcia Dickson. Portsmouth, NH: Boynton/Cook-Heinemann, 1991.)
Gardner, Howard. *Frames of Mind: The Theory of Multiple Intelligences*. New York: Basic, 1983.

Kirschenbaum, Howard, Simon Sidney, and Rodney Napier. *Wad-Ja-Get? The Grading Game in American Education.* New York: Hart Publishing, 1971.

Lewis, C.S. *Studies in Words,* 2d ed. London: Cambridge UP, 1967.

Portfolio Assessment Newsletter. Five Centerpointe Drive, Suite 100, Lake Oswego, Oregon 97035.

Portfolio News. c/o San Dieguito Union High School District, 710 Encinitas Boulevard, Encinitas, CA 92024.

Smith, Barbara Herrnstein. *Contingencies of Value: Alternative Perspectives for Critical Theory.* Cambridge: Harvard UP, 1988.

White, Edward M. *Teaching and Assessing Writing.* San Francisco: Jossey-Bass, 1985.

Zak, Frances. "Exclusively Positive Responses to Student Writing." *Journal of Basic Writing* 9.2 (1990): 40-53.

Selected Bibliography

Creating Writing Assignments and Sequences

Bartholomae, David, and Anthony Petrosky. *Facts Artifacts and Counterfacts: Theory and Method for a Reading and Writing Course.* Portsmouth, NH: Heinemann, Boynton/Cook, 1986.

Bartholomae, David, and Anthony Petrosky. *Ways of Reading: An Anthology for Writers.* New York: St. Martin's, 1987.

Coles, William E., Jr. *Composing II: Writing as a Se;f-Creating Process.* Upper Montclair, NJ: Boynton/Cook, 1980.

Donovan, Timothy R., abd Ben McClelland. *Eight Approaches to Teaching Composition.* Urbana, IL: NCTE, 1980.

Klaus, Carl H., and Nancy Jones, eds. *Courses for Change in Writing.: A Selection for the NEM/ Iowa Institute.* Upper Montclair, NJ: Boynton/Cook, 1984.

Moffett, James. *Active Voices: A Writing Program Across the Curriculum,* 2nd ed. Portsmouth, NH: Boynton/Cook, 1992.

Ponsot, Marie, and Rosemary Deen. *Beat Not the Poor Desk.* Boynton/Cook, 1982.

Conferencing and Evaluating

Connors, Robert J., and Andrea A. Lunsford. "Teachers' Rhetorical Comments on Student Papers." *CCC* 44.2 (1993): 200-223.

Elbow, Peter. "Ranking, Evaluating, and Liking." *CE* 55.2 (1993): 187-206.

"Evaluating Instruction in Writing: Approaches and Instruments." *CCC* 33.3 (1982): 213-29.

Harris, Muriel. *Teaching One-to-One.* Urbana, IL: NCTE, 1986.

Haswell, Richard, and Susan Wyche-Smith. "Adventuring into Writing Assessment." *CCC* 45.2 (1994): 220-236.

Heller, Dana A. "Silencing the Soundtrack: An Alternative to Marginal Comments." *CCC* 40 (1989): 210-55.

Lawson, Bruce, Susan Sterr Ryan, and W. Ross Winterowd, eds. *Encountering Student Texts: Interpretive Issues in Reading Student Writing.* Urbana, IL: NCTE, 1989.

Robertson, Michael. "Is Anybody Listening?" *CCC* 37 (1986): 87-91.

Shaw, Margaret L. "What Students Don't Say: An Approach to the Student Text." *CCC* 41 (1991): 45-54.

Sommers, Nancy. "Responding to Student Writing." *CCC* 33 (1982): 145-56.

White, Edward M. *Teaching and Assessing Writing.* San Francisco: Jossey-Bass, 1985.

Portfolios

Belanoff, Pat, and Marcia Dickson, ed. *Portfolios: Process and Product.* Portsmouth, NH: Heinemann, Boynton/Cook, 1991.

Belanoff, Pat, and Peter Elbow. "Using Portfolios to Increase Collaboration and Community in a Writing Program." *Journal of Writing Program Administration* 9 (1986): 27-39.

Clark, Irene L. "Portfolio Evaluation, Collaboration, and Writing Centers." *CCC* 44.4 (1993): 515-524.

Hamp-Lyons, Liz, and William Condon. "Questioning Assumptions about Portfolio-Based Assessment." *CCC* 44.2 (1993) 176-90.

Metzger, Elizabeth, and Lizbeth Bryant. "Portfolio Assessment:Pedagogy, Power, and the Student." *Teaching English in the Two Year College* 20.4 (1993): 279-88.

Portfolio Assessment: An Annotated Bibliography of Selected Resources. Comp. Betty Hayes and Karen Johnson-Kretschmann. Madison, WI: Madison Area Tech College, 1993.

Tierney, Robert J., Mark A. Carter, and Laura E. Desai. *Portfolio Assessment in the Reading-Writing Classroom.* Norwood, MA: Christopher-Gordon Publishers, 1991.

Yancey, Kathleen Blake. *Portfolios in the Writing Classroom: An Introduction.* Urbana, IL: NCTE, 1992.

FURTHER SUGGESTED READINGS

BIBLIOGRAPHIES ON TEACHING COLLEGE COMPOSITION

CCCC Bibliography of Composition and Rhetoric: 1987- . Carbondale: Southern Illinois UP, 1988- .

ERIC: Educational Resources Information Center. National Institute of Education. US Department of Education.

Hillocks, George, Jr. *Research on Written Composition.* Urbana, IL: NCTE, 1986.

Longman Bibliography of Composition and Rhetoric: 1984-85, 1986. Ed. Erika Lindemann. New York: Longman, 1986-87.

The Present State of Scholarship in Historical and Contemporary Rhetoric. Ed. Winifred Bryan Horner. Rev. ed. Columbia: U of Missouri P, 1990.

Research in Composition and Rhetoric: A Bibliographical Sourcebook. Ed. Michael G. Moran and Ronald F. Lunsford. Westport, CT: Greenwood, 1984.

Teaching Composition: Twelve Bibliographical Essays. Ed. Gary Tate. Fort Worth: Texas Christian UP, 1987.

TEACHING INTERNATIONAL STUDENTS IN COMPOSITION COURSES

Byrd, P., ed. *Teaching Across Cultures in the University ESL Program.* Washington: NAFSA, 1986.

Connor, U., and R. Kaplan, eds. *Writing Across Languages: Analysis of L2 Text.* Reading, MA: Addison-Wesley, 1987.

Hamp-Lyons, Liz. *Assessing ESL Writing in Academic Contexts.* Norwood, NJ: Ablex, 1992.

Johnson, Donna M, and Duane H. Roen, eds. *Richness in Writing: Empowering ESL Students.* New York: Longman, 1989.

Kroll, Barbara, ed. *Second Language Writing: Research Insights for the Classroom.* New York: Cambridge UP, 1990.

Leki, I. *Understanding ESL Writers: A Guide for Teachers.* New York: St. Martin's, 1992.

Nelson, Marie Wilson. *At the Point of Need: Teaching Basic and ESL Writers.* Portsmouth, NH: Boynton/Cook, 1991.

Purves, Alan, ed. *Writing Across Languages and Cultures: Issues in Contrastive Rhetoric.* Newbury Park, CA: Sage, 1988.

TEACHING STUDENTS WITH DISABILITIES

Graham, Steve, Shirley S. Schwartz, and Charles A. MacArthur. "Knowledge of Writing and the Composing Process, Attitude Toward Writing, and Self-Efficacy for Students With and Without Learning Disabilities." *Journal of Learning Disabilities* 26 (1993): 237- 49.

O'Hearn, Carolyn. "Recognizing the Learning Disabled College Student." *College English* 51 (1989): 294-304.

Scott, Sally S. "Determining Reasonable Academic Adjustments for College Students with Learning Disabilities." *Journal of Learning Disabilities* 27 (1994): 403-12.

SOME COLLECTIONS OF READINGS

Brooks, Charlotte K., ed. *Tapping Potential: English and Language Arts for the Black Learner.* Urbana, IL: NCTE, 1985.

Caywood, Cynthia L., and Gillian R. Overing, eds. *Teaching Writing: Pedagogy, Gender, and Equity.* Albany: SUNY P, 1987.

Chappell, Virginia A., Mary Louise Buley-Meissner, and Chris Anderson, eds. *Balancing Acts: Essays on the Teaching of Writing in Honor of William F. Irmscher.* Carbondale: Southern Illinois UP, 1991.

Coles, William E., Jr. *The Plural I--and After.* Portsmouth, NH: Boynton/Cook, 1988.

Cope, Bill, and Mary Kalantzis, eds. *The Powers of Literacy: A Genre Approach to Teaching Writing.* Pittsburgh: U of Pittsburgh, 1993.

Corbett, Edward P. J. *Selected Essays of Edward P. J. Corbett.* Ed. Robert J. Connors. Dallas: Southern Methodist UP, 1989.

Dickson, Marcia. *It's Not Like That Here: Teaching Academic Writing and Reading to Novice Writers.* Portsmouth, NH: Boynton/Cook, 1995.

Emig, Janet. *The Web of Meaning: Essays on Writing, Teaching, Learning, and Thinking.* Ed. Dixie Goswami and Maureen Butler. Portsmouth, NH: 1983.

Fontaine, Sheryl I., and Susan Hunter, eds. *Writing Ourselves into the Story: Unheard Voices from Composition Studies.* Carbondale: Southern Illinois UP, 1993.

Foster, David. *A Primer for Writing Teachers: Theories, Theorists, Issues, Problems.* 2nd ed. Portsmouth, NH: Boynton/Cook, 1992.

Graves, Richard L., ed. *Rhetoric and Composition: A Sourcebook for Teachers and Writers.* 3rd ed. Portsmouth, NH: Boynton/Cook, 1990.

Hurlbert, C. Mark, and Michael Blitz, eds. *Composition and Resistance.*.Portsmouth,   NH: Boynton/Cook, 1991.

Laurence, Patricia, Peter Rondinone, Barbara Gleason, Thomas J. Farrell, Paul Hunter, and Min-Zhan Lu. "Symposium on Basic Writing." *College English* 55 (1993): 879-903.

Lindemann, Erika, and Gary Tate, eds. *An Introduction to Composition Studies.* New York: Oxford UP, 1991.

Lu, Min-Zhan. "Conflict and Struggle in Basic Writing." *College English* 54 (1992): 887-913.

Lunsford, Andrea A., Helene Moglen, and James Slevin, eds. *The Right to Literacy.* New York: MLA, 1990.

Miller, Susan. *Textual Carnivals: The Politics of Composition.* Carbondale: Southern Illinois UP, 1991.

Moffett, James. *Teaching the Universe of Discourse.* Portsmouth, NH: Boynton/Cook, 1983.

Murphy, Christina, and Joe Law, eds. *Landmark Essays on Writing Centers.* Davis, CA: Hermagoras, 1995.

Murphy, James J., ed. *The Rhetorical Tradition and Modern Writing.* New York: MLA, 1982.

North, Stephen M. *The Making of Knowledge in Composition: Portrait of an Emerging Field.* Upper Montclair, NJ: Boynton/Cook, 1987.

Odell, Lee, ed. *Theory and Practice in the Teaching of Writing: Rethinking the Discipline.* Carbondale: Southern Illinois UP, 1993.

Olson, Gary, ed. *Writing Centers: Theory and Administration.* Urbana, IL: NCTE, 1984.

Rankin, Elizabeth. *Seeing Yourself as a Teacher: Conversations with Five New Teachers in a University Writing Program.* Urbana, IL: NCTE, 1994.

Smith, Louise Z., ed. *Audits of Meaning: A Festschrift in Honor of Ann E. Berthoff.* Portsmouth, NH: Boynton/Cook, 1988.

Tate, Gary, and Edward P. J. Corbett, eds. *The Writing Teacher's Sourcebook.* 3rd ed. New York: Oxford UP, 1994.

Wallace, Ray, and Jeanne Simpson, eds. *The Writing Center: New Directions.* New York: Garland, 1991.

Williams, James D. *Preparing to Teach.* Belmont, CA: Wadsworth, 1989.

Winterowd, W. Ross, and Vincent Gillespie, eds. *Composition in Context: Essays in Honor of Donald C. Stewart.* Carbondale: Southern Illinois UP, 1994.

Witte, Stephen P., Neil Nakadate, and Roger D. Cherry, eds. *A Rhetoric of Doing: Essays on Written Discourse in Honor of James L. Kinneavy.* Carbondale: Southern Illinois UP, 1992.

Yancey, Kathleen Blake, eds. *Voices on Voice: Perspectives, Definitions, Inquiry.* Urbana, IL: NCTE, 1994.